SELLING

PRINCIPLES AND PRACTICES

McGraw-Hill Series in Marketing

SELLING

PRINCIPLES AND PRACTICES

THIRTEENTH EDITION

Richard H. Buskirk
University of Southern California

Bruce D. Buskirk
Bryant College

McGRAW-HILL, INC.

New York   St. Louis   San Francisco   Auckland   Bogotá
Caracas   Lisbon   London   Madrid   Mexico   Milan   Montreal
New Delhi   Paris   San Juan   Singapore   Sydney   Tokyo   Toronto

SELLING

Principles and Practices

Photo credits appear on pages 541–542, and on this page by reference.

1 2 3 4 5 6 7 8 9 0 DOC DOC 9 0 9 8 7 6 5 4 3 2 1

ISBN 0-07-009356-3

This book was set in Palatino by Better Graphics, Inc.
The editors were Bonnie K. Binkert, Mimi Melek, and Peggy Rehberger; the production supervisor was Kathryn Porzio.
The cover was designed by Karen K. Quigley.
The photo editor was Elyse Rieder.
New drawings were done by Fine Line Illustrations, Inc.
R. R. Donnelley & Sons Company was printer and binder.

Library of Congress Cataloging-in-Publication Data

Buskirk, Richard Hobart, (date).
    Selling: principles and practices/Richard H. Buskirk, Bruce D.
      Buskirk.—13th ed.
      p.   cm.—(McGraw-Hill series in marketing)
    Rev. ed. of: Selling/Frederic A. Russell, Frank H. Beach,
      Richard H. Buskirk, with Bruce D. Buskirk. 12th ed. © 1988.
    ISBN 0-07-009356-3
    1. Selling.   I. Buskirk, Bruce D.   II. Russell, Frederic
    Arthur, (date).   Selling.   III. Title.   IV. Series.
HF5438.25.R87   1992
    658.8'5—dc20   91-23393

ABOUT
THE AUTHORS

RICHARD H. BUSKIRK is professor emeritus, University of Southern California. He received his Ph.D. from the University of Washington, and his M.B.A. and B.S. in business from Indiana University. He has taught marketing for over thirty years, and his extensive academic experience includes serving on the faculties of the University of Southern California, Southern Methodist University, California State University at Fullerton, the University of Colorado, the University of Oklahoma, the University of Washington, and the University of Kansas. He was director of the entrepreneurship program at the University of Southern California from 1980 to 1988 and has served as marketing consultant or director at a variety of businesses, including Weyerhaeuser Company, Staar Surgical, Premier Entrepreneurial Programs, and The Springs Homeowners Association. He has contributed numerous articles to professional and academic journals such as *American Salesman, Journal of Education for Business,* and *Journal of Marketing,* and is the author or coauthor of over 25 textbooks, handbooks, and audiotapes, including *Management of the Sales Force,* (with William Stanton), *Retailing* (with Bruce Buskirk), *Principles of Marketing, Managing New Enterprises* (with Percy Vaughn), *The Entrepreneur's Handbook, Modern Management and Machiavelli,* and *Writing Winning Business Plans.* In addition to his experience as a teacher, Professor Buskirk cites a wide range of marketing and personal selling experience—including real estate, investments, and advertising specialties. Professor Buskirk is listed in *Who's Who,* and has lectured at various business organizations. He has been a guest on many radio and TV programs, including the Public Broadcasting Series on Marketing. In his free time, he most enjoys playing golf, and has been known to say that he is really a professional golfer in disguise.

BRUCE D. BUSKIRK is an associate professor of marketing at Bryant College. Professor Buskirk received his Ph.D. in marketing from Michigan State University, an M.S. in marketing from Louisiana State University, and a B.S. in marketing from the University of Southern California. He has served on the faculty at Northwestern University, Kent State University, Case Western Reserve University, Michigan State University and the University of South Carolina. His business experience includes the Manhattan Shirt Company and Health Wheels, Inc., where he served as General Manager. Professor Buskirk worked as a subcontractor on the USAID project in Jordan, and has contributed articles to various professional and academic journals and proceedings, including the *Journal of Education for Business, Journal of Direct Marketing,* and *Proceedings of the Northeast Association of Decision Sciences.* In addition to *Selling,* 13/e, Professor Buskirk is the coauthor of *Retailing* (with Richard H. Buskirk) and *Readings and Cases in Direct Marketing* (with Herbert Brown). He is currently working on an upcoming text in strategic retail management. In his free time, he enjoys playing tennis.

To Brian Scott, Robert William, and
Katie who can sell us anything

CONTENTS

PREFACE

This book is tailored to the college student with a serious interest in selling, or to the professional who wants to learn how to sell more proficiently. Key topics of selling, such as how to locate, qualify, and approach prospects, how to make the sales presentation believable, how to meet objections, and how to close the sale, are presented in considerable detail. Because success in selling lies not so much in possessing certain sales techniques as in knowing both oneself and consumer behavior—and having the ability to use such knowledge advantageously—abundant material on the behavioral aspects of selling is included.

Ever since Drs. Russell and Beach created this time-tested material for teaching selling, we have tried to keep its main features intact, improving it where we could and keeping it abreast of the times. The thoroughness of coverage and the depth of discussion of each selling topic that have been hallmarks of the book since its inception remain.

This book is really a blueprint of sales concepts and techniques, and is as capable of helping the self-taught entrepreneur as it is the student in a classroom. As such, it has always had a wide audience. It continues to be an eminently teachable textbook that also can be used for independent, professional study.

SELLING: Principles and Practices prepares today's students for the exciting world of selling by providing them with a solid foundation in selling theory and practice backed by examples of tried and true methods of selling. In the thirteenth edition we offer the following tools for success:

- Real world examples drawn from the authors' vast personal experience in sales.
- Chapter opening vignettes that involve the reader in concepts and examples covered in the chapter.
- Interesting case materials after each chapter that highlight the concepts covered and offer thought-provoking questions to encourage classroom discussion.
- Real-life profiles of professional salespeople and self-starters to provide students with insights into successful sales strategies and techniques.
- References to current readings in selling to encourage students to research topics of interest.

• A new chapter entitled "The Job" (Chapter 2) that gives students a complete explanation, with relevant examples, of what it means to be a salesperson in the 1990s. This chapter stresses that there is much more to the job than simply knowing one's product.

• A new chapter on negotiations (Chapter 13) that represents the next logical step in handling objections. It expands upon the already thorough coverage of objections, including tactics and strategies for anticipating and answering customer concerns.

• A new chapter (Chapter 15) introducing students to account management, which has gained importance in light of increased businss-to-business selling.

• A broader coverage of business-to-business selling (Chapter 21). This sector of the economy has grown in recent years and, in fact, most students will be in sales positions that sell to commercial firms, nonprofit organizations, and government agencies. This chapter emphasizes the increasing importance of the follow-up, and the necessity of providing quality service to business customers.

The Instructor's Resource Manual offers the following materials:

A comprehensive instructor's manual with suggested answers to all end-of-chapter questions, analyses of all end-of-chapter cases and case questions, supplemental material, and examples for classroom discussion.

A complete test bank with true-false, multiple-choice, and essay questions that test students' comprehension of text material. Each question lists a correct answer as well as references to the text page where the material is discussed.

Transparency masters, which include a selection of valuable figures and diagrams from the text to aid students' recollection of important concepts as well as additional figures and tables that extend the material covered in SELLING: Principles and Practices.

We would like to express our thanks to the reviewers of the twelfth edition and the thirteenth edition who provided us with excellent suggestions for revision:

Troy Festervand, Middle Tennessee State University
Jon M. Hawes, University of Akron
Ernest L Maier, Lawrence Technological University
Henry W. Nash, Mississippi State University
Rick E. Ridnour, Northern Illinois University
Pierre Rothstein, Oakton Community College
David J. Urban, Virginia Commonwealth University
Anthony Urbaniak, Northern State University

Richard H. Buskirk
Bruce D. Buskirk

SELLING

PRINCIPLES AND PRACTICES

CHAPTER ONE

SELLING—BASIC

HUMAN BEHAVIOR

CHAPTER ONE

SELLING—BASIC

HUMAN BEHAVIOR

The customer is not your adversary.
Anonymous

After studying the material in this chapter you should:

☐ Understand that selling—persuasion—is a basic skill underlying not only successful living but all aspects of business

☐ Be free of the myths about selling that most people believe

☐ Know about careers in selling and various career paths that can be taken

PROFILE OF A CORPORATE
PRESIDENT WHO
DOES A LOT OF SELLING

William Lennartz

President, Debon Corporation
Los Angeles, Calif.

"Just about everything I've been able to accomplish I owe to my IBM training. I worked for IBM for 4 years after I graduated from the University of Colorado in 1963. I learned the computer business there. Then I saw an opportunity in the computer industry and started my own company. I sold it a few years ago to start my present business of selling power filtering and distribution units to computer users. I do a lot of top-level selling, and I feel that it is directly responsible for much of my success."

Bill Lennartz does much more than just sell computer power units. He was on the 1984 Olympic committee responsible for licensing and merchandising relationships. He is also chairman of a group of citizens organized to raise a considerable sum of money to help support the Palos Verdes (California) public school system—a real selling task if there ever was one. In his "spare time," Bill is active in the Young Presidents Organization, which has resulted in his playing a most active and supportive role on the Advisory Council to the Entrepreneur Program at the University of Southern California.

Top-level selling, Bill says, "can be very effective or very detrimental to your organization. The fact that the president of the company is involved establishes the seriousness of the company in wanting to establish a relationship; and if the president of the selling company is talking to the president or high-level management of the buying company, then the middle- or lower-levels of management often react much more positively and quickly. If the president of the selling company is not successful in establishing a good relationship, then normally everything backfires."

You're a salesperson already. You've been selling since you were born. Remember when you talked your parents into giving you a new bicycle? Salesmanship. How about that time you talked the teacher into giving you a higher grade? Salesmanship. You sell many times each day. The question is whether you are good at it. Your success in business, and in life, depends largely upon your ability to sell yourself, your firm, your services, your ideas, and your products to others. Adept persuaders generally do quite well in life. They possess the ability to motivate others to do what they want them to do.

The American Marketing Association defines *selling* as "the personal or impersonal process of assisting and/or persuading a prospective customer to buy a commodity or a service or to act favorably upon an idea that has commercial significance to the seller."[1] But selling really has a far broader scope.

We prefer to define selling as the art of persuading another person to do something when you do not have, or do not care to exert, the direct power to force the person to do it. Selling *is* persuasion.

PERSUASION—EVERYBODY DOES IT!

If you owned a business, you would be continually trying to persuade other people to do what you wanted them to do: lend you money, buy from you, sell to you, work for you properly, pay you promptly, or grant you whatever governmental permissions you might seek. Persuasion is the fabric of daily business operations. It is perhaps the main implement in the entrepreneur's toolbox.

Moreover, you use persuasion all the time in daily living. Whether you're on the job, at school, or at home, or even when you are shopping, you are continually trying to get other people to do what you want them to do.

Leadership Requires Persuasion

The ability to handle people is the foundation of leadership. Men and women in managerial positions in government, education, labor, the armed services, medicine, and business are constantly confronted with the need to get along with others—to handle people.

And here's the point: This ability to handle people is little more than persuasion under another name. Great leaders are great salespeople.

It is this universal application of the principles of selling which justifies its study by those who never expect to be professional salespeople. You probably aspire to leadership in some area. You can achieve it by mastering the art of handling people—selling ideas to them. A leader is a leader only if there are followers, and the main task is to persuade the followers, by one means or another, to strive to do what the leader wants done.

Bill Lennartz rose to the top largely on the basis of his persuasive skills. (See the Profile at the beginning of this chapter.)

The Uses for Selling

Push

You may ask, "Why should I study selling? I'm never going into sales." Perhaps not, but who knows? Millions of people have been unexpectedly thrust into jobs demanding the ability to sell. Even though a person may not engage directly in any kind of selling work, the hard fact is that one can find virtually no occupation or profession that does not demand selling skills.

Many talented physicians, architects, engineers, scientists, musicians, and lawyers have not advanced professionally because they have failed to recognize the selling aspects of their work. A brilliant electronics engineer, a man who developed numerous valuable patents for his employer, not only was unable to advance into management but was eventually fired. After hours of venting his frustrations to a confidant, he concluded, "I've never been able to sell myself or my ideas to other people."

Frequently someone who has no intention of going into sales enters some other department of a business only to discover that some sales work is expected. "Every Employee a Salesperson" is a slogan of a number of businesses, and it can work wonders. The modern marketing concept now embodied in the management philosophies of most leading corporations claims that *all business is selling*.

Two engineers employed by Beech Aircraft approached one of the authors with a problem for which they found themselves unprepared: "How can we persuade our top management to expand our efforts in manufacturing cryogenic hardware?" They continued, "We are convinced that the market for cryogenic hardware will grow rapidly in the next decade. If we don't expand our facilities now, in advance of the market's needs, we will be left behind by our competitors. Presently, oceanography is the prime market we would like to develop. But how can we persuade our top management to make the necessary financial commitments to go after this market?" A problem of salesmanship!

Alcy Grimes thought she had accepted a job with Carnation Company as a product manager trainee when she graduated with her MBA degree. Management, however, told her that she first had to learn how to sell and sent her to Phoenix for 6 months of sales training.

An electrical engineer working full time for a small electronics company while studying for his master's degree was dismayed when given full responsibility—the product managership—for a small line of instruments that the company made for analytical chemistry teachers. On returning from a short trip during which he visited several colleges in the hope of selling some sets, he confessed, "I couldn't sell a one! I just didn't know what to say or do. It was awful! I thought they would just order the sets, but all they did was ask questions." He was quickly taken aside by the boss, who suggested that even engineers should know how to sell something.

This same firm had to dismiss a purchasing agent who lacked sales skills. That's right, even purchasing agents must sell! Prompt deliveries of critical items are crucial to a project's profitability. This person had so alienated suppliers that it was impossible to persuade them to do any favors when the need arose.

Mack Davis (see the Profile at the beginning of Chapter 20) rose to the presidency of Synergetics, Inc., of Boulder, Colorado, from his beginnings as a retail menswear salesperson largely on the basis of his persuasive abilities. The high-tech companies he headed needed his selling and marketing skills.

In 1985 the top management of General Telephone of California wanted to encourage entrepreneurial ventures within its huge organization. To effect that goal it hired outside consultants who, after much research, identified 12 areas within the GTC organization that could be expanded in separate businesses. The people managing those activities were given a short course on how to start up and run their own enterprises, as well as an incentive plan that strongly encouraged them to be successful in doing so. The ventures were started with great enthusiasm, but soon the manager-entrepreneurs were calling for more training. They were having problems. Business was walking out the door. They did not know how to make sales. They wanted sales training, a lot of it. They got it, and it worked!

Top Management and Selling

It would be difficult to find a chief executive who has not spent some time in the sales field and who does not even now spend a good portion of time daily selling something.[2]

Certainly

Indeed, in this age of large-scale manufacturers selling to equally large mass distributors, the importance of *top-level selling* has greatly increased.

Therefore

• As firms grow larger and larger and buying becomes more centralized, the individual transaction has become much larger; thus, it has become far more important to the seller.

• The decision makers for large buyers are often inaccessible to anyone other than top-level executives of the company trying to sell to them.

• Industrial buyers have a tendency to "marry" suppliers of regularly purchased commodities. Such sales contacts are usually made at high levels.

All of this simply means that in many situations a firm's most important and effective salespeople are its top executives—and you are not apt to become one without selling skills.

The Entrepreneur and Selling

If you plan to own your own business, be assured that your success rests heavily on your selling skills. The biography of Charles Revson, the founder of Revlon, makes it quite clear that the enterprise succeeded because of Mr. Revson's adept skills at selling his new concepts in nail enamel to beauty salons in New York. "Mr. Charles was always out selling."[3]

Convencer

The Entrepreneurship Program at the University of Southern California provides its majors with a thorough preparation in persuasion skills because the 20 members of its advisory board unanimously believed that such training was critical to the success of each of them. As we learned in the Profile at the beginning of this chapter, Bill Lennartz began his career selling for IBM. His success in selling computers provided the basis for his later successes as an entrepreneur.

SALESPEOPLE—THEIR ROLE IN SOCIETY

1- intense

2- trying

Competition is keen. We must recognize that most businesses are in competition—a competition that is often fierce—with many firms striving to sell a similar product to the same buyers for essentially the same price.[4]

It is the persistence of this competition which makes selling necessary. An economic society in which much of the business is done in a free market is a

"Like they say, K.V., nothing happens until someone sells something."

marvelously complex network of individuals and institutions whose relationships with each other are maintained in such a way that the system functions as desired with a minimum of friction. Each cog in what we call "society" performs definite necessary functions. When certain cogs no longer do things that society values, they are discarded—witness the near demise of rail travel.

Salespeople are an economic institution in our society; selling is a service that society has found must be done. Society is both ruthless and benevolent: ruthless in eliminating unwanted firms, activities, or people; benevolent in rewarding those who give it what it wants. Thus salespeople must be performing functions which society values or they would have been eliminated. Some have indeed been eliminated by other selling methods that are more cost effective. Vending machines, self-service, telecommunications, and computer buying systems have had a significant impact on selling.

However, the duties of salespeople are forever changing, and some commentators on modern marketing suggest that unless salespeople change with the times, they may find themselves nonessential. What factors are operating to bring about this change?

First, there is the massive advertising of manufacturers' brands which establishes a preference for these brands among millions of consumers. When this is accomplished, dealers are virtually forced to carry such brands, and little salesmanship is required to persuade them to do so.

But, interestingly, the world's largest advertiser, Procter & Gamble, also has one of the world's largest sales forces. Advertising doesn't eliminate salespeople—it makes their jobs easier and those of the competitors more difficult.

Second, the gigantic retail organizations are buying more and more through committees instead of through departmental buyers. The manufacturer's sales rep finds it difficult to get through to these committees. The decisions of these committees are being governed more and more by the answers given by a computer which has been fed data concerning sales of each item, profit margins, turnover, shelf space needed, etc. It is difficult to do much creative selling to a computer. But the clever sales rep finds ways to influence the situation.

Third, in the largest chains the buying decision may rest with the very top executives, and these people may prefer to deal with their counterparts in the manufacturer's organization rather than with some sales rep. Even the purchasing agents of some big manufacturers may not possess final buying authority on important items. This authority may reside at a higher level, to which a salesperson may not be able to gain access. But there is still much sales work to be done at lower echelons.

Despite the varying demands placed upon selling by the changing times, several definite functions will always remain. The salesperson must dispense innovation, possess technical knowledge, act as a channel of communication with the market, facilitate consumption, and serve the trade (see Figure 1–1).

Dispenser of Innovation

In our society we welcome the new rather than venerating and clinging to the old. Compared with the past or with many other countries today, our rate of innovation is staggering. The life cycle of products is growing shorter. As fast as one new item reaches the market, two things to do the job better are coming out of the laboratory.

But innovation is of little value until it is brought out of the laboratory and the warehouse. New products and services are of value only when knowledge of them is dispensed to those who need them.

How can a shipping room supervisor keep up with all the new techniques and products that will help to handle goods more easily and cheaply? How can the accountant know about all the innovations in data processing? How can the marketing manager learn the latest developments in packaging materials? How can the electronics engineer keep abreast of the availability of the latest developments in various components? How can the physician keep up

FIGURE 1-1   The salesperson's roles in society.

with the latest drugs? The answer to all these questions is the same: These people cannot, by themselves, possibly stay informed of all the innovations affecting their fields.

The pharmaceutical rep calls on physicians to inform them of new developments and products. The busy MD depends upon this representative to keep abreast of new drugs, their characteristics, and their side effects. The sales reps for packaging concerns call regularly upon marketing managers and other executives connected with the packaging of products so that they can consider the latest packaging ideas for use in their businesses.

Without selling, the process of introducing innovations would be greatly impeded, because people have neither the time nor the inclination to be continually seeking out the newest developments in their fields. Emerson was wrong when he said, "Build a better mouse trap and the world will beat a path to your door." Without salespeople, the world will not know of your latest mouse trap, let alone the location of your door.

Innovations, no matter how meritorious, do not sell themselves. Eli Whitney could find no buyers for his cotton gin and was so poor at one time that he was compelled to borrow a suit of clothes to make a public speech. Edison was compelled to install his incandescent lights in an office building free of charge to persuade anyone to give them a trial.

Few business executives would undertake to produce any new product if they did not have available the means to sell it. Without aggressive selling our economy would bog down, and new and improved products and services

Physicians and pharmacists rely on pharmaceutical reps for information on new developments and products.

would not be brought forward for the betterment of our lives. No manufacturer would take such a chance, and no investors would risk their capital in such a hopeless venture. Venture capitalists shun new enterprises whose management teams lack people with proven selling skills. They know that somebody has to sell the new concept.

Possessor of Knowledge

Salespeople should know more about their products and the problems those products will solve than any other person. But product knowledge is only part of the story. The seller must also know the products' applications and how the products will solve the customers' problems. An Apple Computer sales representative might know the computer inside out, but how many sales would be made if the rep were unable to show how the computer could be used in the customer's business?

Demonstrating computer hardware and software are important in securing sales, but effective reps will also be able to offer customers suggestions about how to integrate a system with individual business needs. What types of issues might this computer salesperson discuss with his customer?

Catalytic Agent in the Consumption Process

Considerable friction exists in the marketplace, thus stifling consumption. People want all sorts of goods and services, but many times natural inertia keeps them from satisfying these desires, and this slows down and disrupts our economy. If goods and services are not bought in sufficient volume (and today that necessary volume is extremely large), people producing them lose their jobs. Consumption is necessary for employment. Selling lubricates and stimulates consumption by reducing the inertia inherent in people. Not only do the persuasive powers of the salesperson attempt to overcome such inertia and encourage people to go ahead and buy what they want, but in many cases these powers make buying easier for consumers.

Channel of Communication

One of the growing problems in our huge, complex society is that of communications between the market and the maker. In olden days the shoemaker knew the market personally; his customers told him exactly what to make for them. Today, wholesalers, advertising agents, retail clerks, etc., have been inserted between the shoe manufacturer and the shoe consumer. Yet the basic problem of communicating consumer desires back to the maker still exists. This essential function is performed largely by salespeople. One manufacturer of men's pants for the collegiate market was caught napping one year when styles changed. College men wanted pants with a distinctly tapered look, but he was producing one with a full leg. The manufacturer detected the problem when retailers told the reps; the retailers had learned of it from their clerks, who were continually in contact with the ultimate consumer. Ideas should flow from field sales representatives to sales management to engineering.

Firms without sales representatives in the field may not know what is really going on in the market. One firm selling supplies to floral wholesalers by direct mail was being run out of the market by a competitor who was giving an additional 10 percent free-goods deal under the table to key wholesale accounts which agreed to handle its products exclusively. The management knew its sales were dropping but did not know why. Fortunately a friend of the company eventually explained the competitor's practice, and the firm was able to counter the problem before it went bankrupt. However, this delay seriously injured the firm. A sales rep would have uncovered this practice quickly when calling upon a friendly wholesaler.

Service Function[5]

The selling job does not end once the prospect has given an order. Any great salesperson knows that the work has just begun when the order has been taken. And a salesperson may perform many services for a prospect *before* making the first sale. As is stressed throughout this book, people do not buy *products*, but rather they buy *benefits*. If they do not get them, they will stop dealing with that source. A corrugated box sales rep found out early in her career that her customers weren't buying only boxes when a purchasing agent angrily admonished her for recommending a lightweight box to save a few pennies. "I am not just buying boxes. I am trying to buy a damage-free delivery for the products we ship. The box you suggest won't give us the results we want."

A sportswear sales rep called upon a small apparel firm with a serious overstock of outerwear which reduced its open-to-buy budget. The representative spent no time trying to sell the line but rather spent hours planning a promotion that reduced the dealer's outerwear inventory, thus creating a loyal customer.

A sale has been defined as "a solution to a problem." The buyer is not looking for a product or a service but rather is seeking a solution to a problem. Salespeople who carry in a helpful idea to the prospect are likely to carry *out* an order for their products.

Of an outstanding salesman who sold to repeat customers it was said: "He didn't have any customers—he had only friends." To this man's customers he was never a salesman—just an always-helpful friend.

Service to the buyer may be big: "Here are the plans and specifications for that blasting job you have to do," said the industrial sales rep to the contractor working on the new state toll road through the hills, laying out the complete picture of the placements of the blasts with full details of needed supplies and with all costs estimated.

Or service to the buyer may be small: "You told me this morning that you were having trouble with that spring on your big machine," the saleswoman told a customer. "As soon as I got back to the plant I asked one of our people about it, and he says it can be fixed with only a slight adjustment. If you'll have one of your people call him in the morning, he will be very glad to give instructions on exactly what to do."

Big or small, the spirit of service was at work, making friends and making sales.

THE MYTHOLOGY OF SELLING

All of us have dealt with salespeople, heard stories about them, read about them. Many of us have even tried to sell something at some time in our lives. From all these experiences we have garnered some perceptions of selling and what it is like. Most of such perceptions are myths. Many people shun selling careers because they believe the mythology that surrounds sales jobs (see Figure 1–2). Let's examine and debunk these myths. When we finish, you should have a better idea of what selling is all about.

Myth One: Salespeople are Born, Not Made

The adage that salespeople are born and not made has caused untold damage because it leads the uninformed to believe that all you have to do is to grab some firm's sample kit and go into the field. If one is a born seller, then success will quickly follow, and if one is not so endowed, it will quickly be found out. This is utter nonsense. Such people are usually doomed to failure before they make their first call. Selling is a complicated art, which takes several years to master.

It is incredible to observe the egos of many would-be salespeople. The doctor, lawyer, CPA, and plumber all realize that they must spend years studying and practicing their trades before they can be considered proficient. Not so the "born" seller, a superhero who can give the product a quick once-over and sell it right away. Of course, this attitude gets neophytes into trouble quickly. They learn the hard way that they must study and practice their art, just as other professionals must, before they gain proficiency.

The *principles* of salesmanship can be taught and learned just as surely as those of agriculture, engineering, law, or medicine. As in these other occupa-

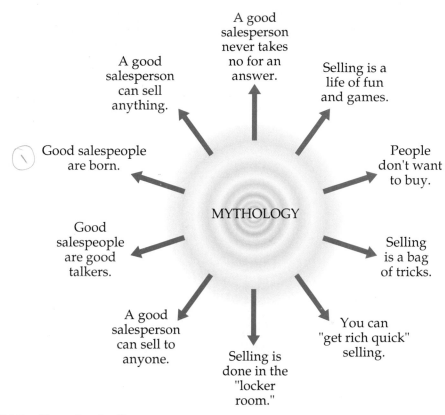

FIGURE 1-2 The myths of selling.

tions, the student is not a skilled practitioner without a wholesome amount of practical experience. But a student will become adept much more quickly by absorbing the principles and not by attempting to learn entirely by trial and error, a method likely to be rather rough on both parties.

 In replying to those diehard souls who cling to their beliefs about the genetic foundations of selling skills, the best answer is found in the experience of hundreds of well-managed corporations which have for many years trained or taught their salespeople by every device known to educators. They have demonstrated over and over again that the trained salesperson can far outsell the untrained one.

Would such firms as IBM, Xerox, NCR, Armstrong, and Procter & Gamble maintain expensive sales-training schools for their people if they were not convinced that people can be taught how to sell? Many of these concerns prefer to hire bright young people who have had no selling experience in the belief that they can more easily be taught to sell properly if they have not had their minds confused by some misguided "salesman" of the old school.

The "get rich quick" ads for sales jobs have given people the wrong idea about selling. Many who would have otherwise made excellent salespeople

Most companies offer sales training classes for their new sales representatives to acquaint them with the company, its products, and its market, and to review the basic principles of selling.

essay have been shunted into other fields of endeavor because of unfortunate experiences on their first sales jobs. Without proper training, they were thrust into the field, only to experience humiliating failure for which they were not prepared.

Myth Two: Good Salespeople Are Good Talkers

facile Everyone "knows" that you have to be glib to sell. Right? Wrong! Good salespeople are good listeners. Selling is the art of asking the right questions—questions that lead the prospect to think that your sales proposition will solve the prospect's problem.[6]

When the customer talks, you gain several advantages:

- You learn what the customer wants.
- You learn what the customer is thinking about.
- You learn what the customer is like.
- You have time to think about the sale and develop some ways of satisfying the prospect's desires.
- The customer feels that you are really trying to learn about his or her problems and respond to them with specific recommendations.

• And, the most significant point, the customer feels important.

When you, the salesperson, talk, you lose the advantage:

• Only you feel great.
• The customer is apt to get bored.
• You are not learning much that will help you get the sale.

So learn how to get the customer to talk with you. An entire school of selling has been built around asking questions and letting the prospect sell himself or herself. It's called "consultive selling." We'll be referring to many of its techniques throughout the book.

Myth Three: The Good Salesperson Can Sell Anything

There are all sorts of top-notch industrial salespeople who would do badly in retail selling. Just because an individual is great at selling used cars does not mean that the same person would be able to sell steel with equal success.

You should find some goods about which you can develop enthusiasm. If you don't like what you are selling, then stop selling it and find something you do like. If you can't find anything you enjoy selling, then perhaps another profession would be advisable. Life is simply too short to do something you dislike. And if you do go into sales, you'll do far better if you sell something in which you have confidence and interest.

Myth Four: A Good Salesperson Can Sell to Anyone

A good salesperson does not even try to sell to everyone. Good professional salespeople spend their time with good prospects—people or companies that need their products and can afford to pay for them.

The salesperson who insists on trying to twist the arm of some poor person who neither needs the goods nor can afford them is not a salesperson but a con artist.

Myth Five: Selling Is Fun and Games—Traveling, Wining, and Dining

Folklore perpetuated the myth of the traveling salesman who was continually on the road, flitting from one tryst to another and partying every night. While some salespeople must travel, most don't. Since industrial selling is largely concentrated in large urban centers, the amount of traveling by the average industrial salesperson is modest. As for the jokes . . . you know better than that.

Some entertainment is required in some selling jobs. Unquestionably, entertaining some prospects and customers is good business. But several factors limit the amount of entertaining most salespeople must do. First, because of the absurdly high costs of entertaining, companies are doing far less today than previously. Second, bribery and buyer-seller relationships are

Inspect

now carefully scrutinized. Sellers are being far more discreet. Moreover, many buyers discourage salespeople who call upon them from offering entertainment. Third, tax regulations have had a significant impact on entertainment practices. The income tax people dislike the fact that some taxpayers have been overly extravagant in entertaining customers. Tax agents have been carefully auditing expense accounts and examining entertainment expenditures to determine the purpose of the entertainment, where it took place, who was being entertained, and the amount spent. The days of the unaudited expense account are over.

There's one other important factor—most salespeople who must do a lot of entertaining report that it gets to be a burden fast. Spending night after night out on the town may sound like fun to you, but you don't *have* to do it. Even entertaining can sometimes become "hazardous to your health."

Myth Six: The Good Salesperson Never Takes No for an Answer

There isn't a salesperson alive who makes a sale every time. People will turn your proposition down—and rightly so if it is wrong for them. At other times people who look like prospective clients for your goods really won't be. Don't feel you have failed when someone refuses to buy your wares. It happens!

Myth Seven: The Locker Room Syndrome

Many people think that the successful industrial salesman does most of his business on the golf course, at ball games, or around the poker table. The image of the hard-drinking, sports-loving, card-playing male chauvinist has permeated the sales world for years. And it is largely nonsense.

Many women sell industrial goods by simply calling on the right people in prospective companies and selling their goods on their merits. Now, isn't that a quaint way to do business? Moreover, men do the same thing—call on people in their offices and sell their wares on the basis of what those products will do for the customer.

Myth Eight: Selling Is a Bag of Tricks

True, there are sales techniques. After all, that is what this book is largely about. But success is not merely a matter of mastering them. Take any one sales technique we will cover in the book. Some of you will be able to use it successfully; others will not. The technique does not determine success. You do. You will learn what works for you and what doesn't. It's called experience.

Myth Nine: People Don't Want to Buy

Many sales managers are guilty of planting the idea in the heads of their salespeople that people don't want to buy; therefore, you, as the salesperson, must beat them over the head to make a sale. What nonsense.

majority The vast bulk of goods and services are bought, not sold. There are all sorts of people and firms out there who need all sorts of things and are waving their money around trying to buy them. To a large extent, your job is to locate such people and sell them what they want. If people didn't want to buy, most of the people who are passing themselves off as salespeople would starve to death. They aren't selling their wares because of their talents but rather because the market wants what they are selling.

Myth Ten: The "Get Rich Quick" Illusion

Some people do make a lot of money quickly in selling. And some people win in Las Vegas. But it doesn't pay to bet that way. More often, money will come to you after you learn your trade and your territory. Don't expect to be an immediate success in sales. If you are, that's to your credit. But if you're not, don't be discouraged. Give yourself time to develop your selling skills and work habits.

A SALES CAREER FOR YOU?

Is selling for you? Can it provide you with what you seek? Oh, you can learn to sell if you want, but do you? Such questions may be bothering you, as they do countless others who have contemplated a business career. We hope we'll shed some light on sales careers that will help you answer these questions.

Characteristics of Sales Careers

Sales careers possess some distinctive characteristics which set them off from most other vocations. And yet, *selling is not a homogeneous activity.* There are tremendous differences among sales jobs which make it almost impossible to generalize about them. No "sales type" of individual will succeed in all lines of selling. The person who is an outstanding success in one field of selling may fail miserably and be extremely unhappy in another. These things being true, we must keep in mind that to nearly every broad statement exceptions maybe found.

Relatively High Earnings Most studies of business incomes indicate that selling is one of the better-paid vocations. Not only is the average income of sales reps higher than that of other personnel at the same organizational level, but the salesperson can aspire to a much larger income than can most other workers. It is not at all uncommon to find salespeople earning more than their managers; many sales representatives have refused promotions into management because they could not afford the pay cut. Some IBM salespeople earn between $100,000 and $200,000 a year; a man who dealt with one large customer earned $75,000 in a single year. Several sales reps for Florsheim shoes earn in the neighborhood of $150,000 a year. A representative for Lanz dresses in a sparsely settled western territory makes about $180,000 a year.

One more point concerning sales incomes: The college senior who goes into engineering or accounting work will perhaps start at a slightly higher salary than those who choose sales work, but figures show that in most cases the sales reps are earning more than the others after a few years. While an accountant can go into a job and quickly produce results, sales is often a different matter. It takes time for the salesperson to gain the experience, make those valuable contacts, learn the territory and the line, and develop sales know-how. Thus the typical sales rep earnings continue to grow with experience and are usually proportional to his or her productivity, while the incomes of most other people are governed by the going market wage rates for their callings.

Larger earnings are mostly accounted for by compensation plans with strong incentives. The apparel and furniture industries rank at the top of the earnings scale, largely because straight commission plans dominate in those industries. Experienced salespeople have always known that good sales reps who want to make a lot of money work on commission. If you are considering a career in selling, it would be wise to take a second look at firms recruiting on campus, because many of them are in product groups not paying at all well. Apparel, furniture, leather products, or textile firms seldom recruit on college campuses. The significance of this is rather clear; if you want these top-paying jobs you will have to actively pursue them yourself because such firms will not come begging for your services.

Ability Quickly Recognized   In many fields of endeavor it requires considerable time to prove one's worth, and promotions tend to be based on seniority. Not so in selling! If you can sell, you can prove it quickly and clearly. If you are working on a commission basis, your pay is directly proportional to your sales. The salesperson need not wait until old age to earn recognition and a larger income. One eighteen-year-old was earning $2,500 a month selling kitchenware before she decided to go to college; while she was in school, her pay varied between $500 and $1,000 a month for selling only part-time. On the other hand, if a person lacks talent or is lazy, there is no place for him or her to hide. Sales tell the story.

Do not jump to the conclusion that success in selling automatically comes quickly to the trainee. Most beginning sales reps must learn the trade just as doctors or lawyers must learn theirs—by hard work. Many sales situations are so critical to a firm's success that the company simply cannot let inexperienced people deal with its customers—a company's most valuable asset. It is comforting to know that if you work hard and produce results, substantial financial rewards can be yours. This is not always the case in other jobs.

Freedom of Action   While most businesspeople spend most of their time in the office, salespeople spend most of their time in the field. They are

Leana Grandy began her selling career as an account rep for the Xerox Corporation, selling to public school systems, from kindergarten through high school (K–12). She quickly became top sales producer for Xerox in the United States. In 1986, she sold 404 percent of her quota. By 1987, her earnings were into six figures.

seldom subject to much direct supervision but are relatively free to get their jobs done in their own way, as long as they show satisfactory results. Salespeople can usually arrange their time as desired. Should you want to see a ball game or a fashion show, you may find some prospect who would enjoy sharing the experience.

This aspect of selling appeals to people who value their freedom and like to operate in their own manner. However, this freedom carries with it tremendous responsibilities to manage time wisely. You must be able to manage yourself. Many people can't.

As an example of this aspect of the sales job, the author was invited to play in a Pro-Am golf tournament at Oklahoma City by a former student now a sales rep for a Caterpillar distributor there. While the sales rep was able to arrange his time so that he could participate in the tournament, he still had to get up at 5:30 two mornings and travel 100 miles to see some prospects who would not wait. (He got the orders.) He also went to the office on two nights to catch up on some paperwork. But that is just the point! A good salesperson will get the work done, but has some control over *when* it gets done.

Mobility Salespeople enjoy almost unparalleled mobility. This high degree of job mobility is one of the factors underlying their relatively high earnings. If you can sell, you'll have a job. If your employer goes out of business or for some reason cannot keep you on the payroll, you can make a connection with another firm more readily than many types of workers. Moreover you can change jobs without a long period of retraining unless your new job is too technical and different. Salespeople are less at the mercy of managerial whim than most workers whose value to the firm is not so clear and who can be more easily replaced. New enterprises, in particular, seek out successful sales reps for their fledgling sales forces. Many of these recruits become sales managers. Since the number of new enterprises each year is large, this creates many opportunities for salespeople.

Changing Philosophies of Selling

Not too many years ago when we wrote about selling we would discuss so-called high-pressure sales techniques largely focused on the ultimate consumer. Times have changed.[7] Selling has matured. Salespeople feel more self-assured, more needed, more professional.

Our emphasis has shifted from the problems of selling to consumers to the problems facing sales reps calling on industrial, commercial, professional, and distributive businesses. With this shift comes a change in selling techniques and processes. These new selling systems can be referred to by different names. Some people call it consultive selling; the rep plays the role of a consultant calling to solve some specific problem facing the businessperson. Others call it conceptual selling; the rep is not selling a product but a concept that will solve the prospect's problem. These different approaches to selling will be incorporated into our time-tested selling processes.

Actually, the nature of selling has changed greatly in many firms. Centralized sales management has taken over tasks formerly done by salespeople. While prospecting was traditionally the responsibility of the sales rep, with increasing frequency companies now furnish sales reps qualified sales leads generated through telemarketing or direct mail programs: such reps do no prospecting. Some firms, particularly in business-to-business selling, furnish their sales force with such polished audiovisual presentations that the reps are reduced to closing and answering objections.

SELLING—THE TACTICAL IMPLEMENTATION OF THE PERSONAL SELLING STRATEGIC PLAN[8]

Throughout your business studies the importance of planning has been emphasized. Indeed, strategy and strategic planning dominate our studies of business administration almost to the exclusion of tactical implementation. However, be aware that the success of any strategy depends greatly upon the skill with which it is implemented. It is fine that marketing management decrees that a firm shall develop and use its own sales force in personally selling its wares to its targeted customers, but its success depends upon the adeptness with which the sales managers and salespeople carry out their mission. Thus selling is essentially the tactical arm of marketing.

CAREER PATHS

The profession of selling encompasses thousands of jobs that differ in many significant ways—difficulty, pay, nature of job, travel, working conditions,

Steven Cullers is an account development rep for Xerox Corporation, Twin Cities District. He earned National No. 1 ranking in 1989 during his first year, and repeated this achievement again the following year. His winning strategy: customer satisfaction.

challenge, fun, independence, opportunity for promotions, opportunity for entrepreneurial spin-offs, physical demands, location, security, and fringe benefits. Within this vast array of selling jobs many different career paths can be developed.

The concept of the career path merely extends to you the same planning that underlies most successful enterprises. One of the authors used to challenge his second-year M.B.A. students by asking, "Now that you future business moguls have been properly instructed in the niceties of strategic planning in your management classes, where is the strategic plan for yourself? How many of you have planned your career paths?" The blank looks on their faces revealed their answers.

"Think about it for a minute. You are a business! You hope to sell your services for a goodly sum over the next 40 or so years in some manner that suits your pleasure. You want to make certain things happen. You want to control your destiny. How do you plan to do it? That's all! How do you plan to do it? That is your career path, your plan."

And so we urge you, our readers, to begin thinking about your career paths. What do you want to happen to you? How are you going to make it happen?

We have stressed the many different selling careers that are available to you; still there are a few generalized models that are so commonly followed that there is virtue in studying them here.

The Career SalesPerson

This individual decides that he or she wants a career as a sales rep only and has no other ambitions. There are two major subsets of this group. One plans to go to work for one company, usually some substantial corporation and stay there. Recently, one of the authors encountered a Yale graduate of the late 1940s who went into sales with General Electric and stayed with the company as a sales representative for his entire career. He wanted nothing to do with management. He wanted to sell and was happy with the pay and lifestyle.

The other group of people become itinerant sales reps working for any number of firms, changing jobs for one reason or another as the markets change. They, too, can do well depending upon their skills and the wisdom they use in changing jobs. Some of these people choose this career path so that they can remain in one location. In working for large corporations, one is often forced to accept a transfer to keep the job.

The Sales Management Path

Many sales- or marketing-oriented people use an initial selling career as a rung in the ladder leading to a job in sales management, either as the general sales manager or as some regional or district manager. Some sales experience, hopefully successful, usually is required as a basis for going into sales management.

The General Management Path

Many college graduates who seek careers in top management recognize the need for and importance of selling experience in their personal development. They recognize that sales can be a good foundation for a general management career.

Some of those in this group of aspiring managers plan to begin their careers selling for some large, noted corporation such as Xerox or IBM and then transfer into the general management of a smaller concern when the opportunity arises. Many presidents of smaller concerns began as IBM sales reps.

The Entrepreneurial Path

Many individuals use a selling career as a springboard into their own businesses. (See the Profile on William Lennartz at the beginning of this chapter.) As a salesperson out in the market every day contacting many businesspeople, you will encounter numerous opportunities for going into your own business or buying some existing enterprise. The action is in the marketplace, not in the home office.

SUMMARY

The need for persuasive skills permeates society. We continually need to motivate people to do all sorts of things for us. Anyone hoping for a successful business career will be well rewarded for acquiring selling skills. Mythology blocks much understanding of the real nature of selling. Selling can be learned. It is not a matter of being glib; listening is the key skill. No one can sell anything to anybody. And selling is not a life of wining, dining, golfing, and poker playing. It's not a bag of tricks.

Selling offers relatively high rewards quickly for those who produce: good financial returns, mobility, freedom of action, and plenty of customer contact in the field. Selling can be just as challenging as you want to make it.

DISCUSSION QUESTIONS

1 In what situations would a company's chief operating executive be called upon to sell?
2 Why is getting along with people essentially a matter of selling?
3 Recall some salesperson who has impressed you. Why were you so affected?
4 Why are sales jobs relatively well-paid?
5 Why does an entrepreneur need selling skills?
6 Why must Procter & Gamble support its huge advertising campaigns with a large sales force?
7 Why is listening so important in selling?
8 What products do you think you could sell? Which ones would you avoid?
9 Is there anything about a selling career that does not appeal to you?
10 Begin developing a career path for yourself.

REFERENCES

1 *Definition of Terms*, American Marketing Association, Chicago, 1988.
2 Louis Boone and John C. Milewicz, "Is Professional Selling the Route to the Top of the Corporate Hierarchy?" *Journal of Personal Selling and Sales Management*, Spring 1989, pp. 42–45, report that the career paths of chief executives usually did not include an entry-level job in sales. The study found that the fastest way to the top is to found the firm.

3 Andrew Tobias, *Fire and Ice* Warner Books, (New York, 1977). One can learn much about selling from this work.

4 "Business is Salesmanship—Do You Get Your Message Across?" *American Salesman*, November 1989, pp. 10–11, stresses that business is selling.

5 Eric Egge, "Word Gets Around," *American Salesman*, March 1986, pp. 16–20, stresses the need for service in modern selling.

6 Ed Cerny, "Listening for Effect," *American Salesman*, May 1986, pp. 26–29, emphasizes that hearing and listening are not the same. He maintains that salespeople must "see" with their ears to learn what benefits the prospect seeks.

7 Robert Rohrer, "Can You Pull the New Wagon?" *American Salesman*, December 1989, pp. 16–19, outlines some of the ways selling has changed, stressing the need for service and product knowledge.

8 Ronald K. Taylor, "Manufacturers' Representatives: The March to Professionalism," *Journal of Personal Selling and Sales Management,* Winter 1990, pp. 53–55. This work stresses that changing market conditions and increased costs are causing firms to alter their strategic use of agents in their sales programs.

CASE 1–1: Bobby Dogan—Sell What?

"I now know, from today's lecture, that the career path I want to follow is the one you described as the professional sales rep," said Bobby Dogan to his selling professor. "I have sold various things for the past four years putting myself through school, so I know I am good at it and I like it. I also had a look at management, and I didn't like what I saw. Never mind the details, I want nothing to do with managing other people."

"So what do you want to talk about?" the professor asked.

"I'm not sure who to go to work for. I have an offer from a large business equipment manufacturer better known as Big Blue (IBM). Good training, good pay, and looks good on the résumé. I know all that."

"Sounds good, so what's the problem?" the prof asked.

"I don't know. It just doesn't excite me. It's too big. For some reason it seems too common to me. And where is it going? It's growth is behind it. The excitement in that company happened 30 years ago. I want today's company. Tomorrow's winner." Bobby explained.

"If you want me to pick a winner, you came to the wrong guy. When I was in college right after Big Two, Big Blue was just getting under way. They had that old 714 plugboard thing they called a computer at the time. If I could have picked winners, I would have put all my paltry savings at the time into its stock. I would be a multimillionaire today. So I can't pick such winners." He added, "You're on the firing line now. *You* pick one. What's going to be hot in the next two decades?"

"Environment, energy, offshore operations, and finance are the trite answers to that. But what companies are there in those industries that are going to be a good place for salespeople? I don't want to sell securities or investments. I don't want to travel the world. Energy—come on, that means oil and gas. Environment—translate *that* into a sales job. I've been down this road for several weeks. It's a dead end.''

The professor thought for a few moments, and then said, ''Why don't you advertise your plight, and see if anyone comes forth with anything of interest?''

''What do you mean?''

''Advertise for a job. Tell the market what you have to offer, and see who wants it.''

''Hmmmmmm.''

1 You are Bobby. How would you react to the professor's suggestion?

2 If you chose to advertise, where would you do it? Make up such an ad for yourself.

3 Do you think Bobby should accept the offer from IBM?

CASE 1–2: Sandi Beach—Born Salesperson

''My father is a born salesperson. He's sold everything, cars, real estate, siding, appliances, health insurance, you name it. He's always made good money doing it, so I guess he's good. At least that's what all his rowdy friends say. And he keeps telling me that either I can sell or I can't. Now you say in class that I can learn to sell if I want to. I don't know what to believe.'' Sandi Beach was talking with her selling professor after the first class session, at which the born-salesperson myth had been discussed.

''So? What do you want me to tell you? Believe what you will. Figure it out on your own. That's one aspect of being grown up,'' the professor replied. ''But something must be bothering you or you wouldn't be here. And would you have registered for this class if you really believed the genetic theory of selling skills? It's not a required course, you know.''

''I know. I guess I am bothered by my father's way of life. I don't want to go from job to job every few years. I don't think he has ever kept the same job for more than 3 years, and that was when he was selling Jaguars. He did love those Jags. Kept bringing home something with 12 cylinders. Then he got talked into selling siding with one of his poker-playing buddies. That was a terrible time in our lives. When I saw that movie *Tin Man*, I couldn't stand it. It only lasted 3 months but it seemed like 3 years for us.''

''Why does he keep changing jobs?''

''Oh, somebody comes along and sells him on how green the grass is in the other pasture. And I think he gets bored awfully quick. He's always so happy the first month or so with a new job. Then the new starts to wear off of it, and you can see him start to look around for something else to sell. It's always something to sell.''

''What does your mother think about all this?'' the professor asked, more out of curiosity than a need to know. He knew that he shouldn't be probing into the student's private life.

"Oh she's been resigned to it for 25 years. She keeps telling me to relax and enjoy life, that we have always had all the money we needed and she doesn't have to work to get it. She just says that everyone isn't made to make their way through life in the same way. Sometimes she says that our big problem is that we live in the wrong neighborhood. All our neighbors are either some sort of executives with large corporations or owners of their own businesses."

"How about your father? Does he want his own business?"

"No way. He says those guys work too hard."

"I still don't know what you want from me?" the professor said.

After some thought, Sandi replied, "I guess I am trying to figure out if my father's career path is going to lead to disaster for our family."

1 What would you tell Sandi?
2 Can Sandi learn anything from her father about selling?

CHAPTER TWO

YOU

CHAPTER TWO

YOU

—that you alone are you?
Shakespeare

After studying the material in this chapter you should:

☐ Understand the role of personality in selling and know some of the more important characteristics that lead to success in selling

☐ Have some ideas about how you can develop your talents

☐ Know some of the things you can do to become a winner

PROFILE OF YOU

IN THE YEAR 2000

When the 2000 A.D. edition of this book is being prepared, what would we say about your career? Write it for us!

inevitable

Perhaps one of the more difficult realizations for us is that we can control our own destinies. We are responsible for our fates. Your success in life depends upon a multitude of decisions you make and actions you take. You are continually involved with career decisions. Even now, in school, you have many opportunities to enhance your prospects for a successful career and life. This is one of them. We strongly urge you to do some serious evaluation of yourself and your career plans. Now!

When an outstanding sales manager was asked, "What do you think is the most important factor leading to success in selling?" the reply was, "The person's character." When studying successful selling careers, you cannot help being strongly impressed by the importance of personal character traits as a major factor supporting success. Indeed, many people with severe handicaps have overcome such barriers by great determination or by other strengths of character. Unfortunately, far more frequently a person with great natural ability fails because of deficiencies in personality or character. So it seems proper to begin by studying ourselves.

abilities
@deteriore

IMPORTANCE OF YOUR PERSONALITY[1]

"All I am looking for is an honest person who is not afraid of hard work." "I am mainly interested in someone who can sit down with me and carry on an intelligent conversation." "Our firm simply wants people with good work-able intelligence who can get along with other people." "We want people who make a good impression on those whom they meet." "I keep asking myself, can our people live with this person for the next 20 years?" These were the replies given by sales managers visiting a college campus when asked what they were looking for in the students they interviewed.

When choosing people for sales work, sales managers look for personality rather than for specialized training. IBM's policy for hiring salespeople is to seek a person with certain fundamental characteristics and then furnish the necessary sales training. Companies regard these beginners as raw material rather than as finished products. No candidate whose personality or character fails to measure up is given a second chance with most firms.

The earlier in life you realize the importance of this fundamental, the easier it is to develop the desired traits. Whether or not you contemplate a career in selling, these same traits are invaluable, because they contribute to your ability to make and hold friends, to gain social prestige, to adjust to your environment, and to influence others in any field of activity.

WHAT PERSONAL CHARACTERISTICS
DO GOOD SALESPEOPLE POSSESS?

What traits, qualities, characteristics, aptitudes, attitudes, and abilities make up the effective salesperson? As a chef would put it: What ingredients must be used and how much of each?

One fact should be made clear at the outset: *There is no such thing as one ideal sales personality.* There is no need to force yourself into a mold. People with a wide range of personalities are successful sales reps. But experience clearly indicates that the possession of certain traits greatly enhances one's chances for success in selling. Some of the more significant of these traits are discussed below.

Before we launch into this sermon, a word of warning—or apology, if you prefer—about the obvious nature of the following material. Frequently students complain that they do not need to be told these simple truths—"Any idiot knows that stuff!" We only wish it were so. Happily, most people *do* know these things, but observation clearly indicates that a sufficient number of people evidently do not. Consequently some mention of "this stuff" seems advisable for those few souls who seem to be in need of it.

Appearance

Fortunately for most of us, perfection of figure or feature is not essential to an effective sales personality, nor, for that matter, to a winning personality quite outside the selling field. However, conscientious people make an effort to present themselves favorably to prospects.

Much has been written and said about the importance of making a favorable first impression on people you want to influence. If you don't make a good first impression, you'll not likely get an opportunity to make a second one. And upon what does that good first impression depend? Largely, your appearance.

This has an effect not only on the prospect but also on the salesperson. People who know that their appearance is above criticism radiate a self-confidence which cannot exist when the buyer's eyes focus on some neglected imperfection in dress or grooming. One salesman relates the harrowing details of how he lost a sale when he disclosed an unsightly tear in the lining of his coat while he was searching his pockets for an important paper. He was keenly aware that the prospect had noted it, and this knowledge upset him completely and ruined his presentation. A salesperson must present a good appearance, not to *flaunt* it, but to be able to *forget* about it and *sell.* Let us now observe the seller through the prospect's eyes.

Clothing   Appropriateness is the keynote—appropriateness for the occasion and perhaps for the type of selling work you will be expected to do. Conspicuous clothing attracts attention to itself and away from the message you are trying to put across. Thomas J. Watson, longtime IBM president, insisted that his sales reps wear dark suits, black ties and shoes, and white shirts. On the other hand, many salespeople make a practice of wearing unusual clothes in the belief that people will remember them for it, but this may not be so smart when trying to make a favorable first impression.

Dress according to the expectations of your customers. This farmer would not feel too comfortable around someone dressed in a suit and tie.

It should not be inferred that every salesperson must *always* be so attired. One Southern Purina feed sales rep claimed that it was the kiss of death for him to wear a suit while calling on a farmer. He maintained that salespeople should be dressed much in the same manner as the people upon whom they are calling lest they make them feel inferior or self-conscious. Good advice!

Women in selling may have a more difficult problem than men because they have more dress options from which to choose and they may find their prospects more opinionated about what is appropriate for them to wear.

Rather obviously, a saleswoman usually should not dress as if she were attending a cocktail party or an evening social function. On the other hand, to avoid looking feminine, some women have gone to the other extreme and have tried to dress too severely, thus giving rise to further criticisms. However, one young woman who was selling cars said, "Around here I gotta wear slacks all the time. Practical clothes for working outdoors, getting in and out of cars, and even doing some dirty work. Dresses don't make it selling cars." And no doubt there are other woman car sales reps who would declare otherwise.

One excellent book on the subject of how to dress for business, *Dress for*

Success, has been a best-seller in recent years, indicating the widespread interest in the subject.[2]

Grooming At this point we used to delve into a long list of personal cleanliness habits, the lack of which can interfere with the persuasion process. However, reading about these matters evidently bothers students as much as the reality bothers customers, so let us just say that many sales are lost when some aspect of the salesperson's personal cleanliness or grooming is such that the prospect's mind is blocked from considering the sales proposition.

One college graduate found it impossible to get the selling job he wanted (selling menswear for a manufacturer) because he was overweight—250 pounds and 6 feet tall. During college he had successfully sold men's clothing in a retail store, but even with the contacts made during that time and the strong recommendations supporting him, no manufacturer would hire him because of his appearance.

Unquestionably the sharp-looking, well-dressed, physically fit individual finds the total impression created by a good appearance of great assistance in making a sale, particularly in selling to customers for the first time. The adage about first impressions is not idle prattle.

Voice and Conversational Habits

While appearance partly determines the first impression created, one's voice and conversational habits are also important in gaining acceptance. Although movies, radio, and television have done much to improve our speaking voices, many people still suffer from speech defects of some kind.

Speech clinics have made tremendous strides in correcting many of these defects, so that even rather serious faults may be eliminated by a person willing to work at the problem. Improvement can be attained in enunciation, tone placement, timbre, unpleasant mannerisms, stuttering, stammering, pitch, and other characteristics of faulty speech. Stagestruck teenagers can learn to speak beautifully; the aspiring salesman or saleswoman can do it too. Speech is more important in business than it used to be; for we now conduct more business verbally and less through letters. The telephone, especially long distance, has made it possible to talk with almost anyone, and soon we may be able to *see* the person at the other end of the line. Air travel can bring people together so easily and quickly that business which formerly required perhaps weeks of correspondence is now done face to face. Facility in using the spoken word is spreading, so it behooves the salesperson to keep abreast of the times.

Many people use a video tape recorder to learn just how they look and sound to others. A common reaction is one of incredulity, not only at the tone quality but also at other unrealized defects and mannerisms. With the weaknesses thus revealed, the determined individual can attack them.

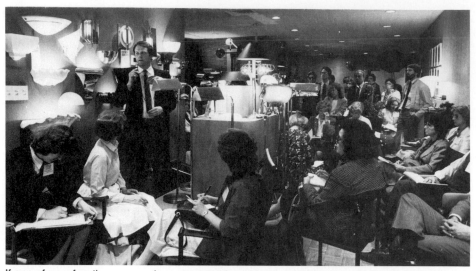

If one of your functions as a sales representative includes speaking to groups of potential buyers, a pleasant speaking voice and professional yet relaxed manner are effective.

Some voices lack friendliness, warmth, personality. Lower tones sound warmer than higher tones; they have a richer timbre. People are likely to let their voices rise in pitch when they try to emphasize a point. Your voice, as it rises, grows thinner, more shrill, less impressive, and less forceful. It indicates that you are under considerable tension. When you are obviously tense, the prospect will usually grow tense also. This is bad, for the prospect should be relaxed and receptive.

Certain speech characteristics seriously detract from one's effectiveness. Among the more common problems are mumbling, talking in a monotone or too fast, mispronunciation, overuse of slang, and unenthusiastic delivery. The professional carefully develops good speaking techniques, realizing that a clear, enthusiastic voice that can be varied as the need arises conveys meanings and thought to the prospect apart from the words spoken. It is difficult for the prospect to believe that the product is the best one made if the salesperson's voice lacks the enthusiasm and earnestness that should be associated with such claims.

By all means avoid using the clichés, as well as various sloppy speech habits such as the phrase "you know" that has infected the conversation of all too many people today. It conveys to the knowing listener that the speaker does not have a good grasp of the English language.

Manners and Mannerisms

Let's observe the salesperson's manners and mannerisms through the prospect's eyes. Some of these observations relate directly to speaking habits and manners, while others are physical actions.

Is she a good listener, or does she interrupt me constantly?

Does he speak disrespectfully of his employers, company, or friends and acquaintances? If so, he will probably ridicule me when I am not present.

Is she vulgar?

Is he natural, or putting on an act?

Does she appear relaxed, poised, comfortable, and confident, or nervous, ill at ease, and tense?

How about the handshake? While the way one shakes hands should not be given undue emphasis, still it is one way to create a good impression—or, if improperly done, a bad impression. Just consider your own reaction to a stranger who gives you the wishy-washy dishrag handshake or the fingertip grip. Just as bad is the bone-crusher handshake of the "muscleman."

Does the person have any nervous little gestures, habits, or mannerisms betraying a lack of experience, poise, and social maturity? Such things as rubbing hair, forehead, face, or chin, pulling at tie or collarband, drumming with finger tips, and tapping floor with toes, which may irritate others, should be noted and corrected. These habits divert attention to the person and away from what is said.

Common courtesy is an increasingly rare commodity. And as commodities become rarer, they become more valuable. Dick Sewell comes to mind as a case in point. Dick was only 2 years out of college when his sales record rapidly advanced him from a part-time clerk in a college men's shop to manager of a large Denver men's store. In the beginning there was real doubt among the owners of the chain that Dick would make it. He missed too many sales and did not seem to have the natural flair for clothing sales demonstrated by some young men, but he dug in! He applied himself and mastered the task. What supported him through his difficulties was his manners. Many customers voluntarily commented favorably on Dick's unfailing courtesy. The rudeness that seems to be so much the order of the day only makes courtesy more effective. Simple things like thanking the customer for coming in or saying "good morning" can set an entirely different tone to the relationship between the salesperson and the customer. The art of selling is the art of pleasing people, and this starts with the way you treat them. So seldom do shoppers have a pleasant experience in most stores that, when they do, they respond most favorably.

Smoking

You lose no sales by refraining from smoking, but you may lose quite a few by smoking while trying to sell. One real estate salesman had the dubious pleasure of smoking a $7500 cigar, for that was the commission he lost on a $250,000 sale when he lit up his stogie inside a car on a cold winter day. It took the couple (prospects) only 2 minutes to remember an appointment they had "forgotten" which had to be kept immediately. They bought one of the houses the salesman had intended to show them that afternoon but from *another* salesperson that evening. Make no mistake about it: Nonsmokers resent the lack of consideration of people who smoke in their presence. Have you ever heard of anyone buying something *because* the salesperson smoked?

The problem is aggravated in retail stores, since personnel (because of their continual exposure) become insensitive to how the store smells to people entering it. The smell can cling to the merchandise. Few people like to shop in a store that reeks of stale tobacco smoke.

Some Helpful Personality Elements

Let us examine a few of the personality elements that seem to be important in selling.

Intelligence and Alertness   Speaking broadly, the better selling jobs demand reasonable intelligence. The salesperson needs to be quick-witted, able to think fast. It doesn't do much good to think of what you should have said to the prospect an hour after the presentation. You must think on your feet.

Social Intelligence and Tact   Social intelligence is the ability to say or do the right thing, one that facilitates the social intercourse between the people present. Almost needless to say, this trait is essential in selling. The person low in social intelligence and unable to develop it should seek other fields for earning a living.

The tactful person has the knack of putting others at ease, never saying or doing anything to wound their sensibilities. It can be so easy to do. A simple thoughtless statement, not intended to offend, not even directed at anyone, can alienate a person. You may be talking about new cars and say something like, "Anyone who would pay that much money for that car must be desperate for status and recognition." Guess who owns one of those cars? Or you may make some derogatory statement about some college or company or city or neighborhood. Guess what? That's why many people vow to never speak ill of anything. "If you can't say something good, don't say anything at all."

Many stores instruct their clerks to refrain, even by implication, from pointing out a customer's mistake. There is a strong temptation to correct the customer who mispronounces the brand name of a product requested, but to do so would not be tactful, for it would make the customer feel inferior.

People are especially sensitive about their speech and educational backgrounds. Any disparaging remarks about them will meet with hostility.

Tact is called for in dealing with those who may feel inferior because of a different background. For example, people lacking education may suffer from a feeling of inadequacy. A university graduate was working in a meat-packing plant and was being shifted from department to department while he learned the business. At one stage he found himself working between two people who had never finished high school. One of them asked him where he had gone to school, and he replied that he had attended a certain high school for a while. That was tact and good sense; that young man became a very suc-

No, this isn't Korea. It's Koreatown, Los Angeles. If this is your territory, it would be a good strategy to be well-versed in and sensitive to the culture and traditions of Korea.

cessful salesman and the president of a corporation. This aspect of tact is closely related to what is often referred to as "sales sense."

Tact may be displayed as emphatically by what a person *refrains* from saying as by what the person *does* say. Often a prospect may drop some remark that invites a crushing rejoinder, but the tactful person bottles up the impulse to make a blasting retort.

People who feel compelled to prove their mental wit and quickness at the expense of others seldom do well in sales. You make no customers by trying to make yourself look better. Your job depends upon your making the customer look better. As one prospect said, "Don't tell me how good your product is; tell me how good it will make me."

One of the important elements of a good personality is the ability to listen courteously. It is a tragedy of life that a baby takes approximately 2 years to learn to talk and then requires the remaining 65 or 70 years to learn the importance of keeping still. Although this remark may seem facetious, its point is serious. How many times have we conversed with people who gave us the impression that they were paying no attention whatever to what *we* were saying because they were so intent upon what *they* were going to say the moment they could interrupt us? To the salesperson this is especially important, because the prospect or customer invariably likes the person who is not only a good talker but also a good listener. Being a good listener involves listening with attention, with evident understanding, and without interruption—especially not to put words in the speaker's mouth. The speaker may be a slow talker, and maybe you could say it better—but don't do it!

If we cultivate the knack of letting someone else have a say, then that person is much more inclined to let us have *our* say. Furthermore, the more the other person talks, the more we can learn that may be used effectively later in the interview. It has been truly said that few people learn much while their mouths are open.

Tact is founded not upon hypocrisy but rather upon a genuine liking for others. Most top-flight salespeople are inclined to see the good points in others and to overlook their weaknesses. They are charitable and tolerant because they *like* people; we do not seek out and stress the flaws in those whom we like. And this liking for others can be cultivated and developed by anyone who really wishes to do it.

We devote quite a bit of space to this matter of social intelligence for two reasons. First, it is essential for success in the higher levels of selling; second, it is a trait which can be developed more easily than can most of the other qualities usually possessed by good salespeople.

Social intelligence comes pretty close to being the heart of sound selling. When you possess it, people say that you are a "natural-born salesperson." But nothing could be further from the truth; we repeat—social intelligence is almost wholly acquired. Small children possess little or none of it, and their parents, teachers, and doting relatives expend much energy, time, and thought to teach the elements of social intelligence to their small charges. Some children have better teachers than others—that is about the only difference.

Dependability   This is basic, especially in selling. If you say, "I'll have that in your hands before noon on Friday," you must keep your promise even if you have to deliver it yourself and drive all night to do it. If you say your machine will turn out 450 units an hour, it had better turn out 450 and not 449. This theme might profitably be elaborated upon because it is so fundamental to a sound sales personality. Honesty, integrity, and care to avoid exaggeration—these are the foundations upon which long-term relationships with customers are built.

A retailer who had bought from the same salesperson for 32 years stated, "In all those years, I never went wrong on any goods Bill sold me. If he didn't think they would sell to my trade, he wouldn't let me buy them. I depended on his judgment, and he never let me down."

When a buyer knows that what you say can be depended on, it is hard for a competitor to crack that account.

Laughing at the Right Time   Laughing at the mistakes or misfortunes of others makes no friends. But laughing *with* others, when they want you to laugh, feeds their ego, and they like you for it. Greet their attempts at humor with a "dead pan," and they dislike you because you have wounded their egos.

Assertiveness   A good salesperson is in control of the situation. Though prospects may be encouraged to do most of the talking, still they are speaking on the topic the salesperson has chosen, and matters are well in hand. Many people confuse assertiveness with an aggressive, perhaps overbearing, forceful personality, but the two are not the same. In many sales situations, the highly aggressive person loses control of the interview by antagonizing the prospect.

In selling, assertiveness is not achieved by force but rather by behavior that clearly establishes in the prospect's mind that you are master of your area of competence—you know what you are talking about. Authority and assertiveness need tact and finesse.

Self-Confidence   Self-confidence is developed as you gain experience and as you learn that you are able to do what has to be done. Neophytes don't have much confidence in themselves; they haven't had the experience on which to base it. As you learn your trade, confidence will develop. You will know it when it happens; you'll have the feeling that you can handle whatever problem is cast in your path. You can cope! You can get the job done. It is a most satisfying feeling, one that will develop, but not without time and effort.

One women's apparel sales rep, in discussing confidence, said, "I'd been working my territory for about 3 years. As I was returning home after a particularly successful trip, I began thinking about the successes I had and remembering the failures I had experienced on earlier trips. Suddenly it came over me that I was now good, able to win, that the world was now mine. It made a new man of me."

Buyers are likely to take you at your own estimate. They earnestly hope that you can help them solve their problems. And yet, while you radiate confidence and force, you must also cultivate patience and tolerance. Out of regard for the feelings of others, the successful sales personality will naturally avoid dogmatic utterances, especially on controversial subjects. It is true that the good sales rep serves and counsels, but the recipient is conscious of the *manner* in which the counsel is given. Flatly positive statements repel rather than convince. One can have definite opinions without stating them in a dogmatic fashion. An opinion offered modestly and as a personal judgment can be defended on the grounds that it is a conviction, without insistence that it is always and unalterably right or that the listener must concur in it. This does not apply to statements concerning the merits of your product, for here you are expected to hold strong convictions.

Someone may object that the person without strong opinions will not be considered to have much force, yet few people have been more highly esteemed in their own time than Benjamin Franklin, and few men's opinions have been more respected. He seldom made positive statements, preferring to say, "It seems to me . . ." or "Under the circumstances it appears. . . ."

If you are interested in getting along with people, take care to say, "This is my opinion under these circumstances." Your words will carry as much weight as those of the person who is dead sure he or she is, was, and always will be right.

Vocabulary   It has been remarked by many authorities that intelligent people rate high on vocabulary tests. So do executives. Apparently there is a close connection between the possession of a good working vocabulary and getting on in the world. Certainly salespeople should be able to express themselves clearly and effectively; and the higher the level of selling, the more important this becomes. Painting word pictures, conveying ideas, addressing a board of directors or a committee of executives, or merely carrying on a conversation intelligently—these are done with words. Words are tools. We do our thinking in words and sentences.

Imagination   Imagination is needed to enable one to see problems through the eyes of the prospect and to devise means for solving them. This ability to originate ideas of value to their prospects is a trait of most successful salespeople. For example, a sales rep for a paper products manufacturer sold a huge order of containers to a manufacturer solely on the strength of an imaginative approach. The prospect was of European origin, so the rep wrote to a European genealogist to obtain a copy of the coat of arms of the manufacturer's family. This was incorporated in a package design which the prospect immediately favored; he gave this sales rep all his business.

The imaginative real estate salesperson reaps large rewards for ideas on taking an idle property or one that is not being employed optimally and devising ways to increase its value. The client of one real estate saleswoman was stuck with an empty, unsalable 25,000-square-foot industrial building. She devised a means by which the space was divided into smaller parcels that would rent at attractive prices, and she arranged to finance the remodeling from the leases.

Determination[3]   Sportswriters, in referring to rookies trying to make a major league team, often comment favorably on their "desire." Every coach values this trait in a player and every sales manager values it just as highly in salespeople. It refers to one's determination to succeed, to make good. The determined individual will study the fine points of the game, practice long and hard, and accept coaching eagerly and not sullenly. In short, this individual will do everything possible to become a top-flight player. This attitude is noticeable in those who excel in any line of activity and certainly in selling.

The term "mental toughness" is often used to describe the person who refuses to allow adversity or failure to affect his or her determination to get the job done—to win. You'll not go far in selling without considerable mental toughness. You cannot allow the obstacles you encounter in the field to affect you in any way other than positively. As football coaches love to say, "When the going gets tough, the tough get going."

Self-Management Salespeople usually work without close supervision and must be able to manage themselves. This aspect of selling work is treated more fully in a later chapter, so it will be only mentioned here. Many salespeople fail because they cannot manage their time. They yield to the temptation to take a long lunch or to start their working day late and end it early. Good work habits are critical to success in any endeavor.

Responsibility Self-management and good work habits depend upon a sense of responsibility. You must realize that you are fully responsible for everything that is going to happen in your territory—good or bad. If you don't, you won't be able to do what must be done to achieve success.

When you fail to get an important account, it is easy to place the blame elsewhere. "The competition was too tough." "Our support staff didn't come through." "The purchasing agent was on the take." "Our product was just not right for them." Losers are never at a loss for excuses to explain why they lost, and there is never a shortage of excuses. But excuses never change the results.

The truth was that the sales rep failed, as we all frequently do, but refused to accept responsibility for it. Until you accept the responsibility for doing something, it will not likely be done.

Empathy[4] Empathy is the ability to feel what another person feels. They are in sorrow over some loss; you also truly feel that sorrow. You see someone hurt, and pain flashes through your system. You wince at a particularly vicious tackle while watching a football game. Empathy!

Similarly, in selling, empathy allows you to feel what the prospect feels, and this tells you what you must do to make the sale. Many cloddish salespeople ramble right through their presentations or sales interviews with few perceptions about how the prospect is reacting to the appeals. The empathetic sales rep instinctively knows how the prospect is feeling about the sale.

Enthusiasm[5] The apathetic, the indifferent, salesperson will not last long or sell much. Enthusiasm is contagious. If you're not enthusiastic about your proposition, your firm, or your wares, why on earth would you expect your prospect to become so? Why would the prospect believe what you say if you lack zeal? If you're not really enthusiastic about your job and what you sell, then you'd better find other work.

Laziness Plain, unadulterated laziness is the downfall of more people than any other personality trait. Selling is not a haven for those seeking an easy berth in life. No purpose would be served in flogging this point, so we just mention it.

DEVELOPING YOURSELF

Undoubtedly, you have been urged repeatedly to devote your college years to developing yourself. There is so much to know and so many aspects to your behavior that it takes a great deal of time and effort for you to become the person you seek to be—a winner.

You may be lucky. Perhaps you'll come under the influence of some person—professor, employer, colleague, or friend—who is interested in helping you develop yourself and who has the talent to do it. But don't count on it. Such mentors are rare. The average person encounters an environment that is hostile to self-development. All sorts of demands are placed on you that make it difficult.

You must work to live, and your employer may not be interested in investing in your development. Your family may demand much of your time. A basic predisposition toward laziness may discourage your efforts to improve yourself. Money may be scarce. Previous self-improvement activities may not have been as rewarding as had been anticipated. There are many roadblocks in your path to success, but if you want it, you'll have to find ways to batter down the barriers.

If you are to develop into the person you want to be, you will have to do it by yourself. True, here and there you'll get some help. Yet be aware that the responsibility for your development rests squarely on your shoulders. Or as a highly successful entrepreneur has said, "My development started the day I realized that no one was going to do anything for Bob Teller but Bob Teller."

Coachability

Are you coachable? Do you learn from other people's experiences? Many people just won't listen and learn. They fight the suggestions of others and yell, "Let me alone. I'll do it my way." Perhaps, but don't bet money you'll succeed. Most people need help in developing themselves. Fortunately, there are many people waiting to help you if you seek their assistance and give evidence that you are worthy of their time and efforts.

Examine yourself for the following blockages:

- "I already know it all—don't need or want help"
- No confidence in the coach
- No concept of the future—training is an investment in the future
- Impatient for results

Some Winning Behavior

Some guidelines for developing a winning behavior pattern are given below:

- It takes great effort to be a winner. Winning has a price and you'll have to pay it to achieve your goal.

"Miss Kaye, send in the company optimist."

• If you don't like to gain material advantage over other people, then perhaps you'd be happier in social work or the ministry. Successful salespeople don't feel guilty about earning money.

• Seek the company of winners. You can learn much from them. You are usually judged by the company you keep, both the people with whom you associate and the firms for which you work.

• Do things you are good at—things at which you can win. Give it your best shot, but don't fret over things at which you can't win. Johnny Carson quit golf and took up tennis when he discovered that he was much better at tennis than golf.

• Don't belittle yourself. Project a winning attitude. If you don't exhibit self-esteem, why should others hold you in high esteem?

• Recognize how lucky you really are. Have you ever noticed how losers blame their plight on "bad luck"? Most winners believe they are lucky! We could delve into this attitude toward fortune at some length, but it comes down to the observation that losers seem more comfortable blaming their losses on misfortune and winners are fond of consoling losers for their "bad luck."

• Winners reject failure. Losing is totally unacceptable, even hateful, to a real winner.

• You can become a winner. It is learned behavior. Do not for one instant believe that fate has decided your plight in life. All you have to do to win is work for it.

You Need a Plan[6]

Your self-development may happen by accident, but don't bet on it. It's wiser to make plans. Of course, plans begin with some goals: What do you want to be at various stages of your life?

To reach each level of development, what will you need to learn? Constant vigilance is needed to make certain that you're learning what you must. It is all too easy to let the months and years slip by while you rest comfortably in some rut, learning little. A plan with a timetable will help prevent such stagnation.

SUMMARY

You are the key ingredient in the formula for your success in selling. Your personality and characteristics play critical roles in your selling career.

You should adopt the philosophy that you can develop the traits you need to become successful, to make the things happen in your life that you want to happen. Granted that it takes time and effort, still you should undertake at this time a self-development program that will allow you to become what you want to be.

DISCUSSION QUESTIONS

1 Develop a plan for your career.
2 Which of your personal characteristics needs to be changed the most?
3 Can social intelligence be developed? If so, how?
4 Can an introverted person be successful in selling?
5 To what extent can a person alter personality traits?
6 How would you go about altering the biggest weakness you perceive in your personality?
7 Why is assertiveness important in selling?
8 Determination is highly praised as a character trait, but how does one go about acquiring it if one does not already possess it?
9 What, in your opinion, would be the most serious personality defect a salesperson could have?
10 Let's get this matter of winning and losing out on the table, because many people are uncomfortable talking about it. How do you feel about it?
11 What is a winner?

REFERENCES

1 Russell Jacobs, "Just Who Are You, Anyway?" *American Salesman*, March 1986, pp. 27–29. This work stresses the role of personality in projecting a professional image.
2 John T. Molloy, *Dress for Success* (Warner Books, New York, 1975).
3 See Thomas N. Ingram, Keun S. Lee, and Steven J. Skinner, "An Empirical Assessment of Salesperson Motivation, Commitment, and Job Outcomes," *Journal of Per-*

sonal Selling and Sales Management, Fall 1989, pp. 25–33, for a study of the relationship between job commitment and success.

4 See Janet M. Durgin, "Empathy: Your Secret Weapon," *American Salesman*, September 1990, pp. 3–5, for a discussion of the importance of empathy in selling.

5 Mark Skipworth, "How to Be a Salesperson When You Don't Like Selling," *American Salesman*, October 1987, pp. 16–18, discusses the problems facing people who find themselves in selling but are not enthusiastic about it.

6 Eric Egge, "Selling Is No Place for Pollyannas," *American Salesman*, July 1986, pp. 13–15, insists that there is no place in selling for people who trust in luck. A plan is needed.

CASE 2–1: Frank Lane—Development of Career Path

"I didn't get much sleep last night thanks to your lecture yesterday on career path planning. It struck a few nerves that my dad has yet to find and work over." It was Frank Lane, senior marketing major at a major West Coast university, who poked his head into Professor Hite's office. He continued, "Can we talk about it for a few minutes? I'll bring the diet colas."

Hite laughed, "Sure thing! Sit down and tell me what's bothering you."

Frank started, "Seems like every prof in this place is telling us that our future in the first quarter of the 21st century will be focused around the Pacific Rim countries, that our future lies offshore, that corporations of the future will be multinational. If that is so, and I think it is, then why wouldn't I be smart to begin my career with a stint in offshore sales based in some Far East location such as Tokyo, Hong Kong, Singapore, or whatever?"

"Sounds like good thinking to me. Exactly how are you going to do it?" Hite asked.

"I met this Japanese-American, Victor, last night at a party. He calls himself an expediter in doing business with Pacific Rim countries, particularly Japan. Right now he is selling fish from Western Samoa and Jamaica into Japan. He seems to be in the fish business, but he says he will deal in anything that makes sense. We got along all right, and he asked me to look him up at work, that he might have a deal for me to develop. What do you think I should do?"

"As long as all you do is talk and listen, you might learn something. What do you know about him?" Hite asked.

"Nothing."

"What is an expediter?"

"I think it has to do with politics, getting government approvals to do business in those countries. He seems to have some contacts in those governments." Frank replied. "I need to know more about him, is that it?"

Hite nodded.

Frank suddenly changed the subject. "I have a friend who said that I should try to get a job with Bank of America in one of their Far East branches, that it would be a good place to learn about doing business there. What do you think?''

Hite asked, ''In what language other than English are you fluent?''

''None.''

''Is that going to be a problem?'' Hite asked.

There was no answer as Frank sat for a while thinking. Finally, he said, ''I'd better start doing some research on this because I see I really don't know enough to make a career plan right now. Gee, this is no different than writing a business plan; it takes a lot of work, doesn't it?''

The professor said nothing as he went back to grading papers.

1 How should Frank go about evaluating Victor? Should he talk more with Victor before investigating him?

2 Would a bank job in the Far East be a good first job for Frank?

3 What are some of the alternatives Frank has in his career path? What should Frank do first?

CASE 2–2: Marty Steele—Developing Selling Skills

Marty Steele had undertaken her new position in the Universal Telephone Company with great anticipation of success and financial reward. She had been head of the large telephone company's scrap disposal operation. Each year the company generated millions of tons of scrap copper and aluminum as well as other materials. She was in charge of a large facility that processed the scrap into resalable ingots. Scrap worth about 20 cents a pound was converted into metal worth about 55 cents a pound. With about 5 million pounds of scrap a year going through the yard, Marty generated about $1,750,000, well in excess of the operation's direct costs.

Top management had retained a consultant to assist in developing some internal venturing enterprises. The Supreme Court decision forcing the telephone companies into competition had freed management to pursue non-telephone economic ventures. Indeed, there was a real need to do so. Profits from telephone operations in the future would be under great competitive pressures.

One of the most attractive internal ventures, the consultants found, was Marty's operation. If she could make so much money on Universal's scrap, why not process other companies' scrap? No additional investments were needed.

To that end, Marty was put through a short training course on how to be an entrepreneur and told to go make some money for the company. She was able to make an incentive deal with top management in which she was to share in the operation's profits.

Eagerly she ventured into the market. She contacted the executives in charge of scrap disposal at three other regional utilities, including another telephone company. No sale! She struck out. Even though she offered them a deal that seemed to be unassailable, they were not interested. She was offering to pay them more for their scrap than they were getting. It was a no-lose proposition. Or at least that was the way Marty saw it. She was quite upset.

She confided to the consultant that she felt that perhaps she needed some training in selling techniques. Marty and the consultant talked a bit about selling and how to develop her persuasive skills.

1 As the consultant, what would you tell Marty to do to acquire the selling skills she needs?

CHAPTER THREE

THE JOB

Where the willingness is great, the difficulties cannot be great.
Machiavelli

After studying the material in this chapter you should:

☐ Understand that there are a wide range of sales jobs that have little else in common than that they are responsible for bringing revenue into the company

☐ Realize the wide range of activities, both selling and nonselling, that salespeople may be called upon to do

PROFILE OF A WOMAN WHO

KNOWS HER GOODS

Denise Neill

Staar Surgical, Inc.
Monrovia, Calif.
Territory: Southeast U.S.

"I spent 13 years as a registered nurse before it finally dawned on me that I wasn't going anywhere in that profession. I was at a dead end, so I became a sales representative for Iolab [a manufacturer of intraoccular lenses for use in cataract surgery]. We had a lot of fun in that company when it was small. I did very well. I'm really very good at what I do. I know the people and I know the medical profession. The job really made those two traits come together quite well. But that came to an end when Johnson & Johnson bought the company. The fun stopped. Instead of the personal contact we had with the owners, all we got were the corporate memos and all of the company procedures. I just couldn't take it anymore and was looking for a way out. John Wolf came along with his new company, Staar Surgical, and asked me to be a sales representative in the Atlanta region, so I grabbed the opportunity. Now I am having fun again. We've got a great product line and a great group of people."

When asked why she was good at her job, she replied, "Because I really believe in the product. These are excellent products we're selling. I really feel that I am doing people a favor making them aware of Staar intraoccular lenses. You have no idea the satisfaction I get from talking with people who couldn't see before their operations but come out with perfect vision with our lenses in their eyes. I really cry with joy when I meet our satisfied customers."

When asked how she was doing, she replied, "Well, as you know, things are tough getting started. After all, this is a new company and the FDA limits how much we can sell. So financially I'm not as well off as I was before. But it is going to be OK. I'm willing to pay the price for what the future holds."

Denise was at her best aboard the Staar Express, an excursion train going to the American Association of Ophthalmologists meeting in San Francisco. She was standing on the rear platform of the train, enjoying every minute of her conversations with the ophthalmologists, who had been invited on a wine-tasting trip through the California vineyards on the way to the trade show.

The sales job is rather simple in concept—to generate revenue for the firm. Sales reps go into the marketplace to compete for money, customer's money, with other sales reps, who seek the same thing. At times such contests can be most fierce. If a company's salespeople fail to win a sufficient number of these competitions, the firm's employees and owners may not eat too well. Everyone in the firm depends on and lives off of the sales—the money that the reps bring in.

A business must have customers, enough of them that it can continue to meet its obligations. Thus in a very real way our business enterprises are totally dependent upon someone selling something to someone else who will pay for it.

So much for the simple concept. In reality the sales job seems to most people to be far more complex than that. An entire book could be written on the different types of sales jobs that are to be found in American industry and all the different things sales reps do to earn their keep. Here we will just try to give you a taste of the diversity of sales tasks most commonly encountered.

TYPES OF SALES JOBS

Perhaps a short description of various ways we classify sales jobs will help you understand this work we call selling.

Single Transactions versus Account Management

Many salespeople deal with a customer only once, while others try to maintain a long-term relationship with an account, two entirely different situations that require different selling tactics. A one-shot deal such as a jewelry salesperson on 47th Street in New York selling a diamond ring to a tourist is a totally different selling job than that of the New York diamond wholesaler upstairs who sells to retail jewelers around the country. One-shot sellers do not build a clientele or develop a customer base from which future revenues will flow.

Salespeople who are account managers look upon each customer as an annuity, an earning asset. It is from such annuities that experienced sales reps gain their fortunes over time. Certainly the job of managing a group of accounts differs significantly from the job of continually seeking new customers. The salesperson in the latter situation is denied the benefits flowing from long-term relationships with clients.

Types of Customers[1]

Not surprisingly the nature of the customers upon whom one calls dictates the nature of the job. The seller of heavy-duty earth-moving equipment such as Caterpillar who calls on earth-moving contractors lives a considerably

Some examples of intangible goods are insurance, investments, services, and consulting. What strategies and techniques might this stockbroker use to sell his services?

different life than the sales rep who sells high fashion womenswear. About the only thing the two jobs have in common is that the salespeople are trying to persuade people to buy their goods.

Types of Products

Traditionally, much was made of the differences between selling tangible goods, things that can be touched and seen, and selling intangibles, such as insurance, investments, services, and consulting. It was thought that selling intangibles was more difficult than selling tangibles, but there is now much reason to question that conventional wisdom. Usually your stockbroker has a far easier task selling you securities than does the car salesperson trying to put you into a new super turbo Zoomer. It just requires different selling strategies and tactics. A prospect can see the product being considered but relies on what the salesperson says and does to visualize the intangible benefit under consideration. Consider this: If it is true, as marketing dogma insists, that people don't buy products but rather benefits (that is, they buy what the product will do for them), then how does that differ from buying an intangible? Benefits are intangibles that the salesperson brings to the prospect's attention. Perhaps we all sell intangibles. Only our props differ.

Inside versus Outside Selling

Inside salespeople work from an office or in a store. Perhaps they are part of that new industry telemarketing. Either the customers come to them or they must call them. In any event, they don't travel and they don't do their work in the prospect's environment.

Outside salespeople enjoy many freedoms usually denied the inside seller. In return they need more self-discipline and self-management. Certainly their working environments differ from the controlled surroundings of the inside seller.

Creative versus Order-Taking Selling

In the early days of teaching personal selling, much was made of the differences between the so-called creative salesperson and the person who routinely called upon a route of customers picking up their orders, such as a person working for a drug wholesaler. A creative sale was one in which the prospect had no perceived need for, or interest in, the proposition offered by the rep. No demand for the product existed. The sales rep had to create it.

Naturally, many sales jobs fall between these two extremes. What about the industrial sales rep who seeks the paint contract from a large manufacturer. The demand is there: It is an order-taking job? Hardly! In truth, this dichotomy is of little use to us in understanding sales jobs, because many jobs that seem to be order-taking still require selling skills.

Scope of Operations

Some sales reps operate around the world. They travel extensively. Others never leave home. Some reps have territories limited to a small portion of some large urban area, while others travel around several states.

WHAT "SALES" PEOPLE ACTUALLY DO

The people who compose a firm's sales force perform a wide variety of tasks for their pay. Let's break down sales jobs by considering what various sales reps may find themselves doing. These tasks are listed in no particular order, and salespeople may work at any, all, or a combination of the following tasks:

- Locating prospects
- Obtaining interviews with buyers
- Making sales presentations
- Working at trade shows
- Obtaining orders
- Negotiating deals
- Rendering technical assistance to customers
- Educating or training customers

- Aiding the distributive system in merchandising
- Performing credit duties
- Delivering goods
- Managing a territory
- Doing repair work
- Doing market research
- Gathering information about competitors
- Fielding complaints
- Expediting the order

No doubt many other "selling" activities could be added to this list, but you get the point: Salespeople do much more than just "sell." They represent the company to the customers; they are the major communication system between company management and the market. Let's examine some of these activities in more detail.

Prospecting

Traditionally, sales reps were supposed to go into the market and locate people or firms that would likely buy the company's wares. Find prospective customers! Drum up trade! That's why they were called *drummers* in the old days. To some extent, that function of selling has been transferred to marketing. Leads to prospective customers are now often generated through direct mail, advertising, or telemarketing programs much to the relief of many salespeople. Prospecting was never one of the sales rep's favorite jobs.

Obtaining Meaningful Interviews

The operative word is meaningful! Anyone can talk to people who don't make the buying decisions. We call these people *conversationalists*. The key is to get interviews with the people who will be playing a role in making the buying decision. Sometimes it's easy, other times it's not. It may require some solid networking contacts to get a sales interview with some CEO.

Making Sales Presentations

Now we're into what most people think sales reps do all day long—sell. Actually, some sales reps are fortunate to be able to make one serious sales presentation each day. Others may be lucky enough to make one presentation each week. In truth, most sales reps make fewer sales presentations than one would think and far fewer than they would like to make. Much personal work and management effort is focused on trying to make it possible for the sales rep to spend more time actually making sales presentations and less time doing all the other things that we are describing.

Many industries participate in trade shows, which are important promotional events usually well-attended by good prospects. How might you, as an automobile sales rep, differentiate serious prospects from those who are just looking?

Working Trade Shows

Trade shows, market weeks, conferences, or conventions are one of the realities of sales life. They are important promotional events at which many good prospects come to one place at one time. Properly managed, such trade shows can be powerful selling tools for the rep who is skillful in quickly separating the good prospects from the lookers. In some lines of selling, working trade shows is a major part of the sales rep's job.

Obtaining Orders

Completing the transaction! Let us never forget or underemphasize the importance of closing the sale, getting the order, and everything that goes with it. Some fortunate salespeople do little more than make transactions—fast food counter workers. Yes, they also sell. And much money is made or lost depending upon their transactional efficiency—how quickly and accurately they complete each transaction.

Negotiating Deals

Some transactions cannot be made without some negotiations, sometimes extensive ones. Negotiating skills are essential for such salespeople. They are so important that Chapter 13 is devoted to the subject.

Rendering technical assistance to customers is an essential function of the business-to-business or industrial sales representative.

Rendering Technical Assistance to Customers[2]

Often industrial sales engineers must render considerable technical assistance to their customers. Jim Perkins, an industrial adhesives sales rep, continually has to develop or recommend special products or processes to meet the adhesive requirements of his customers.[3] In business-to-business or industrial selling, customers often rely on the suppliers to provide the technical knowledge they need. The president of a textile mill in South Carolina bragged, "I have the greatest research facilities in the world. I call them DuPont, Dow, Monsanto, and Chemstrand." He was naturally referring to the fact that he depended on the sales engineers from these companies to provide his firm with whatever technical help he needed in using the products he bought from them.

Educating or Training Customers

Staar Surgical sells silicon intraoccular lenses for use in cataract surgery. The company's sales reps must train the doctors in the proper use of the lenses. Similarly, computer salespeople often must do some training while selling their systems. Norman Hilton, a men's apparel manufacturer, trains the retail salespeople working for Hilton's dealers how to sell expensive suits. Selling can require teaching skills.

Aiding the Distributive System in Merchandising

Many salespeople spend considerable time working with distributors and dealers in merchandising their goods—building displays and developing promotions and in-store demonstrations.

Performing Credit Duties

Some people who want to buy your goods can and will pay for them, while others either can't or won't. Often the sales rep must provide management with some assistance in the granting or evaluation of credit risks.

Delivering Goods

Some salespeople physically deliver the goods they sell. Sometimes the task is burdensome: if you're looking for a workout, try selling bottled water.

Managing a Territory

Sometimes the sales rep is, in all but title, the company's manager for a territory. Everything that happens in that area is under the direct control of the territory's representative.

Doing Repair Work

Things break! The local sales rep may be the only person around who can fix them. Or the repair people may be expected to sell: the broken article is beyond repair so sell the person a new unit.

Doing Market Research

Management wants to know some things about the market, so who better to turn to than the people who are in contact with that market? The sales force is often asked by research for information. While sales managers usually do not

Repair work is important! Good customer service will often lead to additional sales in the future. What might be the benefits for a sporting goods store that offers free repair services to its customers?

like to have their salespeople turned into field researchers, there are times when it makes sense to use them as such.

Gathering Information about Competitors

Although similar to doing marketing research, the gathering of information about competitive conditions and the activities of competitors is a little different and decidedly important. Markets can change rapidly. Competitors can make sudden changes in their policies or prices that can catch a firm unaware if no quick market feedback mechanism is in place. The sales force *is* that market feedback system.

Fielding Complaints

The customer is not happy with the firm. Something is wrong. Often it is the salesperson's job to handle the complaint and to try to make the customer happy once again.

Expediting Orders

The order is not progressing as promised. What's wrong? Where are the goods? Salespeople often have to expedite orders for customers who have special need for them.

SOME OTHER WAYS OF LOOKING AT IT

So far we have been examining the various aspects that make up the jobs we call selling. But in many respects that is like trying to describe a car by describing each of its parts—the tires, the engine, etc. When the task is done, the reader would still have little idea what a car looks like. So perhaps we should consider the job of selling through the eyes of some salespeople.

Bear in mind that a sales career is not for everyone. One of the reasons for delving into the nature of sales jobs is to help you decide if it is a calling that has something that you want from your work, from the way you intend to make your living. Sales is for you if:

• You like to meet and interact with people! Selling is about people, learning about their problems and figuring out how you can help them.[4]

• You have the self-discipline to work with little supervision. It's up to you to do the things that are necessary to be successful.

• You find money a strong incentive. Selling is about money: Getting it from customers by selling them what they need or want. You will usually be paid in proportion to the money you bring into the firm.

• You are competitive. Good salespeople want to win. They want to be the best at what they do.

SUMMARY

Sales jobs vary tremendously in the details of the salesperson's daily routine. Some people work outside, others inside. Some sell to the same accounts repeatedly, while others engage in a continual series of single-contact meetings with prospects. Some sell tangible products, while others sell intangibles. Some travel the world, while others seldom leave a store. Some sales amounts to millions of dollars, while others are for but a few pennies.

The scope of what a salesperson actually does is wide and far exceeds just the activities usually encompassed by the selling process. Often sales reps must render technical assistance, do repair work, do market research and credit work, adjust complaints, educate distributors and customers, work trade shows, do sales promotional work, and negotiate deals.

Finally, there are some people for whom sales jobs hold little interest. They do not believe that their interests in life can be attained by selling. But don't jump too quickly to this conclusion without giving the field careful consideration.

DISCUSSION QUESTIONS

1 What are the advantages of a sales job in which you sell to an established list of accounts?
2 Why do many people believe that it is easier to sell tangible products than intangible ones?

3 What types of customers do you think you would most like to sell to? Least like to sell to?

4 Why do most salespeople dislike prospecting for customers?

5 What is a meaningful sales interview?

6 Why are trade shows important to salespeople?

7 Why might the sales rep handling an account prefer to provide all technical and service assistance to the customer rather than having the work done by other people?

8 Why is it important for customers to be properly trained in the use of your product or service?

9 Under what circumstances is the building of in-store displays and promotions an important part of the sales job?

10 Why might you want to respond to customer complaints yourself?

REFERENCES

1 See John Hafer and Barbara A. McCuen, "Antecedents of Performance and Satisfaction in a Service Sales Force as Compared to an Industrial Sales Force," *Journal of Personal Selling and Sales Management*, November 1985, pp. 7–17, for some insights into the differences between the two types of sales jobs.

2 Kenneth N. Thompson, "Monte Carlo Simulation Approach to Product Profile Analysis: A Consultative Sales Tool," *Journal of Personal Selling and Sales Management*, Summer 1989, pp. 1–10, discusses the use of a computerized simulation to assist technical buyers in making a buying decision.

3 John Nemec, "Knowing Merchandise Thoroughly," *American Salesman*, January 1987, pp. 10–13, stresses the need for product knowledge in selling.

4 Frank Vander Wert, "Learn New Skills," *American Salesman*, February 1989, pp. 9–11, discusses the continual need for learning new skills if one is to keep abreast of what is going on in the world.

CASE 3-1: Desert Fountain and Beverage Supply—Delivery Salespeople

"It's asking too much of our truck drivers to deliver and serve our customers *and* also be responsible for making sales." Dan Cruz was talking to his partner, Art Hand, about what Hand saw as the lack of aggressive sales effort by the three delivery-sales-service people the company employed.

The Desert Fountain and Beverage Supply Company served the Coachella Valley in Southern California's lower Mohave Desert. While its customers were largely the restaurants and clubs in the Palm Springs area, the firm also delivered to a significant number of private residences whose owners maintained bar units that required syrups, CO_2, and servicing.

Art countered, "I just know that we haven't touched the market potential that we're sitting on. Our people are just serving the business that we have. Nobody is drumming up new business except us, and we have limited time to recruit. It's a mistake to expect Larry, Moe, and Curly to sell as well as deliver the goods."

"Nobody questions that, Art, it's just that we can't afford to support a separate salesperson with the 37 percent gross margin we get," Dan responded.

"Maybe we should try some of this telemarketing that I've been reading about. Let's get on the telephone and start dialing for customers. Or how about direct mail?" Art persisted.

"Or how about that plain old advertising in the *Desert Sun* that you keep resisting. And how about the home show? Let's get a booth there, if you want some new customers. Do *you* want to go stand there for 2 days over the weekend? I don't! I want to go to the river and kick back." Frustrated, Dan heaved a deep sigh. He and Art had been having this discussion each week for 2 months without finding a solution.

Art looked at Dan for a few moments, then asked, "How are we going to settle this? We have to do something to make this business grow, or we're dead in the long run. Right now we're just floating down the river."

The two partners had at times talked about dissolving their partnership but had dismissed the idea because they really enjoyed working together and neither one of them wanted the full responsibility for running the business.

"I don't know how we're going to settle this," Dan answered. "But I agree we must do something."

1 What is the basic problem in this situation?

2 Dan and Art come to you asking what they should do. What advice would you give them?

3 How much sales volume would a sales rep have to generate to justify a total cost of $40,000 a year if the partners were willing to pay 10 percent of sales for the additional volume? Should the 10 percent commission be paid on just the new orders the sales rep takes, or should the rep get 10 percent on all future sales from each new customer?

4 Develop a new-customer generation program for this company for a budget of $10,000.

CASE 3-2: Electroptics, Inc.—What Should the Reps Do?

"Welcome to our 1991 Sales Jamboree. The next 3 days should be exciting. They may well change the way we will sell our products in the future. We may even manage to get in some solid work sessions between our sets of tennis." Bill Wooden, president of Electroptics, smiled at the forty-one sales reps attending the company's annual sales conference at Marriott's Grand Isle resort in Honolulu, Hawaii. The reps had gathered to plan the company's sales efforts for the coming year. The firm's management believed and practiced a form of participatory management that had proved successful over the previous 12 years of the firm's existence.

Electroptics had been formed in 1978 by Bill and Nancy Wooden to commercially exploit some of Nancy's discoveries in the field of optics and laser technology. While Nancy confined her efforts for the company to research and development, her husband threw himself into the commercialization of the enterprise.

Originally, the firm sold mainly to research organizations. However, with the commercialization of laser equipment, the company's growth was based largely on sales to manufacturers that incorporated the optics or laser devices into their products. For example, the company's largest customer was a Japanese manufacturer of compact disk players. The rapid expansion of laser technology in the medical field was also providing the company with much new business.

Bill Wooden continued, "While you're out playing tennis this afternoon I want you to think about a problem of which you are all well aware. How can our overworked sales force cope with the increasing demands being placed on it? Our difficulties with locating new customers for our technology—which is enjoying a rapid expansion in usage in a wide variety of industries—combined with the increasing amount of time that we must spend giving much needed technical assistance to our customers poses a dilemma. We see two possible solutions: First, we can hire more sales reps. Second, we can split off the prospecting and technical service tasks from the sales rep's job. Perhaps there are other solutions. If so, I am certain you people will come up with them. We'll meet this evening after dinner for a late-night session on this matter. I'd like to leave here Sunday night with a decision on the problem. We'll meet here at 8 tonight."

Bill personally favored splitting up the sales rep job. He thought that prospecting should be done by the marketing organization using public relations, advertising, and trade shows to generate leads to prospects. He thought that technical service should be rendered by a separate set of people hired specifically to do that task.

However, "Big Red" Ryan, the sales manager, disagreed with Bill's plan. "Let's leave well enough alone. If it ain't broke, why fix it? We're doing great right now. Let's just hire some more reps, and let them keep doing what they have been doing all along."

Nancy Wooden, as a company director, had suggested that perhaps it was time for the company to hire a marketing manager to handle problems such as this one. But Bill was not enthusiastic about taking on the additional overhead posed by a marketing manager.

The discussion that evening failed to resolve the question, since the sales force was evenly divided between the two alternatives. One group wanted to divest itself of prospecting and servicing responsibilities, while the other group wanted to hire more reps, thus allowing them each to have smaller territories. One comment by a sales rep seemed to reflect the feelings of the latter group. "I want to do more than just sell. I like being the total manager of my territory. I don't want other people into my accounts. And I don't want to lose an account because some other guy messed up on some technical problem."

Questions arose about which strategy would be easiest to execute. Would it be easier to hire more sales reps or more technical assistants? What would the cost implications be?

The group of reps who wanted to divest itself of prospecting and servicing tasks seemed to be saying that they really did not like doing those things anyway.

One rep suggested that whatever action was taken should be done slowly, one region at a time. That comment was countered by Big Red's observation that a sequential policy might not be possible for prospecting, that if the company were going to make a change, the new policy would have to be enacted for the whole operation.

At the end of the evening, the problem seemed to be dumped back into management's lap, since there was no consensus of opinion.

1 Evaluate each of the alternatives.

2 What would you recommend the company do about the problem?

CHAPTER FOUR

WHY PEOPLE BUY

CHAPTER FOUR

WHY PEOPLE BUY

When a fellow says it hain't the money, but the principle o' the thing, it's th' money.
Abe Martin

After studying the material in this chapter you should:

☐ Realize that a thorough understanding of consumers and why they buy is essential for the truly competent salesperson

☐ Grasp the essentials of the various theories of motivation, particularly the self-concept theory

☐ Know that a person will not buy a product that is incompatible with, or threatens, some aspect of his or her self-concept

PROFILE OF A MOTIVATOR

Marlin Hershey, marketing student

Bryant College, Smithfield, R.I., 1991

Marlin started a lawn care business in high school by selling the service door to door each spring. He hired his classmates to do the work while he supervised and collected the money. Because mulch prices were rising so rapidly, he started ordering it wholesale by the truckload and selling it to his customers slightly below the going retail price.

At Bryant, he started a T-shirt business using trendy school designs and had his fraternity brothers selling them room to room in the dorms. He also produced designs for sale on the Florida beaches during the spring break. The project financed his vacation and helped pay for school.

Marlin then began selling for Nu-Skin, a multilevel direct sales organization with a product that seemed to appeal to some segment of the market. Marlin's income from the reps working for him was $1,000 a month. The commissions on his own sales added to that. His goal was to earn more than $2,000 a month by the time he graduated which would support him while he pursued entrepreneurial ventures. Marlin works hard, is persuasive, and is able to get people to work with him and buy from him. He's a motivator.

Your product was the best for the prospect's application. Your price quotation was the most competitive. You worked hard on the formal proposal and the presentation went well. By all logic, the purchasing agent should have bought your goods, but it didn't happen. The firm stayed with its supplier. If you don't understand it, then you don't understand the real reason why people do the things they do—why they buy or don't buy.[1]

Perhaps you underestimated the strength of the bond between the buyer and the existing supplier. Perhaps your firm somehow poses risks to the buyer. Perhaps the buyer just did not like you. Perhaps the benefits you offered weren't enough to overcome the inertia preventing a change in vendors. While the list of possibilities is lengthy, you should be able to pinpoint the real reasons blocking the sale.

The past two decades have seen a tremendous increase in the study of human behavior as it affects marketing. We now realize that the behavioral sciences have much to contribute to the study of marketing and to its practice. One of the areas of greatest importance is that of motivation.[2]

The essence of selling is motivation: the motivation of someone to do what you want—obey you, hire you, promote you, or buy from you. While you no doubt have learned much about motivating human behavior from your daily dealings with people, still you can sharpen your motivational skills by examining some of the material recently provided by the behavioral sciences. Much of this chapter is based on such research.

Most sane behavior is motivated. Though the actual motives underlying human activity may not be readily apparent to an observer, people do have reasons for their actions. When a prospect buys something, the action is motivated behavior; people do not buy things without reasons. Typically, a good persuader attempts to ascertain the major or strongest reason which will motivate the desired behavior in the prospect and then concentrates the presentation on it to keep the prospect's attention on the things which are evidently most important. It is a serious mistake for someone selling tires to keep stressing their low price if the prospect is most interested in safety. Such an emphasis on price may lose the sale, because the prospect may believe she would be giving up what is most desirable—safety—for the low price.

NO SELLING WITHOUT BUYING

In any study of selling, the words that should be emphasized are "buyer," "buy," and "buying." The modern viewpoint approaches the subject by regarding the selling process as a buying process. Strictly speaking, the salesperson does not *sell* anything but merely helps to condition the mind of the prospect so that the latter *buys*. There is no change in the mind of the salesperson regarding the merits of the proposition. But, if the sale is to be made, the *prospect's* mind must undergo a change.

A sale is made, not in the mind of the salesperson, not over the counter or desk, but in the mind of the buyer. The seller's every word, every gesture should have only one objective—the making of the right impression on the mind of the prospect.

This is merely another way of saying that every persuader, whether selling in person or through the written word, must cultivate the knack of penetrating the prospect's mind and trying to fathom what goes on there. This habit of giving consideration to the other person's reactions benefits you also by making you a more agreeable person, more popular, more highly regarded as a friend. And it definitely helps to make you a better seller. As the Spanish writer Baltasar Gracián (1601–1658) put it,

> First, guess a man's ruling passion, appeal to it by word. Find out each man's thumbscrew. You must know where to get at anyone. All men are idolators; some of fame, others of self interest, most of pleasure. Skill consists in knowing these idols in order to bring them into play. Knowing a man's mainspring of motive, you have as it were, the key to his will.

PEOPLE ARE DIFFERENT[3]

Not all prospects are alike, nor will they react in the same way to the same stimulus. Their *backgrounds* are different, so they have differing sets of values. One person has been taught to be thrifty, while another thinks of money as something to be spent as quickly as possible. One has a burning urge to study, to learn, to acquire knowledge; another has never entered the world of ideas and lives for the satisfaction of the senses.

These basic differences are fundamental, permanent aspects of the buyer's personality. They influence behavior in about everything we do. They have been termed by some psychologists "frames of reference" and include such behavior tendencies as conservatism or radicalism, optimism or pessimism; they are deeply rooted and generally guide our actions.

People Communicate Who and What They Are

You can tell a good deal about a prospect's frames of reference by closely observing his or her previous purchases, because the factors which influence a person to buy or not to buy a particular article are basically similar to the factors which have influenced previous purchases. We may go even further and say that they are similar to the factors which influence *general* behavior. For example, a man has owned a succession of medium-priced black cars, although he could afford a dashing model of a more expensive make. This puzzled his friends until he chanced to let drop a remark that his mother had drilled into him the attitude that he should always "stay humble." And he stayed humble in *everything* he did. His cars matched this personality trait, as did his garb, his office, his home. A person's desk will usually reveal similar inner attitudes.

Figure 4–1 illustrates the forces which forge your frame of reference. They are a complex combination of your total experiences in life, which you at best

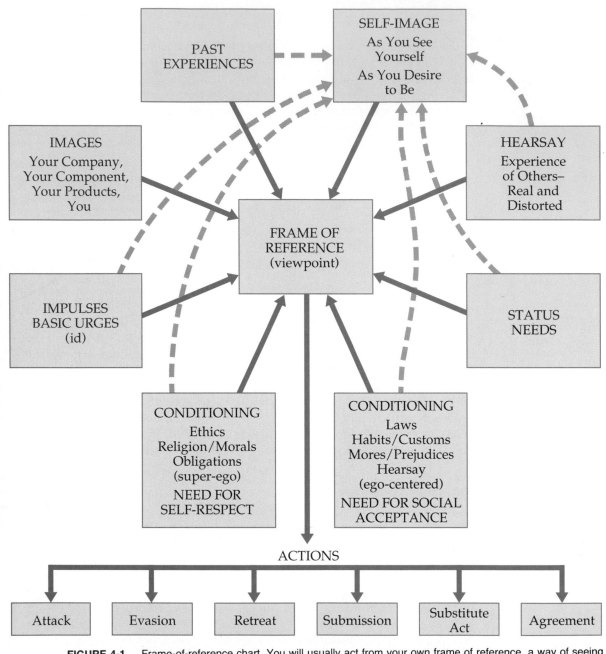

FIGURE 4-1 Frame-of-reference chart. You will usually act from your own frame of reference, a way of seeing things that is conditioned by many factors: status needs, past experience, and so on. Most important of these, however, is your self-image, which changes as you mature and grow. (*Sales Management*, June 1, 1967, p. 49)

can only partially comprehend. But it is not necessary to understand a prospect's complete frame of reference in order to make a sale. Many times you need know only one small aspect of the prospect's motivational structure. Just knowing that an executive wants to be modern and progressive may be enough to sell him some new equipment.

People Are Different at Different Times

People are different from each other, but also the same person is different under different conditions. Conditions such as the following may cause a person to react differently at various times:

- Environmental factors, such as temperature, humidity, altitude, ventilation, illumination, distraction, or other stimuli
- General organic states, such as fatigue, hunger, sleepiness, moodiness, comfort or discomfort, anger, anxiety, frustration, or triumph
- Specific conditions induced by chemicals, such as alcohol, tobacco, caffeine, morphine, medicine taken for pain or hay fever
- Previous events, such as a job loss, a traffic ticket, or a fight with a spouse
- Incentives and motives, such as praise, reproof, rivalry, reward, or punishment

If you have just returned from a vacation, you're in no frame of mind to talk vacation tours with the representative of a travel agency. The minimum-wage earner who has just inherited $100,000 is a very different person from the one he was a week before. If you've recently bought a home, you'll now react very differently to certain sales stimuli than you did while you were a renter. After a poor night's sleep or an indigestible meal you will find your reactions changed.

The purchasing agent for a factory which has suffered from breakdowns in machines will respond positively to claims that the seller can give quick service on repair parts. The buyer who has had an accident of some sort will be in the mood to listen sympathetically to an offer of a product guaranteed against such accidents. An element of timing exists in many sales situations.

One young man selling auto insurance called only on people who had just had an accident—the event had prepared their minds to accept an appeal to buy better coverage. He was most successful.

One must analyze the prospect to determine just how he or she is likely to react to certain stimuli at one particular moment. Although a knowledge of former behavior may serve as a valuable guide, the salesperson is not safe in assuming that a prospect will invariably react in the same manner to the same stimuli. Indeed, the prospect is never entirely normal when in the presence of a salesperson. People interact in sometimes unpredictable ways. A normally easygoing person may suddenly change when confronted with a salesperson whose behavior in some way is particularly irritating. Such a person may throw up defenses, be hypercritical, or be more sensitive to imagined insults.

Or the same easygoing prospect may suddenly become aggressively belligerent.

There are also inhibiting factors to consider. We sometimes refer to an individual as "uninhibited," but everyone is restrained by a variety of constraints. For example, one person may be restrained by a reluctance to do anything dishonest, while another might feel no such compunction.

The salesperson learns to observe and size up her prospect, to discover what causes him to act favorably on a suggestion and what holds him back. The salesperson's approach to this problem may be strictly common sense and not couched in scientific terms.

Glance back at those five sets of conditions which may influence the prospect's reaction. Salespeople have little control over the first four. To be sure, you may be able to interview the prospect in a salesroom where lighting and temperature are favorable and where distractions are absent. You may buy the prospect a dinner. You may time a call on an important prospect so that as many of these factors are in your favor as possible. But generally speaking, you are forced to take these things as they come, recognizing them and handling your presentation accordingly.

The fifth group is different. This area involves motivation and it is in this field that you must be something of an expert. You *can* control your appeals to various human motives that prompt action. Various incentives to action can be utilized. In other words, you *can* control the stimuli which act on the prospect to induce the desired reactions.

DRIVES

These reactions to stimuli are of two main kinds: (1) inborn or innate reactions or reflexes and (2) conditioned reflexes, which are acquired during one's life.

Early psychologists used instinct to explain nearly everything that people did; we behave as we do because we are born that way. Various lists of instincts were compiled, but no two of them were alike. Some mentioned only one instinct—self-love. Others suggested two—egoism and altruism. Some distinguished 50 or 60 instincts. Actually, thousands of "instincts" have been listed by one psychologist or another. Certain writers refer to "neural predispositions" as equivalent to instinct.

Psychologists have engaged in fierce debates over whether certain human reactions are inborn or acquired. Admittedly, it is sometimes difficult to distinguish between them. In an effort to find a term sufficiently general to gain wide acceptance, psychologists have adopted the word "drive." In the strictly psychological sense, drive is a motivating factor of personality—such as wish, purpose, ideal—which regulates and directs one's conduct. Human and animal activity contains countless goals and hence innumerable drives.

Some of these drives are clearly physiological: hunger, thirst, sex, need for rest, and the desire for the most comfortable bodily temperature. Food and drink satisfy a fundamental demand. Stoves and refrigerators are sold because they appeal to the human being's desire for good food and drink. But by no means are all the efforts of salespeople directed at appealing to these primary desires. Enough food and water to sustain life, a rude shelter from the elements, and clothing sufficient to keep one warm are not too hard to obtain—the inmates of properly managed prisons have these.

Clearly, the persuader is mainly concerned with our learned wants. And these wants may be powerful driving forces, sometimes more powerful than instinctive urges, especially when instinctive wants are pretty well satisfied. The well-to-do couple who *must* have a luxurious home in the right part of town is not simply providing shelter for their family, yet the strength of their drive for that home may far exceed the drive of others who merely seek a functional house in which to live. On the other hand, those who seek fame in business have a multitude of other drives—power, wealth, self-esteem, and so forth.

THEORIES OF MOTIVATION

No one overall theory of motivation has been universally accepted. Various authorities have taken slightly different approaches to the problem. As a result, it is necessary for us to approach this discussion of buying motives from several directions in the hope that you can thereby obtain a more comprehensive understanding of the topic.

Semantics are a barrier to the study of motivation when you compare the writings of one authority with those of another. Frequently two writers are talking about the same basic forces but use different words to describe their concepts.

The three approaches to understanding buying motives which seem to be most fruitful for salespeople are: (1) the traditional emotional-rational approach, (2) the problem-solving approach, and (3) the self-concept theory. Each of these is discussed below.

TRADITIONAL APPROACH

The traditional marketing approach to buying motives divides them into two major groups: (1) rational and (2) emotional. The terms "rational" and "emotional" permeate practically all discussions of buying behavior; therefore, it is necessary to understand them before going into the more modern, more complex theories of motivation.

Rational Buying Motives

Rational buying motives concern such matters as price, cost-in-use, durability, servicing, reliability, length of useful usage, and, in general, *any consideration affecting the full long-run cost of the article to the purchaser*. Classical economists predicated much of their theory on the basis of the so-called "economic man," who was a sort of ambulatory computer, able to feed into his brain a mass of cost and performance data and produce an answer—that is, the most economical behavior pattern he could follow. Obviously, this is too much to expect where the factors are numerous and complex; the human brain is unequal to such a formidable calculation. The rational motive, however, does play a role in practically all buying. As was noted previously, many times a salesperson's problem is to select the appeals that will most effectively stimulate rational motives, even though the prospect may already desire to buy to satisfy emotional drives. This is called *rationalization* of one's behavior. Many, if not most, people like to believe that they are behaving rationally even though the real drives underlying their actions are emotional.

This definition of the rational buying motive may appear narrow, but if we are to attempt a clear-cut distinction between rational and emotional motivation, it seems that we must make it on this basis. We should bear in mind, however, that this factor of long-run cost is not limited to dollars-and-cents cost. It may involve cost in time or in degree of labor, in surrender of security. But the fact remains that a rational decision even in such matters is made on the basis of long-run cost compared with the long-run benefits.

In general, business executives attempt to buy as rationally as possible, but they, too, frequently fail to be completely rational. Personal friendships, prestige names, reciprocity, and status symbols may influence their buying decisions. The industrial sales rep must never be deluded into thinking that there is a completely rational individual across the desk, for that executive or purchasing agent is moved by emotions just like anyone else, and many times these emotions take precedence over rational pressures. Many industrial transactions can be explained only in terms of personal friendships or other emotional buying motives which are more fully discussed in the next section.

One noted authority on power (defined as the ability to control the behavior of other people) is the psychologist J. M. Jellison, who insists that people behave as they do because they perceive external rewards for doing so.[4] If you want people to buy from you, then you must somehow communicate to them some future rewards for doing so.

Emotional Buying Motives

Long lists of emotional motives, like security, comfort, ego, emulation, pride, sex, recreation, and many others, have been compiled by various authorities. Although it is helpful to study such lists and discussions, you must realize that a complete classification of *all* emotional buying motives is impossible. Our emotions are so complex that it is difficult to isolate each motive and classify it. Two executives may purchase exactly the same luxurious office furniture for ostensibly the same emotional motive of ego gratification. However, the "motive mixes" underlying these two purchases could be quite different. The first executive may have purchased her furniture to prove to her fellow employees that she possesses certain status *within* the organization. The other executive may have purchased his office furnishings to impress such *outsiders* as competitors, other business executives, and customers—to convey an image of success, largely for business reasons. The salesperson must be able to detect these differences in buying motives, because it is a serious mistake to appeal to the first executive in terms of external prestige when internal status is desired. Similarly, the second executive would not respond to appeals dealing with internal prestige alone. Some of the more common emotional buying motives follow.

Physical Pleasure, Comfort, Avoidance of Effort   Every human being has the same physiological needs. Humans require food, drink, sleep, and a temperature that is not too hot or too cold. Many humans spend most of their effort in acquiring these basic necessities; others are able to satisfy these with a portion of their efforts and go on from there to acquire other desirable things. This urge is basic and accounts for the purchase of food, an easy-riding car, a good mattress, a comfortable lounge chair, shelter, clothes, and conveniences about the home or place of work. Washing machines, vacuum cleaners, automatic dishwashers, elevators and escalators, beverages, ranch-style houses, and precooked foods, as well as cars with automatic transmission, power brakes, air conditioning, and power steering, are all examples of things which we value because they satisfy this urge.

The absence of something that gives us pleasure may cause discomfort or pain. Perhaps this discomfort or pain is merely the necessity of putting forth physical or mental effort—but to many of us effort is akin to pain. This is a generalization that has exceptions. Lots of people enjoy physical effort; their muscles seem to demand it.

Play and Relaxation   The drive for play is basic in both humans and animals. Psychologists have developed a theory of play; they believe it to be mentally therapeutic. Children are encouraged to play out their troubles in "play therapy." There is much evidence that adults seek play as relief from stress, frustration, aggressive pressures, and inhibitions. The vacation with pay is a routine fringe benefit of nearly every job. Parks and playgrounds offer recreational facilities; the automobile and airplane afford means of reaching these and other places; movies, radio, television, and athletic events cater to the urge for play. Books and magazines satisfy this urge, too. Clothing manufacturers are turning out very successful sportswear lines; catalog retailers such as L.L. Bean and Land's End that specialize in sportswear and sporting goods have had phenomenal success. Winter and summer resorts have mushroomed.

The desire for play is manifested in many ways in our society. Note the success of stores decorated in some make-believe decor; erect a play house, and customers will come play with you. Witness the success of many nonsense advertising campaigns; Mother Nature reacts adversely to being fooled by margarine, while the Jolly Green Giant goes "Ho Ho Ho," and the Ener-

Winter and summer sports of all kinds appeal to our drive for recreation and physical well-being. The market for sports equipment and sportswear has grown tremendously in recent years as most families and individuals pursue an interest in some form of physical activity.

gizer Bunny makes unscheduled appearances. Say "Come with me to Fantasyland!" and step aside lest you be trampled by the horde. Disneyland does not make its money on children; they are simply the excuse for millions of men and women who want to escape the realities of their boring or harried lives by "taking the kids" to Disneyland.

Play theory leads to some rather useful ideas for the salesperson. Obviously someone who wants to play needs playmates. Many successful sales reps owe their fortunes to their social abilities. Successful executives have a limited number of people with whom they can relax. Their own people in the organization are usually precluded because of managerial considerations. They may prefer not to let their hair down with peers in the business community for image reasons. They often have few acquaintances from whom to choose friends. The adroit salesperson may be able to fill just the right role for such individuals. If the executive wants to escape to the ski slopes, a short vacation to Sugarbush may develop a lasting relationship that would never be achieved in any other manner. But remember that people must play; the sales rep's problem is to discover just what form that play takes in a customer's behavior pattern.

This aspect of selling has bothered many women who were considering a sales career. It needn't! Most male buyers don't expect or want to socialize with saleswomen beyond a friendly business lunch. It would pose problems for them.[5]

Esthetic Pleasure We derive strong satisfaction or pleasure from the impact of the beautiful on our senses and emotions. This may be beauty of form or color or sound. It may be found in art, music, literature, or nature, in the home or at work. We have only to look about us to realize how strongly this motive has influenced the design of thousands of items, such as auto-mobiles, washing machines, kitchen sinks, stoves, furniture, architecture and landscaping, clothing, and interior decorating of home, factory, office, and store. The purely utilitarian and functional approach has been modified by this determination to produce things that will also appeal to the esthetic motive.

The ascendance of these three motives (comfort, play, and beauty) is a result of our discarding the harsh ethics inherited from our pioneer-Puritan ancestors. For them life was hard, work was arduous, conveniences were few, and leisure was almost nonexistent. Idleness was a sin, pleasure was achieved only by ceasing work; so pleasure was almost sinful too. Traces of this older thinking persist but are diminishing.

The smart salesperson capitalizes on this drive by selling particularly well-designed products and by displaying them in such a way that these virtues are brought out. And it does no harm to point out to the prospect, "Isn't it beautiful? It's the best-looking widget made!"

Self-Esteem, Pride, Ego Striving, Power, Status   Whatever we call it, all of us have it. We want to be appreciated, to be complimented, to be made to feel important. No salesperson can afford to forget this motive; indeed, many authorities on salesmanship assert that this is the most powerful of all buying motives.

Not only must we feel important but we crave recognition from others. Robinson Crusoe may have felt a satisfying sense of personal adequacy before his man Friday appeared, but it obviously was tremendously enhanced by the gratitude and veneration displayed by his faithful servant. This desire for the approval of others leads us to do things merely because society has laid down certain behavior patterns as correct. We strive to climb in society or to earn election to exclusive clubs or college organizations; we labor diligently to become proficient in athletics or music; we seek the spotlight by becoming entertainers; we cultivate acceptable social manners.

Why do rich people occasionally leave thousands of dollars to elevator operators, taxi drivers, or waiters? Simply because these people have been kind or have shown respect or affection, thus helping the benefactor feel that he or she was appreciated and liked.

Surveys indicate that people who stop trading at certain stores do so because the salespeople have shown indifference, which is simply another way of saying they act as if the customer were unimportant. Perhaps their offense was merely being slow to greet the customer, but this wounded the latter's self-esteem.

An appreciation of this very human trait makes it natural for the salesperson to use indirect methods in place of the often-offensive direct methods. It is more tactful to use indirection, because this recognizes the right of the other person to feel important. We therefore merely *suggest* instead of *dictate*. In the long run, people like to make their own decisions, at least in matters that concern them intimately and on which they feel competent to decide. We all resent backseat drivers. So always try to present your views so that prospects can buy without feeling that they have been forced into it. They must be made to feel that they did the buying, that they made a wise decision of their own free will.

The smart salesperson, willing to cater to the prospect's desire to feel important, will not do all the talking. This seller will learn to listen, acknowledging with courteous deference the opinions of the prospect. Be careful not to show off. Don't claim to be the final authority on the subject or boast that you will tell the prospect something which the latter does not know. Thus you should shun such introductory clauses as, "Maybe you never thought of this angle, but—" or "You probably didn't know this before, but—." Rather, be quick to impute your own ideas to the prospect or to someone else. If you can say, "As you remarked a few minutes ago" (or "the last time I was here"), the prospect will more readily accept the idea.

The common clause, "See what I mean?" irritates many listeners, who mentally react, "Of course I do. You think I'm a moron?" The frequent use of the words "you know" can be equally irritating, particularly to people who are proud of their language. It is a careless habit that has seemingly swept the nation. It is the result of thinking that you must keep talking even though you have nothing particular to say. Silence is a much better alternative.

The wise person utilizes praise judiciously. It has been said that praise is one of our least developed resources. It costs so little and pays such huge dividends. In passing, note that it usually pleases a person to be complimented on some less obvious skill or trait, as when a beautiful woman is told that she has a wonderful mind. Someone said, "Make a man like himself a little bit better, and he will henceforth like you very much."

Imitation or Emulation

Pure imitation, such as that displayed by monkeys and small children, is found to a certain extent in adult human beings, but most people imitate others in the purchase of certain things with the idea that by so doing they are showing themselves superior to others. To this extent, then, this motive is akin to the urge for self-importance, because we imitate those who are, in our opinion, more important in this respect than we are. Teenagers dress and style their hair in the way that is currently popular with their reference peer group; their mothers labor to master the system of the currently accepted bridge authority; Dad buys a more expensive car than he can afford because many men whom he admires drive that make. This is emulation.

You can utilize this buying motive in the sale of many things but must always be certain that the person or persons whom you are suggesting that the prospect imitate are among those to whom the prospect looks up. Only then will being like them satisfactorily inflate the buyer's ego.

Usually this motive is automatically working in the mind of the prospect and little may have to be said about it during the sale. If one chooses to bring this motive into the open, one must do so with care, because people do not like to talk about it.

In the selling of fashion goods, appeal to this motive is important. It can be utilized best, also, in selling to prospects who are not entirely sure of their own judgment. Skilled purchasing agents and experienced buyers for retail stores may resent a sales rep's use of this appeal, feeling that it implies a lack of knowledge on their part; they prefer to use their own judgment. In selling to any opinionated person, you will be well advised to soft-pedal this appeal.

Financial Gain This is probably the motive to which most salespeople appeal, especially those selling to manufacturers or to merchants who resell the product.

It may be argued, and with some logic, that this is not a genuine *emotional* motive. And sometimes it is not, as in the case of the purchasing agent for a manufacturer or the buyer for a chain of retail stores. Their objective is simply to make more profit for the corporation which employs them, and they have no knowledge of or interest in what is done with the money they thus help to make. It is not theirs to spend, and it does not satisfy any emotional yearning except to make them feel they have done a good job.

But many people have formed a *habit* of trying to make or save money, without giving much thought to what they will do with that money after they have it. Through years of directed thinking and action, the money has become an end in itself. This is not rational behavior. When the buyer's attention is focused on what she plans to buy with the money saved or made, her emotions may play an important part in her decision, if she hopes to satisfy some emotional urge by the purchase.

Admitting all this, it is still smart salesmanship to point out, when practicable, the wants which can be satisfied with the money gained by accepting the salesperson's proposition.

This motive of money gain has two phases. The one prompts the buyer to *make* money; the other emphasizes more strongly the *saving* of money. Buyers of the first class are willing to *spend* money to make *more* money. They are large-visioned people whose aim is not *saving* money—there is nothing of the miser in them. The making of money is more of a game, a competitive sport, than a mere accumulation of wealth. Money is the symbol of power, of success, which is their real aim. Such people are more willing to take a chance with their money than are people of the "saver" type.

Statements such as "Nothing ventured, nothing gained!" or "It takes money to make money" may strike paydirt with such prospects. Many door-to-door sales propositions appeal to this desire when they promise to pay the buyer for every name furnished to the sales rep if that person later buys the deal. The success of such propositions indicates the effectiveness of the money-gain appeal. The appeal of something for nothing is still strong. In the early 1980s real estate agents in many parts of the country seldom failed to mention to prospects that the property they were considering would be a good investment. "It will appreciate over the next few years."

To the buyer of the second class—the saver—you should use a different appeal. This individual *saves* rather than *makes* money. The saver's outlook is narrower—he is more cautious. To him a bird in the hand is likely to be more desirable than two in the bush. Business is not a sport to be pursued for the thrill of winning but merely because it may add something to the wealth already accumulated.

Statements such as "A penny saved is a penny earned!" or "Why pay more? This will do the same work for less money," or "Why should you have to pay for their advertising?" will often hit home. This desire to save money can be effective in many sales in which the circumstances might indicate otherwise. One man of means purchased a Lincoln Towncar rather than a Cadillac simply because he could save $1,000 for an equivalent model; he would have preferred the Cadillac but could not see paying $1,000 extra—he did not like it *that* much better. Many people with money do not like to feel "ripped off." With those of little means, the saving appeal can be explosive; just the illusion of a saving can bring forth a sale. Witness the success of many so-called discount houses whose prices are frequently little, if at all, lower. The word "discount" can work wonders, as can the word "wholesale."

Acquisitiveness   The acquisitive or possessive urge may manifest itself in many ways. A few of us hoard things, more of us collect things, and most of us like to own things. We seem to have an urge to possess, to call things "mine."

Much of the underlying motivation toward home ownership is the basic desire of people to own land and property; to rent makes them feel rootless, homeless, insecure. The ownership of property is one avenue people travel in their search for security.

The retailer who refuses to stock a new line of goods until the salesperson threatens to give the exclusive agency to the storekeeper's competitor is allowing her action to be governed by this trait.

When the prospect who has had a computer on trial for 30 days confronts the painful prospect of surrendering it, the instinct of possession comes to the front and insists upon the article's being kept. The automobile saleswoman plays upon this motive when she allows her prospect to drive the car. Once behind the steering wheel, the average driver imagines himself the owner of the car and rebels at the idea of giving it up.

Romantic and Sexual Drives, Companionship Needs   The desire to be with, or to appeal to, members of the opposite sex accounts for the purchase of many things such as cosmetics, clothes, tours, hair styling, and tickets to movies and concerts.

Market researchers predict that the youth-oriented focus of advertising campaigns over the past several decades will give way to sales appeals directed at seniors and baby-boomers now approaching middle-age as the percentage of the population in the under-thirty age bracket diminishes.

People of all ages have a need for companionship and romance; successful sales strategies are often geared to this need. Many times, illustrations showing the presence of the opposite sex in some relationship to the product will do the job better than words. For instance, over the years diverse products such as hair tonic ("There's something about an Aqua Velva man!"), automobiles (magazine ads or billboards with images of attractive women in open convertibles or alongside shiny sportscars), and carbonated soft drinks ("the Pepsi generation") have been sold with great success without much of a verbal sales message.

Sales campaigns in the seventies and eighties typically targeted youthful markets and often relied on the use of sexual inferences to catch audience attention (for instance, magazine and tv ads for Calvin Klein jeans).

In recent years, advertisers have become more conscious of the buying power of the post-war "baby-boom" generation, now approaching middle age, and of seniors, who are often financially well-off and living longer and healthier lives than ever before. Both groups represent a lucrative market for cosmetics, vacation packages, health-care products and services, restaurants, home-exercise equipment, recreational vehicles, and entertainment. Consequently, many recent sales messages aimed at companionship needs have focused on people of all ages just being together.

Physical and Mental Health, Physical Fitness   People have an inborn urge to live as long as they can; suicides are still rare enough as to be genuine news. It still holds true that "all that a man hath will he give for his life."

As young people, we do not worry much about dying or being ill. We have many years ahead of us, so each year is taken for granted. We may eat

People today are far more health-conscious than ever before and have demonstrated a growing interest in products and activities that promote good health and physical fitness. If you were planning to open a natural foods store, what motivations might you satisfy with the products you offer to your customers?

unwisely, sleep too little, and generally abuse our bodies, because the consequences are not yet evident. But after forty, it is different. Then we begin to watch our health, cut down on alcohol and tobacco, visit the doctor more often, and take vacations for health instead of purely for fun. We tend to rationalize, to explain our purchases on the grounds that they will promote health. We join golf or fitness clubs; we eat a more balanced diet; we buy "natural foods"; we force ourselves to run one more mile; we visit the dentist regularly. The fewer our probable remaining years on earth, the more jealous we are of each one and the harder we struggle to prolong our stay. The shrewd salesperson never overlooks this urge, knowing that it is powerful. Without it, humans would have vanished from the earth.

This desire for health may not be an end in itself; that is, health may be sought as a means to an end. In fact, it usually is, but this does not lessen its force as a buying motive.

It should be pointed out that in discussing health we include not only the negative aspect of avoiding illness but the *positive* aspect of physical fitness, of a condition in which we possess energy and zest for living. Life yields far more pleasure to people who enjoy abounding health than to those who are merely well enough to be "up and around."

A statement such as "You really ought to get more exercise" may sell a set of golf clubs or an exercise bicycle.

In the 1980s, health appeals have gained considerable strength. We are spending more money on preventative health activities—health spas, vitamins, and exercise equipment. People today are far more conscious of health than were their parents. It's a powerful motive.

Curiosity or the Desire for New Experience   We like to go places and do things, to travel and visit new scenes, to extract new thrills from life. This urge is found more strongly in the young than in the old. The salesperson often appeals to raw curiosity to get initial attention and interest but does not utilize this appeal so often in closing the sale, as it is rarely the motive that finally prompts the purchase.

An illustration of the use of curiosity in the narrower sense is found in the technique of a costume jewelry salesman who carries a small paper bag with samples he plans to show the next buyer he calls on. The buyer usually declares that she is not interested in looking at his line, whereupon he sets the bag on the counter and chats a few minutes. When the buyer asks him what is in the bag, he tells her that it contains some samples he is going to show another customer—some stuff she probably couldn't sell. At this stage he dashes out to check the parking meter. When he returns, the samples in the sack are out on the counter and the buyer is demanding just why he thinks she could not sell them.

The Urge to Create   People build rockets and model airplanes, design dresses, decorate their rooms, write poems, paint pictures, invent gadgets, grow flowers, make home movies. Football coaches devise new plays and systems of defense. All these activities and scores of others are creative. Many people who spend their working hours at some uncreative task find an outlet for their creative bent in hobbies. One of the rewards of gardening is the satisfaction of this urge.

One of the biggest obstacles that confronted the manufacturers of cake mixes was the reluctance of many homemakers to abandon the pleasure of exercising their imagination and skill in baking a cake. They wanted to *create*.

Desire for Justice and Right, Sense of Duty, Love of Others   These may be acquired motives, but we cannot deny their power. People have died for what they thought was right; they fight to obtain justice for themselves or others; they forgo pleasures for the higher satisfaction of feeling that they have done their duty. In the average adult, a sense of duty and the desire to be of service are intermingled with the wish to play a conspicuous role in public affairs, and the salesperson can utilize both appeals with success.

The appeal to such a motive yields better results when used on a conscientious prospect. Parental or romantic love, a selfless devotion to others, is a motive prompting millions of purchases daily.

The sales rep for room air conditioners calls on a family that already has one in the master bedroom. She says: "Like yourselves, my husband and I slept better after we bought our first conditioner." She then pauses and looks her prospects straight in the eye before continuing, "But it's a funny thing— since we got a second conditioner for the little ones' room, well, . . . now my husband and I can *really* sleep."

Fear or Caution   This motive is listed last because it is the antithesis of all the previously listed motives. All those motives are based on the search or desire for pleasurable results. Fear is simply being afraid that we cannot attain those results or that we may lose those pleasures after we have enjoyed them for a while.

We fear the loss of life, of health, of friends, of reputation, of security, of job, of money, of freedom, of comfort, of everything which we value. To fail to gain the things we crave or to lose them causes pain. Thus we conclude that we chiefly fear pain. It may be physical or mental, but it is pain and we strive to avoid it.

Fear is nature's way of preserving us from pain and even from destruction. Animals (including members of the human species) who are devoid of fear usually die an early and often violent death.

The fear motive is closely allied to caution and the desire for security. People buy insurance, homes, and bonds and stocks, or put money in the bank because they are trying to gain security for their old age or for a "rainy day." Fire extinguishers and sprinkler systems, locks for doors and windows, railroad signal devices, and a thousand items are bought because the buyer fears the consequences of not buying them and prefers the security she hopes to gain by having them.

As people grow older, the fear or caution motive becomes stronger. The twenty-year-old would choose a motorboat for its speed, while her father wishes to be assured that it will not easily capsize. Some salespeople believe that this motive of caution is stronger in older sections of the country than it is in those more recently settled.

Pension plans and the Social Security system help satisfy a yearning for security. We all would like to feel reasonably sure that we will not go hungry in our old age, that we will have a decent place to live. We want our children to have an education. We demand hospital care when we are ill. We are beset by doubts and fears for the future, and if sellers can dissolve these and reassure us that we are taken care of by their propositions, they have a good chance to sell because they are satisfying a real need.

THE PROBLEM-SOLVING APPROACH

The best way for the practical salesperson to view buying behavior may be to consider that all purchases are made to solve some problem. Homemakers must prepare attractive, palatable meals for their families approximately 20 times each week. They buy food products and kitchen equipment in the hope that they will solve the problem. Executives have a multitude of problems, such as controlling the operations of the firm, increasing sales volume, lowering costs, decreasing personnel turnover, bringing out new products, and increasing the effectiveness of subordinates. They may buy new computers in the hope that they can obtain better control over operations. They may buy new plant equipment in the hope of lowering production costs. They may buy better office equipment and furniture in the hope of improving morale and lowering turnover. They may even buy a new plant location in the hope that all their problems will be solved.

One corporation president was persuaded to move his research and development laboratory from Chicago to a small western town largely on the basis that it would solve many of the personnel problems in the Chicago plant. He felt that he had considerable deadwood in the Chicago organization and that by moving west he could select only the key people he wished to keep, thereby pruning the corporate tree. While this was the basic motive behind his decision, he sold the idea to the board of directors on the basis of lowering overhead costs and through other rational aspects. He pretended that the major motive was merely incidental.

The salesperson should never forget that the main things to be sold to any prospects are solutions to their problems. This is actually only a slight variation of the consumer benefit theory of marketing. It is axiomatic in all marketing that *one does not sell products but consumer benefits*. The homemaker isn't buying a vacuum cleaner for the metal, bolts, and motor it contains but because it delivers certain benefits, such as a cleaner house with less work. Since the benefits to the business executive are usually solutions to problems, the industrial salesperson should look for problems to solve.

On first obtaining the name of a prospect, you should immediately start looking for various problems which your product can best solve for that prospect. Walk in and ask an executive if such-and-such a problem is troubling the company. When the executive admits that there is indeed such a problem, ask for permission to make an intensive study of it to see if your product offers a good solution. After such a study has been made, present your recommendations showing how your product will solve that problem.

One system of selling, sometimes called the *consultative approach*, insists that its adherents never try to begin a sales presentation until the prospect's needs have been clearly identified and agreed upon by the prospect. Thus the first part of the sale is to ferret out problems.

This is one reason industrial selling is attractive to the college graduate. If you are selling a product which solves certain problems, the sales presentation will be more effective and pleasant than if the need for the product is somewhat questionable. Most of the time in industrial selling, the sales rep is making money for the customers.

Many products and services solve more than one problem. The installation of a computer system in a company may solve a serious shortage of adequate secretarial help, but it can also save executive time in getting out correspondence and communicating with people in the field. In general, the *more* problems a product solves, the stronger its appeal. Also the *seriousness* of the problem solved directly affects its attractiveness. Prospects seldom buy items which solve only minor problems; they must use their limited funds to solve the most pressing problems.

THE SELF-CONCEPT THEORY

The self-concept theory of buying behavior is closely tied to the emotional buying motive of ego gratification. However, it furnishes a much more definitive explanation of the consumer's behavior than just the simple assertion that you buy a given product in order to gratify your ego. This last statement is subject to the additional question, "Just how does it gratify your ego?" The theory of the self-concept is probably the best-integrated thought on buying behavior to date because it nicely combines the rational-emotional approach, the pleasure-pain theory, and the problem- solving approach into one unified concept. In addition, it is equally applicable to nonbuying behavior.

This theory of behavior is a contribution of behavioral scientists and is consequently being continually refined and supplemented. It has some semantic problems. Dealing with anything as complicated as a person's behavior involves many new concepts; unfortunately, different scientists have assigned slightly different tags to essentially the same concept. The terms "self-image" and "self-concept" are two examples. Others talk in terms of your perceptions of yourself. Clearly, the student of behavior must be well versed in terminology in order to comprehend what he or she reads.

The Different Selves That Determine Buying

The term "self-concept" is a bit misleading, for it implies that a person has but one self-concept. Actually, buying is strongly influenced by several different selves which each individual conceptualizes in the mind.

The Real Self   Your Real Self is what you think you really are. It is your concept of your abilities, personality, character, and other factors which go to make up your total existence. You could spend hours trying to list and describe this tremendous complexity that you believe to be you and still only scratch the surface. You may be only vaguely aware of some elements.

The Ideal Self   Your Ideal Self is how you would like to think of yourself. It is your personal goal. Much of your behavior is directed toward making your Real Self coincide with your Ideal Self. One small portion of a man's Ideal Self might be that he is a great football player. With the help of his coach his Real Self screams that he is only an average player. His Ideal Self would drive him to perfect his football skills and participate in the game with extreme vigor. Another player whose Ideal Self claims only average talents would behave differently.

A young woman might harbor as one facet of her Ideal Self that she owns her own business, yet her Real Self might be that she is an assistant store manager. She would do many things to move closer to her Ideal Self. If you could show her how she would move closer to her Ideal Self by buying from you, she would do so gladly.

The Real Other   The Real Other is your perception of others' perception of you—what other people think of you, your abilities, and your personality. Notice that this has nothing to do with how other people actually *do* see you; your Real Other may be far out of tune with reality. You may believe that other people see you as a social lion, while in reality they see you as an utter bore. The entire self-concept theory is based on how you perceive yourself and what *you* think others think of you. You can only translate, to the best of your ability, what others actually think of you by their actions around you. Unfortunately, many people have faulty translating devices. In protecting their Real Other from damage, they will either refuse to acknowledge many messages from other people or will mistranslate them into whatever they wish to hear. Never underestimate the power of the mind to screen out or distort messages it does not want to receive.

The Ideal Other   The Ideal Other is how you want other people to think of you. A man may want others to think that he is a good husband, a kind father, and a wise homemaker; he will buy and do many things to create this impression among the members of his reference groups. The woman who wants others to think of her as a successful business executive will not behave like the woman who wants others to see her as a good mother and home-maker.

The Ideal Other and the Ideal Self do not coincide completely; they can differ significantly. An executive may wish to be thought of by others as a generous employer, while secretly wanting to be as tightfisted as possible. Another person may wish others to believe him to be religious, but his Real Self has no religious feeling; this is hypocrisy. Most people want others to think of them as honest, but experience indicates that many harbor no such restrictions on their behavior in their Real Self.

In theory, individuals have many different Other concepts, as many as they have reference groups. That is, they want different groups to see them in different ways. Let's take a successful executive as an example. On the job she wants her work group to see her as an enlightened, intelligent, responsible executive. This Other will vary between subordinate and superior groups; she will want her subordinates to see her differently than her superiors do. She will want her peers to see her in a different light. At the country club she wants her friends to see her as a certain sort of person, while at home her family will have still different ideas about her.

Behavioralists have assigned the term "Generalized Other" to denote a total overall Ideal Other when discussing an individual without connection to a reference group. In strict theory, it is difficult to consider the behavior of an individual outside of a reference group.

Impact upon Behavior

People express themselves to others and to themselves with the goods and services they buy as well as through nonconsumptive activities. However, it should be pointed out that there are few activities in this society that do not require the consumption of something. The individual is constantly trying to bring the Real Self and Ideal Self closer together and to make the Real Other and the Ideal Other coincide.

Think of the impact of driving a new Mercedes upon your self-concepts. What are you trying to say to yourself and others? Wouldn't you receive much satisfaction from it even if others did not perceive your ownership— frequently the situation in large cities? Think of the effect upon your self-concepts as you stroll around a luxurious home among your fine furnishings, even though few people may be aware of your fortunate situation. All of these tangible symbols reinforce your self-concepts. Of course, when a purchase affects the Real Other also, then far more satisfaction is obtained. But the point is that many seemingly ostentatious purchases are made partly for purposes other than that of impressing other people. A wealthy man may buy expensive silk underwear solely for the effect it will have on his Real Self. It will serve to remind him constantly that he is highly successful. Perhaps nowhere are the differences in behavior between people with different self-concepts so evident as in the case of women who perceive themselves primarily as homemakers and those who see themselves primarily as professional career women.

The professional woman would want to join the clubs, associations, and organizations that were important in the industry and profession in which she worked. The homemaker would most likely be active in church, school, and civic organizations.

The key point is that the mind continually requires evidence of who and what it is. It is not enough to be highly successful if there is little or no evidence of it which can be perceived by oneself and others. You may be bothered by the constant reference herein to the desire for success. Remember that the mind seeks the knowledge that it is adequate; this drive for personal adequacy is basic. A person is successful when this adequacy is achieved. Success can be obtained at any level; it is a reference word denoting how close you are to your goals.

People constantly tell the world who and what they are by the various things they do, say, and *buy*. Most college students shout to all their status through their clothes, speech, and other less subtle forms of behavior. They want to make certain that no one confuses them with high school students or with working-class people of their own age. Similarly, members of the motorcycle set clearly proclaim their allegiances. This symbolic communication is

As a member of a gym or health club, you might acquire a number of valuable sales contacts. What would you say were the benefits of networking with individuals in your own reference group?

not in the least foolish, it serves as a silent but speedy means of communication. Walk into most offices and the boss can usually be identified by some symbols of the office. This saves embarrassment to all.

The Role of Reference Groups

Reference-group theory is extremely important to motivational analysis because of its effect on the individual's self-concepts.

Every person is a member of several sociological groups. You may be a member of a neighborhood, work, musical, religious, fitness, square-dancing, or golfing group. Your role in each of these groups may differ considerably. In some you may be a leader, while in others you may be a follower with little stature. In addition, there are usually groups which you wish to join— you are not now a member but wish to be. The price of admission to and dues for a group is conformance to its standards. You must behave within certain limits to be a member. Groups vary in their pressures for conformity. Some are quite strict and maintain narrow limits for behavior, while others are relatively permissive in the behavior they will tolerate, but all of them have some standards which must be observed if you wish to stay in the group's good graces.

These reference groups interact with the individual's self-concepts. You select your reference groups largely on the basis of your self-concepts. A man may visualize himself as a sportsman and join several athletic groups such as a country club, a rod and gun club, and a football booster organization. Once he is in those organizations, their memberships will sharpen his ideas about himself, his golfing buddies will let him know exactly how much of a hacker he is.

Study people's key reference groups, and you will know a great deal about them. With whom do they spend the most time? Whose company do they seek?

Your persuasive efforts will be most effective when you are dealing with those people in reference groups with which you are familiar. You will know and understand their values.

Four Levels of Abstractions

The self-concept is such a complex phenomenon that it is almost impossible to chart it completely. You can observe about four levels of abstraction in the self-concepts of most people (see Figure 4-2).

First, people have broad general feelings about themselves, such as, "I am a good husband and father. I am honest and law-abiding. I am rather shrewd, and no one puts anything over on me. I am athletically talented," etc. These are the broad, overall generalities which guide most of the individual's behavior, but one should not jump to the conclusion that all people hold these same general concepts.

The second level becomes a little more specific under each of these general categories. The man who visualizes himself overall as an athlete might see himself as a good runner, poor bowler, good skier, fair at football, and a totally disinterested hunter. A woman holding the general opinion of being a good business executive might qualify that thought with the ideas that she was good at selling, poor with paperwork, but great at managing people.

The third level becomes considerably more detailed. The athlete who believes he is a good skier might know as a Real Self that he is only an adequate skier while harboring an Ideal Self that he is an Olympic contender. These specific concepts will strongly influence his buying behavior. He would buy and use equipment similar to that used by other world-class skiers. He has to buy equipment and clothes that will help push his Real Self closer to his Ideal Self. He could not possibly appear before members of his immediate reference group wearing or using the "wrong" gear.

The fourth level becomes quite specific. He might see himself as great in the downhill but only passable in the slalom event. He will buy equipment that will reflect those thoughts.

While we have devoted our illustration to developing some of the ramifications of the self-concept of a skier, this same exercise can be repeated for each of the other segments of your self-concept. Naturally, you can become aware of your self-concept only with experience; experiences tell us what we can and cannot do successfully. Hence, it is only natural that the older you

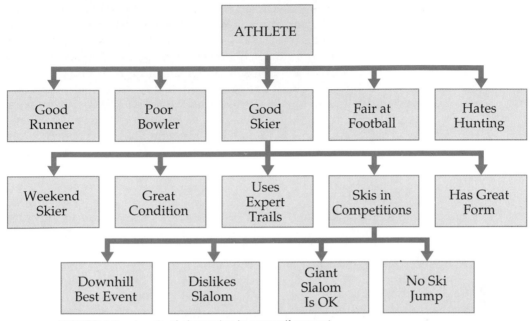

FIGURE 4-2 Levels of abstraction in your self-concept.

become, the clearer your various selves become to you. A young person has difficulty with the self-concept theory because such concepts are not yet clearly formed. Research on this theory has indicated that young college women have a far more definite idea of who and what they are than do their male counterparts.

Perhaps the foregoing appears forbiddingly theoretical and complex—too much so to be practical. Most people are likely to view with scorn academic theories. They avoid the use of the word "psychology" and prefer to use the term "human nature."

But this self-concept *is* human nature. And it is not so complex. It merely lets you ask these questions: What sort of person does this prospect think she is, and what would she like to be? What kind of person does she believe other people think she is? What would she like to have others think about her?

Of course, no one expects to obtain a complete self-concept of any prospect. But this is not necessary, because you need only a segment of the whole—the segment which affects the prospect's attitude toward buying what you are selling.

Naturally, the self-concepts of every individual are constantly changing, but this is not too difficult to detect. The small child abandons a dream of being an astronaut and settles for playing forward on the school basketball team. Later he or she erases this picture and imagines being at a drawing board designing buildings or at a 7-foot-long desk with an intercom, three telephones, and a framed picture of the family.

Too, some people formulate these self-concepts earlier in life and in more detail than do others. They are more introspective and imaginative. You may find it necessary to *help the prospect to formulate a self-concept* which has been vague or even unformed, as when the sales representative awakens some youthful prospect to the possibilities of climbing out of his humble environment and becoming a person of consequence.

But even with all these qualifications, this theory will be found practical and helpful because it forces you to *focus your attention on your prospects* and their hopes, needs, and aims in life. Only when you do this can you present your proposition most effectively.

Merchandise as an Aid to Focusing Self-Concepts

People use merchandise and other purchases as a means of superimposing their Real and Ideal selves over one another while strongly affecting the Other selves. The woman who buys a mink coat is using it to help move her Real Self closer to her Ideal Self and at the same time move the Real Other Self closer to the Ideal Other Self. The manager who feels that she is an important executive will frequently surround herself with many symbols of her status, such as luxurious office equipment and furniture, so that other people will recognize her high place in the hierarchy while she is continually reminding herself that her Real and Ideal Selves are now quite close. This executive for the same reasons may prefer to drive a Jaguar and to live in the most desirable section of town and may regard with satisfaction the swimming pool in her yard. All this consumptive behavior is designed to serve the same end—to help her superimpose more of her Real Self on her Ideal Self. These goods serve as a constant reminder to her and to others of what role she is playing in life and what goals she has attained.

Using the Self-Concept

Quaker Oats capitalized upon the self-concept theory in advertisements by portraying a homemaker as saying that when she feeds her children Quaker Oats for breakfast, she "knows she has done her best for them."

If a woman sees herself as a socialite, the social aspects of the purchase should be presented with emphasis on the fact that women whom she recognizes as social leaders have bought the product, proving that it is the fashionable thing to do. On the other hand, if the woman sees herself as being essentially a homemaker, such appeals could be disastrous. Instead, the salesperson should emphasize, "You owe it to your family!"

A word processor saleswoman can tell much about the concepts of the business executives upon whom she calls by observing the environment in which they work. One executive may have surrounded himself with modern equipment and a fine working environment, while the next works in some dingy hole with outdated equipment. The saleswoman now must vary her presentation to take into consideration these obviously different self-concepts. The first prospect probably sees himself as a progressive and successful business executive. He can best be sold by implying that a word processor is the mark of a truly efficient modern office, that typewriters are passé. The second executive seems to be of the old school—those who pinch pennies and discard machines only when they wear out; she probably believes that she runs an efficient operation and prides herself on her low overhead. She can best be sold by stressing the actual out-of-pocket costs which can be *saved* by operating with smaller office payroll.

Barriers to Buying

To continue with the self-concept theory of buying behavior, it becomes logical that barriers can prevent a prospect with purchasing authority from buying a given product. There are three such barriers: (1) incompatibility of product with self-concept, (2) risk of moving away from Ideal Self, and (3) guilt.

Incompatibility with Self-Concept   People may refuse to purchase a product because its purchase is simply incompatible with their self-concept. It does not fit into the role which they are playing in life. A successful business executive will seldom wear shoddy clothing or allow his personal appearance to deteriorate because such behavior is incompatible with his role. A par-shooting golfer would be unable to bring himself to use certain brands of balls. An intellectual would be incapable of reading trashy magazines. A landmark motivation study on the purchase of instant coffee discovered that one of the barriers to women's use of the product when it first came out was the fact that they considered it incompatible with their concept of themselves as diligent homemakers and good cooks. A woman active in the woman's movement may find many of the symbols of the homemaker totally incompatible with her self-concept.

Risk of Moving Away from Ideal Self or Ideal Other   We are constantly striving to bring our Real Self closer to our Ideal Self and our Real Other closer to our Ideal Other, and we will want to buy any goods which we believe will facilitate this movement. However, if the purchase of an item involves some risk that it may move us *away* from our ideals, we usually will not buy it even if ultimately the purchase might prove to be a wise one. We prefer the status quo to moving away from our ideals or jeopardizing our self-concept. The sales of new products suffer because many people are uncertain of the new item's impact on their self-concepts.

Purchasing agents often fear the new supplier. If an untried firm fails to deliver as promised, the purchasing agents' careers may be jeopardized, thus moving them away from their Ideal Selves. The new firm, product, salesperson are all viewed as risks to the buyers' self-concepts.

Guilt[6] Not all aspects of one's self-concept are completely harmonious with one another. The man who visualizes himself as an excellent athlete may have difficulty reconciling this concept with another—that he is a good husband who spends considerable time with his family. Similarly, a business executive may believe herself to be exceedingly shrewd, able to extract the largest profit out of a given level of sales, while at the same time considering herself a good person to work for. There are many areas of business operation where these two concepts would come into conflict. Her union, for example, might propose a substantial pension plan which she feels would unduly lower profits while definitely providing her employees with an attractive retirement system. The final choice between conflicting concepts, if one is free to choose, usually is in favor of the concept which ultimately is more important to oneself.

Although a person might like to own a sports car, the desire is not fulfilled because it creates guilt feelings. It is in conflict with more dominant concepts. A sports car is a selfish purchase for a family because there is room for only one passenger; the family cannot enjoy the purchase. Hence, a woman who values her relations with her family may find it difficult to buy one. Along comes the four-seat sports car to allow this person to satisfy her sporting urge and yet rationalize that her family can also enjoy the car. Similarly, a man who wants to buy a luxury car may refrain from doing so because he knows that if he spends his money for it, he will have to penalize his family in other areas.

On the other hand, if you can rationalize your buying behavior in terms of a socially accepted concept, buying becomes quite easy. It is easy for parents to rationalize the purchase of a pool or camper and other recreational goods on the grounds that they are trying to maintain their health and want to have fun with the family at the same time. You may desire an expensive camera and may rationalize the purchase on the basis that you want to keep a pictorial record of your beloved family. Though an inexpensive camera would probably do the job, you might nevertheless spend several hundred dollars for elaborate equipment.

In conclusion, you must do everything in your power to remove guilt-causing appeals from your presentation. You must frame your appeals around rationalizing reasons for purchase. In selling photographic equipment to a parent of limited income, the wise sales rep would play *down* the hobby aspects, since they tend to be selfish ones, and would play *up* the love-of-family appeals. A sales rep for appliances, instead of telling the homemaker that she will have more time for relaxing, socializing, and jogging if she buys a dishwasher, should tell her that she now will have more time to spend with her family.

Every purchase creates some guilt. By spending money, you must forgo other pleasures. Thus the rewards of purchase must exceed the guilt it creates.

Distinction between Buying Motive and Talking Point

It is very important to distinguish between a buying motive and a talking point. A *buying motive* is an inner urge that makes us desire the proposition that the salesperson presents. It is a psychological concept, not a material one. *It is in our minds, not in the product.*

One model of a Carrier home heating and air conditioning system has an efficiency rating of 13.5. This is a talking point for it, not a motive for buying it. The sales rep might translate that talking point into several motives by saying, "Compared to the 9.5 efficiency factor of your present system, your power bills will drop significantly next summer." Thus an appeal is made to the motive of money gain.

The rep continues, "and you'll be saving lots of gas next winter too. You know what that means to our energy conservation program." Thus, an appeal is made to the prospect's sense of social responsibility.

In these various appeals the talking point is the same—air conditioning. But quite different buying motives are stimulated.

Some writers have failed to distinguish between buying motives and talking points, sometimes listing such qualities of the product as *dependability* or *performance* or *style* under the head of buying motives. Clearly they are no such thing. They are talking points which may be presented in such ways as to appeal to different buying motives. Why does a buyer desire good performance in the article to be bought? Because it will give less trouble (comfort or ease or security), or because it will be economical to operate (thrift or gain), or because it satisfies a desire to feel important, as in the case of a fast car. *Performance* is such a vague quality that it ought never to be listed even among talking points. In an automobile, for example, what do we mean by performance? Power or gasoline economy? We cannot have both. Ease of riding or ease of parking? We usually must sacrifice one to obtain the other.

Style is no more a buying motive than *red* or *big* or *sweet*. *No quality of a product is a buying motive.* The buying motive, we repeat, is in the mind of the buyer and not inherent in the product. The failure to distinguish between these has been evident in many poor sales manuals and training courses.

It may be a good idea to mention again that any talking point is likely to appeal to more than one buying motive. For example, a window air conditioner may be sold with the talking point that it filters incoming air. This talking point may be presented by a clever salesperson so that it will appeal to several buying motives. The seller can point out that it keeps the room cleaner and saves frequent dusting; that it is a boon to sufferers from hay fever or asthma caused by inhalant allergens; that it filters out smoke and dust which are bound to come in when the window is open for ventilation; that walls and curtains will stay clean longer.

Concentrate on the Strongest Buying Motive[7]

Study the motive most likely to move a prospect to buy and then concentrate on that particular motive, much as a boxer concentrates his attack on his adversary's sore nose or cut eye. But it is not necessary to consider the sales interview as a battle. The sales rep should look at it in this way: "Here is a prospect who is eager to make money. By showing him how my proposition can make money for him, I will be doing him a real service. The satisfaction of this want will mean more than anything else I could do for him."

When the sales rep discovers that no progress is being made by an appeal to a certain motive, the appeal can often be shifted to another motive without any change in the talking points being used. For example, the sales rep for a medium-priced automobile was attempting to sell a car to a family consisting of a husband, a wife, and an eighteen-year-old daughter. He felt the sale slipping away from him and knew from the conversation that his prospects were probably going to purchase another car costing $500 more. He had learned that neither the husband nor the wife knew much about the mechanics of a car, and he rightly reasoned that they were buying the more expensive car to satisfy their pride. He therefore casually inquired, "Have you joined the new country club, Mr. Andrews?" "No," was the reply, "we would like to but feel we can't afford it." This gave the salesman the opening for which he had been sparring, and he proceeded to emphasize the improved social standing that membership in the club would confer on Mrs. Andrews and their daughter, the opportunities to mingle freely with the elite of the community, and the business prestige that would come to Mr. Andrews. He so stimulated this same buying motive—pride—although with different talking points from those used by his competitor, that he persuaded his prospects to buy his car so that they might invest the amount saved in a country-club membership.

This is only one illustration of a big principle in selling. The salesperson can frequently transfer an appeal to new talking points while still playing upon the very buying motive that seems to be operating in favor of a competitor. Whenever the salesperson is offering a proposition that will save time or money for the prospect, this should be borne in mind. The desire to make or save money may not dominate this particular prospect, but perhaps the prospect can be shown what might be done with the money saved through its purchase. The prospect should be shown how this money can be used to satisfy some other buying motive or desire.

The appeal to saving used by the agent selling bonds, for example, is weak unless at the same time she conjures up in the mind of her prospect the use that he could make of the money thus saved or made. This offers unlimited play to the saleswoman's power of description, as she calls up the pleasures

of a winter in California, an automobile trip through New England, the delights of books long desired, the possibilities of sending the children to college, the desirability of employing additional help for the household chores, the added prestige that financial success would bring in the eyes of business associates, the satisfaction of gaining on a business rival. The seller is moving that prospect's self-concept much nearer the ideal.

This line of reasoning also applies to the saving of time. Time may be "the stuff life is made of," but is of no value if merely *saved*; in fact, it is impossible to save it in the sense of hoarding it. Time can merely be *spent* in another way, and it is the task of the salesperson to show the prospect, in as alluring a way as possible, just how this saved time may be spent to bring the greatest satisfaction. When one considers what a multitude of things are sold on this basis—the saving of money or time—it will at once be seen that unlimited opportunities are opened to the salesperson who is sufficiently alert to seize them.

That this discussion of buying motives is not wholly theoretical and academic is proved by the experiences of many concerns. The general sales manager for a company selling fire extinguishers says in the company house organ: "From many years' experience in this business, meeting hundreds of successful fire extinguisher salesmen, I am convinced that our most successful men use the 'fear of fire' appeal. . . . After you have sold him on the 'fear of fire' and the value of fire protection, the order will come easy. In fact he will do the buying."

It is good strategy to cover all the possible buying motives early in the sale, not dwelling too long on any one of them, until you can determine which of them is most likely to interest the prospect. After you have touched on them and made up your mind as to the ones that you wish to stress, you can spend the balance of your time on those.

If you have done your homework and are properly prepared for the sale, you'll have a good idea of what motives will move the prospect to buy. Focus on them until you have reason to believe that other motives are stronger.

SUMMARY

The sale is made in the buyer's mind. It is a buying decision, and it is motivated. People buy things for their reasons, not yours. Thus the salesperson should closely study buying motives and behavior.

While psychologists have studied motivation both extensively and intensively, they have yet to develop one comprehensive theory of buyer behavior. There are many approaches to the subject all of which have some merit. There is something to be learned from all of them.

First, there is the traditional shopping list of motives that is divided into two categories—rational and emotional. Rational motives are thought to be those that somehow involve consideration of long run costs. Emotional motives are the non-cost-based reasons.

Most purchases are made to solve some problem of the buyer. The problem may be a physical one, but often it is a mental, emotional, or cultural need.

Finally, the self-concept theory of motivation holds that people behave as they do in an endeavor to make their Real Selves coincide with their Ideal Selves. They buy many goods and services in the hope of realizing these concepts of themselves.

DISCUSSION QUESTIONS

1 The term "perceived risk" is used in marketing to describe the mental evaluation people make of a proposition that is made to them. If the perceived risk is sufficiently low, they buy. How does perceived risk fit into the self-concept theory?

2 How may salespeople make prospects think they are buying instead of being sold?

3 Is one ever justified in appealing to fear as a buying motive?

4 Sometimes a person is prompted by one buying motive to make a purchase while being restrained by a different motive. A homemaker might like to buy an automatic dishwasher for its convenience. What motives might restrain the person from doing so?

5 What are some of the more common self-concepts American men and women have about themselves?

6 How can one appraise a prospect's self-concept?

7 Carefully diagram your Real Self, Ideal Self, Real Other, and Ideal Other in every category you feel is appropriate to you. List various purchases you have made and describe their impact on these selves.

8 You are selling for Norman Hilton, a manufacturer of expensive ($350 to $450) suits. What buying motives would you use in getting a fine menswear store to carry your line?

9 You are the retail clerk selling Norman Hilton suits. What buying motives would you use in selling the suit to a customer who has been buying in the $175 price line? Why might you buy one as a customer? What might restrain you besides lack of money?

10 Frequently, one encounters a prospect who has been premotivated (conditioned) by previous experience to do certain things. Perhaps he has previously owned a television set that required frequent repair and is now motivated to buy a trouble-free set. How should such instances be handled?

REFERENCES

1 Ted Pollock, "Sales Ideas That Work," *American Salesman*, November 1989, pp. 22–27, maintains that understanding why people buy helps the reps adapt their sales efforts.

2 Russell W. Belk, Jr., John F. Sherry, and Melanie Wallendork, "A Naturalistic Inquiry into Buyer Seller Behavior at a Swap Meet," *Journal of Consumer Research*, March 1988, pp. 449–470, reports on a research technique for motivational studies.

3 Lawrence B. Chonko and Marjorie J. Caballero, "The Mature Consumer," *Baylor Business Review*, Winter 1989, pp. 9–13, reports that a study of Americans over fifty years old disclosed several destructive tendencies in their shopping compared to younger people.

4 J. M. Jellison, "Reconsidering the Attitude Concept: A Behavioristic Self Presentation Formulation," in J. Tedischi (ed.), *Impression Management Theory and Social Psychological Research*, Academic Press, New York, 1981, pp. 107–126.

5 Richard H. Buskirk and Beverly Miles, *Beating Men at Their Own Game—A Woman's Guide to Successful Selling in Industry*, John Wiley & Sons, Inc., New York, 1980, p. 182.

6 Robert E. Hite, "Psych Out Your Customer's Buying Hang-Ups," *Business Marketing*, August 1987, pp. 70, 72, discusses cognitive dissonance in selling.

7 David W. Thompson, "Reading Customer Behavior—Does Your Sales Force Really Know the ABC's?" *Bank Marketing*, November 1985, pp. 46–52, urges that the salesperson pay close attention to the prospect's actual behavior rather than to what is being said in attempting to understand their motivational drives.

CASE 4-1: The Earthquake People—Understanding Prospect Disinterest

Don and Della Leone had opened their earthquake preparedness business in response to a mass media campaign in Southern California urging people to acquire certain supplies and equipment that would allow them to sustain themselves for 72 hours in the event of a major quake. Don and Della put together various kits that met these needs, both for the home and business.

While they had achieved some success in selling to business firms, they experienced difficulty with the home market.

1 Why would selling to businesses be easier than to homeowners?

2 Make a motivational analysis of the homeowner's attitudes toward earthquake kits.

CASE 4: The Ryebold Group—Motivational Analysis of Buyers

All the partners and top management team members of the Ryebold Group had assembled for the firm's annual meeting at the Silverado resort in the Napa Valley of California. (The Ryebold Group was one of the world's largest executive search firms, with offices in every major city in the world.) Mr. Ryebold, the founder of the firm and chairman of the partner's committee, insisted that the meetings not only cover all the usual legal and financial formalities but directly discuss the major problems facing the firm. The agenda for these problem-solving sessions was developed from suggestions submitted by the partners.

This year many partners asked for a session on how the partners and the associates could better understand the reasons why they were experiencing some difficulties with some of the people in charge of human resources for some of their prospective accounts. Although the buying decision was usually made by the prospective firm's CEO or board of directors, the vice-president of human resources was usually delegated the task of acting as the contact person for the Ryebold representative, whether partner or associate. It seemed that the firm was meeting resistance from these vice-presidents, some of whom had taken searches from Ryebold and done them in-house instead.

Mr. Ryebold retained a noted sales and motivation consultant to moderate a session at which the motivations of these vice-presidents of human resources would be examined.

1 You are the expert—what is your evaluation of the situation?

CHAPTER FIVE

THE ART

OF PERSUASION

CHAPTER FIVE

THE ART

OF PERSUASION

Don't tell people how good you make your goods. Tell people how good your goods will make them.

Kenneth Goode

After studying the material in this chapter you should:

☐ Understand that selling is essentially a process of persuasion

☐ Realize that during the sale you should try to integrate the interests of the prospect with your own interests

☐ Appreciate that selling uses the principles of suggestion to lead the prospect into doing what is wanted

THE PROFILE

OF A PERSUADER

Jack Fishbaugh

Treasures from History
Modesto, Calif.

They had no intention of buying anything, anything at all. They were just browsing through the aisles of a small antique show looking at this and that when they saw the small glass display case that housed a collection of perhaps thirty ancient coins, all authenticated, that had been tastefully converted into simple jewelry—earrings, necklaces, and so on.

It was Jack's display, and he gently responded with little prodding to the couple's interest by bringing out a necklace that featured an ancient Greek gold coin in fine condition with a bust of Alexander the Great on it. He told a tale about it and its companion piece, which featured Philip of Macedonia, Alexander's father. There were others all with accompanying tales of historical interest. But then why not? Jack is a retired history professor from Chabot College. As he tells about the shekel from biblical times or the Carthaginian coin of gold and silver alloy he conjures up images of ancient times.

Little is said of prices until the couple starts to bargain. Jack lets them win a bit, but not much. They get 10 percent off by buying two coins. A substantial sale results with nothing being said that resembles a sales presentation, just some stories about ancient times; persuasion occurs in the minds of the buyers, as Jack well knows. "I just show the goods and give them a life, a history."

Selling is essentially a matter of persuasion, persuading others to accept your proposition. Persuasion involves *motivation* aimed at inducing *action*. When we persuade people, we do not merely change their thinking; we cause them to *do* something.

In selling, efforts to persuade are based on an understanding of buying motives (Chapter 4). The *action* which we seek to induce is that of *buying*.

In this chapter we shall consider a few of the fundamental principles which underlie all persuasion, whether utilized by salesperson, lawyer, politician, preacher, advertising writer, labor negotiator, or public relations executive. They may be applied daily by everyone.

PRINCIPLE OF CONTINGENCY BENEFITS

People are persuaded to do things because they come to believe that a package of benefits awaits them for doing so. People are motivated by their desire for the future benefits you offer them. Thus your sales presentation must convey to the prospect most clearly the benefits you can provide them.

And what are those benefits? The answer to that question is not always readily apparent. It would appear that purchasing agents would buy from vendors who quote the lowest prices. Not generally so! Visions of irate bosses maddened by vendor failures race through the purchasing agent's mind. Careers are on the line. The continued smooth flow of goods through the company means profits and jobs. Thus, as you speak with a purchasing agent, be aware that the benefits you offer go far beyond the product or service you apparently sell. You're selling jobs, profits, happy bosses, successful solutions, peace and contentment, whatever. Paint word pictures to help the prospect visualize such intangible, yet important, benefits.[1]

A sales rep for a trucking company related this experience:

> I was assigned to see a family which was moving from Cleveland to Los Angeles, their expenses to be paid by their employer. They had already signed up with another company at a price lower than I could quote. I was never more astonished in my life than when the woman announced that she would switch the job to us and pay the difference out of her own pocket. I couldn't help asking her what I had said that caused her to change.
>
> She answered: "When you told me how your truck would back up in front of our new home in Los Angeles, and how your men would carry those containers with my dresses in them up into my room, and when you pictured how nice and fresh my dresses would look when they came out of their special containers—well, that was when I decided to let you handle our goods."

Another effective word picture is painted by the saleswoman for a microwave oven: "You've had a hard day and left the office late. The bus was crowded, and you had to stand up all the way. Your feet hurt and your head aches, and you actually *dread* the prospect of getting home and tackling the job of getting up a meal. Has that ever happened to you?"

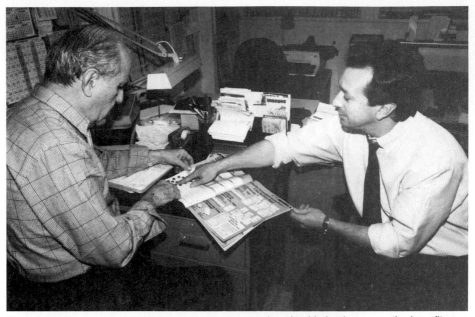

If you are selling to a purchasing agent, your presentation should clearly convey the benefits your product or service will provide. How would you try to pinpoint exactly what it is the prospect is seeking?

The answer will be "Yes," whether it has or not. So the saleswoman unfolds a large color poster of a gorgeous microwave oven, with the door open and a mouth-watering, fully cooked, ready-to-serve meal just begging to be put on the table. "Wouldn't it be wonderful to come home to *this?* Dinner cooked to perfection—hot and ready to serve—in a few minutes?"

The encyclopedia salesperson inquires of the parent: "What do you do when your daughter looks up from her homework and asks, 'What's the principal product of New Mexico?' Do you send her out to the library? Is it still open? Wouldn't it be a lot easier for you if your children just went to this beautiful encyclopedia and turned to the correct answer?" That's putting the prospect into the picture—with words only. But the picture is credible; it is in the circle of the prospect's experience. And it *is* dramatic.

The bond trader doesn't sell a piece of paper but an income and the satisfaction it will bring the purchaser. The agent for a cottage in a summer resort does not sell housing. She sells the pleasures of boating, bathing, golfing, camping—with the prospect in the foreground of the alluring picture.

People do not buy camcorders; they buy family memories. They don't buy ¼-inch bits; they buy ¼-inch holes. They don't buy a television set; they buy entertainment.

Never, never lose sight of the fact that you aren't selling things; you're selling benefits. What benefits does the prospect seek? Pinpoint that, and then show how those benefits can best be realized by dealing with you.

PRINCIPLES OF SUGGESTION

There are two methods of inducing action by another person. The first is by suggestion; the second is by logical reasoning. Some psychologists insist that many people reason scarcely at all—that practically all their acts are the result of imitation, habit, or suggestion. Most of their actions are only *reactions*. This being true, you should understand and use suggestion.

Here are seven principles you should master:

1 People *accept* as true any idea that enters their minds unless a contradictory idea blocks its acceptance.

2 The acceptance of a suggestion depends upon the source of the suggestion.

3 The acceptance of a suggestion is influenced by the intensity with which it is made.

4 People are more apt to accept a recent suggestion than one made earlier.

5 A suggestion is more apt to be accepted if it is repeated.

6 People will believe a suggestion if they want to believe it, regardless of its merit.

7 A suggestion that appears to be natural and spontaneous is more likely to be accepted than one which is apparently planned or contrived.

Blocking Ideas

The prospect's mind is not an empty cupboard; it contains many ideas—some true, some not—gleaned from experience. The car dealer suggests to a prospect that if a trade can be made immediately, a higher price can be given for the trade-in because the dealership has an immediate customer for it. There seldom is much truth to such a suggestion, but it will be believed unless the prospect has previous knowledge of this tactic. Also the prospect may believe it because he wants to believe it—he not only wants to trade cars but wants to believe that he is getting a good deal.

If there are no blocking ideas, a suggestion has a good chance of acceptance. The salesperson suggests that the company is a reputable supplier by referring to its long relationship with other well-recognized customers. Unless the purchasing agent knows something to the contrary, a favorable image will likely result.

If blocking thoughts prevent the acceptance of a suggestion, try to bring those thoughts to light and correct them. Often a sale will be stymied solely because the prospect harbors some blocking idea. We deal with this problem in detail later in Chapter 12 when discussing hidden objections.

Source of Suggestion[2]

The authenticity of the source of a suggestion must be considered. If a nontechnical person suggests to an engineer that he can solve some sticky technical problem, he is not as likely to be believed as someone who possesses technical qualifications. You need to establish your expertise early in the sale so that your suggestions will be considered authentic by the prospect.

One young retail men's clothing salesman was having trouble selling suits to men older than himself until his boss spotted the problem: The older customers were not receptive to his suggestions because they had no reason to believe that he knew his trade, and his age suggested that he didn't. Thereafter this young man would make a remark early in the sale regarding some problem the customer had in obtaining a good fit, thus establishing his technical knowledge in the prospect's mind. It worked beyond all hopes. Often one little comment or observation in the opening moments of the presentation will do the job. Just showing that you are familiar with industry jargon can help establish your expertise in the prospect's eyes.

Intensity

Yell "fire" at the top of your voice, and you'll more likely be believed than if you say it calmly. The way you deliver your lines affects their believability. This is not to suggest that you should shout. Words delivered in a firm, intense voice, with feeling, strongly suggest not only that you know what you are talking about but that you also believe it yourself. Many salespeople work hard to develop a sincere earnestness in their voices. They may even practice before a video camera recorder for hours to perfect their vocal intonations.

Recency and Repetition

You have little reason to expect that the prospect will act on a suggestion made much earlier in the sale. Key suggestions should be repeated for maximum effectiveness. But disguise such repetitions by rewording them lest the more perceptive prospect detect them and see you as a "broken record."

Some salespeople write key suggestions down in large boldface on paper so that the visual impact of the suggestion is continually before the prospect.

Desire to Believe

People will believe whatever is told them if they are of a mind to do so; this is the basis of the "big lie." If a man wants to believe that getting a phone for his car will impress his boss with his diligence and further his career, he will believe it no matter what physical evidence exists to the contrary. Tell a woman that a Jaguar is her best buy, and she'll believe it if she wants to do so.

If you are ever puzzled about how some people can believe some outrageous lies, just remember that they want to believe them. We all harbor and cherish many lies because we want to do so. The truth could be too painful to accept. The cosmetic saleswoman suggests to her prospect that the nightly application of Alligator Oil will make her look 10 years younger; the prospect wants to believe her.

Spontaneity

The strength of a suggestion varies directly with the degree to which it seems to be made on the individual's own initiative. People are more prone to act on autosuggestion than on suggestions from external sources. They tend to resent any attempt by others to dominate their thinking.

It is important to realize that many prospects are already under suggestive influences from advertising, window displays, neighbors, or other sources. The main task in such instances is to reinforce such suggestions and proceed to guide them into the desired channels. It can be difficult to alter the prospect's train of thought. You have seen a particular London Fog coat that appeals to you; you walk into a store and specifically ask for that garment. In many instances, only a skilled salesperson can switch you to the brand in stock even though the two may be practically identical. One sales rep asked such a prospect, "I've heard a great deal about that coat. Have you seen it?" When the prospect replied that he had he was asked, "Could you do me a favor? Come over here and show me how it differs from the coat that our buyer bought. I want to be able to tell him about it." When the prospect started comparing the coats, he discovered that the one carried by the store had more features and was a better value than the one he had in mind, so he bought it. But all the time he thought he was making up his own mind; that is *spontaneity*.

All of us see suggestion at work every day. The waiter suggests the swordfish. A colleague stops by and suggests, "Let's go get a cup of coffee." Your spouse innocently remarks, "The Smiths have a new VCR. They think it's wonderful."

Suggestion through Action[3]

You can use action-based suggestion throughout the presentation. Suppose you wish to convey to the prospect the idea that a machine is quite durable. You could treat it roughly, drop it, and pound it. Suppose you wish to suggest that it is time to sign the order. The simple act of handing the order blank and a pen to the prospect may suggest the proper action.

One salesperson of plastic dishes selling to retailers would deliberately drop several dishes on the floor, ostensibly by accident, to convince the prospect of their unbreakability. Actions speak infinitely louder than mere words.

Direct Suggestion

A direct suggestion is one which is made in a straightforward manner. The salesperson urges, "Will three shirts be sufficient?" or "Would you care to purchase a handbag to go with the shoes?" or "Feel this material, notice its high quality."

It is considered sound selling to suggest directly such items as the type of product you feel is most appropriate for the prospect, the quantity you feel this prospect should buy, the proper distribution of sizes or colors, and other factors on which the buyer may be depending upon the seller for advice.

Indirect Suggestion

Indirect suggestion is used by salespeople who do not wish prospects to realize that they are being subjected to a suggestion. It must be subtle and not easily detectable.

Indirect suggestion should be used when prospects are mentally alert or feel themselves superior to the salesperson.

Suppose you wish to suggest that the competitor's product, which the prospect is about to buy, is inferior to yours. In most instances, you should not directly attack the competitor's product; however, most salespeople agree that there are times when you must take *some* positive action to counter a competitor's claims. You might ask, "Have you talked with any of the users of the Apex machine?" or "Just the other day a client walked into the office and purchased our machine without even so much as a demonstration. He explained that he had bought an Apex a few months before and wanted to trade it in. Naturally we tried to give him as much as possible, but you know how it goes with used equipment of this type." There are many similar statements which, in varying degrees, plant seeds of doubt in the prospect's mind concerning a competitor's wares. Great care must be taken lest the prospect be offended by an exaggeration or adverse comment that reflects on the prospect's judgment.

Positive and Negative Suggestion

A positive suggestion suggests that the hearer *do* something (buy the product) or *say* something ("I like the product").

The positive suggestion implies that the prospect is moving toward a favorable decision on buying. The negative suggestion implies moving in the opposite direction.

Positive: This certainly is a wonderful value, isn't it?
Neutral: What do you think of this proposition?
Negative: You couldn't use this, could you?

These are all stated as questions, because the salesperson is always trying to induce a reaction of some kind to the presentation. A sales rep might say,

"You won't find a better value anywhere." That is a positive *statement*, but it suggests no *action* on the part of the prospect, not even an affirmative nod of the head. The prospect is supposed to agree with a positive suggestion and indicate agreement in some way.

In short, we are thinking about the reaction of the prospect. Is it positive (favorable) or negative (unfavorable)? Any statement or question or action that invites a favorable response is positive. The retail clerk's "Will that be all?" is negative. Be a bit more positive and ask, "What else?"

Often the negative suggestion is *concealed*. "The chances are only one in four that you will lose" is negative. It suggests losing. If the same thought were put "Your chances of *winning* are three to one," the suggestion would be that of winning and therefore positive.

The salesperson who says, "This roof won't leak during the next 5 years: We guarantee that," is suggesting a leak and all the attendant damage it brings. If he had said, "This roof is guaranteed to stay tight for at least 5 years," the suggestion would have been positive.

The automobile salesperson might say, "This car will give you little trouble." Buy why suggest *trouble?* The prospect may start worrying about the trouble and postpone the purchase, perhaps permanently. The positive and negative aspects of suggestion can be illustrated by analogy. The man who asks the woman of his choice, "You wouldn't want to marry me, would you?" virtually compels the woman to do the proposing, which she may consider a bit out of place even today.

Throughout the entire sales process imply, wherever possible, that you *expect* the prospect to purchase. Say, *"After* you have had this car a year . . ." and not *"If* you should decide to get this car you would find. . . ." Say, "You *will* have a lot of comfort in this chair, I'm sure, on the long winter evenings," or "You *will* find that these goods will move off your shelves almost as fast as you can unpack them." Care must obviously be exercised to avoid making these suggestions too early, as some prospects would resent the implication that they had reached a decision when they had not.

And real salespeople should never permit themselves to use the word "regret." It is easy to say, "You will never regret this purchase," but why suggest regret? It would be better to suggest the positive satisfaction to be derived from possession, "I know you'll love it!"

Using Emotional Words to Stimulate Prospects

Many times salespeople deliberately choose words which they know will stimulate certain desired emotional reactions in the prospect. You must remember that when you call on a prospect you are not calling on a dull, neutral machine devoid of memory and emotions. On the contrary, the prospect has had a rich background of experiences, all of which have shaped attitudes, opinions, and feelings about various subjects. He or she is not a pawn to be manipulated. What you are and think today is largely a result of your previous experiences. During those experiences various values have been implanted in you by your culture.

Suppose a sales rep says, "Our machines are used by more successful executives than all other equipment combined." The word "successful" stimulates favorable responses in most business executives, since success is a goal they are striving to reach. The statement couples the product with the pleasant concept of success. Some oil companies have discovered that the word "power" touches off a favorable emotional response in their customers. The same word used by an automobile salesperson stimulates strong, favorable reactions. Hence the sales rep for a hydraulic press might stimulate a favorable response in a prospect by making a statement such as, "Just look at the massive power of that machine at work."

Or the seller of an automatic machine might be able to stir up an emotional response in an executive by "This machine will remain *loyal* to you 24 hours a day, 365 days a year. It will never go on strike or slow down. Can you say the same of all your human employees?" The words "loyal," "strike," and "slow down" are the fuses that ignite emotional bursts—to the advantage of the sales rep. There is an old saying in selling that the marketer should aim at the heart instead of the head because it is 12 inches closer to the pocketbook. Emotional words are aimed at the heart instead of the head in line with the principle (developed in a previous chapter) that emotional appeals are more forceful in most instances than rational ones. Emotionally laden words make emotional appeals far more effective.

LOGICAL REASONING

When salespeople use logical arguments in selling, they expect the prospect to reason, to think, to compare. This type of selling implies the formulation of a logical syllogism in the mind of the buyer. A "logical syllogism" is merely an argument consisting of three parts: a major premise, a minor premise, and a conclusion.

1 Major premise: All humans are mortal.
2 Minor premise: I am human.
3 Conclusion: Therefore, I am mortal.

In selling computers to an office manager, such logic might be:

1 Every able office manager wants to maximize productivity.
2 My computer will maximize productivity.
3 Therefore, you must buy my computer.

Putting an argument* in this logical form may make it unanswerable, but it does not always make sales. It savors too strongly of the debating attitude and

---

*The author dislikes the word "argument" in a book on selling, but it is widely used. It smacks too much of debate and acrimonious difference of opinion. It is best never to argue with a prospect.

is likely to place the prospect on the defensive. You don't like to be convinced against your will; in fact, this rarely happens. Prospects will agree with everything you say and the inescapable conclusions of your logic but still stubbornly say, "I don't want your blasted product." Most people prefer to do their own thinking or at least to be treated as if they are capable of doing it. Most salespeople avoid the syllogistic form of reasoning with their prospects, using instead either suggestion or an abbreviated syllogism which permits prospects to draw their own conclusions. For example:

1 Every driver likes a car that is economical on gas.
2 You are a driver.
3 Therefore, you want a car that is economical on gas—this car delivers 47 miles to the gallon.

But the salesperson skips part of the syllogism and simply says: "This car will give you 47 miles to the gallon." The prospect can fill in the omitted steps. Logic used in selling implies an act of deliberation on the part of the prospect. The prospect must have the point at issue clearly in mind; she must catalog and weigh the arguments pro and con and reach a decision. This all takes time, and the salesperson should not attempt to hurry the process. Indeed, quick selling is seldom accomplished by logic. Suggestion is a faster method.

Sometimes a seller will attempt a sale by the use of suggestion, only to find that the prospect is growing thoughtful and reluctant to make a commitment. Perhaps the prospect is merely trying to think the proposition out along logical lines. Where this seems to be the situation, it is wise to slow down and resort to logic, permitting the prospect to deliberate carefully each point. Or a prospect may want to buy; his emotions impel him to want the proposition. But reason whispers "No!" The task here is to provide the prospect with reasons for buying—to appeal to logic. It is necessary to help the prospect rationalize the urge to buy. One of the best ways to accomplish this is to present the alternatives to buying. When you reason the way to a conclusion, you must weigh various alternatives and ultimately choose one of them.

In making many purchases, you don't do this. You merely buy on impulse. But in buying something involving a substantial amount of money, you are more likely to consider the alternatives available. Let's say a prospect is looking at a new car and eager to have it. But the old car is still running well and the prospect knows that she does not *need* the new one very badly. So the salesperson tries to present alternatives. Obviously, there are only two: to keep the old car or to buy the new one. So the rep concentrates on the first, pointing out that if the prospect keeps the old car, she will have to get new tires shortly or risk an accident, will have to take less for it when she trades it in next year, will have to pay for various minor repairs during the next year, and will have to forgo such features as air conditioning and the new brakes. If she waits a year, she will have larger monthly payments on account of the lower trade-in value on the old car. Thus the salesperson provides the pros-

Selling the right automobile to a prospect involves persuasive skills and sensitivity to the needs of the customer. As a customer who is considering the purchase of a new car, what sales approach might persuade you to make the purchase? What might send you to another dealer?

pect with logical arguments to support the desire to get the new model. The main purpose and objective is to help the prospect rationalize spending the money now. When should logic be used? There are a few general rules:

• In selling to professional purchasing agents or buyers. These buyers are too experienced to be moved by suggestion alone; they want sound reasons. Besides, they are not buying for themselves.

• In selling to buyers with trained minds, especially those trained in engineering or the sciences. These buyers think logically by habit.

• In selling complicated articles or propositions. It may not be used exclusively even here, as suggestion may help in the sales process, but few complex propositions can be sold without the use of facts and logic.

• In selling propositions involving a large expenditure. Most buyers deliberate longer over a large outlay than over a small one.

• In selling something that is new to the prospect. Anything that involves a radical change in habit, thought, or style requires argument to support its introduction.

If—Then

The "if—then" technique simply states an assumed premise and then reasons from that. An apparel rep might say to a wavering dealer who had been carrying the line, "*If* you drop our line, *then* I hope you realize that we will have to find other distribution in your trading area and you will then be selling against our advertising and merchandising campaign." Or "*If* you wait another 6 months before buying this item, the price could go up and *then* you will end up paying more." Arguments such as these are logical if you accept the assumed premise. Therefore, be careful not to exaggerate this premise, thereby losing the confidence of the prospect.

NEED FOR RATIONALIZATION

Even though your prospects' behavior may be basically emotional, they will still feel a need for rational motives for their behavior, in case they are ever called upon for an explanation, and to satisfy themselves that they are rational. Throughout the whole persuasion process you must be conscious of this fact and must stand ready to provide reasons which prospects may seize upon to justify any actions. The Cadillac salesperson may have to show customers how small depreciation is in comparison with low-priced cars, enabling them to rationalize their behavior in terms of cost. Many apparently illogical arguments are never seriously questioned by prospects. They do not want to question, since they need reasons to justify the emotional behavior they have in mind. Cadillac owners want to believe, no matter how illogically, that the Cadillac is their best low-cost purchase, all things considered. They want to believe this so strongly that they make no serious effort to discover discrepancies in the argument. Many faulty persuasion techniques succeed because prospects want them to succeed; they are eager to believe the things the sales rep says. Hence the salesperson may use rather lame or leaky arguments to help the prospect rationalize the act of buying emotionally.

SUMMARY

Selling is a process of persuasion; thus the principles of persuasion pertain to it. While logical reasoning plays a role in many selling situations, more commonly the salesperson must use various principles of suggestion to persuade the other person to do what is wanted.

The seven principles of suggestion can be useful tools: (1) People will accept suggestions if there are no blocking ideas in their minds. (2) The credibility of the source of the suggestion affects its acceptance. (3) The intensity with which the suggestion is made affects its approval. (4) Recent suggestions are more effective than those made earlier. (5) A suggestion is more apt to be accepted if it is repeated. (6) People will believe what they want to believe. (7) A natural, spontaneous suggestion will be acted upon more readily than will a contrived one.

Emotional words play an important role in motivating the prospect, so salespeople should practice their intonation. However, despite the frequent success of an appeal to the prospect's emotions, the salesperson often needs to help the prospect rationalize a purchase that is being made emotionally.

DISCUSSION QUESTIONS

1 Devise a logical argument for selling an income tax service to a small retailer, and then illustrate how each point could be made either by suggestion or by other emotional persuasive means.

2 List various words which are usually loaded with favorable responses.

3 Rephrase each of the following statements which you think is negative into positive terms:
  a Our widget is not complex to install.
  b This grass seed does not take long to germinate.
  c This fabric won't wear out soon.
  d Your spouse won't have to work as hard with this machine.
  e Your in-store theft losses will drop when we install our protection system.

4 As a service station attendant, you notice that a customer's tires are bald. Develop selling sentences using direct, indirect, positive, and negative suggestion.

5 How would you go about helping a homemaker rationalize the desire to purchase an expensive ice-dispensing refrigerator rather than a more moderately priced model that would be more appropriate, considering the family's income?

6 Suppose you have developed the following logical argument:
  • You want the lowest-cost product.
  • My product is the lowest-cost one.
  • Therefore, you want to buy it.
  But the prospect tells you to get lost. What might have gone wrong with your logic?

7 By what means can you indirectly suggest to the prospect that your product is of the highest quality?

8 As a salesperson for Hertz, you are trying to sign up a large firm that is now buying its own cars for salespeople and executives. Devise a logical argument to support your contention that the firm should be renting its cars from you.

9 In the car-rental situation above, devise various suggestions to accomplish the same objective.

10 You wish to impress upon your prospect the fact that the company you represent is a reputable concern with a record for quality and performance. How would you suggest this indirectly?

REFERENCES

1 Susan Shulman, "Spectacular Spiels . . . Knowing Your Stuff is Not Enough— You've Got to Communicate It," *American Salesman*, December 1986, pp. 13–14, discusses techniques that can be used to communicate more effectively with prospects.

2 Trust is essential in most persuasive situations. The following articles provide some interesting suggestions on how to trust: Ronald E. Milliman and Douglas L. Fugate,

"Using Trust-Transference as a Persuasion Technique: An Empirical Field Investigation," *Journal of Personal Selling and Sales Management*, August 1988, pp. 1–7, and Jon M. Hawes, Kenneth E. Mast, and John E. Swan, "Trust Earning Perceptions of Sellers and Buyers," *Journal of Personal Selling and Sales Management*, Spring 1989, pp. 1–8.

3 For some different views of the persuasion process, see Kerry L. Johnson, "Persuading People to Buy," *Broker World*, May 1988, pp. 124–134, and "The Touch of Persuasion," *Broker World*, April 1988, pp. 100–104.

CASE 5-1: Universal Telephone Company—Persuading a Threatened Telephone Company Executive

Marty Steele (see Case 2-2) had been given the responsibility for developing a large scrap retrieval business within the organizational structure of the Universal Telephone Company. It was an extension of the work she had been doing solely for the company. However, she had developed a capacity for handling far more scrap than the company generated. As part of the firm's internal venturing program, management had encouraged her to expand operations by soliciting scrap from other firms. Marty's main interest was in copper and aluminum. There was little money to be made in steel, and she was not equipped to handle the rare metals. Unprocessed scrap wire brought 20 cents a pound from local scrap dealers. Marty stripped the wire, separated the copper from the aluminum, and melted each metal into resalable ingots, for which the company received 55 cents a pound for copper and 50 cents a pound for aluminum. The company generated about 20 million pounds of scrap a year; thus Marty contributed about $6,000,000 a year to the company's profits. She planned to handle about 150 million pounds of scrap in 1987. Once Marty had been given the green light to go ahead with the internal venture, operations were begun to recruit customers. Marty's first target was the region's other large telephone company, Pacific Bell. To that end, she made an appointment to see the man who was in charge of Pac Bell's scrap disposal. Pac Bell did not process its scrap but instead sold about 60 million pounds of it each year "as is" to local dealers who bid on each batch. The meeting did not go well. The man heard Marty's proposal and said that he would have to discuss the matter with top management. "We'll let you know." The next week Marty received a brush-off letter. The firm was not interested. The next potential customer, Southern California Edison, operated in much the same manner as Pac Bell. The executive with whom Marty talked was a bit more open in his manner. He said, "That's a great idea you have. I think I'll do the same thing." Marty fled to her office to rethink her selling tactics. She had thought it would be easy. After all, she was offering to make those firms a lot of money. She asked her mentor, "What went wrong?"

1 What *did* go wrong?

2 Can these executives be persuaded to join Marty's scrap disposal system? If so, how could it be done?

3 What appeals would you suggest she use?

CASE 5-2: Home Sweet Home Realty—Developing a Realtor's Lexicon

"I just heard a prof from the college talk at Rotary about the power and hidden connotations of words, and it hit me that we need to do some thinking about some of the words we use." Harold Ricker, owner and manager of the Home Sweet Home real estate agency was talking to several agents who were lounging around the office on a dull Tuesday afternoon in December. They agreed with what he said, but then they had to—he was boss. However, one new agent was particularly responsive to Harold's observation. She had been a high school English teacher for more than a decade before she realized that she could make more money selling real estate than she could trying to sell high school students on the virtues of using the language properly.

After a short discussion she said, "I am going to prepare a lexicon for us to use in our work. A realtor's lexicon."

One of the other agents blinked at her and asked, "Betty, what in blue blazes is a lexicon?"

In her best tutorial manner, she somewhat disdainfully replied, "Here's a dictionary, Ed. Look it up."

Ed turned away to get another cup of coffee as Betty continued telling Harold what she planned to do. "Tomorrow morning at our sales meeting I'll have a list of good words for us to use and a list of ones that we should avoid using."

Harold smiled and nodded his assent.

1 Develop such a list of good and bad words for the real estate agent.

2 Why do certain words conjure up a favorable image while others create negative thoughts?

CHAPTER SIX

PROSPECTING

Gold is where you find it.
Anonymous

After studying the material in this chapter you should:

☐ Understand that successful selling is based on successful prospecting

☐ Know that a prospect is someone who needs and can afford your proposition

☐ Realize that successful sales organizations develop prospecting systems that keep the sales force fed with an ample supply of good prospects

☐ Understand that customer database management has become an important aspect of sales operations

☐ Know that well-qualified leads cost money, but unqualified leads cost even more

☐ Realize that lead generation programs may use several media—newspapers, magazines, direct mail, or television.

PROFILE OF A MODERN

PROFESSIONAL SALES

REPRESENTATIVE

J. Philip Clark

Vice-President, Sanford C. Bernstein & Co.
Los Angeles, Calif.

The words flowed quickly and smoothly. Phil knew exactly what he wanted to say. "I joined IBM in 1974 and resigned at the end of 1980 to become a real estate broker. I was tired of moving, and we were facing a move to Atlanta. Since we like it here in Dallas, and I wanted to make more money, I thought the time was ripe for a change." Phil at the time was manager of the Fort Worth sales office. He had joined IBM immediately after graduating from college.

"IBM provides very thorough training. They say that the company invests more than $100,000 in you, so I was the recipient of a very fine education that refined and honed my selling skills."

Replying to a question about what personal attributes he thought were responsible for his success, he said, "Drive, a sense of hunger, really having to work for whatever you've accomplished in life. I guess you'd call it a drive for fulfillment. Persistence is in there, not necessarily working hard, but working smart. I think that one of the biggest areas differentiating successful from unsuccessful salespeople is the ability to qualify quickly the people they are dealing with.

"Are you dealing with a decision maker? Do they really have a need? Do they have a desire to buy within a reasonable time frame? You simply cannot afford to spend much time with people who are going to buy in 4 or 5 years. In sales, the person who is the most productive is the one who calls on the most highly qualified prospects. A lot of people spend a lot of time running around doing all sorts of things that look like work yet are unsuccessful because they are not channeling their efforts properly.

"One of the areas I was very involved with at IBM was mass selling. I think in a lot of ways IBM pioneered the concept. When I was manager, I would use the analogy to the people who worked for me that you have to stand on a high peak overlooking your territory and then ask everyone in your territory who is thinking about buying a computer to raise their hand. Then those are the people to go after. So we spent a lot of effort on the telephone, writing letters, and advertising, asking people to identify themselves. I would literally make 80 to 90 telephone calls a day. I hired some students to work 4 hours a day making calls just to locate good prospects. We furnished them with a polished spiel. Then when a good prospect was located we would send out our 'killers' to concentrate just on the people who had identified themselves.''

Phil changed subjects. ''Another point I want to make: phraseology. I am careful of the words I use. I don't want to appear pushy or obnoxious. I found that when it came to closing, I used the phrase ''What do I have to do, or what factors do you need, to make you feel comfortable to make a decision? I never say 'Sign the order' and I never use the word 'contract.' It is always an agreement. I need to write a mini-directory of all my little 'soft' words.

''In my next venture, Invequest, we carried good prospecting one step farther. We based the enterprise upon it. Our concept was to develop investment packages for investors who are looking for real estate deals with short-time turnarounds and high yields. We pinpointed our target market to one type of investor. It made our marketing effort simpler yet more effective. Pinpoint your prospects!''

John Wolf, sales manager for Staar Surgical (see Chapter 16) ''Profile of a Selling Sales Manager''), when asked to explain the quick success of the Staar sales reps, replied, ''They concentrate on the top-notch ophthalmologists who do lots of operations. They go where the business is.''

The importance of prospecting, the first step of the selling process, is often overlooked by the uninitiated. Many good salespeople maintain that the key to effective selling is prospecting. Unquestionably, the route to an order begins with it.

Good prospecting means more sales because it allows you to spend your time with people whose probability of buying is high. One reality of selling is that you spend a small portion of the working day in contact with potential customers. Much time is spent traveling, waiting, and servicing accounts.

Many salespeople make only one or two calls a day. If those few calls are not made on good prospects, the day is wasted. Your performance will be seriously impaired if you waste time trying to sell to poor prospects. Let's examine the numbers.[1]

Suppose two people of equal persuasive abilities each make 500 calls on potential customers. Pam is a better prospector than Gus; she has selected 500 prospects who, on the average, have a 50 percent chance of buying, while Gus, on the average, will only be able to get orders from one-third of his prospects. Moreover, Pam's calls were made on potential accounts which were larger than Gus's accounts. Pam's average order was $700 compared to $500 for Gus. Now let's see what this means in sales volume.

	Pam	Gus
Calls	500	500
multiplied by		
Probability of order	× 0.50	× 0.33
Orders	250	167
multiplied by		
Average order	× $700	× $500
Sales volume	$175,000	$83,500

While these figures are hypothetical and there may be no such thing as two people of equal ability, actual sales experience indicates that the differences in the potential payoff of various prospects is much greater than that assumed above.

Remember the disparity in size among businesses. You can call on hundreds of small concerns all year and still not bring in the volume that would be available from one large corporation. One important factor in Leana Grandy's success with Xerox (see Chapter 1) was that she was selling to one of the world's largest customers, the Los Angeles school system.

Some people believe that a good salesperson is someone who could sell ice to an Eskimo—get an order from someone who neither needs the product nor can afford to pay for it—but that is a mistaken idea. Such a person is not a good salesperson; he or she is little more than an extortionist. The great salespeople call on good prospects, not caring to squander their time on poor ones.

Frequent use has been made of the word "prospect" in referring to the potential buyer for a product or service. Let's define this and some other terms.

PROSPECTS, LEADS, AND SUSPECTS

A *prospect* is a person or institution who can both benefit from buying the product and afford to buy it. Note that two conditions must be met before one can classify a lead as a prospect. First, the person or organization must be able to benefit from the product; those who have no use for it are not prospects. Second, no matter how badly they may want the product or how much they can benefit from it, if they cannot pay for it, they are not prospects.

The word "benefit" is used instead of "need" to avoid difficulties in attempting to determine exactly what anyone truly needs. The important thing is whether the product or service will furnish sufficient utility to the individual to warrant his buying it. A *lead* (pronounced *leed*) is a person or an organization who might possibly be a prospect. A lead must first be qualified before it can be considered a prospect. Sometimes the term "suspect" has been applied to a lead to indicate that the name is suspected of being a prospect.

QUALIFYING PROSPECTS[2]

Once you have a possible prospect—a lead—it is necessary to qualify it. Is that person or firm a good prospect or not? Is there a need and sufficient money to satisfy it? Has the person the authority to buy? The answers to these questions may be obvious or they may require considerable investigation. It would not take much imagination on the part of a drapery salesperson to realize that the people who have just purchased a new home will probably need drapes and will probably be able to pay for them; they are good prospects.

On the other hand, someone selling swimming pools is not as fortunate; good prospects are not as obvious. This salesperson will have to dig a bit, for there are no observable facts to indicate if someone in the family is interested in swimming. Perhaps some observable factors would indicate if they could afford a pool—cars, furniture, price of house, etc.

The same situation exists in industrial selling. A 3M sales rep selling sandpaper knows that a furniture factory is a top-quality prospect but would have to qualify a firm called the Acme Manufacturing Company. What do they make? Do they sand or polish anything? Fortunately, all the rep has to do is ask the company's purchasing agent for the answers.

If the salesperson has been unable to qualify a name prior to making the call, often two or three screening questions right at the beginning of the interview will quickly weed out weak prospects, thus saving time. Sometimes industrial sales reps must gain permission from a company to make a study of the firm's operations in order to determine whether the company needs the seller's goods. In the consultative selling system the sales rep is severely admonished first to get prospects to clearly and freely admit that they have a problem which the rep's firm may be able to solve. Moreover, the prospect must affirm that there is an adequate budget available for solving the problem. This system stipulates that under no circumstances should the rep proceed with a presentation until the problem and budget are established.

SOME COMMON PROSPECTING SYSTEMS

Several so-called systems have been worked out to make the salesperson a more efficient prospector. It should be emphasized, however, that no system guarantees successful prospecting unless it is followed intelligently and consistently so that it becomes an integral part of the salesperson's work schedule. Every successful sales rep develops individual methods which are probably combinations of the plans here suggested. The important thing is to follow a plan that proves effective in supplying a constantly fresh list of live prospects; any system that does this is a good one.

No effort has been made to discuss different systems in the order of their effectiveness. Some may be better adapted to certain types of selling and kinds of products than are others. Ten prospecting systems are used widely enough to justify some explanation and comment. These are (1) endless chain, (2) center of influence, (3) personal observation, (4) junior sales rep (sometimes called "spotting"), (5) cold canvassing, (6) parties, (7) walk-ins and call-ups, (8) farm system, (9) telemarketing, and (10) direct marketing techniques (discussed at length later in this chapter).

The Endless Chain or Referral Selling

This system is based upon the idea that at each interview the salesperson should secure the names of additional prospects for future interviews. Most salespeople who employ this method attempt to get from each person *interviewed* (not just called upon) the names of two or three friends who possess the same needs for the product or service. Naturally, the plan is more effective when the salesperson has been successful in selling the prospect just interviewed, as the new buyer is probably enthusiastic about the purchase and may believe that some friends might like to consider the same proposition. However, even when the sale has not been made, the plan can work. The prospect was probably interested in the sales offer or would not have consented to listen to the salesperson's story. Even though he was unable to act immediately, the prospect should still be able to suggest two or three acquaintances who would have the same need for the product and might be able to act at once.

The sales rep may say to such a person, "I understand why you feel you cannot buy just now, but I'm sure you can think of three or four of your acquaintances who could use my product to advantage."

Occasionally the prospect will object, "I wouldn't want to inflict you on any of my friends." A reply is, "All right [with a broad smile], how about giving me the names of a few people you don't like very well?"

An encyclopedia sales rep, using a flattering technique in getting referrals, says: "The recommendations I'd like to get from you are not recommendations of just anyone, but of those who *share* your appreciation for an educational program of this caliber." He says that more than one-third of his sales are from referrals.

Many companies have trained their salespeople to use parts of the endless-chain plan for securing prospects, but only a few companies have applied the plan in its fullest extent. One company conducts a Good-Will Club, with special privileges and gifts for those who cooperate by turning in names of others who might be interested in the product.

The endless-chain method is especially effective in the development of prospects of intangibles like investments and insurance. In the sale of such services, it is necessary to establish a feeling of confidence and goodwill between the prospect and the seller early in the sales interview. If this is not done, the prospect may be unwilling to discuss private financial problems with a comparative stranger. However, if you come bearing a short note or card of introduction from a friend of the prospect, it is more likely that you will be accepted on a basis of friendship and confidence. Although you have not actually been *recommended* to the prospect, still the introduction carries with it an element of recommendation because (the prospect reasons) unless the friend had felt confidence in the sales rep, the introduction would not have been given.

This constitutes what is called a *referred lead*. It is the best kind of prospect, because a basis of friendliness and mutual interests has been established between sales rep and prospect. However, it is not any guarantee of success in the sale; that will depend upon the skill of the sales rep in discovering the real problems of the prospect and solving them.

In industrial selling the endless-chain prospecting system is widely used. Who is in a better position to know other business executives who might be prospects than the business executive with whom the sales rep is talking? One sales rep of inexpensive men's slacks called upon a small dealer handling men's apparel, one who carried only quality lines. While he quickly turned the sales rep down, he did refer the rep to the stores in town which would be the most likely to take on the line.

Center of Influence or Networking

In this system the sales representative in a community or territory develops a group of people who serve as "centers of influence." These people may be customers of the salesperson or influential friends who are willing to cooperate.

As an illustration of how this system might function, let us assume that an investment counselor returns to build up a business in the town where he attended college. He was a prominent athlete and a member of a fraternity as well as other college organizations. He starts to develop several centers of influence to aid him in obtaining good prospects. He gets in touch with his former professors, his coach, his fraternity adviser, and two or three well-known business executives who remember him. To these centers of influence he explains what kinds of people he hopes to do business with, what his investment service offers, and to what extent his knowledge and experience could benefit his clients. He persuades them to assist him in meeting good prospects. Probably he will try to make clients out of as many of them as possible, although that is not necessary to the success of the system.

For many salespeople, bankers prove helpful. They have more contacts than most people and know just about everything that is going on in the business community. The larger banks have officers who are highly specialized in their training, one being an expert on the steel industry, and others who have spent years learning about oil or textiles or paper. A wise sales rep cultivates a close friendship with a knowledgeable banker.

Executives in an industry are usually the best source of information as to what is going on in that industry, for they must keep abreast of current developments. They have lunch with other executives and pick up many bits of information that may be of value to salespeople. Who is thinking of

Business luncheons and dinners provide busy executives with an opportunity to exchange ideas and keep abreast of current developments. The more relaxed atmosphere of a business lunch or dinner often encourages people to talk more freely about their industry. Information exchanged at such gatherings can be valuable to salespeople. What types of useful information might an executive pass along to sales representatives assigned to call on their organizations?

remodeling the office, who is looking at computers, who is having packaging problems, who is unhappy with trucking connections, who needs a new conveyor system? Naturally, some executives are more in the know than others. Many sales reps make it a point to become good friends with executives who seem to know what is going on and who like to talk about it. Those who wonder why people will give such information to sales reps should realize that in doing so they make themselves feel more important, and they hope to enhance their prestige with the salespeople; they like to give the impression that they are industry bigshots.

Salespeople employing the center-of-influence method usually make an effort to repay the services of their contact group by periodic expressions of appreciation, such as gifts during the holiday season or cards on anniversaries. They make frequent calls to thank them personally for a recent courtesy, to explain a new service or feature of the sales rep's line which might reawaken their interest in it and in the rep, and to elicit the names of new prospects. These calls take little of a salesperson's time if planned for regularly, and they are essential to the success of the plan. No one is going to give much thought to helping a salesperson unless that salesperson proves to be a grateful, helpful friend. In addition, many business executives expect information in return. They expect the sales rep to let them in on prospects who would be helpful to them.

Management researchers have recently discovered the power and importance of networking to the businessperson. Sales reps have known it for years. It's called making *contacts*—knowing people, knowing who to see in each prospective firm, knowing that you can easily telephone or drop in to see someone.

Such contacts can pay off handsomely. For example, Tom Walthen, founder and CEO of California Plant Protection, learned that Pinkertons, the world's largest detective agency with revenues of over $500 million, was for sale. He wanted to buy it. He called Lloyd Greif, then senior vice-president of Sutro & Company, an old West Coast investment banking house, a person he had come to know and respect through their membership on the advisory board of a local university. Greif put together the multimillion-dollar deal, then later in 1990 took the resulting company public. Sutro's fees in the deal were in the millions. Not only did Greif enjoy a big paycheck from the deal but he was promoted into top management. Bear in mind that when the two men first met in 1980 neither of them had any idea that he would play such an important role in the other's life. Of the people with whom you network, you never know who will be important to you in the future.

You won't develop such a network overnight. You do it over the years with countless days and nights at trade shows making meaningful contacts with people who may be important to your future.

Personal Observation

Personal observation is used by most salespeople. Some call it the "intuitive" or "eyes-and-ears" system. It consists of being constantly alert to recognize prospect leads no matter where one is or with whom one may be talking. This ability to discover prospects in the routine of daily existence is much more highly developed in some people than in others.

Newspapers are filled with news items which are leads. Some of these items are useful to certain salespeople and of scant value to others; hence it is necessary to evaluate each one in terms of your prospecting problem.

For example, the insurance agent notes news of promotions, engagements, weddings, births, and deaths and stories dealing with business and finance. The sales rep of machinery and factory equipment watches for news of contracts for roads or buildings or building permits, for classified ads seeking additional workers, for fires or other catastrophes involving factories, for news concerning new products. The society page contains many items of interest to salespeople for home furnishings, clothing, jewelry, etc. The route person driving a milk delivery truck notes births and marriages in the paper. The real estate broker is keenly interested in approaching weddings, transfers of executives to or from the community, expansion plans of local business concerns, and promotions of personnel to better-paying jobs. A change in a zoning ordinance or a legal inquiry concerning eviction of tenants is grist for the broker's mill. Just about every salesperson can find items of real personal value in the local newspaper and should learn to read it carefully.

The industrial sales rep and the sales engineer will find that trade publications in their industry and industries of their potential customers are filled

News stories about business and finance and notices in local newspapers about promotions, engagements, weddings, and other social events are rich resources for leads. Salespeople can identify potential customers for home furnishings, real estate, insurance, and other services.

with news that will provide good leads. Certain firms are expanding their operations into new fields. A company is building a new plant in West Overshoe, Montana. An advertisement announcing a new product may suggest additional needs this item will create for its buyers, as many products complement each other. A merger may free a customer from a reciprocity buying arrangement with a competitor. Every action in the business world creates markets for many different firms. Every business start-up, expansion, or demise brings forth demand for certain products. Think of all the goods and services required by a new company just getting its operations under way.

Many rather ingenious prospecting methods based on using one's eyes in coordination with the brain have been developed by resourceful salespeople. Sales reps for printing paper scan magazines for poor halftones, uneven opacity, or lint buildup on printers' presses. They find in these and other signs evidence that the publication is using the wrong kind of paper and is therefore a prospect for a paper that will give better results.

One insurance agent uses this system to locate male prospects he can call on at home during the day: He stops at factory parking lots in the evenings and jots down license plate numbers of cars. Then he checks them with a listing for the names of the owners. Since they're working on the swing shift, he can see them late in the morning or early in the afternoon.

Real estate salespeople cruise the streets looking for clues to prospects: houses with "For Sale by Owner" signs, empty buildings, new "For Lease" signs, new construction, etc. One enterprising real estate salesman who specialized in industrial properties developed a particularly effective way of discovering manufacturers who were thinking of moving to a larger building. He would drive around industrial areas looking for plants whose parking lots were overflowing. He reasoned that if the company had outgrown its parking facilities it might also have outgrown its plant. He was usually right.

If this method of personal observation is followed to its logical conclusion, the salesperson will be on the lookout for bits of information while on the way to work, in the office, on the street, waiting to interview prospects or actually talking with them, at lunch, or at home listening to the conversation or reading the newspaper. Prospects are everywhere; all you have to do is keep your eyes and ears open and learn to recognize the signs.

Junior Salespeople (Spotters) and Bird Dogs

Some concerns use junior salespeople—sometimes called "spotters"—to locate prospects, thus relieving more experienced sales reps of prospecting so that they can spend more time actually selling.

The spotters usually research a likely new area under some guise—making a survey or a free service call. When they encounter a person who seems to have a need and the money, they may make arrangements for the senior sales rep to call or they may just pass the name on to the boss.

A variation of this method is found in the use of "bird dogs." These helpers are not employed by the company but by the salesperson. For example, the elevator overseer in an office building knows a good deal about the tenants. In sales situations where prospects are located only after a search, such bird dogs may be valuable.

A more dignified and tactful name for these bird dogs is "sales associates." These persons usually operate on a paid-on-delivery basis, provided the sale is made within a stipulated time. It is essential that you maintain close contact with them, telephoning them or meeting them personally at frequent intervals to keep them on their toes. You must *expect* some good leads from them and let them know that you are depending on them to come through. When they have helped to bring about a sale, you should not only pay them promptly but praise and thank them as well. The understanding as to payment must be clear.

In the financial world, people who introduce investment bankers to prospective deals are paid finders fees when the deals are completed. The old Lehman Brothers formula of 5 percent for the first million dollars of commissions, 4 percent for the second, and on down to 1 percent for everything over 5 million dollars would mean that a finder of a deal that netted the banker 10 million dollars in fees would receive over $100,000. Good prospects are worth knowing.

If you were a sales rep for Xerox and downtown Denver was your territory, you would do well to spend some weeks carefully researching these buildings to find out who and what is in them. Metropolitan areas provide opportunities for a great deal of business.

Normally, the sales rep tries to retain bird dogs who are in positions to naturally intercept people who have a need for the rep's services or wares. An investment banker might like bird dogs who work in banks, accounting firms, and law offices.

Cold Canvassing (or Cold-Turkey Canvassing)[3]

These are calls made with no advance knowledge about the person called upon. Calls upon all the dentists or lawyers in the community or upon each resident in a certain section of the city would be cold-canvass work.

While most sales reps usually dislike cold calls and believe they are a waste of time, there is still a place for them in sales operations. Sometimes it makes sense to go office to office in a large building looking for prospects. The reps most likely to profit from cold calls are those selling goods or services that are used by almost every firm—paper, adhesives, light bulbs, office supplies, janitorial services, and the like.

The key to successful cold canvassing is to develop a quick screening question that allows rapid determination of the firm's needs.

Cosmetics, jewelry, housewares, specialty foods and various other products have been sold successfully by companies such as Avon and Tupperware through party selling—a system of selling at home. Home parties allow the salesperson flexibility and the shopper an opportunity for making selections in a relaxed and convenient setting.

Parties

Party selling has been proved by such firms as Avon, Mary Kay, and Sarah Coventry. It works, if done properly. It capitalizes upon some strong buying motives while appealing to people's social drives.

The investment community uses the same system in its cocktail party circuit. A broker with some paper to sell throws a cocktail party to which likely investors are invited to meet and hear representatives of the venture that is selling the paper.

Party-plan selling has even moved into the workplace as workers have become increasingly reluctant to hold such sales gatherings in their homes.

Walk-Ins and Call-Ups

A lot of business is done with customers or clients who either come to your place of business or call you. Yet often such prospects receive shabby treatment. A person with little training and even less sense meets them at the door and quickly frustrates them.

It is appalling to discover how many concerns are unprepared to do business in their place of business. They just aren't set up for it. Yet a real sales-oriented firm will quickly make a sale whenever anyone comes in the door waving money or something that looks like it.

Many sales reps list their firms in the Yellow Pages even though they work from their homes. Sometimes they use answering services so they can be sure that they don't miss any call in business.

A transaction is a two-party deal. While sales reps are busy beating the bushes for prospects, there are many prospects beating the bushes for suppliers. There's a lot of business to be done on the street if the seller can just get in the way of it. So let people know who you are, what you sell, and where they can reach you.

The Farm System

A "farm" is a relatively small territory assigned to the salesperson in which no other salesperson with the agency can operate. The salesperson is supposed to confine her activities largely to the homes in the farm. Nikki Wichert relates her successful experiences with the farm—she works selling real estate in Long Beach, California. Nikki found that her concentrated effort of calling on *each* home in her area, just to introduce herself and her service, paid huge dividends, since a large number of people are involved in some way in buying or selling property at any one time. (See the Profile on her at the beginning of Chapter 14.)

Telemarketing

Telemarketing's role in selling programs has increased to such an extent that Chapter 19 is devoted entirely to that subject. Suffice it to say here, that the telephone plays a key role in most sales programs today.

Other Sources of Prospects

Different kinds of salespeople find prospects in different ways or from different sources. To every kind of sales rep certain prospect sources are available; usually the firm has ample instructional material guiding its own salespeople to prospects for its products.

Old Customers Old customers are frequently the best source of new business. This is particularly true of industrial selling. After all, these people have been using your product; *ergo,* they should like it. Such people may be willing to tell others of their happy experience. Your old customers know *you,* and you have had a good chance to build up their confidence in you; hence there should be no barrier between you that would make them reluctant to cooperate. The rep who is so devoted to seeking new accounts that he or she fails to get all the volume available from old customers is making the job unnecessarily difficult. It is usually easier to get an order from an old customer than from a new one, and that order will often be larger if the sales rep has won the buyer's confidence and the product has given satisfaction.

Service Personnel Companies maintaining service departments often find that the mechanics can furnish excellent leads. A serviceperson is one of the first to know when someone needs replacement equipment. One TV repair shop sells such leads to an appliance store that sells a high percentage of televisions. One Oldsmobile dealer in Miami, Florida, has a person stationed at the drive-up islands at which patrons stop to have their sick vehicles diagnosed who says, "While you are waiting, why don't we go for a drive in a new Oldsmobile?"

Naturally, service reps should be given an adequate incentive to keep their eyes open for such opportunities. Some firms give their service reps sales training to maximize their effectiveness as prospectors.

Classified List and Directories Among the more important sources of leads to prospective buyers are various classified lists and directories which are available in great quantity. Starting with the largest prospect list of all, the telephone directory, the parade of such lists goes down to such specific ones as the membership rosters of various small organizations and lists of club members.

Practically every industry has one or more trade or professional associations connected with it. Such an organization usually has available a roster of its membership. These rosters are indispensable prospecting and preapproaching aids.

Exposure[4] A basic tenet of selling could be stated as, "Your productivity varies directly with your exposure in the market." You cannot sell if you are hiding in the office or at home. You must get out and meet people. Most productive salespeople obtain maximum exposure of their personalities and products by joining a number of clubs and participating in a variety of civic activities on the general thesis that they simply cannot know too many people. Rare is the rep who cannot honestly say that some of the best leads have come during an idle conversation at some party, luncheon, golf match, etc. Leads can come from anywhere at any time, and one is never certain when any given individual is going to be in need of one's product or service.

This factor of exposure is one of the reasons why it takes time to become a top producer. You don't obtain widespread exposure and establish the necessary number of contacts in a few months or even a few years. It follows that more experienced salespeople generally have higher productivity; they simply have more contacts. This is also one strong reason why a good sales rep should not be hasty in changing an employer or product line; many contacts may be lost and the rep may be forced to spend considerable time establishing new ones.

EVALUATION OF PROSPECTING SYSTEMS

We have seen that there are many sources from which prospects may be obtained. From these, how can you go about determining the best prospecting system to use?

First, realize that your system should be tailor-made. Because someone else uses centers of influence for leads, it does not follow that this will be the best source for you. One person's food is another's poison; there is no one best way for everyone to operate. It is not unusual to find successful salespeople with the same firm using different prospecting methods. Hence, in the early stages of your development, try all systems and keep records on every name, where it was obtained, and the outcome of the contact with that prospect. You will be able to determine what your best source of leads is, measured by sales performance. Thereafter you can weed out the poorer sources of leads and concentrate on those that pay off best for you. Develop your own system for obtaining leads to good prospects.

Second, with new products it is wise to do some experimenting to learn where the best prospects are. One sales rep selling food freezers and food to families went against the boss's advice and reaped large rewards. Normally, the presentation was built around the alleged savings which the family would realize should they buy a home freezer. The boss recommended concentrating on blue-collar workers to whom the freezer would represent a sort of safety deposit box of food upon which they could fall back when not working. Also, the boss thought the savings appeal was most effective with this group. After working in this market for a short while, the new rep had sold nothing. He began thinking. The people upon whom he was calling simply did not have the $1,600 which the program required; they could not really afford the product. Besides, he doubted that they really appreciated the quality of frozen food; they were not used to it. He reasoned that wealthy suburban areas might be the best territories to work because the two advantages of a freezer were (1) convenience and (2) quality of food. His analysis was that the people in the suburban areas need the convenience of the freezer because of their distance from supermarkets. Higher-income families would not only be able to afford the freezer but would appreciate quality food. He shifted his operation to a wealthy suburb with outstanding success. He said that every buyer just wrote a check for the amount; there was no struggling with credit reports and collections.

Often a sales rep has hundreds, even thousands, of names of people who are prospects. Some are customers, some have been customers, and some may be customers. But how is the rep to remember even their names let alone anything about them. Files! It used to be card files, but now it is computer files. Professional salespeople keep records, excellent ones, on their prospects and customers. After all, these are the rep's earning assets. The advent of the portable computer has provided the sales rep with a powerful selling tool. Before making a call, the rep can pull up the file on the account and learn much about it.

The importance of maintaining a fat prospect file is strikingly proved by the experience of John Williams, an automobile sales rep in Chicago, who sold in a year more General Motors cars than any other salesperson in Illinois. He maintains a file of more than 2,000 prospective buyers, makes 50 telephone calls a day, and has a group of bird dogs who keep him informed about possible prospects. His file is further fattened by his record of his customer's children; and as each comes of age, the name is placed in the prospect file. It is evident that Mr. Williams owes much of his success to vigorous and intelligent prospecting.

LEAD GENERATION SYSTEMS

Top advertising agencies are now discovering what top-notch salespeople have known for a long time: customers are best solicited when addressed as individuals rather than personalities. Good sales reps keep records of each customer or account. Memory is a poor tool upon which to base your customer relations—and career. There is too much to be remembered, about customers, their buying preferences, their needs. Customer files have grown significantly in importance in recent years with the application of the computer to sales operations. Moreover, new terminology has renamed these files *customer databases.* "Database management" is the updated term and concept for this old activity.[5]

But how are customer databases accumulated? Of course, the old, well-established accounts are plugged in at the start. But attrition erodes such computer bases. New customers must be generated, not only to replace those that fall by the wayside but to make your business grow. To get new customers, either management or the sales reps should develop a process that systematically generates leads to them.

The Need for Cost-Effective Lead Generation

Traditionally, salespeople have been responsible for marketing efforts in their territories. The only help they could expect would be from the firm's advertising. Seldom would the marketing department be active in sales operations; marketing *was,* and often still is, a staff function.

Management tended to treat the commissions paid to its sales force as a variable cost; sales costs were proportional to sales volume. How nice! But that was then. Now, not only has the cost structure changed but the costs of making a sales call have increased significantly. The costs of keeping a salesperson in the field have soared. Those costs now tend to be fixed rather than variable with sales volume, as the sales reps demand more salary and their expenses dramatically rise. Many firms can no longer afford inefficient and ineffective lead-generation systems.

Firms are turning to direct-marketing techniques such as direct mail, direct-response advertising, and telemarketing for lead generations.[6] Some have reduced the size of their sales forces yet increased their workload and productivity by providing sales reps with an ample supply of well-qualified leads.

Products and markets have become more specialized and segmented. With an increasingly large number of products sold to progressively smaller market segments, a salesperson must use outside sources to generate and qualify leads. The old "endless chain" and "center-of-influence" methods fail when prospects are dispersed, separated by geography, or in differing industries.

Direct marketing can reach tens of thousands of suspects each month, asking them to stand up and qualify themselves as prospects worthy of an expensive sales call from one of the firm's valuable sales reps. Moreover, direct marketing can place literature and information in the hands of the prospect in preparation for the sales presentation. Much time can be saved in making the sale.

For example, an owner of a home with a swimming pool received in the mail a "package"* about a new device trademarked Kreepy Krauly, which automatically cleans the pool floor. (He received the package because his name was on a mailing list of people who own swimming pools. Such lists are readily available, as are lists of just about every imaginable classification of buyers. Indeed, the quality of such lists is the key to effective direct mail programs.) It so happened that the recipient of this package had just purchased the home and had no intention of cleaning the pool himself. Moreover, he had had previous experience with such devices and could appreciate the product's attributes. He immediately called the number on the brochure. An appointment was made for a sales rep to call. The rep appeared on schedule with a unit which he attached to the pool for a demonstration. The owner liked it, wrote out a check, and the sale was made in less than an hour. A good direct-mail program made the sale. No salesperson would have ever discovered the prospect; the home was isolated in a hilly area.

If you are selling a product that solves some clearly identified problems for its buyers, a direct-marketing program can effectively identify excellent prospects, prospects who will be ready to buy if the claims made for the product are borne out by personal inspection and demonstration.

Industrial buyers now face more salespeople than ever. The number of firms competing for their business has grown significantly. Buyers now want to check out the salespeople who call on them as much as the sales rep wants to qualify them. They don't want to waste their time listening to an irrelevant sales presentation. Neither person benefits from an unnecessary sales presentation. The sophisticated buyer requires literature in the mail before scheduling a sales call. Firms which fail to supply well-presented literature may never get to see the inside of the buyer's house or office.

---

* *Package* is the term used in the trade to designate the entire pack of materials sent to a suspect.

The Value of the Leads Generated[7]

Not all leads are created equally. Judging the effectiveness of a direct-marketing lead-generation program can be surprisingly difficult. Simply computing the percentage response rate to a mailing or an advertisement is *wrong*. Other factors must be considered.

First, in addition to computing the percentage response rate to the mailing or advertising, calculate the percentage of leads that result in a sales. A mailing list may produce a large number of leads, but those responding are poor prospects for any number of reasons. It is obviously much better to get a 1 percent return on a mailing with a 50 percent close rate than a 2 percent return with a 10 percent close rate. Furthermore, poor leads waste sales reps' time and money.

Second, the dollar sales volume of those sales should be examined. Some buyers buy more than others. A list containing relatively large buyers is obviously more valuable than one containing small buyers.

Finally, in cases in which the price obtained from the customers varies, management will want to examine the gross margin obtained from buyers on different lists.

Further, a lead-generation program should yield a steady flow of leads. Too many leads swamp the sales force and customer perception of the company drops as they wait. Too few leads . . . and your business fails.

No one measurement tells the whole story. Repeat business and the purchase of parts or accessories may increase a customer's value to you. A potentially large account may justify an initially low profit; you may be willing to cut your initial profit to secure the customer's future business.

While sales volume is most commonly used in evaluating the effectiveness of a direct-marketing lead-generation program, gross margin may be a better index of profitability. However, some serious obstacles often block its use. Accounting departments are often unable to provide the sales department with gross margin figures, unencumbered with overhead allocations. Contribution to overhead accounting is not often encountered. Moreover, management may prefer that the organization not know its profitability. Sales volume, on the other hand, is easy to obtain and difficult to manipulate. While the goal of the firm is to make a profit, the goals for the sales managers and their reps are most often sales-based. Since the reward structure is based on dollar sales volume, this volume is most often the yardstick for measuring the success of the lead-generation program.

Effective Lead Generation

The objective of direct-marketing lead-generation campaigns lies somewhere between providing raw prospect names and closing the sale. This leaves ample room to maneuver. Firms seeking to generate only names do not understand the need to qualify those names. Let's examine some commonly used qualifications.

First, there is the choice of lists. All direct-marketing experts insist that the key to effective direct mailings lies in list selection and testing. No matter how good your offer or package may be, it's useless if you send it to the wrong people. Take the swimming pool example. If Toyota owners had been used, disaster would have been certain. Focus on the lists. They're the secret of success in direct mail marketing.

Second, the offer may significantly bias the quality of the resulting leads. Be especially wary of programs that offer your leads a gift if they will listen to the sales presentation. For example, many real estate sales programs for recreational properties offer the recipients of the mailing a substantial gift if they will only drive out to view the property and take time to listen to the sales presentation. There is much mischief afoot in such programs. But many poor prospects will take the bait and run, wasting the realtor's time and money. Recognize, however, why such bribes are made in these industries. It is the only way they can get people out to look at their properties, and the high cost of wooing them with such bribes is factored into the price.

Third, often gift offers are made to help sell products that solve problems of which the suspect was unaware. But this means two sales, not one. The suspect must be convinced that he or she has the problem and then persuaded that the product will best solve it. It is similar to betting on the daily double at the racetrack: Both horses must win.

Direct marketing addresses the two-step selling process by first convincing suspects that they have the problem. Once persuaded of this fact by the direct advertising, the suspects *request* a call from a sales rep—a step which drastically increases the close rate. Let the suspect review the ideas suggested by the direct-marketing message before the sales rep arrives. Establish the key visuals in the prospect's mind beforehand. Identify yourself; don't leave the prospect wondering who you are and what you want.

Management must carefully study what part of the sales presentation can best be accomplished by the direct-marketing program and what should be performed by the sales rep.

DIRECT-MARKETING MEDIA

Five major media will be discussed here. They are:

Mail
Radio
Television
Newspapers
Magazines

A sixth, the telephone, is so important to today's sales world that a separate chapter on it is included later (Chapter 19).

Mail

Direct-mail advertising is a huge business. While much of it is aimed at generating immediate revenue from the package, a large portion is designed to generate leads to good prospects. There are many excellent books on direct-mail advertising and experts who specialize in developing direct-marketing lead-generation programs for you. This is not the place to dig deeply into development of such programs. Instead, a brief overview of the principles of direct-mail advertising may be of help.[8]

We know a good deal about direct-mail, about what works and what doesn't. Don't try to reinvent the wheel. Seek the help of professionals who know the technical details and have contacts with the numerous support organizations servicing the field. There are good list brokers and bad ones. And the good list brokers have good lists and bad ones. Moreover, the good lists can be badly handled by inept managers.

If it's dawned on you that lists are critical to your success at direct-mail, you have been paying attention. It all starts with list management, a science and art acquired only with experience. Many direct-mail programs fail simply because unwise list choices are made. Given strong strategy and work tactics, the effort will succeed. Different lists yield quite different results from identical "packages."

List Enhancement   Lists are compiled from specific demographic, psychographic, and lifestyle information. If a particular list doesn't have the selection criteria you want, list enhancement firms can generate the selections needed. These companies add information to the basic list. If you know the profile of your target customers, you can rent a list that will focus on them.

Testing   Testing is a must. Direct marketers test all critical aspects of their work, and lists are certainly critical. Send a random sample of a prospective list and track the end sales result.

One of the advantages of direct-mail programs is that they are measurable. You know your costs and your results. If the program pays, you continue it; if not, you quit or change some variables. Suppose your mailing piece (the package) costs 50 cents each. Assume that the gross margin on your proposition, after deducting the direct cost of the salesperson, is $500. You would need five sales from 5,000 test mailings to break even: a 0.1 percent response rate.

Response rates naturally vary with the proposition offered. The product and its price are critical. No reputable direct-marketing professional will promise any response rate. They have been fooled too many times. A great-looking program that should be tremendously successful can bomb out, while some seemingly mundane campaign may go crazy. That is why we test and track, test and track, and test some more, trying to find the key that will unlock the market.

Qualifying Questions   The recipient of your package is somehow asked to respond to telephone questions or mark off squares on a response card. If your list is not specific enough, some qualifying questions will help the sales reps not only evaluate the suspect but prepare for the presentation. If you are selling a photocopier, it's helpful to know:

- Does the suspect now own a copier?
- If so, what type?
- What is the nature of the work?
- What volume will there be?

While the goal of direct-mail sales is to make it easy to respond, lead-generation programs strategically create a barrier designed to exclude all but sufficiently "hot" prospects. For example, don't supply an 800 number; just give your regular phone number. If they're eager to buy, they'll pay for the phone call.

In particular, industrial salespeople often have no better cost-effective media for lead-generation than direct-mail.[9] Naturally, it all depends on the situation. Some industrial reps need only use the Yellow Pages for their prospecting. A most economical prospecting system.

Capacity Planning   One of the significant advantages of direct-mail lead-generation is that the manager can, and should, plan carefully how many mailings should go out each week to generate the number of leads required to keep the sales force operating at full capacity.

Suppose a sales force had 20 reps, each of whom could make 10 calls a week. Also, suppose that to make those 10 productive calls, the rep needed an average of 30 leads to contact. Moreover, assume that the response rate to company mailings was 2 percent. Then you would need to mail a total of 30,000 packages each week to keep the flow of leads coming fast enough to keep the reps busy. A larger mailing would be a mistake because leads don't keep. A good prospect does not stay that way. The "hot ones" will likely buy elsewhere.[10]

Radio

Radio is a creative challenge. It has a low cost per thousand contacts, delivers a great psychographic profile of station listeners, and has manageable geographic reach. The problem is that most radio advertisements go unnoticed. Even worse, telephone numbers heard over the radio are difficult to remember. (Matching the target sales territory with the radio coverage can also be a problem.) Obviously, radio is not widely used for generating sales leads.

The use of 800 numbers in newspaper ads is an alternative to direct-mail selling and a popular means of lead-generation. What are the advantages of placing an ad of this type in a local newspaper? What are the disadvantages?

Newspapers

Newspapers provide an excellent alternative to direct-mail for lead-generation. Short lead times allow quick placement of the ad and quick results. Local papers can cover selected smaller markets. Large papers offer area editions plus positioning in selected sections such as sports, business, auto, etc. The cost per thousand (CPM) is low, but the waste is significant, since most readers do not fit your customer profile.

The manager should compute such indices as:

- Costs per inquiry
- Cost per sale
- Total sales per ad
- Gross margin per ad

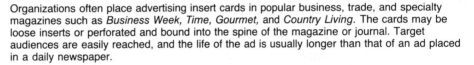

Organizations often place advertising insert cards in popular business, trade, and specialty magazines such as *Business Week, Time, Gourmet,* and *Country Living.* The cards may be loose inserts or perforated and bound into the spine of the magazine or journal. Target audiences are easily reached, and the life of the ad is usually longer than that of an ad placed in a daily newspaper.

In many instances, the present value of new customers should be calculated as a decision-making benchmark.[11] How much will a new customer spend with our firm over the next 5 years?

While newspapers are usually oriented toward the ultimate consumer, do not overlook such highly effective business newspapers as the *Wall Street Journal.* Moreover, many industries have daily or weekly newspapers, such as *WWD (Womenswear Daily)* and *Variety,* that go right to specific target markets and are well read.

While the use of an 800 number in newspaper ads greatly increases the leads generated, it does affect their quality. It is too easy for only mildly interested people to call.

Magazines

Every trade, industry, and special interest group has one or more magazines. They can be quite effective lead generators. The quality of the ads is high; thus a quality image can be transmitted. Moreover, most magazines rent out their subscription lists. You can therefore back up a direct-mail program with ads in the magazine.

Fortunately, many subscribers keep their magazines as a library item, thus giving the ads a long life. Sales can come from the ad for years. Many periodicals bind into the spine of the magazine postcards which interested prospects can use to ask for more information. Guess who provides the requested information—the sales rep. Such cards can be most effective. However, the jury is still out on the use of "Bingo Cards"—postcards that allow the reader to request information on many companies or products on one card. Many reps report bad results from contacting leads furnished by the magazine from such response cards because they take so long to arrive— sometimes 1 or 2 months. An 800 telephone number can overcome this problem.

SUMMARY

Effective selling begins by finding people or firms that are good prospects for your sales proposition. A good prospect is someone who both needs what you are selling and can afford to buy it. Most highly productive salespeople have learned to spend their time with good prospects. To this end, they have developed systems for generating leads to such good prospects. The 10 commonly used prospecting methods are the endless chain, center of influence, personal observation, junior sales rep, cold canvassing, parties, walk-ins and call-ups, farm system, telemarketing, and direct marketing.

Sales calls cost too much to waste on unqualified leads. Management should support the selling effort with a program that will provide excellent leads to prospects to the sales force.

A well-designed lead-generation program can get the sales reps in to see people not normally available to them. Moreover, such prospects can be primed to purchase from the sales reps by the advertising the prospects have received.

DISCUSSION QUESTIONS

1 You are a highly paid manufacturer's rep for business computer software in Chicago. You want to develop a lead-generating system for yourself, but you know little about direct-marketing techniques. How would you proceed with your task?

2 Your sales manager keeps sending you names of people who have responded to the company's advertising requesting more information. They have been sent literature. Your experience from contacting them is that they are exceedingly poor leads. You stop calling on them. Your boss is unhappy about it. What should you do about the situation?

3 If you need to make three sales a week and usually close one-third of your presentations, how many direct-mail letters would you have to send out each week to suspects if your mailing list resulted in a 5 percent response rate?

4 By what means can you improve the quality of the responses to a direct mailing?

5 You sell an expensive line of home exercise equipment. Your average sale is $2,500, for which you receive a commisison of $800. How much would you be willing to pay for good high-quality leads from which you closed one out of three presentations?

6 You have just completed sales training for a large manufacturer of a wide line of adhesives (glues, cements, epoxies). Your assigned territory is in the Los Angeles

area. With it you have inherited a few good accounts from the former salesperson; however, you are expected to start building new accounts immediately. How would you go about discovering prospects? Be as specific as possible. Make a list of the types of firms you believe would be your best prospects.

7 Describe the best prospects for buying an industrial building for investment.

8 You are the regional salesperson for a quality line of garden tractors and riding lawn mowers. You do not have representation in the town you are now in. Survey all possible outlets, and qualify them as prospects. Which outlet would you most want to get your line into? Why? Justify the placement of each name on your prospect list.

9 If you are a sales rep for a home security system, who would be your best prospects? How would you reach them?

10 How might cocktail party prospecting be applied to real estate?

REFERENCES

1 Stephen Schiffman, "Avoiding the Ups and Downs of Sales," *American Salesman*, September 1989, pp. 3–5, suggests the salesperson plan, monitor, coach, and avoid the fluctuations in the sales cycle.

2 Marvin A. Jolson, "Qualifying Sales Leads: The Tight and Loose Approaches," *Industrial Marketing Management*, August 1988, pp. 189–196; Peg Fisher, "It's a Problem! (Or, Is It?)," *American Salesman*, April 1987, pp. 12–15; and Eric Egge, "Second Guessing May Be Bad Guessing," *American Salesman*, April 1986, pp. 3–6, suggest that highly qualified sales may not be as effective; that loose leads produce more sales volume; that one should gather pertinent information, conduct follow-ups, and qualify a buyer correctly.

3 Mark Skipworth, "Take the Chill out of Cold Calling," *American Salesman*, February 1987, pp. 16–19, and Lee Boyan, "Skill in Cold Call Selling Boosts Sales Productivity," *American Salesman*, October 1989, pp. 10–13, discuss overcoming fear and background research.

4 Schiffman, "Generating Sales Leads," *American Salesman*, December 1989, pp. 7–8, discusses word-of-mouth, joining organizations, public speaking, and mailings.

5 Robert H. Collins, "Microcomputer Applications: Mastering Inquiries and Sales Leads," *Journal of Personal Selling & Sales Management*, Summer 1989, pp. 73–75, treats the use of microcomputers to follow potential customers through the sales cycle and manage the communications between sales representative and prospect as inquiries are developed into satisfied customers.

6 Donald L. Brady, "Determining the Value of an Industrial Prospect: A Prospect Preference Index Model," *Journal of Personal Selling & Sales Management*, August 1987, pp. 27–32, suggests using the discounted value of expected revenue less expected cost, which is divided by the cost of conversion multiplied by the prospect's strategic value to determine a prospect's value.

7 Ray Jutkins, "Lead-Generation Planning: Part I," *Target Marketing*, January 1990, p. 63; Ray Jutkins, "Lead-Generation Planning: Part II," *Target Marketing*, February 1990, pp. 52; and Libbie Bramson, "Make Sales a Partner in Lead Generation Programs," *Sales & Marketing Management*, July 1990, pp. 94, 96, suggest that qualifying all leads is important and that one should use a direct marketing advertising lead program.

8 See Robert Stone, *Successful Direct Marketing Methods* (Chicago, National Textbook Company, 1989).

9 Jim Morris, "Low-Cost Direct-Mail Provides Ticket to High-Tech Sales," *Direct-Marketing,* September 1986, pp. 48–50.

10 For an excellent, detailed discussion of how to manage a lead-generating program, see Robert Stone, *Successful Direct-Marketing Methods,* National Textbook Company, Lincolnwood, Ill., 1986, Chapter 14.

11 See Julian Simon, "Calculating the Dollar Value of a Customer," *How to Start and Operate a Mail Order Business,* 2d ed., McGraw-Hill Book Co., New York, 1975, pp. 109–119.

CASE 6-1: The Copy Master Corporation—Selection of a Prospecting System

Jack Adams, sales manager; Harv Michaels, marketing manager; and Sue Lund, sales training director, had been in conference for more than 5 hours planning the company's forthcoming national sales-training program for the 83 new salespeople it had hired from the nation's business schools the preceding June.

All had gone well in the planning session until they started talking about the subject of prospecting. A serious disagreement arose among them about the content of the prospecting portion of the program.

Copy Master was a large, nationally known company with a fine reputation for its wide line of printing and reproducing equipment sold directly to business and professional concerns throughout the world. The firm had its own sales force working out of sales branches located in almost every major city in the world.

The company had just developed and introduced to the market a new copier much like the famous Xerox machine that would make dry electrostatic copies on whatever paper was fed into it. Management had decided that as a matter of policy, this new line of equipment would be sold by a sales force hired and trained to sell it exclusively. It was felt that if the new copier was to achieve its target share of the market, such aggressive sales effort would be needed. The existing sales force, with its many other responsibilities, just would not be able to devote the needed attention to the copier.

After more than an hour of discussion about prospecting methods, the group was still unable to agree on the system that would be taught to the new salespeople. Jack Adams, the sales manager, felt that the best prospects, the ones that the new sales force should focus upon during the first year of operation, would be the company's existing customers for its other equipment. "After all," he reasoned, "these people already know us and are happy with us. We know them, and we can penetrate this market, with a minimum out-of-pocket cost."

Harv, the marketing manager, did not totally rule out existing customers as prospects, but he did not want to limit the firm's marketing efforts to them. He said, "But look at the opportunity this gives us to get our feet in new doors. We cannot just sit still and feed off one set of customers. We've got to get some new blood into this game. Our existing equipment goes to firms who do a large volume of in-house printing and reproducing. They already have reproducing equipment. The customer for our new copier is a smaller outfit whose reproducing needs are less than those of our present customers. The market is different."

Sue, the sales-training director, had still another approach. "Let's go after Xerox customers. Xerox has pioneered the market and has shown us where it lives. We can go after the big Xerox customers because we have a cost story to tell. Our service is cheaper, and we'll sell the equipment for less than will Xerox. I think our best prospect will be using a Xerox machine, or an IBM one, and will be unhappy about its costs."

The two men disagreed with Sue. They were reluctant to go head-to-head with Xerox for fear of retaliation. They did not want to get into a dogfight with the other companies.

But Sue continued, "I can hear the pitch now. 'Let's pull out your last month's bill from Xerox and see what you would have paid if you owned our machine instead of renting theirs.' It would be powerful selling."

The men were adamant. They did not want to start a fight with the other firms. Finally, Jack suggested that they contact the branch managers to get their opinions on a prospecting system for the new copier. They all agreed to do so and to get together in a week to complete the program.

The sales department staff was busy the next week gathering the opinions of the branch managers concerning the upcoming sales-training program. In particular, their opinions about the best prospecting system for the new copier were solicited. At the end of the week, Sue threw up her hands in despair; seemingly every conceivable prospecting system had been mentioned. More important, there was little agreement. Many agreed with Sue about going after existing users. Others wanted to focus on new users and businesses. Some felt that the company should concentrate on the professional offices—lawyers and doctors—because the machine seemed ideally suited to their needs. Many simply said that all business and professional people were prospects and that the company should not concentrate on any one market.

Sue reported the results of the survey to Harv and Jack. They sat silently contemplating the way to go.

1 Evaluate each of the prospecting systems that were proposed.

2 How should they go about determining the most effective prospecting system?

3 What prospecting system would you recommend? Why?

CASE 6-2: The Home Beverage Dispenser—
Generating Leads to Thirsty People with Money

Charlie Ross had retired from a large marketing corporation as regional sales manager for the Dallas territory. He chose to stay in Dallas and play some golf between fishing trips to Lake Sam Rayburn, where he had a small house and a boat. Life was good. After a few months it was also boring. He had to find something to do with his time.

It so happened that Charlie drank a lot of soft drinks. So many that he had found it not only convenient but economical to have a home beverage dispenser installed in both his house and cabin at the lake. Each dispenser cost about $2,000 installed and used 5-gallon syrup containers, costing about $22 each, which yielded 27½ gallons of soft drink (3,520 ounces). Since the retail price for a 12-ounce can was around 30 cents, Charlie figured he got about $88 worth of soft drinks from the $22 syrup, or a contribution of $66 a container toward the machine. The machine was paid for after he used about 30 five-gallon cans, which he easily did the first year.

Charlie thought that was a neat trick—saving money and not having to worry about lugging cans of pop home from the store. He got to talking about it with his supplier. He asked, "Why don't you have more of these machines around here?"

The owner of the distributorship replied, "I don't have time to mess with it. I'm making good money just distributing the syrups. I don't want the headaches that go with the hardware end of the business. You've got to install the blasted things and fix them when they go out. And, boy, do these customers want them fixed in a hurry—I mean right now. They are dry and don't like it one bit."

Charlie thought a bit and asked, "What would you do if I started a business selling and servicing the machines?"

"I'd be tickled pink! I'd love to have you do it. I'll throw everyone your way who asks about them" was the reply.

With that encouragement Charlie set about to study the business and see what it might take to do it. He wrote a modest business plan for his own use. He had sufficient money to start the business, so he did not need outside capital. When he came to his marketing plan, his experience with his former employer had taught him well the need for detailed plans on how to penetrate the market. He first profiled his target customer:

Upper 5 percent income bracket

Socially active with home entertainment

Large family usage

35 to 65 years old

Male

He realized that his profile was little more than an educated guess. He did not really know who would be the best prospect for the beverage dispenser. However, he recalled a young college graduate specializing in direct marketing whom he had hired for his former employer. They were on good terms, so he called to ask how to use direct-marketing techniques to find good customers for the home beverage dispenser. Morever, he hoped that his friend would help him devise a lead-generating system. Charlie thought he would need 10 good leads a week to start with.

1 You are Charlie's friend. What would you tell him to do to solve his problems?

CHAPTER SEVEN

PLANNING THE SALE

Nothing is so difficult but that it may be found by seeking.
Terrence

After studying the material in this chapter you should:

☐ Understand that it is folly to go into a sales interview unprepared

☐ Realize that good planning minimizes the chances for serious errors in the sales interview

☐ Use the planning stage not only to qualify the prospect but also to gain more information about the person's needs and problems

PROFILE OF

A GREAT PLANNER

Mike Markulla

Former CEO, Apple Computers
Silicon Valley, Calif.

"**I** attribute much of my success to my five 'P's. *Prior Planning Prevents Poor Performance*," said Mike Markulla to a large group of college students assembled to hear his inspiring story.

After Mike graduated from the University of Southern California with both his B.S. and M.S. degrees in electrical engineering, he worked for 4 years at Hughes in defense electronics. While he loved the work, it bothered him that he could not reveal to other people what he was doing. Top secret and all that! So he cast about for another job. Intel, the microcircuit manufacturer, was just getting started. He joined the firm but not as an engineer. Someone had to do the marketing for the new concern, and Mike was the one. He became a salesman and evidently a good one, too, as the fabulous success of the venture attests.

Mike made his fortune with Intel and retired for a while. Then he was asked to help two kids, Steve Jobs and Steve Wozniak, with their new venture. It was called Apple Computer, and Mike became its CEO and driving force.

Mike wrote the 5-year business plan for Apple and then made it become a reality. The plan called for the firm to become a Fortune 500 company within 5 years. It did. The plan was executed almost to the numbers. It is not surprising that Mike believes in planning. Planning prevents poor performance!

A young book rep whose future career seemed in jeopardy began the presentation to the author by asking, "Now, what's your name?" After the author replied, the rep continued, "Now, what do you teach?" With patience greatly taxed and with a keen curiosity to see what was going to happen next, the author answered, "Salesmanship."

The rep then began extolling the alleged virtues of the salesmanship book published by his employer. Finally he got around to asking what text was being used. Upon being quietly informed that the prospect was a coauthor of the "chosen" text, the lad came unglued, quickly retreated in confusion, and forgot all about the other books he had to sell. Had the rep taken the trouble to read about the importance of the preapproach, he could easily have avoided embarrassment. He hadn't given any thought to the interview. He hadn't planned the sale.

The professional book sales rep learns the prospect's name prior to making a call and looks at the schedule to see what the prospect is teaching and what book is being used. The real pro will also know a great deal about the prospect's background. Plan the sale properly, and such incidents will not happen. Good plans are based on information. You need information about the prospect and the situation to figure out what to do and what not to do.

In this chapter we take up the preapproach to a *specific prospect*, the facts about that individual which the sales rep would like to learn in order to bring to bear the most effective appeals. The question arises: When is the task of prospecting completed, and at what point does the preapproach begin? The only way to answer this is to point out that the selling process is a continual one with no sharp lines of demarcation between the stages. To put it broadly, the prospecting job is finished when you feel that you know enough about a person to believe that there is a chance of making a sale.

The objective of the preapproach is to enable the rep to *plan the interview intelligently.* This information can be used in planning the approach. The rep is eager to avoid getting off on the wrong foot and to start the interview as favorably as possible.

When they meet, the seller will continue the preapproach by shrewd observation and asking questions in the early phases of the interview. Thus the preapproach merges into the approach, the two actually overlapping somewhat. No matter how much a salesperson may know about the prospect in advance of the call, it is wise to use the first few minutes of the approach to check the accuracy of the preapproach and to enlarge upon it. The seller may find that ideas concerning the prospect must be revised and the mapped-out sales plan must be altered.

Conceptual and consultative selling systems also rely heavily on information gathered in the first phase of their programs, which are, not too surprisingly, called *getting information.*[1] These selling systems rely heavily on questioning the prospect for needed information. The first set of questions verifies what the sales reps think they know, and the next set asks for new information.

Effective, successful sales representatives take the time to map out their sales plans. They plan their interviews and sales strategies in advance so that they can tailor their presentations to the needs of each prospect.

What is meant by "the mapped-out sales plan," mentioned above? In brief, we can point out that any *good* salesperson plans the interview in advance, just as a coach formulates a game plan. Focus the presentation on the benefits that seem most likely to appeal to this particular prospect. Appeal to motives that seem most likely to move the prospect to buy. Avoid discussing matters which may irritate the prospect. Adjust the speed of the interview to the prospect's mental tempo. Plan answers to the objections which the prospect may raise. In short, the entire presentation is tailored to that particular prospect. This could not be done without a careful preapproach.

OBJECTIVES OF THE PREAPPROACH

The preapproach has six objectives: (1) to provide additional qualifying information, (2) to gain insights into how best to approach the prospect, (3) to obtain information around which the presentation can be better planned, (4) to keep the sales rep from making serious errors, (5) to give the sales rep more confidence, and (6) to impress the prospect that the sales rep is diligent and professional.

Additional Qualifying Information

Although the salesperson may believe that certain people or organizations are prospects, closer examination of the circumstances may disclose that such is not the case. They may already have the product. They may be financially unable to buy. They may have a relative or close friend who sells the same thing. All sorts of conditions can exist which would *disqualify* the lead. Therefore, the first thing the salesperson tries to learn is whether the lead really *is* a good prospect.

Approach Strategy

A good preapproach should provide some insights into how best to approach the prospect. Should you stress savings or durability? Focus on the prospect's major interests right from the start. Some like a direct businesslike approach, while others are best approached indirectly. Timing is important in some cases and not in others.

An unfortunate book sales rep approached the author with the statement, "You should give serious consideration to [a new book being introduced] because it has the most advanced quantitative treatment yet given the subject." Now, a good salesperson with some simple preapproach work would have discovered that this prospect had no interest in the latest quantitative treatment because he was a behaviorist. No doubt the youthful representative is still wondering just what went wrong.

On the other hand, another book rep was spectacularly successful in the same region by his adept approaches to various professors. He would discover each one's particular interests and approach them through that avenue. The head of an English department was seriously involved with the campus international club. The representative attended several evening meetings of the group and met the prospect on a social basis. Small wonder he cracked the English adoption on that campus for the first time. This man now owns his own publishing company.

Planning Information

A sales presentation can take many forms and go in many directions. Some are built around cost savings, others around certain unique product features. Obviously, if the prospect is most interested in low cost, it would be a mistake to dwell on quality features with scant attention to the economic aspects. Similarly, if the prospect is most interested in acquiring status, appeals to economy may fall on deaf ears. A good preapproach should furnish the salesperson with some insights into which motives are most likely to move

A well-prepared sales approach may include the use of storyboards or other visual aids. The effective use of visual aids will signal that the rep is a knowledgeable professional who is well-prepared for the presentation, and will instill confidence in the sales message.

the prospect to action and what appeals would prove most effective. A good sales presentation should be tailor-made for the prospect in hand on the basis of the information uncovered in the preapproach.

Avoiding Serious Errors

People have idiosyncrasies which must be humored if a presentation is to be successful. Some people dislike overly aggressive individuals and react unfavorably to anyone who tries to overpower them. Some people will react negatively to a person who smokes during the interview. One hat company executive, quite understandably, would throw out anyone who arrived bareheaded. Many times great rapport can be established if you are able to play up to some of the prospect's pet ideas. Perhaps a purchasing agent with a large firm is known to become quite perturbed with sales reps who directly contact anyone in the company without first going through the purchasing department. The sales rep who explains, "I always believe in first contacting a firm's purchasing agent before seeing anyone else in the company," may be hitting a responsive chord with the purchasing agent.

A sound preapproach also helps avoid errors in handling objections. A salesperson was trying to sell a photocopier to a small merchant who was protesting that not only didn't his office need a copier but he couldn't afford it. The salesperson destroyed the first objection by citing the number of copies the merchant's secretary had to make during the past month at a nearby copy shop; she had found this out in her preapproach. She ignored the latter objection because information obtained in the preapproach indicated he had a profitable store and could well afford whatever he wanted.

Confidence

The unknown breeds fear and uncertainty. The person who walks into the presentation completely ignorant of the prospect's nature and situation is likely to become uncertain, hesitant, and fearful of making mistakes. Such a person seldom knows what to talk about and is afraid to bring up certain subjects lest they offend or antagonize the prospect. However, the salesperson who has done a complete preapproach on the prospect is confident that the sales talk is right and is the key to selling this prospect. Experienced salespeople know that this factor of confidence is extremely important. They reason: "How can prospects buy from me if they have no confidence in me, and how can they have confidence in me if I show no confidence in myself?"

Professionalism

Most buyers want to make purchases from professionals, people who obviously are competent in their fields. Few of us relish dealing with amateurs. Spending money is much too important in most industrial transactions and significant consumer purchases to be treated lightly.

Professionals do their homework before going on stage. They don't walk in and "wing it." The prospect who sees that you have taken a great deal of time and effort preparing for your interview will likely give you the full hearing you deserve. But if it is evident that you walked into the presentation unprepared, the prospect may conclude that the matter you want to discuss is not all that important. In most large industrial sales, the rep spends much time preparing a written proposal for the prospect. The presentation is then built around that proposal.

EXTENT OF THE PREAPPROACH

By this time it is clear that the amount of time and thought which should be devoted to a prospect is governed by the importance of making that sale. Nowhere is this principle more clearly evident than in the preapproach. A sales engineer may spend months preparing data to use in presenting a proposition. The representative of an advertising agency may, together with colleagues, work out a complete advertising campaign for a prospective client, making the presentation of the proposed campaign purely "on speculation" in the hope that it will be accepted. If it is not adopted, the work of this very elaborate preapproach, perhaps involving extensive and expensive research into the prospect's marketing problems, has failed in its purpose. On the other hand, the house-to-house sales rep for brushes cannot afford to make more than the scantiest preapproach, perhaps merely inquiring at each house the name of the family next door.

The point is this: Most salespeople fail to make an adequate preapproach. They neglect to learn vital facts which might have helped them make the sale. They are like the life insurance agent who tried to sell a man a policy by appealing to the buying motive of affection—pulling out all the stops on the "Mary and the baby" appeal. His prospect remained coldly unmoved, a fact which puzzled the agent until he learned that the man was living apart from his wife and suing for divorce. Their only child had died 3 years previously.

Another factor bearing on the extent of the preapproach is the difficulty encountered in obtaining an interview with the prospect. Where there is a serious problem, the salesperson will be well advised to make a careful preapproach and utilize the information gained thereby in the planning of an unusually effective approach.

What the Preapproach May Include

The information gathered in the preapproach will differ with the selling problem facing the salesperson. If selling to an individual for the latter's own use, confine investigations to the prospect as a person. On the other hand, if the prospect is buying for a business, broaden the preapproach to include facts about that business also.

To the Prospect as an Individual Many of these items should also be checked when the prospect is buying for a business, as most buying is done by individuals.

Name[2] Learn to spell it and pronounce it correctly. People are sensitive on this point, and a mistake can be costly. People with names that are difficult to pronounce are likely to react most favorably to salespeople who have taken the trouble to learn the correct way to say their names.

Age Older people respond to the respect they feel is due them. Younger people in high positions appreciate a recognition of the fact that they have climbed fast.

· *Education* This may provide a topic of conversation. A college graduate usually likes to have this fact recognized. The self-made person is proud to have won a position without much formal schooling. If the prospect and the sales rep share a common educational background—and it does happen frequently—a useful common bond can be established.

Place of Residence This may reveal something of the person's social position or friends.

The Need for What You Are Selling If the product is needed, you should learn how the person can best use it. If it is not needed, the person is not a good prospect.

Ability to Buy   Many inexperienced reps have taken orders from poor credit risks only to have them turned down by the credit department. It is not good sense to try to sell someone a Cadillac when you know the person can afford nothing more costly than a bicycle.

Authority to Buy   Does the prospect have to ask another person? Is the prospect only an agent for the real buyer?

Facts about Family   Many purchases are made in the hope that it will make the spouse or children happy. The latter often exercise a strong influence in many purchases for a home. You may also find that the person likes to talk about his or her children; most parents do.

Reference Groups   Rotary, church, temple, country club, trade association, etc. Very helpful information to have!

The Best Time to Call   Every person has a routine and probably dislikes to have it disturbed. You will get a far better reception if you call when the prospect is not in the habit of, and eager to be, doing something else.

Personal Peculiarities   Every one of us has them. The salesperson caters to these—if they are known. Ellen had learned that the prospect had strong dislike for smokers. She found a way to communicate to the prospect that she had a similar disdain for smoking.

Occupation   What does the person do for a living? Is he self-employed? In what business? For whom does she work? In what capacity? For how long? These are critical questions in many sales.

Recreation, Interests, and Hobbies   This point merits elaboration. Some sales reps feel that the most effective way to get by the "cold spot" in the first minute or two of a sales interview—that moment when the prospect first learns that you are selling something and tries to get rid of you—is to discover a particular hobby or interest and utilize it to promote the interview upon a friendly basis. Although this seems to be something to consider in the approach rather than in the preapproach, it will be discussed briefly at this time because the salesperson must learn about the hobby in the preapproach if it is to be used later. The importance of this phase of the preapproach is brought out by a long time sales rep of magazine advertising.

My old professor of psychology told me that every man has two minds, so that in my first job I asked for the hundred men in New York City whom nobody had been able to sell on the magazine, which paid me the handsome remuneration of $40 a week "to start." I was looking for the "yes" mind—the mind that could say "I will take it," not the mind which sat back all ready to say "No."

The question naturally arises as to how to find out the customer's "yes" mind, the things that he will shut down his desk for and talk about to the exclusion of all business.

There was a man I remember well, who at the words "There is open water this week up in Maine and I'll bet the trout will take a fly," would close his rolltop desk, turn around in his swivel chair, and send out word that he couldn't see Mr. Anybody from Anywhere, as he was very busy for the next half hour.

I never will forget the way old John Scullin's eyes flashed when I dropped in one morning with a chisel that I had picked up at a pawnshop. It had a fine, broad blade, a fluted wooden handle, and the initials of some carpenter or cabinetmaker who had used it. Scullin was advertising manager for a food product house, and a classmate of his at Purdue had told me of the workshop down in his cellar and the furniture which he spent all day Sunday working on.

A little inside information about Charles XII of Sweden would sell almost anything to one of the hardest men to sell in the agency field. Any talk of a walking trip through the Berkshires could secure the favorable attention, interest, desire, and sometimes action of the vice president of a motor-truck company in Newark. No matter how unpromising a prospect looked on the first five visits, a little work would always result in finding his particular hobby and the things he liked to talk about. This information once secured, the sale was easy if it was in any way possible to link up his hobby with what you had to sell.

My sources of information were all kinds of people in all kinds of places. I would first list the college and class of the man, if he had such a thing; his golf, tennis, fishing, or hunting club; his church; the school his children attended; whether he had ever lived on a farm or any facts of a similar nature about his past; the names of his neighbors; where he kept his automobile and the kind of car he drove; where he spent his vacations. From these sources, somehow or other it was always possible to find out the story of his hobby.[3]

But let's not go overboard on this hobby matter! It is well to hold in mind that such preapproaches are abnormal, suitable for prospects who are hard to see or hard to sell and who can place large orders. They should be used mainly as a last resort unless the preapproach has revealed that the prospect likes to discuss his hobby with callers. Most business executives would rather discuss their business than their hobbies—at least during business hours. The salesperson who can offer a way to make that business more successful may be accorded a more cordial hearing than the one who tries to talk hobbies. Besides, most salespeople are not well enough versed in the prospect's hobby to discuss it intelligently. A clumsy attempt to drag it into the opening conversation is so transparent that it is likely to defeat its purpose.

It is safe to say that the *obvious* hobby should be approached with extreme caution by the sales rep. The bag of golf clubs in the corner will be spotted by most reps, and all too many of them will waste time trying to talk golf before getting down to business. The salesperson who does get down to business at the outset may be mighty welcome. One prospect had a huge sailfish mounted and hanging above his desk. He was inordinately proud of it, for it represented the high spot of many years' fishing. But he was finally forced to take it down because too many salespeople wasted valuable time talking about it. One business executive solved a similar problem by posting a sign just under a mammoth muskellunge on his office wall. It read: YES, I CAUGHT THIS. BUT PLEASE DON'T MENTION IT UNLESS I DO!

One other observation on this hobby question: The more salespeople a prospect sees in the course of business, the less the prospect is likely to respond to the hobby approach. The person who sees few salespeople, on the other hand, may be glad to talk about a hobby.

To the Prospect as a Business Executive   In addition to the facts about the person as an individual, certain facts about the person as a business executive are pertinent. These chiefly concern the business with which the person is associated and cover matters such as those revealed by the following questions.

Company personnel (assuming the person is employed and not self-employed):

* Who owns the company?
* If a corporation, who is on the board of directors?
* What are the business affiliations of these directors?
* Do I know any of them personally?
* Who has the final word on purchases?[4]
* Who else has an influence on purchases? Many salespeople insist that it is a waste of time to talk to subordinates; they prefer to go straight to the top. Others find it helpful to enlist the cooperation of personnel in the lower echelons. Whichever policy is followed, the salesperson should definitely know who has the final buying authority.
* Who is in charge of the department that will use my product or services?

The company in operation:

* What does it make or have to sell?
* What market does it logically reach?
* Is the product top grade, medium, or cheap?
* What is the capacity of the plant?
* What parts of the finished product do they make, and what do they buy?
* What processes of manufacture does the company employ?
* What type and make of machines are used in production?
* How about raw materials? Kind and amounts? Sources?
* What schedule of maintenance does it operate on?
* Do seasonal factors affect its operations?
* Where does the company rate in its industry—in volume of output?

Buying practices of the company:

* What systems and procedures are followed by the purchasing department?
* Does the company buy from a few sources, or does it diversify more?
* What is its credit rating?
* When does the firm buy my product?
* How much do they buy at a time?
* From whom are they now buying and why?
* Is the firm happy with its present sources of supply?
* What problems has the firm encountered with its present supplier?

- Does the firm practice reciprocity?
- Basically, will the company benefit from buying and using what I am selling?

The Preapproach for Regular Customers—Account Management[5]

In the foregoing discussion prospects and customers have been treated alike, since the careful sales rep takes as many pains to keep informed on regular customers as on prospects. It is as important to keep present customers as it is to secure new ones, so the salesperson should exercise every precaution in the care and feeling of existing accounts.

Since most sales reps have hundreds of accounts, and there are several people involved in each of those accounts, memory becomes a problem. How do you remember the information you know about the people you are calling on that day? Clearly, files are needed. Keep records on each of the people you call upon. Portable personal computers are ideal for this use. Just before you go in to see a customer, call up on your computer the appropriate files for review. Refresh your memory. You may have written yourself a note about something you want to do or to talk about with this customer. Good records pay off in more sales and better relationships. After all, one of the main advantages of account management selling is that you have a longtime relationship with the account and have learned much about it. So why lose some of this advantage by forgetting relevant information?

While one might think that it would be difficult to gather information about a prospect, actually much is publicly known about most people, particularly those in top management positions. Moreover, people love to talk about other people. It does take some time to develop background information on a prospect, but it is time well spent. Consider it homework.

Other Sales Reps

It pays to cultivate relationships with other salespeople. Every buyer has peculiarities that are known to the salespeople who call on him or her, and such facts may profitably be exchanged. These hints will come mostly from noncompeting sales reps, who can be mutually helpful without injuring their own chances. A saleswoman selling fuel oil to a factory purchasing agent could safely give a suggestion to a salesman for office machines. Even competitors may occasionally divulge valuable information, especially if they have failed to sell the prospect. They are likely to feel that they have already lost and have nothing more to lose. Or perhaps the competing salesperson, when led to talk freely about a prospect, may inadvertently drop hints that can be utilized. Conversations overheard in hotel lobbies and dining rooms, on planes, or in prospects' waiting rooms may yield suggestions of value.

A salesperson who receives information of a confidential nature should never divulge it. If a confidence is betrayed, the salesperson will receive no

Portable personal computers or laptops provide easy access to client files as well as to stored information relevant to your clients' accounts. What information might a contractor access on site?

more information from that source. The salesperson who earns the reputation of being discreet and close-mouthed will be told a lot more than one known to be loose-tongued.

Customers

Much can be learned from customers about prospects yet to be seen. People who have just purchased usually wish to vindicate their judgment by having others buy too. They are likely to feel they're doing them a favor, so they suggest that the salesperson call on some of their friends. Fortunately, there are customers who love to talk and who are sufficiently well wired into the industry or community that they can be of great help. Such sources of knowledge should be cultivated.

Bird Dogs and Centers of Influence

The person providing the lead should also be pumped for all possible preapproach information. Frequently, he or she can provide almost everything you want to know. Hence develop the habit of questioning the source of any lead at the time the lead is given.

The Local Newspaper

A source not sufficiently utilized is the local newspaper. It should be emphasized that the sales rep's preapproach consists not merely of gathering personal facts about the prospects but also of building up a background for each of them. It may help to know something of the town's activities and interests when calling for the first time on a prospect. Such knowledge furnishes just so many more points of contact upon which to establish friendly relations.

The industrial salesperson can establish common interests with a prospect by reading articles and advertisements in technical and business journals, especially those containing stories about or advertisements by the firm one is trying to sell. It is not merely a coincidence that most good salespeople are prolific readers of the trade press.

Go to the library to study the past issues of your industry's trade journals and those of your key customers. You will be surprised by the large amount of useful information you will gather.

Directories

Many directories provide personal data on people of some position in practically all fields of endeavor. There is a *Who's Who* in each of many areas, such as business and industry, education, science, various states, and America. If the prospect is of sufficient stature to be listed in one of these directories, much personal information can be easily obtained by going to any good library. Various industries frequently publish rosters of and biographical data on the executives or personnel of various companies.

Observation

As the salesperson enters the prospect's place of business, many things can be learned. A sales rep calling upon a retailer carefully notes the brands carried in stock, for they indicate a great deal about the policies and philosophies of the dealer. You can tell whether the prospect is enterprising or conservative by noticing stock display, fixtures, and the general atmosphere of the premises. You can observe the attitude of subordinates toward their employer and thus learn the employer's real disposition. A man may appear to be a bully and a tyrant to the salesperson, but if his employees treat him without fear, it is safe to assume that the attitude of gruffness is merely a pose.

The industrial sales rep can determine many things about a prospect by simply observing the person's immediate environment. Is she playing the role of the big business executive? The appearance and formality of her office should give some indication of this trait. Is she a hard worker? Again the condition of the person's desk and office may provide insights into her

What can you learn about the owner of this office from observation?

working habits. How modern or up-to-date is she? Look at her present equipment for the answer. What do the pictures on the wall tell about the executive? Is he sports-oriented? Does he smoke? His ashtrays may tell a story of his smoking habits. Is he prosperous? What school did he attend? Any class rings, diplomas on wall, or fraternal insignia visible? What clubs does he belong to? Look at his lapel or on his wall or desk. And so it goes; every bit of material around a person can tell the astute individual something about the nature of its owner. You must be a good detective to put together the clues and come up with a composite image of what the prospect is really like.

The Prospect

Last, but certainly not least, is the prospect. Much critical information is known only by the prospect, so only she or he can provide it. While some skeptics may question the practicality of obtaining information from the prospect, actually it is quite common to do so. It must be remembered that in most sales you are there to solve the prospect's problems. The prospect wants these problems solved most efficiently and effectively and is therefore highly motivated to give you complete cooperation.

Sometimes you can get some needed information over the telephone, but more frequently the first part of the sales interview—or even all of it—is devoted to extracting it. Indeed, there are frequent instances in which people spend a considerable amount of time gathering information in preparation for the ultimate sales presentation. Such would be the case of a computer sales-

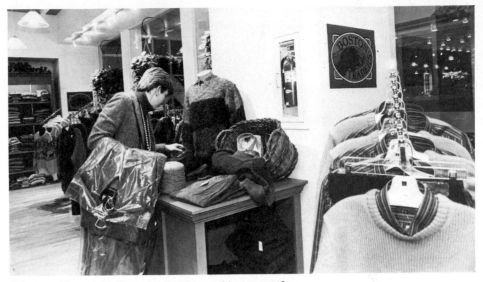

What would you infer if you were sizing up this prospect?

person who would study the various systems of a firm to determine if it could profitably use the hardware that he or she is selling.

Never be bashful about asking the prospect for helpful information, even though it may be personal or confidential. The prospect can choose not to talk, but more frequently people enjoy talking about themselves. The sales rep who commands confidence and maintains confidence will be privy to a great many useful secrets.

As we have mentioned several times previously, the consultative sales rep relies heavily upon the prospect for needed information. The first phase of the "consultation" is devoted to getting information. Understand that this process of bringing information to light is not only for the purpose of enlightening the sales rep but also for crystallizing the information in the prospect's mind. Moreover, it is often helpful during the sale if the prospect knows that the sales rep knows certain information. For example, if the rep knows that the budget for a project has been set at $500,000, then it is pointless for the prospect to play games with the rep about the project's funding.

SIZING UP THE PROSPECT

One of the most debated practices of selling is sizing up the prospect. Don't make up your mind early in the interview that the prospect is *not* going to buy.

A farm equipment dealer in Oregon sadly related:

We'll be pretty careful in the future to see that everyone who comes in here gets attention. The other day a guy came in, looked around, peeked under one of the machines. He was an odd-looking character, so we figured he was just curious. Finally he wandered out. We learned later that he went across the street to another dealer and, when a salesman asked him what he wanted, said he was interested in log haulers. After the sales pitch and a few questions, he placed an order for four. These haulers cost around $8,000 each, but the salesman merely inquired, "How would you like to arrange payment for them?" The "character" muttered, "I'll pay for them now." Whereupon he dug into his various pockets and came up with the full amount in cold currency.

Every veteran salesperson can recount cases like these. One Atlanta furniture salesperson learned the hard way when she avoided a customer who looked like a poor prospect—work-torn clothes, callused hands with fingernails none too well manicured. But an old-timer in the store waited on the man and soon discovered that he had walked out of a competitor's store because the salesman there had tried to high-pressure him into making quick decisions on a few items. So the veteran sales rep remarked, "Take your time and I'll just sort of trail along to answer questions. The boss says that my job is to help our customers find exactly what they want, and I'll try to do that." That customer was furnishing a new motel which he had built with his own hands. When he had finished shopping, he wrote a check for $3,450.

A large wholesale dry goods house in St. Louis has had difficulty in impressing upon its house salespeople the desirability of *trying* to sell every prospect who comes in. Some time ago a rather unpromising-appearing individual strayed in, and all the salespeople promptly busied themselves at something to avoid waiting on him. That is, all but one. This young rep tackled the apparently hopeless prospect and eventually sold him $18,000 worth of hosiery. He turned out to be a buyer for a foreign government, but he dressed in such a manner as to deceive the average salesperson. Indeed, this was his purpose, for he feared that if his identity were known it would cause the sellers to quote him a higher price.

These observations apply to traveling salespeople as well as to retail clerks. The sales rep who relies too strongly on the hasty "size-up" is likely to be whipped without putting up a strong fight. Often the prospect's exterior belies her or his ability to buy. Clothes do not make the man or woman, as the experienced seller has discovered.

Your task is to learn where the prospect is likely to stand in each of these three scales: need for the product, perception of the product, willingness to pay for the product. Even after you come face to face with the prospect, this effort continues.

There is not much point in trying to sell a prospect at the negative extreme of all three scales. But the in-between prospect may be worth working on. However, you want to know whether to spend time trying to awaken a desire for the product in general or to stress the particular product you are selling. Perhaps it will be necessary to justify the price if the purchase involves more money than the prospect had planned to spend. It comes down to putting the selling emphasis in the right place for the given prospect, thereby saving time and making it more likely that a sale will be made.

The order in which these three factors are presented here indicates the order in which you should check on them with a prospect. If the prospect feels no need for *any* car, there is no point in demonstrating that your car is the best and that the price is right. The first task is to make the prospect want a car.

Prospect's State of Decision

There is still another evaluation of prospects, this one based on how far the prospect has traveled mentally toward the decision to buy. Some prospects are already partially, or even completely, sold, while others have not even the slightest intention of buying. The preapproach should tell you about how far the prospect has progressed and, therefore, what sales tactics should be employed.

There are three separate prospect decisions that should be appraised. First, to what extent does the prospect recognize the need for the product? A Xerox sales rep should first determine if the prospect feels any need for a photocopier before beginning to worry about selling a Xerox. In marketing terminology, the primary demand for a product must exist before selective demand (brand) can be stimulated. The prospect's perception of need varies from nonexistent to an outright confession that the prospect not only needs it badly but fully intends to buy something to satisfy that need.

Second, how does the prospect perceive your brand of the product? This, too, can vary from "I want nothing to do with your machine!" through "I've never heard of it," to "I will buy only from you."

Third, how much is the prospect planning to pay to satisfy this need? The prospect who feels a *powerful* urge to buy will probably be willing to pay more than one nearer the other extreme who feels only a *mild* urge to satisfy a need. Some prospects are limited by the money they have available, while others feel more flexible as to how much they can pay. Again, we find variations or gradations here.

In selling to businesses, it is quite proper to inquire about the budget for accomplishing the project at hand. The consultative salesperson, after gaining the prospect's acknowledgment of the need being considered, then asks, "How much has been budgeted for solving this problem?" If the prospect replies, "$3,000" (or any sum that is inadequate for the job), the consultant can say, "We have a problem. The job cannot be done for that amount. Shall I leave?" The business executive with a problem will not want the person to leave, but will want to know more about what it is going to cost to solve the problem.

It is quite critical to the foundation upon which consultative selling is based that the consultant not proceed into the sale until the prospect agrees to spend sufficient money to get the job done. If the prospect refuses to admit that it has the money in its budget to buy from or hire the seller, then why waste time making the presentation?

SUMMARY

One mark of the professional businessperson and of modern business enterprises is their emphasis upon planning. They don't just "put the ball into play" and hope for the best. So it is with highly productive salespeople; they plan their work, plan their sales, and plan their careers.

Effective planning requires good information. The sales rep needs information about the prospect who is about to be called upon. If the upcoming sales interview is to be made upon an old account or some prospect previously called upon, then the rep's prospect or account files can furnish the needed information. If the call is to be made upon someone not previously contacted and the sale is significant, then the salesperson is advised to do considerable preapproach work in order to avoid mistakes and to tailor the interview to take advantage of what is known about the prospect.

Information can be obtained from directories, other people, observation, and directly from the prospect. You should attempt to elicit the prospect's needs, ability to buy, present status in the decision process, and likely motives.

DISCUSSION QUESTIONS

1 Is the concept of the preapproach applicable to any other human activities besides selling?

2 If you were selling mutual funds, what prospect information would you want to obtain prior to making a sales presentation?

3 Under what conditions will a prospect willingly provide considerable preapproach information about herself or himself in the early part of the sale?

4 If you have been unable to obtain certain critical preapproach information about a given prospect prior to the presentation, how could you go about getting it from her in the interview? Exactly what would you say to the prospect?

5 You are a manufacturer's agent representing several lines of quality men's apparel. A store that has heretofore refused to buy from you has just been sold. What information might you want about the new owner?

6 If you were a Xerox sales rep, from what source would you obtain most of your preapproach information on a prospective client?

7 You are a book representative for McGraw-Hill. You have heard that the psychology department at Big State U. is not happy with its present adoption for the beginning course. What preapproach information would you want before you attempted any interviews?

8 From what sources would you seek such information about the psychology situation above?

9 You are a manufacturer's representative handling a line of ice cream equipment and flavorings. One of your customers for flavorings looks sufficiently large that he could profitably make his own ice cream by buying a machine from you that costs about $5,000. What additional information would you want about the prospect before attempting a presentation?

10 You are a sales engineer for a line of compressed air tools used in manufacturing. You have learned that Teakwood Desks, Inc., is planning to build a new plant in your territory. How would you learn of their plans, and most importantly, who would be making the buying decision?

REFERENCES

1 One excellent book on consultative selling is Robert B. Miller and Stephen E. Heiman with Tad Tuleja, *Conceptual Selling*, Warner Books, New York, 1987.
2 Charles J. Smith, "The Art of Name Calling," *American Salesman*, November 1989, pp. 20–21, discusses ways to help remember names.
3 From the recollections of Frederic Russell.
4 Josef Adams, "Be Sure You Are with the Decision-Maker," *American Salesman*, August 1988, pp. 25–27, suggests some ways to find out who is the decision maker in the prospective firm.
5 Gregg Cherry, "How Well Do You Know Your Customers?" *Mid-American Insurance*, April 1990, pp. 20–21, suggests the use of multivariate regression techniques to help in identifying the customer profile.
6 Douglas M. Lambert, "The Accuracy of Salesperson's Perceptions of Their Customers: Conceptual Examination and an Empirical Study," *Journal of Personal Selling & Sales Management*, Winter 1990, p. 1–9, and John Nemec, "Hazardous Challenges," *American Salesman*, Nov. 1989, pp. 3–6, suggest that the accuracy of the salespersons' perceptions of their customers is related to both the sales situation and the background of the salesperson.

CASE 7-1: Ocean Cannery, Inc.—Planning a Consultative Sales Interview

"Many thanks, Vejay, for the introduction into the Ocean organization. I appreciate everything you've done. I'll keep you informed of how things go." Ted Zuggren, business consultant, had just finished talking with his old classmate from graduate school, Vejay Rajah, who now owned and managed a fish exporting company in San Pedro, California. Vejay had contacted Ted 2 weeks previously about his possible interest in helping one of Vejay's suppliers, Ocean Cannery of San Pedro, out of its financial difficulties.

According to Vejay, Ocean Cannery would be bankrupt within the year if some significant changes in management strategies and tactics were not made. Vejay thought that Ted was just the person to advise the two Cappelli brothers who operated the cannery. He had asked for Ted's permission to talk with the Cappellis. Ted indicated great interest in the project. Vejay had just called to tell Ted that a meeting had been set up for Ted to meet the Cappellis the next day at 10 A.M.

Vejay had provided Ted with much information about the Ocean Cannery operation and about the Cappelli brothers. Vejay did not think much of their managerial skills. The $20,000,000-a-year operation did not even have a budget system. It had been unable to obtain a working capital loan from its bank, Wells Fargo. Its fish supply was uncertain. Offshore competition was fierce. Sales to the domestic fish companies such as Seakist were under heavy price competition from foreign sellers.

Ted relished the contemplation of working with such a client, for it presented him with a wide range of serious problems. If he could salvage the operation, his reputation would be vastly enhanced. Perhaps there might be some equity participation for him if things went well. However, Ted immediately recognized that he had better start planning for the next morning's meeting.

1 What did Ted want to accomplish with this first interview with the Cappellis?

2 What information did he want to get from them?

3 What commitments did he want from the Cappelli brothers before proceeding with a sales interview?

CASE 7-2: The Metal Finishing Company— The Selling of a Business

Fred Sanders was ready for retirement. He had formed the Metal Finishing Company of Chicago, Illinois, in 1952. It had served him and his family well, providing them with a comfortable living, but he was tired of it. "I want to go play some golf in Florida." But Fred had a problem. He could not openly advertise the business for sale. His 25 employees would get upset, his banker might pull the line of credit, the vendors would tighten their credits, and his customers would start looking for alternate sources of supply. Fred knew he would have to be discreet in trying to sell a business of which he was the sole shareholder.

The company had earned an average net income after taxes of $165,000 a year for the past 5 years. Sales were a stable $2,000,000 a year. Fred drew a total of $160,000 in salary and expenses from the company and paid his wife and children $75,000 a year for their efforts on the firm's behalf.

Fred had confided his desire to sell to his CPA, who had indicated that she might know some people who would be interested in buying the business. He had set a price of $2,000,000 with a large cash down payment depending upon the buyer. Fred had heard horror stories about what happened to people who sold their businesses in exchange for someone's paper.

Subsequently, the CPA called Fred to tell him about Paul West, an engineer recently retired from the Air Force, who was looking for a business. The CPA asked if Mr. West could come to the plant for a visit. Fred responded, "I'll call you back in an hour to tell you how I want to handle this matter."

Fred had been caught by surprise. He had no idea how the sale of his business should be handled. He wanted that hour to plan the sale. Particularly, he wanted to think about the information he wanted to get from Mr. West and the CPA.

1 What would Fred want to know about Mr. West before proceeding with the sale?

2 If you were Paul West, what information would you want to know before proceeding with negotiations?

CHAPTER EIGHT

THE APPROACH

After studying the material in this chapter you should:

☐ Understand that a good approach should get the prospect's undivided attention, spark an interest in hearing what you have to say, and provide a smooth transition into the interview

☐ Realize that among the many approaches that can be used the product and consumer benefit approaches are the most important ones to master

☐ Discern that duplicity and deception are poor tactics to use in approaching prospects

PROFILE OF A LUGGIES

SALESPERSON

Nicole Frank

President, Luggies, Inc.
Los Angeles, Calif.

Nicole, a 1989 graduate of the Entrepreneur Program at the University of Southern California, took the business plan she had developed for class and made it a reality—an attractively decorated line of children's luggage. Although she had to design the product line herself and have it manufactured in Korea, still her main job was to sell it. And sell it she did: to A. E. O. Swartz, Saks Fifth Avenue, Bloomingdales, and other leading department stores across the nation. Her approach was simple: Show the product! She had a winner.

The curtain rises. Your prospect is before you. You need an approach. Make no mistake about it, your approach is important. Numerous studies over the years have indicated that sales are won or lost in the first few minutes of the interview—in the approach. This will be a long chapter, for there is much to discuss about how to get the sale started off on the right foot.

OBJECTIVES OF THE APPROACH

The approach has three main goals: to gain the prospect's attention, to stimulate an interest in learning more about the proposition, and to provide a smooth transition into the presentation, or interview.[1] In some situations, the sales rep uses the approach to qualify the person as a good prospect. Is there a need and the money with which to satisfy it?

Attention

The sale will go nowhere until the prospect focuses attention on what you say. This is a larger problem than you might suspect, for prospects are frequently in the midst of doing something else. Their minds may be dwelling upon any number of other problems with which they are plagued. Under no circumstances should you be lured into proceeding with the sale while the prospect's attention is diverted. Many times an executive who is busy will say, "Go ahead and talk! I can listen while I finish signing these papers." Don't do it! A person can attend to only one thing at a time. Your approach must gain the prospect's *undivided* attention. You may do this by handing the prospect something to examine.

Interest

You may gain a prospect's attention for an instant but quickly lose it if she decides that she is not interested in hearing more from you. People's interest in your proposition can be fleeting if you do not quickly give them a reason for listening further. The prospect thinks, "What's in it for me? Why should I give you more of my valuable time?"

A good approach provides the prospect with a reason for listening. Tell him how he will benefit, what problems you can solve, why he will be in a better position for having met you, or how much money you are going to make for him.

Transition

The third, and often unrecognized, objective of the approach is to lead easily and smoothly into the presentation. The transition should be so smooth that the prospect scarcely feels it, much as the passenger in a fine automobile can barely detect the automatic shift from one gear to the next. You could win

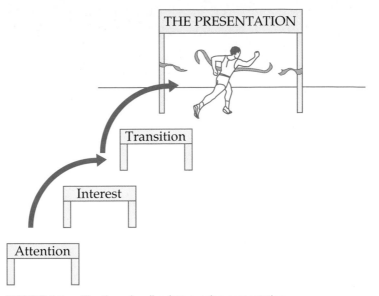

FIGURE 8-1   The three hurdles into a sales presentation.

attention and interest by pulling a gun on the prospect, but you would find it rather rough to swing from there into your presentation (to make the transition).

As we discuss various approaches in this chapter, watch for this transition or final phase. It is often the weakest part of the approach, especially when it appears strained, forced, and irrelevant to what has just preceded it.

Qualifying

You may be uncertain of the person's need for your proposition or ability to pay for it. Before proceeding with the sale, find out how good a prospect the person really is. Some salespeople open the conversation by asking some fairly blunt questions concerning the suspect's needs. Such an approach can be useful even when you have already determined the prospect's needs. It focuses the person's mind on those needs and lets the person know that you are aware of the problems.

The consultative salesperson uses the approach as an information-gathering, or qualifying, opportunity. First, the consultant asks a series of previously developed questions to confirm what is thought to be known about the situation, thus verifying information gathered in the preapproach. No consultant wants to start with bad information. Conditions, people, and situations change quickly in business. Thus the second step is to find out what changes have occurred in the company since the consultant's last contact with it. Again, a series of questions may be in order.

These questions are usually developed to discover the firm's needs, buying procedures, budgets, and decision-making apparatus. Ultimately, the consultant wants to establish the prospect's needs, budget, and timing plans and identity of the decision maker.

IMPORTANCE OF THE APPROACH

Naturally the importance of the approach varies with the type of selling. It is most critical when you are calling on the prospect for the first time to sell a fairly big proposition. It is least important when calling upon regular customers with a relatively minor product or service. In the former situation, a careful approach should be worked out, because if the approach fails to do its job, you may be ushered out of the prospect's presence without getting the chance to tell your story at all. A sale may be likened to a chain; break one link, and it falls apart.

GETTING THE INTERVIEW

In many lines of selling you have little difficulty seeing prospects or customers. Either they have invited you to call or the call is a routine matter. Sometimes the status of the selling company is such that prospects find it difficult not to give the representative a reasonable hearing. A busy executive called upon by an IBM computer rep will usually give an interview. However, in certain situations the sales rep's first problem is that of obtaining an interview with the *right* person. This is most frequently encountered when you are selling something the firm is not now buying or buys only on occasion. Salespeople for services and intangibles may encounter problems with seeing the right person. On a busy day the last person in the world a corporate controller might want to see is some insurance agent or representative of a tax service. Such salespeople have problems seeing the right executives, the ones who have the power to buy.

Many young salespeople have returned to headquarters from their first trips discouraged with the job, chiefly because they were not able to see many of their prospects. "I knew what to do all the way through after I had said 'good morning,' but I couldn't get a chance to say 'good morning,'" one sales rep complained when his manager took him to task for his lack of success on his initial trip.

One sales manager claimed that her salespeople spent more time in reception rooms than with prospects and that more than one-half of their calls failed to become interviews. One prospect had been called on 26 times in 2 years, yet was never seen. But this is unusual. Clearly, this sales manager needs to do considerable work on developing a better approach system for her sales force. Some managements have found that a letter from the firm's president to the prospect asking for an appointment for the firm's sales representative will gain the desired hearing.

In other situations, sales representatives who have difficulty seeing people in their offices arrange to see them outside their offices.

* Invite the prospect to see a demonstration in your office.
* Invite the prospect to some social event which your preapproach has indicated he or she would be interested in attending.
* Work with firm appointments.

Really important business executives are compelled to conserve their time for important things; they properly expect protection from useless interruptions, including salespeople. They surround themselves with secretaries and subordinates whose duty it is to keep out those callers who seemingly have nothing of value to offer their bosses.

Gaining the Interview Is Actually a Selling Process

You should regard gaining the interview in the same light as making a sale. The task is *to sell an idea* to the person who has the power to grant the interview.

Unquestionably the salesperson's *attitude* is of prime importance in convincing the assistant that she should admit the sales rep. If the rep *looks* important, the chances of being admitted are improved. Poise, dignity, a direct glance rather than a secretive one will help. The way you occupy your time in the waiting room is a factor. The salesperson who merely loafs or reads a magazine does not make the same impression as does one who pulls from a briefcase a copy of a leading business journal or studies an important-looking report. If you *act* as though your time is valuable, the assistant will probably *think* it is.[2]

There is another reason why you should be occupied while waiting to see the prospect. It can help to keep you calm and to prevent you from developing high blood pressure as you brood about being kept waiting when you could be earning money elsewhere. A salesperson who has been sitting in a waiting room for an hour or so will probably find it hard to conceal irritation when finally going in to see the prospect, even while knowing that this feeling will communicate itself to the prospect and probably result in a thoroughly unsatisfactory interview. Hence it is better to keep busy at something, even if it is only filling out a report to headquarters. Even a pleasant conversation with another sales rep is far preferable to seething with anger.

Some sales reps ask the receptionist for reading matter about the prospect's company, which often makes a good impression and may provide the rep with valuable information.

Some salespeople feel so strongly about not waiting to see prospects that they place a limit on the time they will wait, especially if they have appointments in advance. Even some sales reps calling cold advise against waiting if it appears as if a long wait is likely. One industrial equipment salesman claims,

I never wait more than 20 or 30 minutes to see a prospect. If he is tied up, I simply ask for another appointment later and go out and make some cold calls on nearby smokestacks. I think it is a mistake to wait too long to see a prospect. First, it puts me in a frame of mind that prevents me from making my best presentation. I get mad, and I can't hide it. Next, it gives the prospect the idea that I have nothing else to do. I want him to know that my time is valuable too. Finally, it keeps me from wasting time sitting in a chair. While I may spend 2 or 3 hours waiting to see some clown who is playing hard-to-get, I can be out taking orders from someone who is more accessible. Another thing, I have detected that when I do call back on a prospect who could not keep his original appointment, he is sort of apologetic about his behavior and willing to give me a fair hearing.

METHODS FOR APPROACHING PROSPECTS

There are 11 methods by which the prospect may be approached: ((1) the introductory approach, (2) the product approach, (3) the consumer-benefit approach, (4) the consultative approach, (5) the shock approach, (6) the showmanship approach, (7) the question approach, (8) the statement approach, (9) the premium approach, (10) the survey approach, and (11) the compliment approach. Many times a sales rep will use a combination of several of these methods. You may start with an introductory approach but swing into a consumer-benefit one to facilitate easy transition into the presentation. Or you may open with a product or curiosity approach and then shift into a statement.

The Introductory Approach

The introductory approach is by far the most frequently used technique. Unfortunately, it is also the weakest for it does little for the salesperson. You walk into the prospect's office and say, "Hello, I am Lee Buffalo representing the Black Ball Express Company." Now what?

This approach gains little attention. Interest will be minimal unless there is a previously recognized problem which this company may help solve. Finally, transition is sometimes awkward if the prospect's mental reaction is, "OK, so what do you want?" Therefore, most salespeople use one of the other approaches immediately after introducing themselves. One purchasing agent reacted to this approach by saying, "I don't care who you are or who you represent. I only care about who I am and what you are prepared to do for me."

The brutal truth is that most introductions at the beginning of a sale are worthless, since the prospects miss the name and have to ask again or look at a card *after* they have decided that they are interested in hearing what the proposition contains for them.

In some situations, it is best to leave the introductions until after a successful approach has been made. Once the prospect has decided to hear more, then a proper introduction can be made.

The Product Approach

The product approach consists simply of thrusting the product into the hands of the prospect. One costume jewelry agent would merely hand the buyer one of his most attractive and salable items without saying a word. The buyer would naturally look at the merchandise, and if it interested her, she would ask, "Where's the rest of your line?"

One baby-furniture rep also used the product approach very effectively in selling a new lightweight aluminum baby walker by simply handing the walker to the buyer without saying a word. He relates the story of one sale to a Macy's buyer in New York City. "I walked into the department and saw that it was the largest operation I had seen in a department store. It carried a full line of baby walkers. I had the buyer's name from a directory, but I verified it with a clerk when I asked where the buyer was. She said he was back in his office, so I went back and walked right into his little cubicle. He said, 'Well, what do you want?' I handed the walker to him without a word. He said, 'How much?' I laid before him our full price list giving all the details. He said, 'Send me six dozen, all blue.' I asked, 'Don't you want to hear the story?' He replied, 'This product and the price list is all the story I need. This is the way I really like to buy. Come back anytime; it's a pleasure to do business with you.'"

The product approach is best used when selling a product that is unique, possesses considerable eye appeal, and tends to tell its own sales story. It works because the merchandise itself attracts the prospect's attention and interest, and it provides the best possible transition into the presentation.

One sales representative for a manufacturer of military electronic equipment carries with him a variety of exotic hardware that his firm has made for various branches of the armed forces. This hardware does three things. First, it gets him by the purchasing agent to see the person in the firm who makes decisions on such items, because the p.a. quickly realizes that he cannot deal with the rep technically and so promptly refers him to the proper engineer. Next, he has found that engineers love to handle such items; they are greatly interested in complex electronic devices. This gives him the entrée he needs to gain the engineer's confidence, for many engineers are antagonistic to salespeople who lack the proper technical credentials. Finally, they give the engineer in the clearest possible way some idea of the firm's capabilities. In general, people like to handle and examine products; they like to opreate them and take them apart. The product approach capitalizes on this urge.

The Consumer-Benefit Approach

The consumer-benefit approach consists of opening the interview with a statement or question which directs the prospect's thoughts to the benefits you propose to furnish. Sometimes the statement is one designed to whet the prospect's curiosity. Other times it is a declaration designed to shock the prospect, thus getting attention and interest. However, often it is simply a

Let the product do the talking by showing it to the prospect. This stand-alone store display makes an eye-catching sales approach.

question or statement designed to make the prospect think about the problem which the sales rep proposes to solve.

An ice cream purveyor addressed the manager of an ice cream parlor with the question, "How would you like to save 40 cents a gallon on all the ice cream you sell?" Needless to say, the manager wanted to hear more about it, so he was told about the virtues of making his own ice cream from a mix that the salesperson sold.

An insurance agent handed the prospect a facsimile check made out to her for $2,000 and asked, "How would you like to receive that check each month upon retirement?" The prospect admitted that she would like it very much and asked to hear more.

An offset press rep began, "Your letterhead will cost you about $10 a thousand with this press. What did you pay last? $60?"

The Consultative Approach

As was previously mentioned, the salesperson using the consultative or conceptual selling systems asks a lot of questions right from the start. One extreme example was a sales training consultant who would, upon being shown into a prospect's office, look at a piece of paper in her hand and ask, "I was given your name to see this morning. Why would I have your name? I am from the National Sales Training Institute." The name was a response from the prospect to some direct-mail promotional material. Thus someone in the firm had furnished the name.

If the prospect acknowledged that he had indeed called for more information, then the consultant would ask some question such as, "Then you have some problems that perhaps our sales training programs can help you with?" After getting the prospect to admit a need for sales training help, then the consultant would ask, "What is your budget for solving this problem?" Until the prospect admitted to having a problem and was willing to spend enough money to solve it, the consultant would not proceed into the sales interview.

Thus the consultative approach is a variety of the question approach in which the questions are aimed at establishing the need for the product or service and the ability to pay for it. It not only validates the prospect but focuses his or her mind on the problem.

The Shock Approach

An insurance agent obtained a picture of a prospect and had a photographer retouch it to make the prospect look much older. He walked into the prospect's office, handed the prospect the picture, and asked, "What are you doing for that old person today?" Variations of this have been employed using pictures of a prospect's spouse or family. The idea is to shock some stubborn prospects into thinking about reality, thinking about things they prefer not to think about.

Such an approach is valuable in getting the attention and interest of a prospect who is not inclined to treat the sales proposition seriously, someone who refuses to become emotionally involved with the problem at hand. Amazingly, some people refuse to come to grips with critical problems; psychologically, they seem to feel that if they ignore a problem, it will go away. Shock treatment may get through this defense mechanism, thereby allowing the salesperson to get on with the presentation.

The Showmanship Approach

There have been numerous shows put on for the benefit of some important prospect who appreciates imagination and showmanship. One young man seeking employment with an advertising agency was having great difficulty getting an interview with the top executive; so he had himself boxed up and delivered into the inner sanctum by an express company. Another salesperson took space on a large billboard on the route his prospect took to and from home. It declared, "Mr. E. Duncan: You are losing $150 every day you fail to see me! Signed: R. Huff, Acme Tool Company." There is no limit to what an enterprising person can do to dramatize an approach when the situation warrants it. But it is important to realize that showmanship can backfire if used in the wrong situations or on the wrong people.

The Question Approach

The use of a question to open an interview is an art. It can be used in conjunction with other approaches, particularly the consumer-benefit approach, or it can stand on its own. "What will you be doing in 2030?" just might lead a young person into talking about retirement planning. "Are you big enough to use automated production equipment profitably?" might cause the president of a growing manufacturing company to answer, "I don't know. How big do I have to be?" And then the two can get right to the heart of the matter.

Psychological questioning immediately gets the prospect's attention, interest, and participation in the affair. It focuses the mind on an essential element in the proposition and gets the presentation off to a good start.

The salespeople for one firm are taught to say, "If you will just answer a couple of questions, I'll know whether my product can help you with the packaging of your goods." This is really a question and usually elicits the reply, "What are your questions?"

A woman selling a collection service used an approach consisting of the simple question: "I'm not sure if you're the person I'm looking for. Have you 20 dead accounts on your books?"

A vending machine company instructs its salespeople to carry a piece of heavy paper about 2 by 3 feet in size, which they unfold and spread out on the floor or counter, saying, "If I could show you how to make that space worth $5,000 a year to you, you'd be interested, wouldn't you?"

An agent for an investment service inquires, "If you save as much in the next 5 years as you did in the last 5, will you be satisfied?"

Of course, the questions must be well framed. Too many salespeople fall into the slack habit of greeting their prospects with, "How's business?" The space buyer for a large advertising agency kept a record of what sales reps said to him when they first approached. Out of the 14 so-called sales reps who called in one day, 12 opened the interview with "How's business?" "How do things look?" "Things picking up much yet?" The sales manager of a large furniture company says that four out of five salespeople open their talks with "How's tricks?" or "How's business?"

Such an approach may suffice in prosperous times, but it is loaded with dynamite when business is not so good. And when did anyone ever find prospects enthusiastic about business? It is a part of the buyer's defense to scowl and insist that he cannot afford to buy. To ask a buyer how business is only invites trouble.

Other approaches are equally ineffective. "Well, anything new since I saw you last?" "No, I guess not, Jane." And that's that.

One industrial sales rep selling forklift trucks would open an interview with the question, "Would you like to save $6,300 on your warehouse handling costs this next year?" What executive could say no to that question? The sales rep had, of course, determined the figure from a preapproach survey.

A representative for a manufacturer in the electronics field catches a purchasing agent's attention and interest by asking, "What one electronic item that you now buy is giving you the biggest headache?" He had found that most p.a.s have many headaches for which they are seeking the right analgesic. This opening allows the seller to dwell on the problems the prospect feels are most serious and about which he is most apt to do something. Sometimes the rep asks, "What electronic equipment you are now buying do you feel is most overpriced?" The point of this additional question is to find in what areas the rep would meet the least pressure on prices and could be most competitive.

This art of asking the right questions serves several purposes. It forces the prospect to talk in the areas chosen by you. It elicits information of tremendous value, thereby pushing the preapproach to satisfying depth. It focuses the prospects' attention on the problems they are most eager to solve, thus guiding the salesperson into the shortest path to a sale.

You will find that the hours spent formulating these "right" questions will be time well spent. Notice that the word is "hours," not "minutes," for it takes considerable time to develop properly worded questions.

There are some basic principles you should observe in phrasing these questions: First, the more specific the question, the better. Compare these questions: "Would you like to save several thousands of dollars in labor costs?" and "Would you like to save $15,500 next year on your costs of handling goods in process?" Which is most likely to whet the interest of the prospect and move smoothly into the sale of conveyor systems?

Second, whenever possible, the question should be tailored for the prospect's situation, based on data obtained through a good preapproach.

Third, the question should be aimed at the major consumer benefit in which the prospect will be interested. Aim at the major buying motives rather than the minor ones. If you are convinced that the prospect is most interested in saving money, then your question should be directed to that motive. If you feel that status is the most important motive, then your question should suggest that your product will help the prospect to gain status.

Fourth, there are some areas in which you should be extremely cautious about asking questions. There are some things which people will not talk about even when asked. Generally, people are hesitant to talk to strangers about their finances. Before you can elicit such information, you must establish your need to know the data for the good of the prospect as well as your ability to respect confidences. You must establish rapport, and this may take some time. Sometimes you can probe these areas by using hypothetical data which you believe approximate the prospect's situation, but which allows the buyer to keep the exact data confidential.

The Statement Approach

The interview can be opened easily by a statement. Sometimes the statement concerns something which the salesperson has done for someone else; other times it may simply be some declaration of fact about the product or what it can do. Frequently these statements are concluded with a question which asks for the prospect's reactions.

One container sales rep opens an interview with a statement such as, "I was able to save the Martin Company $450 a month on their shipping boxes by showing them a new item we have added to our line. Would you be interested in finding out if I can save you some money too?"

Notice that all these statements are aimed at one thing: to drive home to the prospect quickly some major point that is strongly in favor of the product, and it may include the consumer-benefit factor.

The Premium Approach

In some situations, sales reps virtually bribe prospects to give their attention for a few moments in exchange for something of nominal value. An electronics rep sometimes uses a small printed circuit board on which the prospect's name has been etched in copper. This is so unusual that the prospect always listens attentively to what the sales rep has to say.

Frequently, salespeople use advertising specialties such as pencils, cigarette lighters, memo books, ash trays, and so on, for premiums. The success of this approach rests in the human urge to get something for nothing; it puts people in a good frame of mind and creates a more permissive atmosphere in which to operate.

The Survey Approach

Unfortunately, this approach has been badly misused by unscrupulous door-to-door salespeople posing as researchers. Such operators claim that they are making a survey of furnaces or appliances or some other product related to whatever they are selling. Once inside the door, they attempt to qualify the suspects through the use of the questions in the "survey." If the people are prospects, the "researcher" either slyly drops the disguise and goes into a presentation or turns over the qualified lead to another salesperson.

However, this survey approach has its legitimate uses. In many industrial sales situations the rep must obtain the permission of the suspect to do some type of research before knowing whether the product can be of use.

Actually, all the salesperson is doing is asking to be permitted to collect preapproach information within the organization before actually making a sales presentation. Hence the survey approach is not a full-fledged opening into the main presentation; however, when completed, it does provide easy access to the executive and a smooth approach, such as this:

"As you know, you gave me permission a month ago to make a survey of your outgoing correspondence for the purpose of determining whether your firm could profitably use an electronic word processing system. I now have that study completed and ready for your inspection."

The survey approach works in industrial situations because the executive recognizes that no salesperson can know the firm's specific problems without

Sales reps frequently use the premium approach—giving away advertising specialties such as keychains, mugs, or pencils—to catch a prospect's attention. (Courtesy of ASI/The Advertising Specialty Institute, Langhorne, PA. The products in the photo are from the Specialty Advertising Evans product line.)

considerable study. Every executive is sure that her or his business is different and likes the idea of the salesperson tailoring a presentation to the company's specific needs. Also, many executives are glad to get expert help on some technical problem they have not fully solved.

The Compliment Approach

If it can be accomplished sincerely, some expression of appreciation may be used to get the interview started. "Wonderful lighting you have in here. No glare, no shadows. How do you do it?" "That's one of the most beautiful desks I have ever seen. How many varieties of wood are in that inlaid section?" Don't push this approach too far over the line into flattery, although some people can absorb generous doses of the insincere compliment. Jonathan Swift wrote:

'Tis an old maxim in the schools,
That flattery's the food of fools;
Yet now and then your man of wit
Will condescend to take a bit.

All the approaches discussed have one factor in common—they contain something of *interest* to the prospect. Put yourself in the prospect's place when planning your approach in person and ask yourself, "Would this interest *me* and cause me to like this person?"

OTHER ESSENTIALS OF A GOOD APPROACH

After the method of approach has been selected, other important details should be observed. Summarized, they are:

- Making and keeping appointments
- Timing the approach
- Use of the business card
- Avoiding the early dismissal
- Never apologizing for taking prospect's time
- Relieving or removing sales tension
- Using the call-back

Making and Keeping Appointments

Most purchasing agents strongly favor having salespeople call at some specific time by appointment or during certain hours set aside for interviewing salespeople. One IBM computer rep starts each morning and afternoon with a definite appointment with an important, high-quality prospect. Not knowing how long her call will take, she schedules no more definite appointments for the day but fills in any time left with cold calls on likely prospects.

Above all, salespeople should not keep prospects waiting, for when they arrive late, they will encounter real hostility. However, it's not that easy. The sales rep often is unsure about how long a sales interview will take. In some cases, the interview may not last long, either because the prospect or account was ready to buy and did not want to waste time or because the rep was quickly dismissed for one reason or another. In other cases, an interview that would normally take about an hour at best may turn into a marathon session, as the prospect turns into a significant customer who requires considerable attention at that time. There may be no graceful way of getting out of the interview while keeping the customer. Clearly, sales reps are limited in their ability to predict how long it is going to take to make a sales call. Thus they like to build consider flexibility into their schedules; they don't like to be tied down to a fixed timetable. These are problems that salespeople work out as they adjust to their situations.

Timing the Approach

Rather obviously, the timing of calls can be critical to the success of the interview. A firm that is experiencing financial difficulties may not be particularly receptive to an interview with an equipment sales rep. On the other hand, the same rep may be most interested in talking with a representative of an investment banking house.

Even the days of the week must be considered. Some executives are particularly harried on Mondays, while others try to avoid seeing people on Fridays. This is all valuable preapproach information that requires attention.

Japanese businesspeople never begin a sales interview without the exchange of business cards, a protocol to which they attach great significance. In what other situations might a sales rep benefit from using a business card?

Use of the Business Card

The Japanese have given new significance to the use of the business card. All interviews with Japanese businesspeople begin with the business card ceremony, which has a definite protocol that should be observed. Much thought should be given to the content and design of business cards. They often are filed by the prospect for future references when the need arises.

When the salesperson is representing a firm whose name carries weight with the buyer, it may be wise to use the card in opening the interview.

You may attach a small article to your card. An automobile sales rep buys tiny autos at the variety store and fastens them to his cards. Many people devise unusual cards—oversize ones, odd-shaped ones, strikingly colored or illustrated ones. A sales rep for a plywood company has cards printed on a thin sheet of wood veneer. One steel sales rep had cards made of thin stainless steel upon which his name and address were engraved. True, these are not the cheapest cards available, but where the stakes are high, you don't win the pot with penny-ante tactics.

Many people prefer, when possible, to hand the buyer the card at the close of the interview rather than at the beginning. This serves to impress the names of firm and salesperson upon the buyer, who may file the card for future reference, and the card does not distract the buyer's attention from the proposition.

Avoiding the Early Dismissal

Many salespeople with both good products and good information about their lines complain that prospects dismiss them soon after they have started their presentations. What accounts for this unwillingness to allow deserving salespeople an opportunity to explain worthy propositions?

The plain fact of the matter is this: The prospects are not refusing to *buy*, because they do not know enough about the offer to decide whether they want it. What they are really refusing to do is *to give their own time and attention to something that they think they are not interested in at the moment.* A woman may refuse to see a computer sales rep because she does not consider herself in the market for a computer. Another prospect says "Not interested" to a bond sales rep because he has no funds to invest. Another flatly refuses to talk to a life underwriter because she feels that she is "insurance poor" already. Yet these prospects might be sold if the sales rep quickly pointed out a real need and explained how it could be satisfied.

You must anticipate and prepare for the prospect's effort to dismiss you prematurely by making a quick and potent appeal to an important buying motive so that the prospect will make two important decisions—to see you and to listen to your story.

It was previously mentioned that the consultative salespeople refuse to begin the sales interview until the prospect admits to the need and the ability to buy. They may even encourage early dismissal if the prospect refuses to admit a problem and a budget with which to solve it. The coy prospect who tries to play games with the consultative sales rep may hear, "Shall I leave?" Most true prospects won't allow such a departure because, down deep, they want their problems solved. They want to hear what the consultant has to recommend. Thus one school of thought is that the sales rep should not be afraid of early dismissal. Why waste time trying to play games with someone who won't play fair with you, who lies to you?

Never Apologizing for Taking Prospect's Time

The inexperienced seller, confronting a prospect who gives the impression of being busy, can feel an impulse to apologize for taking up valuable time. Such an apology would be unwise, as it places you on the defensive at the start of the interview. Although an apology is not required, this does not mean that you should force your way in where you are not wanted. If it is obvious that the prospect is occupied, you might properly apologize for calling *at an inopportune time* and offer to call again when the prospect could receive you more conveniently, but if you expect to stay and try to sell, you should not offer an apology for so doing, as this weakens your case. Salespersons who apologize for their presence are admitting to the prospect that they feel guilty about making the call, thereby indicating that even they themselves have reason to question the soundness of their proposition. You must believe that you are doing the prospect a favor. With such an attitude there is obviously no need to apologize.

Relieving or Removing Sales Tension[3]

A sales manager in Philadelphia who employs a number of salespeople made a study of more than 500 actual interviews conducted in the general office, without either the salesperson or the prospect being aware of any observation. He discovered that in the great majority of instances there was a noticeable *tension* on the part of the prospect. In other words, the buyer sensed that the salesperson was trying to "sell something" and instinctively put up a barrier of resistance that interfered seriously with the progress of the interview. How may this tension be relieved?

One plan is to talk about hypothetical situations rather than the prospect's own. Thus the prospect is led to think that he or she is not the object of the sales rep's efforts. Some skilled salespeople state that they commonly tell prospects right at the start of the interview that there need be no fear of high-pressure tactics or of difficulty in getting rid of the salesperson at any desired moment. The sales rep must give an impression of absolute sincerity in this statement to make it effective. Lastly, the approach is facilitated and tension is reduced if the salesperson can convince the prospect quickly that an interesting or profitable idea will be the reward for granting an interview.

Several suggested methods for mitigating the initial tension of the sales interview are based on untruths. "I only want your opinion on a matter." (Sure you do!) "I am not here to sell you anything. I only want to acquaint you with our program." (Oh, really?) No doubt there are prospects who initially believe such statements, but it is difficult to gain credibility when you've started out with a lie.

Most professional sales reps reduce tensions by their relaxed manner, smile, and easy-going behavior. They don't charge at the prospect. They control their aggressive ways. One of the reasons the old-time sales rep opened a sale with some stories and good-humored bantering was to reduce tensions. The idea was to get the prospect to laugh and loosen up a bit.

Today's sales reps often manage to stage the sales interview in a place where tensions are low, perhaps during some form of entertainment or over a meal. Try to remove the prospect from stressful environments.

Using the Call-Back

The call-back is a technique that you use on the second or subsequent attempt to sell a prospect. A seller of advertising space called a second time on a space buyer for an advertising agency who had turned him down previously. He opened his call-back with "Good afternoon, Mr. Agate. You remember I was here a couple of weeks ago to see you about an advertising contract and you said you couldn't see your way clear to use my publication at that time. I called today to see if, after thinking it over, you didn't want to try it."

Such an opening only invites a second turndown. It gives the buyer time to frame a reply, while it presents nothing new or interesting. The technique of a call-back opening is *to swing at once into a presentation from an entirely new angle* without giving the prospect a chance to think up another turndown. For instance, the advertising salesperson might open the second interview something like this: "Good afternoon, Mr. Agate. You folks handle the Star Tire account, don't you? Well, I got to thinking the other day that the Star firm must sell a lot of tires in the territory covered by my publication, so I wrote them. They have agencies in every town in which my paper circulates, and it is a sure thing that there would be no waste circulation there." In this way you can start the sale without being turned down before you get going.

Or you might say, "Mr. Agate, since I saw you last I've been kicking myself because, for some unaccountable reason, I forgot to tell you the thing about my paper that you would be most interested to hear. The circulation by lines of business runs like this . . ." And you are started again with a fair chance of completing your presentation. The whole problem is to get started. Best method: new information!

SUMMARY

The success of the sales interview may depend upon how the prospect is approached. The approach has three basic purposes: to gain attention, to stimulate the prospect's interest in hearing more, and to make a smooth transition into the interview.

There are eleven basic approaches that are in common use. They are the introductory, the product, the consumer-benefit, the consultative, the shock, the showmanship, the question, the statement, the premium, the survey, and the compliment approaches.

The handling of appointments, call-backs, and timing of the call and the reduction of tension are all important aspects of getting the sales interview off on the right foot.

DISCUSSION QUESTIONS

1 You are selling Sony products. Devise a product approach, a consumer-benefit approach, and a question approach you could use. Which do you feel would be best?
2 Devise two consumer-benefit approaches for selling a Polaroid camera.
3 Under what circumstances is the product approach best used?
4 You are a salesperson for McGraw-Hill calling upon a trade (noncollegiate) bookstore to get them to stock this book. Exactly how would you approach the buyer?
5 As an account executive for Prudential Securities, a stock brokerage firm, devise some approaches that can be used on middle-management executives.
6 You are working for a technical supply and equipment wholesaler calling upon a professor of analytical chemistry to sell a line of electronic instruments for use in teaching. Exactly how would you open the sale?
7 You sell air conditioning. You have learned that a well-to-do executive is thinking of air-conditioning her home. You plan to call on her cold in January. What approach would you use? Word it!
8 (a) A hunter is fondly examining a Browning Automatic shotgun in your sporting goods store. What do you say as you approach him? (b) Another patron is carefully

looking at the gold-plated Winchester 30-30 classic rifle made in limited numbers to commemorate the anniversary of its first production. How would you approach that patron?

9 As the founder, owner, and manager of *Golf News*, a monthly magazine distributed free of charge throughout the Palm Springs, California, trading area, you are also its major sales rep. The firm's total revenue is from the advertising you sell. You have excellent statistical data showing that just about every golfer in the region picks up and reads the magazine each month. You have many case histories of advertisers that have had excellent results advertising in the magazine. Yet one of the region's golf discount houses has not advertised in the magazine despite being a big advertiser in all other appropriate media in the area. You have an appointment to meet with the store's manager and owner tomorrow at 9 A.M. in the store. How would you approach the prospect?

10 Why do salespeople using the consultative system insist that it is a mistake to try to make a presentation until the prospect admits a problem and admits that there is money to pay for solving that problem?

REFERENCES

1 Bill Palmroth, "The Creative Approach in Selling," *American Salesman*, April 1990, pp. 7–9, discusses five main points: get prospects' attention, relax, obtain prospects' confidence, find buyers' benefits, and arouse interest.

2 Robert L. Carl, "Getting Past the Secretary to the 'Boss,'" *American Salesman*, July 1987, pp. 16–18, suggests using assertive behavior, not aggressive.

3 Patricia Lu Pillot, "Your New Role as Salesperson," *American Salesman*, January 1988, pp. 3–6, discusses recognizing clients' signals to determine approach to use.

CASE 8-1: Tot, Inc.—Approaching Chain Store Buyers

Some years ago, Bruce Johnson, salesperson for the Tot line of juvenile equipment (e.g., strollers, playpens, and high chairs), returned from a trip of 2 months during which he called on large chain and department store buyers for the purpose of pushing the new item in the line, the tip-proof lightweight aluminum baby walker. Now that this trip was completed, he had time to reflect on his successes and failures, to see if he could learn something from them. Bruce always conducted a mental post-mortem on his sales presentations in an effort to improve his performance. He found that when he lost a sale he could usually locate the errors.

Overall, this trip had been successful. However, two failures particularly bothered him, both of them with the central buying offices of large chain store organizations in New York City.

At the first office, he had no trouble seeing someone in the juvenile-furniture buying section. He was ushered into a showroom without an appointment one afternoon at about 1:30. Shortly after, an Ivy-League-type young man entered and introduced himself as the assistant buyer, explaining that the buyer was not in at the present time. He said that he had the power to buy and would look at the merchandise.

In selling the lightweight walker, Bruce used a product approach which consisted of merely handing or tossing the unit to the buyer, depending on the latter's personality. He handed the unit to the assistant and said nothing.

After a careful examination of the merchandise, Mr. Boyer asked, "What's the price structure?"

Bruce replied, "Retails for $7.95. Your cost is $4.75 laid on your dock, 2/10, net 30."

"It's a $5.00 item if I ever saw one. Never would bring $7.95 no matter how hard it was pushed. I won't touch it for more than $3.00 on our dock and that's final," was Boyer's declaration.

Bruce answered, "I can well understand why you would like to retail it for $5.00, because so would I. I would love to be able to get it to you for that price, but I can't because of costs. Those ball-bearing casters alone cost 90 cents in volume purchase. The aluminum tubing is not cheap. The lowest bid we have been able to get from outside experts in aluminum fabrication has been $3.95 unpackaged. When I first saw the unit, I had exactly the same reaction as you just had. It was a $5.00 item; no use trying to sell it for more. However, I have really been fooled. It is moving at $7.95 both in your own stores and in Sears. We have sold several of your own managers directly, and their experience has been very favorable. Mr. Gerry out in your Oklahoma City store moved 36 units last month, which is almost unbelievable, but it is a matter of record. Sears in the same city sold 480 units during the past 8 months. So it has *proven* that it *will* move well at $7.95. I think it is the eye appeal that has done it. People are really attracted to it when it is displayed. It's unique."

The buyer repeated, "I don't care what it sells for, I'll only pay $3.00 and that's that."

"But it is a proven seller in your own stores at $7.95. How can I give you better proof than that of its sales appeal?" Bruce was now almost pleading in his frustration.

"Don't care about that at all. I've got to go now. Good-bye," were the buyer's final words.

Bruce realized at the time that he had got off on the wrong foot with Boyer; their personalities seemed to clash. He sensed during the attempted sale that this buyer would not buy the walker regardless of price or other considerations. Bruce was at a loss to diagnose his trouble. Where had he erred? He formulated several hypotheses but found it hard to figure out anything that might help him in his efforts to sell similar buyers in the future.

He reviewed another interview with anguish. At 2 P.M. on a hot June day he had entered the main New York office of another department store chain. He was calling on Mr. Anthony, head buyer for juvenile furniture. Bruce had called on Halliburton's of Oklahoma City earlier in the year only to be told by the woman in charge of the juvenile-furniture department that she had no authority to buy, that Anthony in New York did all the buying.

On the elevator to the buying office, a young woman commented favorably on the walker which Bruce was carrying. She showed great interest in it and asked on whom Bruce was calling. When told, she said, "That's who I guessed. I am his secretary. I'll take you right in. I think he will be really interested. Follow me."

Bruce was now inwardly jubilant; selling to this large chain would be a significant accomplishment. He stood just outside a small glass-enclosed cubicle while the young lady said, "There is a young man out here with a baby walker that looks real good. Can you see him now?"

"OK, send him in." As Bruce entered, he was greeted with, "When are you jerks going to learn that I only see salesmen on Tuesday?"

Bruce replied extra politely, "I am sorry. I didn't know your days. I am just in from Chicago for today only. I have to go on to Boston tonight. I can come back next month on my return trip if you would prefer."

Mr. Anthony grunted, "Forget it, kid. Let's see your mousetrap."

As he handed him the walker Bruce said, "Miss Starr, the buyer in your store in Oklahoma City, referred me to you because she was interested in getting this unit into her department."

Mr. Anthony countered, "Miss Starr is not a buyer. She is a department head. I am the buyer."

While the item was being inspected, Bruce noticed that Mr. A. was sloppily dressed, was reclining with feet on desk and cigar in mouth. He had been looking at a batch of little girls' dresses on display around the room. The entire room was in a state of chaos.

Anthony asked, "What's the story on this?" After hearing the presentation, he said, "Not interested. It's not for us."

Bruce started to ask some questions for the purpose of discovering Anthony's objections but was quickly interrupted, "Look, kid, there is no use arguing with me. When I make up my mind, it's final. Now get out of here, and let me work." Bruce fled the scene.

Bruce was really perplexed by this call, for it was the first time he had encountered such rudeness. Most buyers had been polite and considerate and generally were favorably disposed toward the walker. He could not figure Anthony out.

1 Make some hypotheses about what went wrong in each of the above instances.

2 How could Bruce improve his approach to avoid the situations which developed in these interviews?

3 After he found himself in these predicaments, could Bruce have done anything to salvage either sale?

CASE 8-2: The Simshingle Company—Approaching a Board of Directors

Kyle DeVos, owner, manager, and sales rep for the Simshingle Company of Corona, California, had an appointment to make a presentation for his new roofing product to the board of directors of the Palms Association of Indian

Wells, California. The Palms Association was a condominium community of 1,000 homes that had been built in the early 1970s. The roofs on the homes were thick cedar shake shingles. According to the rules, it was the responsibility of the association to maintain the roofs in good shape and replace them when needed. In early 1991, a few of the roofs were in need of replacement. More would follow. It was thought that all of the roofs would be replaced in the next ten years. The average roof required about 20 squares of shingles (2000 sq. ft.).

The directors were most aware of the fire hazards posed by the cedar shingles and did not wish to replace them with more cedar shingles. Yet they wanted to keep the same appearance. To that market, a number of firms in Southern California had developed shingles with the appearance of thick cedar shakes but made of a fireproof wood fiber–cement combination. Not only were these shingles fireproof but they would not wear out with time. Unfortunately, they cost $3/sq. ft., about 50 percent more than cedar shakes. Thus the board was going to be asked to pay a one-time expense of 50 percent more than had been anticipated in the association's reserves of $4 million. Each resident paid $405 a month for the association's costs, of which a portion was put into reserve for replacement of pools, streets, roofs, and other association property. The board had the power to assess the members for more roof costs if it so voted, but its member-directors were reluctant to make such assessments, particularly since it had just the previous year voted a $2,600 assessment for new landscaping and lighting of the community property.

Kyle's inside champion, Billy, had shown the board the new shingles, and the other directors were most interested in learning more about them. Kyle had been invited to make a presentation.

Kyle was undecided about his approach. On one hand he wanted the board to see some of his installations, but on the other hand such a trip posed logistical problems. He usually opened up with a product approach by handing the prospect the shingle, but the board had already seen them. Since there had been no fires in the Palms area for its entire existence, he questioned the wisdom of using his scare approach which was built around a videotape showing how quickly homes with cedar shake shingles on them went up in flames from the slightest exposure to fire. One spark from a fireplace could torch a complex such as the Palms in which all the homes were built closely together.

He thought that perhaps a benefit approach built around the long-run costs of his shingle versus the shake might be called for in this instance. Kyle summoned his assistant and directed that a cost approach be developed for use the next morning.

1 You are Kyle's assistant. Develop the cost approach he requested.
2 Evaluate the use of a cost approach in this instance.

CHAPTER NINE

THE SALES INTERVIEW I

CHAPTER NINE

THE SALES INTERVIEW I

It takes two to speak the truth—one to speak and another to hear.
Thoreau

After studying the material in this chapter you should:

☐ Realize that one critical aspect of selling is gaining the prospect's confidence—you must build credibility.

☐ Know the many ways in which you gain the prospect's confidence.

☐ Learn the advantages and disadvantages of the prepared sales presentation.

PROFILE OF AN

INDUSTRIAL REP

John Cunningham

B.S. in Marketing, University of South Florida, 1978

John began his career selling industrial lighting for Westinghouse from 1978 to 1983, and later for Phillips when it took over the company. He won an award for creative selling when he obtained an account from a large highway barricade manufacturer who insisted that he was perfectly happy with his existing supplier of lamps, since they never burned out. John asked some questions and obtained a sample of the product, which required two batteries to operate. He retired to his office and, drawing on the knowledge he had acquired at night studying with the Illuminating Engineering Society early in his career, he designed a product with the same lumen output whose lamp would burn out only once but that only needed one battery, a big overall cost saving to the manufacturer, whose business he captured for the company. His outstanding sales record was noticed by management and resulted in his being sent to the company's management training program. However, no promotion was forthcoming.

He accepted a job with Mitsubishi to launch and set up distribution for a line of energy-efficient light bulbs. He was successful in setting up the system, but unluckily the product was found to violate patents held by Phillips and was withdrawn from the market.

He then was assigned to sell the huge Diamond-Vision television screens in sports stadiums. After a successful stint in that exotic world, he was placed in charge of selling all of the company's consumer electronic products to industrial firms for industrial use.

It's time for action. If you're properly prepared, there'll be few problems you can't handle. Your sales interview depends upon you, what you are selling, and to whom you are selling it. It is not possible to provide a model for you to follow. Some interviews are quick and simple. Get the order and get out. Others are complex, time-consuming processes that stretch out over months of negotiations. Here we will focus on the fundamentals underlying most sound sales interviews and presentations.

Note that two terms are used for this interface between you and your prospect. Traditionally, it was called a sales presentation. It was showtime. You put on a presentation. However, in recent years, with the increase in business-to-business selling, the sale is less of a presentation and more of an interview. The consultative selling system positions you as a consultant who is interviewing the other person to determine if there is any basis for a mutual business relationship.

OBJECTIVES OF THE SALES INTERVIEW

A sales interview usually has four basic objectives:[1]

* To make the proposition aware of a problem or a need
* To prove that your proposition will solve that problem or meet that need
* To prove that you and your company are worthy suppliers
* To motivate or persuade the prospect to act promptly to solve the problem

You must meet these challenges in that order. First the prospect must admit that a problem or need exists. Often the prospect is well aware of the problem, so little needs to be done in this regard. But it is sound policy to bring out the prospect's problem loud and clear right off the bat and never to let the prospect's mind wander far from it. The essence of your position should be, "Here is your problem and the most important thing for us to do is to solve it so you can get on with other things."

While the prospect may be aware of a general need, you may have to devote some time to focusing it in such a way that your sales proposition fulfills it. For example, the owner of a small manufacturing plant is unhappy with the high cost of workman's compensation insurance. He is looking for a new insurance company. You are trying to get a production subcontract from him. So show him how he can cut payroll costs (and therefore his insurance costs) by subcontracting labor-intensive jobs to you. Shift the focus from insurance to payroll costs.

Once the need is clearly proved to and acknowledged by the prospect, you can proceed to show how your proposition will solve it. This is the very heart of most interviews: making the prospect believe that what you say is true.[2]

Coupled with credibility is the building of confidence in you and your firm's ability to perform according to expectations. A prospect can see that she needs a photocopier and agrees that yours looks good, but still she may

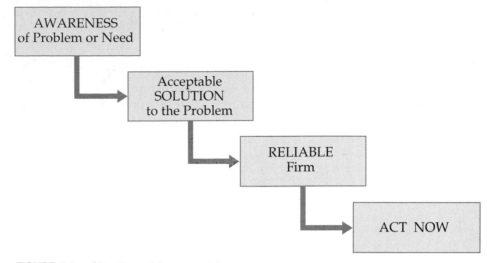

FIGURE 9-1   Objectives of the presentation.

not buy from you because she does not want to deal with either you or your company.

To illustrate these two goals, let's look at the sale of an accounting service to a small business executive who is currently doing the work himself. First, the accountant (the saleswoman, in this case) must stimulate within the prospect a desire to divest himself of the work. This may not be as easy as it seems, for he may firmly believe that he should keep the books in order to understand better what is going on in his business. The very fact that the man is keeping his own books indicates some desire to do so, for a business executive who did not want to keep them would have already sought the services of a public accountant. So, early in the presentation, the accountant will have to discover the man's present feelings toward keeping his own records—the time it takes, the work, and the worry. The accountant will probably suggest that the enterprise will make more money if its owner spends his time managing the business rather than accounting for it. Naturally, the owner's desire for keeping close track of operations will have to be satisfied. Perhaps he has a hidden objection—he is playing tax games. If so, early in the presentation, the saleswoman should show how she has saved her clients much tax money—all legally.

Until the prospect *wants* to stop keeping his own books, it is pointless to extoll the virtues of the accounting service. When the prospect indicates that he is dissatisfied with his present setup, then the accountant can begin to relate the excellence of her service.

Finally, there's the question of time—when to buy. Buyers naturally want to procrastinate. You must build into the interview sound reasons why they should act promptly to solve their problems. You should endeavor to trigger the purchase immediately. These techniques will be covered in detail later in Chapter 12 when we discuss overcoming procrastination.

BUILDING CREDIBILITY

Any way you look at it, credibility is the essence of persuasion. It depends on two major factors: (1) your behavior and personality and (2) your sales techniques. This credibility may derive from the goods or product being sold, from the maker, or from the person or dealer selling them.

Credibility is critical. Indeed, many sales are made solely because the prospect has such confidence in the salesperson that little actual selling needs to be done. The prospect does what the sales rep suggests. Of course, such confidence is not developed easily, but must be earned over time. Since there is little point in giving a presentation unless confidence has been developed, this chapter will be devoted to it and to some other basic strategies of making a sale.

Nothing you say or do will move prospects to buy unless they believe what you say. You may be earnestly and truthfully talking to a prospect, but that person may simply not believe you. Just remember that all of us have been lied to over and over throughout our lives. The newspapers are full of articles about how this or that person lied to gain some business or political advantage. Can you blame the people to whom you sell for being skeptical about you and your claims? The burden is upon you to gain their confidence.

It takes only one statement that the prospect does not believe to taint the prospect's attitude toward the entire interview, just as one drop of ink clouds a glass of water.

The foundation of your believability lies in your personal behavior; the superstructure can be erected by the various techniques discussed below.

Personal Behavior

Your behavior affects your credibility. Prospects seldom separate you from the statements you make; they judge all the evidence at hand, which includes both your statements and your personal behavior.

Perhaps no one thing does more to build confidence than a display of genuine unselfishness on your part. The person who really has the buyer's interest at heart, and proves it, gains the buyer's confidence. "I'd like to sell you that Model 104 motor that you have specified. It's more profit for us. But your situation just does not warrant a motor that large. Model 102 will do the job for you just fine, last longer, and cost less to buy and operate. It's your choice!"

And you should be telling the truth! If you saddle dealers with bad goods, all they will think about every time they see them gathering dust on their shelves is "That no-good rascal stuck me with those dogs!" Those who call regularly upon retailers know that their long-term success depends upon

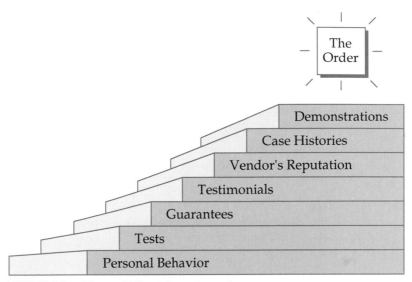

FIGURE 9-2   The credibility stairway to a sale.

gaining the dealer's confidence. This is not likely to happen if you fail to deal fairly and truthfully.

One electrical equipment sales engineer said, "In all my dealings with purchasing agents and engineers I have one overriding thought in my mind at all times. If our position were reversed, how would I want them to treat me?"

"Would you want someone trying to squeeze you into a suit two sizes too small or hang a tent from your shoulders, then try to tell you that it fits fine? Of course not! Well, neither do our customers, so don't you dare lie to them. If you can't fit them, tell them so," said the owner of a successful menswear store.

The way you talk, the way you dress, the way you look at the prospect, your whole attitude, affect how the prospect will perceive your truthfulness. Develop an earnest, sincere tone of voice, not a careless, flip, offhand way of speaking. It wasn't whim that caused IBM to require their sales reps to wear conservative suits, white shirts, and traditional ties. Your body language and appearance are as important as your spoken language. Work on them all.

Confidence-Building Techniques

Besides one's overall behavior, there are some specific things that can be done to instill confidence in the prospect.

Don't Knock the Boss   At times one is tempted to take the side of the customer against one's employer in the mistaken belief that doing so gains the favor of the customer. But it doesn't work out that way. It can destroy the buyer's confidence in the sales representative's firm. Let an experienced purchasing agent state this attitude:

> Do not appear to be disloyal to your company in your effort to be accommodating to your customers. I like to meet the man who "pats himself on the back" because he is with some particular concern, who is glad he is working for the "old man," whoever the old man may be. That man does more than printed advertising can ever do. His loyalty inspires the buyer's confidence in the firm which he represents. He sells not only the manufactured goods but also the reputation of the company.

> In our plants we use a good many scales for weighing our products. These scales must be accurate at all times and require the care which all well-constructed mechanisms should have. Sometimes they get out of order—that is to be expected. It happened that we were using a new type for the first time, and, of course, we had some trouble with it. We sent for a representative of the selling company. No sooner did he arrive than he began to apologize to me that we would not have had any trouble with the scales if the men at the factory had known their business. Their design on this particular type was not what it ought to be, and they might have known that the mechanism would give trouble. In fact, he attempted to console me with the statement that Smith and Jones were having the same difficulty with the new scales.

> There was nothing radically wrong with those scales, and that salesman did not believe what he was telling me, I am sure. He was so afraid of antagonizing me that he took pains to agree with me at every turn and even went one step further by adopting a conciliatory attitude of self-condemnation. That was an error, and a bad one, for it made him appear disloyal to his firm. The reaction on me was a loss of confidence in the company and its product. I stopped buying its scales as a consequence.

This statement needs little comment. Criticizing the company results only in a loss of business through loss of confidence.

This does not mean that you should not represent your customer's interests to top management when the customer has been mistreated. If the customer has the legitimate claim, help press it.

Tests as Confidence Winners Another method of winning the buyer's confidence is through tests. "Just taste that. Did you ever taste anything so good?" the enthusiastic sales rep for grape juice exclaims. The clothing or textile saleswoman submits her product to well-known tests. The paper sales rep has the customer tear the product, hold it to the light at certain angles, and test it in other ways.

The willingness with which you submit the product to testing is a factor in gaining the prospect's confidence. If you are eager to have your product thoroughly tested, the prospect will be impressed by your attitude. Some tests, however, although impressive to the unskilled prospect, are unconvincing to the expert buyer. With an experienced buyer it may be best to permit the buyer to conduct his or her own tests.

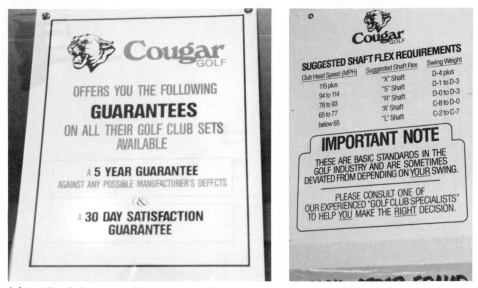

Informational signs, especially those that offer guarantees, help the salesperson by adding credibility. People tend to believe what they see more readily than what they hear. Signs like these that list features or benefits help establish confidence in the product or service.

If the product has been tested by the U.S. Bureau of Standards or by some store that, like Macy's, maintains its own testing laboratory, the results build confidence. Reports from commercial testing firms, paid by the manufacturer, may carry little weight.

The Guarantee   This is a powerful sales aid, particularly in selling a new product or to a new prospect. Of course, the guarantee is of value only insofar as the company issuing it is reliable, but even with this qualification, the guarantee makes it easier to win the confidence of buyers.

Guarantees are of varying strength, some being absolute (like those used by the big mail-order houses), while others cover only certain matters such as material and workmanship. New products will often sell more readily if they are warranted; established products of good quality require less support. Guarantees should be in writing, for many prospects have had unfortunate experiences with oral guarantees.

While most guarantees focus on the quality of the product or service being sold, other types of guarantees can be of even more help to the salesperson. Some people are reluctant to buy a product because they think they can buy it cheaper elsewhere. So some firms guarantee that they will meet any *bona fide* price on the same item offer by any other seller: "We guarantee that you cannot buy it for less elsewhere. We'll meet any other dealer's price."

Some dealers are reluctant to buy a line from a manufacturer because they fear that the seller will also sell the same line to one of the dealer's competitors. They want a guarantee of some exclusivity.

Sometimes buyers fear that the seller won't be able to deliver on time. "That pool must be completed by June 1st. Will you guarantee it with a built-in penalty clause if you fail to perform?" Some sellers will and some won't. Such performance guarantees are dangerous, but they can make a big difference in making the sale.

The Use of Testimonials True, the testimonial has been grossly abused and overworked, but this is only because it can be so effective. It is still sound in principle: "A satisfied customer is the best advertisement."

The testimonial is often used in *advertising* to gain *attention* rather than confidence. We like to read about well-known personalities, even if we do not always believe everything we read about them. In *personal selling*, the testimonial is used for the purpose of inspiring *confidence* instead of attracting attention.

One must know how to use the testimonial. First, it should be from someone whose problems are similar to those of the prospect. Telling the proprietor of the crossroads general store that Marshall Field and Bullocks use the same system of accounting or window lighting would mean little. It would be more effective if the sales rep for a retail accounting system said, "You know George Anderson over in Lincoln. His store is about the size as yours, and he says that his profits have increased 12 percent since he installed this system."

A testimonial will also carry more weight when its author is known to the prospect—and known to be reliable. The experience of a local woman with a new type of clothes dryer may be more convincing than a testimonial from a famous actress who obviously does not do her own wash. Sometimes the source of the testimonial is a group or a society such as a trade association or regulatory authority.

Case Histories A case history is simply a story of someone else whose situation was similar to that of the prospect explaining how that party handled the problem. The inference is that if the prospect does the same thing, the same results will be forthcoming. The prospect may believe the story even if conclusive evidence is not available if the sales rep uses the right tactics. First, insert details to show that you are familiar with the situation. Names, places, and dates are all valuable. Second, if the prospect is somewhat aware of the situation, so much the better. Better yet, if the prospect knows the person in the case history, a telephone call can verify the information if need be. Finally, any documentation such as newspaper articles, pictures, letters, records, that certify the story are most helpful.

Inspection of Previous Sales A contractor wished to convince the president of an electronics company that he was the best contractor to build a new factory. He had previously built a plant for another research firm in the same area, so he took the prospect on a detailed inspection tour of the previous job.

Case histories help provide prospects with an opportunity to evaluate work previously completed. What better way to show future clients the quality they can expect from your firm than with excerpts from articles that profile your successful interior design services in prominent trade publications?

In industrial selling, it is common to take prospects on trips to inspect previous work or the operation of new equipment. Seeing the equipment in actual use on the job is likely to be convincing if the prospect's problems and operations are similar.

Show Records   A women's ready-to-wear rep proved to a small-town merchant that the firm's line was really moving by showing *bona fide* reorders placed by merchants known to the buyer. An industrial machine sales rep wanted to convince the prospect that the firm's turret lathe required a minimum of repair. He produced records for a sample of installations showing each repair call the firm had received from the customers.

Plant Tours   An electronics firm was attempting to convince a large prime contractor that its quality control system was excellent so the firm could be approved as a supplier. Several executives of the prime contractor were flown to the plant to inspect the facilities and quality control methods in operation. They were convinced.

In industrial selling, allowing prospects to inspect previous work or observe the operation of new equipment is a competitive selling technique.

Many food manufacturers encourage plant tours to convince the public of their cleanliness. Meeting and talking with the seller's personnel may increase the buyer's confidence in the firm.

Talking with Customers   This is akin to reading testimonials yet more effective. Suggest to a prospect, "Just pick up the phone and call So-and-So and ask her about it."

Sometimes one is at a loss to know which method to use in gaining the prospect's complete confidence. To save time you might say: "I know that I make statements that may sound too good to be true. If you have any doubts about something I have said, what would convince you of its truth?" Perhaps the prospect is thinking of a free trial or some particular test or demonstration and will tell you. If you can go along with the suggestion, you may make the sale right there.

Visualization[3]   Don't tell about it; show it. Seeing is believing. Key selling points should be visualized. If you claim your product uses heavier gauge steel than its competitors, show cross sections. Don't just say, "Ours is 1.2 mils thick, while theirs is only 1 mil." Much time and effort can go into developing the visuals to communicate each key selling point.

Demonstration   Since much more will be said later about the demonstration, it is enough to understand that a good demonstration is the backbone of believability. A poor demonstration can ruin all your other efforts. Indeed, your presentation is often built around the demonstration.

The qualities of a product are often best conveyed through demonstration.

OTHER BASIC STRATEGIES OF THE INTERVIEW

Although you must devise many specific strategies and tactics for selling your products, there are some general strategies which are applicable to most situations. So let's set the scene early.

Selling Should Not Be a Battle

"Keep arguments out of the sale" is one of the best pieces of advice given to beginning salespeople by their managers. One famous salesman, Rube Wardell, used to say, "Sure, you can prove to the buyer, and to anybody that's around him, that he doesn't know what he is talking about. But what does that get you? There's no nourishment in showing the buyer up. He isn't going to thank you for it. More often than not he'll remember the incident, and sooner or later it will cost you business."

Some salespeople seem to go out of their way to arouse the antagonism of the buyer. One of the commonest forms of this reverse technique is to make a remark to this effect: "Well, sooner or later you are going to buy from me. I'll be seeing you." You must constantly maintain the attitude, "I am here to serve you, not compete with you."

Keep the Interview Friendly[4]

Buyers are not computers who arrive at a decision by feeding facts into their brains and turning out the right answers. They are human beings and, as such, prefer to do business with people they like. If a buyer likes a certain salesperson, she will give that person a longer interview, will listen more sympathetically to the story, and is more likely to give the person repeat business. While it is not good business to buy from someone just because of friendship, if other factors are equal the friend will usually get the business—and should.

Bear in mind that the buyer is often glad to stop a few minutes and talk with a friendly soul. It may have been one of those days when everything goes wrong, one full of unpleasant decisions or arguments with too many people. Nerves are on edge, blood pressure is up, and the buyer wants to quit for the day. Then a smiling sales rep is ushered in, bringing a new idea that promises to help solve some problem confronting the harassed buyer. You bring in a breath of the outside world, together with some trade gossip and *always* helpful ideas. The buyer may act tense at first, but this may be a holdover from previous hassles. The buyer who feels you are really friendly relaxes for a few minutes and is glad of the chance.

We have said many times that a sales interview should never be an argument. Rather, it should take on the aspect of a friendly conversation on a topic of mutual interest. With a friend, we do not quibble over some minor point; we feel an urge to agree. The interview moves smoothly.

If the buyer is already a customer, you must work hard at the job of *retaining* the friendship. Watch out for that customer's interests in every way, such as pushing for prompt deliveries, careful packing, or selling aids that have been promised. You must be dependable—absolutely.

A buyer related to the author an incident which had stuck in his memory for 20 years. He had placed an initial order with a certain sales rep and had been promised delivery on January 15, as the goods were needed January 16. At 4 P.M. on January 15, the buyer's phone rang. It was the salesman who had promised to make delivery that day. ''I'm at Jonesville only 120 miles away. I'm driving a company truck with your stuff in it and I'll get to your place by 8 P.M. We ran into a lot of unavoidable delays, and the roads are slippery, but we'll beat that deadline. Will someone be there to take the stuff inside at 8 o'clock?'' That buyer, after 20 years, feelingly commented, ''That salesman kept my business as long as he called on me. And *he never let me down* in any way.''

Controlling the Interview

Some people strive too hard to control the interview; they try to keep the conversation from straying to subjects other than the business at hand. But this may not always be the smart thing to do. Perhaps the sale is dragging, failure is imminent, when the prospect suddenly thinks of something of personal interest and starts to talk about it. The only hope for the seller is to listen sympathetically and search for a means to connect the prospect's expressed interests with the proposition to be sold. Even when this cannot be accomplished, one must listen with interest; often the customer will return to the subject of the sale voluntarily, reciprocating your courtesy by listening to you for a while.

There are, of course, buyers who purposely break the thread of the interview and then turn the proposition down before the conversation can be resumed. Such persons must be held more strictly on track. Other buyers are prone to let their thoughts wander afield from any subject under discussion and must be gently guided back to the main topic.

As with other problems arising in the sales presentation, there are useful techniques. Many salespeople rely on questions, believing that the one who asks the questions controls the interview. This is often similar to taking the pulse of the interview, although at times it may differ from this. For example, one might ask, "Did you ever see a valve that operates on this principle? It's really revolutionary."

Occasionally, you may have failed to make the presentation clear on some point, thereby prompting the prospect to ask about it. This may be just what you want, but again it may embarrass you if the question is a deliberately nasty one. The prospect asks: "Have you people ever solved all your quality-control problems?" It is like the oldie, "Have you stopped beating your wife?" You hesitate to answer either yes or no, so you regain control of the situation with something like, "I wonder if perhaps you aren't thinking about some other company. If we ever had any quality-control problems, it was before I came aboard."

If the prospect's questions reveal a genuine interest in the proposition, they are, of course, welcome and do not jeopardize your control of the interview. Generally speaking, the salesperson prefers to ask the prospect if there are any questions about the point just covered. In this way one can elicit questions and still retain control.

The salesperson may lose control of the interview through statements that are open to challenge. It matters not whether such statements are made as deliberate lies or through ignorance. An inexperienced sales representative for a small plane, designed for the use of executives who travel quite a bit, called on a prospect, unaware that the man was an older flier. The latter asked, "How many feet per minute will it climb on one engine?" The sales rep chose to guess, and guessed wrong, thereby completely losing control.

Timing

There are wrong times to try to make a sale. Prospects can be so busy or preoccupied with other problems that they have no time for the proposition. Someone whose plant has just burned down is in no state to listen to anything unless it is something that will directly alleviate the disaster.

Prospects can be in unfavorable mental or emotional states during which it is difficult to communicate with them in any rational manner. A person who has just had a death in the family is not in the mood to listen to someone extolling the virtues of a turret lathe.

The financial abilities of prospects vary with the times. The person who has just heard the accountant report a large increase in profits is a different buyer than one who has been told that the company suffered a loss last quarter.

Obviously, you should take this factor into consideration if you discover some significant event during the preapproach. You must be prepared to bow out quickly and gracefully upon encountering some unexpected event which places the prospect in an unfavorable frame of mind.

A Good Listener May Sell, Too[5]

Many salespeople seem to feel that it is necessary to keep up a constant flow of talk, that the prospect must be pinned down by an oral machine gun. More experienced reps have learned that it is wise to let the prospect do quite a bit of talking, especially if the person appears favorably inclined toward the proposition. If the prospect wishes to elaborate on some advantage of the product, it is good strategy to keep silent and let the buyer do the selling.

Indeed, many skilled persuaders make a practice of presenting their claims in a rather sketchy style, allowing their prospects to fill in the gaps and arrive at their own conclusions. Under such circumstances the prospect is likely to exclaim, "Then this would be true, too, wouldn't it?" This is precisely what the salesperson is striving for—to help the buyer reach the same conclusions. When these tactics are employed, the buyer feels smug, having figured the thing out more or less independently, and forthwith embraces the new idea. Thus the prospects sell themselves on the proposition. Obviously you can use these methods only when the prospect is not firmly in opposition and has sufficient mental agility to fill in the gaps in the presentation and reach the desired conclusions without being led step by step.

In selling to the opinionated buyer, you may fare better by not talking much. Also, when two people are shopping together they may wish to discuss the articles without interference from the salesperson and are likely to appreciate being allowed to make their own decisions. As long as they are interested in the article and are talking it over, you can afford to wait until it may be necessary to put in a word to save the sale. If this does not prove necessary, all is well. Many buyers prefer to be allowed to consider a proposition carefully without being pushed.

If you insist on doing too much of the talking, several things are likely to happen:

Prospects lose interest. They can keep their minds moving better if they are moving physically. It is always the students in the lecture who fall asleep—never the professor. A prospect who is allowed to talk a share of the time will be more likely to grasp quickly what is said.

Prospects brood. Prospects mull over the things that they would like to say, instead of paying attention to the things that you are saying. This is fatal to successful selling.

Prospects' obstacles grow. The longer prospects are forced to bottle up their questions and objections, the more inflated they become. Permitting prospects to do their share of the talking often discloses the obstacles to buying; it brings out objections and airs opinions on the proposition. With this knowledge the sale can be more intelligently planned.

Prospects feel pressured. Letting prospects talk makes them feel that they are not being pressured. It gives them the impression that you are trying to learn all about their problems so that you can render them a real service. It builds confidence and relaxes tensions.

The Art of Listening

There is a good deal more to listening than merely keeping your mouth shut. You must make it plain to the prospect that you are *listening*.

Mildred says to John: "You aren't listening to a word I'm saying!"

What's the matter here? John isn't saying a word. Why does Mildred feel so sure he isn't listening? Well, he may be doing something, such as

- Glancing at the paper he is trying to read
- Letting his gaze wander to activities or objects other than her
- Appearing to be thinking about something else

How can you give the impression that you are *really* listening? *Listen with your eyes*; look directly at the speaker. Let your facial expression respond to the statements of the speaker. Smile, compress your lips, raise your eyebrows, nod your head, or reflect a moment on some point. Comment occasionally on a statement made by the speaker: "so that's why they use aluminum in that part." "Yours is a larger firm than I realized." Anything like this will show that you *are* listening. Use a rising inflection, questioning some point. Be careful not to interrupt with some off-beat comment or remark, thereby revealing that you are not in step.

By listening—*really* listening—you accomplish several desirable objectives:

- You compliment prospects and build up their egos.
- You impress them with your intelligence and interest.
- You learn something. Nobody learns much while talking. But while your prospects talk, you learn.
- You make them like you and put them in a mood to be helpful.

This doesn't mean that you need do little talking at the opening of the interview. It is usually necessary to talk long enough to get the interview well under way and to ensure against being turned down before having a chance to present the proposition. After the interview is off to a start, then let the prospect take part in it.

Notice that you do not lose control over the situation by allowing the prospect to talk; the sale is going as planned. You can maintain control even while listening.

Listening is the essence of consultative selling, which begins the presentation by having the prospect describe the problems he or she wants solved. The consultant must first grasp clearly and accurately the prospect's situation. Only by careful listening can this be done.

THE SETTING FOR THE PRESENTATION

Sometimes the smallest details can influence the outcome of a sale. Certainly the immediate environment in which the presentation is to take place most definitely affects it. For that reason, some forethought should be given to where you want to make the presentation. Many times it is wise to avoid making sales presentations in a prospect's place of business—confusion and interruptions can be ruinous to the train of thought required for the transaction. Pick a place where both you and the prospect can meet in comfort and in privacy. Frequently a prospect's behavior becomes more sociable when not in a business setting.

People tend to behave according to the roles into which you cast them. If you want them to be friendly and sociable, put them in a social environment. The boss will be boss as long as he or she remains in the office.

As you enter the presence of the buyer, try to size up the situation, and plan quickly how to arrange things to your advantage. Some buyers try to make salespeople tell their story while standing in the outer office or doorway. The salesperson should request a better chance to make the presentation, perhaps basing this on the need for a place to show samples, set up a projection machine, etc.

Once inside the buyer's office, quickly appraise certain factors. Lighting is one of these, as you wish to show your samples or photographs in the most favorable light.

Noise is likely to interfere with the interview, unless it is noise to which the buyer has become so accustomed that he scarcely notices it. If it can be eliminated by closing a door or window, perhaps this should be done. Normal factory noises, for instance, cannot be entirely excluded although they may be minimized. Sometimes it is necessary to shift the scene of the interview to a hotel room or other quieter spot, but this possibility should be anticipated rather than left to the last minute. The very fact that you are forced to raise your voice to be heard reduces your effectiveness. The interview loses the desirable relaxed conversational tone. Your voice usually becomes more strident and unpleasant under these conditions, and this may jar the sensibilities of the prospect and cause him or her to cut short the interview. Noise can ruin a sales presentation.

How might this environment influence the outcome of these possible sales and how can the salesperson best handle the situation?

A Contrast in Settings

A menswear buyer, in New York for his semiannual buying trip, called at his appointed time of 9 A.M. at the offices of the manufacturers of Cricketeer, a line of medium-priced suits and sport coats. He had been carrying the line for several years and consequently was well-acquainted with the firm's personnel. He was greeted warmly and ushered into a showroom. The showroom was divided from the other showrooms by plastic folding room dividers, and noise filtered through them. It developed that no showroom had the complete line of models for the season; salespeople kept running in and out asking for such-and-such a model. The sales rep attending to the buyer often had to leave the room to locate something that she needed. There were constant interruptions. The sale dragged on hour after hour. The buyer had planned to spend the morning with Cricketeer, have lunch, then "work another line" in the afternoon. Noon passed, and a new problem arose; another buyer was scheduled in the room at 1 P.M. After much ado, other arrangements were made for the afternoon shift.

The real victim of this situation was a young salesperson who was trying to introduce Cricketeer's new line of slacks to the buyer. The rep was brought into the showroom and introduced to the buyer at 11 A.M. Given the confusion, the buyer's growing impatience, and the interruptions, it is no wonder that the rep failed to make a sale. Afterward the buyer confessed that he would probably have bought the slacks under better conditions, but he did not want to take time to make fabric selections and size the order. It was 2:30 P.M. when he went to lunch.

Next, the buyer proceeded to the offices of Norman Hilton, a high-quality suit and sport coat manufacturer. He was ushered into a private, beautifully decorated showroom. The "sales rep" (who happened to own the company) ordered that under no circumstances were they to be disturbed, nor would he take any phone calls. The room was completely equipped; he made the entire sale without leaving it and was finished in a little over an hour. It was a great presentation.

DEVELOPING THE PRESENTATION

Only people who have had to develop a sales presentation appreciate the difficulty of doing so. Presentations don't just happen. Only rank amateurs walk unprepared into a sale, with the intention of "winging" it. While it might seem to the casual observer that the professional sales rep is not following a plan, years of preparation, training, and experience, combined with talent, give the performance a deceptively natural appearance.[6]

Effective sales presentations are developed over time using proven techniques. All presentations should be planned; only the extent and rigidity of the plans are in question. Some interviews can be held to a fairly rigid pattern, while others must be conducted with great flexibility.

Prior to about 1890, the attitude prevailed that a sales rep had to possess a fluent tongue, a "gift of gab," in order to succeed. Extemporaneous eloquence was the mark of successful salesmanship. But in 1894, John Patterson, president of the National Cash Register Company, insisted that his representatives memorize the contents of a little book, which he rather tactlessly called a "primer"* and which contained the sales arguments for the product. It resulted in greatly increased sales, which led other manufacturers to insist that their salespeople should also memorize their presentations. The theory was that there must be one best way to sell a thing, just as there is one best way to handle a piece of work on a lathe, and that if this were true no other way could be so good—the notion of "scientific management."

Few speakers can make as effective an appeal extemporaneously as after careful preparation. Actors feel the necessity for preparation and rehearsal;

---

*Patterson had not been happy with the overall sales performance of his reps. One, however, had an outstanding record. He called that man into his office and directed him to write down his sales presentation. After looking it over, he directed the rest of the sales force to use the same presentation. The results were remarkable.

teachers memorize their lectures and constantly aim to improve their diction; debaters gather arguments and commit them to memory; and even preachers know that "the Lord helps those who help themselves" in preparing a message for their flocks.

Advocates of the prepared sales talk claim that the salesperson is able to deliver the talk more spontaneously and with more fire if free to devote attention to the *method of delivery* rather than to a *search for words*. You can size up the prospect as the sale proceeds and plan your campaign as you talk. Without a prepared sales talk you could not do this.

Additional points in favor of the presentation are:

• It covers all the ground, leaving no gaps. It does not leave persuaders wishing they had remembered to bring up certain points which might have clinched the sale. It is complete.

• It ensures a logical order in the sales talk. The prospect is led from one point to another easily, the whole presentation building itself up into an effective pattern.

• It saves time for both the sales rep and the prospect.

• It enables beginners to sell effectively, whereas they might fail if left to their own devices.

• It gives salespeople more confidence to know that they are prepared for a complete presentation.

• It has been field tested and it works.

Developing a Planned Presentation[7]

Progress in planning the sales talk has been rapid in recent years. Sales consultants can help sales managers develop presentations. These consultants operate something like this:

They accompany the salespeople in the field, listening to their every word and watching their every move. For example, in working with the sales rep for a food company the consultant broke down their operations into 354 different elements—different things that the salespeople did and said.

After this list was compiled, the next step was to reduce it to a code, for the company did not want the salespeople to know that their performance was being checked. Experienced observers then memorized this code. When they had mastered it, they went into the field. An observer would spend a day with a sales rep, recording in code everything that the salesperson did and said at each stop and what sales were made.

Next, the consultants tabulated all the individual results—that is, how often each rep did each of these 354 things. This determined the average frequency for each point.

Then the consultants compared the sales volume of the reps who did that thing more frequently with the volume of the reps who did it less than the average. They carried out this comparison for each of the 354 items. And 95 percent of them turned out to have no direct relation to the size of the order. But when this study was finished, the company got a brief, simple list of 16 selling methods that were important—the key methods that, beyond any question, really controlled the sales volume of their salespeople.

For example, they found that salespeople would do better if they suggested to a food jobber the quantity that ought to be bought instead of leaving the decision up to the dealer. Only 15 percent of the reps made a practice of offering this suggestion, but the average order of these reps was 300 percent larger than the average order of the salespeople who failed to employ this method.

Other planned presentations have been worked out by having some of a firm's best salespeople dictate their sales talks to tape recorders, then picking out the best features of the various efforts and combining them into one strong presentation. Others have merely adopted the sales talk of their best salespeople. This is not recommended, as it will probably reflect too strongly the personal traits of the salesperson. Also, a sales rep may have the best sales record because he has the best territory or gives the best service, not because of the sales techniques used.[8]

On the Other Hand . . .

Arguments *against* the standardized presentation are advanced by many successful salespeople who contend that committing a sales talk to memory is suicidal, that it turns a person into a phonograph, that it destroys initiative and places a premium upon mediocrity. They insist that a memorized, recited sales talk lacks punch and is likely to be delivered in a mechanical, singsong manner which robs it of vitality. Further, they point out that the salesperson who depends on a memorized presentation will lack the ability to meet interruptions and will be thrown off stride by the buyer who insists on asking questions and raising objections. But their chief criticism is that selling can never be standardized, because conditions are seldom the same. They claim that it is necessary to vary each interview considerably to meet differing conditions, that no two buyers can be handled alike.

SITUATIONAL SELLING

While some sales interviews may run smoothly, with the salesperson following an organized presentation, often it is necessary to depart from the routine. Sometimes you can foresee this if your preapproach has been carefully done, but frequently you must change your strategy and tactics to meet some sudden and unexpected development. Perhaps you had planned to conclude the sale after several interviews only to find upon calling that the prospect is on the verge of buying a competitor's product. An immediate change of strategy is called for under those circumstances. Perhaps you were anticipating a tough time for some prospect who seemed to be highly sales resistant, but midway through the presentation you sense that the prospect is ready to buy. This calls for an immediate change in plans. Never allow yourself to become so chained to your presentation plans that you ignore all signals warning you to change them. Flexibility is a *must* in selling.

The term for this philosophy is *situational selling*. It means that you must be prepared to meet any situation encountered and that you cannot become so attached to a certain pattern of action that deviations in the prospect's reaction will throw you off stride. This concept of situational selling is in sharp contrast to *canned selling*, in which you follow a certain preset course of action and try to force the prospect to go along with it.

The element of *timing* may force you to change strategy. The call may not be well-timed; the prospect may be in a violently unreceptive frame of mind. A steel sales rep told of the occasion when he nearly lost an old account because he was unfortunate enough to be calling upon the purchasing agent after the p.a. had been severely reprimanded by his superior. The purchasing agent began berating the rep for not giving him a better deal; he was attempting to transfer the blame for his troubles to someone else. The rep began to defend himself, but quickly realized that the man merely wanted a scapegoat and that it accomplished nothing for him to defend the company's policies. Instead, he wisely withdrew as gracefully as possible, carefully avoiding any argument.

SITUATIONAL STRATEGIES

Certain out-of-the-ordinary situations arise often enough that you should plan your strategies for handling them. Flexibility is necessary here, too, because given identical situations with different customers, you should vary the way of handling them because of personality differences, your rapport with the customer, and the particular circumstances of the customer. Suppose that an order is 2 weeks overdue, and the customer calls to complain about it. Depending on the customer's need, in one case you might be safe by simply giving the reasons for the delay, while in another you would be wise to immediately take action to expedite the order.

Ignore the Static

There are situations in which you would ignore a prospect's offhand remarks and go right ahead with your presentation. Many times this is the proper course to follow with people who are not serious about what they say or whose statements have no relevance to the presentation.

A tough old construction superintendent might growl, "If I bought any 'dozer that looked that pretty, the boys would think I'm gettin' soft and senile." Knowing the personality of the buyer and the way in which the statement was made, the sales rep might feel perfectly safe in ignoring the comment. Or he might acknowledge that he is listening by remarking, "You getting soft and senile? Everybody knows that'll happen when hell freezes over!" and then go right on with the presentation.

A cosmetic sales rep walked into a buyer's office only to be greeted with a blast, "You have your nerve even showing up here again after what you did to me last time." Lesser individuals might quake and run, but this one knew better and waited for what came next. "You know that new lipstick you sold me? Well, it's no good! I can't keep it in stock. Fool customers keep buying the junk for some weird reason. What are you trying to do? Work me to death?" Yes, some customers do have peculiar senses of humor. Many just like to give you a lot of flak, and you must learn to go along with it.

Agree and Act—Take a Strong, Positive Action

Many times you should agree with the prospect and do something about it. Suppose the cosmetic buyer followed up her opening blast with, "You know that new lipstick you sold me? Well, it melts! Here, look at this!"

The situation calls for action. The representative should say, "You're absolutely right. Lipstick should not melt like that. Send it back and I'll have a credit memo made out to you. Or would you prefer that I take it with me? I'm eager to find out exactly what happened with this shipment because I know for a fact that the company thoroughly tests it for just such environmental factors as heat, cold, and dampness. I really appreciate your bringing it to our attention." This strategy should be used whenever possible, for it makes the customer a hero; people like to be told they are right and have others take strong positive actions on their complaints.

It was related in Andrew Tobias's excellent book, *Fire and Ice*, that Charles Revson would personally act quickly and forcefully the instant a customer voiced some complaint about a Revlon product. Customers like action. They hate being ignored or put down.

The Challenge

Sometimes it is best not to let the prospect get away with irresponsible statements or complete untruths; the sales rep should challenge such claims. While great care must be exercised in using this strategy, there are times when it is needed.

A loud-mouthed prospect shouts, "I heard you guys give rotten service." The salesperson knows that this is not at all true, and so might say, "I would appreciate it if you would tell me from whom you heard such an outlandish statement. I am not worried about your now holding that view because I know I can prove to you beyond any doubt that we have excellent service, but I want to find and rectify whatever misunderstanding someone else has about our service." Usually the prospect will fold in the face of such a statement because he was bluffing, trying to throw the sales rep onto the defensive and confuse the issue.

Why might having a customer service desk such as this be a good idea?

Care must be taken not to criticize prospects; never call them liars no matter how clear-cut a case of prevarication it might be. Once you challenge their integrity, people are not likely to buy under any circumstances. Let the other person save face by blaming a third party for planting "misstatements" in their minds.

There are times when an account or prospect will persist with a lie. "I tell you these things were damaged when they came in! We didn't touch them." If the salesperson wishes to keep this account, it will be necessary to give the customer credit despite the fact that the goods had obviously been tampered with. It is not good salesmanship to go around proving your customers are liars and cheats. However, you'll have to reconsider selling to such an account if such incidents occur too often. There are some customers you do not want. Their business is not profitable.

The problem in such confrontations lies buried deep in the nature of most people—they refuse to admit they were wrong or that they lied. They will go to extreme lengths to avoid exposure. One of those lengths is to throw the salesperson out of the office to save face. Don't place customers in such positions.

Mitigating Circumstances

Many times, what the customer or prospect says is true as far as it goes, but there are other aspects to the situation. "I heard that your firm gives lousy service." You might have the reply, "Yes, I suppose that is one way to look at it. But we do it with your interests in mind. You know service costs money; it takes lots of people with lots of parts waiting for something to go wrong. Well, things don't seem to go wrong all that often with our product. We've found that we can provide service from headquarters for the relatively few repair requests we have and save you a lot of money doing it. You know X company's price is higher, and they have an annual service fee after the guarantee runs out. Let me show you the dollars you will save by doing it our way."

There almost always are mitigating circumstances involved in any situation, and if you are sufficiently adroit, you should be able to show a reasonable buyer the reasons for anything without making them sound like weak alibis.

An actual example: The sales rep for Wall Streeter men's shoes was calling on one of his dealers. During the sale the merchant complained, "You know delivery of our special orders has really been bad these past 2 months."

The rep calmly explained, "Yes, I know they have, and I think I can assure you that the situation will be cleared up shortly. As you know, we are only a small shoemaker, so when the boss saw that business was slowing up a few months back when he had $900,000 in inventory, he shut down the plant. If your orders were not in stock, they couldn't be shipped until the plant reopened. But on top of that, he found out that his shutdown cost him some good men who went to work elsewhere. So he has been having trouble getting the plant going again when business picked up. He now knows he was wrong to push the panic button so soon, but I guess it wasn't our money sitting in inventory."

The merchant smiled and said, "I want to thank you for the first straight answer I have heard all week. We've been involved in negotiating some leases in a shopping center and are tired of lies. Thanks for the fresh air." Needless to say, this sales rep's rapport with the merchant was greatly strengthened by his honesty.

Withdrawal

Sometimes a strategic withdrawal is called for when a situation looks particularly explosive. It may be wise to let a person cool off before proceeding with the deal. Perhaps the buyer has just had a battle with a superior which has left the buyer looking for a scapegoat, and you happen to be next in line. He may transfer the blame for his failure upon you and your products. You can't win in such situations; better run for cover. Get out before you say something that you will later regret.

This is not a recommendation to run if the problem involves your products or your firm. In this case, you had better be on the scene to defend yourself and your wares.

Play for Time

Frequently it is wise to ask for more details and encourage buyers to relieve their minds. This is the best strategy for handling serious statements made by responsible people. It helps focus the discussion on the actual facts and gives the salesperson time to think. Also, it lets the buyer unwind a bit and almost forces a reexamination of the whole picture. Frequently, after blowing off a lot of steam, the buyer will calm down and not demand any action: "I just wanted to let you know how I felt about it."

The strength of this strategy lies in its protection for you; it keeps you from attempting an answer without complete information. Many times the buyer misstates his true feelings or thoughts, leaving you to tackle a phantom problem while the real one still blocks the buyer's mind. The more the buyer talks, the more likely it is you can weather the storm.

Be a "Whipping Boy"

Your buyer errs; he ordered too much and now is on the hook with his superior for overstocking. A sales rep, able to place that overstock elsewhere, might offer, "I'm sorry. It's my fault. I should have caught that for you. How much do you need to get rid of? I'll try to place it for you." How can a buyer fail to like such a salesperson? Don't be afraid to take the blame for something, whether or not it is your responsibility, if the matter is relatively insignificant or can be easily remedied.

The Interrupted Interview

In spite of your efforts to stage the interview favorably, the prospect may be interrupted in the midst of it. The telephone will ring, a subordinate will ask for instructions or make a report, a customer will enter the store. This break may be disastrous, as it pulls the attention of the prospect elsewhere and halts the journey from decision to decision.

Picture the prospect at a big desk listening to your sales presentation. The telephone rings. A 5-minute conversation, evidently of considerable importance, ensues. At its conclusion the prospect swings back to face you, but it is apparent that she is still pondering the matter discussed over the telephone. She cannot immediately transfer her attention to the sales message, even though she is willing to do so. You must recognize this mental condition and make allowances for it. If you do not handle this situation intelligently, your presentation will be incomplete, because the prospect is preoccupied during part of it. This gap must be filled.

One method of handling the problem is to start the presentation again at once, but instead of continuing from the point at which the interruption occurred, *to review briefly the points last made*. This brings the prospect back gradually to the subject without leaving a gap in the presentation. Care must be taken to rephrase the repeated points so that the statements will not sound like repetition. When it is evident to you that the prospect's mind is again on the right track and traveling at the proper speed, you may proceed.

If you can pick up a sample or an exhibit or a chart and hand it to the prospect, it may serve to pull her attention back to the matter in hand. An *action* may be better here than *words*.

When it appears that the interruption will offer the prospect an excuse for ending the interview, you should have ready some forceful statement to ensure that the interview is resumed. Indeed, the interruption is likely to prove permanent unless you take command of the situation *immediately* in a decided fashion, for the prospect is apt to feel that the break has given her an advantage, of which she is often quick to avail herself. If you permit her to take the offensive after the recess, you are allowing yourself to be put on the defensive—not a good strategic position.

A question may be used at this point. It operates in the same way as a question put by a teacher to a student whose attention has been distracted. It serves to bring back that wandering attention to the subject as effectually as any device known in pedagogy and may be applied with equal success by the salesperson.

There will be times when the interruption has so distracted the prospect that it is hopeless to proceed. Under such conditions it is wise to stop trying to sell and to make an appointment to see the prospect later, perhaps at home or at lunch—some place where interruptions are less likely to occur.

SUMMARY

The sales interview, or presentation, is at the very core of the selling process. Its objectives are to convince the prospect of the need for the product or service, to prove that the selling proposition will meet that need, to prove that the seller is worthy of the order, and to convince the buyer to act now.

Credibility is the key to persuasiveness. Not many buyers will trade with people they distrust. Thus many things are done in the interview to gain the confidence of the buyer. While personal behavior is critical to the rep's credibility, there are other actions that can also be taken to enhance credibility, including the use of case histories, guarantees, testimonials, tests, demonstrations, plant visits, visuals, and records.

Some effective basic strategies are to listen carefully to what the prospect says, avoid all conflicts with the prospect, place the interview in a setting conducive to the sale, avoid situations in which you are likely to be interrupted by third parties, and, above all, keep the interview friendly.

The popularity of the so-called canned or prepared sales presentation has waned in these days of consultative selling. The philosophy of the sales interview obviates a canned pitch. Today's sales reps are involved in situational selling, in which they must be flexible and responsive to the demands of the situation.

DISCUSSION QUESTIONS

1 What are some of the things that can happen during a sale that can cause the prospect to lose confidence in you or your product?
2 How can you get an otherwise silent prospect to talk?
3 What are some of the factors that can cause you to lose control in a sales interview?
4 If the prospect continues to disbelieve you after you have done everything you know to prove your claims, what would you do?
5 How can you determine the prospect's state of mind?
6 If you were assigned the task of developing a prepared sales presentation for your company, precisely how would you go about it?
7 How can you avoid third-party interruptions?
8 Your sales manager has provided you with a sales presentation with which you are most uncomfortable. It has you saying things that you feel are not quite the truth. Its words are stilted. You would never use words that appear in the presentation. What should you do?
9 How do you become a good listener?
10 How can you best avoid making the sales presentation a battle with the prospect?

REFERENCES

1 Bill Palmroth, "The Perfect Presentation," *American Salesman*, August 1989, pp. 16–19, suggests investigation and demonstration.
2 E. J. Knudsen, "Selling Unseen Values," *American Salesman*, September 1988, pp. 9–12, suggests finding a hidden key to desire that unlocks the door to the sale.
3 Milt Grassell, "Sales Presentation Skills: How to Make Sales Presentations Come Alive with Simple, Easy-to-Use Visuals (Part 1)," *American Salesman*, November 1987, pp. 16–20, and "Sales Presentation Skills (Part II)," *American Salesman*, December 1987, pp. 3–9, suggests using visual aids to get customer's attention.
4 John Franco, "Side-by-Side Selling Endears Salespeople to Clients," *American Salesman*, June 1986, pp. 23–26, suggests the salesperson and the buyer should not have an adversarial relationship.
5 Morgan P. Miles, "Adaptive Communication: The Adaptation of the Seller's Interpersonal Style to the Stage of the Dyad's Relationship and the Buyer's Communication Style," *Journal of Personal Selling & Sales Management*, Winter 1990, pp. 21–27, suggests selecting the appropriate communication style: discrete transactions or relational exchanges.
6 William S. Pierson, "Presenting the Benefits," *American Salesman*, February 1986, pp. 3–6, asserts that preparation does not have to be a long, tedious process.
7 Mark G. Gilbert, "How to Prepare an Effective Sales Presentation," *American Salesman*, December 1988, pp. 7–10, suggests using a printed sales presentation.
8 There is evidence that structural inflexibility of a sales presentation does not necessarily inhibit its persuasiveness. See Marvin A. Jolson, "The Underestimated Potential of the Canned Sales Presentation," *Journal of Marketing*, January 1975, pp. 75–78;

Robert H. Collins, "Unleash the Power of Desktop Presentations," *Journal of Personal Selling & Sales Management*, Spring 1989, pp. 70–75, discusses the effectiveness of computerized desktop presentations.

CASE 9-1: Inez Angelo—A Matter of Credibility

"I just received notice from my boss that if my productivity doesn't improve in the next 6 months, I'll be fired." Inez Angelo had called her closest friend, T. Harry Uppington, from graduate school days for consolation as well as some advice on what she should do.

Inez had graduated with high honors from a noted graduate school of business with an emphasis in finance. Her career plan was focused in the investment industry. She had accepted a job as account executive with a large nationally known stockbroker. After 6 months of intensive training in the New York home office, she was assigned to the San Antonio, Texas, office, since she was fluent in Spanish and well as English. She was not overly enthusiastic about her assignment but accepted it as a price she would have to pay in climbing the corporate ladder.

She had called Harry, whose family owned a smaller Wall Street investment banking house whose major customer seemed to be the Uppington family trusts, because she and Harry had worked closely together on many class projects and had become good friends. Harry had been impressed with her ability to make case presentations before the class. She was good on her feet. Harry had proven that he had a good understanding of the investment business.

"Harry, I just don't seem to be able to persuade the men with money around here to let me help them with their investment problems. Even my Spanish doesn't seem to help. My gross commissions are the lowest in the office and are not going anywhere. I don't blame them for giving me notice. I'm not doing the job. But I can't quit a loser. I've got to do something."

Harry said, "I was afraid that this was going to happen to you when you took that job. You need a lot of credibility to get rich people to let you work with their money. Where's your credibility? You're a young woman just out of graduate school. You should work on the money management side of this business. Get a job with a mutual fund or manage some institutional money. There's all sorts of jobs that are begging to be filled in that area."

Inez was silent for a moment and then replied, "I know you're right, but I still want to leave here with a success. I will not leave whipped. That word 'credibility' hit home. I know it. They just don't think I know what I am talking about. They don't believe me. And some of them just can't let a woman tell them what to do with their money. What can I do to change that?"

Harry replied, "Several things come to mind right off the bat. First, . . ."

1 What are some of the things that Harry told Inez to do to help her build up her credibility?

CHAPTER TEN

THE SALES INTERVIEW II

CHAPTER TEN

THE SALES INTERVIEW II

Talk of nothing but business, and dispatch that business quickly.
Placard on the door of a Venetian publisher, ca. 1490

After studying the material in this chapter you should:

☐ Understand the role of showmanship in selling and the use of demonstration

☐ Know how to handle competition

☐ Know how to use effective figures of speech to make your point clearer to the prospect

☐ Know how to prepare a formal sales proposal

PROFILE OF A TELEMANAGER

Joe McCormack

American Mirrex
Wilmington, Del.

"I went to work for Richards Merrill Pharmaceutical right out of college, and they gave me great training and experience. Then in '76 I went to work for Continental Can selling highly engineered films used for clear wrappers or blister packages.

"I think that the greatest thing about selling is the freedom that it gives me. It's a license to be creative and entrepreneurial. I think that the reason I have done so well is that I am good at getting the order. I can close the sale."

In 1991, Joe lives in E. Greenwich, R.I. while functioning as vice-president of marketing for American Mirrex in Delaware thanks to our electronic toys—computers, FAX, mobile telephones, etc. He believes that with the high costs of relocating and employees' reluctance to move, we will see an increasing amount of business done by telephone, FAX, and overnight delivery. "There will be a lot less face-to-face selling in the future."

The sales proposition must be *clear*—so plain and understandable to the prospect that not one vestige of doubt remains about either the disadvantages of rejecting the proposition or the advantages to be gained from accepting it. Clarity means not merely being clear enough to be understood, but being so clear as not to be *misunderstood*. Often there is a distinct difference.

Moreover, prospects must be *convinced* by the presentation, convinced that the proposition you offer will solve their problems or meet their needs.

How can we make our interview clear and convincing? Here are six suggestions:

- Use showmanship! Dramatize! Visualize!
- Take the pulse of the interview often; make sure that the prospect comprehends what you have said.
- Handle the competition.
- Talk the prospect's language.
- Demonstrate.
- Put it in print.

SHOWMANSHIP

Everyone likes a good show. It's fun. It keeps the audience interested. Showmanship in selling is dramatization, visualization, and demonstration—all keys to good selling. It grabs and keeps the prospect's attention while you deliver the message. Of the hundreds of ways to introduce showmanship into a demonstration, we will mention only a few.

Dramatization

It is often necessary to emphasize certain points in the demonstration by being dramatic. Some illustrations will provide insight into the area of dramatizing your statements.

An average tire sales rep might say, "These tires are built to take it; they're tough!" A more imaginative salesperson might try to be dramatic by saying, "You're driving 55 miles per hour down the road with your children in the car. Suddenly some jerk swerves over into your lane, forcing you onto the shoulder. You hit a big pot hole . . . jars every bone in your body and every bolt in the car! But you only have to worry about your steering, not about your tires. These tires can take everything the road hands out!"

Now let's examine what such dramatization tries to accomplish. First, it tries to project the prospect into an emotional setting—for example, to relate the tires to the safety of the car's occupants. We have previously discussed how people are more apt to buy because of emotional forces than rational reasons. Dramatization tries to cast rational talking points into an emotional framework.

Second, people like stories, so we create a plot with characters and make our product the hero of the action. It's entertaining.

Whether you are buying a car,
an rv, or a motorcycle, there
is no substitute for the test drive
as a means of checking
performance.

Finally, people will more likely remember the point if it is dramatized than
if it is simply stated. Any talking point can be dramatized with the assistance
of a bit of imagination.

Tests as Means of Dramatizing the Presentation   Tests are a method of
dramatizing the presentation. They should relate closely to the use of the
product. The test should be a performance of the product at some stage of its
legitimate use. Many tests are dramatic but prove nothing about the actual
performance of the product. Showing that a ballpoint pen writes underwater
may be dramatic, but it's also irrelevant. How many people write underwater?

The best tests are simple. The prospect may easily become skeptical of a
test that seems too complex. If the prospect is supposed to perform the test,
there is a possibility of an error being made if the test is not simple, thereby
ruining the chance of a sale.

*Wherever possible, the test should be performed by the prospect rather than by the
salesperson.* It not only interests the prospect more but inspires greater confidence. When the prospect is allowed to conduct the test, it is wise to tell the
prospect in advance just what results to look for. In this way the prospect's
attention is focused on the right features of the test.

One sales rep for a plastic material used for upholstering furniture carries a swatch of the product mounted on a stiff card. The prospect is handed a nail file and challenged to scratch the material.

A salesperson for Corning Glass carried a hammer with which to hit the glass, thus proving it unbreakable. That worked pretty well, but she had a better idea—she let the prospect swing the hammer. That really convinced the most skeptical buyers and sales shot up.

A sales rep for a new adhesive snips a shoelace in two and applies adhesive to the ends, holding them together while delivering the sales talk. Then, handing the shoelace to the prospect, the rep invites him to pull it apart.

Revere Copper & Brass, Inc., wants to prove that the copper-clad stainless steel they use in their cooking utensils transfers heat more quickly than ordinary steel does. They give each salesperson a "heat stick," which is merely a rod, one-half of which is ordinary steel and the other half their Copperclad. The prospect is asked to take hold of it, one hand holding each end. The salesperson holds a lighted match or a cigarette lighter under the middle and waits for the prospect to let go of the hotter end of the "heat stick." This is always the Copperclad end, and prospects are convinced by the evidence of their own senses.

The sales rep for a roofing cement takes an ordinary handkerchief, coats it with cement, and then uses it as a dish to hold water. When the handkerchief proves watertight, he has scored his point more emphatically than if he had quoted any number of statements from scientists or testing laboratories.

Owens-Corning Fiberglas Corporation stages a dramatic demonstration for its insulation. At the beginning of a typical show, the master of ceremonies asks a member of the audience to come up on the stage and light the oven of a kitchen range. As the oven preheats, the M.C. displays a roll of Fiberglas, the same as that used to insulate the range. Next, he wraps a quart of ice cream in the insulation and pops the ice cream into the oven. Beside it he places a cherry pie ready for baking.

Then a pot of hot coffee is wrapped in a blanket of Fiberglas and placed in a refrigerator on the stage. The show proceeds, the pie, ice cream, and coffee apparently forgotten. When it is time to take out the freshly baked pie, out comes the ice cream, too. A member of the audience unwraps the quart of ice cream and finds it frozen as firmly as when it was inserted in the oven. The pot of coffee is taken from the refrigerator and sampled by the amazed spectators, who find it still hot. Other equally dramatic tests are carried out, at the conclusion of which not the faintest doubt of the product's insulating qualities remains. Splendid dramatization and showmanship—and it sells.

How about visualizing a cooling fluid—a nonconductor—guaranteed not to cause short circuits if it leaks into electronic equipment? Its maker took the cabinet off a television set and placed the set inside a large glass tank filled with the fluid. Prospects saw the set working in it. Heat from the set's components boiled the coolant in places, causing bubbles to rise, but the set continued to operate perfectly.

Some companies give samples to the prospect to test at the prospect's leisure, in the absence of salespersons. It is wise to give the prospect a clear idea of the product's limitations, if any, and strong points before turning it over. These products to be tested may be offered free, or they may be loaned, as in the case of machines.

Care Must Be Taken   Considerable care must be taken that the tests do not fail or backfire. One salesperson demonstrating a new dictating machine took pains to bang it around with great gusto, but when the demonstration began, the machine would not work properly. You should always check out a demonstrator to make certain that it is in operating order before attempting a demonstration. A faulty demonstration or test is worse than nothing at all.

It is usually unwise to subject the actual product which you hope to deliver to very rough tests, for it will upset the prospect who is already thinking possessively. Customers prefer new, perfect products.

In planning to use showmanship, two facts should be remembered: Some prospects don't like it, and some salespeople can't use it effectively. Sales managers say that buyers in large cities rather expect it, but in smaller places they react unfavorably to it. Individual buyers are different in their reactions, also.

If you are not much of an actor and find it difficult to use showmanship, perhaps it will be better to simply say, "Now I'm supposed to be very dramatic here and to use a lot of showmanship, but I just don't feel comfortable doing it." Then you can go into a sincere, quieter demonstration. Perhaps the prospect will accept your statements with even more confidence than if you had tried to be dramatic.

Visualization

The old-style "barehanded" selling is virtually obsolete. Salespeople are now equipped with sales aids designed to tell the story quickly through the eye. When using visual material, you should talk less.

The Product   The product itself is one of the best visual aids you can use, so use it. Whenever possible, show the product. But there are times when that is not possible, so other techniques are needed.

An agent for the Clary militarized printer was perplexed when the engineers to whom he had been lecturing about the product's ruggedness showed no response. Their reaction seemed to be, "Ho hum, so it prints when it's sitting on a nice quiet table. Big deal." He got mad. He started pounding on his boxful of electronic equipment while it was running; he picked it up and let it fall a foot; he took off his shoe and whaled away. The printer was jumping all over the table, all $12,000 worth of it. The audience crowded around the table to see what the madman was going to do next. One engineer growled, "Let me see that tape. . . . Well, look at that! It didn't miss

Visual aids such as slides or video demonstrations help the prospect visualize the product and better understand each selling point.

a digit." It took a dramatic visualization of the printer's ruggedness to make the audience believe what he was saying. Thereafter, the sales rep developed a shock test kit containing a rubber mallet.

Pictures   Pictures of the product can be used for those items too bulky to carry. Furniture, machinery, and many other products can be shown fairly well in this way. The old method used to be to turn the pages of the catalog or to toss out pictures from the briefcase. Today, it is the custom to have these pictures arranged in the best order and frequently displayed on an easel built for the purpose. This makes them easier to look at and also helps to hold the sales rep to the standardized presentation.

Portable automatic slide projectors with small self-contained screens can be effectively used to visualize not only the product but your talking points. Many organizations coordinate a series of such pictures with the sales talk so the two work hand in glove. Each selling point has a visual to support it. Moreover, the series of pictures helps the salesperson remember the presentation in a complete, orderly manner. Such visual programs are particularly useful for inexperienced salespeople.

Video   Modern electronic technology provides salespeople with wonderfully effective devices for visualizing, dramatizing, and even demonstrating the proposition being sold. Video cassette tapes, video cameras, and portable television units allow the filming of the product or presentation for showing to the prospects. No need to relate a story about some previous installation—show it.

The Sales Portfolio This is usually a collection of illustrations, graphs, letters from satisfied users, records of tests, and other material which the company believes will help make an effective presentation. The pictures may be of the production processes for making the product, showing the size of the plant, special machinery used, careful inspection, cleanliness of the factory, packaging processes, assembling techniques, etc. Or they may show the product in use, as the Caterpillar Tractor Company does. For bulky products, a portfolio shows all pertinent facts about the product—facts which would be difficult to present in any other way.

One type of portfolio deserves mention. This is the book which has a number of pages printed on transparent cellophane so that they can be laid one on top of the other, letting the reader see the various parts of an automobile engine or a gas stove as it is assembled. Even though a part or all of one section may be later covered by another, the prospect can see each clearly as it is put in place. There is something fascinating about such a portfolio. However, its chief function is to make clear the features about the product which are ordinarily hidden from view, even in the product itself.

Sales reps for the best-managed companies are usually provided with carefully prepared "visuals." All the salesperson has to do is to learn to use them effectively. But sometimes it may be necessary for salespeople to devise and make their own visuals. They may not be quite as professional looking as those put out by the company and its advertising agency, but they may work just as well.

Visualizing Intangibles Intangible products or services, such as insurance, investment bonds, and various services, need effective visualization even more than tangible products, which may be shown and tested.

How can you visualize such concepts as security, protection for loved ones, capital appreciation, and a full, rewarding retirement? Pictures can help, particularly if they allow the prospect to be easily projected into the scene. If you wanted to visualize the annuity a person would receive each month upon retirement, show a facsimile check for that amount, made payable to the prospect. Tire manufacturers portray their safety claims by showing their tires in action as they are being severely tested.

Salespeople of intangibles value the frequent use of pencil or pen during the presentation. Many times a simple chart or graph, completed as the interview progresses, aids clarity and maintains interest to the end. Casually jotting down a figure or a fact on a pad also utilizes eye appeal successfully. Many salespeople write down the key word of each talking point given, both to emphasize and to help the prospect retain the point by hearing it and by *seeing* it. If certain psychologists are correct in saying that 87 percent of all impressions are gained through the eye and only 13 percent through the

Attractive displays help catch the eye and encourage prospects to handle and "try out" the products. Bookstores, museum gift shops, toy stores, and other retail establishments often arrange books and toys on related themes to attract the imagination of both children and adults.

other four senses, it becomes immediately plain how essential it is to use eye appeal as much as possible in selling.

The Display of Goods   To ensure a good impression on the prospect, it is vital that the goods be displayed under the most favorable conditions.

One principle concerning product display always holds true: The salesperson should handle the product with respect, as though its value is appreciated fully. If you are selling shoes, wipe them off carefully before letting the customer handle them; do not *toss* them carelessly on the floor but *lay* them down. If you sell textiles, you must show a genuine pleasure in feeling their fine texture. You should not throw a coat down on a pile carelessly without straightening out the sleeves. If you don't value what you sell, why should the buyer? Unless the salesperson appears to like the product, a similar feeling cannot be generated in a prospect. This is not to imply that every article must be handled as though it were delicate or fragile. The farmer who buys overalls may want to see the salesperson try in vain to tear them in two; the vacuum bottle salesperson hurls her sample to the floor to prove it unbreakable. These rough methods of handling, however, only emphasize the salesperson's respect for the merchandise. The sales rep for the filing cabinet who jumps on the opened drawer to prove its sturdiness can be just as enthusiastic about the results of the test and treat the product with even more regard because it stood up under severe strain. In this way, salespeople create their own favorable conditions.

Bakeries sell products that appeal to the senses of taste and smell. Mrs. Fields has used these senses with great success to bring customers into her stores. Not only do Mrs. Fields' baked goods smell delicious, but samples are often available to reinforce customers' interest.

When showing an article to a prospect, it is often a good idea to move it a little. Movement catches and holds attention. A rabbit "freezes" to escape detection. In comparing two items, a sales rep often holds the larger or better one *over* or in front of the other, thereby making it look somewhat larger and bringing it more prominently to the buyer's attention.

Where possible, it is wise to show the goods as they will appear when actually in use. The salesperson for shoes or clothing tries the article on the prospect, of course, but some products do not lend themselves so readily to this purpose. In selling yard goods to be made up into a dress, it is often necessary to drape the material on the customer in the fashion in which it is to be made up. In selling house furnishings, some enterprising firms arrange complete outfits for a room, working out a harmonious combination of floor covering, draperies, and furniture for the customer. Most people are deficient in imagination and need help from the sales rep to visualize how the product will appear in use.

The senses of smell, touch, and taste are powerful pathways to the brain. You can talk your head off about how great your new food product tastes, but why waste your breath? Just let the prospect taste it. Bakeries sell products that appeal to the sense of taste; an exhaust fan is often placed in an aperture in front of the salesroom so that passers-by will catch the aroma of fresh cookies and pies. A department store found that sales of women's hose were stimulated by faintly scenting them with perfume. Apparel sales reps appeal to the sense of touch in selling fine fabrics. Quality has a distinctive feel.

Demonstration

As with testing, it is wise to let the prospect play an active role in a demonstration. Picture someone selling a shotgun or tennis racket to a hunter or tennis player. The person would stand a very slight chance of selling the prospect unless the latter were allowed to handle the product. These illustrations are purposely extreme in order to bring out the principle, but there are hundreds of products whose appeal would be greatly strengthened if made through the sense of touch as well as the senses of sight and hearing.

Why merely *tell* homemakers how easily a vacuum cleaner rolls when they can prove the point for themselves by operating it a few seconds? Many retailers have discovered the necessity of permitting customers to handle certain goods if sales are to be made. The variety chains in particular have learned that it is often better to take a loss from theft or breakage than to place the goods out of reach. An outstanding example of this principle was the experience of one of the great chains in selling cheap flashlights. If they were left out on the counter, people would handle them and try them. They could not seem to keep their hands off, and the result was broken bulbs and exhausted batteries. So the flashlights were placed under glass. The breakage ceased, but so did sales, and the flashlights were once more placed within reach of the shoppers.

Demonstration is such an important topic that we will discuss it more thoroughly later in this chapter.

TAKING THE PULSE OF THE PRESENTATION

To learn just how clearly you have been putting across your selling points, you will find it helpful to ask questions of the prospect as you go along. There is a technique in asking these questions that it will pay you to study.

You might phrase them in such a way as to disguise them slightly. Ask "This proposition certainly gives good value for the money, doesn't it?" *before* you mention the price. If the reply is either affirmative or negative, the prospect has not been attending carefully to what has been said. Or you might drop the innocent query, "What do you think of that last point? Does it appeal to you?"

Some sales reps make a practice of injecting a "See what I mean?" or "Do you understand?" into the presentation at various places. Although the purpose is good—to keep the prospect nodding in agreement and presumably listening to the arguments—the query can be better phrased. Nobody likes to be asked if he has sufficient intelligence to comprehend a thing. The tactful salesperson shoulders the burden of making the proposition clear and inquires, "I wonder if I made that point clear. I'm afraid I stated it awkwardly." This not only makes the prospect feel more comfortable but also opens the door to a fuller discussion on any points that may remain unsettled in the prospect's mind.

Pulse-taking questions serve more than one purpose. First, they can reveal which features or arguments are most effective with that prospect. When the salesperson asks, "If you owned this machine, would you find this feature useful?" he should watch keenly the *way* the prospect replies. If she says, "Oh, yes," the sales rep knows that this point should perhaps be stressed again, if necessary. If the reply is "Not very," the salesperson should hurry on and not bring that point up again.

Second, by getting an affirmative commitment on each point along the way the salesperson keeps the prospect from raising objections later in the interview. This makes the task of closing the sale much easier, as when you say, "You have said that you liked this feature."[1]

Often it is wise to begin a sale with some question to discover just where the prospect is in the buying process. If there is reason to believe that the prospect is ready to buy, it would be foolish to launch into your presentation when all you need do is take the order. Ask "Have you seen our line previously?" and take it from there. Some people have looked at you and the competition and are ready to buy.

The consultative or conceptual sales systems call this final stage the commitment stage or phase of the interview. The salesperson must discover to what extent, if any, the prospect has made a commitment to buy. Consultative sales reps often encounter what they call incremental commitments to buy. Perhaps the company is committed to study the problem but has decided nothing else. If the sales rep is asked to make a proposal about the problem, a *conditional commitment* should be sought: "What will you then do with my proposal?" asks the consultant who wants some commitment from the prospect about what will happen once the proposal has been submitted.

Most prospects clearly signal their commitment to buy if the salesperson only has sufficient sense to recognize the buying signals, which are usually focused around questions about how the deal will be implemented.

At market times, sales reps often bluntly ask the visiting merchant, "Are you ready to order or do you want to look and talk awhile?" When the prospect gives clear-cut positive answers to your questions, stop your presentation and go into your close.

If prospects refuse to make commitments, it is because they think that they will lose by doing so. They do not see the proposition as a win-win deal. Usually some basic issue is blocking the transaction. Chapters 11 and 12 discuss how to handle such objections.

HANDLING COMPETITION

Few sales are made without encountering competition of some sort. You must be prepared to handle it, because if you're not, the prospect will think that you can't. Certainly the prospect is aware of some competitive offers in most instances, but it is surprising the number of times a salesperson will encounter a prospect who is unaware of some of the leading competitors in the field. Hence wise salespeople are reluctant to bring up the matter of competition for fear that they will be telling their prospects about something they do not know.

A business executive was shopping for a car for his son as a high school graduation present. He had been attracted to Volvo by advertising, so he dropped by a dealership for a demonstration. Throughout the presentation the sales rep stressed how superior the car was to Honda. It seemed to the prospect that this sales rep considered the other car serious competition, so the prospect decided to check it out for himself. He ended up buying an Accord.

Praise and Pass On

Of the three views on handling competition, the first holds that salespeople should not mention their competitors except in praise. When and if the prospect brings up the matter of competition, praise it and pass it on. "Yes, that is a good product. But ours is better!" By ignoring competition entirely, the prospect is not led to consider the other fellow's proposition. The motto of the group seems to be, "Sell your own goods, and let the other reps sell theirs."

Unfortunately, this may not always be the best strategy. A competitive brand may loom large in the prospect's mind, and ignoring it will do little to dislodge its place in the picture. In fact, some prospects will not bring up a favorite product for fear that the sales rep will show them the folly of their ways. *There is security in silence.* If you are to handle that competition, first get the prospect to talk about it. Smart car salespeople determine their competitors early in a sale. They ask, "Of all the cars you have seen so far, which one do you like best?" The answer to this question provides a great deal of information to the perceptive person. If the prospect answers, "The 300 ZX!" then it would be folly to try to push a sedate four-door sedan. Most car sales reps dread prospects who have only begun to shop for cars because they know that no matter how good a deal is offered such prospects, they will still feel it necessary to look around. The wise car salesperson prefers to get prospects *after* they have seen the other brands; then there is hope of closing a sale.

Meet It Head On[2]

The second viewpoint is that competition must be recognized and combated, that it cannot gracefully be ignored. Indeed, some advocates of the theory want a return to the day when competitors were not afraid to point out the weaknesses of the other's products. These stern old warriors feel that business has perhaps become too effete.

When it seems necessary to make a comparison between your product and a competitor's, such a comparison should not try to cover every point. Rather, discuss only those features which seem to interest your prospect the most. To cover *every* comparative advantage is to confuse the prospect.

Some people believe that it is shrewd to plant a seed of doubt concerning a competing product. They may do this adroitly by telling something they have heard about it. Or they may come out more frankly with their own opinion. If the salesperson and prospect are well acquainted, the salesperson may be more frank than when they are strangers. But a seed thus planted may grow into a big doubt—big enough to prevent the purchase of the competing product.

However, this adverse comment by the sales rep *must* have a basis in fact. Frequently the prospect may ask the competitor about this point and may receive such a convincing reply that all faith in the other sales rep is shattered. But, if the reply is *not* convincing, the first sales rep may gain the prospect's confidence and make the sale.

Recognize but Handle with Care

A third view lies somewhere between the extremes. It is doubtless wise to avoid attacking competitors, and yet it seems impossible to ignore them completely. Knocking competitors creates the impression that the seller is finding the competition strong. The inference is that you feel antagonistic toward the other company largely because you have suffered much at its hands. The next step in the prospect's reasoning is, "If this seller loses so much business to that competitor, probably the competitor has a good proposition. I ought to look into it."

The principle also applies to retail selling when salespeople attack the reliability of their competitors. A young man lived in a small town that supported two jewelry stores. He wanted to buy a diamond ring—*the* diamond ring. Each dealer cast so many aspersions upon the integrity of his competitor that the young man concluded that since he knew so little about diamonds and since both jewelers were probably dishonest, he would do better to go to a jeweler in a neighboring city.

A purchasing agent relates an incident of a sales rep's knocking a competitor with disastrous results:

> I was in the market for a supply of shipping cases. Bids were received, including one from a firm with which I had done considerable business and one from another company with which I had not so good an acquaintance but which bore a fine reputation. A salesman from the first firm put in his appearance and asked me what concerns were bidding. I told him, although I refrained from mentioning prices. Immediately he started in, "Well, of course, you know Jim is a good fellow, but can he deliver the goods as you want them? His factory is small, and I am not too sure

of his methods. Can he give you what you want? You know he has not had much experience with our product." And so on.

Good-natured knocking in a way, but knocking nevertheless. What was the result? I was filled with curiosity to see the inside of Jim's factory and to talk it over with him, so I made an inspection tour. He got the order and, incidentally, did a good job. There was a simple case of a man selling his competitor's goods, for it was really his discouraging comments that created in me a curiosity to go and see for myself, with the outcome extremely disappointing to the knocker.

The Deadly Comparison

Some manufacturers of mechanical products train their sales reps to make a point-by-point comparison between their product and the competing product which stands highest in the prospect's opinion. They sometimes write down each point, putting a check mark by one of the points in the two columns to show which of the two products is superior. When the process is finished, it is expected that the sales rep's product will have more check marks in its column than the competing product does. This is bare-fisted selling, but it is sometimes necessary and effective, especially if the comparisons are made in a fair and objective manner.

A variation of this method is to take a sheet of paper and draw a line down the middle, making two columns. Put the name of the competing product at the top of one column and your product at the top of the other. Then put the price of each—in this case, $220 and $250—in the proper column. The competing product is the cheaper, so the sales rep's task is to justify the higher price. She therefore mentions one *exclusive* feature of her product and says, "Would you say that this feature would be worth $1 a year to you? That's a very conservative estimate, isn't it? All right, this product will last much longer than 10 years, but let's be conservative again and say it will last 10 years. That's a $10 benefit you get from this feature." Thus the salesperson proceeds feature by feature until she has built up value exceeding the $30 difference in price.

In cases where the prospect has already bought from a competitor, the salesperson must exercise care in making comments on the competitor's proposition, for to criticize it is to question the taste or judgment of the prospect who purchased it. Tact must be used, as a sales rep for office filing equipment realized when she tried to persuade a prospect to change his system completely and install a new one costing nearly $2,000. She did not make the prospect feel that he had shown a lack of acumen in installing the first system; rather, she complimented him on it, but showed tactfully how enlarged business, changed conditions, and new inventions in the way of equipment now made a change desirable.

Transfer Blame

Perhaps the blame for a previous poor purchase may be placed on the competitor or the competitor's sales rep, thus making it appear that the former did not have the true interests of the buyer at heart. The shoe sales rep, finding a customer wearing a shoe a size too short and a width too wide, might win the confidence of that customer by commenting, "The person who sold you these shoes must have been short of time or of shoes. You have an aristocratic foot; narrow and with a high arch. Let me show you the difference between this shoe and the one you need."

Testimonials

Testimonials may perhaps be used in combating the claims of competitors or in proving that the sales rep's product is superior to a competing one. Office appliance sales reps are compelled to meet inquiries about competing devices. The sales manager equips each sales rep with a loose-leaf binder filled with facsimile letters from satisfied users. When a prospect asks, "But will this stand up under hard use like the Blank machine?" the salesperson merely has to open to the testimonial letter from a shoe manufacturer who wrote that, "After using both machines for several years, we have standardized on [the sales rep's machine] because of its relative freedom from trouble." It is better to let some qualified outsider claim superiority for a product than for the sales rep to do so. Tests by universities, the U.S. Bureau of Standards, and similar institutions are effective when used in this connection.

Tests

Sometimes, if competition grows keen, it is necessary to resort to an outright test of merit between the competing products, as is done in selling agricultural implements, paint, calculators, etc.

Nothing is as effective in selling as a side-by-side test of products, provided that your product's superiority is relevant. It would be rather pointless to prove that one car was faster than another if the prospect had a dislike of speed.

But tests can be unfairly rigged. Motorola's policy on buyers' tests of its two-way radio communications equipment was to allow prospective purchasers to select the unit to be tested from Motorola's stock on hand and then perform whatever tests they desired with their own people at the controls. However, Motorola's main competitor (an extremely large corporation which will remain unnamed) would use for such tests units which they had "doctored" to give the desired performance. Moreover, Big Company's representatives, not the prospect, had to administer the tests.

From bitter experience, Motorola instructed its sales representatives never to allow Big Company's representatives to be in the same room alone with Motorola test equipment. Peculiar things had happened to such equipment in those circumstances. Yes, tests have their hazards.

Some General Observations

With a bit of experience, sales reps quickly learn which competitive products pose the most potent threat and are made aware of their good's competitive

Prominent and well-written information on packaging helps consumers make a well-informed choice when comparing products. It is especially important to distinguish your product if the market is crowded with other competitors.

strengths and weaknesses. Thus it is possible to anticipate and forestall competitive arguments during the presentation. If you know that your product is relatively high-priced, you will continually build up the product's value—higher quality, additional features, etc.—during the interview. You can meet the claims you know will be made—meet them with talking points showing the superiority of your product in those very particulars or in offsetting advantages. In this way you can shrink those competitive advantages or claims in the mind of the prospect before they are brought out into the open. This can be done without mentioning the competitor by name, thereby avoiding arguments or engaging in a rough knocking session.

It goes without saying that a thorough knowledge of competing propositions must underlie any such effort to eliminate them. This knowledge should include such matters as: sales trends, how current models are catching on, service given, delivery performance, value of their dealer help, advertising and sales promotion programs, various trade practices, and their *real* price. It is helpful to know just where your competition is most vulnerable. Talk with owners of competing products.

Be familiar with your competitors. Watch their advertising; get hold of their sales literature; visit their salesrooms or showrooms if they have any. Ask your good customers what they hear about competitors.

Learn what your competitors are saying about *your* product. Get competitors to try to sell you, if possible. Make a list of their claims against your product, line, or company.

Finally, it will help if you can identify where your chief competition lies in each particular sale. Then you can slant your demonstration accordingly.

It is hard to remain silent in the face of unfair competition. Indeed, it may be a sound idea to fight back vigorously when a competitor tries by unethical means to ruin you. This is just about the only time it is wise to mention a competitor by name, and even here it is usually better to wait until the prospect has brought this competitor into the conversation.

If your prospect has a good friend who is in competition with you for the prospect's business, it does not pay to criticize that friend. Rather, it is wise to present your own proposition so effectively that the prospect's self-interest overcomes the desire to buy from the friend. If the question is raised, you can point out that a true friend of the prospect would want the prospect to buy the product which would best serve the prospect's purposes. Sometimes the alleged friendship may not be so warm as you imagine it to be; perhaps the prospect is really eager to end the arrangement, as the "friend" may be selling on friendship alone and not providing the best service or the best product. It is by no means a hopeless situation.

One reason for keeping on as friendly terms as possible with competitors is that the nasty things said about them always get back to them and cause them to be even more vigorous and active in their efforts to win business. If your adverse comments are not true, they may retaliate.

Salespeople will therefore do well to avoid mentioning their competitors as far as possible; if they must make comparisons, these should be made in a spirit of fairness; and no statements should be made that cannot at once be substantiated. The ethics of business are improving, and salespeople should help to lead the way.

Unethical Competitive Tactics

Unfortunately, there are still far too many instances of unethical competitive behavior for it to go unmentioned. If you do not learn how to handle such tactics, your firm's reputation may be severely damaged without your knowing the real reason for it.

One salesperson for a baby-food manufacturer confessed that he planned his route so that he would be in each store the day after his major competitor serviced it. While the store manager was not present, he managed to "steal" a few baskets from the competition by combining their contents, and he would place them in a disadvantageous position on the shelves. He was rather clever at sabotaging the other's efforts.

A beer sales rep trying to get his brew into a tavern admitted to several interesting tricks. He "sandbagged" an owner by having several phone calls made to the owner, requesting one brand of beer and emotionally refusing any substitution. The rep would manage to be in the tavern during the last phone call so he could take the order. When one owner would not order the salesman's brand of beer, he sabotaged the other brew by slipping a little grease into the nozzle of the spigot, thereby causing the beer flowing through it to become excessively foamy. He would do anything to make the buyer dissatisfied with his present supplier.

Eventually these tactics catch up with most salespeople using them, but in the short run they can cost the innocent salesperson much grief—and money. You must learn the tricks of the trade in order to recognize when they are being used against you.

The best protection against such tactics is a smart, alert customer. Once the customer discovers such tactics, the salesperson is through in that account. Help the customer discover them! But be sly about it, or it may appear to the buyer that it is merely a case of "sour grapes."

TALKING THE LANGUAGE OF THE PROSPECT[3]

It seems so obvious to state that you should talk the language of the prospect that the reader might well remark, "Why bring that up?" The fact of the matter is, however, that many of us do not do it. The importance of using short, simple words that convey meaning and weight cannot be emphasized too greatly.

Examine Lincoln's Gettysburg Address, and you will find that it contains 268 words. Examine it more closely, and you will learn that 196 of those words are of one syllable, 52 are only two syllables, and only 20 have three or more. Lincoln used short, simple words to construct one of the finest speeches ever delivered.

This does not mean that words of more than two syllables are ineffective. It does suggest a careful selection of language appropriate to the prospect in every different interview. A good illustration of the use of language fitted to the prospect is obtained in the account of a life insurance agent's effort to sell a policy to a young man and his father who were trying to build up a dairy farm. The son managed the farm while the father worked as a carpenter, putting all surplus funds into building up the herd, on which they both hoped to retire some day. The prospects admitted that if something should happen to the father in the next 10 years the family would not be able to reach its goals because the dairy now needed the extra funds he provided; it was not yet self-sustaining. However, when the sales rep mentioned the annual premium for life insurance to provide the funds needed to bring the herd up to a profitable operating level if the father died, the family threw up its hands and claimed that it was impossible. The agent then made his appeal in other terms. "In order to make certain that you reach your stated goals should something happen to your breadwinner, would you be willing to give me the milk from those two cows? Just pretend that you don't have those two cows; their milk will ensure that you will have your dairy no matter what happens." He made the sale.

A real estate agent said to a prospect:

"I've been wondering why you don't buy that property on Elm Street that I showed you. You told me that it suited your needs and that the price was right. I felt that you wanted it, and I still do. Yet you don't buy. The only answer is that I've fluffed the presentation somewhere and failed to make some point clear. Maybe you have some question in your mind that I didn't answer. Would you just forget that I have been trying to sell you this property and tell me frankly where the obstacle lies? Maybe we can straighten things out."

So the prospect accepted the invitation:

"You're right; I do like the property and want it. But I don't understand your financing plan. I'm hazy about that second mortgage you mentioned. Until I know where I stand on that, I'm not going to buy it."

A purchasing agent with a sense of humor relates his experiences with a young seller who had not learned to speak the language of the prospect:

Having had occasion the past 3 months to purchase a great variety of office building supplies, this hitherto unsuspected condition has been effectually demonstrated in my own case.

The first disillusion came with the salesman who represented letter-filing cases. Having heard our requirements, in terms of approximate number of letters daily, the young man looked wise, considered a minute, and decided what we needed was their CSI.

"What is CSI?" I inquired.

"Why," came in a somewhat grieved and condescending tone, "that's our letter file you want."

"Is it made of paper, metal, or wood?" I ventured.

"Oh, in case you are considering metal you want our FDX, and probably two NCOs for each FDX."

"Some of our manuscripts are pretty long," I confessed.

"In that event you will need FDX with two NCOs for transfer for ordinary correspondence, and PL1, with RIP transfer for manuscripts."

By this time I recovered a little of my lost nerve and remarked, "Young man, what you say strikes me as ROT. What I am trying to buy is office furniture, not alphabets. If you will only talk Greek, Armenian, or Western Chinese, our translator can probably get a little intelligence out of it, as to the material, size, operation, capacity, color, and price of your goods."

"But," quoth he, "Those are our catalog numbers."

After a questioning that would have done credit to a lawyer on cross-examination, I managed to worm out of him the size, capacity, material, color, and cost of his various file cases, but it was like pulling back teeth with tweezers, and he seemed to think he had grossly betrayed secrets belonging exclusively to his firm.

If he had been the last and only one, these lines would never have been written. But unfortunately, he merely opened the ball. They came in droves: fine, clean, bright-faced, earnest young fellows; every one good to look at, and all talking the same catalog lingo, which, of course, was unintelligible to me. Even when I got down to scrubbing brushes, one tried to sell me FHB, which turned out to be "fiber and hog's bristles"; and when the stuff came, C18 turned out to be some kind of a mop.

With scarcely an exception they all reeled off yards of (to me) utterly meaningless trade letters and numbers with a confident air of profundity which at first was amusing but quickly became exasperating. My conclusion was that if these young salesmen were selling my goods, I would get some friend to send for one of them, and I would sit concealed where I could hear their puzzle talk and then go home, call the boys all in, and give a few first easy lessons in salesmanship or buy a course in some correspondence school for each of them, or both.

Indeed, companies whose sales forces cover a wide area make an effort to choose their salespeople partly on account of their ability to talk the languages of the various territories. Likewise, occupational backgrounds of the salespersons are considered. Thus people with a farm background would be chosen to sell in agricultural sections, individuals with retail shoe experience would be picked to sell to shoe retailers, etc.

DEMONSTRATE

At the very heart of sales is the demonstration. A good, effective demonstration is perhaps the single most persuasive tool in your sales kit. When in doubt, demonstrate.

And when you get into trouble, go back to your demonstration. "Let me show you how that works again." Don't be afraid to repeat.

Plan Each Demonstration

It is easy to fall into a rut when one goes through the same routine time after time, but the astute salesperson tries to alter the demonstration to fit the particular circumstances of the situation. The computer sales rep will have to alter the demonstration when selling to a private individual rather than a purchasing agent of a corporation. A seller of home stereo systems would devise different demonstrations for different types of customers; an elderly couple probably would not be interested in listening to a heavy metal group any more than a teenager would want to hear Lawrence Welk. And each would be interested in different aspects of the units.

When you fail to tailor your demonstration to fit the situation, you lose one of your major advantages over advertising. You can shape your sales appeals to fit individual needs, while advertising cannot.

Sequence of Points

As just pointed out, people are interested in different things about a product. One person may be most interested in its performance, while another is more concerned with safety. One prospect may be price-conscious, while another wants quality merchandise. If you do not quickly focus your presentation on the points that are most important to the prospect, you may *never* get to talk about them. Once the prospect loses interest, it may be difficult to reattract his or her attention. By leading off with the strongest features, the sales rep may get the prospect so excited that the sale can be closed before the weaker points arise. One car salesperson almost lost a sale because she waited to the last to take the prospect on a drive into the country to test the car on the open road. The prospect was sold the instant he took a particularly bad curve at a rather high speed without any effort.

Applications

When possible the demonstration should be relevant to the prospect's particular application. Obviously, a customer shopping for a family car is unlikely to be interested in having a demonstration of its powerful accelerating capabilities.

The engineer buying computer workstations may not be particularly impressed with a demonstration involving an accounting application. Focus on the prospect's problems, the prospect's applications.

Pace

Some sellers make the mistake of rushing through the demonstration. Because they thoroughly understand the proposition, they assume others must understand it. No matter how alert buyers may be, if the proposition is a new one, they will need to be shown point by point just what it should mean to them. When the concept is *new* to the prospect's mind, lead *slowly* along until each idea has been assimilated thoroughly.

However, if the prospect is familiar with the product, the demonstration may move faster. A man is buying an electric razor as a gift. If he uses one himself, little demonstration is necessary; if he has never used one, a thorough demonstration may be in order.

Repeat the Talking Point It is usually helpful to *repeat* the outstanding talking points about the proposition. The prospect may not grasp the point on hearing it the first time or may be thinking about some other feature of the proposition. It may be wise to state the talking point in different words the second or third time. All educators know that repetition is an indispensable teaching device. No youngster ever learned the multiplication table after reading it through once. Repeat your best points.

DEVELOPING FORMAL SALES PROPOSALS

Professional salespeople selling significant products or services must often prepare formal written proposals. The sale often depends more upon the skill with which the proposal is written than the intrinsic merits of the proposition. A deserving product can be sabotaged by an inept proposal writer.

The typical Xerox sales rep presents an average of 100 sales proposals per month. Some are simple routine proposals using standard forms, while others can be complex custom documents requiring much preparation time. The simplest proposal may only consist of a letter outlining the terms of the offer. Other proposals may be hundreds of pages long.

The written proposal serves two other purposes: It backs up the sales rep's statements and verbal proposals, and it minimizes misunderstandings about what was said. Good businesspeople put things on paper. It is sound business to do so.

Whatever the length, the basic elements that require coverage remain the same. A formal sales proposal should contain the following six elements:

- Title page
- Cover letter
- Table of contents
- Body of the proposal
- Summary
- Contract

Title Page

Start off on the right foot: Give the prospect a good-looking professional title page that clearly identifies what the proposal is about, to whom it is addressed, and from whom it comes. Dates can be important. When is the proposal made and for how long is it valid?

Cover Letter

The cover letter summarizes what's happened with the sale so far and lists what's being sent to the prospect. Make sure the letter is appropriate to the situation. How can you grab the reader's attention?

Table of Contents

Make it easy for the reader to survey the report to see what it contains. All tables and illustrations should be listed.

Body of the Proposal

The body of the sales proposal should outline the prospect's present situation before introducing the proposed system or product. Then the benefits and features of the proposed products or services should be clearly spelled out. Next, the cost justifications must be presented along with the investments needed. Prove that the proposal will somehow save the prospect money.

Above all, it is imperative that it be clearly shown just how the proposal meets the prospect's needs or specifications. One NCR sales rep was emphatically told by a merchant that under no circumstances should the company's proposal for a computerized control system use a cash register for inputting data into the system. A small input keyboard was wanted. The rep came into the interview pushing a cart with a cash register on it. The proposal was for a cash register system. He was physically pushed out of the store. The rep thought he was going to be able to "sell" the merchant on his way of doing things. This merchant had been successful by doing things his way and he had no inclination to change.

In Conclusion

The proposition should be summarized in a concise statement that will allow the prospective firm to grasp it quickly. Not everyone wants to wade through the whole proposal. Get to the bottom line as succinctly and quickly as possible.

Contract

Finally, make it easy for the prospect to buy. Give him or her a firm legal document to sign or discuss.

SUMMARY

Communication is the essence of selling. The rep must develop techniques that allow clear communication of the points to be made. Thus much use is made of visuals, demonstrations, showmanship, and dramatization.

It is important that the rep continually be alert for commitment signals from the prospect. It is important to get commitments throughout the interview. Usually commitment questions focus on matters of implementation—delivery, terms, conditions, etc.

The issue of the competition can arise at any time and must be handled in some manner. It is usually wise not to knock competitors. However, at times a head-to-head comparison of competitive units is unavoidable.

The formal sales proposal is often needed. Properly done it can be an effective selling tool. It should lead to a contract.

DISCUSSION QUESTIONS

1 Why is showmanship effective in stimulating sales?
2 If you are making a presentation of an office photocopier to a lawyer, what questions might you ask to take the pulse of the sale?
3 If you were selling landscaping, what might you include in your sales portfolio to make it more effective?
4 What visuals might you develop if you were selling water softeners?

5 When should you bring up the topic of competition?

6 You have finished with your presentation of the office photocopier to the lawyer and have discovered after asking your pulse-taking questions that she is about to buy another machine that is particularly subject to servicing troubles. How would you make the lawyer aware of the other machine's defects?

7 You learn that one particular sales rep for a competitor in your territory has continually made disparaging remarks to your customers about both you and your wares. What would you do about it?

8 A prospect says that he is about to buy another brand that is much cheaper. While your product is fine, he says, it is just too expensive. You know the other machine is junk. How would you convey that information to the buyer?

9 You are selling insulation to homeowners. What demonstrations of your product's virtues might you want to develop?

10 You are a small electronics manufacturer who is trying to gain acceptance by a large prime contractor for the government on a big defense contract. This contracting firm is afraid that you and your firm will not be able to perform according to specifications. What methods might you use in your presentation to make the prospect believe that you will meet your promises?

REFERENCES

1 Jim Lorenzen, "How to Quit Presenting! . . . And Start Selling!" *American Salesman*, December 1986, pp. 6–8, suggests getting commitments on each benefit.

2 Amanda Burnside, "Exhibitions: Taking the Stand," *Marketing (UK)*, June 28, 1990, pp. 31–32, says that the advantage of exhibitions is that the seller comes face to face with the potential buyer; the disadvantage is that the seller normally shows wares alongside competitors.

3 "Handling Customers," *American Salesman*, May 1989, pp. 20–22, suggests using an actual story to support each point.

CASE 10-1: Mountain Glass Company—Developing a Short Presentation

Tom Scott, a sales representative for the Mountain Glass Company, had just received a sudden special assignment from his boss—to sell a new line of safety plate glass patio doors and windows to people whose homes had suffered glass breakage during a particularly heavy windstorm the previous night.

The Mountain Glass Company was located in a western city of 85,000 which was usually buffeted several times each winter by extremely high winds. Glass breakage during such windstorms was always extensive. Homes in the area, almost without exception, had both large patio doors and large picture windows because of the spectacular views.

During such windstorms, which usually hit at night with velocities in excess of 130 miles per hour and could last up to 12 hours, families would abandon all rooms with windows facing the west—the direction from which the wind would come but also the direction of the view. The windows were usually shattered not by the force of the wind itself but rather by some object—rock or wood—picked up by the wind.

Once shattered, slivers of broken glass would fly all over the room. If the doors to the room were not closed, the sudden increase in pressure inside the house, combined with the low pressure on the sides of the house where the wind was at high velocity, frequently blew out the windows on the sides of the house.

These windstorms were fearsome affairs, particularly to homeowners whose houses were exposed to their full force.

The glass damage had been especially heavy the previous night; the firm's telephones had been busy since dawn. The company had a policy of going to work the minute the wind subsided sufficiently for work to begin.

Tom's boss had called to say, "This time let's sell these people some safety plate glass to replace the junk that keeps blowing out. Develop a short, hardhitting pitch that'll do the job. Then go see everybody who got clobbered last night."

Tom realized that the main barrier to selling the safety glass was that insurance companies would only pay damages based on the cost of the cheapest glass available. The excess cost had to be borne by the homeowner.

Tom wondered just what he should put into the presentation.

1 Develop a step-by-step outline of a presentation that Tom could use.
2 Develop a few key selling sentences for him to use.
3 Develop an approach for Tom to use.

CASE 10-2: Staar Surgical Company—Handling Unethical Competitive Tactics

Staar Surgical was a small firm, with $3 million in sales, that manufactured and sold a patented intraocular silicon lens used by eye surgeons in cataract-removal surgery. It replaced older types of hard plastic lens.

As the firm's market penetration increasingly cut into the market shares of its competitors, word began filtering back from customer-physicians that the salespeople for the other firms, one large competitor in particular, were saying disparaging things about Staar as a company and its products. These comments were hurting sales, because doctors did not want to buy from a company that might not be around to honor its commitments.

John Wolf, sales manager, brought the issue to the attention of the Staar board of directors. He proposed several courses of action.

"First, we could take legal action. This is an unfair business practice. Second, we can get out some letters to the trade to counter what is being said. Third, we can advertise in the trade journals to counter their claims. Fourth, the sales reps can aggressively seek to undo the damage that has been done."

The board instructed its legal counsel to pursue whatever legal recourse the company had in the matter. Then one director asked the company's lawyer, "What information should the sales reps seek in helping you with your job?"

Counsel replied, "I need proof of what was said. I need names, places, and dates. I need cooperative witnesses. What can you do for me along those lines, John?"

"We'll get on it. But you realize that this is ticklish business. Customers don't want to get drawn into what looks like a dogfight. What's in it for them?" John observed. "I'll have to be real careful here and figure out how we can do it."

1 How should the sales manager handle this matter?

2 You are a Staar sales rep. A prospect tells you that the sales rep for a major competitor has told her that Staar won't be in business 2 months more. How would you handle that comment?

CHAPTER ELEVEN

A MASTER SALESPERSON

CHAPTER ELEVEN

HANDLING OBJECTIONS I

The nail that sticks up gets hammered down.
Proverb

After studying the material in this chapter you should:

☐ Know what to do when the prospect says no

☐ Understand how to forestall commonly encountered objections

☐ Have a grasp of the various ways you can handle objections

PROFILE OF

A MASTER SALESPERSON

Mack Frasier

NBI
Boulder, Colo.

NBI of Boulder, Colorado, is one of the nation's most famous entrepreneurial start-ups. It makes and sells word processors—one tough market cluttered with competitors and the bodies of the vanquished. Anyone with the foresight to buy one $10,000 investment unit when the company began would have been a millionaire 8 years later. Such was the success of the company. And Mack Frasier's sales abilities were one of the main forces underlying that phenomenal story.

Mack is the master of using a lead blocker to overcome an industrial buyer's natural reluctance to buy equipment from a new, untried company. When NBI began operations, all it had was high hopes and a word processor that few people had ever heard of, let alone used. As one of the firm's original founders, Mack was assigned to open up the San Francisco market. He discovered that a certain large insurance company was planning to buy 500 word processors. He obtained an interview with the person who would be buying them and made a deal that the buyer could not refuse. Part of the deal was that the buyer would accept telephone calls from other industrial buyers on whom Mack was going to call and would tell them that the NBI machine was fine equipment. Mack had provided the proper motivation for such testimonials. Seventy calls later, Mack had penetrated the San Francisco market and established NBI distribution there.

Up to this point a person with a bit of training can proceed through the sales process somewhat as a mechanic fixes a car—do this and then do that. While a good "mechanic" can make a lot of sales, and the mechanics of selling are important, still many professional salespeople maintain that real selling starts when objections are encountered. When the prospect says "No!" real selling begins.[1]

Unfortunately, too many salespeople are unable to cope with even the simplest objection. Should the prospect say "I'll think about it," many salespeople don't know what to do. You cannot consider yourself a proficient, professional salesperson unless an objection triggers a competitive reaction in you that results in your digging in with vigor, confident that you know how to handle it. So let's get on with studying objections.

ATTITUDE TOWARD OBJECTIONS

Objections are an integral part of the sales process. Once you accept the idea that objections are to be expected and are normal, you will have a much sounder philosophical attitude with which to approach them.

Bear in mind that when you try to sell something, you frequently ask the prospect to change his or her behavior. A business executive has a traditional accounting system, and you are asking him to change to your computerized system. People seldom change behavior without resistance. The old way is the easiest, the old brand a trusted friend. We fear the new, the untried.

Almost instinctively, prospects assume a defensive attitude. The more often they have to meet the "attacks" of salespeople, the more pronounced this attitude becomes, until it may develop into an antagonism toward anyone trying to sell them anything. In fact, the much-tried buyer may actually take the offensive with the intention of forcing you to assume the defensive and thus placing you at a disadvantage.

How should salespeople regard objections? If they are beginners, they may feel disheartened when an objection is raised. To them it may appear to be a refusal to buy—an insuperable obstacle to making the sale. Sometimes it is, although usually it need not be.

After all, you know the company is a good prospect because your preapproach qualified it as such. You know your product meets its needs and that the firm can afford it. So why fear an objection?

Veteran salespeople welcome the expressed objection. They know that it is a sales aid, not a hindrance. One of the most difficult prospects to sell is the "clam" who shows no interest in the proposition, does not comment upon it at all, but sits in stony silence while the sales rep strives to pierce this armor of indifference. Sales reps trying to sell to such "clams" cannot tell whether or not they are making a favorable impression and wish fervently that the prospect would give some clue to how the sale is progressing and what the prospect is thinking about.

"Yes, but does it have a graphic equalizer *and* automatic reverse function?" Potential customers who readily voice their questions and reservations while inspecting a product provide salespeople with important clues about possible objections and how to overcome them.

Objections Are Guideposts to Prospects' Reactions

Prospects who voice honest objections are assisting you by disclosing how far away you are from a sale. They are also providing more valuable information about what it will take to make the sale than all the preapproach data you have assembled. Proper interpretation of objections should reveal a great deal.

During the sale you should try to determine the prospect's reactions to the points being presented. Ask such questions as "That makes sense, doesn't it?" "You'd like that, wouldn't you?" "That's what you want, isn't it?" "Would that feature be useful?"

But no matter how careful you may be to gain assent and agreement, as prospects begin to get more familiar with the proposition, they are likely to pose objections. These, however, may serve as effective guides to the alert salesperson.

Sometimes prospects remain unconvinced simply because you have failed to meet one objection or to answer one question. When that point is raised and cleared up, they may be ready to buy. A prospect being shown a forklift truck fears that it may be too small to handle the loads in the warehouse. Otherwise it looks good. A demonstration that the truck can handle the job may get the order right there.

A veteran sales representative commented that he always looked upon an objection as a request for information. "Objections arise," he declared, "for one of two reasons. Either the prospect does not understand what I have told him, or he does not have enough information to grasp the significance of my point. So I consider objections as requests for more facts and respond by giving the information desired." "I'm glad you brought that up, because I was going to explain it anyway," is an excellent way to make the prospect feel that objections are welcomed. "That is a good question,* and I'm glad to give you full information about it" is the way many salespersons approach important objections. Thus the prospect is assured that the sales rep has no fear of objections and accept the rep's answer as a simple reply to a request for information. It should be pointed out that if a salesperson replies in the same way to every objection the prospect makes, it soon becomes monotonous and somewhat phony. However, with variations in language, these methods may be used successfully in most instances.

OVERALL STRATEGY FOR HANDLING OBJECTIONS

The successful handling of objections requires certain attitudes and methods. It should be observed that many of these can be applied to advantage in numerous human relationships other than selling.

Avoid Arguments in Handling Objections

This is not the first time that the importance of avoiding arguments has been mentioned. However, there is probably a greater tendency on the part of people to indulge in arguments when answering questions or objections than in other parts of the interview. It is so easy to do and so disastrous. You can suddenly realize you have slipped into an argument with the prospect, yet not know how you got there. *No matter how violently your prospect disagrees—or directly contradicts you—or persistently tries to argue—don't argue.*

You should think of your position as being in cooperation with the prospect and not in conflict. This attitude helps you to keep in good humor and aids in maintaining friendly relations with the prospect. If you think of yourself as an ally and not an enemy, it gives the prospect a similar feeling. As long as you stay out of the fight, both you and the prospect will avoid injury. Let prospects fight the battle out internally, so that, when it is over, they will not feel that they have been forced to make a decision but rather that they have arrived at their conclusions independently. If they are allowed freedom, they will be more likely to stay sold and not regret their decisions when you have gone. Few are really convinced by argument.

---

*Observe that the salesperson does not refer to an objection by that name. Rather it is called a "question" or a "point." In fact, many objections are offered in the form of questions, and it is usually good practice to try to treat actual objections as mere questions and not as firmly held objections. Some salespersons try to restate many objections in the form of questions.

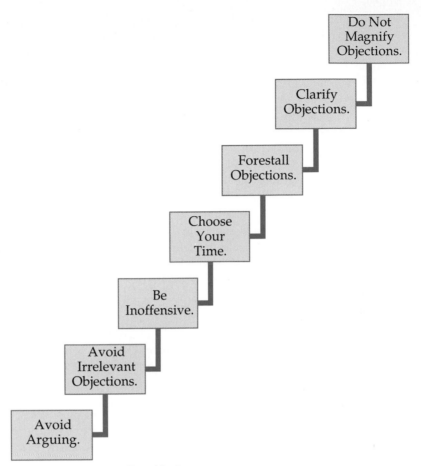

FIGURE 11–1 Overall strategy for handling objections.

The oft-quoted experience of Benjamin Franklin serves to stress the value of the proper attitude:

> A Quaker friend informed me I was not content with being in the right when discussing any point but had to be overbearing and insolent about it—of which he convinced me by mentioning several instances.
>
> Endeavoring to cure myself of this fault, which I now realized had lost me many an argument, I made the following rule: to forbear all direct contradictions of the sentiments of others and all overpositive assertions of my own.
>
> Thereafter, when another asserted something I thought an error, I denied myself the pleasure of contradicting him abruptly and of showing immediately some absurdity in his proposition. Instead, I began by observing that . . . in certain cases or circumstances his opinion would be right . . . but in the present case there *appeared* or seemed to me some difference, etc.

I soon found the advantage of this change in my manner. The conversations I engaged in went on more pleasantly. The modest way in which I proposed my opinions procured them a readier reception and less contradiction, I had less mortification when I was found to be in the wrong, and I more easily prevailed upon others to give up their mistakes and join with me when I happened to be right.

Franklin's philosophy is echoed by a present-day paint manufacturer which advises its salespeople to "use anti-argument phrases" in handling questions and objections. For example: "Don't say, 'This paint has the best reputation in town.' Do say, 'From what others tell me, I'm led to believe that this paint has the best reputation in town.'" When the prospect objects, "Your price is too high," the salesperson is instructed to reply, "I don't blame you if you doubt what I am going to say, but this will save you a lot of money." These are sample "anti-argument phrases."

Many salespeople listen intently to a prospect's objection and try to find some point in it with which they can agree. They *restate* this point of agreement and then proceed from there.

Avoid Irrelevant Objections

Too often salespeople permit themselves to be led into a controversy on a point unrelated to the proposition they are selling. If the buyer is prejudiced or holds odd ideas, the salesperson's business is not conversion. The sales rep is interested solely in the buyer's opinion of the proposition and should not be concerned about anything else.

Of particular importance are the matters of politics, religion, local issues, controversial persons in the news, and other "hot" topics. Usually little can be gained and everything can be lost if you allow yourself to be drawn into such discussions. Even if the two individuals are of the same party, they can easily fall into disagreement on minor issues and each leave the interview wondering about the other's basic intelligence and intellectual integrity. Unless the objection directly deals with the proposition at hand, the salesperson is wise not to take issue with the prospect's statement. If the prospect says that the world is flat, agree that a good deal of it sure looks that way, and go on with your presentation. One office machines salesperson lost a sale by getting into a discussion with the prospect over the appearance of the seller's new quarters. The prospect stated that he did not like the looks of the firm's new building. The salesperson flew to her firm's defense, and the fat was in the fire.

Remove Objections Inoffensively

The essence of the Franklin theory is that the seller must learn to remove the objection or the "objectionable idea" from the mind of the prospect without giving offense. That is not always an easy thing to accomplish, depending upon the tenacity with which the person clings to the objection raised.

However, a number of ways to do this without jeopardizing the sale are available.

Exoneration from Blame It is within your power to exonerate the prospect from blame for expressing an objectionable idea. You can give such excuses as "I see that I did not clearly explain that feature." Or "I'm sorry that I misled you into thinking that. . . ." Or "It is quite easy to get that idea because of the complexity of factors." The strategy behind this tactic is to allow the prospect to save face and to minimize the chances for ego involvement when you say, in essence, that he or she is wrong.

Concessions You can take the sting from a rebuttal by making some concessions before giving an answer. You might allow, "There is a great deal of truth in what you say. However . . ." Or "I really do think you have a good thought there. That's a new point! I wonder if . . ." People like to be told that their ideas are great, and they are not apt to be as resentful when the sales rep subsequently points out how their thoughts just aren't quite appropriate in this instance.

Deliberate Attitude No one likes to be lightly dismissed; people want their ideas taken seriously and not passed off without due consideration. So the wise seller will say at such times, "I'd like to mull that over a minute." Or "That's worth thinking about!"

Others Who Agree Somewhat in the same vein, sometimes the salesperson is able to point out that there are many other people who agree with him; he is not alone in his misconception. "You know, a great number of people believe that. However . . ." Or "Under similar circumstances, many people take your view. However . . ." are statements typical of handling objections by this means.

Paying Tribute At times the salesperson can pay tribute to the prospect in several ways, thereby erecting a buffer to protect the prospect's ego when the rebuttal is made. The salesperson may note that the prospect's motives are worthy by saying, "I admire your idealism and know that you are sincere, but . . ." Or "I know that you are honest and fair-minded, so allow me to observe just where our discussion went astray." Other times the salesperson can tell the prospect that she is generally right by saying, "I know that you are an authority on this and are seldom wrong. However . . ." Or "I seldom hesitate in taking your advice, however . . ."

When Should an Objection Be Answered?

Most authorities agree that an objection should usually be handled the moment it is raised. Several logical reasons support this policy.

Assume that the prospect raises an objection which the salesperson promises to answer. Not wishing to forget the objection and thinking that the salesperson may neglect to come back to it, the prospect concentrates upon the point and is so preoccupied with it that he does not hear what the sales rep tells him in the meantime.

The prospect may get the impression that the salesperson does not have a valid answer and hopes the prospect may forget the objection if it is passed by for the moment. Confidence is shaken if the salesperson replies, "I'm glad you brought that up. I will come to it in just a few minutes."

Deferring the answer also makes the prospect feel that the salesperson is just speaking his piece and that he is unable to reply to an objection without throwing himself off stride. The desired impression of spontaneity is destroyed; also it is likely to draw the prospect's attention to the salesperson's technique rather than to the points he makes.

When an objection has been met effectively, it may turn out to have been the only obstacle to the order. Many salespeople seize upon a well-met objection as a good closing time. They ask prospects whether that is the only matter about which they want information. They make it a focal point and try to set it up as the one deciding factor that, if answered, will lead the prospects to buy.

It may be concluded, therefore, that in most instances it is better to answer objections the moment they are raised by the prospect.

When Should an Objection Not Be Answered?

However, certain specific situations may be mentioned which seem to justify postponing the answer. These are as follows:

When a price objection arises early in the interview.

When the objection raised will be answered more effectively later in the salesperson's orderly presentation of the proposition.

When the objections raised are so frequent or so petty that the salesperson becomes convinced that they are simply an effort to disrupt the presentation and slow up the sale.

Each of these three situations deserves brief consideration.

The Early Price Question   The first situation—the price objection—frequently comes up in an interview before the seller has awakened a desire for the proposition or shown its value. It is often used by prospects as a stall to avoid listening to the proposition at all. When this objection is raised early in the interview, it may be postponed until the prospect has enough information about the proposition to be able to decide intelligently.

The sales rep of air-conditioning equipment for the home defers the premature question about price in this manner: "I can't give you the price until I've made a detailed study of how best to make your home comfortable in hot,

Prospects will often raise the issue of price early during a sales interview. In what situations might it be best to provide cost information when requested? Why is it advisable in some circumstances to temporarily delay answering a price objection?

muggy weather. There are many ways we can do it, but they vary greatly in price, so it takes some work to figure out how to do it for you for the lowest cost." Note how she has turned the question into an opportunity to make a sales point. Also note how she uses the words "home," "comfortable," "lowest cost," "hot," and "muggy" to stimulate the emotional reactions she wants in the prospect's mind.

Premature Question   The second situation permitting postponement of the reply is where the objection is concerned with a different subject from the one then being discussed but one which is being approached.

Admittedly, from a purely psychological point of view, it would be advantageous to answer the prospect's question immediately, thus removing it from his or her mind. However, to do so many times disrupts the point that the salesperson is trying to make and perhaps sidetracks the presentation into fruitless channels, thus bogging matters down.

Even in consultative selling, prospects can get ahead of themselves. "What is it going to cost us?" may be heard before anything has been established. The rep replies, "Until we determine your needs there is no way of quoting you a figure." This sounds smooth enough, and often it is enough to allow the rep to proceed. But sometimes the prospect persists, "I know that, but give me a ballpark figure." The rep may be forced to give some sort of answer just to get the prospect's mind off of it. This behavior is not as irrational as many salespeople insist. The prospect is just trying to save time. There's no point in going for a ride in a $50,000 car if all you have to spend is $20,000. Many propositions cost so much in excess of the funds budgeted for them that the prospect may feel that there is no point in listening. However, the wise prospect with some time may listen to a proposition that she well knows she can not afford to buy just to gain some ideas and insights into the problem's solution.

Thus the consultative salesperson may reply in several ways. "It may be that you cannot afford us. [Note that the word "afford" conjures up some strong emotions in many people who do not relish the thought that they are so impoverished that they can't afford something.] However, why don't we look at your problem and see if we can figure out something for you. You may get some ideas from it that will help you."

Another approach is to provide the prospect with a range of your prices. "We did a small job for the ABC Company for $10,000. Our work for the XYZ Company exceeded $100,000 last year. So it all depends on what you want done."

Of course, if the rep finds out that the firm just cannot afford the proposition, then perhaps the rep should make an early departure.

Suppose a men's apparel representative is in the midst of presenting a fall line of sport coats when the dealer asks, "When am I going to get delivery on that last fill-in order I sent you last month?" Yes, prospects do throw in such *non sequiturs*, much to the sales rep's dismay, but they can be handled. "I'll go get my invoice book after we finish working this line." It is important that the delaying answer be logical and reasonable, lest the prospect be irritated by nonsensical replies.

Trivia The last situation in which postponement of the answer to an objection is advisable is when the question or comment is so trivial that you are certain that the prospect is trying to delay the interview. When such is the case, you may use the following strategy to justify a refusal to answer: "I appreciate your interest in this proposition, and I certainly want to answer all your questions before I leave, but it has been my experience that most of these questions on details will have been covered when we are through with the presentation. I am sure we could save time (and I know you are busy) if you will just wait a few minutes and then ask your questions about anything that I have not covered." Most prospects are fair-minded enough to go along with such a suggestion if it is offered with a smile.

A situation demanding postponement of some answers arises when the prospect rattles off several objections without waiting for a reply. The answers to some of them must obviously wait until you have answered the others, so smile and say, "You're going too fast for me. Now tell me which one of these points you would like to discuss first."

Forestalling Objections

It is not possible to lay down an inviolable rule on the matter of meeting objections promptly or postponing them; the decision will depend on the circumstances. One general proposition can be laid down, however: Many objections can be forestalled. The principle previously stated, that it is wise to keep prospects from placing themselves on record as opposed to the proposition, is well proved. With experience you will learn when certain objections are usually raised. The same objections are raised in most cases at about the same time. A knowledge of the prospect helps in anticipating the objections that will likely be brought up. The preapproach should aid you in preparing to answer those stock objections. When this is done, it is not uncommon to have the prospect say, "I was just wondering about that."

Just what is meant by "forestalling" objections? It does not mean first stating the objection and then answering it. No mention of the objection is made, but the counterargument is presented in such a manner as to preclude the objection.

Suppose you are selling some equipment that is seemingly high-priced. You know that you will encounter a price objection. Then head it off at the pass—forestall it. From the outset, prove the equipment's quality to show its value. Show the prospect early in the sale why he wants to buy the quality, why he needs it. Even go so far as to try to make your machine look as if it is a bargain, considering everything.

Sometimes the consultative salesperson asks the prospect for a brief history of the procurement to date. "What have you looked at? What problems did you have with those proposals?" Find out what objections have blocked other propositions. Chances are those same objections will be uppermost in the prospect's mind when evaluating your proposal.

Other objections may be similarly preempted. For example, many buyers want to "think it over." You may forestall this by saying: "I know you are a busy person, and I'm not going to waste your time. If I explain how my proposition will make you real money and if I prove every point to your satisfaction, will you tell me today how it strikes you and not ask me to come back next week? That's a fair proposal, isn't it?" After this it is difficult for buyers to say they want to think it over.

When the sales rep for a small car wishes to forestall the objection that the size of the tires is too small, he points out early in the interview that the light weight of the car makes it possible to use smaller and less expensive tires, although these tires are as large as stipulated by the Tire Manufacturers' Association for cars of this weight.

The anticipated price objection is often dealt with like this: "You are thinking that a product with all these new features will cost you at least $300; so you'll be happy to know that we're selling so many that production costs have been driven way down and we can let you have it for only $197.50."

One securities agent constantly encountered the two objections, "I haven't got any money" and "I've got to talk it over with my wife (husband)." He whipped these obstacles by opening the interview with the question, "I am interested in talking with a person who has at least $10,000 to put into a sound business venture and who makes decisions without having to consult someone else. Are you such a person?" Once the prospect admitted to being qualified, he or she could hardly use those excuses as objections later.

When you have a particularly forceful answer to some common objection, it may be good strategy not to try to forestall it but to let the prospect raise it, so it can be used as the basis for a "trap close" in which you respond in effect to the prospect's objection, "If I answer your objection, will you buy?" Naturally, few salespeople would use those words, but they would try to get the prospect committed to buying upon meeting the objection. More is said about the trap close later.

Before Answering an Objection

No matter how you plan to handle an objection, it will be wise to do these things first:

Listen carefully before answering. Let the prospect state the objection fully, even though it is one you have heard a thousand times. Do not interrupt! This courtesy places the prospect under the obligation to accord you similar attention when you answer the objection. It also helps to keep the interview friendly, thus avoiding tension.

Act interested in the objection. Don't attempt to belittle it. Pay the prospect the compliment of receiving her opinion with respect. Appear to regard it as one worth voicing.

Don't hurry the answer too quickly. Pause long enough to seem to weigh it carefully, even though that objection may be old stuff and the answer memorized. This pause flatters the prospect and, at the same time, prevents a feeling of being pressured.

Sometimes it is good selling to restate an objection before answering it, because:

You can sometimes restate the objection a trifle more favorably to your own case. This can often be done by putting it in the form of a question rather than a declarative statement. But the restatement should be honest and not twisted out of its original meaning.

The prospect is assured that you understand clearly the exact nature of the objection.

It gives you a moment in which to consider the best method of answering the objection.

If the prospect has offered the objection in an effort to break up the continuity of the presentation, the restatement of it enables you to retain control of the interview.

In opposition to these reasons, however, there is the danger that restating an objection may tend to give it greater importance in the prospect's mind than it really deserves. The prospect may feel that he has hit upon something that puzzles or surprises the salesperson and may be less apt to forget the objection than if it had not been thus emphasized. In general, restating objections may be good policy in cases where the objection is somewhat vague or may be restated so that it can be met more easily.

Restating the question slows down the progress of the presentation and may waste time. And it becomes monotonous if done too often.

Never Magnify an Objection

Too much should not be made of any particular objection; it should not be exaggerated in the eyes of the prospect. It is just as fatal to make this mistake as it is to ridicule an objection or pass over it too lightly.

You should answer each sincere objection clearly, emphatically, and in a straightforward manner, making sure that the answer is intelligible to the prospect and that he or she agrees entirely with the way of meeting it. It may be wise to comment upon every answer by saying, "Isn't that the right way to look at that point?" or "Have I answered that question to your complete satisfaction?" If you have, then forget about that one, and get on to something else.

To linger too long over an objection is to magnify it. "When the baby goes to sleep, you had better quit singing," counsels the experienced parent. "You might wake him up again." Or, to change the figure of speech, objections have been likened to stepping-stones through a bog. If you just keep going, you're all right, but if you stop and stand on one of them, you'll sink down into the mud. The more the objection is discussed, the more important it becomes in the prospect's mind until finally it may seem much bigger than it did at the start.

DETERMINING HIDDEN OBJECTIONS

Up to this point we have assumed that the prospect overtly states an objection and the sales rep answers it. But it is not that simple. Prospects are often reluctant to bring their objections out into the open, thus forcing the sales rep to ferret them out before they can be dealt with.

To make the problem even more baffling, a prospect may offer a false objection, thereby wasting your time while not advancing the sale at all. Why do people behave this way?

Basic Issues as Hidden Blocking Objections

The consultative salesperson realizes that some basic issue must be blocking the sale when the prospect refuses to make a commitment to buy after an interview in which everything went well. Such basic issues may have little to do with the matter at hand. Perhaps the executive is about to change jobs and is just going through the motions of working for the present employer.

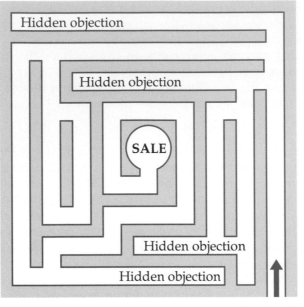

Road to Sale

FIGURE 11-2   Hidden objections waiting to block a sale.

Perhaps the company is secretly being sold, and is not buying anything until the sale is completed. There are few limits to the basic issues you can encounter. Your insights into some of the more common basic issues that may block a sale, as shown below, may help you salvage some sales.

SOME BASIC ISSUES

- Threat to career
- Loss of power
- Less leisure
- Lack of skill
- Decrease of personal productivity
- Would have to change
- Not seen as a problem solver
- Lack of recognition
- Decrease in growth potential
- Lose social/professional status
- Less time with family
- Less self-esteem
- About to retire
- More work
- Loss of flexibility

- Lose security
- Being seen as a malcontent
- Not invented here
- Seen as poor performer
- Loss of leadership
- Loss of credibility
- Seen as me-too
- Incur indebtedness
- Decrease responsibility/authority
- Lose freedom of choice
- Pigeonholed
- Not fun anymore; no laughs
- Lazy
- Animosities

If a potential buyer's objections to closing a sale seem vague and general, asking direct questions may help pinpoint the nature of the problem.

A common example is found in people who cannot afford to pay the price. They are embarrassed to confess their poverty and so offer some other reason for not buying. Other prospects are afraid of being influenced by you, so they pose as tough, hard-nosed buyers who challenge almost everything said. Sometimes a prospect is too kind to come right out and say she thinks the product is junk. Or the prospect may simply say nothing at all, thus effectively concealing all her reactions.

Consequently, the real professional sales rep develops the skill to nose out the hidden real objections blocking the sale. Because this art is so important let us discuss it in considerable detail.

Asking Questions

Questions encourage the prospect to talk and, sooner or later, to reveal what is really stopping the sale. Sometimes you may say frankly, "I feel that we aren't getting anywhere in our conference, and I'm afraid it is my fault. There must be something that I have failed to bring out clearly. If you would just tell me what it is, it might save us both quite a bit of time."

If the prospect is inexperienced or unwary, or if she feels the urge to level with you, she may state her objection. If you can meet this objection, the prospect is almost committed to buy.

Some sales reps carry the practice still further. When the buyer says that he does not want the proposition, the salesperson queries, "Just what is your reason?" The prospect will offer an objection, in reply to which the sales rep asks, "Is that your only reason?" If the prospect says, "Yes," he has eliminated all others and virtually promised to buy if the obstacle to buying can be removed.

Another argument in favor of asking for the objection is that it speeds up the interview by making it unnecessary to present many talking points which may be utterly beside the point. If you could talk right to the big point, you could perhaps close the sale.

If you are reluctant to ask the nature of the prospect's objection, how can you discover it? Perhaps you can use slightly indirect questions, hinting at the probable objection and watching closely to see what effect the question has upon the prospect. You might say, "The other day I was talking over my proposition with another client and we couldn't reach any conclusion until I had made clear our guarantee. Maybe you, too, would like to have me go a little further into that?" Then you could see if your remarks were well directed, for the prospect would be likely to give some sign that would enable you to know whether or not you had hit upon the right objection.

Unquestionably, the adroit asking of questions and the perceptive observation of the prospect's reactions to them is the key to uncovering most hidden objections.

"What Else Is Bothering You?"

You may even pry more forcefully into certain touchy areas in which you have learned that objections frequently lurk, thereby encouraging prospects to talk about what is bothering them.

One common technique is asking for the additional objections. After the prospect has voiced objections, you then say, "Now then, what else is really bothering you? Isn't there something else you don't like or want to know about the proposition?" The prospect is encouraged to reply with the real objection, having seen you have not been fooled.

The theory is that if you keep pushing for more objections, eventually they will run out of phony objections and be left with only the real one to disclose.

"Honest John" Technique, or the Appeal for Fair Play

One insurance agent developed an effective method for handling the hidden objection. He called it his "Honest John" method. When he suspected that some hidden objection blocked an order, he said, "If I am ever invited to your office again, it will be for only one reason—you believe that I am an honest man. That is the way it should be. If you feel that I am dishonest, you should throw me out quickly and never see me again. After all, you have every reason to expect to do business with an honest man. Isn't that right? . . . Well, in return haven't I the same right? The right to sell to an honest person? Now I have a feeling that you are not being completely frank with me. There is something bothering you about this deal that you are not telling me. Be honest with me, and tell me what is really on your mind." He claims this appeal to honesty and fair play works almost every time. This basic tactic is not limited to the insurance field. Most people respond to an appeal for fair play.

The basic tactic is to cast the prospect in the role you want to have him play—that of the honest person.

"Habeas Corpus" Technique

One industrial equipment sales rep has developed a special method for ascertaining a prospect's objections which she calls her "habeas corpus" technique. When she sees that some hidden objection is preventing a sale, she relaxes the prospect by certain movements to indicate that she is leaving. Then she says, "Suppose two police officers walked into your office right now and hauled you off to jail without so much as a word about what charges are against you. You would be fuming mad at the injustice, and your lawyer would without doubt obtain a habeas corpus to force them to produce you in court and charge you with *something*. Well, Mr. Jones, our legal system makes certain that you know what you are charged with, and it allows you to retain the ablest defense lawyer you can get. Unfortunately, I am not being given the same rights. You have some charges against my proposition which you are not bringing out into the open so its best defender [smilingly tapping herself] can cope with them. Go ahead and prosecute this product all you want, but please let me be here to defend it against the charges so we can reach a decision as to whether it is guilty or innocent."

The Four Nos Technique

An industrial supplies sales representative claims that there are four nos which are encountered in selling: no need, no want, no money, and no hurry. He uses these to help him dig out the hidden objection by saying to the prospect, "It has been my experience that there are only four basic reasons why people don't buy my supplies. They think they don't need them; they don't want them; they don't have the money; or they are not in any hurry." As he is saying this he writes down each item.

NO NEED   _____
NO WANT   _____
NO MONEY   _____
NO HURRY   _____

He then says, "I would deeply appreciate it if you would place a check mark after the real reason you are not buying." He claims that people will frequently be willing to do this when they are reluctant to say it orally. Once the prospect has indicated the area in which the hidden objection lies, you can begin probing to determine its precise nature.

Perception—Insight

Many hidden objections are uncovered mainly through insight or perception. A run-down office, store, or factory would suggest a lack of working capital. Sometimes it is just the sales rep's shrewdness that turns the trick. One paint salesman selling to a large corporation was at a loss to understand why he was not getting at least his share of that firm's business. His company was the largest local manufacturer. He knew that his price was right and that there was nothing wrong with the paint, particularly in comparison with the paint they were buying. He knew that his firm had given good service and had a fine reputation in the industry. He felt that he had done a good job selling to the purchasing agent, who had the authority to buy. He concluded that someone was being paid off under the table. He slyly made a few remarks one day to the p.a., indicating in a noncommittal way that the company might be willing to contribute a little extra to the p.a.'s personal welfare fund. The p.a. responded with unwise candor, and "the cat was out of the bag."

It may be that from the prospect's actions in handling the samples or the merchandise the salesperson could tell easily that price or quality was not satisfactory. If, for example, a customer in a retail shoe store appears interested in a pair of shoes until the price is mentioned, whereupon he transfers his interest to other, lower-priced shoes, the salesperson does not need to be told that the objection is "too high a price." But it is better to learn this without having allowed the customer to take a definite stand on the matter, for it will be much easier to show him the superior value of the higher-priced shoes and finally to sell them to him if the customer has not already declared that he wants something cheaper.

If an interview was almost satisfactory but the buyer seemed to cool off inexplicably during the presentation, the rep should mentally retrace the interview to discover just where he made a statement or asked a question that showed a lack of tact. It may have been a critical reference to competing goods already purchased by the prospect; perhaps it was a lack of knowledge concerning the prospect or the prospect's business. The chances are excellent that some unfortunate remark created an antagonism that acted as a hidden objection or obstacle to the sale.

It may be advisable to face such a prospect frankly a second time and apologize for what you must have said. It will often thaw the prospect to the extent of talking business on a new and friendly basis.

BASIC METHODS FOR HANDLING OBJECTIONS[2]

In most interviews the prospect will raise some objections which cannot be anticipated or forestalled. These objections constitute *reasons for not buying,* and they are brought up to justify the prospect's unwillingness to buy.

The next step is to examine some of the ways by which one can handle important objections that are neither concealed nor too trivial to merit consideration, and which are not common enough to be forestalled. (There are half a

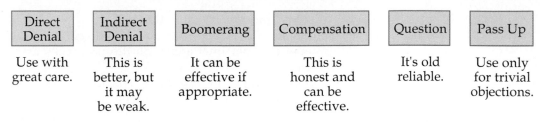

FIGURE 11-3   Six basic methods for handling objections.

dozen distinct methods of handling the honest objection, *after* it has been raised. Obviously these do not include the method of forestalling, which must be employed *before* the objection is raised.)

There are six ways to handle objections:

The *direct-denial* method, also called the head-on method or the contradiction method.

The *indirect-denial* method, also referred to as the "Yes . . . but . . ." method or the sidestepping method.

The *boomerang* method, called the reverse English method, translation method, or capitalization method. It capitalizes on the objection, translates it into a reason for buying and returns the objection, boomerang-fashion, to the prospect as a talking point *for* the proposition.

The *compensation* method, called by some the superior-point method or the offset method; outweighing the objection with advantages that more than compensate for it.

The *question*, or interrogation, method.

The *pass-up* method, used only where the objection is flimsy or unimportant.

The Direct Denial

Many sales trainers contend that the salesperson should never contradict the buyer in any circumstance. They point out that a contradiction stirs up antagonism and makes the interview acrimonious, thereby rendering more difficult the task of obtaining the prospect's complete agreement. The view is generally correct, but there *may* be times when the direct method is effective, although such occasions are rare.

The realtor is showing a house to a prospect who objects, "I hear the taxes on this property are over $5,000. That's too high." The salesperson might reply, "The taxes are $3,724.50. We can verify it with the county treasurer."

Under conditions such as those outlined, what is the effect upon the prospect of the direct denial? When handled properly, it may well impress the prospect with the salesperson's absolute sincerity and belief in what she is selling. It is possible to be too agreeable, with the result that the prospect gets the feeling that you are insincere.

It is probably wise to soften the impact of a direct denial a bit. Avoid projecting a "No, you dummy, you're all wet!" attitude. You do not want the direct denial to be interpreted as a personal attack on the prospect's mentality. Four warnings are needed.

First, a word of caution concerning the *manner* in which you state the denial: You must be earnest but not offensive—smile and not frown. You must not appear to lose your temper, or you weaken your cause. Only a skilled salesperson should attempt to use the method, for in the hands of a bungler it is suicidal.

Second, if the prospect is extremely sensitive or fond of his or her own opinions, direct denial will probably give serious offense.

In the third place, the direct denial is better in reply to an objection put in the form of a question than to one phrased as a declaration of opinion or a statement of fact. "Won't that color fade in the sun?" asks the anxious prospect. The salesperson replies, "Definitely not. Tests prove it and we guarantee it."

Finally, a direct denial should never be used if the objection has any ego involvement in it. You should never place the prospect in a position of having to defend some erroneous opinion. The prospect objects, "Your motor looks too small for that car." He has stated an opinion and to deny it directly questions his intelligence and will only serve to make him hold his opinion more firmly. This is especially true when the point at issue is important. The direct denial should usually be confined to answering minor objections.

The direct, or head-on, method of meeting objections, therefore, should be regarded as a "desperate remedy for a desperate disease," not to be attempted except by an expert salesperson under circumstances where it would be likely to succeed.

A careful study of scores of sales manuals and instruction courses for salespeople reveals few cases where the direct-denial method of meeting objections is recommended. There is a tendency for the sales rep to use this method too often, to use it without thinking. Hence, the warnings and the small number of illustrations of its use.

The Indirect Denial

The second, or indirect-denial, method of meeting objections is unquestionably the most widely used. It fits more situations and can be used with more types of prospects than any other.

It recognizes the fact that most people resent being flatly contradicted. They prefer to have the sales rep bend a bit. Analogies are not difficult to find. The baseball player permits his hand to give way slightly before the ball as he catches it, rather than to allow the ball to inflict a painful bruise, as it might if he held his hand in a tense position. The boxer tries to roll with his opponent's blow to lessen its impact. The sales rep does not usually meet the prospect's objections head on but gives ground a trifle before replying, saying, "You are quite right in saying that this is often true, but in this particular case . . ." etc. Or, "There is a lot of truth in what you say, but don't you think also that . . . ?" Or, "I'm not surprised that you feel that way about it at first; I did myself, but when I had time to go into the matter a little more I found that . . ." How much more comfortable the prospect feels than if the sales rep had said, "No, I can't see your point at all," or "It may seem that way to you, but as a matter of fact . . . " or "You are wrong there," or "That's not so."

Often the use of the indirect-denial method may be exaggerated in dealing with buyers who hold an unusually good opinion of themselves. With such prospects you must give them credit for having given birth to a real idea. Here you may pause a bit when the objection is raised, may perhaps appear puzzled over it. The plan is to convey to the prospect the impression that the prospect has thought up a reason that is not commonly raised, that requires consideration to answer. He is subtly flattered by the thought that he has rather "stumped" you; he feels that you are properly giving him credit for possessing a keener insight than is enjoyed by the average person. After you have thus given due weight to the objection, you can answer it with a reasonable assurance that the prospect will in turn give *you* credit for *your* ideas and will be more likely to view the matter fairly than he would have done had you belittled his objection. When the prospect states his objection flatly as a declaration of belief, the indirect denial is more tactful than the direct denial.

In selling steel pipe to oil companies, one sales rep would occasionally encounter a purchasing agent who objected, "I think I can find some of that pipe a bit cheaper than what you're quoting me."

The rep would reply, "Perhaps if you look long and hard enough somewhere you will turn up something cheaper. However, I don't think so. I am here now and have a load of pipe ready for delivery. You need it, so why not do it the easy way?"

Sometimes the indirect denial is less obviously tactful. That is, the sales rep does not noticeably yield ground to the objection and yet does not directly deny it. Here are a few illustrations:

The prospect for a lot in a new subdivision may object, "Your lots are too far out of town." The salesperson is taught to answer, "That is what some people thought of every subdivision we ever put on the market. Many of the sections that we opened up years ago are all built up and would be considered close in now, but they were called too far out by people then. It pays to look ahead a few years when making investments."

This method is sometimes referred to as the "Yes, but . . ." method. Some prefer "Recognize, but . . ." The word "but" should be avoided whenever possible. The word is filled with negative connotations; it arouses antagonism. Frequently the word "and" can be substituted. Try this and note how it softens your answer.

While we are on the subject of semantics, the word "unless" is a good one.

Prospect: I don't want to pay so much.

You: Neither do I . . . *unless* I know I'm getting full value for every penny of it, as you are here.

We should keep in mind that both this method and the previous one are *denials* of the objection's validity.

The Boomerang, or Translation, Method

The third method of handling objections is often called the boomerang, because the objection hurled by the prospect comes back as a reason why he *should* buy. It is also sometimes referred to as the translation method because it translates an objection into a reason for purchasing. To illustrate in a general way: The prospect raises an objection, and the sales rep immediately replies, "Why, that's the very reason I think you need it!"

To illustrate more specifically: The IBM salesperson, when the prospect objects, "But my business is different," replies "The IBM AT is particularly adapted to people who believe that their businesses are different. The more important it is for a business to have its letters correctly written, the greater the value of the AT system."

The well-drilled sales rep for a book sold to mothers of grade school children provides another example of this method. When the prospect objects, "My boy takes no interest in his schoolbooks. I doubt if he would read it if I bought it," he replies promptly, "Right there you have voiced the strongest argument I can think of in favor of this work. Why doesn't he like his schoolwork? Because he had not been encouraged in his studies. We both know that he has a good mind, so why don't we help him develop it? Don't we owe him that much at least?"

Or when the rep for a highly advertised line of clothing meets a dealer who objects, "Your firm spends too much for advertising. If you would cut out some of that expense and give us retailers a wider margin of profit, I might handle your line," the rep uses the boomerang method. He says, "It is the advertising that makes it easy for you to sell this brand. Your customers are already sold on its quality before they come into the store, and it is our advertising that brings them in." He continues to talk quick turnover, small selling cost per garment, and total profits, until this objection is thoroughly laid to rest.

The prospect for a fire extinguisher may object, "I can't afford it." The salesperson may reply, "I'd rather hear you say that than anything else that you could say. If you can't afford to invest a few dollars in positive fire prevention, you surely couldn't afford to have a fire."

The prospect for an office appliance may object, "I'm a busy woman; can't take time to talk to you." The sales rep turns the objection into a reason for buying with "If you are a busy person, then I am just the one you want to see, because busy executives know the value of time and are eager to discover new ways to save time. I have a real time-saver."

The boomerang method is useful in meeting excuses that are not strongly backed by facts. The excuse is thus disposed of before facts or reasons can be marshaled to support it. Care should be exercised to avoid giving the prospect the impression that his or her objection is of no consequence. The manner of the salesperson is important in this connection; for if you allow the least hint of a sneer to creep in or appear to be enjoying a triumph over the luckless prospect, your chances will be ruined. Your manner must be friendly and sincere; a smile must dull any edge that the words might in themselves seem to possess. Above all, it is necessary to avoid giving the prospect the impression that one has "shown one's hand" or "led with the chin."

The Compensation Method

The fourth way of handling objections—the compensation method—admits the validity of the objection but points out some advantage that compensates for it. The prospect for a pair of shoes might object that the leather did not seem to be of the best quality. The clerk might admit the fact that the leather was not the highest grade but tactfully point out that, if it were, the price would be much higher. The low price compensates for the lower quality. This method of meeting objections is based on the broad principle of compensation, made famous by Emerson and other philosophers and epitomized in "You can't have everything." If the wheelbase of the car is too short for easy riding, the vehicle handles and parks more easily.

Always remember that there is no perfect product. All of them have limitations and features to which someone can legitimately object. The compensation method is used in handling valid product objections. The only possible defense against a valid objection made in good faith is to point out the compensating features which outweigh the mentioned deficiency. The salesperson must simply make the prospect desire the product's advantages more than he or she dislikes its disadvantages. It does actual harm to try to beat down a legitimate objection, for the prospect may lose all confidence in the sales rep who refuses to acknowledge valid objections.

Usually there are good reasons why a product is designed as it is. One sales rep for baby equipment often encountered product objections from department store buyers such as: "Why don't you put a handle on it so it can be used as a stroller?" or "Why don't you put some beads on the front of it?" or "Why don't you put rubber bumpers on it?" The answer always was: "That does sound like a good idea, and we did give it careful consideration. How much more do you think your customers would pay for it with these features? . . . Well, that's just what we found out; they wouldn't pay any more. So we just could not do it and keep the price down to a level where it sells in good volume." A product's compensating advantages and relative disadvantages can be visualized by listing each point with possibly a picture or diagram explaining it. Fundamentally, what the salesperson tries to convey is that the product will give the prospect what is really needed, and that what it does not give is not really important.

The Question Method

The question affords an excellent means of answering objections. When a prospect has raised an objection, an answer is just about necessary, yet a statement of fact is likely to open the way for further objections. The question form of answering the objection not only does not invite objections but makes the prospect answer her or his own objections.

Suppose a prospect says to a computer salesperson, "You have a marvelous machine and I would love to own it, but I just can't see putting $3000 into it." A great many questions can be asked to attack this objection, ranging from a simple, "Why do you feel that way?" to such queries as, "Are you willing to invest $3000 in an asset whose rate of return exceeds 100 percent a year?"

One of the most exasperating excuses a salesperson has to answer is the statement that "All our buying is done through the home office at————." To most sales reps this is *finis*, and many buyers use the excuse even where it is not true. One sales rep has developed an effective method of handling the situation. When he finds that he is talking with a prospect who thinks that he is not a prospect because someone else will have to OK the requisition, he says, "Would the home office [or the boss] allow you to consider a plan for improving any detail of the work at your branch [or in your department]? Can you look into any plan that *might* help you, provided the home office [or boss] doesn't have to buy anything in advance?

"Wouldn't it be possible to consider my plan, and if it pleases you, then you can recommend its adoption for all branch offices [or departments]? If we can work out a plan that is really good, we'll present it to the home office [or the boss] as *your* plan and help you sell it to them. Or would you rather have some other branch manager [or department head] sell *his or her* plan to the home office [or the boss] for *you* to use?"

One of the most valuable words in the sales rep's vocabulary is the little word "why." It's true for a number of reasons:

It forces the prospect to talk. This gives you information, especially about why the prospect is not buying yet.
It forces you to listen.
It takes you off the hook, and gives you time to think.
It pushes the prospect to examine his or her reasons.

Many common objections can be met with "Why?"
I'm not buying now. . . . I think prices are coming down. . . . Sales are falling off. . . . I don't like your price. . . . I want to think it over. . . . I want to look into some other deals. . . . I've always bought from the ABC company. . . . I'm not interested in having you make a survey. . . . My business is different. . . . I want to talk this over with a friend first. Why? Why? Why?

You can take any one of these and build an imaginary but probably little conversation growing out of the powerful "why." Such a conversation can be channeled to an agreement on that point.

If a customer says to the vacuum cleaner sales rep, "Your machine is too heavy," the salesperson asks, "Too heavy for what?" Usually the prospect has no sound reasons for her statement; she had heard rumors. The salesperson can then more effectively meet the objection, for its weakness has been exposed.

The question engages the attention and thought of the prospect. It is specific. It ties the prospect down to brass tacks. No matter when it is used—whether in the approach, during the opening argument, in the presentation, or in the closing arguments—the question can be a strong form of delivering a selling talk.

In many circumstances asking a question will cause the objection to evaporate. The baby-equipment buyer might want more colors in the line; the sales rep would ask, "Why do you want to complicate your inventory with a multitude of colors?" The buyer would then admit that the thought did not appeal to her; the objection would evaporate.

Frequently it is wise to combine this method with others in answering particularly difficult objections. You should first ask questions to focus the prospect's thoughts and clarify the exact nature of the objection. Then you can proceed to use some other technique for answering it if it still exists after the questioning.

The Pass-up Method

Some salespeople attempt to smile and pass off many objections, particularly if there is reason to believe that an objection was not made seriously or it is such that it deserves no recognition.

A buyer for a regional grocery chain kept muttering complaints about how much he hated the appearance of a certain character featured in a soap company's TV commercials. The firm's representative would just smile, agree, and go right on selling. Why bother trying to squash the buyer's plaint with a "But we know he sells a lot of product for both of us?"

Other reps pretend not to have heard the objection, passing on rapidly to the next point. Dodging the issue may be effective now and then, but it is not recommended for use when the objection is a valid one. When the prospect has offered an obviously flimsy excuse, the method may be justified.

SUMMARY

Although it is impossible to state definitely that one method should be used in one situation and some other for another, certain general conclusions may be drawn concerning the use of the various ways.

Direct denial may occasionally be employed when the objection raised is a *false* one.

Indirect denial is the chief weapon used in meeting most important objections. It removes the idea from the prospect's mind *inoffensively* and courteously. It is used in all cases where the objection may be shown to be *inapplicable* to the product or proposition offered by the salesperson.

The boomerang method should be used carefully, since few prospects relish having their objection thrown back at them as a reason for buying. However, in some situations it offers an effective reply to objections that actually constitute reasons for buying when properly presented.

Compensation should always be used where the objection is perfectly *valid* and *true* and must be admitted.

The question method is used in three situations: (1) When the objection is so vague and general that you are not sure just what is in the prospect's mind, it may be employed to force the prospect to qualify the objection further. (2) It is used frequently to show the folly or lack of logic in the objection raised. (3) It can be used to have the prospect answer his or her own objections.

The pass-up method is used only when the objection is too trivial or flimsy to deserve a careful answer. It does not actually *meet* or *answer* the objection.

DISCUSSION QUESTIONS

1 "We used to do a lot of business with your firm, but we became disenchanted with you." How would you answer this purchasing agent's objection?
2 Can procrastinations be forestalled?
3 What objections cannot be met?
4 How does one know there is some hidden objection blocking the sale?
5 You sell new cars. You constantly encounter objections to their high price. How would you forestall this objection?
6 How do arguments occur in a sale when the salesperson has decided in advance not to get into one?
7 A sales engineer for a small machine tool company was constantly meeting the objection that his firm was unknown. How could he forestall this objection?
8 As a salesperson of office equipment, you suspect that a prospect is keeping hidden a price objection. What questions could you ask to determine if price was the real barrier to the sale?
9 You are an account executive with an advertising agency that is making a presentation to a large national food account. The president states that she likes your work but that she thinks your agency is really too small to service the account properly. What method would you employ to meet this objection? Give an example of what you would say if you used each of the different methods.
10 A large food processor tells you, a container sales rep, that he has been doing business with his present supplier for a long time and that he is perfectly happy with him. He is not about to change suppliers. What method would you use to meet this objection?
11 Why are a prospect's real objections likely to be kept hidden?

REFERENCES

1 Robert Rohrer, "No!" *American Salesman*, July 1986, pp. 6–8, suggests a refusal should be countered with perseverance.

2 Robert Stanley, "Break Down the 'No' Barrier," *American Salesman*, June 1989, pp. 3–5, suggests continuing questions to which the prospect can give only an affirmative answer.

CASE 11-1: Windsor Associates—Seminar on Hidden Objections

John Windsor, principal partner of Windsor Associates, after carefully reviewing the organization's disappointing sales performance over the past 3 years, had called a meeting of the firm's 66 managing partners. They flew in from the firm's offices all over the world to meet at Palm Springs, California, for a week of serious work and play.

Windsor Associates was one of the world's largest and most successful executive search firms. Called "head hunters" in business jargon (much to the chagrin of the people in the industry), the demand for their services had grown greatly over the previous two decades. While Mr. Windsor acknowledged the industry's growth and that of his firm, he said, "But there is still much to do. Many firms do not use us who could profit greatly by doing so."

The firm's sales curve had leveled off. The company was not growing. Worse, the revenues of Korn Ferry, Windsor's leading competitor, were still rising. Something was wrong, and that something was to be the major topic of the Palm Springs meeting.

The meeting opened at 8 A.M. on Monday morning. Mr. Windsor spoke for 90 minutes about the problem and about how critical it was to the firm's future that revenues be increased in accordance with the firm's rolling 5-year plan, which called for a 15 percent increase in revenues each year.

At the conclusion of his speech, Mr. Windsor distributed a list which divided his 66 partners into 6 groups of 11 each. Each group had been assigned a room in which to meet. He said, "At 10 o'clock you will meet in the assigned rooms to discuss what you perceive the problem to be. Why aren't we selling more? What's going on? Don't you dare tell me that it's the market. We know it isn't! The market's there. Our competition proves it each day. Don't tell me that we have been rendering poor service. Our surveys of our customers say that they are quite pleased. And they do stay with us. So what is it? We will meet here tomorrow morning at 8 and you will tell me what each group has decided." With that declaration, Mr. Windsor walked out of the room, not to be seen again that day.

The groups met and collectively agonized about the problem. No one disputed the facts. Their partnership earnings statements told the story. They talked, many of them late into the night and early morning. At 8 the next morning they assembled for the presentations. There was a surprising consensus of opinion as to the root of the problem—the persuasive skills of the firm's representatives had not been up to meeting the increased competition in the market.

The scenario went something like this: In the early years, selling the new concept of executive searches was difficult, but it was accomplished through great effort. Sales increases were large because the base was small. Once the concept was accepted by business, it grew rapidly as responsive executives found the service useful. However, the "easy sales" had been made. They were established customers. Now growth had to take place through sales to prospects who had been resisting the concept. The "hard sales" were not the target market for growth.

In particular, the groups focused on the problems they were having with corporate "human resource managers," formerly called personnel managers. While top management was often most receptive to the concept of executive searches, the human resource manager was often not. The groups concluded, "We must find some way to overcome their objections."

1 What hidden objections might human resource managers have to using executive search firms?

2 How could you determine such objections?

3 How would you try to overcome them?

CASE 11-2: The Dobbs Company—What's the Problem?

Glenn Kroy had been working with the contracting officials of the General Systems Company, a large aerospace-defense prime contractor, for over a year about a contract from them for his employer, the Dobbs Company, a software developer. He was experienced in using the consultative sales system. He had obtained a very clear statement from the purchasing officer that the company had a great need for a particular software program for a space probe program for which General Systems had been awarded the prime contract.

Glenn had also gained a firm commitment from the firm about the budget for the software program. It was right in line with Dobb's estimates. There were no budget problems.

Glenn also had obtained their commitment to let the contract on the first of the month, 2 weeks hence. He had also gotten their agreement that the Dobbs Company had done excellent work for other firms and was well qualified to do the job. Dobbs did have an excellent reputation in the field, although it had never done any work for General Systems.

Glenn had obtained a meeting with the group charged with procuring the software program. He felt that he had them properly prepared over the past year so that they could make a commitment to the Dobbs Company that day.

The meeting began most cordially, with Glenn reviewing all the information that was known and agreed upon to that point. There seemed to be no new information. Consequently, he pressed for a commitment to buy, to award the contract to Dobbs. The group began to squirm. Its leader said, "I'm not sure we are ready to do that."

Glenn asked, "What is the problem? Has something changed?"

"No. Everything is the same."

"Then let's get to work on the software. We need all the time we can get, and you can work on some other things."

"It's not quite that simple. Top management still wants to review everything before we let the contract."

Glenn winced as he recognized the old "higher-authority" negotiating tactic. However, he had previously moved to block that tactic by getting an agreement from the purchasing official that the final authority for making the contract was with the buying group he was now meeting with.

Glenn said, "Who is going to make the final decision, then?"

"Oh, we are. We have the authority. It's just that we think it is good policy to clear it with top management" was the reply.

Glenn quickly reviewed what he knew about prospects that refused to make a buying commitment when everything on the surface seemed to be going toward a sale. He recalled a lecture he had once heard about basic issues. He heard the lecturer's loud voice boom out, "If the prospect keeps refusing to make a commitment for some hidden reason, then some basic issue exists that is blocking the sale." Glenn wondered what the basic issue was in this sale. He knew it was not himself, for he really got along well with the group.

He knew that he had competition for the contract from the software firm that had been doing much of the outside programming work for the other projects the company had in-house. However, he had an agreement with the group that the people Dobbs would put on the contract were without doubt the best in the world at what they did. They were perfect for this work.

Glenn was uncertain what the basic issue was, but he had some ideas.

1 What were some of Glenn's perceptions of the basic issues that were blocking this contract?

2 How could he validate these perceptions?

CHAPTER TWELVE

HANDLING OBJECTIONS II

There is no excellence without difficulty.
Ovid

After studying the material in this chapter you should:

☐ Understand the various types of objections encountered in selling

☐ Comprehend the various ways each type of objection can be handled

☐ Appreciate that procrastination can be a particularly deceptive objection to overcome

PROFILE OF AN ADVERTISING
SALESPERSON AND
ENTREPRENEUR

Beverly Miles

Parkhurst Publications
Dallas, Tex.

When asked to explain her success, Beverly Miles, owner and manager of Parkhurst Publications, publisher of a newspaper supplement called *Intowner*, said, "Persistance, belief in my product, and a strong desire for success."

Beverly started selling advertising space in Montana many years ago. Through the school of hard knocks she learned how to sell and how to survive, particularly how to survive. After selling space for the *Dallas Times* for several years, she saw the opportunity to develop a special newspaper supplement for the *Dallas Times*. Its distribution is only in the North Dallas area and covers only firms located there. While she still does much of her own selling, she is helped by several saleswomen.

In 1980 she coauthored a book on women in selling (How to Beat Men at Their Own Game—A Woman's Guide to Successful Selling in Industry) and now gives seminars to women who are interested in sales careers, a subject she taught at Richland College in Richardson, Texas.

Beverly strongly believes that women have a great future in selling. She sees their major problem as one of gaining self-confidence. "They have got to come to believe in themselves and that they can sell. They can't let themselves be intimidated by the business environment."

Because the handling of objections is one hallmark of the adept professional salesperson and because the subject seems to pose more than average difficulty for the sales trainee, let us delve even deeper into the matter.

Chapter 11 was devoted to an overall look at the nature of objections and some basic strategies for handling them. It took the broad view. This chapter focuses on how to deal with specific objections.

TYPES OF OBJECTIONS

Objections can be classified in various ways. There are stated and hidden objections; these were discussed previously. Then there are valid and invalid ones. Objections may also be classified according to the phase of the sale to which they apply (which buying decision the prospect is *not* ready to make). There are objections to the product, to its price, to the terms of sale, to its source, to the salesperson, and to the time when the purchase should be made. Each of these types of objections will be discussed here in detail.

Valid versus Invalid Objections

Many objections are perfectly valid; the prospect is speaking the truth. Some of these valid objections are answerable, while others are not. The unanswerable objections generally take one of two forms: (1) no money or (2) no need for the proposition.* Unfortunately, these are often used as excuses to cover some hidden objections; hence the salesperson must immediately determine whether they are valid or are merely excuses.

Of course, there are limits beyond which a prospect is truly unable to pay. It would be useless to try to sell a new Rolls-Royce or a million-dollar life insurance policy to some poor soul trying to eke out a living on $200 a week. He cannot pay for them, and you would be unethical, as well as foolish, if you tried to force such a sale.

Lack of buying power and lack of need are problems that are practically hopeless for the average salesperson, although the resourceful individual will sometimes find a way out. If you are selling a production good—something which will make or save money for the purchaser—you may yet sell it and let it pay for itself over time. However, where the article is not capable of producing anything for its owner, there may be no sensible means of selling such a person.

Even where the salesperson finds the need for the product is apparently well satisfied, one can sometimes persuade the owner to make a change. The fact that a person already owns a certain make of automobile or carries a certain brand of canned goods or cutlery in stock does not necessarily deter

---

*Speaking accurately, the person without money or without need is not a true prospect. The work done by the salesperson in prospecting and in the preapproach will eliminate many of them, but it is impossible to screen out all of them.

the enterprising sales rep from making an effort to persuade the person to change. True, sales can usually be made to better prospects with less effort, but perhaps the satisfaction derived from inducing these users of other products to change may make the effort worthwhile. An indictment frequently directed against selling is that there is too much competitive (and hence unproductive) effort.

The professional salesperson will, however, avoid selling where there is no need, since this only creates dissatisfaction which will hurt the future chances to sell to this person or to friends.

Valid objections can be voiced about many aspects of the proposition. No proposition is perfect. The prospect may object to one of its shortcomings. Or the prospect may have a good reason for not buying immediately. Sometimes the prospect has a real objection to the item's price or its term of sale.

These will be discussed in detail later. However, a word of caution is needed. There is a tendency among salespeople to treat all objections as invalid. This is unfortunate, for it frequently injects antagonism into the interview as the prospect realizes that a perfectly reasonable objection is being treated lightly by the salesperson.

An executive objects, "I've heard too many bad reports on the service your company gives. I am afraid that I just can't see giving my business to you." Many salespeople would treat this as an untruth, but maybe he really *has* heard bad reports.Notice that he says he has *heard* bad reports, not that the alleged poor service is a fact. The sales representative may be convinced that her firm gives excellent service, so immediately labels the objection as invalid. This is a mistake, for the prospect believes it to be true, and it may block the sale if not successfully answered.

OBJECTIONS TO SPECIFIC BUYING DECISIONS

When a prospect raises an honest objection, it informs you that the person has not yet made one or more of the buying decisions which must be made before he or she is ready to accept the proposition. Every objection can thus be related to some buying decision, and your task is to go back and gain that decision before you can make the sale.

Buying decisions 1 and 2 have already been gained when the prospect agrees:

1 I want to see you.
2 I want to year you.

The other six decisions involved here are:

3 I realize the disadvantages of my present position; I am dissatisfied with things as they are.
4 I see that this proposition would improve my position and make me more satisfied.

5 I approve this proposition, including price, terms, service, etc.
6 I like the firm.
7 I like this salesperson.
8 I want to buy now.

Now let us examine some of the more common objections and see where they fit into this classification. We shall also discuss some suggestions for handling these objections—suggestions collected from the experience of thousands of salespeople over many years.

Objections Blocking Buying Decision 3—No Need

The prospect raising an objection in this category does not yet feel a need for the proposition. The salesperson has failed to arouse a desire to own it. The prospect is cold to the whole matter.

The objections in this group frequently require careful study for their answers, because no sales rep can say with certainty that a prospect *does* need his or her goods unless some thought has been given to the needs of that prospect. As discussed earlier, you may be able to show the prospect that he or she needs the proposition, even though no need has been felt before. We will discuss a few typical objections of this type.

We Are All Stocked Up, and Until This Stuff Moves I'm Not Going to Buy Any More

(A retailer is speaking.) This may be a difficult objection to meet satisfactorily. The salesperson may offer suggestions for moving the goods or may reply, "Let's see just how overstocked you are and then figure out what we can do about it."

If the buyer's excuse is a bluff, it will be quickly disclosed. Be not misled; dealers are frequently mistaken about their inventories. Many use the "over-stock" ploy routinely as a shield against naïve or inept sales reps. One Lanz dress rep said, "Early in the game I learned that my dealers loved to say that the line wasn't moving well, that they were overstocked. So I started keeping records on what each had bought, and then I would take inventory of my line first off so I would know exactly what had and had not sold. Now when one of those rascals tries that old line on me I just say, "Let's take a look at the records. . . . They've stopped trying to bluff me since they know I have the facts."

If investigation proves that the dealer is indeed overstocked, the truly great sales representative will try to work out some solution for the dealer's problem if one is possible. One Levi sales rep made two solid friends on one day. He was calling on the buyer for a large Denver department store who complained that her jeans inventory was badly out of balance. She had far too many wheat-colored jeans, and she said that they were reducing her open-to-buy to the point that she could not give the rep an order for fill-ins (sizes and

Good retailers keep merchandise moving so that fresh goods can come in. How might a salesperson determine whether a retailer is overstocked or simply well-supplied with inventory that moves well?

items out of stock) that were badly needed. Fortunately, the previous day the rep had called upon a sizable specialty store whose owner was pleading for more goods immediately. He was out of and needed jeans. The rep arranged a transfer between the accounts that made both dealers most happy.

Bear in mind that merchants will not prosper if they allow goods that are not selling well to block the purchase of merchandise that will sell. Good retailers keep the goods moving so that they can keep fresh goods coming in. So the clever sales rep finds a way to drive this merchandising principle home to the merchant.

No Room for a New Line This objection is usually an excuse, for any dealer has room for a line or product that will make money. When this objection is offered it simply indicates that the dealer is not thoroughly convinced that another line is needed.

Inasmuch as this objection is merely an excuse for not buying, it cannot be answered directly; you cannot answer an excuse, because the prospect will simply think up another excuse. You must get at the root of the problem—the hidden real objection.

However, unquestionably space is scarce in any well-managed store. Efficient retailing demands that the merchant use the square footage in the store to the utmost. This situation provides the basis for one means of dealing with the excuse. A sales rep for kitchenware would say, "Of course, you don't have room. If you did, you wouldn't be as good a merchant as you are. People don't have room for a new item until they see what it will make them per square foot. When you see the annual return on our line, I think we can find some space for it. We are only talking about 12 square feet. And for those 12 feet, you'll get $3,600 a year. That's a lot more than you're making on most lines you are carrying, isn't it?"

Your Product Duplicates Brands We Are Already Carrying. It Wouldn't Add to Our Sales, Only Switch Them, So We Would Be Carrying Two Items to Make One Sale   Dealers are understandably reluctant to carry brands that duplicate market coverage. Each brand should appeal to its own market segment—should add to the merchant's total sales volume—not just steal volume from some other product. Thus the salesperson has two ways to go in handling this objection: (1) Prove that it will bring in new sales or (2) prove that the brand will outsell the merchant's existing brand and thus should displace it. This is not an easy task to accomplish, but it can be done with some help from management. You need sales statistics and market research information on your product's markets and sales performances ranked against those of the competition. Then you can say something like, "Let's look at the sales experience of our line in comparison with your present lines in other stores such as yours." And then proceed with your proof.

We Like Our Present Supplier and See No Reason to Change   This objection may be offered either by a retailer or by a manufacturer and is a tough one to get around, for the buyer sees no need for buying your line. The sales rep's strategy must be aimed at persuading the prospect that it is good business to have alternative sources of supply for an item just in case something happens to the present source. You might say, "There is no question that they are a good company. In fact, most of our customers also buy from them. For example, just last week I was talking to Mr. Diamond, the buyer over at Acme Steel, about pooling all his business with us instead of splitting it. He shot me down real fast when he reminded me of the time that Acme couldn't ship because of a strike. He declared that it was the policy of his firm to maintain multiple sources of supply so they can minimize their chances of having their supply cut off should anything happen to one firm. Don't you think that makes sense?"

In other situations, the best strategy is to obtain a small trial order, get the product in on a limited basis, and then slowly expand the beachhead by giving excellent service and waiting for the competition to make a mistake. This can be a waiting game but well worth it for a large account, because it is surprising how many times the competition will make some mistake that changes the balance of trade between suppliers.

My Old One Will Last for a While Longer   Many prospects are reluctant to abandon their old possessions in favor of the new. "Sure it will. You can make about anything last as long as you want to, but at what cost?" That is the point of attack for the salesperson—the cost: the cost in dollars for increasingly frequent repairs, the cost in time lost while repairs are being made, the cost of not enjoying the many modern features now available. Usually prospects voicing this objection are somewhat small-visioned and penny-conscious. Therefore, appeals to savings and sometimes profits are likely to be effective.

Sometimes social pressure or an appeal to pride can be used to advantage. One might reply, "Certainly it will! Your old coal furnace would still heat your house, but you installed gas. And your old suit is now at the thrift store. And your old car is now driven by someone less fortunate than you. But you got rid of those old items for better ones. So it is with this product."

Old industrial equipment can actually be most costly in terms of unit production costs. The industrial sales rep must be ready to prove the cost saving of the new in comparison to the existing equipment.

Objections Based on Buying Decision 4—Product

When an objection in this group is raised, you may assume that the prospect recognizes the need, feels dissatisfied with things as they are, but is not yet sure that your proposition will best satisfy it. These objections, if valid, may most frequently be met by use of the compensation method. Use the indirect denial if they are not valid. If the goods are not of the best quality, you usually have a lower price to offer as a compensating inducement. It may be that the compensation method can be used in another way. Sometimes the prospect compares one aspect or characteristic of the goods with the same aspect or characteristic of a competitor's product—a point-for-point comparison. Few products can win all the points in such matches, but be prepared to minimize the significance of those in which your product compares unfavorably. If the sales rep has reason to fear that her goods will not stand the closest scrutiny as to quality, she must avoid making extravagant claims early in the interview, for these will be thrown back at her later. The presentation should rather be devoted to pointing out what other advantages the product possesses.

If the product actually is a second or an irregular, this should be admitted at the outset before the prospect calls attention to it, thus disposing of the objection that it is not up to standard.

The use of analogy is sometimes resorted to in meeting the quality objection. "You can't buy a Lincoln for the price of a Ford, although the same company makes them both. And more Fords are sold than Lincolns."

In other instances you may be able to show the prospect that the several features or qualities he prizes in other products are, in reality, superfluous for his applications—they are not needed. "Certainly, another product has a much heavier-duty motor, but it is not needed in your situation. Why pay for something you don't need?" Here the *concept of useless quality* can be brought forth: All parts of a product should be designed to give the same length of life. It makes little sense to design a motor to last 10 years if the gear mechanisms are designed to last only 5: the customer pays for 5 years' quality that he won't get. A paint sales rep claims that this paint will last for 10 years. But if the customer is going to repaint in 5 years because of soot and dirt, he needs only a 5-year paint. How many "lifetime" guaranteed pens are still in use? Few people have any desire to use something for a lifetime; this is one of the bases for the success of Timex watches. These are some of the arguments that can be put forth in trying to meet a quality objection.

I Have a Friend Who Bought Your Product and Was Unhappy with It You cannot deny this statement; so try to learn more about it. Urge the prospect to tell you all about it. Often this will reveal that the complaint is trivial and sounds silly when brought out into the open. If it is not then disposed of, you might say, "This is the first I have heard about this and I'll take it right up with my company and with this friend of yours. Could I use your phone to ask him what he thinks we ought to do about it?" This may serve to screen out the false from the honest objection and certainly impresses the prospect with the salesperson's eagerness to do the right thing.

The embarrassed sales rep might be able to take some of the sting from the customer's barbs by saying, "Obviously it is disturbing to learn of such occurrences, but you will have to admit that such things happen in all companies and with all products. They can happen to you no matter from whom you buy. The important things to remember, however, are: How often do such mistakes happen and, when they do occur, what kind of service and factory support will be forthcoming? So let's go right into our total performance record." With that statement try to convince the prospect that your firm gives excellent service to back up its relatively few mistakes. Guarantees, case histories, testimonials, personal telephone calls to satisfied users, repair records, and visits to facilities are all techniques that can be used.

I've Used the Ajax Machine for a Long Time, and I Simply Like It Better Than Yours Many times product objections are broad-based attitudes solidly backed with strong prejudice. This situation frequently is based on sheer unfamiliarity. People are comfortable with the familiar; the new and unknown frightens them. A secretary learned to type on an IBM Selectric in high school; she is familiar with its workings and used to its touch. She will have product objections to changing to a Wang word processor. The best strategy for overcoming this type of broad product objection is to get the prospect to agree to a trial usage. Leave the machine, and let her get used to it.

A man has been wearing H. Freeman suits for several years and is thoroughly satisfied. Changing his buying habits will be difficult. You can't offer him a free trial! So you may ask questions such as, "I am interested in knowing exactly what it is you like about these suits." By getting the prospect to outline the features he likes about the competitor's product, you can learn what to stress in your product. Also, such questions will aid in determining if the preference for the other product is based on solid reasons or is only prejudice or habit.

About the only workable strategy available to the enterprising salesperson in such cases is an appeal for open-mindedness and fair play in giving the product a fair trial. If the sales rep is confident that the product will sell itself if used by the prospect, all efforts should be focused upon getting the prospect to try it, with no obligation. Since most people believe that they are open-minded, they should respond when the salesperson says, "Yes, I heard that the Ajax machine gives good results, but I would like to know more about it. As you are an open-minded, objective individual I would really appreciate it if you would give my machine a fair trial and then tell me just how it stacks up against Ajax. This would help me considerably because right now I am not as well acquainted with the Ajax as I would like to be."

I Like Your House, but I Need a Double Garage Instead of the Single One You Put on All These Models Frequently a product objection can be answered most simply by giving the prospect what she or he wants. Many builders are in a position to answer, "Fine, let's get everything down on paper to see what it will cost. I personally agree with you; a double is a good investment and a real improvement over these models."

A customer of a men's apparel store complained that a certain sport shirt was not tapered sufficiently around the waist to suit his tastes. The owner said, "We can have our alterations shop take it in to suit you for a slight alteration charge." As money was not important to that customer, the sale was made. Normally, that owner gives free alterations on all major items of apparel as a means for meeting objections as to the fit of the suits and coats. Other times he meets objections about the design, color, or fabric of his garments by offering to order from the factory exactly what the customer wants. Sometimes they take him up on it; at other times the objection evaporates.

It is in this field of objections that a salesperson's imagination can save many lost causes. A motorist wanted a peculiar shade of pink paint on a new car she was trying to buy. She had been to several dealers, and none of them had the color in a car line. Our hero took the color swatch from the woman and asked her to pick out the *model* she wanted. He merely figured into the deal the cost of a repaint job and made the sale.

You should always examine your position carefully to see if it is possible to actually give the customer the exact product wanted. Can the product be altered in some way to meet the objections? A clerk in a women's ready-to-wear department claims that she frequently has to rearrange the dress to conform to the customer's desires. She snips off unwanted flowers or buttons, adds a different belt, or perhaps puts some costume jewelry on it.

The salesperson who is willing to go out of her or his way to give the prospect what is wanted, will find closing the sale to be easier and the customer appreciative. People like to be catered to.

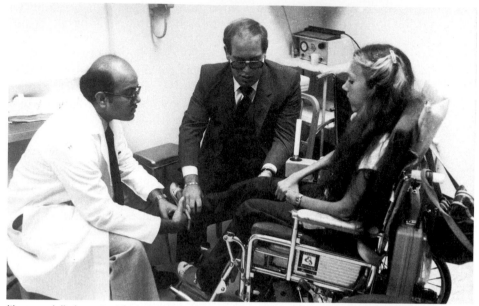

It's especially important for representatives of hospital or home health-care equipment manufacturers to ensure that their products are tailored to meet the special needs of their clients.

Objections Based on Buying Decision 5—Price

These objections cover those aimed at such matters as price, terms, delivery, advertising allowances, services, and many other factors that directly bear on the out-of-pocket costs of the product.

When the prospect says, "Your price is too high," this may mean any one of several things.[1] First, it may mean that your product is not worth the price you are asking; it is not a good value. Or, he may be saying in effect, "I haven't enough money to pay your price." This, of course, is a different matter, for it assumes that if the prospect did have sufficient money he would buy. Naturally, the approach used in handling this type of price objection is entirely different from that required to answer the first. In the latter case, the salesperson would attempt to work out some plan of payment that would meet the prospect's financial requirements. In the former case, he would use one or several of the various techniques, discussed later in this section, for building up the value of the product in the prospect's mind.

In other instances, the prospect may be saying, "I think I can buy your product elsewhere for less money." The prospect is sold on your product and would buy it at your price if it weren't for these other opportunities she has in mind. The techniques used to handle this type of objection naturally vary still further from those previously used.

A price guarantee is often used. "We will meet any verifiably lower price you are offered in the next 10 days," responds a camera salesclerk.

In conclusion, before you can hope to answer a price objection, you must first ascertain exactly what the prospect is objecting to. It is necessary to determine whether the price objection is one of value, lack of money, or competition.

Now let's discuss several methods of meeting these different types of price objections.[2]

Hidden Quality or Merits The classic answer to value objections has usually been to try to increase the merits of the product in the eyes of the prospect. Many times the reasons for an item's higher price are not obvious but must be specifically pointed out. After all, if a product carries a legitimately higher price, there must be some reason for it; therefore, prove the reasons.

Sales representatives for a check writer, designed to prevent checks from being fraudulently increased in value, use this method effectively: "I have a watch here. What would you estimate it is worth? . . . you don't know because you have not examined the works. That is true—you cannot tell whether it is worth $20 or $1,000 merely by looking at the outside. What is true of this watch is even more true of our machine. Inside this machine are seven segments, each with 10 individual dies of a hard composition, besides an oscillating and two stationary dies, making 73 in all. Every character must be true to the thousandth of an inch. This means the finest kind of workmanship." From here the sales rep goes on to explain the other hidden parts of the machine, stressing quality all the way.

The salesperson for a manufacturer trying to sell to a purchasing agent of another manufacturer may find it effective to say, "No doubt your own salespeople have to meet the same objection every day and they answer it in the same way I'm going to answer you. You believe that your product is good—that it is worth what you ask for it. You could probably cheapen it in places, but you don't want to sacrifice quality to do it. We are in exactly the same boat, and I know you understand."

Nearly 100 years ago, John Ruskin wrote, "There is hardly anything in the world that some man cannot make a little worse and sell a little cheaper, and the people who consider price only are this man's lawful prey."

A sales rep for Head skis justified the higher price asked for them over those of a competitor whose skis are quite similar in appearance by showing the prospect a cutaway cross section of the two skis. He pointed out certain details of construction which obviously were superior to and more costly than the competitor's wares.

Sometimes the idea that the product is truly of high quality can be established if the sales rep focuses the prospect's attention upon one key part or component and proceeds to prove its quality beyond doubt, thus suggesting that the rest of the product is similarly constructed.

If you sell a relatively high-priced product, then take great pains to learn as much as possible about its quality and why that quality is of value to the prospect. Know that in every sale you'll have to prove the value of your wares early in the presentation, for most assuredly the prospect will almost instinctively feel from the first a price objection.

All of which proves that a customer's idea of price depends entirely upon the ideas in his or her mind. The more you know about what you are selling—whether it is a supercomputer or potatoes—the better able you will be to overcome price objections. Customers should not be allowed to feel that a price is too high. They won't feel prices are high if you know the fine points of your merchandise.

But, you protest, suppose the product really *is* overpriced?

Overpriced? In whose opinion? Yours or your customer's? It's time to examine this issue of price in some detail. It is usually difficult for people with scant funds to understand other people to whom money has little value. The latter have so much of it or care for it so little that the price of goods means little to them. They buy what they want.

Moreover, the professional salesperson understands that many people buy things for reasons other than price. Indeed, sometimes they buy something because it is high-priced. They want to buy a recognized high-priced product—they're buying the price tag. Other times they are buying some nonprice qualities that they seek such as store image, convenience, or to impress some shopping companions with their affluence. Consequently, it is a mistake for the salesperson to project his or her own values into the prospect. Under-

At $135, the Reebock Pump is a high-priced sneaker. What hidden merits could the Foot Locker salesperson highlight to help his customer overcome his objection to price?

stand that Rolls Royce, Mercedes Benz, Jaguar, and Cadillac sell very well even if you can't afford to buy one of them.

And if you still think that what you sell is over priced or a poor value, then don't sell it. Work elsewhere!

Savings or Profits   Many times, particularly in selling to industrial concerns or middlemen, the qualities or merits of the product may be completely beside the point. The important factor business executives look for is the product's ability to save them money or make them a profit. Suppose a certain product cost but $100 to make and was of obviously cheap construction; however, it would save the prospect $6,000 during the first year. Would the buyer refuse to pay $1,000 for it? In pricing theory, *costs* do not determine prices; the *market* does. Costs determine profits and therefore who stays in business. Do not get into the habit of thinking that the price of your product must be justified on a cost basis, because often it will not be possible to do this. After all, it is often impossible to ascertain the costs of a certain product. Do forequarters of beef cost less than hindquarters? No, but they have to be priced differently in order to clear the market in equal amounts.

The best justification for a high price is that the product will save or make the buyer more than its price. If you can prove that fact, the prospect will buy. A men's apparel store owner objected to a sweater sales rep that the prices were too high. The sweaters were a highly advertised line which sold for around $100. The seller replied,"Would you rather sell a $100 sweater or a $50 one? You get about 50 percent on each, so why not be making $50 on each sweater sale rather than $25? Besides, it is actually easier to sell our $100 line that is being pushed vigorously than it is to persuade a customer to accept your present unknown $50 line." The merchant bought and was pleased to find that the rep was right; sweater sales doubled that year, with the $100 line leading the parade. It was a much better sweater.

Most industrial sales are built around the profit or savings which will accrue to the buyer. Once this has been convincingly demonstrated, price is seldom a barrier. The Hughes Tool Company was able to obtain a handsome price for its rotary diamond drilling bit because it saved the oil well drilling contractor considerable money as compared with the old cable drilling method.

In conclusion, one of the best methods for overcoming a price objection is to show that the product would not cost the buyer a cent; it would actually make money. If such is the case, you can reply to the objection,"I can't afford to buy it" with "You can't afford not to buy it."

Break Price into Smaller Units   Sometimes the high unit price of an item may scare the prospect into making a price objection without really giving thought to exactly how much is being asked for it.

Big price tags can be frightening regardless of the values they represent. Real estate salespeople continually encounter a great reluctance to make an offer by people who are afraid of the high prices. Such amounts are beyond their comprehension even though they may be quite reasonable for the property involved.

A microcomputer salesperson says, "I have already shown you how you can save money by the purchase of one of our machines, but I see that I have not made myself clear in comparing the cost of this machine and the saving that it will give you. You have already told me that your loss through incorrect additions, etc., totals up to several dollars a day. All right. Let's bring the cost of this machine down to cost per day. This computer costs $3,000. Dividing that by 360, the number of days in a year, we have a cost of $18.33 per day. Your present system is certainly costing you more than that, isn't it?"

Another idea is the breakdown technique: Quote the price on some other basis than the product itself. The price can be related to some short unit of time or to some unit of productivity. A paper sales rep made a sale of quality letterheads to a purchasing agent by saying, "Isn't it worth a cent to you to know that your firm is being represented on the best letterhead paper available? That's all it will cost to give you the best instead of what you are now buying."

Of course, one way to meet the price objection is to offer easy terms of payment, reducing the statement of the price to fractions of the original amounts. Real estate agents often remark that many buyers care little about a home's price: "All they want to know is how much down and how much a month."

An executive complains about the high price of a check writer, to which the salesperson replies, "Our $250 machine will last for 50 years, but let's figure it on the Internal Revenue Service 10-year basis. The other 40 years are for free, okay? That's $25 a year, or about 7 cents a day. Seven cents for the time you save and the protection you gain is a bargain!"

More recently salespeople offer leasing plans to overcome price objections. "Okay, $250 is more than you want to pay right now. I'll lease it to you for $10 a month."

Prestige Appeal   Usually people who are buying a product for its prestige know its price and do not object. J. P. Morgan is reputed to have told a young man who asked him how much a yacht costs, "Young man, if you must ask the price of a yacht, you have no business owning one." The regular customer entering the Steuben Room of an exclusive department store fully expects to pay the high prices asked for that kind of artware. However, many times certain products are on the borderline of prestige, or the prospects are not fully aware of the product's reputation. The salesperson must develop some tactful ways of informing these people of the situation without offending them.

This problem of communicating a prestige price is quite touchy and, if bungled, it can lose the firm a potential customer. People resent being talked down to or insulted by some statement implying that they can't pay the price. Perhaps they can't afford the product at hand, but that is still no reason to alienate them as future customers, for many people acquire money later in life and retain memories of slights.

One dress salesperson frequently used the following reply to objections that a certain dress seemed to be expensive for its quality: "When you buy a dress from us, you are not buying merely fabric and stitching. You are buying assurance that you will be dressed in the best of taste and that no other woman in this city will have a dress similar to yours. You will be unique. The price for high fashion can never be measured by fabrics and workmanship, only by what it does for you. If the dress is not for you, any price would be too high. If it makes you elegant and brings out the real you, the price is low."

One should not overlook the virtue of silence in such situations. You are not required by law to reply to every objection or comment made by the prospect. Sometimes a look can say more than words. Some prospects just like to make noise. They expect no reactions.

Comparison   Many times the prospect reacts unfavorably to price only as the result of not having carefully compared it with other products. A customer objected strenuously to the seemingly high price of a bicycle for his child until the sales rep asked, "How much did you pay for those golf clubs I see in your car? . . . Which do you think it takes more time and effort to make, golf clubs or bicycles?" Since the parent had just laid out $800 for the clubs, there was no alternative but to buy the bicycle.

When the price difficulty seems to be based on a comparison between your product and a competing one, it may be good strategy to get the exact difference between the two and then show clearly just what your product offers for the extra amount asked. In this way, by stressing *exclusive* advantages, the difference in price may be made to appear small.

A potential buyer of filing cabinets complained that he could buy another brand for $10 less than was being asked for a particularly well-known brand. The sales rep replied, "Let's see, you say that $10 is the difference between my brand and the one you have in mind. Let me show you what you are getting for your $10. First, our cabinets are 2 inches deeper, giving you about 8 percent more filing space. On a $50 investment that alone is worth $4. Next, if you will inspect the ball-bearing rollers on which our drawers are mounted, you will find them much superior to the friction roller used in the other brand. Next, look at the way the movable support in each drawer is operated. Ours work much easier. Feel the way our drawers lock shut. It is obvious that this is quality hardware. So, you see, you are getting a lot of quality and superior performance for your $10."

Sometimes the retail shopper objects, "I saw the same thing for sale at a lower price at Blank's." When this objection is raised, it does little good to deny it flatly. It may be true; if it is not, a contradiction accomplishes nothing. It boils down to a matter of the customer's word against yours. The clever clerk, therefore, will not deny the statement but will ask questions with the aim of finding out the facts. "You can doubtless find something at a lower price, but did you notice carefully the material used in the other coat? Are you sure it was as heavy as this, and was it made of virgin wool instead of wool that had been used once before? There are no imperfections in the weave of this one, and the color is very fashionable."

Perhaps the other article was a duplicate design in a cheaper material, often found in leather goods, such as purses, or upholstered furniture. The salesperson who suspects this should set about to educate the customer on materials, so that the latter can tell the difference. The salesperson may compare the article under discussion with cheaper articles carried in stock and point out the differences. "This looks almost identical at first glance, but a closer examination shows that the lining is not so durable and the color is a more ordinary shade of brown."

The customer may, indeed, be wrong, for the goods may be handled only by the one store in the city. In this case the salesperson can point out that the store has the exclusive agency for the city and that it is unlikely that the other store is selling the same article. It occasionally happens that a store will obtain, through devious channels, a small quantity of an article sold by another store that has been given the exclusive agency. The first store then makes much ado about the article, using it perhaps as a loss leader while the stock lasts. This is often done with trademarked clothing or shoes, the practice being to have in stock unusual sizes or styles so that they will not readily sell. The salesperson who suspects that the customer is referring to such a situation might ask, "Were you able to find the size you wanted there?"

Recognize that there are times when it may be best to say to the person, "Sounds like you have found a great deal. You'd better buy it." If for some reason the competition has you beat hands down, you only jeopardize your future business with the person by maintaining otherwise.

The way in which the customer offers the objection will help the salesperson know how to meet it. If it is offered seriously, the matter is worth discussing. If it is mentioned in a casual manner, it is probably a flimsy excuse made by a shopper who has little intention of buying.

Bear in mind that people continually buy items at stores for prices much higher than they know they would have to pay elsewhere. But they aren't elsewhere. They are willing to pay for the convenience of having the goods here and now.

Questioning   The question technique can prove quite effective in handling certain types of price objections. Many times a person believes a price to be high only because they lack information about it or have failed to think about it. The right questions can encourage such prospects to realize that the price is in line, after all. You may ask such questions as "Why do you think the price is out of line?'' or ''What price do you have in mind?'' or ''I wonder what you have in mind when you say our price is too high. High compared to what?''

After getting the prospect to bring out his thoughts on the matter of price, you can swing into one of the other methods for answering the price objection, the choice depending on the particular situation uncovered by the questions.

Adjusting the Price Although most salespeople do not have control over the prices charged for their goods, some are authorized to meet competitive prices under certain circumstances. Some firms have a policy of meeting any legally quoted price lower than theirs if the customer can show tangible proof of that lower quotation. In such cases, you should ask the prospect to give positive evidence of the lower price, and it will be immediately taken up with the home office. However, a word of caution: You should never intimate to a prospect that you can meet such lower prices unless you are certain of it, for to hold out the hope of a lower price only to refuse it later will antagonize the prospect right into the competitor's camp.

Handling the Trade-In In selling many products, such as automobiles, television sets, vacuum cleaners, refrigerators, furniture, and computers, the salesperson is likely to encounter a prospect who wishes to turn in a used article as part payment for the new one. Even in selling industrial equipment, salespeople must be prepared to deal in two markets—the new and the used. They must know how and where their prospective customer can sell the old equipment if its existence is blocking the sale of the new equipment. In nearly every case the prospect places a much higher value upon the old car or stove than its real worth. The sales rep is faced with making two sales—selling the new article and selling the prospect on the depreciation in value of the used article. Because so many sales are ruined at this point, it seems desirable to discuss briefly some of the methods that have proved helpful.

If possible, avoid the whole problem either by not taking trade-ins or by quoting the price on an exchange basis. Modern appliance dealers for the most part have learned to avoid the trade-in problem. Only if the prospect's old equipment has some real recognized value is it really necessary to develop a system for handling it.

It is better not to place a price on the used article until after all the value in the new one has been fully explained. The prospect should be brought to desire the new car before anything is said about how much you will allow for the old one. This principle holds especially true when you are not in a position to allow very much on the old article. Of course, if the firm has a liberal trading allowance and you can appraise the old article at a high price, this fact may be used as a talking point and brought out early in the interview.

When the appraised value will be low, have the old article appraised by a third party rather than by yourself. Thereby, any antagonism aroused by a low price will not be aimed so directly at you.

The appraisal should not be done in the presence of the owner. When it is so done, every point leads to an argument and makes the sale that much harder.

Have a formal appraisal program in which the prospect understands that the possession is getting a complete examination rather than an offhand, eyeball evaluation. The prospect will gain confidence in the firm's integrity and thoroughness.

Have some outside, independent authority upon which to base the trade-in price. Automobile dealers use their red and blue books to give an independent look to their pricing. Many appliance and office equipment manufacturers are furnishing their dealers with such trade-in information in order to support their valuations. You might print up your own trade-in valuation tables to fall back on in case of emergency. Blame the low price on someone else.

Encourage prospects to sell the equipment themselves by showing them how to do it and giving them case histories of others who have done so.

One salesperson developed the following analogy for handling situations in which the prospect's trade-in apparently should be worth more than can be offered. "I know how you feel. I owned some stock in a real good firm, good growth, good earnings. Any way you wanted to look at it, it was worth at least $60 a share. But the market said it was worth only $42. You know, I've never met a person yet who won an argument with the market!"

Many salespeople claim that it is wise to praise the prospect who has a trade-in for the care he has taken of it. Some statement such as, "I see that you have taken exceptional care of your present machine. That's good, for it will allow us to give you top dollar for it." Of course, this tactic should not be used if it is obviously untrue.

Most salespeople prefer to get the prospects to commit themselves on what they think they should have for their trade-in before they commit themselves on its trade-in value. Sometimes the prospect is quite reasonable, and the figure given is one you can close on. For example, you might say, "Then if I can get you $500 for your trade-in you will go ahead with this deal. Is that right? . . . OK, let's write up the deal for the boss's approval and see what happens."

On the other hand, the prospect may give you a figure so far out of line that there is little hope of a sale until the market has pounded some of the inflation out of the prospect's system—until he has shopped around and been educated as to the value of the property. Other times you may see that there is a good chance for a deal if you can only get around the trade-in smoothly. This phenomenon gave rise in the automobile business to the practice of giving the prospect the trade-in asked for but upping the price of the new product commensurately.

Objections Based on Buying Decisions 6—Source

These objections are leveled against the firm you represent. Often they are not so much objections as questions and can be met with a straightforward statement of facts covering such matters as age of firm, its size, its financial standing, affiliation with well-known firms, important customers, rate of growth, patents held, other products manufactured, efficiency of operation, sound labor relations, etc.

This problem is particularly acute among new firms, which continually encounter source objections. The prospects (industrial and commercial buyers in particular) are most reluctant to buy from unproved vendors. They wonder, "Who are these people? Can they be believed? Can or will they perform on their promises? Can we trust them?" Unfortunately, they may be justified in their fears. They have been disappointed and dismayed in the past by the inability of some new firm to perform as promised. A few years ago a small candy company in Manhattan Beach, California, obtained a contract from a large candy company for 5 million cans of carameled popcorn for delivery in 6 months. Five million cans! And this firm has a hole-in-the-wall operation just off the beach! How could it deliver? There was a lot of subcontracting and long hours. It worked out OK but the point is that the buyer risks a great deal in buying from unknown sources.

Your task in handling such objections is to somehow show the buyer that you can and will deliver. Testimonials from previous customers, if you have them, can help. Show the buyer how you plan to do the job. Sometimes you have a silent factor going for you; it is not critical to the buyer's operations whether or not you deliver. If you do, fine; if not, no damage done.

Sometimes, however, the prospect has had unpleasant dealings with the firm and is personally unfriendly. For example, he or she may have had a dispute with the credit department over some claim. In this case you may be tempted to join with the prospect in giving your firm a thorough "bawling out."

Such tactics, however, are bad, for no buyer respects a disloyal representative of any concern. If a mistake has been made, the sales rep can promise a careful investigation and proper adjustment of the difficulty. The use of analogy may also help. Say to the prospect, "You wouldn't refuse to patronize a barber shop just because one barber in it gave you a poor haircut, would you? The other barbers are all good, and even the careless one would probably try extra hard to do a good job on you next time." The sales rep, as the representative of the house, must not be led into taking sides against the employer.

Often, when the buyer has suffered annoying experiences with the firm, the only way to correct the situation is to keep calling until the prospect is convinced that you are a fine person and not in any way to blame for the misunderstanding. These tactics, pursued persistently, have won back thousands of former customers.

The ability of a firm to deliver the correct quantity of goods on time is crucial in selling to a large industry. Many concerns will not deal with a new firm unless it receives a performance recommendation from a well-known respected company.

The two most common causes of source objections are past experiences with poor quality and late delivery. The rep is posed with the problem of proving to the prospect that the causes of those past experiences no longer exist. The buyer must be given reason to believe that things have changed for the better. It is not an easy task in many cases.

Some buyers permit personalities to influence them to an extent that seems ridiculous. The position of an executive of your firm on a political issue may prevent some narrow-minded prospect from patronizing that concern. One answer could be: "Do you refuse to *sell* to everyone who does not agree with you on this question?" Perhaps the best way to meet this objection is to sidestep it: "You may be right, and our president wrong. There seems to be a lot on both sides and I can't figure the thing out. But I *am* sure that you would profit a whole lot from handling our line."

The problem of prejudice is not easy to handle. You can't just smash it with argument. It is often based on emotion or on some experience unique to the prospect. General topics such as politics, personalities, sports, and educational methods had better be avoided by the sales rep. A prejudice based on an unpleasant experience must be treated with sympathetic respect and a promise to set things right, if this is possible.

Objections to the source are most frequently encountered in selling to large industry where the ability of the firm to deliver the needed goods in proper quantities, of specific quality, and on time is vital. Many large concerns will not take a chance on a smaller, unproven firm no matter how good its prices may be. Thus such firms often find it difficult to break into big accounts except after a long period of selling efforts. These larger firms usually maintain lists of approved vendors or sources of supply, and firms are placed on these lists only after a team of the buyer's personnel has visited the seller's plant and investigated its ability to perform as claimed. One small electronics firm selling exotic hardware to defense contractors has a policy of automatically bringing the top executives of buyers' companies to its plant for first-hand exposure to its capabilities.

Sincere testimonials from executives of similar firms can go a long way toward assuring a doubting purchasing agent. Nothing sells such a prospect better than a record of good performance. The fact that the firm is on the list of approved suppliers to certain well-known and respected companies is reassuring to skeptical buyers.

Objections Based on Buying Decision 7—The Salesperson

Here the prospect does not like the sales rep. This is often an objection that is hard to discover. As a matter of fact, the salesperson seldom knows whether the customer is refusing to buy for this reason. Most buyers do not tell the sales rep that they did not like the way he spoke of competitors or the manner in which he "kidded" the switchboard operator or the indelicate stories that he has told. So the salesperson usually is compelled to guess at this objection and should always be on the alert to discover any personal weaknesses or unfortunate mannerisms that result in an unfriendly feeling on the part of the prospects. As a rule, the preapproach will disclose facts about the prospect that should help the sales rep to avoid running counter to a pet hobby or prejudice.

Some salespeople, after being turned down, have asked prospects if the refusal to purchase was based on any personal peculiarity that might be overcome. If the salesperson is sincere in his or her request, the buyer may enlighten him or her and help the salesperson become more efficient.

Obviously, if the salesperson has not played square with the buyer, the objection is valid. For example, if the rep promised advertising aids that were not forthcoming or overloaded the customer on a previous visit or exaggerated the merits of the proposition, there is nothing left to do but acknowledge the error and promise to reform.

Some buyers are cautious because of experiences with unscrupulous sales reps: "I've been stung too many times on propositions that sounded good." A reply, involving a judicious use of compliment and an analogy, may meet the objection: "I suppose that every person who has done much business has made some poor investments at times or at least feels that she or he has. However, if someone had passed counterfeit money on you a couple of times, you wouldn't refuse thereafter to accept any and all money offered you, would you? You would examine it more carefully before you accepted it, which is precisely what I should like to have you do with this proposition."

Personality conflicts do arise occasionally in which you just can't get along with a certain buyer. In such cases you may arrange to swap accounts with another of the firm's sales reps, perhaps thereby benefiting all parties. But this should not be a common situation. Good salespeople are able to get along with almost anyone, especially when they know something about the person in advance.

Objections Based on Buying Decision 8—Procrastination

The motto of many people is, "Never do anything today that can be put off until tomorrow." So it is in buying; prospects frequently want to delay making a decision if they can. It would seem that making a decision to buy is a painful experience. One continually hears, "I want to sleep on it." "I want to talk it over with my spouse." "See me next month, and I'll be ready to buy." "I want to think about it for a while." "I want to look around a bit more." There is no end to the variations of the stall: The prospects just want to avoid making a decision *now*.

Admittedly, some procrastination is legitimate; the prospect has to consult with some higher executive or has to wait for some event to happen. But most of them are just excuses.

Many deferrals are offered as camouflage for other objections. Frequently, when the prospect says, "I think I'll look around some more" or "I'll have to think about it," what she is really saying is, "I don't believe that this is the deal for me." She remains unpersuaded; thus you must go back and discover her real objections.

The person who is unable to cope with procrastination will never be highly successful, for too many sales will be lost to more aggressive competitors. The following is told by a Seattle real estate agent:

I am sitting in the office one Saturday afternoon taking my turn at floor duty when this couple walks in and asks if we will build a house on their lot in the south end. I check and find out that we do go that far south, so I ask some questions to find out what they need in the way of a house. It turns out that they need a four-bedroom house of modest price. We had one about completed for show purposes, so I took them over to the site, and they fell in love with it. The price was right, and we could deliver on time, so it looked like another sale. However, as usual, they wanted a few minor changes made, which required a visit to our architect for cost estimates before we could sign a firm contract. I called and found that the earliest time we could get together was on Tuesday morning, so an appointment was made for then. The couple was extremely happy; they even took me to dinner and spent the hour telling me what a good outfit we were because we would quote firm prices and delivery dates instead of giving them the runaround they had been given elsewhere. Well, on Monday I called to remind these prospects of the appointment and confirm it. I was greeted enthusiastically with a big, "Hello there, Mr. Salesman. Gee. I'm sure glad you called. Guess what happened to us over the weekend—we bought a house!" Some other agent had gotten hold of them on Sunday and sold them a used house, taking their lot in payment. Which all goes to show you that when people are ready to buy they will find someone who will sell them if you are stupid enough to turn them loose unsigned. I made my mistake by not getting them signed to *something* right at the time and then amending it *after* the architects had given the additional cost figures. As a matter of fact, they really got stung, for the old house they bought did not fit their needs at all.

Every salesperson can match that story with some other one about how excellent prospects got away when allowed to delay. You must be prepared to cope with procrastination forcefully, for these prospects are, in essence, agreeing to buy your merchandise but are just arguing over the timing of the sale. If they are that well sold on it, then the present is the best time to close the sale, for the love affair may well wane if another sales rep gets into the act in the meantime.

Fortunately, there are several good ways of handling procrastinations. First, learn to "put a hook in the close," provide a reason for buying *today*. Second, outline the advantages and disadvantages of waiting. Third, use the "Standing Room Only" close to discourage waiting. Finally, use impending events as a good reason for acting immediately.

Put a Hook in Your Close   Give the prospect a good reason for not procrastinating. Many firms selling to intermediaries always have a special deal for the rep to offer, this being "good only on this call." There is ample cost justification for such inducements, for it costs money to have a sales rep make two or three calls to get an order when he might have gotten it on the first call.

One book sales rep would say to the trade-book buyer for a bookstore, "If you give me your order now, I'll send you a couple of extra books for yourself." A bribe? Perhaps! Effective? Definitely!

A machine tool sales rep would, when he could, put the following hook into the close. "There's a firm down in Wheeling that's been looking for a milling machine just like yours. I can unload it for you at a good trade-in if we can get going on this deal. Let me call and put together a proposition for you."

Retailers use "one day" sales to prod the sluggish buyer into action.

What Do You Gain by Waiting?   Many times the prospect will see the light by simply comparing what is gained by waiting with what is lost. Usually the gain is little or nothing, while the use of the product is lost for a period of time, and the price may go up. The salesperson may ask the prospect to write down on paper exactly what he expects to gain by waiting, while the salesperson writes down what may be lost.

A sales rep for an industrial janitorial service told a procrastinating prospect, "You're a very busy person. It's obvious you have many things to do with your time. Well, I'm busy, too, so let's be nice to each other and get this business over with so we can both get on with our other affairs. Sign the order. You're not going to get a better deal if you spend another 100 hours searching for it."

"Standing Room Only" Close   In the next chapter a more detailed discussion of this closing method is found, but here it will suffice to point out that it can effectively prevent procrastination if truthfully used. In many situations the salesperson can truthfully say, "I am sorry, but I can't promise that I will be able to make you this same offer later."

Supplies may be short, prices may be increased, models may change, or delivery dates may be altered. There are many reasons why a sales rep cannot always promise that the offer will be the same at a later date. Some vacillating buyers have to be educated in the realities of the market. In selling real estate one of the big problems is to get a prospect to act promptly on a hot property—one which will move off the market quickly. Experience may indicate that if the prospects don't act now, the property will be sold by the time their decision is made. Many prospects do not believe such assertions, but once a couple has lost a few desired properties to others who were more decisive, it becomes easier to deal with them. Sometimes the agent can help this process along by relating some real case histories of people who lost their "dream house" because they vacillated. One agent would say, "You really love this house, don't you? It's priced right and is attractive in every way, isn't it? Well, I guarantee you that there are 100 couples right at this instant in this city who are looking for a house just like this. They will agree with you, for you are right. Among these couples in the market now are some that know a bargain when they see it and will grab it. In fact, I cannot guarantee you that if you made an offer this instant the owner has not already accepted another offer. If you want this house, then you had better make up your mind right now, for I feel sure that this property will be off the market soon."

In selling real estate, convincing prospects to move promptly on "hot" properties that may not be on the market very long can be a major challenge. How might a real estate salesperson convince a potential buyer that availability is genuinely limited?

Another possible approach is to ask the couple, "Have you seen many properties at this value that you wanted as much as this one?" If they say that they have, then ask what happened to them. When they in effect say that for some reason they got away from them, then you suggest, "Don't let it happen again." If they say that they haven't seen a similar value in something they like, then you should say, "No, and you probably won't for such bargains are rare and don't last long on the market."

Few things will make prospects want to buy quicker than the thought that they might not be able to buy later. One southern California builder of luxury homes deliberately creates a "standing room only" environment around his projects by only placing them on the market in small batches at a time and then arranging it so that most of the homes in that batch have been previously spoken for. When a prospect walks into the "trap" (southern California slang for the model-home sales complex a builder erects from which to sell the homes in the tract), the builder manages to convey the impression that the houses are almost all gone and the prospect is lucky that one or two are left to buy.

Impending Events   Sometimes impending events such as price increases, strikes, upturns in business activity, and model changes will create a situation on which the sales rep can capitalize to forestall the procrastinator. One can calmly mention these events during the presentation, thereby priming the prospect to buy promptly when she is convinced that the proposition is what is wanted.

In inflationary times the threat of a price increase tacitly acts as an impending event urging immediate action. Moreover, never underestimate the power of delivery dates to force buying actions from laggard purchasing agents. Few thoughts put such terror in the minds of purchasing agents as that of not having items in the plant when they are needed. Anything that threatens delivery can be used as an impending event.

Some Procrastinations Are Valid

Not every procrastinating objection is a stall or is insincere. In many industries no buyer would think of giving an order on your first call. This is true in most industrial selling, where it is necessary to make several calls before you can expect even a token order. One firm reports that its salespeople make an average of eight calls before receiving their first order. There are many situations in which the prospect legitimately requires a little time to think and perhaps to discuss the matter with others before he places an order. To pressure such a prospect too hard would lose the sale.

There are other times when the prospect has good reasons for procrastinating. Perhaps some funds are yet to be received. Perhaps the customer, not wanting to carry the goods around while shopping, waits until just before going home to buy them. Perhaps approval must be obtained from some other individual. Whatever the reason, there are many instances in which the salesperson can do little but try to pin down the prospect to a date by which a decision will be made, try to arrange another appointment, or try to extract a promise not to make a decision until the salesperson can see the prospect again.

Once you understand clearly that the prospect is not going to buy immediately, you should start arranging a meeting in the future at which a decision can be made.

SUMMARY

Objections can arise on any of the buying decisions the prospect must make for a transaction to take place. Objections may arise about the prospect's need for the proposition, the nature of the product or service, its price, its source, or the timing of the purchase. Each of these types of objections are handled in different ways.

If the prospect denies a need for the product, then the rep must go back into the presentation to establish the need, if one truly exists. If it doesn't, the rep should leave.

Product objections are usually handled with the compensation technique, in which the product's deficiencies are admitted but shown to be irrelevant in the situation at hand. Or perhaps the product can be modified to meet the prospect's requirements.

Price objections come in several modes. Sometimes the buyer is saying he or she cannot afford the product, while other times the prospect means that the seller's product is a poor value. Each requires a different answer.

Procrastinations can best be handled by giving the prospect a good reason for acting promptly. Source objections can best be met by showing the prospect that the firm has many satisfied customers.

Any of these objections can be either hidden or overt. Hidden objections are particularly difficult to dig out, but they must be discovered if a sale is to be made. Adroit questioning is the most popular way of discovering hidden obstacles to the sale.

DISCUSSION QUESTIONS

1 An industrial purchasing agent responds to your sales presentation, "I'll admit your product and deal are attractive. However, we are perfectly satisfied with our present supplier." How do you answer?
2 Should you ever bring up an objection that the prospect has not mentioned just so you can counter it?
3 It was suggested that one excellent way to avoid procrastinating objections is to put a hook in the close. If you were the sales manager for a manufacturer of office supplies, what kind of bait would you furnish your salespeople for their hooks? How can management assist in closing such sales?
4 Suppose a prospect simply will not believe what you say regarding her or his objections. What should you do?

5 Many insurance prospects claim they have no need for insurance when in fact they are saying that they simply do not care about protecting their family—they are irresponsible. What kind of objection is irresponsibility? How can the agent meet it?

6 What are some of the methods by which the salesperson can meet a buyer's objection to the newness of the salesperson's company?

7 A customer refuses to do business with you again because of an unfortunate experience with the last purchase. What should you do?

8 There is an old saying in selling, "Be your own casting director!" It refers to the strategy of placing your prospects in the role you want them to play. If you want the prospects to be fair-minded, you tell them they are. Why does this frequently work?

9 When meeting a lower price quoted by a competitor, why does a good sales rep get the prospect's signature on an order with the lower price before going to his or her superiors for approval?

10 Under what circumstances does one accept a prospect's objections to buying and quit?

REFERENCES

1 Raymond Dreyfack, "The Selling Edge: 'Your Price Is Too High' (But What Does the Prospect Really Mean?)," *American Salesman*, December 1988, pp. 20–23, suggests educating the buyer and using the powers of persuasion.

2 Ted Pollock, "Sales Ideas That Work—Handling the Price Objection," *American Salesman*, January 1989, pp. 25–30, suggests communicating the quotation as the "good news" and making the price a less dominant factor in the purchase decision.

CASE 12-1: Della Johnson—Going for Money

While attending the business school of a large west coast university, Della worked to support herself by doing freelance designs for various firms in the apparel industry. She was good at it. Her clients came back wanting more of her work. One particular item, a casual sportswear dress for young women, proved to be a big seller. The maker wanted to hire Della full-time as his designer. Della had other ideas about what she wanted to do.

As a major in entrepreneurship she became convinced not only that she wanted to be her own boss but that she wanted to do so immediately. She did not want to work for someone's salary. During her last semester in school, she developed a comprehensive business plan for starting her own company—Della.

The concept was to design trendy sportswear for young active women, particularly for taller athletic women. Della herself is 6 feet tall—a fact which had sensitized her to the opportunities in this market. "I have a difficult time buying fashionable clothes off the rack. They are made for short women. But we are getting taller each year. There's a big market now for what I have in mind. I don't want to make the garments. I will subcontract out the work to a house I have been working with that is eager to do the deal."

Della's business plan called for an initial investment of $100,000 in exchange for 45 percent of the business, with a provision for buying out the investor for a price that would result in a 100 percent return on the investment each year. Or, as an alternative, she would give the investor 5 percent of sales revenue for as long as the investor wanted to stay in the deal. If the investor wanted out after 3 years, the $100,000 would be returned within 6 months. Della could get rid of the investor on a downward sliding scale that began at $1,000,000 during the first year and came down to $200,000 in the 10th year.

She had given her plan to Robert Kane, a private investor she had met while in college. Mr. Kane had spoken to one of her classes and had talked with Della afterward about her proposed business. He invited her to send him the final plan for it, which she did.

It had been returned by Mr. Kane's private secretary with the comment, "Mr. Kane believes that he will pass on this one." No explanation of his decision or any comments were on the plan when it was returned. Della ran to her adviser's office with her problem. She had been led to believe that she would have Mr. Kane's support.

After listening to Della's story, Professor Davis told her to go see the man and find out what he didn't like about the deal. What was his objection to it?

An appointment was made and Della had her interview. It was frustrating. Mr. Kane confessed that he liked the concept, that he thought Della would be able to make it happen, and that much money would be made in the venture. "You'll make a lot of money on this deal, but it just isn't for me." He would say no more nor would his wife, who also loved the concept and thought a great deal of Della.

"They sure sounded like they were telling me the truth, but I just can't figure out what is bothering them," Della complained to Professor Davis.

He replied, "Let's use our imagination for a minute and develop some hypotheses as to what the problem might be."

1 What do you think is Mr. Kane's objection to Della's deal?

2 Make a list of possible objections that may be blocking Mr. Kane's participation in the deal.

CASE 12-2: Winning Images, Inc.—Designing a Sales-Training Session on Objections

"Eighty percent of our sales force has been with us less than a year. They're rookies with only our initial sales-training course under their belt. All we do is give them some product training and a presentation book. We really don't get down into the guts of selling, closing, and objections. Now we're paying the price. We have a bunch of conversationalists out there who aren't making sales they should be making. They can't close because they can't handle objections. They need a lot of work on objections. And that is why I need your firm. We can't do it. Haven't got the people! We're still a small company and have a long way to go.'' Sally Sowinski, sales manager of Winning Images, was talking to Jerry Voll, a sales consultant she had met at a local marketing club meeting.

Jerry asked, ''What's your budget for this?''

She responded, ''Not much. We're still small, but growing. We only have 40 part-time sales representatives in the field now. How much do you charge?''

''$1,000 a day plus all expenses.''

''Gee, that's a lot. How many days do you think it would take?''

''I really don't want to take on a client for fewer than 10 days over a period of a year. It just is not worth my time to learn about your business and think about your problems for less than that,'' Jerry stated.

There was some silence on the line; then Sally said, ''I'll have to check with Mrs. Love about it. I don't have that kind of money in my budget right now. I'll get back to you.''

Sally brought the matter to the attention of Mrs. Love, founder of Winning Images, Inc., a direct home sales organization selling products to career women that made them look professional—cosmetics, clothes, accessories, business appliances. The firm used a party plan; a Winning Image sales rep would be hostess to a number of her acquaintances at an after-work party during which the line was presented.

While operations were profitable and the business was growing rapidly, it was still small and vulnerable. Ten thousand dollars was not a sum that Mrs. Love took lightly. She asked Sally, ''Why can't you prepare a short program for training our people? It would seem to me that we could do it for a lot less than $10,000. Try it anyway, and let's see how it goes.''

Sally returned to her office to ponder the problem. The reps reported several common objections. First, they had difficulty getting prospects to agree to attend the party. All sorts of excuses were encountered: ''I've got a date tonight,'' ''I'm busy,'' ''I've made other arrangements,'' ''I've got to run home to take care of my family.'' Once a woman agreed to attend the party, usually she bought something, even a low-ticket item on which little money was made. The price range of the products in the line was from $10 to more than $1,000. Generally, the main objections heard at the party were: ''I just don't have the money right now,'' ''I really can't, not now. Too many debts as it is,'' ''It's more than I really want to pay.''

Down deep, Sally thought that most of the real objections revolved around the relatively high prices of the goods. It seems that having a Winning Image was not cheap. The goods, while of the highest quality and most attractive, were not inexpensive. Price objections had to be the center of most problems in Sally's opinion.

1 Is Jerry asking too much for his services?

2 Prepare an outline of a sales training program for teaching the Winning Image sales reps how to overcome objections.

CHAPTER THIRTEEN

NEGOTIATIONS

You can get anything you want, but you have to do more than ask.

Roger Dawson

After studying the material in this chapter you should:

☐ Understand the importance of negotiating skills to your career and your life

☐ Know that sound deals are win-win situations—both parties get from the deal what they want

☐ Realize that sound negotiations depend on knowledge

☐ Accept that it requires patience to complete deals

PROFILE

OF A NEGOTIATOR

Tom Knapp

President, Club Sports
Los Angeles, California

While in college in the early 1980s, Tom did a large portion of his studying at the beach where he noted the increasing interest in beach volleyball. It occurred to him that the sport did not have its own apparel. He set about to correct that situation. He did, with great benefit to himself. During his senior year he grossed $800,000 with his Club Sports line of beachwear. As he continued his venture after graduation, he soon realized how much of his time was being spent on negotiations.

"It seems to have become my main job. Dealing with the big buyers takes a lot of skill. And the money guys are something else. If you can't negotiate, they own you."

Negotiating skills are essential in all phases of business and life if one is to be successful.[1] Even in the most routine sales positions, some negotiating is done. Perhaps it is only over a delivery date or some other minor aspect of the transaction. In other instances, the salesperson must conduct extensive negotiations whose outcome vitally affects the firm's profits. If the rep cuts a good deal, the company makes money.[2] Generally, higher-level, better-paying sales jobs require substantial negotiating skills.

Successful entrepreneurs also depend on their negotiating skills. Businesspeople with poor negotiating skills either pay too much or sell too cheaply. Either way, they lose money.

Good negotiators understand the bargaining process from both the buyer's and the seller's standpoints. Buying and selling are two sides of the same coin. You cannot be a good buyer unless you understand the seller's position and tactics, and you cannot be a good seller if you don't understand the buyer's situation and tactics. Thus we will be discussing both buying and selling.[3]

THE WIN-WIN STRATEGY[4]

The strategic position of most modern negotiators is called win-win, that is, both parties to the deal win. They both get what they want from the deal. A win-win agreement stays together. Neither party wants "out," since both of them gain advantage. They both want to deal.[5]

Win/Win Challenge

"If we don't deliver quality glasses in One Hour,* we'll give them to you...FREE!"

*One hour excludes time for eye exam, frame selection, fitting

This store offers a deal phrased in the WIN-WIN tradition. This is the strategic position of most modern negotiators: both parties benefit from the deal. What might be the advantages gained by each party in this situation?

In a transaction in which the sales rep bests the other party, a win-lose transaction, the customer will likely find some way to get out of the deal. The minute customers figure out that the deal is not in their best interests, that they lost the negotiation, they'll try to get out of the deal.

If by chance the sales rep has made a lose-win deal, in which the customer has gotten the best of the seller, several unfortunate things may evolve:

1 The rep's job may be in jeopardy.

2 The seller may find some way to repudiate the contract to the detriment of customer relationships (there is usually an escape clause in most contracts).

3 The quality of the goods delivered may suffer also to the detriment of customer relationships.

4 Or the company may decide to swallow its loss and make it up elsewhere, to no one's advantage.

Sometimes two parties manage to make lose-lose deals, to the chagrin and disadvantage of both of them. The seller's price is too low to allow a profit and the buyer fails to get what was sought. Imagine buying a car only because it was priced below cost? The dealer would lose money and you might end up driving something you hated. Lose-lose! How do such deals happen? The parties lose sight of what they must have from the deal.[6]

THE IMPORTANCE OF KNOWLEDGE

Several years ago one of the authors had the pleasure of appearing on the Donahue television show with several teenage entrepreneurs, one of whom was Jeff Gold. In a casual conversation after the show, Jeff was asked about his father's occupation. Jeff said he was an entrepreneur. He was then asked, "Is he a good one?"

"No!"

"Why not?"

"He's a poor negotiator!"

"And you're a good one?"

"Definitely!"

"What makes you so good at negotiating?"

"Because I know what I want and I won't settle for anything less," Jeff replied firmly.

And there we have the first basic principle of negotiating. You must know what you want from the negotiations before you begin them. Know what you *must* have, know what you *would like* to have, and know what you *don't really need* to have from the deal. Know what you can give and what you can't give!

After beginning with your needs assessment, start learning about the needs of the other party. What benefits does the other person seek? Never mind what they say they want, what do they really want? What's important and what's not important to them?

The owner of a business that was for sale said she wanted $1,000,000 cash up front for it. After some exploration, it was finally admitted that what she really wanted was a secure income of $100,000 a year, a totally different matter than $1,000,000 right up front.

Often people do not know what they truly want from a deal. The skillful negotiator leads them to realize their true desires.

Specific Knowledge Needed[7]

Six important factors should be known by the negotiator:

1 costs
2 time
3 alternatives
4 authority
5 desperation
6 allies

Costs   Cost information is critical to successful negotiations. Surprisingly, many people enter a negotiation not knowing their own costs let alone those of the other party. If you are trying to buy a house, it is helpful to know that its owner has about $200,000 invested in it. This is not to say that costs determine prices. Far from it. However, they do pose barriers that must be overcome. People are reluctant to sell below cost unless they see even larger losses in the future.

Time   What are the time pressures on each party? How quickly must the other person act? If the buyer is in no rush, then the seller has a more difficult task making a deal than if there is truly great pressure on the buyer to buy. The author once sold a difficult house in Boulder, Colorado, to a man who had just 2 hours to buy a house before his flight back to New York departed. He could not go home without a place for his in-transit furniture. He had placed himself in a most disadvantageous bargaining position. Time management is essential to good negotiating. Give yourself as much time as possible; sound deals take time to negotiate.[9]

Alternatives   What alternatives are available to each party? Must the buyer buy from you, or do you have real competition? Must you sell to this one prospect, or are there other options?

One principle of good business is to develop and maintain as many options as possible. Without options, you are at the mercy of the other party. That is why professional purchasing agents seek multiple sources of supply. No one seller has control over them.

When selling a business, never let a potential buyer know that she or he is

Professional purchasing agents use multiple sources of supply when ordering stock for their organizations. It's good business to develop and maintain as many options as possible.

the only person interested in the company. The astute owner projects to the potential buyer that several other options are being considered.

Authority Who makes the final decision? Often the other party takes great care to disguise the true authority. Most negotiating experts recommend that you never let the other party know you will make the final decision. "I'll have to clear this with the committee." Thus the negotiator can play "good guy—bad guy": "I like your deal. I think you people are great, but you know how bosses are. I'll have to get an OK on this." Guess what? The negotiator will come back with some additional demands.[10]

On the other hand, another school of negotiating says that you should never try to negotiate with anyone who does not have the power to make the deal. You're wasting your time and encouraging the nibbling tactics described in the previous paragraph. Consequently, quite a battle can rage between the parties over who can or will make the decision. Sales reps gain protection if management denies them any leeway to bargain. All buyer demands must be approved by higher authority. The rep cannot be portrayed as the bad guy. "Hey, I'd like to give you a lower price. Believe me. I have to live with you. But the boss is the boss. Only he can change a price." Make the boss the bad guy.

Desperation How badly does the other party need this deal? People often get into such desperate straits that they lose all bargaining power. They must accept whatever is offered. Necessity never drove a hard bargain.

Allies It is not unusual in selling situations to have people on the other side of the table who support your proposition. They want it. They will help you sell if you allow them to do so.

Conversely, who on the other side is your foe? Who is against you and will try to stop your deal? Perhaps there is some way to eliminate such foes from the decision or otherwise minimize their impact on the sale.

Disguising the Situation

Naturally, clever negotiators disguise their true situation. The buyer may need to buy your product immediately, but will act as if there is no time pressure, that many alternatives exist. Sometimes people go to great lengths to disguise their true situation. The seller of a near-bankrupt business will do almost anything to avoid tipping off a potential buyer to the true financial health of the business.

Motives Do not jump to the conclusion that price is always the major bargaining issue. It isn't. Often the buyer wants service, warranties, and/or delivery instead. Too many sales reps automatically think the hesitant buyer is asking for a lower price. Consequently, the rep must probe for the prospect buying motives.

BASIC TACTICS

There are hundreds of various negotiating tactics which may help you in any situation.[11, 12] However, a few of the more useful ones will be discussed here.[13]

The Setting

Where should negotiations take place? Your place or mine? Notice how often in international political negotiations the participants choose a neutral bargaining site—Vienna, Zurich, Geneva.

Jerry Murphy, CEO of Early California, tells students that he tries to meet the owner of a business he wants to buy at some coffeeshop that has paper placemats on which he can put together a deal. "There's just something about figuring a deal on a placemat that appeals to people."

Stage management plays an important role in negotiations. Many small business owners have felt at a disadvantage in negotiations when overwhelmed by the buyer's posh executive suites. On the other hand, some people want to project an image of poverty, so they set the stage accordingly.

Negotiation is an art. Negotiating tools and tactics that can help influence the deal include setting, time, asking the right questions and listening carefully, patience, bluffing, stalling, and talking. How might the setting influence this negotiation?

It's difficult to convince anyone that you are strapped for funds after you arrive in a Roll Royce.

Cast of Characters

Who do you want to be present at the negotiations? Sometimes a sales rep gains leverage if the company president, or some other executive, joins the negotiations. Who do you want present for the other side? If you have inside support, try to have it included in the meeting.

Avoid Personalities[14]

Never, but never, get personal with the other party. Never say, "You are being ridiculous." "Your price is too low." Take the personal pronouns out of your speech patterns. Say instead, "That price is too low." Don't call someone's statement "ridiculous." It's usually an affront.

Keep negotiations focused strictly on the issues; separate the person from the issues. Once a negotiation starts involving personalities, it's likely to blow up.

Ask Questions

As has been stressed throughout this book, astute questioning is by far the best tactic for learning what we need to know about the other party as well as leading them to our way of thinking.

Listening

It is pointless to question if you don't listen to the answers. Yet, that is precisely what many people do. Careful listening is a valuable negotiating tactic, because most people reveal their true feelings in some way by what they say or how they say it. The exact wordings of statements are informative.

When people are trying to deceive you they often still try to make statements that are technically true. Should you challenge the statement, they will carefully prove that they told the strict truth even though the result of the statement was misleading.

Other times it is not what a person says but what he or she does *not* say that is most informative. Always search for what is not being said that should be coming into the conversation.

Patience

If you hurry, you'll not likely make a good deal. Often the more patient person prevails. Moreover, in cross-cultural negotiating, impatience is perhaps our national Achilles heel. Americans are so driven by a desire for speed that they find it difficult to settle down to serious negotiations.

One entrepreneur related how he withdrew from a deal in which he and a partner were negotiating to buy a bank. The parties were $500,000 apart and had spent an hour talking about it. His partner then stood up to proclaim, "Gentlemen, gentlemen, why are we sitting here haggling like fishmongers over a paltry five hundred thousand when we could be on the street making millions." The entrepreneur then rose and said, "Count me out of the deal. I am not the least bit interested in being in business with anyone who won't sit here and talk awhile about five hundred thousand dollars." (The grandiose person who was too proud to talk about $500,000 soon went bankrupt. The referree in bankruptcy discovered that he had paid far too much for every asset he owned, and this was the basic reason he went broke.) You must be willing to sit, talk, and wait to be a good negotiator.

The Door Knob

Your best negotiating tool is the knob on the door. Use it. Often, negotiations are broken off several times before a deal is struck. You'll probably eventually get the deal you want just as you are about to slam your car door. Until the other party really believes the deal is about to drive off, the concessions sought won't be granted.

One person negotiating the purchase of a radio station in Montana five times walked out of the room and returned to Denver because the two parties had seemingly reached an impasse—the seller would not budge from some condition that was totally unacceptable to the buyer. Each time, after a month or so, the seller would call the buyer, reopening negotiations. Finally, the station was sold.

Narrow the Field

Don't waste time trying to talk about dozens of different points. You must narrow the discussion down to those important factors in dispute. Try to get the minor points all settled and behind you so you can focus on critical issues.

Bait Your Hook

The prospect just won't make the deal. You wonder why. The answer is: You probably failed to bait your hook. You haven't provided a forceful reason for immediate action. Rewards! There must be some reward for acting now. If the other side isn't buying, it means one thing—they feel that they will not gain in this transaction.

Set Up Straw Men or The Red Herring

Often negotiators insert weak or false conditions into negotiations. They don't expect to have these conditions met. However, they do expect to use those conditions as a means of extracting concessions. "I'll give up this, if you'll forget about that!" People seldom give up anything that they aren't willing to relinquish.

Nose in the Tent or Foot in Door

In industrial selling, the sales rep may just want to get started with a firm, to get on their approved list of vendors. To do so, the rep bargains to be given a trial order. "Just try us. Give us a chance to show you what we can do for you." The rep makes them an offer they can't refuse at a low level of risk for both parties. High risk levels block many deals.

Raise the Stakes

This tactic is sometimes better known as "Buy the Pot." Some firms are able to make a critical deal because of their financial strength. They can finance the transaction or otherwise sweeten the deal in a way that competitors cannot match. Often, extended terms or generous return privileges help make the deal. Bonding requirements often remove from the playing field smaller competitors who are unable to furnish a bond.

Bluffing

Bluffing is not an unknown tactic at the bargaining table. A person may say that he or she will do something if something else happens when that person has no intention of doing it. However, a strong word of caution. Be careful! Be fully prepared to perform if your bluff is called, as it may be. Life is not a game of poker in which your losses are limited to the money you've put into the pot. If you try to bluff your employer that you will accept a job offer from another company if certain conditions are not met, be prepared to move. Your bluff may be called. Bosses don't like to be confronted with such threats.

In negotiations, if you bluff and then do not carry through on your threat when your bluff is called, you lose much credibility. How can the other person believe anything you say afterward? "Say what you mean and mean what you say" has much virtue in business.

However, there are times when a bluff is a sound, low-risk tactic. You're trying to sell your car. A hesitant buyer is trying to get you to lower your price. You don't want to lower the price; you really mean what you say when you tell the person, "Two thousand dollars is as low as I can go. That's it!" He paws the ground, and you realize that he really wants the car. If not, he would leave. So you bluff, "If I can't get $2,000 for it, I'm going to keep it. It's worth that much to me." On the contrary, you really want to get rid of the car, but you've got to do something to move this prospect to action.[15]

On the other side of the deal, if the hesitant prospect was a tough negotiator, he would have made up his mind how much money you would likely accept and lay that amount in cash in front of you. "Here's the $1,800 that I have. That's it. If you want it, let's deal. If not, I'll keep looking." Now that might be a bluff. He might have some more money tucked away just in case, but he knows how to bait the hook.

Keep Talking

As long as two parties are talking, there is a chance for making a deal. When they stop talking, the negotiations may be over. However, there is a counter-tactic—the door knob which was previously discussed.

The virtue of talking is that if it is done wisely the other party's real motives and objections may surface and be resolved. In other instances, some people just weary of the negotiations and give up. There is a theory that a good negotiator should be in excellent physical condition because fatigue alone can cause a person to weaken his or her resolve.

Stall

If you sense that the other party has great need for haste in completing the deal, stalling may bring forth some concessions. In other situations, you may lose bargaining strength as time passes. Things change, and they may change for the better or worse, depending upon which side of the deal you are on. Strangely, some deals drag on for years as both sides think they are gaining strength as time passes.

Make the Future Look More Expensive

One of the best ways to get the other party to make a deal is to convince them that the costs are going to go up. Nothing is to be gained by waiting, and much is to be lost.

STRATEGIES

Most sellers adopt a basic bargaining strategy that they will *not* bargain. One price, that's it! Our business system is strongly based on the one-price policy. It is the only way to deal in a mass distributive society. Can you imagine the chaos if we were to bargain for our groceries as they do in many foreign marketplaces? It takes too much time to bargain with each buyer. Besides how would you train scanner operators?[16]

In reality, however, there is a lot more bargaining going on than most people realize. Once skillful professional buyers realize that a seller is firm on price and will not negotiate it, attention shifts to other aspects of the sale.[17]

They will negotiate the terms of sale. There is an old saying in negotiation, "I'll let you name the price, if you'll let me set the terms." You don't believe that? OK. How much do you want for your pencil? A million dollars? OK, it's a deal. I'll pay you in the year 3000. Price means nothing in a deal if it is not tied to the other terms of contract.

When skillful negotiators sense that the other party is adamant about one factor, they give that away and then take it back elsewhere.

The classic case is in the sale of a business: The owner believes that the business is worth a million dollars and will not listen to any thought to the contrary. The adept buyer, sensing this, adopts the strategy, "OK, now let's see what looks like a million dollars to this guy." So all sorts of different types of paper, besides greenbacks, are discussed. The seller may end up taking a note on the business for a million to be paid out of earnings—an earnout. But he can brag to everyone that he is a millionaire. There is a lot of ego involved in all negotiations. Remember win-win!

On the other side, some buyers adopt the strategy of telling you what they will pay for the item. Either you agree or forget it. "It's my way or the highway!" Many large corporations use this strategy in dealing with small concerns. Such insolence is difficult to counter by the seller with little power. Sometimes the seller uses the nose-in-the-tent tactic, accepting that price and then finding ways to increase it along the way.

Such tactics are frequently used by defense contractors who are forced to give lower-than-cost bids to get a contract; they first get the contract, then find ways of getting relief from it—extras, overruns, accelerations, changes in specifications, etc.

SUMMARY

Negotiating skills are important to develop not only for your success in business but for success in life as well. Sound negotiating starts with knowing what you want and must have from the deal as well as what you don't need. Similarly, you need the same information about the other party. Knowledge, power, and time are keys to successful bargaining. Know the costs, time pressures, options, and motives of the parties involved.

Although sellers try to maintain a one-price policy and not negotiate price, there may still be considerable negotiating about terms of sale.

Negotiating is essentially a tactical art of finding a way that both parties can get what they want from the transaction.

DISCUSSION QUESTIONS

1 How can both parties to a deal be winners? Doesn't one or the other get the better deal?

2 In what way does time affect negotiations?

3 Why do sellers try so hard to maintain a no-negotiations policy ("these are our prices and terms")?

4 As a seller, what options do you have when a buyer refuses to make a deal with you?

5 It is understandable how a seller could be desperate to sell, but why would a buyer be desperate?

6 How can you control the setting for the negotiation?

7 You and the other party have a mutual dislike for each other. How could you handle that situation in a deal?

8 One sales rep said, "If I make more than 50 percent of my deals, I worry." Why worry?

9 Why would you not want a buyer to know that you, the sales rep, have the power to lower price up to 8 percent?

10 What are some of the ways in which you can make the future look more expensive than the present?

REFERENCES

1 Carole King, "Negotiating Skills Agents Need Now," *National Underwriter (Life/Health/Financial Services),* June 11, 1990, pp. 7, 10, advises that the agent must clearly identify the clients' needs and find a mechanism that will both satisfy those needs and meet the agents' goals.

2 Louis J. De Rose, "Negotiating Value," *Sales & Marketing Management,* October 1990, pp. 108–109, discusses that the negotiation process requires (1) discussion in order to gain an understanding of respective positions, (2) analysis to break down problems into component elements so they can be presented in terms more favorable to the seller, and (3) bargaining in order to exchange one objective, issue, or negotiating point for another.

3 Barbara C. Perdue, "The Selling Firm's Negotiation Team in Rebuys of Component Parts," *Journal of Personal Selling & Sales Management,* November 1988, pp. 1–10, recommends that the selling team also be the negotiating team.

4 Roger Dawson, *The Secrets of Power Negotiating,* Nightingale-Conant Corporation, Chicago, 1987, is an audio-cassette program that stresses win-win negotiating.

5 D. Forbes Ley, "What's in It for Me?" *Insurance Sales,* February 1988, pp. 21–22, advises that the agent must find an emotional desire for any satisfaction that may be related to the product, then build up the desire for that emotional satisfaction to the point that the prospect is willing to buy the product immediately.

6 Russell H. Granger, "The Account That Almost Was," *Rough Notes,* December 1988, pp. 31–32, describes negotiation as the process of guiding a discussion of differing wants and needs toward a mutually rewarding agreement.

7 Robert M. Benedict, "Back-Door Selling," *Purchasing World,* September 1989, pp. 44–46, describes backdoor selling as a series of probing questions that salespeople are meticulously taught to ask prior to the formal negotiation.

8 John Lidstone, "Negotiation or Selling? Their Roles in Sales Strategy," *Journal of Sales Management,* vol. 3, no. 3, 1986, pp. 8–18, discusses the fact that negotiating parties are motivated by the effect of the outcome on the profitability or reduction in costs to both sides.

9 Joanna Kozubska, "The Role of Negotiation in the Selling of Industrial Products," *Journal of Sales Management*, vol. 3, no. 3 1986, pp. 3–7, discusses the three primary variables of negotiation: (1) power, (2) time, and (3) information.

10 Sheril Arndt, "The Essential Art of Negotiating," *National Underwriter (Life/Health/Financial Services)*, November 20, 1989, pp. 7–8, suggests striving to reach an agreement on easier issues first, then dealing with controversial issues later.

11 Ray J. Stone, "Negotiating Tactics: Negotiating in the Philippines," *Practicing Manager (Australia)*, Winter 1990, pp. 25–27, advises that it is vital to plan and practice countertactics ahead of time to become an effective negotiator, and that when negotiating with individuals from another culture it is important to recognize the cultural basis for some of their tactics.

12 For a more detailed treatment of tactics see Richard H. Buskirk, *Frontal Attack, Divide & Conquer, The Fait Accompli & 118 Other Tactics Managers Must Know*, John Wiley & Sons, Inc., New York, 1989.

13 Mark H. McCormack, *The Terrible Truth about Lawyers*, William Morrow and Company, Inc., New York, 1987, furnishes insights into some problems encountered with lawyers in negotiations.

14 Russell H. Mouritsen, "Client Involvement through Negotiation: A Key to Success," *American Salesman*, May 1987, pp. 16–18, discusses 10 suggestions for involving the prospect in cooperative negotiation: (1) Separate people from the problem at hand. (2) Focus on interests and not on positions. (3) Establish agreeable objectives. (4) Create options for mutual gain. (5) Move from one plateau to another in negotiations. (6) Start by seeking areas that are of mutual interest. (7) Make sure that both sides participate equally. (8) Handle disagreements on issues with care and tact. (9) Use lateral thinking skills. (10) Be patient and do not move to the bottom line too quickly.

15 Homer B. Smith, "How to Concede—Strategically," *Sales & Marketing Management*, May 1988, pp. 79–80, discusses many concession strategies salespeople can employ: (1) Start negotiations with your highest expectations. (2) Avoid making the first major concession. (3) Ensure that the customer understands the value of a given concession. (4) Make concessions in small amounts. (5) Be willing to admit mistakes and make corrections. (6) Be prepared to withdraw concessions made before the final sales agreement. (7) Avoid jumping the let's-split-the-difference ploy. (8) Be careful not to advertise a willingness to make concessions.

16 Michael Lewis, *Liar's Poker*, W. W. Norton & Co., New York, 1989, presents an excellent overall view of how price is truly negotiable by the salesperson. The writer was a bond trader for a famous brokerage house.

17 Thomas C. Keiser, "Negotiating with a Customer You Can't Afford to Lose," *Harvard Business Review*, November/December 1988, pp. 30–34, suggests the best approach for dealing with aggressive but important customers involves encouraging a joint search for inventive solutions without resorting to fighting or allowing the customer to take advantage.

CASE 13–1: Jayhawk Popcorn Company—Some Negotiating Incidents

Incident No. 1   As a sales rep for the Jayhawk Popcorn Company selling to supermarket chains, you have the power to lower price from the posted list price no more than 1.5 percent. Half of any price reduction is taken from your commission of 3 percent of sales. Or you have the power to give free goods up to 5 percent of the order: if the account buys 10,000 pounds, you can give them 500 more pounds free. Half of the cost of the free goods is taken from your commissions. You can give a price reduction or you can give free goods, not both.

A particularly aggressive buyer for a large regional chain of super stores is buying 100,000 pounds of popcorn split between the 2- and 5-pound sacks, but she won't pay list price. You give her the choice of which discount she would prefer. She says, "I'll take both of them."

You reply, "I'm sorry. I failed to make it clear. We offer one or the other, not both."

The buyer retorts, "I am sorry that *I* did not make myself clear. It is both or forget it."

1 What do you say next?

Incident No. 2   You're still selling popcorn. A buyer wants to purchase 200 or 300 thousand pounds of popcorn (the quantity has yet to be agreed upon) packaged in sacks marked with the store's name. The buyer says, "If you can give us our own sacks at the same price, I'll give you the purchase order right now."

You know that you can accept that offer. No problem!

2 Exactly what do you say?

Incident No. 3   You're still peddling popcorn! A buyer wants to nail down a large amount of your popcorn at the present price because of impending price increases. The weather in the Corn Belt was not everything it should have been. Moreover, the consumption of popcorn is increasing rapidly because of microwave packaging. However, the buyer says, "We can't take delivery for all of it right now. We haven't the space. I want the order split into monthly shipments for the next year. We will pay you for each shipment 10 days after the end of the month in which the corn is shipped."

This poses some problems for you because Jayhawk Popcorn has not given you the power to make such deals. It also poses some financial and storage problems for Jayhawk.

3 Exactly what do you say?

Incident No. 4   More popcorn! A buyer says, "Your price is too high. Corn is going down 3 cents this next week, you just watch. If you want an order now, drop the price 3 cents and we do business."

You know that the facts do not support the buyer's assertion. Prices are not going to go down but, to the contrary, might increase.

4 Exactly what do you say or do?

Incident No. 5   Corn again! There is a penny per pound difference between what a buyer is offering to pay for 1 million pounds of your corn and what you are asking for it. You are thinking about splitting the difference and calling it a good day, but you wonder whether you should spend some effort to try to salvage that money. Moreover, you are afraid to be the first one to offer to split the difference. What if the buyer doesn't go for it?

5 Exactly what do you say and/or do?

CASE 13–2: Troy—Clearance Policy

Troy, an upscale women's apparel store catering to "mature" wealthy women in Palm Desert, California, opened the doors to its new costly store in late 1990. Quickly, it became apparent that customers did not think some of the garments were worth the posted prices.

As a matter of policy, management did not want goods to hang on the racks for long. It wanted to cultivate an image that its garments moved out fast. "Better buy now, it won't be here for long." What to do with the markdowns headed the agenda at the next management meeting.

Four different proposals were put forth regarding how to handle the problem. The manager of the sales floor wanted to be given the power to let the "wardrobe consultants" lower the prices on garments that had been tagged for markdowns as needed when they had a client showing interest in the item. Called an open-price policy, this gives the salespeople some power and helps them solidify their relationships with clients. Since the salespeople were paid a commission of 20 percent of the gross margin realized on a ticket, they would have little reason to cut prices unless it were really necessary.

The sales manager wanted an automatic markdown policy. Goods would be marked down 10 percent each week until sold.

The merchandise manager wanted to put all goods to be marked down in a separate little area in the store with items added to the selection each morning.

The owner of the store wanted to maintain prices, which generally carried an initial markup of 70 percent, and have a clearance sale at the end of each season.

1 Evaluate the pros and cons of each alternative.
2 What would you recommend and why?

CHAPTER FOURTEEN

THE CLOSE

CHAPTER FOURTEEN

THE CLOSE

Never mistake motion for action.
Ernest Hemingway

After studying the material in this chapter you should:

☐ Understand the importance of closing and recognize signals indicating that it's time to close the sale

☐ Know the various closing techniques available to you, particularly the basic assumptive close

☐ Understand that fear of failure is often the force inhibiting the salesperson from closing

PROFILE OF A SALESPERSON

EXTRAORDINAIRE

Nikki Wichert

Long Beach, Calif.

Nikki Wichert became a real estate agent after her family had grown and flown the nest. She is employed by Century 21, for whom she carefully works her "farm" (or territory).

When asked how large her farm was, she replied, "It contains 723 houses and has 14 apartment buildings. However, I only have to send out 681 direct-mail pieces to cover the area because I don't want to send direct-mail pieces to other realtors, and the area is a favorite residential place for them." She obviously knows her farm inside and out. Such knowledge is not acquired by sitting around idly but by hard work—going from door to door and meeting everyone in her territory—the farm.

When asked how often she uses direct mailings, Nikki replied, "In the last 6 months, I've sent out three direct mailings. I don't send them out unless I have something to say about the neighborhood that I know they will be interested in learning. I try to tell them what is going on in the neighborhood, who is moving in and who is leaving. This past week, I've gotten three good listings from the last mailing, one of which is from a person who owns property in another area that I cannot service. I have arranged to have the Century 21 agency nearest to the property sell it for her. Since the woman is also planning to sell her home in my farm, I think she will list with me because of the excellent service I've given her on her other property."

Asked why she was successful, her replies were quick in coming as well as clear and concise. "Because I work like hell. I care about people. And I don't take on a property without doing my very best for it. I don't really consider myself a saleswoman. I prefer to think of myself as a people-helper. I am also great at taking care of all the little details."

She brought up a very important aspect of selling when she said, "You know, oftentimes I am entrusted with hundreds of thousands of dollars of other people's property. I feel very responsible for it. So I feel like I have to be at it all the time to take care of this responsibility."

She lamented that in the past 2 years she hasn't been making as many personal calls as she would have liked. "I really like to greet all the new people who move into the area and give them a neighborhood service directory so that they'll know all the things they need to know about: when the trash is picked up and where the library is and where the best stores are. I just try to help them. There's so much that people need to know when they move into a new house. I simply try to help them the best I can."

That's what we mean when we say that you should try to be of service to your customers.

"Closing should be the easiest, most natural step in selling," stated a highly successful industrial sales rep. "After all, the prospect needs your proposition, can afford to pay for it, and you've done a good job presenting it. So what's left to do? Close the sale. Start writing the order."[1]

It seems so easy. Evidently it isn't. Far too many salespeople have trouble closing the sale. A good salesperson is always a good closer, and a poor closer is always a poor salesperson. Everything that has gone before—prospecting, preapproach, approach, presentation, handling objections—all the preparation and effort have been focused on this objective. The sales rep who cannot close is like the runner who trains faithfully all season, leads the field in the big race until 10 yards from the tape, and then falls down.

Young or unsuccessful salespeople are often heard to say, "I am all right until I start to close. Then I just don't seem able to put it over, like a football team that can make its first downs in the middle of the field but lacks the punch to go the last 10 yards for a touchdown. I'm a good salesperson but a poor closer." There may be *some* truth in this analysis of the difficulty, but more often than not the trouble lies farther back in the sale. The person who is a really good salesperson all the way through the interview will not experience *chronic* difficulty in completing the sale.*

It should not be inferred that every presentation should result in a sale. No one ever made such a record. The best salespeople can sell only a fraction of the prospects called upon. But there is a tremendous difference between a baseball player who hits .250 and one who hits .350. The same is true of salespeople.

Using a golf analogy, the closing effort is like the golfer's effort to hole out. All that has gone before, no matter how brilliantly executed, avails nothing if that final putt refuses to drop. The golfing adage "If you can't putt, you can't win" can be matched by the selling slogan "If you can't close, you can't sell."

People who are uncertain of their closing abilities are handicapped throughout the presentation, for they cannot help being worried about the impending obstacle with which they have so much difficulty. Some people actually develop a fear of closing which eventually drives them out of selling.

---

*This calls to mind the rookie who reported to the sales manager, "I could lead 'em right up to the watering trough, but I couldn't make 'em drink." The boss bellowed: "Whoever said you had to make 'em *drink*? It's your job to make 'em *thirsty*."

This usually comes about through a combination of ignorance of closing techniques and outright bashfulness about asking for the order. Many sales have been made simply because the salesperson had the fortitude to ask for the order.[2]

The consultative salesperson sees the closing stage of the sale as one of ascertaining or gaining the prospect's commitment to the proposition.[3] The consultant asks many of the same questions used by other salespeople: When do you need delivery? Where do you want it shipped? Will a dozen be enough? When can I get your purchase order on this?

REASONS FOR FAILURE TO CLOSE

The difficulty of closing has perplexed sales managers for years. Only recently have we begun to understand the mental barriers that block closing efforts.

Fear of Failure[4]

First is the fear of failure. Most of us are so psychologically programmed toward success as the only worthy goal that the mere thought of failure frightens us into a semiparalytic state in which we are afraid to *ask* for the order or final decision for fear of being refused. We seem to think that so long as the prospect is not asked for the order we have avoided failure even though no sale transpires. We just do not like to hear such awful words as "No," "Not interested," "Sorry, I don't want it." These terms bruise our egos, and that hurts us. This is much the same fear that keeps the man from asking that certain woman for a date even though he is fairly sure she is interested; he is afraid that she just might say "no." But no ask—no date. (The consultative salesperson avoids much of this fear by thinking of this phase of the sale as merely the commitment stage of the interview, not as the monumental climax of an epic struggle.)

Guilt

Some people fail to close because of guilt. They are ashamed of their profession. After much research the Life Institute determined the biggest single cause for failure of new life insurance agents is that they feel guilty about their work. They feel as if they are intruders begging for a living instead of people helping other people solve serious problems. This guilt usually exists in those who do not yet fully understand the proposition they are selling and what benefits it can bring the prospect. Life insurance agents who have delivered many big checks to beneficiaries entertain no feelings of guilt as they see how much good in time of need is accomplished by the insurance policies they sold. Such agents sincerely believe that they may be doing prospects a real favor by being pretty insistent.

If you aren't proud of what you are doing, then you would be better off if you didn't do it. It is important that salespeople understand their purpose in the scheme of things, their importance in our socioeconomic system.

Imperception of Need

Some people fail to close because they feel little need to do so; they think the prospect will automatically buy at the end of the presentation. Of course, some prospects do so, but it has been proved that a larger percentage of prospects will buy if a good close is used than if it isn't. They need a push to get them to act. Natural inertia stops many purchases.

Ineptness

Inept salespeople get so bogged down meeting objections that the thought of trying to close doesn't enter their minds. They are fighting for their lives; they are confused; they have lost control of the sale. The close should be so natural that the salesperson can swing into it automatically.

Cultural Taboos

Our environment teaches us a host of cultural attitudes and behavior patterns. Many people are raised in the tradition that there is something a bit impolite, improper, about asking another person for money or to do something for you. Closing means asking for the order, and this can run afoul of cultural taboos in some circles.

(Again, the consultative sales approach somewhat avoids this cultural barrier because the action of determining someone's commitment to a proposition is acceptable to most people.[5])

BASIC CLOSING TACTICS

Aside from the actual closing techniques discussed in detail later in the chapter, there are certain overall tactics which are helpful in closing a sale. These apply to all sales, whereas a given closing technique has application to certain situations.

Avoid the Interrupting Third Party

It is usually difficult to close a sale when a third party has intruded. The sales rep has succeeded in presenting the proposition so that the prospect is really convinced, only the formalities of closing being left, when a third party drops in. This party is not familiar with the proposition, has no appreciation of its merits, and tends to throw cold water on the whole scheme if the prospect asks him or her for an opinion. For this reason the sales rep should try to close without allowing interruptions to occur. One salesperson tells of a sale that she lost because she forgot to bring a blank contract with her; so, as the buyer was going that way, he suggested that they drop in together at the salesperson's office and close the deal. On the way over a friend joined them and so chilled the atmosphere that the prospective buyer decided not to sign the contract at all. It may be argued that this smacks of so-called "high-pressure" selling and that if a person is thoroughly sold, it will not be so easy to change his or her mind. But it must be remembered that in buying something new, the balance in the buyer's mind is very delicate and has perhaps been turned so slightly in favor of the proposition that it requires little to tip the scales the other way. This may be true, even though the proposition is a meritorious one, for it may require actual trial by the buyer to throw the balance heavily in its favor.

For this reason, when ready to close the sale, many salespeople endeavor to get the prospect isolated in some special office or in a location where they will not be bothered by outsiders. Ever notice the closing booths in automobile dealerships? Many sales are closed at private dinners or clubs where the salesperson has arranged for privacy.

Simplify the Contract

If the seller uses an individual contract form, it should be simple and short. The buyer has not time to puzzle out a complicated legal document and search for a suspected "joker" concealed in the small print. The long order

Privacy helps in most closings. Salespeople often try to isolate the prospect in a private office to avoid interruptions and outside distractions.

blank, which is in effect a contract, tends to frighten the average buyer unless she or he has had dealings with the selling firm.

Although it is undoubtedly wise to simplify the contract, it should not be abandoned altogether. Indeed, many salespeople have far less trouble with returned goods or with failure on the buyer's part to live up to agreements if they go over the provisions of the contract and make certain that they are understood fully. The seriousness of the contract is thus impressed on the buyer, with the happy result that the goods stay sold. If buyers are made to feel that they are *expected* to live up to the contract, they are more likely to do so.

If the buyer hesitates at the actual act of signing, the sales rep should point out that the contract is as binding on the seller as on the buyer. Show the clauses which require the seller to deliver, on or before a certain date, goods of stipulated quality and amount, etc. Sometimes a guarantee is included on the order blank, thus providing a talking point and at the same time furnishing an excuse to bring out the order book or blank.

And, speaking of the order book, it is a good idea to bring it into view early in the interview, to accustom the prospect to seeing it, to convey by suggestion the idea that it is going to be used soon. Various devices are tried to make this act of bringing out the order book less noticeable, but experienced salespeople scorn these and bring it out with no comment or excuse.

The contract or order form may be designed so that one or two specifications are left blank, and the prospect may be asked to fill them in. The salesperson for an air conditioner discusses rather briefly the downpayment and monthly installments, at which point he hands the prospect the order blank and pen, saying, "Just fill in whatever figures would be most convenient to you. You know better than I do what you can do." In this fashion you can get the order blank and pen into your prospect's hands. The proverbial dotted line is located just below the line that the prospect is asked to fill in.

When calling on a new prospect, salespeople like to use an order book in which many orders have been written. The act of thumbing through the carbons of these orders while turning to the right page reassures the buyer. Since many are buying, it must be a good proposition. It appeals to an imitative tendency, also. With old customers it is safe to break in a new book because they know that it is doubtless because of good business and not poor business that the new book is used.

Attitude in Closing

As the sale approaches its close, you are likely to feel an increase in nervous tension. This is natural, yet you should be careful not to reveal it. In most cases—especially when selling an experienced buyer—it is better to maintain a calm and casual attitude, for the appearance of excitement betrays the novice. The buyer may think, "Evidently this salesperson doesn't make many sales, he's so excited about making this one. If he doesn't make many sales there must be a reason. Probably I have overlooked something and had better hold off a bit and check up."

The experienced salesperson approaches the close without fear and maintains an attitude that conveys the impression that getting the order is all in the day's work, a routine matter. Calm assurance leads the buyer to conclude that taking orders is the usual thing—that there is nothing to fear. Say, "If you will just OK it here," handing the order to the buyer, rather than, "Sign on the dotted line." Avoid the word "sign"; say "write" or some more casual-sounding word.

And don't wisecrack when you start to close, as "Now we're coming into the home stretch. Hope I don't have to go to the whip." Spending money is too serious a matter to be treated lightly.

Needless to say, you should avoid such acts as getting out your pen with a big flourish, mopping your brow, wetting your lips, taking a deep breath before the plunge, suddenly whipping out the order blank or contract, putting away your visual aids, or clearing your throat. These things all call the prospect's attention to the fact that you are about to deliver the lethal wallop. You should avoid appearing as if you think you are a victor and the buyer is the vanquished.

This poise comes with experience, but its growth can be stimulated by a conscious effort to induce a feeling of self-confidence. This is accomplished by reminding yourself: "I know this prospect needs my proposition because my preapproach and my interview questions clearly indicate it. I know that my proposition will satisfy that need and make the prospect happier. I have made my presentation complete, clear, and have taken care of competition. I think she has confidence in my proposition and in me. She has made all seven decisions except the final one. It is logical and natural that she should be ready to make that commitment now."

The Right Time to Close

Much has been written about the "psychological moment," when the minds of prospect and sales rep are in perfect accord. It is often assumed that at some moment the two minds are attuned and that if the salesperson does not close the sale at this particular moment, the chance of doing so is forever lost. It is apparent, however, that in most sales there is more than one time when the sale can be closed and, furthermore, this time may be longer than is implied by the word "moment." A sales rep may bring the prospect to the commitment stage and, not realizing it, continue to talk too long while the prospect loses interest. But even under these conditions the sale may not be lost, for you may warm up the prospect once more and close the sale.

In the average sale, however, there is a rising tide of interest which can be detected by the seller who is alert and trained to feel the attitude of others. Any experienced salesperson can tell the signs by which to judge, although some say that they do not know precisely how they tell—they just *feel* it through a kind of sixth sense.

Closing Signals

Some closing signs are voluntary and some are involuntary. If the prospect asks, "How soon could you ship it?" this is a *voluntary* sign of real interest. It signals that it is time to close without going into more detail, even though you may not be finished with your presentation.[6]

Other comments or questions by the prospect help you to know when to close. It has been said that, when the prospect asks the price, she is keenly interested, and that when she inquires about terms, she is practically sold. These are voluntary signs. But it is the *involuntary* sign which you must learn to read.

The attention given by the prospect is one indication. As a meager interest is fanned to the flame of desire by the salesperson's presentation, the air of indifference drops away and the prospect's whole attitude betrays an interest. He leans forward in his chair; his eye indicates a less skeptical or hostile frame of mind. Some salespeople say that they always watch the prospect's hands, for they open and close with his mind. So long as he is unconvinced and unwilling to buy, he keeps his mind and hands closed; but when his mind opens and his mental tension relaxes, his hands relax likewise. The muscles around the corners of the mouth and eyes may also betray the same change in mental attitude. Hunched shoulders may be lowered as the buyer relaxes. Perhaps the prospect rubs his chin or pulls at his ear or scratches his head; he may re-examine the product or sample or contract. Any one of these gestures may reveal an "almost persuaded" attitude.

Possibly the best way to learn the prospect's frame of mind is to ask certain commitment questions designed to disclose it. Suppose you are trying to sell advertising space for *Los Angeles* magazine to the owner of a menswear store which does $5,000,000 a year in sales volume from a Westwood location. To learn the merchant's frame of mind you might ask such questions as: "What particularly new and striking item would you feature in an ad?" "Who would do your artwork?" "The deadline for the next issue is the 26th. Can we get your artwork by then?" The replies to such questions will reveal the state of the prospect's mind. Similar questions may be formulated to meet any situation and are recommended for use by those seeking to avoid the embarrassment which follows an attempt to close too early.

One young sales rep selling refrigerators was so imbued with knowledge of his product and his various presentation techniques that he lost a sale. A young man entered the store with two friends to buy his wife a refrigerator as an anniversary present (a highly questionable decision). After the rep had talked a few minutes, one of the friends said, "Kenny, that box is just right for you." The other agreed and Kenny nodded. And our idiot went right on talking. Several other very forceful closing signs were given, and still the salesperson (?) talked on. He was talking as the trio departed to buy elsewhere.

Don't get so tied up in what you are saying that you don't pay attention to the prospect's signals. By word, facial expression, and body language the prospect tells you what he or she is thinking. You have to learn how to translate the messages. It's really not difficult. Much of it is common sense. You can tell if someone is eager to buy or is resisting you by his or her behavior.

Prospect's "No" Does Not End the Interview[7]

Many people fear that if they attempt to close too soon, they will ruin their chances for making the sale. This trying to close before the prospect is ready may not be a serious blunder.

One of the most successful salespeople on the Pacific Coast makes the statement that only in about 1 sale out of 10 has he been able to close on the first attempt. He expects to be turned down one, two, five, seven, or eight times before he finally makes the sale. He builds his sales talk around the expectation of being turned down, merely adds more value, and tries again to close.

He does not stop to argue the decision; he tries to *figure out which buying decision the prospect has not yet made* and proceeds, "By the way, I should have made another point clear to you," starting off on another selling point.

Some salespeople consider a no merely the buyer's opening position in the negotiation. In essence, the buyer may be thinking, "I'll say no and see what this rep will do to sweeten the deal to make me say yes."

A certain amount of imperviousness to rebuffs is beyond doubt an asset to nearly any salesperson. It may be found helpful to be hard of hearing when the prospect says no. One such sales rep was trying to sell his valves to a Chicago candy manufacturer who had used another brand for 25 years. The rep intercepted the master mechanic at lunch and informed him that he would see him at 2 o'clock that afternoon.

Shortly after 2, the master mechanic stormed into the lobby, glowering fiercely. "Let's sit down here," said Carlson, the salesman. "Do you have any leaky valves?"

"I can't buy valves," shouted the M. M. "The chief engineer buys them."

Carlson's hearing failed him. "Where do you have most trouble with leaky valves?"

"On our caramel steam kettles," the M. M. reluctantly admitted. "But *I* can't buy any valves."

By this time Carlson was demonstrating how his valve's superhard seat and disc were unblemished after smashing a steel paper clip between them. "What size valves do you use on those caramel steam kettles?" he queried.

"Three-quarter inch," answered the M. M. "But it's like I told you—I can't buy any."

At this point Carlson went stone deaf and issued this command to the baffled M. M. "You write out a requisition for one ¾-inch Hardhearted valve and go in and get an order from your purchasing agent. Then you'll see how to get rid of leaky valves. Go ahead!"

The master mechanic went in and got the order for that single trial valve.

Carlson had done in a few minutes what the distributor and his salesmen had been unable to accomplish in 25 years. His ears just automatically tuned out the word *no*.

Eventually a prospect grows weary of saying a thing over and over when it makes no impression. He concludes that the easiest way out is to buy.

TRADITIONAL CLOSING METHODS[8]

There are nine traditional tactics for facilitating the prospect's final buying decision. You may use them in combinations. You may use them as trial closes. You may work out variations of them. But you can't sell without them. While these nine methods will be discussed one at a time, here is a list of them that may help give an overall impression of the closing tools with which you can work:

- Continued affirmation
- Erection of barriers
- Assumptive close
- Closing on minor point
- Narrowing the options
- "Standing room only" close
- Special inducements
- Asking for the order
- Closing on objection

The first three methods are used throughout the interview; they are basic sales tactics and fundamental to the other six techniques, which are used mainly as closes.

Continued Affirmation—Yes, Yes, Yes!

Prospects should never be asked any question to which they can make negative replies easily. Every question should be so framed that it will be answered favorably or affirmatively. The theory underlying this practice holds that by so doing the prospects are encouraged to think positively, to give favorable answers, and that from this force of habit they will more likely answer affirmatively at the time of the close. It is also based on the belief that if prospects have been encouraged to realize that they are favorable toward the various segments of the offer, they more likely will be favorable to the whole proposition when the time comes for accepting it.

A husband and wife walk into a carpet shop looking for a floor covering for their new house. The salesperson is trying to sell them on buying an acrylic carpet rather than the wool one they had in mind. Some of the questions that the rep might be heard asking during the sale could be, "I would suspect that you are looking for a carpet that will take hard wear yet keep its fine appearance. Is that right? . . . Do you want a carpet that can be easily cleaned, even the tough Coke stains that won't come out of wool? . . . Would you like to have a carpet that would not mat down permanently in spots where furniture has been set? . . . Which of these colors do you feel is best for your decor? . . . How much carpet will you need? . . . When will you need it? . . . Which of these two patterns appeals to you most? . . . Which of these two weights do you feel would be most appropriate for you?" Notice that it would not be natural for the prospects to give a negative answer to any of these questions. The good sales rep would never ask, "Do you like this color?" A no answer is highly probable, so rephrase it. Ask, "Which of these colors appeals to you most?" Keep the entire presentation positive!

The purpose of this closing method should be plain by now. It attempts to *make the closing decision only another favorable decision out of many* made during the interview. By pursuing the method here outlined, the salesperson gently leads the buyer to the desired point without a struggle and has gained the buyer's assent to many statements that make it difficult to take a stand against the proposition. This builds up gradually to a much stronger claim than would have been admitted to at first.

Erection of Barriers

The erection of barriers throughout the presentation is closely allied with the previous technique of asking questions, except in this instance the purpose is to block the prospect from using certain reasons or factors as excuses for not buying at the close. The security sales representative who approached prospects with the question, "I am interested in talking with a business executive who has $25,000 to invest in an excellent business opportunity and who

FIGURE 14-1   The closing toolbox.

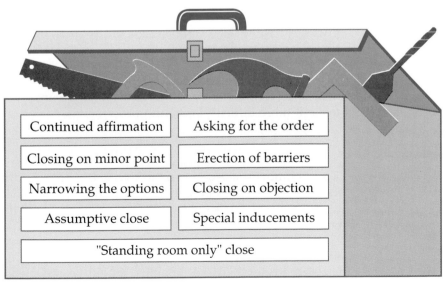

Continued affirmation	Asking for the order
Closing on minor point	Erection of barriers
Narrowing the options	Closing on objection
Assumptive close	Special inducements
"Standing room only" close	

makes decisions without asking anyone. Are you such a person?'' was erecting a barrier right at the start of the sale. To hear the proposition, the prospect had to admit to having money and not needing to consult a spouse. To lean on those lame excuses at the close could be embarrassing.

The auto salesperson tries to block the procrastinator by asking early in the sale, "If I can get you the right deal, are you prepared to act today?" The looker hedges, paws the ground, and plays with his keys, thus telling the sales rep what she wants to know.

The apparel representative could ask the dealer, "Are you open to buy if you see a new style that appeals to you?" to block the old stall, "I'm not open to buy." Even that is a poor question for it can be easily answered with a resounding "No."

Most insincere objections can be blocked early in the sale if you are sufficiently clever to perceive them soon enough. A real objection cannot be blocked so easily.

The good salesperson tries to erect a barrier for every major objection usually encountered. Perhaps he commonly meets a price objection because he is selling a premium product, so he will endeavor to get the prospect to acknowledge during the presentation that the product's features are well worth the price and that he can use those premium features. "Now, our new design has an automatic feed that gives you constant control over input quantity and quality. You would find that profitable, wouldn't you? . . . And the surprising thing about it is that we were able to do it at an amazingly small cost considering what it does for you."

Sometimes when a consumer benefit is priced well below what the buyer would expect to pay for it, the sales rep will ask the buyer what the feature would sell for. Then when the salesperson quotes a lower price, the buyer is even more eager to buy it. At other times the sales rep must structure the buyer's scale of values toward a feature by pointing out costs, or competitor's prices, or some bit of apparent logic so that the product's true value is perceived by the prospect.

Suppose the salesperson senses that the prospect is a procrastinator. She might say, "I have been told that you are a person of action, a person who makes decisions and gets into gear." Has a barrier been erected that may make it more difficult for him to procrastinate?

The Assumptive Close

The assumptive close is basic to every sale and should underlie all actions throughout the presentation, as well as at the time of closing. "The prospect is going to buy. He is going to buy. There is no doubt about it! He is going to buy. I know he is a prospect: He has money and the need. I have done an excellent job selling him. My product is the best and my company the finest. There is no reason in the world why he will not jump at this opportunity. He is going to buy." These thoughts should be reflected in your attitude and demeanor. Not that you should seem cocky or overconfident but that there should be no trace of doubt in your speech or actions that would indicate to the prospect that you feel there is a reason for not buying.

This is nothing more than the principle of positive suggestion applied to the closing of the sale. The salesperson assumes by word and act that the prospect will buy. If the prospect does not stop the salesperson, the sale is made. It might go like this:

An industrial adhesive sales rep to a purchasing agent: "Let's see, you need 1,000 gallons of No. 153 epoxy on the 15th of each month for the next year at 15 percent off our list price. Look over my write-up, and if I have it right, initial it at the bottom."

A box salesperson to a toy manufacturer: "When can we get your artwork for the box?"

Some other assumptive closes:

"Where are deliveries to be made?"

"To whom do we send the invoice?"

"Can we deliver the order Monday?"

Any fact that must be determined to make the deal can be used as the basis of an assumptive close.

Many times *action* without words serves the same purpose, such as clearing a space on the desk to fill out the order blank, getting the pen ready, or merely pulling a chair up closer to the desk.

Perhaps you can do something which the prospect must stop you from doing if he is not going to buy. "May I use your phone to see if we have the quantity you want for immediate shipment?" Unless the prospect stops you, the sale has been virtually closed.

Sometimes such actions are called the "physical action close"—the sales rep by some physical action communicates to the prospect that he or she believes the proposition is acceptable to the prospect and all that remains is to complete the details. The carpet salesperson might stand up, take out a tape measure, and proceed to draw up a schematic. The retail clerk might start wrapping up the merchandise or writing out the sales check. The car sales rep might hand the keys to the buyer. The industrial agent might start drawing up the contract or specifications demanded by the buyer. The essence of this tactic is action: Get into action to indicate to the buyer that the matter is seemingly settled. The buyer has to make a special effort to stop the process, and many buyers will fail to overcome their natural inertia, so the sale is consummated.

It will be recalled that this matter of assuming the prospect is going to buy was discussed earlier. Now we understand why, if the sales rep has used this assumptive technique throughout the interview, it does not shock the prospect to meet it in the closing phase. If the sales rep has said, "You *will* find yourself enjoying many more hours of great music with this stereo than you ever have with your older model," or "When you pull into a motel at the end of a 500-mile drive you won't feel tired with this car." In every interview the salesperson should be assuming that the prospect will buy. Say "when" and not "if." Say "will" and not "would."

Of course, to start out too obviously with this assumptive technique might offend the prospect. But gradually these little assumptive words are slipped in and, if not resented, are introduced more frequently. Then the final assumption seems to come naturally.

Many salespeople use this close by simply starting to fill out the order blank, asking such questions as "Where do you want this order delivered?" "When will you need this merchandise?" "Do you think three dozen will be enough, or should I send you four?" "What is the address?"

There is really no reason to be bashful in using this assumptive close, for in many types of selling the buyer fully expects to give an order. In some instances in which the salesperson calls regularly upon some retailers the entire presentation is built around the filling out of an order blank. One toiletries firm has devised a rather large order blank on which each item it makes is printed. The sales rep merely goes right down the order blank asking the merchant how much of this or that will be needed, making suggestions occasionally.

Closing on a Minor Point

It is easier to make a minor decision than a major one, so make it easier for the prospect by avoiding the *major* decision, "Yes, I will buy," and substituting a *minor* decision.

The industrial equipment representative might ask, "Are you interested in our lease plan or are you thinking of outright ownership?" thereby focusing the buyer's attention on this relatively minor point rather than the major issue of the acquisition itself.

Usually there are many minor issues to be decided by the prospect in a purchase: delivery dates, payment plans, colors, optional features, and quantities required. Any of these factors can be used as a basis of closing.

The brush seller says, "Would you like the extension handle on your wall brush or will the regular handle be long enough?"

The closer seldom asks *if* but asks *which*.

This device is widely used on all types of prospects except those who insist on making their own decisions without any pressure.

Narrowing the Options

This technique is useful in situations where the prospect is offered quite a range of products from which to choose and as a consequence may find it hard to reach a decision. The buyer surrounded by 20 pairs of shoes—all of which he has tried on—cannot make up his mind as surely as he could if there were fewer shoes from which to choose.

The availability of a wide range of products can overwhelm and confuse the prospect, possibly jeopardizing the sale. An effective method of closing is to narrow the options by focusing attention on several choices that best reflect the criteria most important to the buyer.

The smart clerk somehow shoves out of sight the shoes in which the customer has shown least interest, gradually focusing attention on the two or three pairs that seem most suitable and favored.

The industrial machine sales rep would not show the entire line of equipment to the prospect for fear of confusing him. Instead, he would narrow the items down to those that would be best for the application at hand. A prospect's curiosity sometimes encourages her to ask the sales rep about products for which she has no need, if she just happens to see them in the portfolio. This tends to confuse the sale and gets the salesperson off track.

Sometimes prospects can be overwhelmed by a multitude of products to the point that they become apprehensive, afraid of making a mistake by picking one product out of the many, and will flee the scene even though wanting to buy one of the products. A good salesperson will assist buyers by helping them eliminate the products that are not appropriate.

The wise real estate salesperson learns early in the game not to show a prospective couple every house in town but carefully to select only those that seem to meet their stated requirements.

The foregoing illustrations cover situations where the product is tangible and present. But the method of narrowing the choice can be utilized where the product is intangible and not present. The security sales rep could narrow the choice to two or three issues merely by talking about them. And one could still further narrow the choice to one by the same procedure. Often the salesperson's task is to narrow the choice from two to one, as in the case of the prospect who can't decide whether to buy a typewriter with pica or elite type.

Sometimes it is necessary to narrow the choice to the *amount* which is best for the prospect to purchase.

The securities broker, who has presented a plan for investing a fixed sum each month, says, "Do you figure that $2,000 a month is about right, or could you perhaps invest $3,000?" This device helps the prospect make a wise decision by eliminating conflicting and confusing concepts until attention is focused on the final choice. It may render a real service as well as close a sale.

The Standing Room Only Close

This closing method should only be used in complete truth. Often a seller has only one left of the item being offered and if the buyer wants it he or she should act quickly. Or the item being offered is selling so fast that a waiting list is being used—standing room only. If such is the case, then the sales rep should make the prospect aware of the situation and in so doing, help close the sale. "I should tell you that even if you place an order right now, I cannot promise you that we have it in stock for immediate shipment. If immediate shipment is important to you, I'll call our warehouse and find out." Some reps may make such a call even if they are fairly certain the item is in stock. Perhaps asking the prospect, while on the phone, "Yes, there is one in stock. Do you want me to put your name on it?" will close the sale.

Many hesitant prospects are encouraged to buy when they are shown how popular the proposition is with other people. Few prospects are comfortable being the only ones to buy the deal.

Often a line of goods is being discontinued. What is being offered is the last of it. "If you like this model, then you'd better latch on to it right now, for this is the last one. They're changing the models."

Industrial sales reps make frequent use of this technique with complete honesty. In so doing, they furnish information which the prospect needs to make an intelligent decision. There may be some impending event such as a strike, either in the seller's plant or in that of a supplier or a transport agent; inventories may be running short in that particular model; the special deal will be discontinued after this week; or some other event may occur that will prevent the prospect from exercising free choice at a later time.

Offering Special Inducements to Buy Now

This technique was referred to in the previous chapter as putting a hook in your close. It is used widely to encourage prospects to buy now. A gypsum sales rep for a new concern trying to expand its market share offered with each boxcar of "rock" 25 sacks of plaster. The 3M salespeople usually have a special inducement to offer dealers if they will buy some package deal today: On one trip they were giving the dealer a billfold.

Buying inducements such as rebates or giveaways often encourage potential customers not to delay their decision.

It is important not to use this technique as a trick. The same inducement should not be used twice on the same prospect, or the prospect will quickly see that he could have had the premium whether or not he had bought at that time. But, judiciously employed, this is a highly effective way to prod some prospects into action.

Asking for the Order

In discussing methods for closing the sale, we are likely to overlook the perfectly obvious—ask the prospect to buy. Professional buyers declare that it is amazing how many salespeople seem unable to bring themselves to ask for the order. Perhaps they are afraid of being turned down; maybe they forgot to do it.

When the sale has been conducted on a matter-of-fact basis, it is natural for the salesperson to say, "Can I get your purchase order number for my order form?"

Naturally, there are many variations in the way a salesperson can ask for an order, but few of them ask bluntly, "Do you want to buy?" Instead, most prefer to word the question along the lines of the assumptive close, using such questions as: "When do you think we can get your purchase order on this shipment?" or "How much of your business will you give us at this time?" or "It would help our production planners if you could let me know your buying plans as they affect us."

But one sales rep, who knew the prospect well, closed a large sale by saying: "I want you to buy this now so both of us can get a good night's rest.

If you don't, we will both be nervous wrecks." The sale was important to both parties and had been causing worry to both of them.

Under the right condition, a flat statement declaring that the prospect ought to buy may be effective, as "That seems to cover everything. You can OK the order right there." (Pointing to the place.)

Asking for the order can salvage sales that are apparently hopeless. One book sales rep had been having little luck trying to get a professor whom he had known for some time to adopt a certain book. The professor had thrown all sorts of trivial objections into the picture, thus thoroughly muddying the waters. Finally the rep yelled, "For crying out loud, Harry! Stop giving me all this flak and buy my blankety-blank book!"

Harry broke out laughing and said, "Okay, okay, it's yours."

Naturally the salesperson must know the prospect, but it is surprising the results one can get by forceful requests for the order.

Closing on an Objection

Closing on an objection can be effectively used when the prospect voices only one significant objection and the sales rep knows that it can be answered to the prospect's complete satisfaction.

Suppose a salesperson trying to sell an Apple Macintosh computer encounters from the prospect an objection to the incompatibility of its operating system with that of her present IBM computer. The rep knows that an interface is available to allow the Apple to communicate with the IBM machine. That fact can be used for a close. "Is that the only thing between you and all of the things that this Apple can give you?" If the prospect says it is, then close. "Then I'll include the interface that can let this Apple talk to your IBM right into the deal." There is nothing left for the prospect to do except to buy.

These closes are used frequently in handling price objections. It is a serious error to lower price without getting the prospect committed to buy if the price is met, as the prospect may continue to press for even larger concessions if the first demand is met. So the sales rep says, "Let's write up the proposition with the price you mentioned and just see what the office will do with it. You've nothing to lose that way, and, who knows, maybe we can really get you a deal today. Never know how the boss feels; he might accept this contract." Once the prospect has signed for the lower price, if the seller agrees to it, the deal is binding. Real estate salespeople find this technique useful.

A Few Random Hints

A good word to use in the closing efforts is "let's." "Let's start with . . ." "Let's say you want this by the 15th." "Let's just run over some of the points you want to consider most carefully." That "us" identifies the interests of prospect and sales rep; the two of them are trying to work things out *together*;

they are not *opposing* each other. The owner of a collection agency says, "Let's start collecting some of your overdue accounts right away. You can use the money now, can't you?"

The little word "when" is also helpful, especially when attempting a trial close. "When will you be wanting the initial shipment of this order?" "When would it be most convenient for me to take the measurements for the new awnings?" "I can get this heater installed in time for you to enjoy it over the weekend. When would it be better for you—Thursday or Friday?"

Sometimes it is necessary to ask for payment when the sale is made. Here it is essential to appear casual about it. You can continue to write up the order and remark, "If you'll give me your check now, I'll send it right in with this order." Or, "You can be making out your check while I'm finishing up the order. The amount is . . ."

And while we are talking about dollars, some people try to make the amount sound less formidable by omitting the word "dollars." Thus $23,500 becomes "twenty-three five." "Twenty-three thousand and five hundred dollars" sounds like much, much more!

Get It In Writing

The spoken word is a mischievous culprit of misunderstanding. Never trust your ear or your memory. Always, repeat, *always* put the order in writing at the time it is obtained and have the buyer sign it after checking it for accuracy.

To avoid misunderstandings, orders should always be put in writing at the time they are obtained. All details should be specified, and the order checked for accuracy before it is signed.

There are salespeople who are reluctant to go into a great many details at the close for fear that something will come up that will cause the buyer to change his or her mind. The answer to this dilemma lies in the nature of the sale. It is foolish not to make clear certain details that are important in the transaction. Similarly, it is foolish to bring up matters that are of minor consequence. It is a matter of judgment, but bear in mind that just getting the order is not the same as getting a customer. A great deal can happen between the close of a sale and the creation of a satisfied customer. Misunderstanding created at the time of closing can result in order cancellations and, worse, unhappy customers. When in doubt, clarify.

Silence

There is a time for silence during a close. A sales rep for industrial properties related, "I had made all my points, laid out the whole situation, answered the person's questions. I saw he was thinking, thinking hard, so I shut up and just sat there. Seconds stretched into minutes. We just sat there. Pretty soon I sensed that the first person to speak was lost, so I let it ride. We sat there for 15 minutes, not saying a thing. Suddenly he said, 'Let's do it!'' and I had a sale.''

The chatterbox who raves on and on long after he has exhausted his story will be discounted as a fool by the wiser buyer. People don't like to deal with fools.

THE DEPARTURE AFTER A SUCCESSFUL SALE

"And there I stood with the order in my hand muttering something about being grateful while the buyer just sat there giving me a pained look. Finally he said, 'All you have to do, son, is turn around and walk out the door. It's as easy as that!' I was so embarrassed. Nobody ever told me what to do after I got the order,'' painfully related a new representative for an abrasives manufacturer. It had not occurred to him that a graceful departure might be an important part of the selling process. But think one moment! Doesn't a good departure lay the foundation or set the stage for the next approach to that buyer or prospect? It's wise to leave with your fences mended and bridges intact.

When you are ready to leave, one of two things has happened—either the sale has been made or it has not. Assume first that the sale has been made. In this case you must guard against certain dangerous moves. An inexperienced salesperson may suffer a reaction from the nervous tension under which he has been working. In this reaction his prime feeling is one of thankfulness that the interview is over and the order obtained. Under the impulse of gratitude and relief it is easy to grow effusive in thanking the customer for the order; there is a tendency to release the pent-up emotion in a flood of talk, which may border on the semihysterical with a young and high-strung salesperson. Here is the place to keep a tight rein on your feelings and a close watch on your actions. Remember that the sale is a mutually profitable transaction, that the buyer has neither done a favor nor received one, and that the buyer will have less respect for the sales rep and less confidence in the proposition if the sales rep acts as if getting an order is a rare event. Thank the buyer for the order, but not overeffusively. Then turn the conversation into other channels, perhaps regarding the new advertising campaign, successful methods practiced by some other buyer of the goods, or any matter of interest to the buyer. While the prospect is signing, you should not stage a dramatic silence but maintain a conversation—unhurried and friendly—as if the act of getting an order were a commonplace affair.

As you gather up your possessions and are taking your leave, you may remark, "Thank you for your courtesy and for the order. I'll be on my way to get things moving on it promptly." Or "You have made a wise choice. Good-by and thank you." Confirm the prospect's wisdom in buying.

This raises the question as to whether one should depart at once or should linger awhile. This depends on certain factors, but it is safe to say that *the salesperson should always be the first to rise.* If the buyer rises first and shakes your hand while leading you to the door, you've overstayed your welcome. The most important factor is whether the buyer wants you to stay. The merchant, particularly in smaller places, usually appreciates having people display an active interest in her and her problems and rather resents having the salesperson rush off as soon as the order has been taken. The professional purchasing agent, on the other hand, works faster and will appreciate having the sales rep show his understanding of this fact. Here a prompt getaway is advisable.

A second blunder is to assume a superior attitude, as though you have won a victory. There is an air of condescension about such a person which is maddening to the buyer and may result in cancellation and certainly in little future business. Any tendency to patronize the buyer will be resented. The sale should not be thought of as a battle which you have won but as a mutual agreement on a business matter.

The third danger, and one to which the retail clerk is peculiarly liable, is that of indifference. How often have you made a retail purchase only to have the clerk hand you your package without a "Thank you," without a smile, without even a glance, while the clerk turned to greet the next customer? The fact that a person has bought does not remove him or her from the list of prospective purchasers for the future. Here is the time to start the next sale, to leave with the purchaser a feeling of satisfaction that will bring that person back again. This is really the approach to the next sale.

THE DEPARTURE WHEN NO SALE IS MADE

First, it may be laid down as a general rule that the attitude of the salesperson who has lost the sale should be no different from that of the successful person. This is easier to preach than to practice, for it takes a good sport to smile and act friendly after trying in vain to make an obdurate prospect see the light. But it must be done.

After one unsuccessful call on a prospect, a sales rep called a second time. After putting his signature on a liberal order the buyer burst out, "Say, do you know you are the first salesperson who ever went away without an order who actually thanked me for the time I gave him? You sold me these goods when you were here before."

When the interview has resulted in no sale, avoid these three attitudes: scorn, anger, and inferiority. The person who has failed to sell a car may show scorn for the prospect who had too little taste or means to buy. Or he may be angry and show it. Or, lastly, he may feel so defeated that he assumes an apologetic air which is almost equally bad. It is hard to remain pleasant in the face of a turndown, but it must be done, for right there a new sale may be started.

When the turndown is received in the outer office, it is hard to take it without wincing, but this, too, must be done. It does not pay to let subordinates see that one has been humiliated in any way; keep a cheerful self-confidence with poise unshaken. A good final impression on the subordinates will be valuable later.

The real artist will be able to sense the *certain* turndown before it arrives and will contrive to make a getaway unostentatiously. Guide the conversation into new channels, deftly and without a break, finally rising and perhaps remarking, "Well, I've got to be getting on. I've enjoyed our visit a lot and will look in again some day soon. Good-by." The purpose of making some such getaway is to *leave the way open for a return*. Try to prevent the prospect from turning you down flatly. If the prospect has not gone on record, there is a better chance to reopen the sale than if the prospect had been permitted to do so.

Of course, consultative salespeople insist that calling back upon a prospect is no problem because they only make a call if they have a sound reason for doing so, a reason that the prospect should readily realize.

A danger connected with this method is that if you use it too often, you may acquire the "call-back" habit. It is all too easy for a weak seller to "bug out" of a presentation that is not going smoothly by making an early departure, with the mental defense mechanism that you can "call back" later and all will be right. "I'll make this sale later if I don't press this person too hard now. No need to seem irritating," is the way some reps start thinking about such situations. One problem with call-backs is that they are expensive. If it takes two calls to do a job that should have been done in one call, selling costs will soar.

A serious judgmental problem arises in trying to decide when to stay and fight and when to "run away so you can fight another day." There is no way to provide such answers here, for it all depends on the situation.

Where the interview is being conducted under serious difficulties, it may be suicidal to attempt to close and the next best thing is to effect a graceful exit, leaving the door open for another interview.

Capitalize on Defeat

The able tactician endeavors to come away from the scene of a defeat with something to show for it. Bear in mind that often the buyer who has just rejected your proposition in favor of a competitor's deal has some guilt feelings about it if you and the buyer have established a good relationship.

Often buyers can avoid guilt feelings if you have, by some ill-advised personal action, given the buyer an excuse, some seemingly good reason, for rejecting you. But if you have done a good job and have shown yourself to be professional in defeat, the buyer may respond to an appeal for particular consideration on the next order. In one case, the purchasing agent was so impressed with the performance of a sales agent in defeat that he not only provided a lead to another good prospect but telephoned the other party to personally recommend the sales rep. Thus don't let your emotional reaction to rejection cloud your mind. Be alert to discover what else the nonbuyer can do for you.

If you have worked hard for an order yet failed to get it, you may profit handsomely if you can get the buyer to tell you honestly why you didn't get the order. This sounds easy, but it isn't. Most buyers do not want to discuss their reasons. They know that such conversations can lead to disagreeable arguments, and they are not obligated to tell you why they decided to buy from someone else.

However, if you can establish rapport with your prospect, you may be able to obtain some valuable information by saying something like, "I honor your decision and I know that you don't have to tell me anything. However, it would be a great help to my personal development if you would favor me by evaluating my performance. Where did I go wrong? I promise I'll not reply or argue with whatever you say. It's just information I need to improve my performance."

An appeal for help and for candor may work for you if you have earned the buyer's respect. And if you haven't, you may get the information without asking for it.

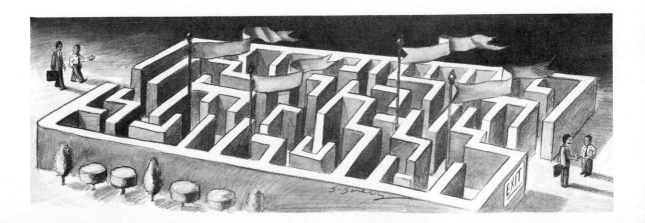

SUMMARY

If the salesperson has performed properly, closing the sale should be the next natural step. After all, the prospect needs the proposition, can afford it, and has been given an excellent presentation or interview. Unfortunately some salespeople are burdened with guilt and fear of rejection, which make them hesitant to close.

While there are many closing techniques, the assumptive close is the base from which most of the others flow. Usually prospects signal when it is time to close by statements they make and by their body language.

The consultative sales rep looks at the closing stage of the sale as getting a commitment from the prospect. Many trial closes are used to find out if the prospect is yet committed to buy.

The end play can be important. Do not gloat or otherwise position yourself as the victor in a battle. On the contrary, the buyer was the winner. Also, withdraw gracefully after a defeat, and be alert to ways to gain some consideration in the future from the nonbuying prospect.

DISCUSSION QUESTIONS

1 It was stated that you can tell by the prospect's facial expressions and body language whether the person is ready to buy. What are some of the specific things people do to signal that they are ready to buy? What does the person do to signal you that you are not near a sale?

2 In what way does the assumptive close underlie all other closing techniques?

3 You are an audio consultant who has been advising the owner of a substantial new home about a complete stereo system in the home. You think it is time to close the deal. What are some of the ways that you could close the prospect that day?

4 You are the manager of a retreading firm that is seeking the business of a large trucking company. You have called on the owner-manager many times but without success. While she has encouraged you on each visit, you still have been unable to get the business; she claims that your prices are a bit higher than those granted her by another concern. Now your top management has given you the authority to meet whatever price is necessary to get that business. What are some of the closing statements you would prepare for this interview with the trucker?

5 As a rep for a large chemical company you are attempting to close a deal with a small plastic-injecting molding company for a boxcar load of a certain plastic. What are some of the closes you could use? Give exact words.

6 You are a CPA who has been contacted by the president of a small manufacturing concern about the possibility of your auditing their books on a continual basis. She has told you that she is looking over all potential accountants for her job. How would you close the deal that day? Give all the possible closes you could use with complete ethical observance.

7 What does the consultative salesperson say to find out if the prospect is yet committed to buying?

8 Why might a no answer just be the beginning of a negotiation?

9 In what ways can you make prospects feel they have won when they buy from you?

10 You have just lost a sale. Another firm was awarded a large contract for lumber. In what ways might you want to try to capitalize on that defeat?

REFERENCES

1 Irvine Feldman, "The Pros Don't Close," *American Salesman*, July, 1986, pp. 3–5, insists that closing is now given too much emphasis, since it should be the natural result of a good sales interview. Feldman maintains that closing should only be a matter of agreeing upon the details of the transaction.

2 William S. Pierson, "The Importance of Closing," *American Salesman*, April 1986, pp. 21–23, stresses the importance of the close but recognizes the need for sound groundwork leading up to it.

3 Tim Connor, "The New Psychology of Closing Sales," *American Salesman*, September 1987, pp. 25–30, stresses the need to ask probing questions in closing along the lines advanced by the consultative salesperson.

4 Gregg Berlie, "Anatomy of a Closing," *American Salesman*, January 1986, pp. 3–6, discusses how to handle anxiety during the latter stages of the sale.

5 See Bob Collins, "Tailoring the Close," *American Salesman*, March 1986, pp. 14–15, for an excellent discussion of the importance of tailoring the close to the prospect's personality and cultural inclinations.

6 See "It's All in the Closing," *American Salesman*, February 1986, pp. 7–8, for a discussion of the role of signals in closing a sale.

7 Ted Pollock, "Getting the Next Best Thing to an Order," *American Salesman*, January 1990, pp. 21–26, recognizes that there are times when an order simply cannot be obtained.

8 See John Nemec, "Toward a Happy Ending," *American Salesman*, May 1986, pp. 10–13, emphasizes the need for a smooth transition from the interview into the close. Nemec's "Do You Have Grand Finales?" *American Salesman*, June 1987, pp. 3–6, discusses the need for mastering several closing techniques.

9 See Nemec, "Innovate Your Closing," *American Salesman*, February 1986, pp. 23–26, for a discussion of the advantages of improvising closes to meet special situations.

CASE 14-1: Northside Motor Sales—Development of Closing Techniques

Because of a number of unforeseen developments, Bill Perry, used car sales manager for the Northside Motor Sales Company, had hired during the previous month 4 new, inexperienced sales reps for his 11-person sales force. While he was rather pleased with their overall appearance and behavior, he quickly realized that they needed considerable sales training, particularly in the closing of sales. He had been especially distressed the previous day to overhear three different salespeople lose what he thought were easy sales solely because they evidently did not know how to close the sale. He vowed to correct the situation.

Mr. Perry invited Walt Kane, his assistant sales manager, to coffee. During the coffee break the matter of training the sales force to be more effective closers was brought up. After a lot of discussion on the problem, Mr. Perry asked Walt to develop a training program specifically designed to make the salespeople better closers. Walt half-heartedly protested that in his opinion the subject of closing could be treated as one of the topics naturally covered in the organization's existing sales-training program, but he was forcefully overruled by Mr. Perry, who insisted that the topic was too important and the need too urgent to have it buried along with all the other things covered in the existing sales-training program.

The Northside Motor Sales Company held regular sales meetings each Monday morning for an hour, and all the firm's salespeople were supposed to attend. However, several of the firm's older, more experienced, and more successful sales reps frequently decided that they could use their time better elsewhere. Seldom were sales techniques discussed at these meetings. Rather the time was devoted largely to product knowledge and company problems. One representative described them as "the Monday morning huddle to get our signals straight."

Under Mr. Perry's directive Walt began contemplating a special training program to teach the used car sales force how to be more effective closers. He first decided to pull the 11-person used car sales force out of the Monday morning sales meetings: "They are a waste of time. Besides, we shouldn't ask our people to go to two training sessions a week, that's too much." He planned to meet separately each Monday morning with the used car people for the next month: "Four sessions should be enough to get the idea across!"

Walt had a copy of a salesmanship book, *The Art of Closing*. He planned to buy a few more copies of it and have the salespeople read the book. Then each Monday they would discuss what had been read.

Upon outlining his plans to Mr. Perry, Walt had reason to worry about his job. Mr. Perry was unimpressed with Walt's plans. All that Walt recalled of the meeting were such words as "half-baked," "unprofessional," and "superficial." But he did recall the parting orders: "I want a well-thought-out, thorough, professional program that will really get our people prepared for closing sales. And I want it by Friday morning!"

Walt had a problem; he did not know what to do next. He thought his program was pretty good, so he did not know how to change it to suit Mr. Perry. As he contemplated looking for another job, Walt thought about asking for help from a friend of his, Sally, who was a district sales manager for a large business machine company.

That evening Walt talked with Sally about his problem. Sally responded, "There are so many things that you could do that I don't know where to begin. Have you ever thought about inviting a number of highly successful car salespeople in to tell your people how they go about closing? How about getting some video equipment and making a video of them in action, then having the group analyze their closing techniques? There is a lot written about closing techniques. I am sure your manufacturer's representative could give you material they have developed. Have you talked with other dealers about the problem? Maybe several of you have the same difficulties and could get together for some common sales-training program. Have you thought about just giving your people some standard closing techniques that you have developed?"

Walt was overwhelmed. He had not thought of any of those techniques. He thanked Sally for the ideas and retired to his den to think everything over. He just did not know what to recommend.

1 Why did Mr. Perry react so adversely to Walt's first program? What was so wrong with it?

2 Develop a program for Walt to submit to Mr. Perry.

CASE 14-2: Sara Bee—No Close, No Sale

After more than a year in her Midwest territory, Sara Bee's performance was so poor as to threaten her career. Sara sold materials-handling equipment to any firm that maintained a warehouse, mainly manufacturers and wholesalers. She had failed to make quota by a large margin for four straight quarters. She was not earning enough to sustain herself, let alone justify the company's keeping her.

Bill Lemon, sales manager, had been carefully evaluating Sara's activities and performance, hoping to help her. He was personally involved with her success because he had gone out on a limb with top management at the time he hired her. The company's president did not believe that a woman could sell materials-handling equipment to the people who purchased it. Hardly a week passed but that the president did not ask Bill about Sara's progress. "Has she sold anything yet?" was his jibe the previous week.

Bill knew that Sara was making the calls and seeing the right people, those who made the buying decisions. He had accompanied her on several calls and satisfied himself that she conducted an excellent sales interview. She was truly professional. She knew both the equipment and how it was used. But he saw that she just could not get the orders. When it came time to make a commitment, the prospects would avoid it by giving some lame procrastinating excuse. Sara would try to attack those excuses but could make no headway. She could not close the sale.

Bill wondered how he could help Sara learn how to close and overcome her problem.

1 Evaluate the situation.

2 What should Bill do to help Sara learn how to close sales?

CHAPTER FIFTEEN

ACCOUNT MANAGEMENT

The most valuable asset of any business is its customers.
Anonymous

After studying the material in this chapter you should:

☐ Understand the differences between a batch and a flow system of distribution

☐ Realize the nature and importance of service in marketing

☐ Know the nature of account management selling

☐ Appreciate the need for following up a sale

PROFILE OF A CHEMICAL

SALES ENGINEER

Gene Urban

Drexel, 1973, chemical engineer
Akronchem Co.
Akron, Ohio

"I never in my life would have thought I would be in selling, but I love it. I could never go back to being a research engineer. When I graduated, the dollars and the jobs for engineering majors were in selling, so I went to work for Columbian Chemical selling carbon black. The product became a commodity, and the company was sold several times in the early eighties so I went to work for Akronchem as a sales rep. I now sell pigments for rubber as well as a full line of other rubber OEM technical chemicals for the production of higher grades of specialty rubber products."

Gene's territory is the United States and Canada. He travels 50 percent of the time and is paid a flat salary plus a portion of the firm's net profits at the end of the year. He says, "I love the freedom I have." Gene is well placed.

Much of what is written about selling assumes that the salesperson goes into the market to locate a prospect for some proposition; then a sales presentation is made, and, hopefully, a sale is made. Each sale is treated as a discrete event. However, that scenario does not accurately describe the situation of most industrial salespeople.

Instead, they work in an assigned territory selling to customers, call them accounts, that have been buying from the company for years. Sometimes a rep will be assigned just one or a few large accounts. An account may be so large that several reps may be assigned to it. Here are a few aspects of the job of such salespeople.

THE ACCOUNT MANAGER'S JOB

A review of what account managers do discloses quickly the nature, difficulties, and heavy responsibility of the job. A customer is an earning asset. Good management is careful what it does with its assets. Sometimes one account manager may alone control so much business that top management is uneasy that so much of the company's volume is in one person's hands. For this reason, some managements retain control of the key accounts for themselves. They are called *house accounts* and are often a source of conflict between the sales reps and management. More than one sales rep has complained, "They give us all the little fish to catch as best we can while they keep the big ones for themselves."

Becoming an Account Manager

In effect, becoming an account manager is a promotion. Only the experienced, the adept, and diligent need apply since the account manager is entrusted with the company's most important assets. The pay is higher, often over $100,000 a year. The work is more interesting. Moreover, most sales reps prefer to deal with the same people over time and not be on the streets drumming up new business.

Consequently, if you want to be an account manager, first you must become a successful salesperson for a company that uses account managers. Many firms are not structured for this type of selling.

Getting New Accounts

Even established account managers are always looking for new accounts. Customer attrition is normal. Things change. Customers come and go. Certainly, losing a large account can be hazardous to one's financial well-being. However, the adept account manager realizes the need for a continual flow of new business into the fold.[1]

Troubleshooting and Expediting

Customer satisfaction with a vendor depends to a large degree on how smoothly everything goes. Buyers want no problems. They want the goods

Account management involves the heavy responsibilities associated with managing some of the company's most important assets. In some cases, one rep may be assigned to a few large accounts; in others, an account may be so large that several reps may be assigned to handle it. If a company is small, the owner may act as the account manager, as does this owner of a construction company.

delivered on time, where designated and as specified. They want them placed into service without undue hassle.

So much for what they want. What they get is often another matter. Deliveries are late. The wrong goods arrive at the wrong sites with improper documentation. Billings are often confusing and sometimes in error. Such aggravations are daily irritants in business. Account managers who shield their customers from such annoyances solidify their relationships with these accounts. Much of the account manager's time and effort is devoted to making certain that everything goes smoothly with the account's orders. When problems arise, the account manager moves quickly to solve them. Large customers expect, even demand, such service. When something is broken, they want it fixed, right now.[2]

Contractual Negotiations

Often large customers contract for their needs in advance, perhaps for a year, or even longer. Some relationships are ongoing, with prices renegotiated periodically. Account managers are usually deeply involved in such negotiations, since they are in the best position to know the account's situation.[3]

Since customer satisfaction is crucial to maintaining a longtime, mutually profitable relationship, especially with larger customers, minimizing service problems through careful scheduling and tracking of deliveries is a necessity.

Schedules

In the management of any significant account, there is considerable work involved in scheduling deliveries. It is critical that the customer have on hand at the time needed the goods required. A vendor that hinders a customer's operations will not be around long.

This is particularly important where the customer does not want to store the goods but wants them to arrive at the plant just as they are needed or put into use.

Customer People

The cast of characters keeps changing. The people working for an account keep getting fired, promoted, or moved or they resign or otherwise have their assignments changed. Just about the time the account manager has established a solid comfortable working relationship with the key people in the account, those people may change. Thus the account manager can never be assured that an account is well under control. There are always new relationships to be developed.

One rep relates the story of how an account that furnished her with a large portion of her income was suddenly bought by another firm. All relationships were suddenly disrupted. The parent company had its own sources of supply, and the rep was cut adrift.

Phil H. was an account manager for Prudential Securities. He had only one account, a big trader, from whom he earned more than $200,000 a year. The market soured in 1990 and so did the big trader's enthusiasm for trading. He took his millions and went off into the real world to play. Phil is now broke, doing something else for a living. Account management has its risks.

Politics

Relationships and power ebb and flow inside organizations. At one time your contacts in the account may be powerful. Suddenly things change. You find yourself aligned with the wrong people in the company. The account is in jeopardy. The account manager must be extremely sensitive to the political winds in client companies.

Blocking Competition

Competitor's sales reps are not sitting idly by twiddling their thumbs while you enjoy the fruits of your business with the account. They are scheming to get it away from you. They are calling on the same people you think are your friends trying to find a crack into which they can wedge a toe. The minute you fail to serve the account, rest assured that they are poised to step in to solve the problem. Sometimes they are willing to spend a great deal of money to crack into a significant account. They look at it as an investment for future income. All they want is an opportunity to show what they can do for the account.

Consequently, the account manager is continually trying to counter whatever the competition is telling the account, some of which may even be the truth.

Coordination

Often considerable coordination is required among the vendor's units serving the account's units. Trainers may have to be in the factory the day new equipment arrives. Perhaps different components from different places all have to arrive at the buyer's designated delivery site at the same time.

The owner of a large home-building company insisted that the lumber company from whom he was buying wood products place all deliveries at the building site precisely where they were to be used. He did not want his highly paid carpenters carrying wood. "I want them to pick it up and nail it down." Since the lumber company's normal policy was to dump each load right at the border to the building site and let the buyer take it from there, a conflict arose that the account manager had to resolve with the lumber company's delivery people and management. It was not an easy task to get the firm to change its policies; few people willingly take on extra work.

Coordination among the account's employees is also often needed. A factory superintendent wants a small change made in a product being supplied. While the idea is excellent, all sorts of permissions from engineering and others in management will be needed. Guess who has to do it?

Innovation

Technology keeps making new products, processes, and materials available while rendering the ones being used obsolete. Clever sales reps use new technology as a lever to pry their way into large accounts. If the rep is able to convince the buyers that the new technology is somehow superior to that being purchased, the account may change suppliers.

Alcy Grimes won her greatest sale when she was a sales rep for The Carnation Company. Pizza Hut, which was not a large customer at the time, had been assigned to her. After a year of skillfully working with the people at Pizza Hut, she finally persuaded them to buy a new cheeselike product to replace the cheese they were using on their pizzas. Such decisions are not easily made. Changing such an important ingredient is a serious matter and not something done without much thought and consideration. Finally, her selling points of lower cost, better taste, and better baking characteristics won the day. It was a substantial sale and served her career well.

Sales-Cost Enhancement

The wise account manager is ever alert for opportunities to help customers improve their profit performance. Perhaps it is some idea for increasing sales; maybe it is just a lead to a new customer for the account. Often it is a cost reduction idea. If you gain a reputation for having the account's best interests in mind, you'll be welcome to call upon them and you'll be given every consideration as a supplier.[4]

The Follow-Up

The follow-up is an important aspect of the account manager's job. The purpose is to make certain that the buyer is satisfied with a purchase. This applies to all buyers, whether they are expected to become regular customers, or whether they will never buy from you again.[5]

Before proceeding, it may be wise to point out some qualifying factors which may govern the scope, intensity, and duration of the follow-up.

The importance of the sale is perhaps the chief factor. Obviously, someone who has just sold a magazine subscription cannot afford to call back several times to educate the customer in how to get the most pleasure and profit from the magazine. But when the sale is a big one, it may be vitally important that the buyer be educated to extract the utmost in satisfaction from the purchase. The price paid probably includes a margin for this service, and the buyer is entitled to it.

A second factor is the likelihood of repeat business. If a long-time relationship is hoped for, with frequent and profitable orders, a follow-up will help develop the desired permanent relationship.

A third factor may be termed "educational." How much does the buyer need to know about the new purchase before it can be used properly? It may be a complicated machine or an office computer. It could be raw material requiring careful and unfamiliar processing. Perhaps it is merely a new line to be sold through retail outlets. Whatever the item, if it needs special knowledge and definite performance techniques on the part of operators or sales clerks, it is the salesperson's job to follow up that sale until sure that the product is being handled *right*. Ignorant or slipshod personnel may ruin the success of the installation and create a most unhappy customer who will go out of his way to know the product and kill chances of making other sales.

It is this last point that makes it important to follow up fully even on buyers who may never buy anything from you again. They can still hurt you badly with other prospects.

With the foregoing thoughts in mind, you must strike a balance between active selling effort and follow-up activities. The test of whether you should devote a given hour to selling or to follow-up is simply which way of spending that hour will result in more sales in the long run, because the basic purpose of any follow-up is to increase sales. A salesperson is not being altruistic; that time is not being given away. Rather, it is being *invested* in the manner which will bring greater sales.

Now let's see what you may be getting in return for an investment of your time in follow-up.

Checking on the Order First, you can gain buyer goodwill by checking to make sure that the order was filled and delivered properly. This is especially necessary when the sale is the first one made to that buyer. Occasionally a sales rep is in a position to personally check the order out of the factory or warehouse or store. A furniture sales rep for a large department store in Kansas City, Missouri, made a practice of personally selecting the pieces from the warehouse when the customer, who may have been furnishing a new home, had chosen certain items from the retail stock. These were treated as samples, and the rep tried to select pieces constructed of fine woods and flawless upholstery from the many duplicate items in the warehouse. He cultivated the friendship of the delivery truck drivers who took pride in careful handling of the merchandise when they delivered it.

The salesperson who took your order for a new car will be on hand when it is delivered in order to demonstrate the controls and go over the owner's manual with you. The salesperson may also have a checklist of tests to run to make certain that the car is in perfect working condition.

Even a professional person can utilize this follow-up idea. A physician in Seattle makes a practice of calling up a patient who is under new medication to inquire how things are going. The physician may be able to suggest a slight change in the prescribed procedure, and often can exhort the patient to follow orders. She is simply checking to see that her "customers" get what they wanted—good health.

Proper Installation or Use

Proper Installation or Use   This has already been touched on. Obviously a buyer who does not know how to operate or use the new purchase will be unhappy and may even return it. Or, even worse, the ignorant buyer may damage the new item and then make claims under the warranty.

Here the problem frequently lies in the salesperson's thorough familiarity with the equipment. The salesperson knows it so well that he or she tends to think everyone else will quickly grasp it with but one explanation. Unfortunately, people are reluctant to admit that they did not fully comprehend the first explanation or do not understand some aspect—a result of ego involvement. It takes a wise person to admit she or he does not understand something. The wise sales rep will understand this and take care to test covertly the buyer's comprehension of the equipment—that is, to make sure the buyer can operate it before leaving!

Getting New Prospects

Getting New Prospects   As we pointed out in Chapter 6, "Prospecting," present customers are a good source of leads for new business. The subur-

The follow-up is a very significant part of account management. Checking on the proper installation of equipment and providing instruction on how to use the product are crucial to customer satisfaction and may even guarantee future sales.

banite who has just bought a new power mower and is riding it triumphantly around the yard is likely to be visited by neighbors who want to see the new contraption and find out how (and if) it works. The sales rep who is on hand when the mower is delivered and is being helpful to the new owner is in a prime position to pick up new prospects.

There is a vast amount of word-of-mouth advertising going on in this land, where every home has a telephone. Employees discuss such matters over lunch and coffee breaks. Employers meet frequently and exchange experiences. The salesperson who follows up promptly on sales can often catch the customers at the time when they can recall easily the names of several friends with whom they have been discussing their recent purchases.

Cementing Friendships[6] One important gain from a good follow-up is the holding of customers in line or keeping them from shifting to another source of supply. But many salespeople are also close friends of their customers. The two parties are seeking the same objectives; they find themselves congenial in personality; they help each other in many ways. Most of us like to do business with friends when it is possible. Time invested in such follow-ups is like investing money in an annuity—it continues to pay off for many years.

Wise reps strive to make friends by sincere and subtle means. They pass along tips on possible new business to their clients. They bring them fresh ideas for making greater profit. They help them obtain efficient personnel for key posts in their organizations. They remember certain occasions, such as a child's birthday, graduation from high school or college, and various anniversaries. In short, they manifest a genuine interest in the customer (or perhaps the prospect), trying to find ways to establish their relationship on a basis of true personal friendship as well as merely profitable business. Such salespeople will go far out of their way when the occasion demands in order to help their customers in some way. They may find a job for someone in their customer's organization who is forced to leave.

One office machine sales agent in a big city has only one customer—a very large bank. She regards herself as a part of that bank's organization and often jumps in and helps with a rush load of work in any department that uses her machines. When she delivers a new machine, she sets up a course of instruction for the employees who will use it, making sure that they all know how to utilize it efficiently and without damage. She sometimes smilingly says: "I think of myself as the bank's vice president in charge of bookkeeping or accounting machines. The other day I recommended that the bank buy a competitor's machine for a certain job because it was better than ours. It was the natural thing to do, and my employer understood." This woman constantly studies the bank's systems for keeping its records and can frequently offer suggestions for improving them.

Another example of efficient follow-up methods is provided by an electrical contractor who calls on every family a week after they have been in a new house (which he wired) to find out how the system is working out. He sometimes suggests changes, like a new outlet or two, which would make the system more convenient. His purpose is not to get additional business but to ensure satisfaction, as he knows much of his business comes through the recommendations of old customers.

Then, 1 year after the house was first occupied, he calls again, just before the expiration of the warranties, to see whether anything should be replaced under warranty and to learn whether anything needs adjusting or minor repair. Of course, he is always ready to respond to calls for emergency service, but he insists that the program outlined above reduces total costs because he catches many little things before they develop into real trouble.

The sales rep for ready-to-wear garments takes his orders months ahead of delivery, but after the goods are in the store he follows up carefully. He wants to know how each item is selling, where the stock is spotty, how the advertising is taking hold, how well the salespeople in the store know the talking points of his merchandise, and a score of little details. He says that these follow-up calls make him a lot of business.

Indeed, this is the purpose of the follow-up—to lead into the next sale to that same buyer. This next sale may come at once or years later, but smart salespeople start in the minute they follow up on any sale. And they never forget that, even though they may not sell this same buyer for a long time, it is important to win goodwill. Truly, a satisfied customer is a firm's best advertisement, and every top-flight sales rep knows that much new business can be traced to the kind words uttered by some customer who appreciated the efforts of the seller to make certain that this customer was completely satisfied with both the salesperson and the firm.

In a survey of 400 purchasing agents, they were asked: "Do salespeople follow up adequately on orders?" Some 38 percent answered yes, but 62 percent replied no. Obviously, there is ample room for improvement in this area.

Just remember that business is largely relationships—relationships between people, between institutions, and between companies. Learn how to develop, nurture, and care for these relationships and you'll do quite well in business.

Servicing Intermediaries   The duties of the representatives who service intermediaries—retailers and wholesalers—involve five functions:

- Building the intermediary's sales of the rep's line by assisting with dealer's merchandising of it
- Training the intermediary's salespeople to sell the rep's lines
- Expediting orders and shipments
- Handling and adjusting complaints
- Providing a communication link between the market and top management

Let's look at each of these tasks in detail.

Merchandising Assistance   Experience shows that most intermediaries can benefit from merchandising suggestions and help from the sales rep, who, after all, has had the opportunity of observing the merchandising schemes of many dealers. When someone has developed a particularly effective promotion or merchandising technique, the rep can relate it to other intermediaries who could likely benefit from it.

A relatively new men's apparel dealer was not doing a satisfactory volume in casual slacks, the Day's slacks rep noted, even though the merchant was most skilled in selling other clothing items. He was clumsy in how his skimpy stock was stored in the store; it was awkward for customers to even look at the slacks. Over a period of 2 years the Day's rep slowly and most unobtrusively taught the merchant the ABCs of displaying and selling them. In the end the merchant built a special casual slacks salesroom and these items became his leading profit maker by a large margin.

Sales Training   The selling skills of intermediaries' salespeople usually leave much to be desired. It's difficult to find good retail salespeople. The wholesaler's sales forces are usually not much better. More to the point, they seldom are inclined to push the wares of any single manufacturer unless they have been given a reason to do so.

Experience indicates that if a manufacturer wants the retail or wholesale salesperson to push a line, continual efforts must be exerted to train them. Several forces are at work here. First, salespeople generally avoid trying to sell goods about which they know little, preferring to concentrate on the wares with which they are comfortably familiar; the fear of looking foolish makes them avoid the unknown. Thus much work should be done to give them the product information they need.

Second, intermediaries do little training on sales techniques; their people usually can benefit greatly from even the most basic instruction in sales techniques.

Third, people tend to do things for their friends; as the manufacturer's rep becomes better acquainted with the intermediary's people, they will naturally do more things to sell his or her line.

It usually falls upon the shoulders of the manufacturer's sales rep to do such training; he or she is the one who is in contact with the customer's sales force.

Expediting   After prospects buy, they usually want the goods delivered as promised. But orders do go astray, and production difficulties delay delivery, much to the anguish of both the customer and the sales rep. Fortunately there are times when, with efforts applied in the right places, the salesperson can do some things to expedite the order.

Adjusting   No business transpires without difficulties; things go wrong. The wrong goods are sent, the invoice is incorrect, goods prove defective, or the wrong quantities are received. Whatever, it usually falls upon the rep to straighten out the difficulty. The customer looks to the salesperson for satisfaction.[7]

Communication Channel   Customers possess all sorts of information that would be useful to management if it could but learn of it. The sales force is one means management uses to learn what transpires in the marketplace. A good salesperson keeps alert to learn market trends, competitive developments, and consumer reactions.

Unfortunately, much of the information the sales rep forwards to the sales manager fails to go any farther up the chain of command. One study indicated that only 20 percent of such data was passed on.[9]

As you can surmise from this overview, the account manager's job is diverse and demanding. Add to this the challenge of coordinating sales to all the units of a national company and you have the job of a national account manager.

THE NATIONAL ACCOUNT

Bear in mind that the 500 largest companies in the nation do about 80 percent of the business. These firms have plants, branches, stores, warehouses, and other operations all over the world, but they often buy as a single customer. For a variety of good reasons the firm buys everything for the system from one central location even though the goods may be delivered to the local units from one of the seller's local units. This is called *national buying*. These companies feel that they can buy more advantageously by pooling the com-

Many Fortune 500 companies, such as the Burlington Industries, practice *national buying*, which can result in billions of dollars in sales.

bined volume for the entire system into one negotiation. Moreover, they gain considerable power in the buyer-seller relationship through national buying. The reps servicing such accounts are called *national account managers.*[9]

Naturally, sales to such national accounts can easily amount to billions of dollars. There is much money involved, and the relationship is important to all parties. The account manager has great responsibility and works hard servicing the account.

To a great extent the account manager is working for the account's best interests, always seeking solutions to the account's problems, and trying to help wherever possible.

Serving a national account requires a great deal of work coordinating units within the manager's company to properly serve all of the national account's units. There may be many different sales reps involved in serving the national account, since the rep calling on the home office cannot be around to serve all the company's units. Thus compensating all the people involved with a large account poses problems to management.

SUMMARY

The account manager maintains relationships with customers that provide a continual flow of business to the firm. Often the amount of business controlled by the account manager is quite large. One account may easily mean millions of dollars in sales to the firm.

Such sales reps perform a wide variety of functions, such as soliciting new accounts, expediting orders, training, negotiating, blocking competition from the account, introducing innovation, maintaining relationships inside the account's organization, scheduling, troubleshooting, and coordinating activities connected with serving the account.

While account managers are particularly adept at following up a sale, other types of salespeople also have need for a sound follow-up after a transaction has been made.

National account managers often handle one or more very large accounts. They must coordinate sales to their account's units, which may be located throughout the country, as well as the work of other sales reps serving the national account.

DISCUSSION QUESTIONS

1 "Account management bores me. It's politics and hand-holding. You're always walking on eggs, afraid that you'll lose a big account and get fired. I want to sell something and move on. I don't want to have to live with my customers." Evaluate that statement made by a recent college graduate.

2 "A good account is like a money machine." What did the sales rep who said that mean?

3 "You know, I don't go to Las Vegas. I don't like to gamble. I put all my money into annuities. I really believe in annuities, money coming in regularly." An account

manager was voicing her basic philosophy of life. She continued, "I guess that's why I really like being an account manager." How are those two thoughts compatible?

4 What advantages does the account manager have over the sales rep for the competition who is trying to take an account away?

5 Your firm has developed a new material, an innovation. It would supplant a material you are now selling to a very large account, but if you suggest that the account consider the new material, the existing contract, which is highly profitable, will have to be renegotiated, with all the risks inherent in such negotiations. Would you introduce your account to the new material?

6 Just how much time and attention can you afford to give an account?

7 A buyer for one of your accounts says to you as you sit down for an interview, "I'm not sure I want to talk to you. You've been neglecting us lately." What do you say in reply?

8 Your firm has been the sole source of supply for one of your large accounts. You hear from one of your contacts in the account that the purchasing agent is about to start buying some of the firm's needs from your major competitor. You immediately get an appointment to see the buyer about it. You open the interview, "I heard that you are thinking of buying some of your needs from X Company. Is there something that we have or haven't done?"

   The buyer answers, "No, not at all. It is just that we think we need a multiple source of supply of this item. Matter of policy." What do you say?

9 You have one national account to manage, a very large one that is most rewarding to both you and to your employer. Your contact in the home office calls you one day to complain that some of the regional branches of your firm have been giving poor service at some of the account's plants in other parts of the country. What would you say and do?

10 Your major account has just hired a new buyer from an outside firm. Your information about the person is discouraging. The person has a reputation in the industry of being tough and somewhat unreasonable. What would you do?

REFERENCES

1 Bill Backvold, "Are They Your Accounts?" *American Salesman*, February 1987, pp. 28–30, asserts that customers see salespeople as protectors and should provide them the services they need.

2 Charles Smith, "Sales Complaint Busters," *American Salesman*, January 1990, pp. 3–5, suggests salespeople should view a confrontation between themselves and clients as a chance to right a wrong or to at least set the record straight.

3 Paul Birchard, "How to Get More (and Larger) Orders," *American Salesman*, November 1989, pp. 12–15, suggests the salespeople should do the groundwork and spend more time developing the account; the goal is long-term sales.

4 John F. Tanner, "Leadership through Quality," *Journal of Personal Selling & Sales Management*, Winter 1990, pp. 49–51, suggests that using the marketing concept of identifying and satisfying customer needs is the fundamental way to expand an account's sales.

5 Josef Adams, "The Newcomer's Page: Follow-Through on New Sales," *American Salesman*, February 1989, pp. 6–8, advocates a personal follow-up after the sale to show the salesperson's personal interest in the account.

6 Milt Grassell, "Remembering Your Customers—It Costs Less to Keep Your Customers than to Replace Them," *American Salesman*, October 1986, pp. 7–10, lists the basics of good customer relations: answer questions; mail materials; handle complaints; follow through on transactions; telephone with helpful ideas; provide clippings of interest; write congratulatory notes, holiday cards, and birthday cards; and write a brief newsletter to keep customers informed.

7 Jacquelyn Denalli, "Dealing with Angry Customers," *American Salesman*, May 1989, pp. 16–19, advises the sales representative to be sensitive to both the customer's emotions and the actual problem.

8 Dave Wayman, "How to Write 'Killer' Sales Letters," *American Salesman*, January 1990, pp. 6–9, suggests that the letters appeal directly to needs that are important to the readers and that they back up that appeal with proof.

9 Edwin Simpson, "The National Account Marketing Association: Turning Silver into Gold," *Journal of Personal Selling & Sales Management*, Fall 1989, pp. 65–66, advises that, through the use of survey and purchasing panels, the organization brings top industry decision makers together on items of professional interest.

CASE 15–1: Prudential Securities Inc.—An Account in Jeopardy

Scott Larkin looked up from his desk to see the large angry face of a client, Dr. Bryan, who was evidently not too happy about the management of his substantial Command account. Scott knew what was going to be said for he had heard it from other accounts. Unisys was the seed of this discontent.

In August, 1990 Scott had called his accounts who were interested in income-producing securities about a strong recommendation made by a stock analyst for Prudential to buy the common stock of Unisys, which was then selling for about $10 a share while paying $1.20 a year in dividends—a 12 percent rate of return.

Dr. Bryan had checked with the trust officer of his bank and had been bluntly told, "It's a dog! It's losing money and will cut the dividend." He had relayed that information to Scott, only to be told the analyst insisted that the company was financially sound and would not cut the dividend. Dr. Bryan acquiesced. In October 1990, Unisys stopped paying dividends and the stock dropped to $3 a share.

A lead story appearing in the financial section of *USA Today* featured the plight of the Prudential analyst who had been proven to be only a bit less gullible than the customers who believed his research. It seemed that the number of Prudential customers who had been burned was substantial. There was no explanation for the error.

Dr. Bryan asked, "How can this happen? I told you what the trust officer said, and you told me not to worry. I'm just glad I didn't buy much of that stuff. What happened? What's going to happen?"

1 What should Scott say to Dr. Bryan?

2 How serious do you think this incident is to the account relationship?

CASE 15-2: The Double Eagle Golf Company— How Much Service?

"Boss, I know our organization is built on service. And you know that I give all my accounts good service. But I've got a problem I need some help with." Buzz Green was not in the manager's office to pass the time of day.

The sales manager looked up, smiled, and invited Buzz to sit down and spin his tale of woe.

"You know old Joe Rule, the pro over at Lakes Country Club, don't you?"

"Yeah, we go back a long way. We both went on tour about the same time right after the war. Neither one of us made a dime at it, but we sure had a lot of fun—and played a lot of golf on empty stomachs. Why do you ask?"

"He's giving me fits. He's always after me to come over to the club to play with some of his cronies or to give an exhibition to the members. It never ends. And you know how little he sells. He's the smallest account I have. I'd be better off if I never sold him a club," Buzz complained.

"Well, such is the price of fame, Buzz. After all, you are a minor celebrity of sorts around here. You were on tour and did win some tourneys. People know you. You can't blame old Joe for wanting to impress his members. He's fighting for his job over there."

"Yeah, I know. But so will I be if I go over to Lakes every time Joe calls. I seem to recall that you stressed that we should spend time with an account in proportion to the potential sales we can make from the account," Buzz countered. "It's hurting my coverage of other accounts."

The manager nodded. "I see where it could, but it still is company policy to accommodate all our accounts regardless of size. All the little 'Joes' in this business add up to big volume for us, so we don't want to alienate them.

"You'll have to handle this problem as best you can without making Joe mad at you and us."

As Buzz left the office he wondered why he had bothered. He still had his problem—Joe.

1 How should Buzz handle Joe's frequent requests for attention?

CHAPTER SIXTEEN

SALES MANAGEMENT I

CHAPTER SIXTEEN

SALES MANAGEMENT I

The whole idea of managing salespeople is to devise a system which, after they figure out how to beat it, will have them doing exactly what you want them to do.

Anonymous

After studying the material in this chapter you should:

☐ Understand that the key to successful sales management rests in one's ability to hire the right people for the sales force

☐ Appreciate that sales training is an important part of the sales manager's job

☐ See that, in training salespeople, realistic role playing is an important skill to master

PROFILE OF A

SELLING SALES MANAGER

John Wolf

President
Staar Surgical, Inc.
Monrovia, Calif.

John was one of the initial members of the management team that founded Staar Surgical in 1982. He was given stock options that would make him wealthy if he accomplished the task set before him. He did and not only became rich but also rose to become the firm's president.

Asked about his success as sales manager, he replied, "I've spent my time in the pit and know what it takes to sell in this business. I know the people and I know the competition. I know who can sell and who can't. When the chips are down, I'm not bashful about getting out into the field to help the reps do their jobs. Some months I have to dial for dollars to make our budgets. But we do make our budgets, one way or another."

John has developed creative promotional programs to help the sales reps do their job. In 1985 he created the Staar Express, an excursion train that transported the sales reps and their best customers from Los Angeles to San Francisco to attend a large and important medical conference. In 1986, at the New Orleans meeting, he entertained the customers on a Mississippi riverboat. Staar customers have fun.

John Wolf, president of Staar Surgical, talks with a sales rep about a problem encountered in the field. For John, primary factors in achieving success as a sales manager include familiarity with the market, willingness to directly supervise the sales force, and a creative and innovative approach to promotional programs.

Thus far the discussion has concerned itself with the relation of the salesperson to the *prospect* and with competitors. But there is another interface of great importance—that with the *firm*. Although admittedly more independent than most workers in other lines, the sales rep is under supervision and owes "the house" certain obligations that cannot be wisely ignored. The typical sales rep is likely to be an individualist but still must work under a boss. Whether selling in a store or on the road, the salesperson is part of an organization and subject to its rules.[1]

A couple of generations ago traveling sales representatives were more independent. Communication with the home office was slower and more difficult; they did pretty much as they pleased, they regarded customers as their personal property, and they went from one employer to another and from product to product as the inclination or the reward prompted them. Today, salespeople are far more closely knit into a smooth-functioning machine, each person feeling a greater dependence upon management in preparing and equipping him or her for the job. Customers belong to the firm;

the salesperson is only the connecting link, maintaining the contact. Adequate compensation, encouragement, and control develop loyalty to the firm and the sales manager. Each person has or should have a feeling of permanence and importance with the company.[2]

The major purpose of this discussion is not to instruct you on how to become a sales manager but rather to provide some insights into the managerial framework within which you will be working. Sales managers have some specially developed managerial tools with which you should be familiar in order to comprehend completely the managerial environment which governs selling activities.[3]

When you understand this, it will help you to get the kind of job in which you'll be most successful and happy, and to approach it more intelligently. We also hope that some things in this chapter may facilitate the adjustment process for the young salesperson just embarked on a "shake-down cruise." The more quickly this adjustment process can be accomplished, the more contented and efficient the salesperson will be. Moreover, you may harbor managerial aspirations. Perhaps you elect sales management as a route to the top. If so, this discussion may provide you with some insights into the nature of the job—what it entails.

GETTING THE JOB

It has been said by some sales managers that the firm should select the sales rep and not the reverse. Of course, the sales manager does the hiring, but this does not mean that you should not exercise your choice as to the firm you ask for a job. You should not sit back and await a summons to appear for your interview.[4] Much thought should be given this aspect of your career planning because it is so terribly important to your success.

By now you should have formulated some rather definite opinions as to your fitness for selling. You should know whether you are best qualified to sell staples or specialties, in large cities or in smaller places, one-time sellers or repeaters, tangibles or intangibles, to retail or industrial firms.

The next step in seeking a connection is to study various firms with which you might find congenial employment. Then consider their history, policies, products, and personnel to determine which of them might offer the best opportunity.

Then you might look into the question of the sales manager. If possible, work for an able one. Under the guidance of a talented sales manager you are most apt to develop your full potential. Just as good coaches get the most from their players, good managers will find and develop the skills of their people. Most ambitious young salespeople aspire to be sales managers or heads of their own businesses. They want to learn how to be good administrators from a boss who is a master of the art.

You can learn much if you will carefully observe a top-flight manager in action. Better yet, get to know the manager well enough so that you can discuss the reasons behind the actions.

It is important to choose your boss carefully. It has been demonstrated repeatedly that a good administrator will build a strong organization, while a weak administrator never can build one or even maintain one that was strong before the changeover.

When seeking your first selling job you will, of course, realize that although you may not be so fortunate as to connect immediately with the precise firm and sales manager that you might have wished, you may be successful in doing so later.

Those of you who have persisted thus far should realize that *obtaining a job is often a selling task* in which you can utilize everything you have learned about salesmanship. You will make a careful preapproach; you will plan your approach and generally bring into play every bit of selling skill at your command.

The one matter most requiring emphasis here is that you should have something to sell, if you present yourself with an *idea of value* to your prospective employer, you are *in*.

Take the young woman who wanted a job on a newspaper. Her first step was to study the paper and compare it with other papers. Presently she noted that it had no department devoted to a discussion of new recordings, a subject of interest to many readers. So she haunted a record store, read up on the subject, and spotted similar departments in other papers (the local library subscribed to these). When she felt she was ready, she wrote several sample articles and took them to the editor. She also pointed out the possibility of stimulating new advertising from stores selling recordings. She had promises of such advertising if her articles were run regularly.

About one applicant in a hundred bothers to present an idea of value to the prospective employer. This one lands the job.

This matter of obtaining a job is only one side of the question. The other side is obtaining a sales representative. That is, it is a mutual problem, of equal interest to applicant and to employer. It costs the employer thousands of dollars to train a salesperson, and employers try to avoid spending this money on a poor prospect. Many firms go to great lengths to tell prospective sales reps all about the company and the work of its salespeople, often stressing the unpleasant aspects of the job. They figure that this eliminates some applicants who feel that they would not fit into the job or fear they would find it too hard.

Where does one find out about the qualities of these potential employers? One good source of information is the firm's own salespeople. The word gets around rapidly in selling circles as to which firms are "good places to work." If a sales rep has a good boss, he or she usually lets everyone know it. Conversely, the reputation of poor managers is usually broadcast widely in an industry. By all means you should talk with the sales reps of a firm that you are considering working for.

Kathryn wanted to sell furniture for a manufacturer—which one she did not know, but she had a plan. She talked with several furniture dealers, asking about which firms were the comers in the market, which seemed to have the best sales force, and which seemed to be the most progressive. Three companies were continually pointed out as excellent operations. She successfully focused her efforts on them.

Jobs vary greatly in their attractiveness.[5] Unfortunately, it is the "bad" jobs that are most readily available, particularly to the beginning salesperson. After all, people do not often quit good jobs, and when they do, the employer has a long list of proven, top-notch representatives who are eager to go to work for the firm. Good jobs do not go looking for you; you must go after them. And that itself requires salesmanship.[6]

RECRUITING

The amount of recruiting that companies do for their sales jobs varies tremendously among firms. Some companies do no recruiting; their sales jobs are so attractive that they have many more excellent applicants than they have job openings. At the other end of the spectrum are firms with such unattractive jobs and their job turnover is so high that they are continually recruiting large numbers of people. A few follow the practice known as, "If the body is warm, hire it."

Not too many years ago recruiting posed far more problems than it does today, because the size of the labor pool from which interested people could be drawn was much smaller. Back then, when most firms only considered hiring men as sales reps, the firms were contending vigorously for the

Major industrialists hold job fairs at university campuses for graduating math and computer science majors. Why might sales be an ideal entry-level position for candidates seeking employment in business and industry?

relatively few talented men who were interested in a sales career. Now that women are freely, even eagerly, recruited for sales jobs, not only is the size of the labor pool larger but its quality is often enhanced.[7]

Recruiters search for new sales personnel in a variety of sources. First, they look within the firm's nonselling ranks to see if there is someone who would like to get into sales and has the requisite talents to do so. This is the cheapest and easiest action the manager can take, and it is good for company morale because many people in the plant look upon being transferred into sales as a promotion. So, if there is a particular firm for which you wish to sell but find there is presently no opening on the sales force, you might well accept employment in another capacity, making your ultimate desire for sales work known at the time.

Second, most good firms have a file of applications from people seeking employment with them. True, the quality of these applications may not be as high as management would prefer, but many times management will still go through them because of the low cost of doing so. However, wise applicants will periodically follow up on such applications to let the firm know they are still interested.

An obviously strong desire to work for the firm must impress management, because in most instances management is saddled with just the opposite kind of person—one who is indifferent or even hostile to management's efforts.[8]

Third, many managers ask their sales reps for leads to good recruits on the theory that good people know and recognize other good people. Again this is inexpensive and relatively easy recruiting. You can take advantage of this practice by letting the sales representatives of target employers know of your interest in their firms.

Fourth, personal contact with the sales manager can be highly effective. Many sales reps owe their jobs to some chance meeting with the sales manager during which the manager became impressed with the person's abilities. Perhaps the manager saw the individual in action selling something. No matter what the circumstances, no one was ever damaged by favorably impressing a potential employer.

Many firms, after exhausting the previously discussed sources for recruits, contact employment agencies, but numerous sales managers avow that a real sales rep should not rely on someone else to "sell" him or her. Really good selling jobs seldom come through employment agencies, but there are exceptions.

Advertising for salespeople is usually the last resort reserved for employers who need a large number of applicants to process. Some fairly decent jobs can be found in this source, particularly in the nonclassified advertising in the financial or sports sections of the newspaper or in trade journals, so job hunters should not automatically ignore this source. But discriminate between advertisements that promise to make you rich overnight and those that offer *bona fide* possibilities with reputable concerns.

Strong verbal and written communication skills, motivation, experience, and education are among the qualifications often listed in ads recruiting potential sales representatives. What criteria would you look for if you were planning to apply for a position listed in an ad?

The best advice that can be given the job hunter is simply this: Choose a firm that you would like to sell for and then directly approach its sales manager for a job. If you locate a job that you really want, go get it. Be aggressive! Sell yourself! But remember that sales managers with highly attractive positions to fill seldom have to recruit; they are usually deluged with voluntary applicants. It may take some time to get in with the firm of your choice, but it is worth the time and trouble to make every effort to do so.[9]

THE SELECTION PROCESS

Six or possibly seven steps are usually followed in the selection of applicants for sales jobs. Each one of these steps should be looked upon by applicants as a separate attempt to weed out the undesirable and to employ only the most qualified person. This is advantageous from the standpoint of the individual, since it is an honest effort by management to improve the quality of salespeople, to hire only those people who can put the work upon a higher plane, and to protect those engaged in it from the encroachment of others who are poorly prepared to work in a professional manner. The basic steps in this selective or eliminative program are (1) the application form; (2) verifying the information provided by the applicant; (3) the personal interviews; (4) tests of various sorts to measure qualities desired in applicants, such as intelligence, initiative, various personality traits, good health, persistence, poise, and aptitude for the particular job. A more complete version of this process can be seen in Figure 16–1.

Bear in mind that in sales management theory nothing is more important to the building of a successful organization than hiring the right people. With the right people, the sales manager's tasks are greatly simplified. With the wrong ones, the manager will know little but grief. The more important selling is to the success of the firm, the more careful management will be in selecting the sales force.

Basic Philosophy

Several philosophies should be continually borne in mind while studying selection processes. First, nothing you as manager can do is more important to the firm's success than how well you perform this task. Thus do not begrudge it the time you will have to spend on it or the seemingly large amount of money it costs. You must do it if you truly seek success.

FIGURE 16–1 Model of employer's selection process.

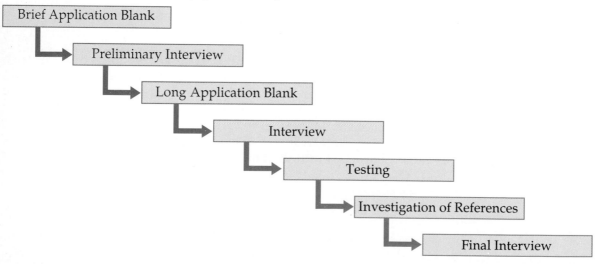

Second, try either to maintain or obtain a sufficiently large pool of fully qualified recruits from which to select, so that you have some choices to make.

Third, try to identify and reject unqualified recruits as quickly as possible so that selection costs are lessened. As long as each recruit is still being considered, it costs the firm money.

Fourth, use the most inexpensive selection techniques first, saving the most expensive ones for late in the process when the number of people has been whittled down to only a few.

Fifth, most managers look upon the selection process in terms of probabilities. They understand that each applicant has a certain probability of failure; they try to select the person who they think has the best probability for succeeding, fully realizing that no matter how good the person appears to be, there is a chance those expectations will not be realized. Even though the chances of success might be good for several applicants, the offer will be made to the person who poses the least risk.

The Applicant Form

The qualified applicant should welcome the opportunity to put his or her record down on paper for the inspection of the employer. Every question should be answered accurately and completely. The manner in which an application form is filled out is in itself an indication of the character of the applicant. Careless, sloppy, and poorly written forms create serious doubts in the employer's mind about the applicant's intelligence and general awareness of what is and is not important in business. Moreover, salespeople must complete sales order forms, expense reports, call reports, and the like, in which legibility is essential. If the applicant can't fill out a job application form neatly, what is likely to happen to the paperwork on the job? Most sales managers do not care to have the person around long enough to find out the answer to that question.

A hesitant, grudging compliance with the request to fill out the form may indicate that the applicant will have the same attitude toward routine tasks and reports that must be filled out. On the other hand, a cheerful and cooperative attitude is apt to indicate a similar handling of unpleasant and tedious duties that must be performed later. The application form furnishes a valuable record of the applicant for future reference in case of employment. It also supplies an effective means of eliminating a number of applicants before the sales manager's time has been wasted in personal interviews.

Many people who apply for a job are unqualified. Normally, these people are detected and rejected by a short screening of their first application form, on which they have been asked to give their basic qualifications.

Some application forms are awesome in their proportions and in the minuteness of the information requested. They pry into the applicant's personal history with a thoroughness that may be irritating if there is anything one prefers to conceal. But one would be wise to fill such forms in fully, with no gaps unaccounted for and no discrepancies or contradictions.

Employers carefully scrutinize application forms to try to discover people who are not what they claim to be. Some recruits claim education or experience they do not have. Others try to hide unfavorable experiences by extending the dates of other experiences. Many sales managers demand a careful account for *all* the recruit's time since entering the labor market.

When these application forms are evaluated after they are filled out, some of the questions are given greater weight than are others. Since the applicant may not know which ones are thus weighted, it is important to answer each question as carefully as possible. However, the section on work experience is almost always an important one. An outstanding work record will usually overcome serious deficiencies in other areas. Conversely, a bad work record can nullify an otherwise outstanding background.

References

Experienced sales managers say, "The person who needs a lot of references will usually have them." If former friends and business acquaintances of the applicant are given as references, they will normally give the person a good send-off just to be helpful. In many instances they will not know enough about the applicant to furnish any valuable facts to the employer. When former employers of the applicant are given as references, two difficulties arise. In some cases the applicant may have been dismissed by the person, and a recommendation will be given out of sympathy. In other cases where the applicant has left the former employer voluntarily, there may be some feeling of resentment or unfriendliness toward the applicant. The most effective use of references is to secure enough of them so that a cross section of opinion is obtained. By this method the practice of "whitewashing" by friends or former employers as well as the tendency to "run down" an applicant usually can be detected. Some reference forms come out baldly with the request for statements about weaknesses and shortcomings of the applicant so that the new employers, knowing them in advance, can attempt to prevent their recurrence in the future.

Most smart sales managers rely more on telephone conversations with references whose opinions they respect. A reference is more likely to disclose pertinent facts about an applicant if not forced to put them on paper, as one never knows who may read what one has written. Also, the sales manager can learn much about potential recruits by the *way* references talk about them. There are many ways of saying the same sentence; little overtones, nuances, inflection, emphasis on certain words, and general attitude reveal much when spoken.

The applicant should try to provide references which mean something. The name of a leading sales executive will carry more weight than that of a neighbor or fraternity chum. Careful thought should be given to the choice of references for still another reason: Many people cannot write effective letters of recommendation, thereby injuring the applicant's chances. The potential employer wishes to hear about a person's work habits, dependability, productivity, loyalty, and ability to work with others, rather than about religion, family connections, how sweet he was as a small child, or what a fine parent she was or is.

While most managers downplay the importance of references, most of them still feel that it is necessary to follow through on them to see if by chance there is anything to be learned about the recruit from them.

Above all, the applicant should have obtained the references' prior permission to use their names.

The Personal Interview

Few salespeople are hired without a series of personal interviews, which are far more important to sales managers making a hiring decision than are resumes, application forms, or references. In the personal interview, sales managers form opinions of the applicant's appearance, voice, bearing, poise, resourcefulness, and general philosophy of selling. They like a person who is well-groomed and who looks as though it is a regular practice to be that way. They like a person who can look them squarely in the eye without embarrassment. They like a firm handshake. They like a person whose voice is pleasant and who knows how to use it to advantage. They prefer someone who cannot be thrown into a display of temper, who does not laugh immoderately at the sales manager's jokes, who, in short, has poise.

Many sales managers make it a practice to draw applicants out, to encourage them to tell their life stores, to state their hobbies and favorite forms of recreation or reading. They claim that more can be learned in this way about someone's real character than by all the application forms in existence. Somewhere in this interview most reputable concerns insert a topic of conversation designed to test an applicant's code of business ethics. They prefer honest people.

The applicant for a sales position will do well to make a preapproach before submitting to this interview. Learn as much as possible about the company, its policies, and its products, so that you can intelligently answer the sales manager who suddenly inquires, "What makes you think you want to work for *us*?" Most of the principles of the preapproach may profitably be applied by the applicant for a selling job. The very fact that you have made such an investigation proves to the prospective employer that you believe in its value and would probably continue the practice in actual selling.

Usually applicants are interviewed several times by the same manager or in succession by several executives. This is done to get a better line on the applicants and to check up on them. For example, a person might bear up well under the ordeal of the first interview but begin to "crack" at the second or third. Also, interviewees who have been careless with the truth are likely to contradict themselves at some point in the various interviews. Moreover, the executives like to have their impressions of the applicant verified by others. It is easy for one executive to somehow get a wrong impression on some critical issue.

Dr. Robert McMurry* described the interview system used by a large national advertiser to uncover traits which contribute to a salesperson's *promotability*. Many of these same questions may also be asked of an applicant *before* being employed. The essential traits which Dr. McMurry endeavored to discover in this interview program were (1) a high development of industry, ambition, loyalty, self-reliance, willingness to accept responsibility, and capability of dealing with and handling people, and (2) a capacity for meeting emergencies and handling situations demanding courage, initiative, and moral stamina. He was also interested in the influence of the person's domestic life. These traits do not lend themselves to measurement as simply and exactly as intelligence or product knowledge, which may be ascertained from tests; there are no written psychological tests which provide insights into one's personality complex or which determine what a person will do under pressure. Personality is a combination of many traits, which may be present in different patterns and configurations in different individuals. A single index that adequately expresses these complicated relationships is, therefore, impossible to develop. The *dominant* traits of a person's personality must be determined because it is these that govern our actions and responses and make possible the prediction of our behavior.

Dr. McMurry concluded that the best way to gain an insight into these dominant traits which make up a person's personality is, first, to listen to the individual's life story from childhood to maturity, stressing social, domestic, and business relationships. Secondly, observe carefully the person's behavior on the job or among friends. Perhaps assign a hard or unpleasant task to perform; then watch the response to it—does the person do it cheerfully and efficiently or try to shift the responsibility to someone else? It is claimed that such a series of tests will invariably provide sufficient material to allow a thorough "personalysis," because it is practically impossible for the person to conceal or change certain conditions. Dr. McMurry described the detailed working of this plan and commented as follows upon its chief aim or purpose:

A program of this type has been in use now for nearly three years with considerable success by a national sales organization. It consists of three parts:

1 *The field interview:* A specially trained representative of the company spends from one to two days in the field with each candidate who is regarded as promising on the basis of production and service records and rating by at least four people. In order to conceal the true purpose of the interview, the home-office representative explains that he is studying sales methods and is interested in obtaining any constructive suggestions the candidates may care to offer.

*Robert N. McMurry, head of the consulting firm bearing his name, is a psychologist specializing in sales personnel problems.

The interview is conducted with the person as he works on the job and with complete informality. This is done partly because many of the candidates are busy and would be reluctant to spare the time; partly because much can be learned by observing someone in action among prospects and associates (even if the person suspects the true purpose of the call and attempts to put on an act for the interviewer, he cannot alter attitudes of others toward him); and partly because an interview in an office is necessarily somewhat artificial and tends to put anyone on the defensive.

In the course of these informal talks, information is obtained specifically upon the following points:

a Early upbringing, with particular reference to formation of habits of industry and self-reliance and ability to get along with other persons.

b Schooling, with special attention to social adjustment and evidences of leadership.

c Work history, with emphasis on attitudes toward work, associates, superiors; the extent to which he has shown initiative, ambition, and creative imagination; and the progress which he has made in gaining increases in compensation and responsibility.

d Social adjustment as an adult, with reference to friendship, hobbies, and modes of recreation; social, religious, and political beliefs; and the extent to which he is respected and a leader in the community.

e Domestic adjustments, with special attention to family relationships; whether he has established a home of his own; whether he is dependent upon spouse or others for a portion of support; the extent to which the spouse may be expected to be a help or a hindrance to him in his work.

2 *Difficult assignments and frustration:* The second step in the program is to subject the person to pressure. Here, for example, he may be required to make an effort to see unusually difficult prospects. Or he may be asked to handle particularly unpleasant customer complaints. In the course of carrying out these assignments an opportunity is provided not only to observe his response to the assignments themselves but also, in those cases where he is unable to carry them through, to see how he responds to disappointment, failure, and frustration.

3 *The home interview:* The third step (the program is not necessarily carried out in any regular order) is the conduct of a very informal interview—ostensibly a friendly call—with the person's spouse, and other family members in the home, preferably at the person's own invitation. Here, however, unless extreme care and tact are used by the interviewer, little of value will be obtained. If it is necessary to apply pressure or use artificial pretexts, not only will little information be obtained but actual ill will may be created.

The person who is eager to obtain a position with a particular organization is well advised to locate someone who has been through the firm's selection process recently to learn of any tricky situations that some managers like to create for the recruit. One sales manager startles applicants by asking them first off, "So you think you can sell? Well, sell me a new car!" Applicants who are prepared for such tactics naturally have a better chance of successfully handling them and still maintaining their poise than those caught by surprise.

The Use of Tests

The application form, in spite of its detail, may fail to disclose weaknesses in the applicant. In some cases the careful checking of references and even the personal interview may not divulge serious shortcomings. For this reason tests of many kinds are sometimes used to further the job selection. Belief in the saying "Poor selection means rapid turnover in salespeople" influences the sales manager to employ every possible device to reduce the number of mistakes in selection that have been all too common in the past.

Space does not permit a lengthy discussion of these tests, but the college student of today is fairly familiar with some of them. While such tests are far from infallible and are usually supplemented by other means of appraising a candidate's fitness, nevertheless they are used by many firms and are being improved steadily. They measure such things as:

Mental Ability or Capacity to Learn If the product to be sold is complicated and the training course long and difficult, people who lack the capacity to learn cannot master the material. It is a kindness to eliminate them before they waste their time and the company's money. In the case of simple propositions, the selling of which demands little mental ability, this test may serve the purpose of eliminating the candidates who are too smart and would soon quit the job because it is below their capacities.

There are several tests that can measure fairly well what is commonly called "intelligence." However, we are beginning to realize that intelligence has many more dimensions to it than were recognized in our traditional tests, which measure largely verbal, math, perceptive, and logical talents. The general assumption is that the individual who possesses these skills will also have other talents; it is true that a high correlation exists between these talents, but it is far from perfect. A person ranking quite low in math or verbal skills might well possess exceptional social intelligence.

Information Acquired in School and by Home Study The prospective seller of accounting machines should know accountancy and business practices, while the sales representative for road-building machinery should have workable knowledge of road-building and earth-moving techniques. Some firms especially favor the applicant who has taken correspondence or night school courses while employed regularly on a job. It is evidence of a desire to succeed, a most important personality characteristic. Such information can be determined by tests or oral questioning.

Personality Characteristics In recent years much discussion has taken place as to the value of personality testing in the selection of salespeople. Many employers swear by such tests, while others swear at them. For the purposes of this discussion it need only be said that a great number of the larger concerns in this country use such tests. How much they really believe in them is another matter. An executive of one of the nation's largest employers of highly skilled sales engineers confessed to the author that for all the time and money the corporation had put behind the development and standardization of their highly regarded testing program, an internal study of its validity had disclosed the disheartening fact that the tests had not distinguished between their successful and unsuccessful sales reps. But the company continues to make use of these tests. So the job seeker had best be prepared for the ordeal by pencil.

Equal Opportunity laws and several court decisions have cast suspicion on the use of psychological tests for selecting salespeople. The courts have insisted that employers be able to show that their testing programs are relevant to the jobs being filled. If the test is irrelevant, then the firm may be challenged in court concerning its validity as a predictor of sales success. Validation is a difficult task. It is costly, time-consuming, and perhaps impossible to do for many sales jobs.[10]

TRAINING

Some training of newly hired salespeople is required in all concerns even if it is no more than a brief introduction to the product line and some information on the firm's policies. But today most large concerns find it necessary to institute formal sales-training programs for their new salespeople, particularly if they hire young people or those inexperienced at selling. However, these training programs vary widely in excellence: Some are good, and some are not so good.[11]

An executive analyzes her videotaped performance at a speech-making workshop in Newport Beach, California. Lectures, conferences, and workshops help sales personnel sharpen their skills and broaden their knowledge.

In fact a young person planning a sales career may be wise to accept first employment with an eye to the firm's sales-training program even though harboring other thoughts for an eventual career. It is usually not too difficult to determine the amount and nature of training offered the applicant; it is certainly fair for the interviewee to ask about such things during interviews.

Wise management usually spreads the recruits' training over considerable time, initially giving only what is needed to get them into the field with an adequate degree of proficiency. Additional training is forthcoming as they gain experience and prove their dedication to selling and the firm.

A word of warning: Although it may not appear so, management is carefully appraising the trainees while they are in training, and the trainees' performance bears heavily upon the type of assignment they will be given upon graduation. The best trainee usually gets the best assignment.

While sales training begins by using conventional educational tools, such as lectures, movies, and discussion, it is difficult to hone one's selling skills through exposure to those methods alone. To learn selling one must sell. And that means role playing.[12]

Role Playing

Role playing consists of placing trainees in realistic situations and allowing them to sell simulated prospects. If the method is to work effectively, care must be taken to make the prospects realistic in their reactions and to place them in a realistic environment. The trainee must be given the preapproach information an actual salesperson would have before calling on the individual.

This type of learning-by-doing education can be highly effective in teaching selling techniques, particularly in initial training programs. The trainees are placed in a situation that subjects them to the many unforeseen developments that always arise in selling. Besides the training the students obtain in handling selling techniques, role playing also allows the instructor to work with each individual on such things as voice, poise, bearing, mannerisms, speech, and movements, which are all highly important factors bearing on the ultimate success of a sales rep.

Many things brought to light by role-playing situations would otherwise remain unknown. Ordinarily calm and collected students have broken down in an actual sale from nervousness or lack of confidence. There is no question that role playing is the best method yet developed for convincing the student of the validity of certain principles. The instructor can emphatically stress the necessity for product information, but let a trainee come before the class in a role-playing situation not adequately knowing the product, and the ridiculousness of the position is brought to the class's attention in an unforgettable manner. In one instance, a student was to sell Pyrex glass cookingware to a hardware store owner. Thinking that the "unbreakable" feature of the product meant that it was literally unbreakable, the student's approach consisted of coming in the door and deliberately dropping a set of Pyrex onto the floor. He had hoped to demonstrate forcibly to the merchant his product's major selling point. This could have been an excellent approach. Unfortunately, as he swept up the broken glass he succeeded only in convincing everyone that he did not know his product—the "unbreakable" feature he had been told about referred only to the application of heat. This demonstration was indelibly etched into the memory of the students; to this day when members of the class see the teacher they laugh about the incident, and many have related just how it taught them an unforgettable lesson. They said they resolved right then and there never to be caught in the same position as that student standing there, embarrassed, sweeping up a pile of broken glass.

Role playing also shows the student in a most convincing fashion that *knowing* what to do is one thing, but *doing* it is another. One of the major weaknesses of most selling courses is that they only teach the student *about* selling, not *how* to sell. Many students can recite all the various methods of approaching prospects, answering objections, and closing the sale. However, many are shocked to learn how much of this knowledge they can forget under the emotional involvement in a sales situation.

In a sales-training program designed for teaching new recruits selling techniques, extensive use should be made of role playing. It takes practice to perfect a sales presentation; one or two attempts are inadequate to accomplish the task. Although it would be impossible to definitely establish any given minimum number of times each trainee should be placed into a role-playing situation, four or five times is probably the absolute minimum.

Observers   Many trainers prefer to have each sales presentation performed before the entire class so that all the students can benefit from it. While this obviously reduces the number of presentations that can be made in a given length of time, it does have much to recommend it. First, many times the students can see a few things that escape the teacher and can recommend actions that may otherwise go unmentioned. Second, the teacher can escape some possible resentment by the trainee by allowing the class to do the major criticizing. Further, if the class uniformly says the same thing, the trainee is more likely to accept it as the truth. Third, while the trainee is learning through role playing, the class learns by watching and often is deeply impressed. They see things that they resolve never to do. For this reason, each presentation invariably gets better as the teacher progresses through the class, even though for each student it is the first sale. The first few presentations are usually very poor: The teacher must take great care to inform the class and the trainees chosen to lead off the series that many mistakes will be made and things will not go as smoothly as might have been expected. However, it should be pointed out to the students that basically they will learn best through making mistakes. Sometimes, the instructor is wise to pick for the first few presentations people who apparently have some skill in verbal activities and selling. This can get the sessions off to a good start and give the completely inexperienced trainees some idea about the entire process.

It is usually wise to prepare some form of rating sheet for each observer to complete on each sale. Otherwise, during the sale observers can forget the points they want to bring out. They should write down immediately any comments they want to make on any phase of the sale. The rating form also serves as a record for the trainee to study in trying to improve. In connection with this rating sheet, the instructor should make clear that no grades are given on any sale—that it is merely a learning device. Grading is usually unfair, since the first salespeople are penalized and the later performers are rewarded because of the learning that takes place during each sale. The last trainee should have learned much about selling by the time his or her turn occurs.

In handling the role-playing sessions, trainers must go to extreme lengths to convince the students of the importance of taking criticisms in the right way. They must convince them that they are there only to help them earn more money and that absolutely nothing is meant personally by any criticism. They must point out that there is no such thing as a perfect sale—that everyone makes mistakes in every sale. They must convince them that for many situations there are no cut-and-dried answers to the problem, and that criticisms on those points are only designed to give them some ideas about other ways of handling the problems.

Role playing without criticism is of limited value, since the trainee has no way of determining what is right or wrong. Although practice without observers may aid in polishing delivery and mastery of the presentation, much more is accomplished when observers are present to react to the performance.

An important fact frequently overlooked by many teachers of selling is that the trainee should be commended on the good features of the sale, and that these can provide as valuable a learning experience as mistakes. In one sale when the prospect was a blustering, loud individual who had strong opinions about the product being sold, the salesperson spoke in a soft, calm voice and allowed the prospect to talk freely about his feelings. Certainly, the interview took more time than usual, but after the prospect had expressed his feelings, the salesperson was able to shape the presentation to fit the man's stated desires and dislikes. Also, the class observed how the prospect quieted down as the rep got calmer, in direct contrast to a previous sales presentation when the trainee made the mistake of getting loud right along with the prospect until they were yelling at each other.

Frequently, the trainer is tempted to concentrate too much on the small details at the expense of ignoring larger factors. One of the first questions the instructor should put to the class is, "Just why did the salesperson fail to make the sale?" or "just why did the salesperson get the order?" It is important for the students to acquire an ability to see just where a sale was made or lost. Frequently, one major reason or event decided the affair. For instance, one trainee did a rather poor job in making her presentation and in attempting to close, but she got the order anyway. It was easy to point out the many mistakes that occurred, but much more was learned by indicating the basic reason why the order was obtained. In this case, it was because the seller had taken the trouble to locate an excellent prospect and had allowed him to do all the talking. She just let the man talk himself into the sale, which is good selling. This one factor overrode the small errors the woman had made.

Importance of the Buyer   In role-playing situations, the buyers should be given specific identities, such as the owner of a certain store actually in existence or the purchasing agent of a real company. Then the buyers should have information about the company they are representing so that they can make the proper reactions to the salesperson's proposition. Without a definite company situation, buyers are unable to answer questions intelligently; they must fabricate answers, and this prevents the salesperson from preparing answers to them. If the trainee is selling Texas Instruments calculators to business executives, the buyer should be told that he is Mr. Jones, who is controller of a given local concern. The buyer then should project himself in the role and try to act just as he would if he were really the controller of that firm. If he fails to do this, the sale is unrealistic and little learning takes place. The trainer should go to some effort to locate individuals who can successfully fill the role of a realistic buyer. Many times, she may find it advisable to act as buyer if she feels she is best qualified for the role. One danger with this is that the trainees tend to think the instructor is being too hard on them when in reality she is only trying to give the trainee a maximum amount of sales resistance. The trainer must convince the trainees that they will never excel in selling by practicing only on easy buyers.

PROGRAM CONTENT

Most sales-training programs focus on four major areas: (1) product knowledge, (2) customer applications and problems, (3) company knowledge, and (4) selling techniques. Traditionally, training programs were heavily slanted toward product and company knowledge with too little attention paid to selling techniques and the prospect's problems.

Product Knowledge

Understandably sales-training programs have been strongly oriented toward furnishing the trainee with the necessary product knowledge because even the dullest of managers recognized that the salespeople had to know about the firm's products if they were to be able to sell them. Fortunately, teaching product knowledge is a rather straightforward matter, but it can be burdensome if the product is complicated, as is the case with computers, or if the product line is large. Sometimes the trainee spends time in the factory or in the service department to learn about the product.

Bear in mind that only large companies hire and train several people at the same time. Large concerns such as NCR, IBM, and Xerox conduct sizable sales-training schools on a formal basis. More typically, in smaller organizations, only one or two people are in sales training at any one time. Much of the time such concerns have no new recruits in training, but that does not negate the need for a sales-training program—a continual one for the existing sales force. As new products are brought forth, the sales force needs information about them. Product knowledge training is particularly critical in the selling of industrial goods, whose buyers expect the sales rep to be a technical expert.

Customer Applications and Problems

We have previously seen that product knowledge is not enough—that one must know how to apply that product information to the customer's problems. The key to selling is proving to the prospect's satisfaction that the product provides the best solution for the application. Thus a great deal of attention should be devoted to the study and solution of customer problems.

Xerox approaches this type of training through the extensive use of case histories, in which its machines are applied to a wide range of needs. For example, if the sales rep is planning to call upon a police department, a reference to the Xerox sales manuals would disclose how one rep applied a large photocopier to the problems of the St. Louis Police Department.

Company Knowledge

The new sales trainee has to know many things about the company: how it operates, who does what, its reporting systems, and its history, plans, and policies. Most of this information can be provided by written material and amplified with lectures.

Selling Techniques

Unquestionably, the teaching of selling techniques is a considerably more difficult endeavor than is instruction in the previous three subject matter areas, in which we were largely concerned with the transfer of essentially factual material. Since selling requires quick reaction to situations created by the prospect, the mere possession of knowledge is not enough. Moreover, the wide variety of situations, combined with the fact that there is no one right way to handle any one situation, means that instructional techniques should rely heavily on role playing (which has been previously discussed) plus roundtable discussions in which experienced people can exchange insights with the rookies.

As sales manager for a company selling a record system for banks, would you assign this account to a man or to a woman? Who might be more effective? Or would it matter?

There is little need to review the subject matter covered in teaching selling techniques, for that has been the topic of this whole book.

SUMMARY

Successful salespeople often aspire to management; the first rung in the ladder upward is in sales management. In large corporations, there are several layers of sales management: district, regional, national, and international. Such jobs can be most satisfying.

Staffing the sales force, which involves recruiting and selection, is a major ongoing task in most organizations and requires much of the sales manager's attention. Fortunately, the size and quality of the labor pool from which salespeople can be hired has expanded in recent decades because of the increased interest of women in sales positions.

Once the recruit is hired, training is needed. Sales training is continual and commands much of the manager's concern. Stress should be placed on role playing in the training program.

DISCUSSION QUESTIONS

1 How could you appraise, before accepting a job, the quality of training that will be provided for you?
2 Since the qualities of your immediate superior are important to your development, how can you determine them prior to working for the person?
3 Suppose you are sales manager for a carpet manufacturer in Georgia. You have a vacancy on your sales force in the southern California territory. From what sources would you seek recruits?
4 Why does the use of psychological tests in selecting salespeople cause controversy?
5 Although many experts consider a recruit's references a waste of time, still most managements require them and contact the people. Why?
6 Why do sales managers place so much value upon a recruit's work experience?
7 What constitutes a good work record?
8 Why is sales training a continual managerial activity?
9 Why is product knowledge a continual sales-training problem?
10 Why do sales trainers rely so much on role playing in teaching sales techniques?

REFERENCES

1 John F. Tanner and Stephen B. Castleberry, "Vertical Exchange Quality and Performance: Studying the Role of the Sales Manager," *Journal of Personal Selling & Sales Management*, Spring 1990, pp. 17–27, describe the interaction process that integrates the salesperson's attempts at influencing the manager with the actual management by the sales manager.
2 Michael H. Morris, Ramon A. Avila, and Eugene E. Teeple, "Sales Management as an Entrepreneurial Activity," *Journal of Personal Selling & Sales Management*, Spring 1990, pp. 1–15, discuss the nature and role of entrepreneurship as it applies within sales and how it affects company loyalty.
3 Jens Maier and John Saunders, "The Implementation Process of Segmentation in Sales Management," Winter 1990, pp. 39–48, discuss eight stages for using segmentation to guide sales-force allocation and selling tactics: enter, agree on focus, identify segments, validate segments, select targets, develop strategy, implement, and track.
4 Donald B. Guest and Havva J. Meric, "The Fortune 500 Companies' Selection Criteria for Promotion to First Level Sales Management: An Empirical Study," *Journal of Personal Selling & Sales Management*, Fall 1989, pp. 47–52, point out that existing lists of desirable attributes for managers typically mix knowledge, skills, and personality traits and fail to distinguish between qualities that must be innate and those that can be developed with training.
5 William S. Pierson, "An Honest Day's Work," *American Salesman*, November 1989, pp. 7–9, states that while sales is one of the most demanding professions, it also is one of the most rewarding.
6 Jeffrey K. Sager and Mark W. Johnston, "Antecedents and Outcomes of Organizational Commitment: A Study of Salespeople," *Journal of Personal Selling & Sales Management*, Spring 1989, pp. 30–41, suggest that anticipatory socialization, along with work and manager satisfaction, are determinants of commitment to the job.
7 The literature on the role and impact of women in selling is substantial. Some of the books and articles worth reading are Myron Gable and B. J. Reed, "The Current

Status of Women in Professional Selling," *Journal of Personal Selling & Sales Management*, May 1987, pp. 33–39 (rationalize the rapid increase of women in selling); Ellen J. Knudsen, "Sexuality in Selling," *American Salesman*, December 1987, pp. 26–28 (discusses the problems associated with sexuality in selling and suggests that the best policy is to keep one's mind thoroughly on the product and its presentation); Darrel D. Muehling and William A. Weeks, "Women's Perceptions of Personal Selling: Some Positive Results," *Journal of Personal Selling & Sales Management*, May 1988, pp. 11–20 (report positive predispositions from college women toward selling); "Rise in Number of Women in Sales Positions," *American Salesman*, May 1986, pp. 14–15 (reports a survey by the Research Institute of America showing a large increase in women in sales); Frederick A. Russ and Kevin M. McNeilly, "Has Sex Stereotyping Disappeared? A Study of Perceptions of Women and Men in Sales," *Journal of Personal Selling & Sales Management*, November 1988, pp. 43–54 (report the results of a study on women's and men's attitudes toward sales positions); and Richard Buskirk and Beverly Miles, *Beating Men at Their Own Game*, Wiley, New York, 1980 (report the results of a field study of industrial saleswomen which indicated that they were highly successful in their jobs).

8 Raymond Dreyfack, "The Selling Edge," *American Salesman*, December 1989, pp. 23–26, maintains that the personal comfort index is highly related to self-motivation, which is an essential ingredient for a successful sales career.

9 Thomas R. Wotruba, Edwin K. Simpson, and Jennifer L. Reed-Draznik, "The Recruiting Interview as Perceived by College Student Applicants for Sales Positions," *Journal of Personal Selling & Sales Management*, Fall 1989, pp. 13–24, discuss the attributes of entry-level selling job offers as perceived by graduating seniors in specific job interview experiences.

10 Lee Boyan, "Who's More Productive?" *American Salesman*, November 1989, pp. 16–19, suggests that saleswomen are more productive than salesmen.

11 "Good Speech Habits," *American Salesman*, July 1988, pp. 9–11, suggests that salespeople who have careless speech habits usually do not get the sale, careless speech suggests indifference, and it takes practice and thought to speak well. These skills should be stressed in training.

12 K. Randall Russ, Joseph F. Hair, Robert C. Erffmeyer, and Debbie Easterling, "Usage and Perceived Effectiveness of High-Tech Approaches to Sales Training," *Journal of Personal Selling & Sales Management*, Spring 1989, pp. 46–54, discusses that interactive video is the most frequently used high-tech method at present, whereas computer-managed instruction (CMI) is the least often used.

CASE 16–1: Stan Wood—Career Path to the Sales Managership

"I want to be the sales manager, I know I can do a great job of running this sales organization. Certainly I can do a whole lot better than the job old man Lockett is doing. He's asleep on the job. He never helps anyone—just yells at them. He doesn't know what is going on in the field. This industry is changing fast. The old-time buyers are gone. The new generation of buyers doesn't respond to the old selling methods. Buying them lunch doesn't cut much ice anymore in this industry. They are too sensitive to charges of favoritism. We need new blood in the sales force and new ways of doing things." Stan Wood, sales rep for the Industrial Fasteners Company in Los Angeles, was venting his frustrations to a close friend.

"You sound just like the young reps on my sales force. They all know more than I do about how to run my company and aren't shy about telling me so. I pretend to listen to them as long as they are meeting their quotas. What's with you guys anyway? You're always popping off about how stupid your management is. Just remember that the same management you're complaining about hired you." Bob Suttle, president of Audio Studios, was none too sympathetic to Stan's plight.

Stan Wood has been the firm's top producer for 5 years. His commissions exceeded $100,000 a year. Management was totally satisfied with his performance and communicated its pleasure with him at every opportunity. He was given every recognition possible. Everything, that is, except promotion.

Every time he asked his boss about it, the reply was essentially the same. "Why would you want to take a pay cut? The sales manager makes $60,000 a year. You make more than $100,000. I can hire sales managers by the dozen. I don't know that I can hire someone to replace you that easily. You're doing a great job. Why should I take you out of a job in which you're great and put you into one in which you're untested?"

When Stan would reply, "But I can get the rest of the sales force up to my performance standards. Pay me an override on all sales increases of their performance and I'll make even more money and so will you."

The president's reply was always the same. "Stan, you cannot expect others to match your performance. Besides, you should seriously ask yourself about the role of your territory in your success. Do you really think that the rep in Salt Lake City can improve sales in that industrial base?"

Nevertheless, Stan still wanted to be sales manager, if not for Industrial Fasteners, then for some other firm. He let his feelings be known in the industry. One day he received a telephone call from a competing company's president inviting Stan to a private dinner at the president's house. Stan accepted.

The net result was an offer to become the sales manager for Fasteners Unlimited, a newly founded small firm in Los Angeles. Stan would be given an incentive contract in which he would receive options to buy 100,000 shares of the firm's stock at 10 cents a share, its present book value. There was no public market for the stock. The president owned 80 percent of the firm's 5 million issued shares. Stan would be paid a salary of $50,000 plus a commission of 2 percent on sales he made, plus an override of 1/2 of 1 percent of all sales of the sales force he would assemble. The firm now had one sales rep who was selling about $600,000 a year and was paid 5 percent commission.

Stan asked that the offer be put in writing and said that he would respond within the week. He pondered his future.

1 What would you advise Stan to do?

2 Would it be ethical to accept this job?

3 Will Stan be able to get the reps to perform to his standards?

4 What do you think of Stan's compensation package?

CASE 16–2: United Publishing Company— The Role of Psychological Tests in the Final Selection of a Salesperson

Mr. Pearson, sales manager for United Publishing Company of New York, was reviewing the documents in the file of Ray Johnson, an applicant for a job as field sales representative. United Publishing Company, one of the largest firms in the industry, published a wide range of textbooks from elementary through collegiate levels and also had a complete line of trade publications and other noneducational programs. The sales force for which Mr. Johnson was being considered specialized in calling on college professors. Mr. Johnson had been introduced to the company by Jerry Newfield, who was presently a highly successful salesperson for the firm in a western territory. Although Mr. Newfield had been with the company but 2 years, his performance in the field had clearly designated him as a man with a bright future. He had tripled sales in his territory in the short time he had been there. Mr. Johnson and Mr. Newfield had been close friends from childhood and had attended the University of Illinois together.

On paper, Mr. Johnson looked like a very poor risk, indeed. Since graduation from college 10 years previously, he had not held a regular job. The longest period he had worked at any one time was 8 months as a waiter in Chicago. He had just returned from spending 2 years on the Riviera, doing little more than keeping alive. While he had no independent money of his own, he had always managed to make a living wherever he was. Hence his employment record was such that in most situations it would automatically disqualify him from consideration. Mr. Pearson decided to give further consideration to Johnson's application, however, largely because one of the firm's leading sales reps strongly recommended him, even though the sales rep was fully aware of Mr. Johnson's record.

Mr. Pearson spent 2 days in Phoenix, Arizona, interviewing Mr. Johnson in the presence of Mr. Newfield and a consultant who was a personal friend of Mr. Newfield. Everyone agreed that the major issue was whether Mr. Johnson was ready to settle down and make something of his life. Mr. Johnson was honest about the matter and admitted that he really did not know the answer. He was well aware of his unconventional employment record, and he seemed to realize that he should soon start making a career for himself if he was ever to have one.

Mr. Johnson seemed to have more than ample qualifications for the job. Both his mother and father were professors in a large eastern university. Since he was reared in an academic environment, he was aware of the various problems involved in selling textbooks to professors. He had an amazing ability to converse intelligently on just about any subject, and made a highly favorable impression on all people who met him. He was a likable, engaging man. Both Mr. Pearson and the consultant agreed, after interviewing Mr. Johnson at some length, that if he would settle down to work he would be an outstanding sales rep. But they both realized that there was a risk that Mr. Johnson would once again get restless and take off for some resort. Pearson tentatively decided to hire Mr. Johnson.

However, part of the company's selection procedure required each applicant to take a battery of psychological tests before final hiring. Some of the tests showed that Mr. Johnson was highly intelligent and was certainly quite adept at social skills. However, the rest of his tests, which focused on personality and interests, yielded a profile unacceptable to the company. The psychologists reported that Mr. Johnson was a highly creative individual who would be unlikely to accept authority and settle down to the work demanded in a large organization. Many other comments were made concerning his personality, but they all added up to the fact that he simply was not the type of individual the company preferred to hire. In view of the test results, Mr. Pearson was uncertain whether to recommend to the president that the company hire Mr. Johnson.

1 What are the pros and cons of Mr. Johnson's case?
2 What should Mr. Pearson recommend?

CHAPTER SEVENTEEN

SALES MANAGEMENT II

CHAPTER SEVENTEEN

SALES MANAGEMENT II

The best fertilizer on a farmer's land is his own shadow.
Hank Hendler

After studying the material in this chapter you should:

☐ Have some idea about how salespeople are compensated and repaid for the expenses they incur in the field

☐ Understand something about establishing sales territories and sales quotas

☐ Know how to stimulate and motivate the performance of salespeople

PROFILE OF A HIGH-TECH

REP—ROBO REP

They called it *RO* in the lab where it was created. It was the result of a research project paid for by a large consumer products company whose management was weary of its sales reps who continually complained about being overworked and underpaid while failing to do their paperwork or meet their quotas.

RO was the first designed to work trade shows, where it would provide product information in response to any question asked of it. It had a built-in thought detector that allowed it to read the prospect's mind and immediately design its presentation around the major buying motives detected while answering the objections that were lurking there. After an assumptive close, it quickly completed the transaction, with all the paperwork in perfect order. It worked around the clock and never took a coffee break or told off-color jokes.

And then the sales manager woke up. "Hm, I wonder . . . ?"

Now that you have hired and trained your sales force, some thoughts about managing them are in order. First, let's examine some automatic supervisory mechanisms, such as compensation plans, sales quotas, and reports and letters. Then some attention will be given to supervising, motivating, and evaluating each person.[1]

COMPENSATION PLANS

There are scores of different plans for paying salespeople, but they all break down into two types of payments: payments for time and payments for productivity. A salary is paid for your time; to receive it, you put in the time your employer tells you to. A commission, however, is paid for selling something—productivity. A bonus, depending upon what it is paid for, can be either a time payment or a productivity payment. A Christmas bonus is a time payment, while a bonus for sales over quota is a productivity payment.

There is no perfect system of compensation. Nearly every plan is a compromise, a combination of time and productivity payments. Each concern tries to construct a plan which will attract the type of people wanted, which will not be too complicated to compute and administer, which will be fair to everyone, which will keep the sales force contented, and which will pay them for doing the things that management wants them to do. This last point is very important. We have already observed that the sales force is usually expected to do many things besides sell. The plan of compensation should reward them for doing these things.

Salary

This is often preferred by the beginning salesperson, as it pays an assured income that may be more than the neophyte is worth at first. Even the more experienced salesperson may like to have a *part* of the pay in the form of straight salary so that it will not be necessary to worry about certain regularly recurring obligations such as taxes, rent, and insurance.

From the firm's viewpoint, the straight-time wage gives the management control over the sales force. They are paying for their time and have the right to tell them what to do, thus making it possible to take care of many nonselling activities. The main trouble with straight salary is that it usually does not provide much incentive to sell. And it does discriminate against the good sales rep in favor of the poor one. Really outstanding people are seldom paid what they are fully worth because some of their productivity must be used to subsidize those salespeople whose productivity is insufficient to warrant their salaries.

Most plans now contain large elements of salary, and if the salary program is carefully administered, it can be made to reward the productive sales rep. However, in situations requiring a high level of selling in which truly professional sales representatives are engaged, commission plans still dominate. Truly great salespeople opt for the commission, for they know they will make far more money by doing so. Almost without exception, the reps who make in excess of $50,000 a year are on some form of commission plan.

Commission

Commission is simple and offers a strong incentive to sell—no sales, no pay. But it does not give the employer much control over the sales rep and does not pay the latter directly for doing nonselling duties. It is easy for the firm to finance, as it does not pay the rep until after the sale has been made.

From the standpoint of the sales force it is uncertain—they never know how much they are going to make. Beginning sales reps often dislike this method, as they are not sure of their ability to make a living. They become nervous and worried, which adversely affects their ability to sell. The incentive is perhaps *too* strong, defeating its own purpose by making the salesperson too tense, too eager. To use a sports analogy, they begin to ''press'' and end up losing. They may also be tempted to concentrate on present sales and neglect the many duties that build for future sales.

As in the case of the salary, the commission is included as a part of a great many compensation plans. The salary is designed to give the house *control* over the salesperson's activities and to offer *security;* the commission provides *incentive* to make more sales.

There are circumstances in which management has good control despite paying a straight commission; the job is so good that the person wants to keep it, and the price for keeping it is to do what management says.

Commissions pose two additional problems to management. First, it is difficult to find salespeople who are willing to work on a commission unless the potential earnings are obviously so large that the recruit feels it is worthwhile taking a chance on the offer. Second, if the potential earnings by commission are that large, management soon realizes that its total sales force costs are much higher than they might be if a salary were paid. In essence, people seem to be willing to accept lower total earnings in exchange for the security of a salary plan. However, consider that the brutal economics of the situation demand that sales reps earn their keep—sell enough goods to pay their salaries. Thus the security of a salary is illusory. You'll be fired if you don't earn enough to pay your way.

Bonuses for Special Services

Offered by many firms, bonuses are sometimes awarded on the basis of points compiled by the salesperson for such things as making collections, opening new accounts, selling special items, setting up window displays, staging demonstrations in stores, cutting down expenses of selling, and exceeding quotas. Bonuses are widely used in paying retail store salespeople also.

If the plan can be kept simple, it may work admirably. The tendency is for it to grow complicated and difficult to understand and compute. Bonuses are sometimes added to a base salary and a commission on sales volume.

One small retail chain paid the 40 people in the sales force a salary based on each person's projected sales volume for the year. Salaries were set to reflect a total selling cost of 10 percent of the salesperson's sales volume. In addition, each person could earn these "fun" bonuses. One bonus was given if the individual achieved the sales projections and another was given if the person's store met its goals. Everyone received the last bonus if the chain achieved its sales projections. The bonuses were trips or merchandise that the person particularly wanted.

Profit Sharing

Profit sharing has never played a large role in the payment of salespeople because it places them at the mercy of the employer's accountant. It may cut down on the salesperson's earnings when he or she is not in any way responsible for decreased profits. Profit sharing works best where the workers can all watch and stimulate one another. Sales reps, usually scattered throughout the country, are far from meeting this requirement. The principle of profit sharing may be sound, but its application has proved difficult. However, one type of profit-based compensation plan that serves well in certain situations is based upon the gross profit realized from a sale.

In situations in which the sales rep has control over price or the value of a trade-in, it would be a serious mistake to pay the person a commission on sales volume. The rep could "buy" sales volume by simply lowering price. In order to motivate such price-setting salespeople to push for as high a price as possible, many managements pay them a percentage of the gross margin obtained from the sale.

EXPENSE ACCOUNTS

Sales reps are among the few corporate employees who spend company money. Make no mistake about it, field selling expenses are substantial. One study reported that per diem expenses for meals and lodging alone average about $31,500 a year per salesperson; the sales reps located in New York City averaged about $63,000 a year with the Southern and Midwest salespeople spending much less.

The additional costs of transportation and entertainment make the total costs to the firm quite large. Transportation costs alone account for more than 50 percent of all travel and entertainment expenses. Thus management is most sensitive to its field selling costs and tries to minimize and control them as much as possible.[2]

Expense Account Policy

Many firms do not have expense accounts. The reps pay their own expenses. The firm includes enough money in the sales rep's compensation package to

Company expense accounts are designed to provide sales reps with flexibility in arranging their activities when acting as agents of the company. Sales reps in large metropolitan areas may average as much as $60,000 per year in travel and entertainment expenses. What are the benefits to the company of client entertainment functions such as business luncheons?

cover such costs. This policy is usually followed when the sales reps are paid on a straight commission basis. Thus such managements avoid the problems involved with administering expense accounts. When possible, this is a wise policy.

However, there are situations in which sales reps simply won't do various things management wants done if they must pay the costs for doing them. Other times the reps don't have sufficient money to sustain themselves in the field. If the rep does not see any prospect of a likely sale to a prospect, then few of them would waste money making the call. Moreover, the reps would not spend their own money doing nonselling work for the firm.

Sales reps who are paid by commission and must pay their own expenses often consider themselves independent agents, not company employees. Much control over them is lost.

Expense Account Plans

Essentially, companies either offer their reps an unlimited expense plan, or they place some limits on what can be spent. The types of limits vary. Some firms set a flat amount of expense money per month, while others limit what can be spent in various categories. No matter what plans are used, problems are posed in auditing those accounts. Much mischief can occur if the sales reps are not honest. The padding of expense accounts is a widespread problem, which is beyond the scope of this discussion. Suffice it to say that managements do not view favorably those employees who cheat. The rep's handling of the expense account is one basis for evaluating the rep's performance.

SALES QUOTAS

Reference has been made several times to quotas. Most concerns use quotas for defining the tasks expected of the sales force. Quotas may be established for number of calls, volume of sales, or other factors, although the most common form is that on sales volume, expressed either in dollars or in units of product.

Some salespeople do not like quotas, but it is an established fact that most of them sell more when they are given a mark at which to shoot. To be sure, the quota is not always set equitably, but the usual practice is to set one that the person can reach with reasonable effort. Frequently the sales manager consults the salesperson concerning a fair quota for the territory.

The quota may be set for the entire year or for a shorter period, the latter ordinarily being the plan. Salespeople are inclined to take it easy during the first part of the year, expecting to start a belated drive that will carry them over the line, but when the quota is set for each month or quarter, such postponement of effort cannot achieve the desired results.

The salesperson's compensation is often based on attainment of some quota, a higher rate of commission or a bonus being offered on sales in excess of the quota. The relationship between one's earnings and quotas can be most complex, depending upon the nature of the situation and management. Perhaps a bonus is paid if quotas are met. One drug company set sales quotas for each of its product lines. The detailer calling on the territory had to meet all those quotas before receiving a bonus, the idea being to encourage the selling of the entire line of products. The results of many sales contests are determined by sales performance in comparison with some quota.

In modern sales management, do not underestimate the importance to the salesperson of meeting, or beating, the sales quotas. All sorts of good things normally happen to people who perform better than expected. The individual who fails to come up to expectations will not like what will eventually happen. And all this is independent of the accuracy or fairness with which the quota is set. One seldom looks good complaining about the unfairness of some quota that one has failed to meet.

SALES TERRITORIES

Most firms assign each salesperson to a definite territory. It is felt that this policy offers a greater incentive to cultivate future business than the policy of permitting representatives for the same firm to compete for business in the same territory. This is especially true in organizations selling a repeat product. Where the proposition is a one-time seller or a slow repeater, salespeople may be permitted to compete with one another on the theory that such competition keeps them all hustling for business. Examples of this are real estate, insurance, and automobiles. Even here, the competition is largely for *prospects,* and once a prospect is on a sales rep's list, competing colleagues withdraw.

The chief factors governing the size of the territory are the number of customers and prospects, the frequency of calls on old customers, and the number of calls that the rep makes in a day.

The assignment of the salesperson is a basic managerial control mechanism by which the responsibility for sales performance in a territory is fixed upon the person. Whatever goes right or wrong there is the salesperson's responsibility. Sales quotas and territorial sales potentials are assigned to the sales rep on the basis of market data pertaining to that territory.

Number of Prospects

There are more prospects in most territories than either the sales rep or the boss realizes. Before the territory is laid out, a careful analysis of it should be made to determine just how many prospects it contains. Most salespeople want a large territory and are deeply offended when they are forced to accept a smaller one. But experience has shown that more sales can often be made in the smaller territory than in the larger one, as less time is consumed in traveling from one prospect to the next. Intensive cultivation of a territory is the modern ideal sought by most large concerns.

One major problem in managing sales territories evolves from the natural growth of successful firms. The synopsis goes something like this: The young firm with scant sales hires a few salespeople with whom to cover a large market area, thus forcing each of the sales reps to cover huge geographical areas. The salespeople like it because large sales can be made with a minimum of effort by skimming the cream from the market. The potential is so large that there is no need to dig to find sales. As the company prospers, it hires new salespeople, but where do they go? Some existing sales rep must give up some territory, and that usually makes the rep unhappy; the reps think the territory belongs to them, not the company.

Thus sales managers usually tend to divide sales territories when one opens up through a vacancy; they let the salespeople alone if possible. But it is not always possible; a promotion or transfer may open up the territory for division. In any case, changing a sales territory is a touchy problem, one that requires great tactical finesse by the sales manager. Some of these problems can be lessened if care is taken in the beginning when the territories are set up. Recognize that eventually the salespeople will have different territorial assignments. One manager with such foresight designed territories as he would want them when the company reached maturity and the sales force was covering each territory intensively. The result was 112 territories; however, since he was starting out with only 10 salespeople, each person was assigned about 11 of those territories with a full explanation of what was going to happen.

Call Frequency

The frequency of a salesperson's calls obviously is a factor only when selling to old customers. Because the emphasis is now placed on quick turnover of stocks by retailers, it is necessary for sales reps to call more often than formerly. Of course, customers can be kept and some orders secured by phone or by mail, but if personal selling is the main means of creating demand, the salesperson must call often enough to hold the business and keep competition from breaking in.

Sophisticated sales managers now realize that customers should be called upon in proportion to their potential business. It makes no economic sense to call as frequently upon a small customer as a large one. Thus we are now classifying customers according to their potential volume. Usually the customers are divided into three or four categories, tabbed A, B, C, and D accounts. Then management dictates a call frequency for each classification. All A accounts would be called upon every week; all B accounts, every two weeks; all C accounts, every month; and the D accounts would be seen only every season. This is all part of an overall effort to get the sales force to exert efforts in proportion to the potential sales volume obtainable from those efforts.

Call Rate

The third factor—the number of calls that a salesperson can make in a day—varies widely with the type of selling. It is estimated that many salespeople spend no more than 2 hours a day in the presence of prospects. Carefully planning the day's work will help in making more calls by saving needless crisscrossing of territory and poorly timed calls. Most sales managers attempt to set a quota of calls for their sales reps, knowing that without some such incentive not enough calls will be made. Much managerial effort is devoted to training the people to make more calls each day and have each of those calls be a meaningful contact. There is much distortion in communication on this matter of making calls. In a misguided attempt to get their people to make more calls per day, many firms set call quotas: Make 15 calls a day! So, to keep the job, the rep sticks her head into 15 different doors, identifies herself, and says hello and good-by. Not much selling takes place. It is just a contact. If that is what management wants, fine, but it is doubtful that that was what was in the manager's mind in setting the quota. If the manager wants a full, legitimate presentation, sufficient time must be allowed for it. The sales manager should make an effort to help the salespeople make use of time that

Keeping track of appointments is critical for sales reps assigned to cover large territories.

is normally wasted—to stretch the working day. There are prospects who get up early and would appreciate having breakfast with the salesperson rather than have their working day interrupted. There are customers who prefer to work with the sales rep in the evening rather than during business hours. Not everyone goes home early in the afternoon. A good preapproach should identify prospects upon whom one could call during such irregular hours.

Another aspect of this matter is the schooling of the salesperson in the recognition of when to spend time with a prospect and when not to do so.[3] One must match the probability of success of a presentation with the time it will likely take to get the order. One seasoned sales rep stated it thus: "I figure it this way. I know that I want to earn $40,000 this coming year. I know that I do not intend to work more than 200 days of 6 hours each to get it, so I must make $33.33 an hour to do it. I am paid a 6 percent commission on my sales, so that means that I must sell $555.50 an hour to get the job done. Unless I think I can see a sale of that size in the offing, I can't spend the hour it will take to get it."

This is just another way of saying what was said in the prospecting chapter: You must spend your time with good prospects. Do not waste it on poor ones. It pays handsome dividends to develop some quick screening questions to use early in the sales interview to determine the probable economic worth of spending some time with the prospect. Caution is required lest the unskilled sales rep misjudge the prospect and jump to the wrong conclusion.

Class of Customer

The assignment of territory is sometimes made on the basis of customer classification, one salesperson being assigned the banks, another the department stores, while still another sells the meat dealers, for example. Geographical lines are partially ignored. There is great tactical advantage to assigning territories by class of customer because it significantly increases the salesperson's effectiveness. It is much easier to sell when one has but one set of customer problems with which to deal and when one can closely associate with only one type of customer.

Trading Areas

Modern sales managers attempt to establish territories on the basis of economic trading areas rather than of political boundaries. It makes little sense to have one person responsible for Kansas City, Kansas, and another for Kansas City, Missouri, yet that sometimes happens when one rep is assigned the state of Kansas and another the state of Missouri. Wise territorial layout can save the agent considerable time in traveling and minimize time away from home. Historically, many firms have failed to realize their full sales potential by assigning too much territory to each person in order to get full coverage with the limited number of people at their disposal.

Personal Considerations

From the salesperson's point of view, the particular territory assigned may have a great bearing upon eventual success. Because of the inadequacies of statistical information on various sections of the nation, plus the ignorance of the impact of growth and stagnation upon consumption in a given area, salespeople assigned to growth territories are given a tremendous advantage over their colleagues in static or declining areas. One miscellaneous group of sales reps was polled concerning contests being run by their employers. One fact uncovered by this study was that invariably the winners in the contests were in growth areas.

If a salesperson is uncertain about which concern to work for, it would be wise to consider the probable territories each firm has available. Also the nature of the territory can have great impact upon one's morale. It is only natural to prefer one area over another. Such preferences should be given consideration. However, salespeople who are too fussy about their location severely limit their attractiveness to employers who look upon their sales trainees as potential managerial talent. Mobility is usually one of the attributes expected of most corporate executives, because in their advancement it is usually necessary for them to move several times.

STIMULATION OF EFFORT

One of management's constant problems is that of stimulating the efforts of its sales force to do a better job. Such tactics as contests, conferences, pep letters, and honor awards are used for this purpose.

Contests

Many varieties of contests have been devised to keep salespeople on their toes. Baseball games, airplane races, golf games, cross-country runs, around-the-world trips, and just plain statements of each person's sales are all calculated to yield the same result—increased selling effort.

Some people consider contests juvenile, holding that no mature person would be inveigled by such childish devices into working harder. These blasé skeptics contend that the contest is too obviously a means of getting *all* the salespeople to increase their efforts, while rewarding only a *few* of them.

There are answers to this argument. First, mature people have participated in contests for years and *do* take part in them with gusto and grim determination. There is in most people, and perhaps especially in salespeople, a competitive spirit that responds to this stimulus. Second, many well-thought-out contests *do* reward everyone in proportion to their success in the contest; they are not all-or-nothing gimmicks. Third, they give management a tool to provide additional incentive to do certain things it wants done without altering the basic compensation plan.

The most potent arguments against sales contests are that they may be followed by a slump in sales and that they may lead the salespeople to oversell in their eagerness to win. If the contest is well planned and managed, however, it need have neither of these negative results.

The best contests try to get the sales force to do the basic work that results in long-term sales, not immediate sales volume. A contest built around getting new dealers or accounts builds long-term volume. A contest that encourages full-line selling may build permanent sales.

But the management of a contest is no easy matter. The weak sales reps, the ones who need the stimulation the most, must be handicapped in such a way that they have a good chance of winning something if they do a good job. Yet handicapping the contest is fraught with danger, for it is difficult not to favor some salespeople while placing others at an unfair disadvantage. Moreover, all sorts of disagreements arise during a contest, and these must be settled.

There are sales managers who feel that there are great advantages to be gained by having many small contests rather than one big affair. The salespeople who barely miss winning a large contest may have a big dent put in their morale. The person who fails to win a pair of tickets to a football game won't get too perturbed.

Conventions and Conferences

Most sales organizations of any size hold conventions or conferences of some kind at more or less regular intervals. These have one or more of three general purposes: education, inspiration, and reward for effort.

The national convention, to which all the salespeople are brought, is not as common as it used to be. It is expensive, it takes the people out of their territories for long periods, it encourages dissipation, and it may be too big to handle efficiently.

For these reasons many concerns have turned to the regional or district conference. Here the group is small enough so that the sales manager, who usually conducts it, can get to know all the people; discussion is free and more to the point, the sales manager comes to know the territories better, the time is better spent, and it is cheaper.

For purposes of education, the district conference is undoubtedly superior to the national convention. But for inspiration and reward the national meeting may be better.

The convention held in the hotel of a large city is probably about the poorest variety, likely to have all the evils and few of the virtues of conventions. For this reason conventions are sometimes held in small towns, on islands, in summer camps, or even on shipboard while cruising. Under these conditions the participants are under better control and the wrong kinds of extracurricular activity are not so prevalent.

Progress has been made in building convention programs so that they are interesting and helpful. Frequently they contain a good deal of showmanship and much of the dramatic.

After the convention is over, the company usually tries to follow it up to cash in on it. Bulletins, letters, the house organ, sales supervisors, and every other medium of communication are used to emphasize and press home the teachings of the convention.

Many sales reps insist that they learn more at conventions through the informal exchange of experiences with fellow salespeople than they do in the formal sessions. But many other places provide this opportunity. The real benefit of the convention is derived from the programs, when they are efficiently planned and staged.

The latter point is very important, yet it is widely violated. The key to holding a good convention or conference is planning and expert execution. Salespeople object to having their time wasted by poor speakers mouthing platitudes and truisms, or by programs that do not move along rapidly to some valid point or that do not deal with the problems salespeople are currently encountering in the field.

Communications

Sales reps are isolated and subject to many disheartening influences. The sales manager would like to be able to meet them face-to-face every week, to inspire them with the sound of her voice, the friendly smile, the warm handclasp, the word of advice. But she cannot do this, so she does the next best thing: She keeps the lines of communication open with letters, bulletins, perhaps a house organ, telephone calls, etc. These communications are of two main types, the purely "pep" talks and the kind that are written with a sympathetic understanding of the person's needs.

Too much "pep" talk has been given by sales managers. A little of this is good, but too much disgusts the sales reps. It causes them to regard their chief as a lazy, swivel-chair hypocrite who dictates a scorching bulletin exhorting the salespeople to quit offering alibis and put in an extra hour each day, and then picks up his bag of golf clubs for a quick 18. A good manager gets out into the field and works with the sales force when the need arises. The new rep in particular needs much personal help in order to develop on schedule.

The kind of communication welcomed by the sales force is the kind that helps them to sell more. This type contains specific, practical suggestions rather than inspirational "fluff." As one watches salespeople toss sales-promotion literature from their firms into wastebaskets, it becomes apparent that not all this literature accomplishes its aim. They want concrete help but not locker-room half-time histrionics.

Basic Motivation

Many sales managers, in their preoccupation with contests, conventions, and sales newsletters, have lost sight of the proven fact that the most powerful motivating force is a good compensation plan backed by an excellent operating organization. The fundamentals are the real key to the sales rep's motivation to do a good job.[4]

REPORTS AND LETTERS

In a small organization it may not be necessary to have a system of reports from salespeople, but as the number of reps increases, it becomes more and more necessary to ask them for a variety of facts and opinions. Some salespeople are antagonistic toward this policy, insisting that they are paid to sell goods, not to make out reports.

Most companies ask their salespeople to send in weekly reports or letters. These usually contain such items as the number of calls made, the names of prospects sold, and names of those whom the representative was unable to sell, together with reasons for such failures, business conditions in the community, total sales for the day, and expenses incurred. A few firms ask their salespeople to fill out reports that are virtually work tickets, accounting for every minute of every day.

Industrial reps selling some proposition of significant size are frequently requested to make detailed reports on each call they make. Management wants to know what is going on with the account. The advent of the small portable cassette dictating device has led some firms to use them for such reports rather than burdening the rep with a long, written document.

There is a tendency for the report forms to increase in size and number as more facts are wanted from time to time by management. They may become a burden to the salesperson, who may be justified in raising the question whether all the facts requested are put to any good use and whether some of the computations could not be done more cheaply by the staff in the office.

One thing more about reports. Sales reps who will not do them satisfactorily are hurting their chances for promotion. They are showing that they do not grasp the problems of management; they cannot view their work from the top. An appreciation of the viewpoint of the sales manager is an indication that one has the qualifications for that post. Management's viewpoint differs distinctly from that of the rank-and-file members of the sales force.[5]

EVALUATION OF PERFORMANCE

Many salespeople seem to be unaware that their selling performances are constantly being evaluated by management. Data gleaned from call reports, invoices, expense accounts, and personal evaluations all help the astute manager evaluate their abilities and weaknesses. The purpose is twofold. First, such evaluations assist considerably in training. It is difficult to know on what aspect of selling a person needs additional training without some clue as to his or her weaknesses. It is insufficient just to scream at someone whose performance is unsatisfactory; the person may have little idea of what should be done or just what is going wrong. A good performance evaluation should pinpoint the difficulties so that training can be focused on them.[6]

Second, evaluations are used as a basis for promotions, transfers, pay raises, and terminations. Fundamentally, each person is compared with a company norm, the performance of the average salesperson. This comparison strongly prejudices management for or against the person, so the ambitious individual will strive to compare favorably with the others.

Management usually develops figures on such factors as calls per day, cost per call, orders per call, average order, cost per order, cost per dollar sales, percentage of market potential realized, sales by product line, profitability of sales by product line, effectiveness by class of customer called upon, and any other index that seems to make sense. These indices usually are the bases around which periodic review sessions between the salesperson and the boss are built.

The basic formula for evaluating the salesperson's performance is:

Sales = days worked × call rate × batting average × average order

This formula can be expanded as follows:

$$\text{Sales} = \text{days worked} \times \frac{\text{calls made}}{\text{days worked}} \times \frac{\text{orders}}{\text{calls}} \times \frac{\text{sales}}{\text{orders}}$$

If someone's sales are unsatisfactory, the problem has to reside in one or more of the four factors that compose the performance equation. Suppose that the company's model sales performance for each rep for a month is:

$$\$25,000 = 20 \times 4 \times 0.25 \times \$1,250$$

Doris wrote orders for only $10,000 last month; her boss wants to know why. The sales analyst prepares Doris's performance equation:

$$\$10,000 = 15 \times 3 \times 0.33 \times \$667$$

Now a picture of Doris's effort begins to unfold. First, she simply isn't working enough days—she is 1 week under, so she is starting out well behind the eight ball. Had she but worked that week, she would have sold $13,206 if she had maintained her other performance factors. Then she made only three calls a day instead of the company standard of four. If she had worked 20 days with a call rate of 4, her sales would have been $17,608.

Her batting average of 0.33 is significantly better than the company model. Evidently she has no trouble closing sales—getting orders. Her manager understands that the call rate and the batting average may be inversely related; if one spends more time with a prospect, the closing percentage should rise. In this instance, it is a matter of indifference. The model salesperson would get one order a day, and so does Doris.

Now we come to Doris's most serious problem—her low average order: $667 versus the model $1,250. To pinpoint her problem further, deeper analysis is needed. The low average order could be the result of:

1 Poor prospecting—she is calling on small concerns
2 Not selling the full product line
3 Settling for small trial orders rather than pushing for full orders
4 Poor selling techniques—she isn't suggesting the right quantities
5 Nature of her sales territory

So her boss hauls out her call reports to evaluate the quality of her prospects and territory. The orders she had sent in were pulled in order to check what Doris was selling. If the answer is not found in these reports, it must be in her selling techniques, in which case her boss would make some calls with her to check out her sales techniques.

But the search was quickly ended when the sales reports showed Doris was failing to sell two major lines of technical equipment. A short discussion with her disclosed that she shied away from bringing up these lines because she was not confident of her knowledge about them. She did not want to be asked questions that she couldn't answer about the equipment. Her boss prescribed a heavy dose of sales training in product knowledge on those product lines.

CAREER MANAGEMENT

There are people who feel that their fate lies in the hands of the gods, that they are tossed on the seas of life, incapable of giving much direction to their search for economic well-being. Well, that is nonsense. It is the thinking of those who want to transfer to others the responsibility for their lives. Perhaps it is easier that way, but it is not a philosophy that is likely to lead to economic success.

Not only *can* you manage your career, you *must* manage it if you want to avoid the hundreds of pitfalls that lie in wait for the unwary individual. While it usually takes many years and much hard effort to build a substantial career, it takes only an instant to ruin one. One error may do it. Sounds overly dramatic? Ask those people whose careers now lie in the dust, destroyed because of the Watergate incidents, about how easy it is to make a career blunder. Ask Jim K., who was president of a prospering subsidiary of a large, highly respected company. He was enticed away from his solid, rewarding job into another organization, only to have it go bankrupt because of contract disputes with some large customers. Jim is now "at large" looking for a way back up the ladder.

But these were people who had made it to the top and blew it. How about the millions of people who never get there because of simple career blunders? Betty B. is now fifty-plus and somewhat discouraged with her career as a public accountant. She had sought bigger game years earlier but had refused to do the work necessary to become a CPA. The lack of those three letters has blocked her from doing many things that she wanted to do. Certain careers require certifications; if they are needed, go get them. Why make it any tougher on yourself than necessary?

Harry didn't need a college degree to make "big money" in selling, or so he told everyone who would listen when he was getting started. He was right, up to a point. You don't need a college degree to be successful in selling, and certainly you can make a great deal of money without college training. It happens all the time. However, after 20 years on the street Harry tired of his life. He was one of the company's top producers and felt that it was time for him to be promoted into management. Not having a college degree was not an absolute barrier keeping Harry from management echelons: The company had made several previous exceptions to their policies. However, Harry's lack of development and his lack of understanding of the whole enterprise blocked his promotion. All Harry knew was selling, so his boss reasoned that Harry should keep on doing the one thing he really knew well. Harry had made a mistake; he had failed to develop his talents. If he wanted to get into management, he should have learned some new things.

Sue was miserable in New York; she hated it—wanted out—but she was stuck. She had built a successful career in the publishing business and was in a position and pay bracket that locked her into her job, just as her boss intended. She could not afford to quit and go live where she wanted. She made the mistake of starting to climb a ladder without first looking to see where that ladder went.

Marty went to work for Maytag and then spent the next 5 years complaining about life in a small town. Well, what did Marty expect? Newton, Iowa, is not Los Angeles. But Marty could not learn to live with that fact, so 5 years later she quit Maytag to return to her Los Angeles home, only to learn that she would have to start all over again at the bottom with another company.

Hank padded his expense account—"After all, everybody does it. They expect it! It's part of the game," Hank rationalized. The only problem was that Hank's bosses were not playing the same game. They did not look with much favor upon Hank's casual regard for the truth, but they did not fire him because he was a good salesperson in other respects. However, they did get the company's money back: Hank did not get the pay increases that would have normally been his, and he was not promoted. Who wants a liar in top management? But Hank was so busy fudging on the expense account and thinking he was ripping off the company that he paid scant notice to what was really going on with his career—it was dead in the water. He stayed asleep for 11 years before asking questions about why he had been constantly overlooked in promotions. No one ever told him. "After all, Hank's a good salesman, so let's just keep him out there selling for us."

These stories could go on and on, each pointing out a different blunder that people make early in their careers, some of which prove disastrous. The point is that your career is affected by almost every decision—the training you get, your first employer, changing employers, choice of professions, and so on. So give these matters the serious thought they deserve.

Important Factors in Career Management

The basic elements in career planning and management are:

- Self-knowledge
- Choice of goals
- Personal development
- Choice of employers
- Choice of environment
- Changing jobs and getting promotions and pay increases

Know Yourself Sound career planning begins with a realistic appraisal of yourself—your skills, talents, preferences, characteristics, and needs. Your plans should accommodate your strengths and limitations. All sorts of grief results when people try to do things for which they have neither a liking for or skill. Your plan should be ''doable.''

On the other hand, a case can be advanced. If you really want something enough, you will find ways to overcome your limitations. Many people opt not to try something just because they think they can't do it. Consequently, self-knowledge can pose some tricky problems.

Choice of Goals Quite clearly those people who have been able to decide what they want to do in life are indeed fortunate. Experience indicates that they are far more likely to achieve success than people who are uncertain about what they want to do. Chances are that you are not sure what you want to do. There is no need to worry about this, for you are normal. Few people have clear-cut career goals, but that does not mean that you should not be trying to develop some.

The fundamental reason people usually have difficulty knowing what they want to do is that they lack experience. They have not had much of a chance to discover their likes and dislikes. Goals usually emerge as you gain experience. Sally thought that she would like to be a fashion merchandiser; clothes appealed to her, and her high school counselor encouraged her toward that goal. During the summer of her freshman year in college she worked for a department store and lost her interest in fashion merchandising. She found out by experience that she just did not like the work, and that was the only way she was going to make that discovery. But look how fortunate Sally was compared with Ed, who thought throughout college that he wanted to be a statistical analyst for a securities firm. He accepted a job with a Wall Street broker after graduation only to discover that he hated the work—''too many figures.''

The chances are that your goals will evolve over time as you gain experience and gather information, but you'll have to work at it. The process is largely one of elimination; you progressively eliminate those callings which for some reason do not appeal to you.

But then, why should your career appeal to you, why should you like your work? Experience clearly shows that not only is your likelihood of success vastly enhanced if you truly enjoy what you do, but your happiness in life is also at stake. And that is most important! Life is too short to spend it earning a living doing something you dislike. The sooner you can make such discoveries, the more likely it is you will be able to avoid ''career traps.''

Yes, people get trapped into careers for which they have little liking. Fred was a dentist of no particular note; he made a living at the calling, but that was about it. One night at a cocktail party he unloaded his woes onto a friend. It seemed that Fred was miserable; he hated his work. ''Have you any idea what it's like looking down people's mouths all day long?'' he asked. And he went on to relate the ordeal in explicit detail. What was he to do? It was the only way he knew to earn a living, and he was forty-five years old. He was caught in a career trap.

When you think that you would like to be something or other, give a lot of detailed thought to exactly what you would be doing. Fred failed to think about whether he would like a life looking into other people's mouths. Sally found out that she did not like waiting on customers.

Personal Development   In a very real sense you must expect to spend the rest of your life developing yourself if you want to achieve great success. There is so much to learn. So far in life your learning process has been regulated by instructors, but that will soon come to an end and you'll have to take over the responsibility for your own development. (It may come as a shock to you to learn that you have had that responsibility all along, but we often fail to communicate that idea.) If you are going to develop your potential—and please be assured that your potential is great—you are the person

Personal career development takes place after work and on weekends and includes reading books, newspapers, and periodicals, and attending seminars and workshops designed either to teach new skills or update current knowledge.

who will have to develop it. While a few are fortunate enough to come under the influence of some great teacher or boss who directs their development, that situation is sufficiently rare that you cannot count on it happening to you. Instead, you should make up your mind right now that if you are to be successful, you will have to be the one to make you so. You will have to develop yourself—with the help of others, of course.

Right now, as you read this book, you are developing your skills. Thus two sources of self-improvement are evident: educational programs and reading. It is not coincidental that successful people are usually avid readers. They are hungry for information, for knowledge. They want to know more. So you should be thinking about your reading program, both books and periodicals. One outstanding sales executive said, "I buy every book on selling and sales management that is published. Most of the stuff I've seen before, but if I can get only one new idea from a book, I have recovered the price of the book many times over. And, you know, I have found out that the review of old material doesn't hurt me either, because I frequently discover that I have developed some bad habits or have forgotten something."

Your job experience is definitely part of your self-development. You learn by doing, so work for someone who can teach you what you want to know. Certain companies are famous for their ability to develop outstanding sales-people. Evidently their sales-training programs are superior to those of other concerns. It may be wise to go to work for a firm that can give you the training you need.

Choice of Employers   The firm you go to work for is important to your career, particularly that first significant job on your career path. You want two or possibly three things from that first job.

Above all, you initially want to work for a concern that will provide the training you need—on-the-job training that experience tells us is so vital to your future productivity. Avoid the firm that hires you and then thrusts you onto the streets, briefcase in hand, to face a hostile world almost defenseless. Such experience can destroy a career. It happened to Dave. He wanted to be a women's apparel salesperson, so he accepted a job with a manufacturer's agent operating out of the Dallas Apparel Mart. He was given 1 day's training, handed a line of lingerie, and told that everything east of U.S. 35, south of the Red River, and west of the Mississippi was his territory. No one had covered it previously. He bravely headed out to meet his future customers. They "killed" him! He couldn't sell a thing. No need to go into the grisly details, but what else could have been expected? Dave had not been trained. He was inexperienced in a job that called for a high degree of experience. It was a tough job. Accept the fact that you need to go to work for someone who will develop your skills gradually and not throw you into a situation that will destroy you.

Second, it may pay to go to work initially for a firm with a good national reputation. That experience goes on your record, which will stay with you the

Trade marts are major factors in certain types of selling, such as apparel, furniture, gifts, electronics, and housewares. Sales organizations selling to these trades must have offices in the marts. While most of the reps are in the marts only during "Market Week," larger sales organizations keep a sales staff on hand to work in the mart showroom at all times.

rest of your life. It is easy to move from IBM or Xerox or Procter & Gamble or any number of firms famous for their ability to attract and train excellent people. But if you go to work for some unknown firm, it may be difficult to move upward to another concern.

It is fortunate if your first job provides you with a lifetime career opportunity; you can stay with the firm and find your success within its organization. Interpersonal relationships are important to most people's happiness, and these are fostered over time. The person who keeps moving around from industry to industry may find it difficult to develop close relationships with other people.

However, that career model is rapidly waning as world competitive conditions no longer allow large firms the luxury of "guaranteeing" their employees lifetime careers. In this age of mergers, bankruptcies, and downsizing, no one's job is secure. Consequently, young people today had better be prepared to work for several employers during their lifetimes if they choose not to be their own boss.

Choice of Environment   There is no law that declares you must live in such-and-such a place. The choice is yours: big city, small town, east or west, north or south. The location is important to your happiness and thus to your performance on the job. It is difficult to be highly productive in a situation in which you are unhappy, and we know that your environment is an important part of being happy.

Perhaps one of the biggest career blunders you can make is to be lured away from a pleasant environment by monetary or positional enticements, only to fail when the new environment proves unsatisfactory. There is nothing at all wrong with approaching the matter of career planning by deciding where you want to live and then figuring out how you can earn the living you want in that location.

Changing Jobs and Getting Promotions and Pay Increases   If you are playing a game and want to know if you are winning or losing, you look at the scoreboard. In business, look at your position and paycheck if you want to know how you are doing. Pay and position are important. It is difficult to believe that you are a success if others, your superiors, do not concur and have not communicated their feelings toward you in a tangible way. Talk is cheap. It is easy to keep telling someone what a great job she or he is doing; it doesn't cost a thing. If the manager really means it, then such feelings will be reflected in earnings or promotions. Many times when the manager says, "You're doing a great job," what is left unsaid is "right where you are for what you are being paid." When pay and promotion don't meet expectations, a job change is usually considered.

Perhaps one of the most difficult decisions, and one containing much risk, is that of changing jobs. You have a good job (perhaps you do not realize it!) but are offered another one that is apparently better. Many people are initially tempted to accept the new job, for several reasons.

First, the grass usually looks greener on the other side of the fence; you know all the disadvantages of your present position but can see only the virtues of the new one. Only after accepting the new job will you learn its drawbacks and realities. All jobs have inherent problems and disadvantages; there is no such thing as a perfect position. Always bear in mind that the job you are considering is not going to be as attractive as you think it is.

Second, people tend to like the excitement of the new. Many change jobs from sheer boredom. Such pressures are unfortunate, for they can easily result in your leaving an excellent position for a poorer one with permanently damaging results.

Third, over a period of time you are bound to accumulate a long list of grievances (real or imagined) against your employer. The mature individual realizes that this is to be expected and counterbalances those grievances with all the good things that have happened on the job. Malcontents see only the negative side of situations. Armed with a list of grievances, it is easy for a person to rationalize why the new job should be accepted.

But changing jobs can be a blunder. Myra was a computer expert with IBM. she had a great job and was making lots of money. A small group of engineers put together a new computer company and invited Myra to join them as a vice president at a salary 50 percent higher than what she was making at IBM. She was dazzled. The picture painted by the entrepreneurs was indeed a rosy one, as it always is when a new venture is being promoted. Myra quit IBM to go with the new outfit. The dream job turned into a nightmare within 4 months as the group fell apart and went bankrupt. Myra was out of work for 9 months before catching on with another firm in a position much lower than the one she had left at IBM.

There are times when you should move on to more fertile fields in which to plant your talents. When it becomes obvious that there is little future with your present employer and you want a future rather than just a job, you should start looking around rather than spend years spinning your wheels in a hopeless situation.

There can be several reasons why a job may develop into a dead-end situation. First, people do get off on the wrong foot. It is easy to make an unfortunate first impression which is difficult to erase. It may be difficult for the boss to forget all those stupid mistakes you made, largely because of inexperience, during the first months on the job. You may have to move on to leave behind such a reputation.

Second, it is difficult to go from the bottom to the top in many organizations because the boss tends to regard you as you were when you came to work. Sometimes the individual rises most quickly by changing jobs, not waiting for promotions. One of the advantages of the large corporation's policy of moving people around is that it minimizes this effect. Each time a person moves into a new location it is almost like going into a new job.

Mark spent 13 years diligently working for one employer, during which time his pay increased from $6,000 to $15,000 and he had one promotion. He was highly productive and well regarded by everyone in the organization. He stayed on for those years because he liked the situation, but finally another employer lured him away—$20,000 was the bait. Once freed from his first job, he changed jobs four times in the next 20 years and is now making $150,000 a year. He knows for certain that, had he stayed with his first employer, he would now be making only $60,000.

It is sad to report that if you expect to be paid the market price for your services, many times you will be forced to place yourself on the market. Your current employer is reluctant to pay you the market price.

Third, management changes can turn a promising situation into a sour one. On her way upward, Irma had accepted a job as assistant to the president of a large, nationally famous organization. She had been tremendously excited about the situation, for the president was a most capable, likable person doing many exciting things. Unfortunately, he was fired about a year after Irma went to work for him, so she had to move on.

On the other hand, some people successfully employ a wait-it-out, this-too-shall-pass philosophy. A situation turns sour, but rather than leave, many people pull in their necks and wait it out, hoping that things will take a turn for the better. It is a brave tactic usually employed by people who, for one reason or another, do not feel that they can find a better job. Sometimes personal considerations make moving impractical, thus individuals feel they have little option other than to just stick it out, come what may.[7]

Changing jobs is serious business, and you should look carefully into the possible consequences of doing so.

SUMMARY

You are now aware of the subject of career management, and if you are interested in it you can delve into its many facets more thoroughly over the next few years as your career aspirations mature.

If you desire a career in the sales field, the capsule advice that summarizes most of what has been previously said is:

• Carefully select an industry whose products and working conditions appeal to you; then try to stay in that industry, making as many contacts in it as possible. Be well known in your industry!

• Select a firm in that industry with the best reputation which provides good sales training.

• Remember that, right from the first day on the job, you are being evaluated for future potential.

• Do not allow yourself to become bogged down in a situation that holds little promise for you. Time can become a foe.

• If money is important to you, select industries and companies that are known to pay high earnings. Do not expect to outperform your industry; if the money isn't there, there is no way you're going to get it.

DISCUSSION QUESTIONS

1 You have just been hired as sales manager for a furniture manufacturing company with 25 sales reps covering the nation. What would be the first thing you would do upon assuming the job?

2 You have decided that you would like to sell women's ready-to-wear to retailers. How would you go about getting a selling job in this industry?

3 What are the earmarks of a good sales-training program?

4 If you were being interviewed for a sales job at the present time, what weaknesses would an astute sales manager spot in your records or background or you? How would you overcome them in the sales manager's mind?

5 You have decided that you would like to work for X company. Its sales manager asks, "Why do you want to work for us?" Along what lines should your answer be constructed?

6 What are some of the differences between a managerial point of view and the worker's viewpoint?

7 Suppose you were the sales manager of a medium-sized printing plant who needed to hire three new sales representatives. Where would you recruit? What characteristics would you look for in them?

8 If a sales rep's call rate is low, what are some of the possible reasons for it?

9 If you are interested in high earnings in selling, tell exactly how you would go about getting them. What type of selling would you enter? How would you go about getting into that field?

10 Would the geographical location of your sales territory make any difference in the nature of your sales job?

REFERENCES

1 Much of this chapter is based on William Stanton, Richard H. Buskirk, and Rosanne Spiro, *Management of a Sales Force.* 8th ed., Irwin, Homewood, 1991.

2 "Annual Cost of Business Travel," *American Salesman*, March 1987, pp. 27–30, suggests that the two biggest travel management problems are confusing air fares and the cost of travel.

3 William A. Week and Lynn R. Kale, "Salespeople's Time Use and Performance," *Journal of Personal Selling & Sales Management*, Winter 1990, pp. 29–37, suggests that sales success is more dependent on specific events that take place during the customer-salesperson interaction than on time management.

4 Raymond Dreyfack, "The Selling Edge," *American Salesman*, December 1989, pp. 23–26, states that the personal comfort index is highly related to self-motivation, which is an essential ingredient for a successful sales career.

5 Don Bauer, "Creative Salesmanship through a Sales Journal," *American Salesman*, October 1988, pp. 16–19, states that a personal journal is the perfect tool for calling on the intuitive senses for specific jobs.

6 Alan J. Dubinsky, Steven J. Skinner, and Tommy E. Whittler, "Evaluation Sales Personnel: An Attribution Theory Perspective," *Journal of Personal Selling & Sales Management*, Spring 1989, pp. 9–21, states that supervisors were more likely to make an external attribution for a poorly performing salesperson with a good work history than for one having a poor work history.

7 Mark W. Johnston; Joseph F. Hair, Jr.; and James Boles, "Why Do Salespeople Fail?" *Journal of Personal Selling & Sales Management*, Fall 1989, pp. 53–58, mentions that lack of enthusiasm, inadequate product knowledge, lack of proper training, lack of initiative, and poor planning and organization are important determinants of failure.

CASE 17–1: The Dress Shoppes, Ltd.—Salary or Commission?

For 20 years, the 40-person sales force of the Dress Shoppes, Ltd., of New York had been paid quite well on a straight salary basis administered by Mrs. Watson, the manager of operations and part owner of the six-store chain. The average salesperson earned $35,500 in 1990, the top producers earned more than $45,000. The store managers earned between $60,000 and $70,000 in 1990. Mrs. Watson felt very strongly about the wisdom of paying a salary instead of a commission. "I want to control my people. I want them to do what I want them to do. When I want them to work stock in the backroom, I don't want them to begrudge me the time because they aren't earning anything doing it. Pay a commission and all sorts of bad things happen. Petty conflicts can arise between salespeople over customers. They will fight over whose customer a particularly big buyer is. Moreover, when a person is paid a commission, they think they are the ones who earned it. Suppose a clerk increased her earnings from $32,000 to $36,000 in 1 year; in her mind she was responsible for it. It wasn't my doing. Now suppose I raise her salary from $32,000 to $36,000. *I* was responsible. She is beholden to me; thus I gain control over her. And I must have control over the sales force to do everything we want to do in this operation."

Mrs. Watson retired in 1990. Her replacement, Miss Newell, had come up through the ranks starting as a part-time clerk while in college 15 years previously. Miss Newell held the opposite view: She proposed to switch the compensation system to a straight 9 percent commission. She said, "It's easier to administer and it's fairer. If they sell the goods, they get their money. They don't have to bargain with me over how much money they will receive. More importantly, it puts a lot more incentive into the picture. They will be motivated to sell harder."

Miss Newell was trying to sell her position to Mrs. Burke, the majority owner of the chain and the chief operating executive. However, Mrs. Watson, even though retired, was still very influential in the organization. She opposed the change. "Newell is just plain lazy, too lazy to administer the salary system. Sure, it takes some work, but it can be quite objective if you use agreed-upon sales goals. And the last thing in the world we want is a lot of aggressive salespeople scurrying over the floor fighting for customers. That's not our operation. That's not who we are! We will drive away our clientele."

Compromise was not to be the order of the day. Miss Newell was adamant. "I am now sales manager, and I want to pay our people a straight 9 percent commission."

Mrs. Burke was hesitant to allow the change in compensation systems. "Things have worked quite well for us for 20 years using the salary system set up by Mrs. Watson. We have grown from $120,000 in sales to over $6,000,000, so I can't see that we need more incentive. And I hate to tinker with anything that is working."

Miss Newell countered, "But that is history. Sales were easy to come by over the past two decades. It was a boom period. Now times are tougher. It's getting hard to sell dresses in our price line. We must change with the times, and the times now call for more incentive to do a tougher job."

Mrs. Burke was torn between her own philosophies and wanting to support her new sales manager. She did feel that she should allow her managers freedom to run their operations as they felt best. If she did not allow Newell to have her commission plan, then Newell would use that as an excuse every time sales failed to meet goals.

1 Evaluate the situation.

2 What recommendation would you make to Mrs. Burke?

CASE 17-2: Caroline Burch—A Place in the Sun

After 5 years of working as a secretary and office clerk for a large appliance manufacturer, Caroline Burch yearned for a more challenging job "somewhere in marketing," as she put it.

Caroline had graduated from a small liberal arts college in the east with an outstanding record as a history major. She had not found her training to be of much use on her job, but then she had not expected it to be, so she was not disillusioned about higher education and its relevance to business operations. She had seen that for some reason the young people who were coming into the company with M.B.A. degrees were being given the "red-carpet treatment" and got good managerial positions after a short time in training. These were the jobs Caroline wanted, so she decided to quit work and enroll in an M.B.A. program. She selected a program at a private southwestern university which provided her with an opportunity to gain some experience in the marketing field.

Caroline's experiences during her year in the M.B.A. program clearly told her that she loved the work involved in most marketing programs. "I even liked selling!" she confessed, as if it would be regarded as a sin. She continued talking with her adviser. "I really think that it would be of immense value to me to start to work in selling so I'd have the type of field experience to take with me into the kind of managerial work I'd like to get into."

The adviser nodded and asked, "And what kind of managerial work is it that you want?"

"Eventually I'd really like to run the whole show. I've met two women here locally who own their own companies and are doing great nationally. I can't tell you how much I admire them. They have it all together. And that's what I want. I know that is a long way down the line, but I'm willing to pay the price to get there."

The professor smiled; he enjoyed watching such ambition in motion. Then he asked, "Well, then, what is it that is bothering you?"

"It's this selling. I don't want the usual junk jobs they throw to women. Cosmetics leave me cold, and you can have real estate. I want some real, hard industrial sales experience, but I don't have any leads. Have you any ideas where I might go?"

"Not offhand, but let's talk about it for a minute," the professor said. "What industry appeals to you? Do you remember our talk about the importance of identifying yourself with an industry and then staying with it for a career?"

Caroline nodded. "That's the problem. I don't really know what turns me on."

"Did you like what you were doing this past year?"

"Not really. Retailing just doesn't have what I want."

"You said you admired these two local women who have made such famous names for themselves. You like their industries?" the professor asked.

"That's cosmetics and real estate. No way! I hate being difficult, but that is just the way I feel," she said.

"No need to feel guilty about it. Most people are in the same boat. Very few people know what they really want to do, what they really like, what industry will satisfy them. The person who finds her real liking is indeed fortunate and rare. But that doesn't mean that we can't work on it and narrow down your choice."

Caroline relaxed and talked a bit about what she liked doing. It developed that she was not overly fond of mathematics, the arts, or sporting events. She seemed to be more people-oriented; they liked her and she liked them. She was a doer; her undergraduate days were filled with activities of which she was usually the leader.

"Why do you think you want industrial selling?" she was asked.

"I just love big, complicated machinery. I don't know why. I just do. It fascinates me. I love to go through factories. Remember when we went through the Ford factory? I loved it."

The professor asked, "Why don't you try for one of the big machine manufacturers? Ingersoll Rand, Link Belt, Keller Air Tool Division of Gardner-Denver, FMC, or the like. There are a lot of them, so you have quite a number to choose from."

Caroline thought for a moment, then asked, "Do you think I could get into selling such things?"

"I just have a hunch that it might not be as difficult as you think. But don't think for one minute that such companies are going to hand you a price list and push you into a territory. It takes a lot of training for such jobs."

Suddenly changing the subject, Caroline asked, "What about Texas Instruments? All that microcircuit business grabs me. Do you know anyone there who would talk to me?"

"That's quite a shift from big machines to very small ones, but you won't have much trouble talking to the people at Texas Instruments. However, they may insist on a degree in electrical engineering. Their products are highly technical. You might run into trouble meeting their job specifications."

For a while no one spoke; then the professor asked, "Have you ever considered such firms as IBM or Xerox or any one of a number of such business equipment manufacturers?"

"Yes, but I don't want to do what most of the others do. It seems as if every other person I meet is working for IBM or Xerox. I want to be different."

The professor declined to comment on her declaration, preferring instead to offer more alternatives. "Where do you want to live? Is location important to you?"

"Not really. I'll go anywhere the job is right." She continued, "Where would I most likely be able to be promoted into sales management?"

"There is no way of answering that, for it all depends upon you, the situation, and the future," the professor answered. "It would be easy to say that your chances of being promoted are greater in industries that sell to women, or in which women are widely employed. For example, you would find it much easier to rise in the advertising industry than in selling men's apparel to men's stores. As painful as it may be for you to hear, there are some situations in which men are distinctly preferred. You might not find much of a reception with a company that sells equipment to football teams, but who knows. . . ."

"But where is this all leading us? I still don't know how to proceed, even though I know the general direction I want to go. Can you give me some specific things to do?"

"Yes, I think I can!"

1 What would you tell Caroline to do in seeking a job in industrial sales?

2 Should she go into industrial sales, where the going may be tough, or should she seek some industry that is obviously more amenable to women sales representatives?

CASE 17-3: Ken Carson—A Change of Jobs

"I've just received a firm offer from IBM to sell their new line of minicomputers, but I'll have to start over at the bottom of the ladder and go through training." Ken Carson, a college graduate who majored in mathematics, had been working for 3 years selling photo copiers for Xerox. "I make good money. I'm one of the top producers in our Orange [California] office. But I don't see myself staying in selling the rest of my life. And selling copiers is getting to be a bore. I want to get into management."

Ken was discussing his plight with his friend Linda, to whom he had gone for advice. Linda asked, "Have you made your managerial desires known to your boss at Xerox?"

"Yes!"

"And what did he say?"

"He told me that when I demonstrated some managerial skills I would be promoted into management."

"And how do you interpret that statement?"

Ken stammered for a while without ever answering the question directly. He was bothered by the large pay cut he would be taking in making the move. "I work on a commission now and make more than $50,000 a year. I start out on a basic salary at IBM until I'm through with training, at which time I will be put on a commission."

"Something seems to be bothering you about your present job or you wouldn't be here. What is it?" asked Linda.

"I'm just concerned about my future. Where am I going if I stay with Xerox?"

1 What do you think about the statement Ken's boss made?

2 What are the advantages and disadvantages of each alternative?

3 What advice would you give Ken?

CHAPTER EIGHTEEN

LEGAL AND ETHICAL

PROBLEMS IN SELLING

When you do it, it's unethical; when I do it, it's competition.
Anonymous

After studying the material in this chapter you should:

☐ Appreciate that the salesperson's job is loaded with legal and ethical dilemmas

☐ Realize that there are some guideposts which will help you to judge the ethics of any situation in which you find yourself

☐ Understand that you have ethical problems with your relationships not only with your customers but also with your competitors and your employer

☐ Understand that salespeople are involved in a process that entails many serious ramifications

☐ Understand that you should be very careful about what you say and what you should put in writing—take great care not to mislead or defraud the customer

☐ Realize that you should not play lawyer

PROFILE OF
AN ETHICAL BROKER

Bill Lewis

Rotan Mosle
Dallas, Tex.

"Right after I graduated from college, I coached football and taught history at Garland High School. I saved my money and started buying some stocks. I did so well that I spent more and more time on my investments and less and less time worrying about Friday nights in the fall. Finally, I cut the cord and took a job with Merrill Lynch. It was good training."

When asked to explain his success, Bill Lewis replied, "My clients trust me. I do my best to shoot straight with them. No deception. No churning the accounts. I'll never recommend something to a customer I'd not be willing to put my own money in. I try to do my best for them. When you're dealing with other people's money you cannot be too careful about what you do."

Bill paused, then added, "You know it's a lot more fun doing it my way. I sleep well at night. And I don't have to cross the street when I see a client coming. Selling is a great life when you play the game honest."

"First the good news: for the second straight year, we've managed to avoid paying taxes."

Now we examine some matters that pose grave risks to both your career and your employer should you handle them improperly. You have only to read the newspapers and trade journals to learn that the legal aspects of business are becoming increasingly important. Almost daily, careers are ruined as businesspeople come afoul of the law. And so many of these tragedies are unnecessary, the result of ignorance and certain attitudes toward the law.

The sales rep not only is an important economic cog in the organization but also plays a significant role in the organization's legal affairs. A great many selling processes have serious legal ramifications. It is prudent, therefore, to spend more time discussing the legal problems the salesperson encounters.

IMPORTANCE OF LEGAL ASPECTS

It seems to be a natural tendency of most people to minimize the importance of the legal aspects of business operations, but that cavalier attitude toward the law may bring about costly legal difficulties.

The fact is that anyone engaged in business will be party to quite a few legal disputes. One must be prepared for them, for they are as inevitable as death and taxes. We mention this because there seems to be a certain mental attitude, a philosophy all too prevalent among many people, that attendance to legal details is somehow unbecoming—not the thing to be observed among friends. Experience clearly indicates otherwise. As a matter of fact, people are more likely to maintain friendships if they closely observe the legal niceties of doing business than if they allow misunderstandings to arise through carelessness about such details.

Cost of Errors

If for no other reason, the sales representative must be aware of the legal aspects of his or her activities because one error can cost the company millions of dollars. An error could bring dismissal, for legal carelessness or oversights are the stuff from which lawsuits are made.

A retail clothing sales rep sold $600 worth of clothes to a nice young man on open-book credit. The customer's credit record was good, and everything seemed in order. The bill became 30 days overdue, 60 days overdue, 90 days overdue, and no record of the customer's whereabouts could be discovered. Investigation revealed that he had moved from Denver to Kansas City, Missouri. He was located there, so the retailer's lawyer sent him a collection letter threatening suit unless the matter was settled. The customer's lawyer answered with a stiff letter, claiming that the individual did not make such a purchase. They demanded proof of purchase—a signed sales slip. A check through the sales slips quickly disclosed that the sales rep had failed to get the customer's signature on the sales slip. The retailer's lawyer advised that he drop the matter, for there was no practical way of proving that the customer ever purchased the goods.

An electronic parts sales rep received a very large purchase order from a small defense electronics manufacturer. The purchase order spelled out in great detail the items ordered, the prices to be paid for them, and the terms under which the sale was to be made. The rep wrote up the sales order on the basis of the customer's purchase order, but changed the terms somewhat to coincide with the company policy. This customer was always pushing for a larger cash discount than the firm allowed, 2/10, net 30, rather than the customary 1/10, net 30. The rep wrote up the order and put it in the mill. The customer's contracts were suddenly cancelled by the Department of Defense, and the buyer had to scramble to cancel out firm orders on the best basis possible, with the Department of Defense picking up the costs of such cancellations.

When the invoice for the shipment came in, the customer yelled, "Foul! We have no contract. You didn't accept our terms and we didn't agree to yours, so it's no deal!"

The supplier replied, "Oh yes, we do have a deal. We merely changed your terms to coincide with the discounts you know we offer. Your attempt to get a larger cash discount was just a cheap trick to squeeze a few more bucks out of us. Besides, it's an insignificant change."

The buyer's lawyers replied, "There is nothing insignificant about 1 percent on a $78,000 order."

The judge was asked for his opinion in the matter, and he said, "No contract. The buyer's offer was not accepted by the firm. The counteroffer was not accepted by the customer."

A salesperson simply cannot go around changing the terms of a customer's purchase order without the customer's approval. The employer was stuck with $78,000 worth of goods and no purchaser.

As a general rule a sales rep is an "order taker" and is not authorized to bind his or her employer to a contract. If the salesperson changed the terms on a written order after the customer signed it, that would void the agreement and no contract would result.

A luggage dealer tended to discount the price of a line of baggage whose maker frowned on such deviation from the firm's suggested retail price. The discount trade was sufficiently large that other dealers in the area continually complained to the sales rep about it. They wanted to have the discounting dealer's supply cut off. So one day the saleswoman strolled into the discounter's store and after a brief talk about the weather and sports on a nice, friendly basis, she delicately opened up the subject of discount sales in the most friendly manner: "Now look, George, I want to go on selling you goods. You are a good dealer and we get along fine. We value your business. But the other dealers in the area are continually complaining to us about your discount sales, and they've shown me a lot of evidence to support what they're saying. They want me to take the line away from you. Now, George, if you don't stop this under-the-table discounting of our line, I'm going to have to stop selling you the merchandise. I don't want to do it, but the other dealers are just going to force the home office to make me do it."

These words were sufficiently unfortunate if they had been spoken alone with the dealer, but, even worse, the saleswoman said them within earshot of a sales clerk and a customer who was lounging in the store—potential witnesses. The saleswoman had just made her employer vulnerable to a suit on conspiracy and restraint of trade. She had admitted in public that she and her company had been conspiring with competing dealers to restrain the trade of this one discount dealer.

The law says that you can refuse to sell your goods to any dealer, but it also clearly says you can't do so when it is part of a conspiracy. You must make up your mind without the help of other companies. This salewoman's attempt to be nice and explain the real world to the dealer resulted in a Federal Trade Commission order against her employer.

Not only is there a possibility of government action against the offending company in such matters but also the antitrust laws offer potential triple damages in a civil suit by the offended party. The sales rep must continually be aware of exactly what he or she is saying and the legal significance of it. In this case, the rep made two classic blunders. First, she threatened the dealer, and second, she did so in front of witnesses. It's one thing when it is the sales rep's word against the dealer's but quite another thing when there are other people to support the other person's contentions. Moreover, it is always bad policy to threaten anyone so overtly. There are ways of getting the point across without such an obvious threat. For example, the sales rep could have related a tale of what had happened to a similar dealer—an analogy. Thus the discounting dealer might get the point without being told, "Look, continue discounting and we'll cut off your supply!"

This could go on at great length, for there is no shortage of legal cases. Rather, we have presented three widely divergent examples to give you an idea of the difficulties that salespeople can easily get into if they are not aware of the legal complexities of their business. Management should include sufficient legal information in the sales-training program so that the sales force is aware of what can and cannot be done.

Sellers of securities must be thoroughly schooled in the complex web of regulations administered by the Securities and Exchange Commission. Violations of the SEC regulations can result not only in heavy fines but also in jail terms. It is a serious matter.

Look at the newspaper headlines. All sorts of high-level salespeople face a bleak future in prison because they dealt too loosely with the truth and the

Michael Milken, the indicted junk bond star of Drexel Burnham Lambert, leaves court with his lawyer after pleading guilty to securities fraud charges. Violations of Securities and Exchange Commission regulations can result not only in heavy fines but also in jail terms.

law. Savings and loan salespeople told their customers things about the junk bonds they sold them that simply were not true. No doubt they did not perceive at the time the gravity of what they were doing, but that is no excuse. Be advised that what you do in selling your wares is serious business. Your career is at stake.

Customer Ill Will

The most valuable asset of any business is its customers. This is a cliché of long standing, but nevertheless it is quite true. Businesses spend a great deal of money cultivating the goodwill of their customers. When a customer is lost through some unfortunate incident not related to the merits of the company's proposition, management usually becomes rather cross with the sales rep.

In a great many situations, salespeople may do things that are illegal, and the customer may know they are illegal but may not be in a position to do anything about it—at that time.

A sales rep for a particularly popular line of blue jeans was making a call on a menswear store that had not previously sold the line. The merchant had contacted the company to indicate his interest in taking on the line. The rep had been told to respond because investigation by the home office had revealed that the store was a rapidly growing, aggressive operation. The sale was taking place rather late in the buying season, and the merchant had already purchased most of his requirements for other items. After he had given the rep a rather substantial order for all sorts of blue jeans—blue denims, wheat, faded denims, greens, etc.—the sales rep asked him for his order on casual slacks, a new line the company had just introduced.

The merchant replied, "Ed, I'm sorry, but this season I've already placed my order for casuals with Days and Haggars. I'm all bought up; I have no open-to-buy in casuals right now. We can talk about it next time around."

The rep replied, "Harry, I don't think you understand. If you're not willing to take on our line of casual slacks, we're not willing to give you the blue jeans."

Whee! Illegal as all get-out! Tie-in sales are in violation of the Clayton Act. The merchant sat there seething, for he knew this was illegal behavior on the part of the sales rep. More importantly, it was exceedingly stupid behavior. Nevertheless, the merchant was over a barrel because he needed the blue jeans, so he threw in a token order for casuals, just enough to get by.

This incident did not end up in court. Rather, the merchant made a point of letting the top management of the blue jeans company know what had happened. The rep was fired. He was way outside company policy, using the cheap tie-in trick only as a last resort to meet his quotas in selling casual slacks. The fact was that the casual line had not been moving as well as management had hoped, and the rep's boss had put a great deal of pressure on him to sell the casual slacks; so he chose the easy way out.

This brings up an important point. When a salesperson is caught doing something illegal, management almost inevitably assumes a "holier-than-thou" stance and punishes the salesperson. However, in most such instances managerial policies that strongly encouraged such illegal behavior were the real culprit. In the blue jeans caper, management's insistence on forcing its reps to sell an unpopular item encouraged the illegal tactics.

Bear in mind that many people will do whatever they perceive must be done to keep their jobs. If management insists that a person increase sales unrealistically, they should not be surprised to learn that the individual uses high-pressure tactics to do it. Under such circumstances, it has even been known for the rep who is under the gun to turn in phony orders to meet the monthly quota, and then cancel the order in the next month.

At one time a large grocery chain refused to recognize that meat lost weight with the passage of time. Thus store managers were forced to shortweight customers to make up for the shrinkage that the home office would not accept. Managerial policy forced the undesirable behavior.

The wise manager should carefully consider the sales rep's probable reactions to a policy before making it.

SOME PRACTICAL ADVICE ON LEGAL BEHAVIOR

As most businesspeople learn eventually, there is a difference between the technical aspects of the law and one's practical behavior in legal matters. The idea is that one wants to conduct daily affairs so as to minimize the chances of ending up in court. The old adage "The only people who win in court are the lawyers" is quite true. Only a masochist would relish going to court. No matter how strong your case might be, you can rest assured that the other person's attorney will do everything possible to make your life miserable. The process will take a great deal of your time and money and severely tax your patience and sanity. Stay out of court if at all possible.

However, that brings up a piece of counteradvice. If you have an unreasonable fear of going to court and your adversary senses it, you will lose most of your bargaining power in transactions, for your opponent will immediately recognize that all that has to be done to make you fold your tent is to threaten to go to court. Thus you will be continually waltzed to the courthouse steps, where you will fold your winning hand out of fear.

You must never fear going to court and must be completely willing to do so, and you must let this attitude be known. Such a stance will usually work to your advantage, for your adversary has little desire to go to court and will thus be more likely to settle disputes to your advantage. Indeed, this is one of the basic tactics lawyers use in writing letters for the purpose of precipitating some action from an adversary. The letter will usually be written in a rather stiff, demanding form and will usually end with the statement that the lawyer has been instructed to file suit if the matter is not settled by a certain date.

On Making Statements

Bear in mind that the evidence in court cases usually consists of statements made in letters, sales orders, purchase orders, and memos; all can be strong evidence substantiating various claims.

What the sales rep says can be easily construed as misrepresentation if careless language is used. Precise and accurate statements go a long way to building the rep's credibility.

Putting Things in Writing

While it is true that oral contracts can be enforced in court as long as the statute of frauds is not applicable, from a practical standpoint it is a most difficult undertaking. Moreover, any documentary evidence is usually considered by the courts to supersede all testimony. Courts are well aware that people lie and twist things for their own benefit; thus they are reluctant to

In certain circumstances, an oral contract is as strong a bond as a written agreement. For these two New York City jewelry district salesmen, a handshake is considered binding.

believe testimony unless it is amply supported by competent, independent witnesses who have no interest in the case.

So from a practical standpoint, oral contacts for the sale of goods in excess of $500 are unenforceable unless there is some memorandum signed by the party against whom enforcement is sought which indicates there has been an agreement between parties. The memorandum does not have to be a complete document spelling out all terms. Moreover, oral agreements are honestly fraught with dangers arising from misunderstanding. You said one thing but your customer heard another. When you suggest to the customer, "Let's put our agreement down on paper so there will be no misunderstanding between us," you are protecting yourself, for inevitably customers have a way of expecting more from a deal than was agreed on.

Put it in writing, but be careful *what* you put in writing. Don't promise something or even suggest something that you are not prepared to do.

Don't Play Lawyer

Average sales reps are not lawyers, have had no legal training, and should not attempt to behave as lawyers. It is sheer folly for them to attempt to draft a contract in legalese with all the "whereases" and "whereofs." All they will do is look silly, and if the matter ever gets to court, judges react severely to amateur lawyers. Rather, a sales rep who must create an agreement without legal advice is advised to write down the matters agreed upon in handwriting, using plain English, and making certain that all the things agreed upon, such as dates, places, amounts, prices, and quality, are clearly spelled out. The court won't try to guess what you meant to agree upon if you fail to be specific. Such a handwritten document in plain English signed by both parties is considered much stronger evidence in court than even the formally drafted contracts prepared by many lawyers.

Traditional or common business practices evolve in every business. When a contract or purchase order is ambiguous, the courts usually assume that the transaction will be governed by the business practices that are standard or traditional in that business.

So don't think you have to be fancy and imitate the lawyers in your business negotiations. Simply learn how to nail down all the details of an agreement in clear, concise English. The salesperson who thinks he or she is a lawyer is a dangerous animal. As the old adage relates, people who act as their own attorneys have fools for clients.

Relations with the Employer

The relationship between you and your boss contains many legal overtones which frequently erupt and cause great discomfort to both parties. A large number of legal misunderstandings may arise at the time the salesperson is hired.

It is not at all uncommon in the courting days, when the employer is trying to lure someone to come to work for the firm, to make promises and statements in the hope of enticing the person into camp. This is especially the case when employers are going after a particularly able individual. They will make promises about high commission rates, protected territories, house accounts, overrides, guarantees of the job for a certain period of time, expense accounts, and other perquisites. In short, the company will usually say whatever it has to in order to get the person to come to work. From your standpoint, get all that talk on paper, even if it is only a letter stating all the conditions under which you're accepting employment. Time and again courts have ruled that a formal contract under such circumstances is not necessary. As a general principle, courts go out of their way to protect employees in such matters; if an employee has a letter signed by the employer promising certain things, the employer will be made to honor these commitments.

So always get the terms of your employment down on paper. If your employer will not give them to you on paper, you have to be very naïve not to perceive what is going on.

Employers, too, should be extremely careful about what they promise. The courts are filled with instances where, in the spirit of enthusiasm surrounding the hiring of a new sales rep who has great promise, the employer makes a number of valuable concessions, only to have later developments prove those concessions to be economically unwise. When the employer tries to rectify the situation, the sales rep brings forth the contract and demands that it be honored. A great deal of grief results.

The classic case usually involves new companies just starting up business. In their desire to procure the services of particularly adept salespeople who can build up the trade, they usually agree to allow such salespeople a large protected territory and a substantial commission. Moreover, they may agree upon a commission for all sales made to customers within the territory.

The salespeople go out and perform admirably, many times *too* admirably. The business grows fast and prospers. Then there comes a time when management wants to put more salespeople into the field in order to achieve a better coverage of the territory—they want to take away some of the agent's territory. Or they may see the sales force making handsome earnings, and they consider cutting commissions. As they move to alter the compensation plan, the sales reps haul out the agreements. Clearly, unless there are some definite termination points placed in the salesperson's contract with the company, an employer may be saddled with initial promises for a very long time.

Naturally, any able lawyer will recommend to an employer that the contract be made good for only a stipulated period of time, such as a year or two. While this sounds wise and prudent and is easy to say, the fact is that if the new firm were to offer such a contract to a top-notch sales rep to lure her away from her present job, she simply would not accept the job. She would leave her present job only for an outstanding deal.

So there are no easy answers to this question, only the admonition that both parties should be careful to ensure that they get everything in writing and that they must be particularly careful about *what* they put in writing.

You might wonder what the sales rep would have to fear in such arrangements. Well, there are ways in which one can be victimized. There is the agreement not to compete. Many times an employer will force the sales rep to sign an agreement not to work for a competitor for a stipulated period of years after quitting a job. Many salespeople blithely go along with such a noncompeting clause, not realizing its seriousness. The fact is that a salesperson has the most value when selling services to a competing firm in the same line of business. After all, if you have spent 10 years selling paint for Glidden you would be more valuable to another paint company than to a manufacturer in another industry. All your know-how, expertise, and contacts are in the paint business, but your employer may ask that you sign away your rights to work in that industry. Today many large corporations require all of their employees to sign such agreements as a matter of routine, but the employee should recognize that these documents can cause them hardship.

Of course, such agreements can give rise to some useless nonsense. One sales rep who was being ardently wooed by a competitor had previously signed an agreement with his present boss that if he, the rep, were to quit, he could not work for a competing firm for a period of 5 years. But the agreement stipulated that if he were discharged, he was free to work for whomever he pleased. So the sales rep created a situation in which he was fired. He simply stopped making sales but still turned in expense accounts and so on. It didn't take long for the sales manager to fire him, thus freeing him to go to work for the competitor, who had been apprised of what was going to take place.

The courts will protect the employee from unreasonable restraints on the right to make a living, but that may be scant comfort to the employee who is dragged into court by a former employer. Moreover, the "reasonable restraints" are the very ones that are usually most binding, for they are ones that usually offer the best opportunity to the person.

FEDERAL TRADE COMMISSION RULES

The recent agitation concerning the protection of the consumer from a wide variety of business practices has not spared door-to-door salespeople. The Federal Trade Commission tries to stop salespeople from using various ruses to gain entry into the home. In the not too distant past door-to-door salespeople were never "selling" anything: They were "making a survey," "introducing a free program," "establishing demonstration homes for advertising purposes." But selling, never! It was only natural for sales reps to resort to such deceptions, for the big problem faced by the door-to-door salesperson is getting into the house to make the presentation. Once the pitch is made, the chances of making the sale are good. Experience had clearly shown that if salespeople made their true mission known at the door, their chances of making a presentation were slim. But promise the customer something free. . . . And this is the crux of the enforcement problem—management claims it has little control over what the salesperson actually says at the door. Be not deceived by this defense, for in fact most door-to-door selling organizations in the past have taught such deceptions to their employees. The tricks are incorporated into the prepared presentation.

Indeed, many such presentations were nothing but a pack of lies from beginning to end. One very large merchandising chain has a division that sells encyclopedias door to door; let's look at its pitch. First, trainees were instructed to gain entry by saying that they were visiting customers of the chain to get their opinion of a new educational program the company had developed. Nowhere in the presentation was the word "encyclopedia" used—it was always a home education program. And it was free. Oh, yes, free. All the recipient of the chain's generosity had to do was pay $17.95 a month for 12 months to cover "research costs."

This is the type of nonsense the Federal Trade Commission and various local governments have sought to eliminate. Now various state and federal regulations try to control the practices of door-to-door salespeople. One key element is the "cooling-off" period in which the buyers have 3 days to change their minds and void the sale. State laws vary in their regulation of all types of consumer sales contracts.

CONFIDENCE GAMES

Some naive individuals are trapped each year in schemes which can result in their criminal prosecution. In some instances they are victims of the confidence game; in other cases they are made accomplices in some scheme to bilk a third party.

Salespeople as Victims

Any time you are asked to invest a substantial amount of money as a condition for employment, you had better investigate the proposition carefully. Sometimes one is asked to pay rather handsomely for a sales kit. Most legitimate firms do not ask their salespeople to "buy" their jobs. When a potential employer asks you for money, you would be wise to walk on. The few exceptions are those in which the salesperson is asked to buy a reasonable amount of salable inventory.

Salespeople as Accomplices

One of the "get-rich-quick" boy wonders built a complex of companies around a stock-selling swindle. The mainspring of his venture was an investment sales company which hired hundreds of salespeople. These salespeople were conned into believing everything was as advertised. But there were

Windmills in the desert were a hot-selling tax shelter a few years ago. Many such investment syndicates were little more than scams devised to get around income tax laws. What about the salespeople who sold them? Did they really believe in what they were selling, or were they con artists? How many customers were seriously hurt financially by these projects? Will time bail them out as energy costs soar in the future?

those who saw through the scheme; a man who had been hired as vice president of sales resigned 3 days after beginning work. He told his family, "This whole operation is nothing but a swindle. I'm getting out quick." He was a very smart person, for many of the people who failed, or refused, to see through the scheme suffered great losses and legal prosecution.

There are also real estate schemes which result in legal difficulties for the people involved.

The real culprit, of course, is greed. The salespeople in such schemes are motivated by the promise of great return for their efforts.

MISREPRESENTATION

It is illegal to lie to the customer in such a manner that he or she is caused to buy when if the truth were told the customer would not have bought. This practice is called "misrepresentation." It can be cited by the customer as the basis for nullifying the contract.

Moreover, silence is not a safe course of action. Courts have held that the representative who fails to disclose a critical factor which, if known, would have caused the prospect not to buy has misrepresented the goods. The contract can be declared void or financial adjustments may be ordered.

In recent years the courts have been particularly severe in holding real estate agents to a strict code of behavior in the representations they do and don't make. Silence is no defense. If the agent knows of some defect in a house being sold, she or he is obligated to inform the buyer of it.

ANTITRUST ASPECTS

The so-called antitrust laws (Sherman Act, Clayton Act, Robinson-Patman, and Federal Trade Commission Act) are so complex and cover such a wide range of behavior that it is not within the scope of this book to cover them completely. Rather, we will just point out a few of the areas in which salespeople may be involved.

Tie-in Sales

The Clayton Act specifically outlaws tie-in sales. The sales rep cannot force the customer to buy some product or service in order to buy some other item. You can't tie two sales together—you can't make one contingent upon the other. The law feels most strongly that the customer should be free to buy exactly what he or she wants and not be forced to buy unwanted goods or services.

Price Discrimination

The law states that two buyers of the same goods in the same quantities should be charged the same price. The general principle is that all customers should be treated relatively the same—benefits should be bestowed in proportion to each customer's sales volume. Moreover, when the customer is given some allowance for doing something, it must actually be done. An advertising allowance must be spent on advertising the seller's products.

It may be some comfort to learn that the buyer who knowingly accepts an illegal price can be held as guilty as the firm offering it. At times this fact can be used to hold off the buyer who demands price concessions. "I would like nothing better than to give you a lower price, but if I did we would both be in violation of the law—it would be price discrimination."

Conspiracy in Restraint of Trade

It is illegal to conspire with others to damage in some way a third party's trade. A sport coat manufacturer had two dealers in one small town in the South; one was large, the other small. One day the manufacturer's sales representative called upon the buyer of the larger store only to encounter the threat that if the company didn't stop selling coats to the other store, the buyer would throw the line out of the store. The two talked about it for a while and came to an agreement that the sales rep would stop selling to the other dealer. Had the other dealer found out about the conspiracy to keep him from buying that line of coats, he would have had the basis for a suit against the company.

Collusion

The law winces when competitors become chummy. In some industries the executives scarcely dare attend the same social functions lest the fact be later used against them in some antitrust litigation. Salespeople should be aware of this situation. One oil company sales rep wasn't, and it resulted in a large antitrust case. One of the rep's customers—the owner of a gas station—complained that he had to charge gas-war prices because another station across the street was charging them. In front of witnesses, the salesperson was able to get the price of gasoline raised in the other station. Competitors should not collude.

Bribes

It is against the law to offer a bribe. The salesperson who bribes a purchasing agent can get into serious trouble. One saleswoman thought she detected a state government official on the take, so she offered a bribe in return for a contract. Instead of receiving a contract, she was indicted and subsequently imprisoned. Be warned that there are dangers other than refusal and rejection connected with offering bribes. (See below for a discussion of the ethics of bribery and gift-giving.)

Exclusive Dealing

The courts have progressively moved toward the position that exclusive dealerships in which the dealer is given a monopoly to sell a product in a certain trading area are illegal. Moreover, a manufacturer cannot insist that the dealer not handle competing lines. An oil company found itself in a losing court case when it tried to force a dealer to sell only its product. An independent business executive is free to buy any desired product, and the courts intend to maintain that freedom. Thus the salesperson must take care to do nothing that smacks of coercion in trying to persuade the dealer to do business only with a particular company.

ETHICAL PROBLEMS

Unquestionably, one of the earmarks of the past decade has been our vastly increased interest in and more critical attitude toward ethics in business and government. While part of our increased social sensitivity can undoubtedly be traced to the strong consumer movement that has come to the forefront since 1970, considerable credit must be given to a change in our basic philosophies about how we want to live and what our responsibilities to each other are. We are simply more conscious of our environment and our relations with other people. So let's examine ethical problems as they pertain to selling.

People in every calling face ethical problems daily which not only have no answers but are also severe tests of character. Discussions about ethics are usually rather fruitless affairs bogged down in platitudes about right and wrong, good and bad, and moral and immoral. Unfortunately, such platitudes are of little use to the person who is in the midst of a situation that contains ethical considerations. Indeed, by their nature, ethics defy answers. Therefore we will try to point out the areas in selling which seem to contain ethical problems. We have few, if any, answers.

It does little good to give you such platitudes as "Honesty is the best policy" or "don't lie." The world is full of people who are careless with the truth but who really believe that they are "straight arrows."

The ethical behavior of salespeople has long been roundly condemned by those who considered them little more than swindlers and thieves. Even today their conduct is subject to steady criticism by the trade press, by government agencies, by buyers, and by each other. Beyond question, this is a live and troublesome problem.[1]

The philosophers distinguish between absolute ethics and relative ethics; the former are inflexible and always applicable, while the latter are somewhat flexible and adaptable to differing situations. The sales rep usually operates under a system of relative ethics, for it is virtually impossible to develop a single code that would cover a significant segment of the situations that arise and still take into account the problems peculiar to each industry and type of selling activity. Practices condemned in one industry are considered permissible in another. Different companies lay down widely varying rulings for their salespeople's guidance.

Therefore, the purpose of this chapter is not to provide an absolute code of selling ethics but rather to introduce you to some of the ethical problems that you will meet and to suggest some of the consequences of dealing with them unwisely.

There seems to be no one simple test or rule that can be applied to all acts of selling to determine which is right and which is wrong. Experience indicates, however, that some standards are more widely applicable than others. For example, a salesperson may evaluate the ethical status of an act by answering such questions as:[2]

- Does this seem sound in the long run?
- Would I do this to a friend?
- Who will be injured if I do this?
- Am I willing to have this done to me?
- If other people learn of this act, what will be their reactions?
- Will I be ashamed to tell others about this?

People who are guilty of some unethical act usually know it. They have inner qualms about it because they are not comfortable with some of the answers they must make to questions such as those above.

But sometimes the pressure on salespeople is tremendous; they feel that their personal interests or those of the firm are at stake. They may revert to the code of the jungle, which decrees that survival may be purchased at any price. Ethical considerations are ignored. It is easy to be ethical when it involves no hardship, and most people prefer to play it that way as long as they can. The real problems arise when it costs something to stick to what is right.

Ethical Problems Involved in Customer Relations

Customer relations constitute a large portion of the salesperson's ethical problems. In the long run it pays to deal ethically with one's customers, as most salespeople find it profitable to build up a large and loyal clientele.

Keeping Confidences   Industrial sales reps, as well as many salespeople selling to retail outlets, call on accounts that are competing with each other. The sales rep naturally learns much vital, confidential information which could be of great value to a competitor, such as plans for new products, volume of sales in various lines and territories, marketing campaigns in preparation, contemplated changes in personnel, and other facts which the executives do not want to broadcast.

Naturally, the salesperson who violates such confidences will no longer be trusted and might not even be welcome to call on that account in the future. It would seem that only the worst and weakest of gossips would succumb to the temptation to tell one customer any facts about a competitor which had been given under seal of secrecy, but the problem is not that simple. Sometimes the sales rep is subjected to severe pressure to divulge critical information as the price for another firm's patronage.

The sales manager of a chemical company was keenly interested in learning the sales volume of a certain chemical compound sold by a competitor, the only other seller of that product. He was haunted by the suspicion that the other firm was outselling him, so he figured out what he thought was a clever scheme to get this information. One of the ingredients in the compound was purchased by both firms from the same source, a refiner of corn syrup. So he pressured the corn syrup sales rep to find out how many carloads of the ingredient his competitor bought each year. He hinted that if the rep failed to come across with this information, he would buy from another corn products refiner. Naturally, no salesperson wants to lose a large-volume account, so these threats were taken seriously. The rep promised to see what he could do, but he stated clearly that such information was not available to the sales force and he might find it hard to obtain. Later he reported back that the other account was handled by a different salesperson, who flatly refused to tell him what he wanted to know. Moreover, his own manager sharply informed him that it was none of his business and that if he valued his job, he had better keep his nose out of other people's business. He produced a memo from the manager to support his story—a wise tactic known as documenting your story. Thus he avoided offending his customer and losing the account. Not all salespeople can evade the issue so smoothly, for the customer may know that they do have the facts that are wanted.

Some salespeople prefer to meet such requests firmly with, "If your competitor asked me to provide the same information about you, what would you want me to do? If I told you what you just asked for, you should throw me out of this plant, for you could no longer trust me. If I would tell *you*, how would you ever feel sure that I wouldn't tell your competitors your secrets? One thing you can be sure of in dealing with me is that your secrets stay secret. I tell *no one*, not my boss or my colleagues or my family. That's one rule I'll never break."

This ethical attitude is not always maintained. In fact, in certain industries it is not expected, and executives are careful not to reveal to salespeople anything they do not want repeated.

Some customers go to great lengths to keep the sales reps with whom they do business from learning much of value. Don't be surprised when your physical movement around a customer's plant is carefully restricted. Often you will be allowed to learn only what the customer thinks you need to know. This is particularly true in selling to high technology businesses.

Bribes An unpleasant fact of the salesperson's life is the practice of bribery. Not that bribery does not thrive in other fields of endeavor, for it does. It is sometimes called nicer names, such as "reward" or "in appreciation for services rendered," and is regarded as standard procedure in some circles. But in selling it is not standard.

However, some firms and some salespeople have found it effective, at least in the short-term. A small business executive selling an item to oil well drillers took an active part in private meetings where field prices were established, all firms selling this standard product at identical list prices. He said, "Everything is billed out at the agreed price, but I manage to get a fair hunk of it back to them under the table to the right men who won't spill the beans."

In other cases buyers request bribes of some sort. The sales manager for a regional paint manufacturer related that he had this problem with a large aircraft company. He said, "They had a purchasing agent who was on the take. He was rather open about it and made it clear that if we wanted any of their business, he had to be paid off. We just won't do business that way, so we pulled out of bidding and stopped calling on them. One day the big brass in the east stumbled onto the fact that the region's largest paint manufacturer was not bidding for their business. I got a call from their executive vice-president, who asked me why we hadn't submitted bids lately. I told him exactly the reason. Now we do business with a new purchasing agent. But I know there are still some buyers out there who are on the take."

Few purchasing agents are so clumsy as to ask for outright bribes. Instead, some drop veiled hints that they are in need of something or other. The sales rep for one electronics firm recalls the time an executive of a potential account mentioned that her family had been pressuring her for a new stereo, a product which just happened to be made by one division of the salesperson's firm.

However, far more clever are the purchasing agents who say nothing of their larcenous inclinations but manage to patronize the perceptive salesperson who senses their bent. These buyers, while not openly soliciting bribes and preferential treatment, nevertheless bestow their business on the firms that are most generous.

One sales manager admonishes his salespeople to start looking for a bribe or for personal friendship somewhere in the background if they cannot understand why some other firm is getting an account's business. He says, "In our industry buyers have good reasons for buying from the sources they do. If none of the usual business reasons are present in a certain situation, then I immediately start looking for the existence of personal friendships, family ties, or bribes. It makes no sense for one of our salespeople to beat his head against a stone wall trying to sell a purchasing agent who is in the control of one of our competitors. Once we find this to be the situation, we simply stop calling on the firm."

It would be nice if there were easy answers to this problem, but unfortunately there are none. A salesperson will encounter buyers who want to be bribed and competitors who are willing to do so. How to handle bribery depends to such a large extent upon the conditions peculiar to the industry and the situation that it is impossible to provide any meaningful rule for action. Many sales reps and firms refuse under any circumstances to be parties to commercial bribery, not only on legal grounds but also on moral ones. On the other hand, some firms and salespeople will not hesitate if they feel that a bribe will gain them what they want.

Gifts[3]   Closely akin to bribes is the practice of giving gifts, particularly at Christmas time. The practice has become so widespread in industry that outcries are being heard from many sectors of the business community complaining of their general ineffectiveness and meaninglessness. Clearly, the dividing line between a gift and a bribe is rather arbitrary at best. Some firms have declared that their executives may not accept gifts over a certain nominal value, thus in effect saying that articles under the amount are gifts while items over it constitute bribes. Salespeople, as frequent bearers of gifts, are caught in the middle of this confusion of top management concerning the role of the gift in business.

Here are some guidelines to keep the salesperson from making too many serious errors in gift-giving. One purchasing agent for a large oil company warned, "Never give us a gift *before* we have done business with you. Use sales ability, not 30 pieces of silver."

A psychologist claims that the way in which a person gives is probably tied in with personality. He says, "The best salesmen do it with finesse. They give unobtrusively; they never talk about it, and they never show signs of expecting a return. If a salesman feels queasy about a gift, it's probably a sign that he doesn't have the right motive and ought to be careful."

According to one buyer, only 5 percent of business gift-giving is done deftly enough to benefit salespeople. What are the mistakes that reduce the effectiveness of gifts? The experts list the following common mistakes made in gift-giving:

1 Any gift that puts the recipient at a disadvantage is in bad taste and a mistake. But if it is clearly symbolic of appreciation, no strings attached, the gift has a good effect.

2 If it is so extravagant as to approach bribery or if it is blatant advertising, it is in bad taste.

3 If an item can be misinterpreted, a wrong connotation put on it, it's dangerous. For example, one man never gives another grooming aids.

4 Another mistake is to overestimate the effect of barroom humor. Just because you think nude figures on the inside of beer glasses are amusing doesn't mean your best customer will.

5 In most cases good taste prohibits the giving of gifts to the purchasing agent's spouse, but gifts to the children are fine and may be especially effective.

The timing of a gift may be particularly critical to its effectiveness. Another box of candy at Christmas time gets lost in the deluge, but the same gift at another time of year—say, the purchasing agent's wedding anniversary— may be deeply appreciated. Many of the most effective gift programs in business are not made routine to the point of boredom but instead are administered by salespeople who attempt to send only appropriate gifts to the right people at the right time. A pair of tickets to a football game may be far more effective in creating goodwill than an expensive portable television set.

The Internal Revenue Service allows the firm to deduct only up to $25 for gifts to any one individual in a year. This ruling has had the effect of placing a ceiling on gift-giving.

Entertainment   The problem of entertainment is in much the same category as bribes and gift-giving. It can be an attempt to influence the buyer on a basis other than the merits of the proposition. Nonetheless, it is a widespread practice, and most sales reps must decide who should be entertained and to what extent.

Naturally, there are problems connected with entertainment. A large portion of the salesperson's expense money may be devoted to it. If it is not spent wisely, if it is wasted on prospects with little potential, productivity will be seriously impaired, and selling costs will be out of line. Indeed, in many industries one of the key factors in a sales rep's success is the ability to know who is the right person to entertain and what the nature of the entertainment

A lot of business is conducted on the golf course. Where else can you get a half day or more with a prospect under favorable conditions? Should you play "customer golf?" That's a question of both ethics and skill. Would it be considered a bribe?

should be. It is a mistake to assume that all entertainment takes the form of eating and drinking. In many circumstances unusual forms of entertainment are far more effective. One book representative was particularly resourceful in his entertainment. He invited prospects to go skiing with him—he would pay for the two tickets—a modest amount compared with a night of wining and dining. His philosophy of entertainment was to do something a little different. He tried to determine what the prospect liked to do best and then treated him or her to it. An invitation to play golf at some nice country club is highly appreciated by the avid golfer.

The Saleswoman and Entertainment One of the early fears of both women and management was that problems would arise between male customers and female salespeople, particularly if the saleswoman had to entertain the buyer. Those fears have now largely subsided. Experience has shown that

> most professional male buyers do not want to be entertained by the saleswoman. It poses them even more problems than it does the woman. The saleswoman does not have to entertain to sell. People will buy on the merits of the sales proposition. If some entertainment seems in order to make the sale and establish relationships with the firm, the saleswoman and her spouse (or date) can entertain the buyer and his or her spouse (or date). Make it a foursome.[4]

Conflicts of Interest   In some cases a salesperson may be faced with a conflict of interest in handling an account. One sales rep selling to an electronics firm proved to all parties his high ethical standards by withdrawing from the account on the grounds that his brother-in-law was the president of a competing firm. He preferred to avoid a position in which he might be suspected of passing along to his brother-in-law information gained from servicing a competitor's account.

Sales reps may have interests in firms in conflict with those of customers or employers. Ethical, professional salespeople will take great pains to make their exact positions clear to all parties concerned, lest their interest be misinterpreted at some later date when they are discovered—as they usually will be.

Hiring Customer's Employees   Most well-managed growing concerns have a great need for excellent people. They are constantly looking for them. Often the sales force is urged to keep an eye open for promising new employees. Sometimes a bonus is offered for each person the sales rep locates who is ultimately hired.

Now comes the problem. You spot someone working for a customer who you think would make an excellent recruit for your company. And you have reason to believe that the person would be available. Should you recruit your customer's employees? Usually not! People have been known to get rather testy about losing a good employee and may retaliate in whatever way is available to them—in your case, by throwing you out. . . . You must be careful in your contacts with the people in your customer's organizations. It is best to get permission from the person's boss before talking with him or her. Even so, it is a most delicate matter, and one fraught with danger to you. Employers can be very possessive about their employees, and should they learn that you are even considering hiring one of them, you may not be welcome on the premises again.

If the customer's employee approaches you, then refer the person to the proper executive in your organization. Most well-managed companies have stated policies to cover these instances. Often the policy is that all such contacts must be cleared with the customer. It usually depends upon the practices in the industry. In some trades these matters are so sensitive that under no circumstances will a firm talk with one of its customers' employees about a job.

Ethical Problems Connected with Employers

Your relationships with your employer are even closer than those with customers and give rise to just as many, if not more, ethical problems.

Changing Jobs   There usually comes a time when you consider changing jobs and must face certain ethical considerations. In some industries the ethical code is so strict that it precludes you from going to work for a direct competitor lest that firm benefit by information and knowledge obtained from the first employer. However, this is the exception. More commonly, it is considered unethical for a competitor to initiate negotiations with salespeople in trying to lure them away from their present employers. However, usually a dissatisfied salesperson may ethically initiate contacts with competitors. In some industries open piracy of salespeople is considered perfectly ethical and is practiced by all.

You are faced with the ethical problem of how much notice should be given the employer, because it may be difficult to find a replacement immediately. It may take several months to train the replacement, and in the meantime the company may be severely damaged should it not have a representative in that territory. Clearly, the ethical person would not want to place an employer in such a position by leaving without notice. Try to reach an amicable agreement as to the date of severance.

However, realists in management know that once someone has decided to quit there is little advantage gained by keeping the person around, and quite possibly there is much to lose. The company may be paying to help set up the former employee in his or her new position in business. Normally, the quicker you get out, the better it is for everyone.

In severance situations there arises the problem of your accounts. Should you attempt to take them with you to the new employer? Accounts have been known to follow the sales rep rather than stay with the house; however, that usually happens in competitive environments in which there is little difference between products and the accounts have been buying the sales rep's services rather than the firm's wares. One survey of appliance dealers directly asked dealers if they would switch lines if their favorite sales rep changed houses. The dealers overwhelmingly claimed they would not follow any salesperson to another distributor but would stick with the lines they were selling. Many agents have been deluded into thinking they had a clientele loyal to them only to be rudely shocked when they discovered that their previous customers had been buying products, not personalities.

Sometimes a firm will lure away key sales representatives of successful competitors for the knowledge they may have of important operational details. Naturally, it is difficult to control the information a salesperson gives a new employer, but there are limits beyond which a sales rep's behavior is clearly unethical. One man resigned as a sales rep to accept the sales managership of a smaller competitor. He managed to get into the files before leaving and take with him important marketing research information and data on the firm's customers. Needless to say, the president of the firm was disturbed by this unethical behavior, but there was little that could be done about it. Some employers take precautions to protect themselves against the risk.

Expense Accounts   Handling expense accounts naturally involves many ethical considerations. For the moment, let's ignore the rare situation in which the company encourages fictional expense accounts and assume that accurate statements of legitimate sales expenses are desired.

The ethical problems connected with expense accounts are not concerned with whether you should abide by the employer's wishes, for that is rather clear-cut ethically. But many little problems arise which are seemingly quite innocent. Suppose the employer has set limits on what can be spent for certain activities. For example, only 15 cents a mile will be paid for automobile expenses. Yet you, in all honesty, have computed the operating costs at 20 cents a mile. Now you may be tempted to pad the mileage to make up the difference between the 15 and 20 cents. In your own mind you may try to justify your actions on the basis that the money was actually spent for business purposes and that the spirit of the expense account was not being violated. You face the ethical problem: Should you manipulate the expense account in order to protect yourself from the stingy policies of management, thereby recovering money honestly spent on the solicitation of business for your firm? Or should you strenuously attempt to get the policies changed, and failing that, change employers rather than commit what you believe to be unethical acts? What are the dangers of such manipulation? Quite simple! Once you find you can manipulate figures with ease for honest amounts, does this not encourage you to manipulate a bit more and increase your earnings? Just where can you draw the line at manipulation?

There is an old story about a sales rep who lost his hat while making a sales call. He thought the company should compensate him for its loss, since it was in the pursuit of business. He put at the bottom of his next expense account, "New hat to replace one damaged while calling on customer: $40." The auditor disallowed the claim. The next week he put it in again and, once again, it was disallowed. The third week, he wrote at the bottom of his expense account, "OK, Wise Guy. It's in there. Try to find it."

Suppose a company allows $40 a night for lodging. Should the saleswoman average out one night which cost $60 with another which cost only $20 by recording both as $40 nights? Should she put overages on one account into others? For example, suppose it costs her $3 more for lodging than is allowable, should she take her $3 from the entertainment fund?

Most unethical expense account practices evolve when salespeople can rationalize them because of some stingy policy of an employer. If they are able to justify their actions by thinking that the amounts they steal on the expense account are justly due, their stealing becomes much easier. It is quite similar to the situation in which the underpaid bank clerk embezzles, rationalizing that it was deserved.

Moonlighting   In some situations a sales rep can quite easily carry additional lines of merchandise other than those furnished by the principal employer. One representative for a manufacturer of women's high-priced dresses carried lines of underwear, lingerie, and sportswear without the approval of the employer. The employer had clearly disapproved of such moonlighting activities when another sales rep in Texas was fired for exactly the same practice. The employer's reasoning was that the agents were making good money, about $120,000 a year, selling the line and that they should devote their entire attention to it. The dress sales rep justified the moonlighting by saying, "It's true that my principal line is making me sufficient money presently. But in this business it is 'here today and gone tomorrow.' While the market is buying our styles in large quantities today, I've got to look ahead because I never know when this line will go sour. So I take on these other lines of merchandise to keep in with my accounts. I don't want to become too identified with one line, so that when it goes bad, the buyers won't look at anything else from me. In this industry you have to take care of yourself. I don't know who they (the management) think they're kidding, for they pay us on a straight commission basis, and we pay all of our own expenses. We have no fringe benefits; really I don't see how we are employees of the company, for they certainly don't treat us that way. We even have to pay our own way back to pick up our samples in New York City. I'm really in business for myself."

This neatly poses an ethical dilemma: How far is a person entitled to go in order to protect individual interests?

Experience has clearly shown employees that employers have little hesitation in letting them go when it is thought to be to the company's advantage to do so. Most employees are firmly convinced that management takes care of itself first. Then, conversely, the employees conclude that they had best take care of themselves first for if they don't who will?

Many sales reps have in the back of their minds that they will someday own their own businesses. Sometimes they even begin them while working for someone else. It may be some business that is somehow connected with what the reps are selling, or it may be totally unrelated. Whatever, it will take time and effort away from their jobs. Thus most employers take an exceedingly dim view of salespeople who begin their own business while on another's payroll. They rightly suspect that they will be paying for much of the new concern's supplies, long distance telephone calls, travel expenses, entertainment, and the like. It's called *conflict of interest* and should be avoided.

Selling Tactics[5]   Suppose you believe that the customer is overbuying. Should you say so? Bear in mind that you are working on commission and need the money badly.

Suppose the customer, a retailer, is about to buy a "dog"—a *bona fide* charter member of the bow-wow club. Normally, you would say something, but this morning your sales manager strongly urged you to push the item and offered you a "spiff" (extra money) on every one you sell. You need the extra money badly. Do you say something about the article's canine characteristics?

Suppose a customer needs an early delivery date on an order. Should you promise to meet the date, and then hope for the best and prepare an excuse for the worst?

If you understand everything we have said about professional selling up to now, you know our answers to these questions. Don't lie! Don't mislead! Serve your customer!

Fellow Salespeople   Your relationships with colleagues are fraught with ethical problems. Although most companies endeavor to minimize conflicts between their reps by assigning specific territories and accounts, ample room still exists for misunderstandings. What about the customer who is a personal friend of the sales rep and is located in another rep's territory? What about prospects a fellow salesperson fails to sell? When is it ethical for another rep to call upon them? Should permission be asked of the first sales rep? Does a salesperson owe a split commission for leads furnished by others? Firms do set policies to handle a few such problems, but naturally they cannot cover all contingencies.

When salespeople are turned loose in an area without territorial assignments, conflicts arise. Suppose prospects contact a realty firm in January about a house, and agent Jones shows them around but fails to close a deal. In September the prospects contact agent Smith, who closes a deal on the house first shown them by agent Jones. Obviously, troubles will arise when Jones learns of this. It is for this reason that realtors have established boards to judge these matters and have set forth fairly clear-cut rules governing such situations. However, in other fields this type of regulation is not available.

Personal Use of Company Assets   One of the unique attributes of sales is that corporate assets are entrusted to you. Cars, expensive samples, or equipment are frequently furnished. Most managers establish policies governing the use of the company cars. A few firms allow the salesperson to use the company car just as if it were personal property, with the company paying the costs, but this is the exception. More commonly, the sales rep may use the car for personal needs but must pay so much a mile to cover direct costs. Some concerns severely limit personal use. Some insist that there be no *long* personal trips, while a few restrict *all* personal usage. Whatever the company's policies on these matters, the salesperson has ample opportunity to violate them.

On the other hand, a slightly different problem arises in the case of samples and equipment. There have been numerous cases in which salespeople have sold samples for personal gain, claiming that they lost them or that they had been given to some customer in furtherance of a sale. Some firms instruct sales reps to sell their samples when they become shopworn or damaged. The result—opportunity for questionable practices. Salespeople for 3M are sometimes faced with an ethical problem in picking up old stock on dealers' hands and writing it off. Top management does not want outdated stock shipped back to the factory; the quicker it is junked, the less it costs. Hence, authority is vested at low levels for writing the stock off as a complete loss. Some salespeople have been known to take such stock home and sell it later for personal gain. This is particularly true with tapes printed for Christmas that the company uniformly picks up after each Yuletide. This behavior is illegal as well as unethical, but it is mentioned to illustrate that these problems do exist.

Contests Contests, and other managerial tools, frequently pose ethical problems because the opportunistic operator can take advantage of loopholes in the rules. For example, one man was able to win a large monthly contest by withholding orders during the last 10 days of the previous month and filing them with those taken during the contest month, thereby significantly enlarging his sales volume. While this is clearly unethical, a sales rep might defend it because management established the situation which fostered it.

And what of the contest that is designed to promote tremendous volume production? Does it not tempt the sales rep to overload customers or dealers to a degree that is unethical? What about the contest that offers great rewards for selling a certain product? Does it not encourage selling it to prospects despite the fact that it might not be the best product for them?

Adherence to Company Policies The typical salesperson operates within a rather formidable framework of policies that attempt to regulate the rep's behavior along the lines desired by management. But these policies do not always make economic sense, nor are they always conducive to selling more goods. Hence one is frequently tempted to deal outside of policy for the sake of either profit or expediency. One office machine manufacturer has a firm policy on handling trade-ins: The price allowed on the trade-in is set forth in a small booklet, at a disgustingly low figure, and the salesperson is not allowed to buy or sell them on the side. But one of the firm's biggest producers has allied himself with an independent office machines dealer who buys at a higher price than the sales rep can allow for the trade-in. Thus the sales rep can be more competitive in selling the new equipment. "The company's policy stinks. They trim the customer on the trade-in, but I won't deal that way. If I can't give a square deal, then they can have my job. And if they learn of my wheeling and dealing they'll can me, but to heck with them. I'm making a lot of money for them and myself now and know where I can earn more any time," explained the rep involved.

Should an agent work for a firm whose policies cannot be followed in all good conscience?

Management tells sales reps to push a certain new product line, yet the reps know that it is a dog; the trade will scream at them next time around if they shove these goods on retailers. To whom do the reps owe their first allegiance? Are they not acting in the best interests of the company by ignoring such orders? These are some of the problems that are encountered frequently in applying company policy to actual field conditions. The problem arises many times because the policy maker may not have a realistic view of conditions or may be strongly prejudiced by personal emotions on a matter.

Many policy makers have never had to face an irate customer cheated by some company policy. It can be a traumatic experience.

Moreover, there is a distinct difference between what is good for the company and what is good for its management. Inasmuch as policy is made by management, many times it is made for its own convenience and purposes and not for the best interests of the concern.

Ethical Problems Connected with Competitors

When a salesperson is accused of unethical behavior, the chances are that the accusations are being made by a competitor. If any particular tactics or tricks were used to gain the victory, the loser is tempted to yell "Foul." However, this does not automatically make it unethical, for the very essence of competition involves certain sharp practices. All too often the price-cutter is called unethical. Yet genuine competition usually involves price variation. The industrial sales rep who persuades a customer's engineering department to establish certain specifications which favor her firm may be accused by a competitor of being unethical, but others would merely consider her an excellent saleswoman. A competitor may claim that it is unethical for one to sell direct to a certain account at a lower price. Yet is not this just a matter of business policy under our competitive system?

There are some competitive practices, however, that *are* clearly unethical. At one time a business machines manufacturer had his salespeople drop sand in competing machines whenever they could. The practice became so bad that finally the Federal Trade Commission issued a cease-and-desist order against this firm, which is in effect today. The order specifically forbids the company's sales reps from dropping sand in competitors' equipment.

Many sales reps admit that if they are forced to make a demonstration against the leading competitor's equipment, they can always make it look bad in comparison to their own. One favorite tactic of vacuum cleaner salespeople is to clean a rug with the owner's present machine first and then reclean it with their own to show the superiority of their cleaner. Just how far can you go in adroitly disparaging the competition? Should you even agree to such tests?

Naturally, these are questions that cannot be answered categorically, for they depend upon the circumstances. In many situations the sales rep must agree to a test demonstration against all the competitive equipment if the prospect demands it. In some instances the competitive equipment may have disadvantages which should be pointed out to the prospect, but the sales rep must remember not to go too far or the word will get back to the competition. A victory gained by an unethical tactic may cost the salesperson dearly in the future as competitors retaliate.

SUMMARY

Sales reps face many legal and ethical problems as they go about their work. The law affects much of what they can and cannot do. Most of the legal aspects revolve around the use of deception, misrepresentation, and unfair business practices. However, in some industries other critical legal issues arise. The real estate agent is strictly regulated in what can and cannot be done in selling real property. Securities brokers must walk a tightrope lest their freedom be impaired. Even door-to-door salespeople must carefully abide by the laws passed to govern their activities.

Sales reps must be concerned with their ethical relationships with their customers, their employers, and their peers. Each has its own problems. Unethical behavior with customers, usually designed for short-term gains, can result in lost customers. Most of the customer-related ethical dilemmas revolve around truthfulness and fair dealing.

Relationships with employers can be fraught with problems. How much effort and times does the rep owe the employer? Changing employers gives rise to a host of ethical problems that center around advance notice and the transfer of the rep's customers and knowledge to the new employer.

This seems to be the nub of ethics in selling. It comes down to how competitive the market is. The more competitive the industry, the more temptations the salesperson will face, the more ethical problems he or she will encounter. It's easy for a sales rep selling for a monopoly to be ethical. Clearly, the classical economist's concept of competition makes no allowances for ethics, for in their theoretical framework the firm must do everything legally possible to get the better of its competition if maximum efficiency and productivity are to be achieved.

DISCUSSION QUESTIONS

1 As a sales rep for a manufacturer of fine men's sweaters you have been trying to get the line into one large men's specialty store for some time but with no success because the line is also being sold to a nearby large department store. "Stop selling to them and I'll buy!" the merchant has continually told you. The department store bought $22,000 of sweaters last year. The buyer for the specialty store will not be pinned down on what his volume would be. What will you do?

2 A purchasing agent for a large aerospace firm was to be laid off at the end of the project on which he was working. A sales rep of a potential subcontractor for a substantial electronic component costing $5,000 a unit—1,000 units were needed—took the p.a. to lunch. Over lunch the p.a. managed to convey that if he were to get $50,000, the contract would be awarded to the salesperson's firm. You are the sales rep. What would you tell the p.a.? Then what would you do?

3 You sell lumber to manufacturers such as furniture makers and builders of various components that go into home construction. You have been calling for 3 years upon the purchasing agent for a large kitchen cabinetmaker but without results. The account is all locked up with another lumber company. One day while relating your woeful tale to a sales rep for builder's hardware, you are suddenly told that the only way to do business with that firm is by bribing management. What would you do? Be as specific as possible.

4 You believe that a competitor's sales rep is being unethical in certain remarks made about your equipment. What courses of action are open to you?

5 You discover that you have significantly overcharged a customer on one item she has ordered. The situation is such that it is unlikely that the overcharge will be discovered. What, if anything, would you do about it?

6 You have been a sales representative for a manufacturer of electronic components for the past decade and are presently earning $38,000 a year. A competitive firm offers you $55,000 but you *must* start immediately. The territory would be the same. You feel that you owe your employer at least 1 month's notice, but the competitor is adamant—it's now or never. What would you do?

7 You have tentatively accepted a sales job selling women's coats in a large western territory. Your compensation will be 5 percent of sales, with you paying your own expenses. What protections would you try to obtain in writing from your new employer?

8 Why are salespeople so often the victims of confidence games built around selling some new device?

9 Just how much time and effort do you owe your employer ethically? Some firms demand one's complete dedication to the job day or night.

10 Under what circumstances would it be ethical for a sales rep to carry additional lines of goods?

REFERENCES

1 Clarke L. Caywood and Gene R. Laczniak, "Ethics and Personal Selling: Death of a Salesman as an Ethical Primer," *Journal of Personal Selling & Sales Management,* August 1986, pp. 81–88, indicate that guidelines for ethics are inherently limited. The "Proportionality Framework" by Garrett (1966) may be useful for issues not covered by a code of ethics.

2 Thomas R. Wotruba, "A Comprehensive Framework for the Analysis of Ethical Behavior, with a Focus on Sales Organizations," *Journal of Personal Selling & Sales Management,* Spring 1990, pp. 29–42, discusses the four major parts of an analysis of how sales organization personnel arrive at ethical decisions and actions: (1) the moral decision structure, (2) the characteristics of the decision maker, (3) situational moderators, and (4) relationships connecting ethical behavior with outcomes.

3 I. Fredrick Trawick, John E. Swan, and David Rink, "Industrial Buyer Evaluation of the Ethics of Salesperson Gift Giving: Value of the Gift and Customer vs. Prospect Status," *Journal of Personal Selling & Sales Management,* Summer 1989, pp. 31–37, suggest that gift-giving to customers is seen as more ethically appropriate than gifts to prospects.

4 Richard H. Buskirk and Beverly Miles, *Beating Men at Their Own Game: A Woman's Guide to Successful Selling in Industry,* 1980, provide a more detailed account of the experience of women in sales work.

5 Ely S. Lurin, "Research and Lead Generation Are an Ethical Mix," *Marketing News,* January 2, 1987, pp. 4, suggests that generating leads during market studies saves time and money, while privacy is not violated.

CASE 18-1: The New England Tool Company— The Care and Feeding of a Large Account

Sam Carbone, sales engineer for the New England Tool Company in the Chicago area, felt he could no longer avoid a problem that had been growing in significance each year with his largest account, the Universal Electronics Company. For 20 years he had enjoyed extremely good relations with the firm's purchasing people and their production and engineering staffs. While tooling purchases varied each year depending upon the business cycle, Sam received orders from $275,000 to as much as $1 million a year from Universal. In 1985 sales to the firm had been $653,000. He had worked very closely with the account and gave it exceptional service whenever it was needed. Naturally, over the years he had entertained Universal's people in meaningful ways in keeping with their importance to him. His gifts at Christmas were in good taste and were appreciated; for Christmas 1985, he had a case of fine California wine sent to each of his important contacts in the company.

In early 1986 a new vice president of purchasing was appointed, Mrs. Devonne Hammersmith. She soon issued a company memo to the effect that the giving of gifts to company employees by vendors would no longer be allowed. Moreover, all entertainment except for nominal business lunches was to cease. The memo was countersigned by the company's president. It was not well received by the rank and file within the company.

Sam strolled into the hornet's nest the day after the memo had been issued. It was, to say the least, a matter of great conversational interest among Universal's managerial staff, particularly the ones who had been the recipient of significant gifts in the past or who were particularly addicted to entertainment on someone else's expense account. The memo had been sent in letter form to all of Universal's suppliers, and a large sign had been posted in the purchasing department's outer office stating the new policy on entertaining and gifts. Sam at first mused that his selling expenses would be dropping rather significantly in the future. He saw no reason not to comply at first. However, in many and varied ways, the people to whom he had given gifts and whom he had entertained began to let Sam know that they had been quite happy with the old arrangements and saw no reason to alter anything just because of the new vice president. They felt that the only consideration now was that such matters had to be carried on discreetly. The vice president of production in particular let Sam know that he really liked his case of wine and expected to receive another at his home for Christmas 1986. The head of production planning asked Sam when they were going to Palm Springs again to play some golf. A few of the discontented buyers openly hinted that other vendors were ignoring the company's policy. "It's just eyewash to keep the board happy. Business is going on as usual," was the attitude.

Sam was perfectly happy to accommodate his customers for he was most adept at using entertainment and gifts to his advantage. He knew the subtle art of the care and feeding of one's customers. But Sam was no dummy. He saw he could get into real trouble should his violation of Universal's policy be discovered. He sought advice from his boss and was told that he was on his own. If Sam violated policy, the boss did not want to know about it. But, most important, he was told, "Keep the account happy!"

Sam became increasingly aware that the dilemma was not going to go away with the passage of time as he had originally hoped. His relationships with several key people in the Universal organization were cooling off as he failed to respond to their somewhat veiled invitations to be entertained. Then one day he was jolted to learn that a good-sized order for a particular tool that he had been selling to Universal for years had been given to a competitor by the vice president of production. Sam did not like the new developments one bit and knew he had to do something about them.

1 Should Sam adhere to Universal's new policy against giving gifts and entertaining?

2 If so, what, if anything, would you recommend he do about the Universal account?

3 If you believe that Sam should find some way to evade the intentions of Universal's policy, how would you recommend he do it?

CASE 18-2: The Alpine Ski Company— A Change of Signals

Bob Turner had accepted the challenge of building up the Rocky Mountain territory for the Alpine Ski Company when it began business in 1980 selling a new type of ski boot. He had been a sales rep for a line of ski products for 10 years, so he was well connected in the skiing industry. He was so enthusiastic about the new boot and the other products the company had on line that he dropped his other products to work for the company full time. However, in exchange he demanded and received a written employment agreement giving him a 12 percent commission on all sales made by the Alpine Company or any of its subsidiaries in Bob's stated territory of the states of Utah, Colorado, New Mexico, Wyoming, and Montana. The contract provided that his territory could not be reduced in the future. His attorney had placed several other clauses in the contract to protect Bob's interests.

In 1990 company management changed when the firm was sold to a large organization. New management took one look at Bob's contract and said, in effect, "No way! Either Bob agrees to a new contract or he goes." Bob was informed of management's attitude toward his previous arrangements at a very pleasant social outing specially set up for the purpose. It was well orchestrated. Management was trying hard to sell its proposal, for it realized the legal problems posed should the contract be breached. In 1989 Bob had earned more than $240,000 from his territory, and since Bob was only 46 years old, he intended to live a while longer.

Management's legal counsel had advised that as employment contracts go, Bob's was well constructed. It would be difficult to attack it in court. Thus management developed a contingency plan to harass Bob.

At the social gathering, when management thought Bob had been carefully primed, they praised him for the outstanding work he was doing for the company and offered him the sales managership. Of course, the job did not pay quite as much—but it would be only a matter of time, since Bob was clearly destined for higher responsibilities. The plan, in reality, was to move Bob into the job for a few months and then fire him. Acceptance of the new job would void the old contract.

Management was elated when Bob indicated he was interested in the promotion. "I've been on the road a long time now and would like to get into management." Management panicked when he continued, "I'll have my lawyer draw up a new contract."

The president replied, "Our management people don't have contracts. I don't have a contract. So I hardly can see how we can give you one."

Bob replied, "Then I doubt if I am interested." The tone of the party suddenly changed.

The president became a bit firmer. "Now I would give this matter some serious thought if I were you. There are ways we can handle your contract. We don't want to do them, but we can and will if you make it necessary."

Bob said nothing. The president continued, "You're not going to last long if your customers don't get the deliveries they need, you know."

"Neither will your company!" snorted Bob. He thought the president was an idiot to try a play like this on him, the company's biggest sales producer. To say he was mad would be a gross understatement. But he remained outwardly calm. Bob had not been tested under fire for years without developing a facade to see him through sticky situations. He kept thinking about the importance of not tipping his hand, not agreeing to anything, and encouraging them to talk to learn about their schemes.

The net result of the evening was that Bob learned that management planned to harass him and make his life miserable. And in the back of their minds seemed to be a plan to fire him for some trumped-up cause and then let him go to court and try to collect.

1 What should Bob do?

CASE 18-3: John and Big Max—A Duel in the Sun, or You've Got 'till Sundown to Get Out of Dodge City

John Weber had learned his lessons well. His professor had told him that one key to success in business was to put your wagon in the way of a lot of potential customers. John followed the advice literally. After graduating from the Entrepreneur Program of a large West Coast university, he outfitted a truck to sell hot and cold food—a mobile food concession. He reasoned that since a lot of hungry people flocked to the huge fast food franchises, he might do well if he parked his truck nearby and tried to service the overflow during rush hours. He picked one particularly crowded location in downtown Los Angeles and parked his truck across the street. The results were fantastic. "I had more business than I could handle."

Then the fun began. The manager got the police to closely examine John's operation for illegalities. But as we mentioned before, John had learned his lessons well. Always touch all legal bases. Be as clean as a hound's tooth. John was! So after all the hassle he was still in business.

In the second round, the manager for the fast food company was able to get the city authorities to paint the curbs where John was parking red—NO PARKING.

Enough was enough. John was ready to declare war. He contemplated giving some of the homeless street people a little money to buy coffee in the fast food outlet on the condition they spend most of the day drinking it. He also knew a young lady who could do some disgusting things with the food she ate; he thought about hiring her to do her act at peak times in the restaurant.

While his friends were all of a mind to help John in his war, there were some who counseled more restraint. "Why fight it? Go to another outlet. There are hundreds of them. Keep moving around. Don't let them focus on you!"

One of John's friends thought he was being highly unethical in what he planned to do. She questioned the legality of his actions. "You could get into big trouble."

1 What advice would you give John?
2 How ethical is the behavior of the fast food manager?
3 Are John's plans ethical? Legal?

CHAPTER NINETEEN

TELEMARKETING SYSTEMS

CHAPTER NINETEEN

TELEMARKETING SYSTEMS

Let your fingers do the walking.
Ma Bell

After studying the material in this chapter you should:

☐ Appreciate the role of modern telecommunications technology in sales management operations

☐ Understand the cost economics that are the foundation for tele-marketing

☐ Know about both inbound and outbound teleselling programs

☐ Perceive the importance of scripting to an outbound teleselling program

☐ Understand the ethical problems posed by telemarketing operations

PROFILE OF

A SALES REP IN 2000

"I should have a telephone grafted onto my ear. I'm on the horn all the time—calling customers and prospects, checking with the office, answering customer service calls, and who knows what. Without my mobile telephone in the car either I would be tied to my desk or no one could reach me.

"Besides, without the mobile phone I couldn't access the office computer with my portable computer to use our customer database and our inventory and order sytems. With my portable computer I can bring up on the screen everything we know about any customer—what they bought in the past and who the players are and our history with them. I can also tell a prospect our inventory position on any item and provide whatever technical information might be needed. I don't have to carry those big technical books around with me anymore. More importantly, I can submit purchase orders immediately and have them confirmed while sitting in the customer's office.

"Paperwork and meetings are much easier to handle. I can file expense accounts directly using the mail feature of the computer. My field reports go directly to the sales manager over the computer. The other day we had a sales training meeting over the satellite television system, with the home office people talking directly with us back and forth.

"When I'm making a presentation I can call on my computer to help me show the prospects the economics of my deal. They just plug in the figures for their operations, and our program feeds back to them what they need to do to maximize their situation. And I have all the financing alternatives in the computer, so I can show the prospect immediately the choices available.

"And you know, I'm now making more money than I ever dreamed I could. I can do so much more business because I don't have to pound the road all the time to call on customers."

While telephone and telecommunications technology plays an important role in lead-generation programs (see Chapter 6), telemarketing differs from those applications in that it is a marketing strategy, not a tactic.

Let's first define what is meant by *telecommunications*. Stone and Wyman, the leading authorities on the subject define it as follows:

> Telemarketing comprises the integrated and systematic application of telecommunications and information processing technologies with management systems to optimize the marketing communications mix used by a company to reach its customers. It retains personalized customer interaction while simultaneously attempting to better meet customer needs and improve cost effectiveness.[1]

Stone and Wyman provide another more pragmatic definition: ''Telemarketing is a new marketing discipline that utilizes telecommunications technology as part of a well-planned, organized, and managed marketing program that prominently features the use of personal selling, using non-face-to-face contacts.''[2]

The key term is ''non-face-to-face personal selling.'' Telemarketing has been developed to counter the vastly increased costs of personal selling in the field. Time is money, and it simply takes too much time to make a sales call for many companies to make a profit doing so.[3] (We use the term ''sales call'' loosely. Any contact with a customer or potential customer is a sales call. You call Avis for a rental car; that is a sales call. You call Microsoft for technical assistance; that is a sales call.) Thus a great deal of sales service and sales promotional work is included in telemarketing, as well as actual sales order solicitations. There is no shortage of success stories with which to fuel the fires that keep the telecommunications pot boiling.

Telephone and telecommunications technology have helped counter the increasing costs of personal selling in the field. Sales reps can save time and money yet still interact with their contacts.

OVERVIEW

The advent of telemarketing strategies was a logical result of significant advances in computer and telephone technology. These allow low-cost rapid access to consumer and product databases as well as quick, low-cost telephone access to the customers and prospects.[4]

The technology has been in place for years, but sales management has not always been ready to use it. Putting new operational systems into place requires much effort and often a change in philosophy. It is not easy for an old-line sales manager who spent years on the road, calling on accounts day in and day out, to accept some of the philosophies inherent in telemarketing programs. Infrequent entertaining, cost-effectiveness analysis, by-the-numbers marketing—these are different skills, used by different people.[5]

Costs

Consider: An average field salesperson might make five or six sales contacts per day, or 25 to 30 a week, while a telemarketing salesperson can make the latter number per day, or 125 or 150 contacts per week, without any field selling expenses.

An effective telemarketing program can be highly cost effective for many firms. Moreover, the costs are predictable and controllable. You can compute them ahead of time and monitor them daily. If someone is not doing the job, you will know it quickly. You know when they are at work and when they are not. This factor appeals to many managers who are certain that their sales force is goofing off, sight unseen, in the field. How do they know it? Simple! That's what they did when *they* were in the field. Teleselling changes the game.[6]

Computer Databases

The existence of huge customer databases, combined with the possibility of programmed, predetermined, automatic calling routines, allows telemarketing programs to service an account base as never before. The firm's market can be covered in the desired manner. Such coverage does not depend upon the whim of field sales reps who might or might not call depending upon how they feel that day.

Changes in Buying Habits

Initially, there was much resistance to telephone selling. Many customers felt it to be an intrusion into their privacy. They had not considered its virtues.

Now most professional buyers prefer telephone buying in situations in which it is appropriate. It is easier and quicker, and the buyer has more control over the interview. It is easy to hang up on the seller if matters get out of control. "I'm not interested!" Bang! and the conversation is over. It's not so easy with a sales rep in the office who may be persistent in pressing a lost cause.

As the buying public becomes more and more occupied with earning a living, there is less time for shopping. Telemarketing is time efficient. As favorable experiences accumulate, the buyer's fears of telephone buying lessen.

BUSINESS VERSUS CONSUMER TELEMARKETING[7]

An individual behaves in a manner consistent with the role he or she is playing at the time. A woman at home may resent an uninvited telephone sales call that tries to entice her to buy something. Yet that same woman at work, in a different role, may welcome an unsolicited telephone sales call; it's part of her job.

While the business teleseller can be flexible in talking with prospects while exploring some problem, the consumer teleseller must follow a rather strict script. Such scripts usually involve a series of questions which can only be answered in the desired pre-established manner and do not allow the consumer to speak for an extended period of time.[8]

The reason for such strong tactics is that experience shows that the longer the consumer is on the line, the more likely it is that he or she will buy. Often the main goal of the script is to keep the respondent from hanging up during the first minute of the call. Thus great care is taken in developing the early portions of the script.

TELESELLING

There are two distinctively different types of teleselling: inbound and outbound. Each has its own use and set of problems.[9]

Inbound Teleselling[10]

A prospect or customer has a problem. Somehow that person gets the idea that your firm may be able to solve that problem, perhaps from an advertisement or the Yellow Pages. In any case, the prospect calls you up, either to buy or for more information. In any case, the game is on. Now, what do you do about it? Many firms botch the opportunity; the telephone call is grossly mishandled. First, the receptionist or operator may be so ill-trained that the caller's desires are frustrated. The caller is unable to penetrate the defenses that the firm has erected to "protect" its executives and to reach the person who should be contacted.

Or, "Sorry, no sales rep is available now. Can you call back?" Maybe the prospect will call back, maybe not. In any case an infuriating game of telephone tag will probably ensue. It is most aggravating to want to buy something from a firm and be totally unable to talk with anyone at the company who can answer even a single question.

Thus one of the first checkpoints for appraising a firm's teleselling system is the way a phone call is first answered within the company. Top management should audit personally on a regular basis just how the firm's telephones are being answered. How are sales inquiries handled? It is inexcusable for a firm to lose business at this point. Yet what attention is paid to the people who are the firm's first line of contact? Not much!

Teleselling can be someone calling out of the blue for information about your offering. It can be someone who is responding to an advertisement. It can be a former customer who wants to do business again. It may be a recent customer with a complaint or request for service. Or it may be a regular customer calling in an order. Each requires different handling.

The 800 Number   In keeping with the basic marketing principle that the more convenient you make it for the customer to buy from you, the more you will sell, firms have rushed to install 800 numbers for inbound teleselling. The public is provided with a toll-free number such as 1-800-555-5555. It can be a big convenience. It can also be a big cost to the company.

While inbound teleselling is often associated with 800 numbers, there is considerable question as to the necessity of the toll-free inbound line. These numbers are most helpful in consumer marketing programs, when the prospect's decision of which firm to call may be swayed by which is the easiest and cheapest to contact. A prominently displayed 800 number in an advertisement may win the day over the competition or otherwise motivate the buying decision.

But many direct marketers have reported that profits rose when they eliminated the 800 number. In business-to-business teleselling, an 800 number is seldom justified. Businesspeople have little hesitation in calling long distance to make their jobs easier.

Traditional Selling   Inbound call handling is selling, not just order-taking. Salespeople can increase order size by systems selling and suggestive selling. The calling buyer has already decided to solve the problem. The inbound salesperson's task is to ascertain the buyer's true problem and make certain the buyer acquires everything needed to solve it. Inbound salespeople must have quick access to a wealth of information. The caller must perceive that the telesalesperson is an expert.[11]

Inbound operations are usually centralized in order to use the central mainframe computers for order entry, access to customer records, inventory status, product specification data, and other such information. However, there are some systems that allow access to such centralized databases from remote terminals.

Above all, inbound telesellers must be listeners. Friendly listeners! There is no need for hard selling. The customer already wants to buy. The customers

Mobile retail and service organizations such as this dog grooming service combine the advantages of both inbound and outbound teleselling.

want assurance that they are buying the right product from the right company for the right price. They eagerly state their problems to solicit advice and suggestions. They are usually ready to buy the system and not just the main component.

Do not for an instant think that everybody can handle inbound sales calls. They can't. They must be trained to do so and then provided with adequate incentives to do a good job of selling.

Outbound Teleselling

There are several types of outbound teleselling varying from cold-calling people or firms, without invitation or advance knowledge of them, to responding on the telephone to highly qualified prospects who have asked to be called. Naturally, each is a different situation.

Cold Calls[12]   First, cold-call outbound sellers need to be talkers, not listeners. Thus they are quite different from the inbound telesellers previously discussed. They need to be mentally tough to handle the continual rejections they encounter from those people who hang up on them. Perhaps the person has absolutely no interest in whatever is being sold. Perhaps the person detests being bothered on the telephone. People may resent the intrusion into their privacy, and many of them will let the caller know it in no uncertain terms. Others are just too busy to listen at the time but have no reason to encourage the caller to try again at a more convenient time. In any case, the cold-call teleseller must not allow constant rejection to affect his or her enthusiasm for, and belief in, the proposition.

The outbound teleseller cannot ask people if they have any problems that need solving. Some problem must be assumed before the call. The outbound cold-call teleseller has one product, one offer, and one script. Suggestive selling is nearly impossible because the customer, when called, does not even plan to buy the original offer.

Warm Calls   The outbound teleseller making "warm calls" is working from a list of people who, it is believed, may be prospects for the offer. The people working in the "boiler rooms" for securities brokerages (see below) have lists of potential investors who they know have sufficient money to invest. Perhaps the prospect has previously responded to some advertisement for some other broker and is therefore placed on a list which is in turn sold to any interested party.

One swimming pool chemical distributor called all people known to own swimming pools in the region. A computer software firm has its telesellers call all attorneys in the area; it was selling a database program developed to provide immediate access to conveniently classified citations. In such cases a forceful opening question can immediately focus the prospect's mind on the benefits being offered.

Often the main problem encountered by the business-to-business teleseller is getting through to the real decision maker. With experience some tactics can be developed that will increase success.

Obviously, this type of teleselling is far more popular than cold-call selling. Lists of specific prospects and telephone numbers are readily available. However, scripts need to be specifically written for each list used.

Hot Calls   The teleseller loves to call people who have indicated in some way that they need the product or service. Perhaps they have answered an advertisement. Perhaps they have approached the company for information, or even a quote. Such sellers are much like inbound tellers. They are responding to stated need.

SCRIPTING

Some of the worst advice anyone can give would-be-salespeople is "Just be *yourself!*" They'll starve if they do. They have little to say, and what they do say few people want to hear. There is much to learn about presenting a proposition to a prospect so that the chances for a sale are excellent. *Yourself* can become terribly bored after the 25th call on a sunny day. *Yourself* can be having some terrible problems that the prospect doesn't really care to know about. *Yourself* probably has different values than the prospect. No, being *Yourself* entices few prospects into buying.

You need a script, a means of controlling the quality of the presentation. While telephone scripts may not produce the optimal sales call, they can produce an acceptable and predictable flow of revenue. Moreover, scripts allow novice tellers to gain results similar to those of seasoned professionals more quickly than if they are left to develop their own sales patterns.

Boiler Rooms

The infamous "boiler rooms" (roundly condemned in the securities business) flourish nevertheless not only in the business of selling securities but in many other fields. Stripped of associations, the so-called boiler room is an outbound telemarketing center where many people are simultaneously selling under close supervision using well-tested scripts. Woe to the teller who deviates from the script. The employer wants assurance not only that the seller is using effective selling phrases but also that no laws are violated or misrepresentations made.

Left to their own devices, one-shot telesales people are likely to say whatever they think will make the sale. Often the truth can be bent or even ignored, since the salesperson is only compensated on the basis of sales made and does not have to live with the ultimate results of such misrepresentations. Legitimate telemarketers who want to stay in business must carefully control the tellers. Thus close monitoring of operations is necessary.

Flexible Scripts

Don't jump to the conclusion that scripts are only for boiler rooms. They're not. They can be most useful to just about all salespeople in making follow-up calls, getting appointments, prospecting, or taking routine order calls.

Scripts need not be used verbatim. They can be flexible; some may be little more than an ordered list of the points to be made. Good salespeople often

Although they are viewed negatively by many businesses, telemarketing "boiler rooms" are common. They usually consist of a closely supervised room full of telesellers simultaneously selling products and services with carefully crafted sales messages.

develop their own scripts simply by keeping track of what works and doesn't work for them.

While the process of developing a winning telemarketing strategy might seem to be logical and linear, the process is actually circular. If you are going to measure your results, you should constantly revise and test new strategies, tactics, and phrases. The process is dynamic. Scripts should be continually evaluated and revised, then tested against the previous script to determine which is more effective.

When starting, even in a small-scale telemarketing operation, we recommend the use of an outside professional sales script writer. Even if you don't like the resulting work, it can be tested against your own effort. If you win, you have at least bought assurance that your work has merit.

ETHICAL PROBLEMS

Few areas in marketing are under stronger attack than the teleselling industry. Its defenders are largely those people who find its use profitable. Profits have been its traditional rationale. Why spend money on advertising if more sales can be made for a lower cost by telemarketing?

Lately, a defense of convenience has been put forth to help buttress the arguments. For many people who have little time for shopping, telemarketing can provide a convenient service. Along with catalog operations, mail-order advertising, and direct mail, all of which are forms of direct marketing, teleselling has grown tremendously in recent years. There must be a good reason for this phenomenon from the buyer's viewpoint.

Still, telemarketing raises many ethical problems that require attention:

- The use of automatic dialing machines
- The hours during which calls should be made
- Misrepresentation
- Fraud
- Sale to minors

Dialing Machines

The advent of low-cost automatic dialing machines that can deliver a computer-programmed qualifying message has made possible a rapid low-cost canvassing of all telephones in an exchange. The machine does not know what or who is being called. People with unlisted numbers or those who for some personal reason do not want to be called on the telephone often get testy when they answer the phone only to discover they are talking to a robot. They believe that it is an invasion of their privacy.

Hours

Many people are not home during normal business hours. To contact them, one must call after hours. But how late should calls be made? Many people go to bed early. They are not happy with telesellers who awaken them. Similarly, how early in the morning should you call? Many people sleep late. They resent being awakened.

Misrepresentation[13]

We have previously alluded to the problem of controlling misrepresentations over the telephone. Many of these problems are inadvertent or the result of misunderstandings. However, many other scripts are deliberately misleading. The entire sales pitch may be based on deception. It is a serious problem and one that must be fought by the industry before it is saddled with restrictive legislation.

Fraud

While misrepresentation and fraud are usually included in the same category, we feel that it is important to separate them here for emphasis. Fraud is illegal. It takes many forms. The most blatant type involves making a sale over the telephone or through the mail, taking money or credit card information, and then failing to fulfill the implicit contract. We have stringent laws against such fraud, but catching up with the perpetrators is often difficult.

While it is of little consolation to their victims, sooner or later such frauds are frequently intercepted by the postal inspectors and convicted of criminal offenses.

Age—Young and Old

How old is the buyer? Many old people who have lost some or much of their mental acuity love to buy things through the mail. They love to receive letters. It's Christmas every time the mail is delivered. Unfortunately, much of what they buy is junk which they have no earthly need for. But who is to say what satisfaction they receive from such purchases? Perhaps they have the money to afford such folly. But what if they don't? Now we get into the sticky territory of values and who is there to make such judgments.

·And what of minors who use the mail to buy things of which their parents disapprove? Clearly, we have many ethical problems involving the capacity of the buyers.

Technological Solutions and Problems

Digital telephone switching equipment will soon provide anyone who can afford the service and equipment the ability to know the calling party's phone number. The device can then be programmed to accept or deny phone calls based on a programmable list. Inbound marketers already use these devices where possible to fight fraud. Callers who provided false phone numbers are immediately detected.

Conversely, customers would automatically have the telephone number of sales callers, thus providing customers with some degree of protection.

SUMMARY

Telemarketing is clearly the wave of the future. Electronic advances have made possible a wide range of non-face-to-face selling. Inbound telemarketing makes the seller accessible to the buyer at a moment's notice. All the modern seller has to do is set up the apparatus to receive the orders and execute them.

Outbound selling allows sales calls to be made for a fraction of the cost of sending a sales rep into the field to make a personal call. Costs are at the root of the telemarketing movement.

However, as is true with just about any other tool, telemarketing is misused. For example, it can be a disguise for illegal operations. The victim never sees the culprit. Misrepresentation is facilitated because the sales rep is not facing the buyer. Moreover, the buyer's privacy may be violated if calls are made during inconvenient hours.

DISCUSSION QUESTIONS

1 The telephone has been around for more than 100 years, so what's so new about teleselling?
2 Why is teleselling increasing in use?
3 Why might a firm choose to automatically call all of its customers routinely in some rational predetermined manner?
4 Why are many customers evidently so willing to buy either over the telephone or from television presentations?
5 Why are businesspeople evidently more receptive to telephone selling than are consumers?
6 What is the role of the person who answers the telephone in inbound teleselling?
7 What are the advantages and disadvantages of an 800 number for inbound teleselling programs?
8 How can you develop a good script for an outbound teleselling program?
9. Are "boiler rooms" unethical?
10 Why do many people consider the use of dialing machines unethical?

REFERENCES

1 Bob Stone and John Wyman, *Successful Telemarketing*, National Textbook Company, Lincolnwood, Ill., 1986, p. 5.
2 Ibid., p. 6.
3 William C. Moncrief; Shannon H. Shipp; Charles W. Lamb, Jr.; and David W. Cravens, "Examining the Roles of Telemarketing in Selling Strategy," *Journal of Personal Selling & Sales Management*, Fall 1989, pp. 1–12, discuss the use of telemarketing either as a replacement of or as a support to face-to-face sales.
4 Richard L. Bencin, "When to Use Telemarketing—And When Not To!" *Sales & Marketing Management in Canada (Canada)*, February 1988, pp. 27–29, suggests that telemarketing, along with other direct marketing techniques, can be helpful for the investigation and sale of new products in new markets.
5 Robin Shaw, "Telemarketing and Marketing Management," *Practising Manager (Australia)*, Autumn 1989, pp. 41–45, suggests that when the implications of telemarketing for promotional management and other areas are recognized, a focus on telemarketing in the options-appraisal process of marketing managers is a desirable innovation.
6 Bencin, "Building a Telemarketing Blueprint," *Sales & Marketing Management in Canada (Canada)*, August 1988, pp. 8–9, 38–39, advises that the company have some person who is able to design, implement, monitor, and evaluate a customized program.
7 Leon Kreitzman, "Telemarketing: Numbers Count," *Marketing (UK)*, July 14, 1988, pp. 43–44, discusses how quickly the market is growing and what it is used for; however, the industry still needs to educate marketers and is in the process of investing heavily in computers.
8 Richard N. Cardozo, Shannon H. Shipp, and Kenneth J. Roering, "Implementing New Business-to-Business Selling Methods," *Journal of Personal Selling & Sales Management*, August 1987, pp. 17–26, suggest that companies guide managers to adopt a new selling mix using seven stages: (1) problem formulation, (2) alternative

analysis, (3) customer classification, (4) mix selection, (5) organizational structure changes to match the selling mix, and (7) payoffs.

9 Eugene M. Johnson and William J. Meiners, "Telemarketing: Trends, Issues, and Opportunities," *Journal of Personal Selling & Sales Management*, November 1987, pp. 65–68, advise that telemarketing is considered a part of an organized and managed marketing program and just one of the tools to be used in direct marketing.

10 "Telemarketing: High-Payoff Communications," *Telecommunication Products & Technology*, November 1985, pp. 42–46, describes telemarketing as a system of communication software, hardware, and phone lines that produces lead generation and revenue generation; it includes inbound catalog orders, customer service, and dealer service.

11 William C. Moncrief; Charles W. Lamb, Jr.; and Terry Dielman, "Developing Telemarketing Support Systems," *Journal of Personal Selling & Sales Management*, August 1986, pp. 43–49, advise that the important issues concerning the development of telemarketing support systems are (1) sales force deployment; (2) telemarketing organization structure alternatives; (3) workload definition, measurement, and rewards for telemarketers; (4) motivational techniques for telemarketers and avoidance of ill-feelings between them and field representatives; and (5) enhancement of job satisfaction.

12 Marvin A. Jolson, "Prospecting by Telephone Prenotification: An Application of the Foot-in-the-Door Technique," *Journal of Personal Selling & Sales Management*, August 1986, pp. 39–42, asserts that this technique's success is brought about by generating initial compliance on a sequential series of requests, with each increasing in importance; the final goal is to obtain a major commitment.

13 Emile van Westerhoven, "Telemarketing: Finding the Needle in the Haystack," *European Research (Netherlands)*, May 1987, pp. 72–76, suggests that in telemarketing, the basic goal is to identify individuals and convert them into effective sales. Also important is establishing an active list of names and addresses of persons open to the purchase of a certain product and the direct sales approach.

CASE 19–1: J. J. and the Telephone—A Better Selling System?

J. J. Schmidt loved both gadgets and selling life insurance. Thus it was inevitable that he and telemarketing would become allies in his quest for new and better ways to sell insurance. Not only did J. J. love gadgets but he wanted only the finest. Naturally, he was an eager prospect for the salesperson who represented the finest telephone marketing equipment available. The device would automatically call numbers in sequence to given telephone prefixes, or it would call a preprogrammed list of numbers. It would call during any selected hours of the day, play messages to which people could respond, and then transfer those people who responded favorably to J. J. for a personal telephone interview. Or it would ask the favorable responders to leave their names and numbers on the tape.

The sales rep demonstrated to J. J. all the possible ways to use the new computer sales system. The machine looked and sounded great. However, once J. J. bought the system and had it at home he wondered how he should use it. What hours of the day should he choose? Should he always be there to pick up the phone when someone responded favorably? Should he use the message to screen people before picking up the phone, or should he let them leave their names and numbers on the tape only while he was out selling? Should he hire a person to supervise the operation and answer inquiries while he was in the field? What information should he seek from the respondents before talking with them?

The phone line cost $20 a month. The machine cost little to run. J. J. wondered about the long-term effect of his new sales program. What will people think of it? Was it ethical? Should he care?

1 How would you use this machine?

2 Design a selling system for J. J. around the use of the automatic telephone machine.

CASE 19–2: Barton Enterprises, Inc.—Improving Customer Services

James Barton, chief executive officer of Barton Enterprises of Chicago, was upset. His company manufactured and sold bar dispensing equipment, compressors, refrigerating equipment, and other commercial food service products. It also made and sold a home soft drink dispenser which had created a good deal of grief for all concerned.

Jim had just received a scathing three-page letter from an obviously unhappy customer. Her new dispenser would not work as anticipated. According to her, the instruction manual was obviously written by someone with only a fleeting exposure to the English language and a single digit IQ. The dealer who sold her the unit was no help.

One such letter would not have disturbed Jim much, but this was the last in a long series of complaints not only from consumers but also from Barton's distributors and dealers. When the company had designed the scaled-down unit, it had tried to cut costs, believing that consumers would not be interested in an expensive machine. The firm was wrong. It seemed that, at least for heavy consumers of soft drinks, the unit paid for itself in very little time. The last product manager doubled the price of the unit in an attempt to get rid of the line; sales simply went up. Now the profits from the home dispenser were greater than those from any other product.

Normally, service was up to the dealers and distributors, who were trained to service all of Barton's industrial equipment. Some dealers insisted on doing all their own service—they wanted to keep their accounts strictly to themselves—while smaller dealers might rely on the distributors, who were forbidden to sell to dealers' accounts. Barton's service record for its industrial products was good.

But the home dispenser was a company orphan. The firm and its distributors and dealers were primarily interested in the food service industry, not in home buyers. Dealers were not trained or prepared to handle service for the machine; they had sold too few units to put much time or effort into service. Now they faced a flood of consumer complaints.

Jim immediately called in his product manager, Jill Bell, for a meeting. The meeting was short and anything but sweet. They had to do *something*, and they had to do it quickly. "I don't want to have to answer another letter like this one," Jim told her. Jill was to develop a program to handle customer inquiries about anything—service, deliveries, instructions, credit, whatever—and Jim wanted the program yesterday, not tomorrow. He told her about a seminar he had attended on direct marketing, given by a local university, which dealt with inbound telemarketing, and he suggested that Jill look up the professor who had taught it.

Jill was as anxious as her boss to set up a consumer program. She, too, was disturbed by the number of customer complaints, but she had been led to believe that the company was not much interested in the problem. Barton's policy had seemed to be "Sell it and forget it." Now it seemed that that policy was to change, that service for the soft drink dispenser was to be more in line with the service for the firm's main product lines. She called the professor to arrange a meeting—tomorrow was none too soon as far as she was concerned. She came away from her meeting with a clear understanding of her options and of the homework she needed to do before she could make a recommendation to Mr. Barton.

The professor outlined several telemarketing alternatives. First, Barton's could set up an inbound 800 service number and assign a trained person to handle all calls and answer all questions. Second, the calls could be referred to the appropriate sections of the organization. Third, calls could be forwarded to the sales reps. There were problems with all three options. What would happen if the trained operator couldn't handle a question, or if the system backed up? People hate being put on hold for 20 minutes. If they chose to refer calls within the organization, what happened if the appropriate person was unavailable? Customers don't want to wait to be called back. Moreover, taking a large number of consumer calls could tie up too much of an employee's time. As for the sales reps, most of them disliked calling on consumers, who tended to live in out-of-the-way places and who often didn't know what they wanted when the reps finally managed to reach them. And the reps disliked the soft drink unit too.

Jill was uncertain what her recommendation should be. She liked the idea of directly handling problems in the field with service calls, but she couldn't ignore the costs and problems of such a program—their dealers would have to be trained to handle problems for a unit which they sold infrequently and to an unfamiliar type of customer. She wondered just how effective an inbound telemarketing program would be.

1 Prepare a plan for Jill to submit to Jim Barton.

CHAPTER TWENTY

RETAIL SELLING

No one returns with goodwill to the place which has done him a mischief.

Phaedrus

After studying the material in this chapter you should:

☐ Appreciate that retail selling can be every bit as challenging as industrial selling

☐ Know that the techniques of suggestive selling are particularly important in retail selling

☐ Understand that the technique of substitution is important to master

PROFILE OF A RETAIL

SALESPERSON

R. Mack Davis

Formerly of The Regiment, Ltd. Boulder, Colo.

There are many people who believe that Mack Davis was one of the best retail salespeople ever to slip a sport coat on the back of a customer. After graduating from the University of Oklahoma, Mack spent a few months in West Texas selling Scotch tape for the 3M Company. When a childhood buddy offered him the opportunity to join forces in a traditional menswear store to be called The Regiment, Ltd., Mack agreed. Starting in a small 1,300-foot store near the University of Colorado, Mack was directly responsible for managing sales operations that ultimately grew to 40 salespeople in six stores in the Boulder-Denver region.

Each of the salespeople had been hired while in college and each developed into an outstanding producer because of Mack's abilities in sales training. Mack claims, "It takes about 14 to 18 months to really train someone to become a professional clothing salesperson. After their initial training they can usually write about $150,000 in volume a year, but they will do about $300,000 after they've been in our continual training program for about 18 months."

Mack relied heavily upon peer instruction for training the new recruit. "It didn't do much good for me to stand up in front of a group of salespeople and preach to them on the right and the wrong ways to do something. I let our senior salespeople do a lot of the training of the new recruits. This did several things for us. Not only did the recruits learn selling, but it allowed the senior salespeople to develop their skills, and we could judge their managerial potentials. If someone's not able to train people very well, then it's unlikely they'll have the skills we were looking for to manage new stores."

Since retiring from The Regiment in 1979, Mack has taught salesmanship at the University of Colorado and has conducted numerous seminars in sales and sales management throughout the country.

While most of you have never seen an industrial sales rep in action, you encounter retail salespeople daily. You will be able to draw on your own personal experiences to a great extent to augment the material that follows.

Throughout this book, where a selling principle was applicable to industrial selling and to retail selling, both aspects have been considered. In this chapter, however, attention will be confined to problems encountered in retail selling.

WHAT IS WRONG WITH RETAIL SELLING?[1]

The distinction between retail selling and other types is not always sharp, and a wide area exists where the distinction is almost nonexistent. A lazy industrial sales rep can wait for business to roll in, while an alert retail clerk can go out after business. Sellers of such items as electrical appliances and automobiles usually work part-time on the floor as store clerks and part-time outside as specialty salespeople. There are good and poor salespeople in both groups.

Many articles regularly appear in the trade press deploring the low estate to which retail selling has fallen. This complaint has been tempered somewhat with the realization that the distributive system at the retail level has undergone a fundamental change toward presold merchandising and mass distribution. The basic marketing strategy for a large number of goods is to move them quickly and cheaply through the retail stage, using low-skilled help who are little more than stock clerks, checkers, and wrappers. For many goods, the demand-creation function has shifted from personal selling to advertising.

For the most part, the large retailing organizations have chosen to focus their managerial strategies not on personal selling but on physical assets, financial power, advertising, and operational systems—things they believe they can manage and control. As one retail executive said, "I put money in a good location, I own it. I put money in a merchandising format, I own it. I put money in people and they leave me for a better job. So we don't invest much in people."

But the large organization's weakness is the small merchant's opportunity. Salespeople can be a good investment and developing good ones can be a sound strategy. Much true salesmanship survives in many small specialty shops not participating in the mass distributive system. In fact, it is doubtful whether selling in the good old days was as good as it is pictured in nostalgic memories. What the critics remember was probably not so much good salespeople as hungry ones—people who had to exert themselves because of a scarcity of customers and of other jobs to which they could flee. It was not a time of plenty.

As these words were written, the author and his wife had just returned from a short shopping trip. As had been the case for the past 3 months, we had to stop at two yet unvisited plant nurseries to look for two or three indoor plants that were needed for the living room. Knowing little about such greenery, we were uncertain about what we wanted or what would thrive in the particular location they would occupy. Without exception, in each of the other dozen or so nurseries we had visited the customers were largely left alone to select what they wanted and take it to a checkout stand. In a few stores a clerk would answer a few direct questions, but none would really wait on you. Finally in one establishment, The Plant Room, a young woman waited on us and escorted us around the premises showing us plants that would prosper in our locale. She knew the plants and was pleasant, helpful, and most understanding of what we wanted. She sold four plants with little effort; it was all so natural. And we'll return there the next time we are in the market. Moreover, we'll recommend the place to our friends.

Lazy merchants and salespeople like to use self-service as a cop-out for not helping the customer. True, many people will buy of their own accord, but many others need help.

Destructive criticism is easy to find and easy to offer, but it does not go far toward solving the problem. An effort to discover the reasons for the situation would be more helpful.

Some store managers insist that the public does not want good service—at least, not strongly enough to be willing to pay for it. Customers are now so used to self-service stores with virtually no service from salesclerks that they expect very little from them in any store.

It has also been pointed out that many customers are responsible for the poor treatment they receive. They are unreasonable and rude, thereby arousing resentment and dislike on the part of the sales personnel. "If customers would treat us with some degree of courtesy and consideration, we would try much harder to please them" seems to be the reaction of many salespeople, for which there is some basis.

Another reason often assigned is that stores simply cannot afford to pay their sales personnel enough to attract top-notch people. The managers of the stores study their "cost to sell" figures and see them steadily rising. It costs more to sell a dollar's worth of goods today than it did some years ago. The natural reaction is to cut selling expense wherever possible—and one place is the wages of salespeople.

Our retail executives see the marketing process growing more automatic year by year; machines dispense coffee, cigarettes, gum, cold drinks, entire meals, and scores of other items. Self-service stores are taking over one field after another; department stores have self-service units. Advertising sells the customer in advance. It is only natural that a retail executive, harried by rising costs of operations, should trim expenses by cutting down on sums spent for salespeople.

This means that many young people are hired who do not regard the job as permanent and who are not greatly concerned with trying to advance in it. They therefore put forth a minimum of effort.

Just what would happen if all retail executives decided to raise the pay of

Good training is of proven importance in retail selling. Sales volume rises sharply when salespeople are knowledgeable and able to answer a prospect's questions.

their salespeople and thereby attempt to attract and encourage more efficient personnel is anybody's guess. But a few stores have done precisely this and have discovered that their sales increased and the cost of selling each dollar's worth of goods dropped.[2] These stores are chiefly those selling "shopping lines" and catering to higher-income patrons. If all stores tried to follow their example, there might not be enough good salespeople to go around. So most stores continue to pay a weekly wage appreciably lower than that paid to workers in other areas.

But the problem of poor selling would not be solved by merely offering higher wages to salespeople. Of equal importance is sound training of all sales personnel in the store. Hundreds of stores have found that the volume of sales per salesperson has risen sharply after a program of training has been put into effect. If the salespeople sell more, they should be paid more, and this could often be done without increasing the cost of selling each dollar's worth of goods. It might actually decrease it.

It is clear that management is by no means free from blame in this matter of inefficient retail selling. New clerks are too often allowed to struggle along, picking up what ideas they can from colleagues, and many of these ideas do not improve their techniques. They deserve better treatment.

Finally, few retail salespeople today perceive themselves as career professionals. Too frequently it is just a job to hold "until something better comes along." With little pride in their work, it is small wonder that their skill at it lies uncultivated.

THE APPROACH

Instead of being obliged to search for customers, retail salespeople rely upon advertising, attractive display windows and counters, and numerous services in the store to bring in buyers. For this reason *the retail salesperson is in the position of a host receiving a guest.* It is important for the seller to extend every courtesy and consideration to make the visitor feel welcome and at ease.

Service Approach

"Do you wish to be served?"

"May I wait on you please?" (This last one is used by a large variety chain and is good for that type of store.)

These service approaches are so similar that they may be considered together. They indicate a desire to be of service, if asked in the proper tone of voice and with the proper expression and attitude. They would, however, be manifestly out of place in a small specialty store where the customer could be plainly seen as he entered the store. It would be evident that he had not received attention, and he might resent such an inquiry as pointless and inane. In the large department store it would be more excusable; but even here, where it is possible that the customer has already made a purchase in another department, there is in it a suggestion that could frighten away the "looker," who might otherwise be induced to linger, look, and perhaps buy. However, it is too easy for the customer to reply no to these questions, then move on without becoming interested.

"Something for you?"

"Something special I could show you?"

"Was there something in particular?"

These questions are typical. The consensus seems to be against them. The reason these greetings are not more popular is their weakness. A petulant customer naturally replies (mentally at least), "Of course there's something, or I wouldn't have come in here!" If the customer is not certain just what she does want, such a salutation places her on the defensive and causes her to hurry on to some other part of the store. The inclusion of the word "special" or "particular" is bad, as it implies a lack of willingness to display goods unless the customer is able to state precisely what is wanted.

"What will it be for you?"

"What can I do for you?"

"What did you want?"

"What was it you wanted?

In this group there is an obvious attempt to utilize the principle of the positive suggestion—that the customer wants *something*. Thus these questions are perhaps better than the previous group. This type of salutation is applicable in a store dealing in convenience goods, such as a drugstore. Here it may more safely be assumed that the customer intends to purchase something than in a store handling shopping lines such as millinery or shoes.

These questions are dangerous ones for uninterested clerks, however, as they may so easily be made to sound brusque and abrupt. There is no suggestion of service in any of them except the second, and this has been so frequently inverted to "What can I do you for?" that there is danger in its use.

"Yes, sir," or "Yes, madam."

This greeting is used in some stores as the salesperson steps up to the customer after having been otherwise occupied for a moment. It is best in the type of store where the counter does not separate the salesperson and customer, although it may be used over the counter. Much depends on the manner and tone used by the salesperson, but properly handled, it is good. Obviously, it could not be used on the casual shopper roaming through the aisles of a department store.

"May I serve you?"
"May I assist you?"
"May I be of any service, madam?"
"May I help you?" (Widely used. Best of the four.)

These are typical greetings that stress the idea of service. They are adapted to use in a high-class store. Many salespeople could not utter such a salutation easily and naturally, and to many customers it would sound forced, almost laughable. In smaller communities where acquaintance exists between customer and clerk such a salutation would appear little short of ridiculous.

When addressed to the casual shopper, such a salutation may cause the latter to say, "No, thank you," and move on. Much depends on the way the question is asked.

Salutation Approach

"Good morning, sir," or "Good afternoon, madam."

In case of doubt this greeting is perhaps the safest to use. Almost any clerk can use it without making it sound brusque, as all of have been accustomed from childhood to smile or at least register good humor as we voice such a salutation. It should not be shouted at the customer. On the contrary, many salespeople murmur it almost inaudibly so that it will not appear to call for an answering "Good morning."

When coupled with the customer's name, as "Good afternoon, Mrs. Bennett" or "Good morning, Mr. McIntyre," it is good. In communities where customers are well known to the salespeople and no social chasm lies between them, the salutation may be familiarized by "Hello, Jim!" or "How are you, Bertha?" without giving offense.

When this "Good morning" salutation is used, it is important to give it a *rising* inflection. Used with a falling inflection, it starts the sale off wrong. It does not sound friendly—and the big objective in the approach and salutation is to start the sale in an atmosphere of friendliness. Whether the customer seems friendly or not, the salesperson *must* be. Smile!

And this is important—*speak the first word yourself* and don't wait for the customer to set the tone of the interview. If you offer a greeting that is genuinely friendly, accompanying it with a smile and a meeting of the eyes, the customer will usually take a cue from you.

Merchandise Approach

Many times it is best not to greet the customer with a salutation or a service approach but rather to use a modification of the product approach discussed in Chapter 8, referred to in retail circles as a merchandise approach.

The merchandise approach is used largely with two types of customers. It is the best way to approach rather uninterested "lookers" and also to handle someone who is ardently looking at some goods with obvious interest.

Retail clerks quickly learn to detect the person who is "just looking." To approach these people with "May I serve you?" always prompts the answer, "No, thank you, I am just looking." After this turndown the clerk will find it embarrassing to reapproach the customer if it appears that the "looker" now wants service. It is best not to approach these lookers too quickly or eagerly.

How does one identify lookers? They usually are wandering with an obvious aimlessness. They avoid the eyes of the clerks. They try to keep at some distance from clerks, for they do not want to be waited on.

A clerk should wait until a looker settles down to look at one item before moving in with the merchandise approach. Suppose a looker stops and examines some sport shirts. One of the following merchandise approaches could be used: "What size are you interested in?" "Is there a particular color you have in mind?" "We have some additional stock if you don't find what you like here." "We just received these new Dacron shirts today. We think they are the best buy we have seen for a long time." "These have a more tapered body that gives a better fit for the man who has kept himself trim."

The salesperson walks up and starts talking about the merchandise without asking the customer whether he or she wants to be waited upon. The comment used in the merchandise approach should be the most appropriate to the situation and should give the looker some information that is not apparent to the eye. More will be said about handling lookers in a following section.

In other cases a customer may speed directly for a certain section, obviously bent on buying something. She picks it up and eagerly examines it, when the sales clerk walks up. A merchandise approach is indicated in such an instance also. In fact, some clerks approach with a trial close in such cases.

Some question such as "Which color do you like?" or "What size are you?" may reveal that the person is ready to buy.

A word about asking for the customer's size. The skilled salesperson can judge the prospect's size by observation, thereby demonstrating experience by saying, "The XLs are all on the top shelf" or "The 46-regulars begin here." If the salesperson is in error, no harm is done, as the prospect will quickly provide the correct information. Admittedly there are instances where tact requires that the size of the prospect be minimized and not brought out so overtly that it might embarrass the customer. Obese people may be sensitive about their size and not appreciate the salesperson who makes an issue of it.

The merchandise approach is particularly adapted to the looker, so let's examine it a bit further. For example, to the customer who pauses before some blouses the salesperson might say, "Those are splendid values at $25.98. Notice the doublestitched seams."

The shirt salesperson might easily offer the comment, "Solid colors seem to be going out this season, don't they? Stripes are good now, though." Such a comment would be more likely to induce the customer to linger and look than a query, "May I show you some shirts today?"

This attitude on the part of the retail salesperson is worth cultivating, as it aids him or her to sell many idly curious shoppers who would otherwise pass on without purchasing. A shopper was standing in a bookstore one day looking over a book with the idea of learning if the vocabulary was too difficult for his children to understand, when a clerk bustled up with, "Did you want to buy that book?" The immediate impulse was to deny any such intention, to lay the book down, and leave. The clerk's attitude and words produced an effect similar to that produced upon a loitering vagabond by a blue-coated officer who prods him in the ribs with his club and exhorts him to "move on, you!" In striking contrast was the skill displayed by another salesperson in the same store, who, under identical circumstances, casually strolled near, rearranging books as he came, and finally remarked, "That's a splendid book you have there for children around 10 years of age. Did you happen to hear the talk by Mrs. Whittier, of the Detroit Public Library's juvenile department, before the Parent-Teacher Association last week? She specifically mentioned it as one of the very best books for children of this age because . . ." This salesperson did not frighten the customer away; he sold the book.

This casual attitude, devoid of all signs of *selling*, has a large part in enabling a salesperson to gain the attention and interest of the undecided shopper. One man, who has made a success of a men's department in a large department store, never goes behind the counter but sells "out front," following the method illustrated by the previous examples.

Sometimes the store has advertised a special offering for the day or week. In this case the salesperson may ask a question such as "Have you seen the new line of sport shirts we advertised this morning for $18.95?" The prospect, although he or she may not have any definite intention of buying, usually replies, "No, I haven't,"perhaps adding. "What are they like?" This question, which carries scant suggestion of either buying or selling, is more effective than one which makes the prospect feel that he or she is being importuned to spend money.

Proper Attitude[3]

Salespeople's verbal greetings are important, but not so important as their attitudes. One of the first points in a good approach is promptness. The salesperson must drop a conversation with fellow salespeople, must stop work with the stock—in short, must show instant willingness to wait on the customer. This point appears self-evident, yet there is a peculiar trait in most of us that makes us like to seem busy. It crops up in the purchasing agent who enjoys keeping sales reps waiting while fussing with papers on the desk and the clerk who exhibits the identical characteristic while diligently rearranging stock after the customer has entered. It is partly mental inertia and partly a desire to appear important. Whichever it may be, no customer likes to wait while the salesperson continues doing something which could easily be suspended.

Promptness is essential in approaching a customer, but this should not be interpreted as meaning *haste*. The speed of the salesperson's approach will be governed largely by that of the customer. If the latter is hurrying, the salesperson will exhibit more alacrity in an effort to accommodate the customer's mental state. In an open department it is safe to time the approach so that the

The first and major responsibility of a salesperson is to wait on customers. Customers appreciate promptness and courtesy.

customer will be met about halfway. At a counter the sales clerk must walk toward that part of the counter before which the customer has paused.

The importance of promptness is not fully appreciated by many salespeople. One authority ventures the opinion that the prompt salesperson gains 25 to 50 percent more trade than a slow one who may in other ways be equally efficient. This does not mean that salespeople should engage in a scramble to wait on a customer, but merely that promptness is appreciated by customers.

Some salespeople seem to forget that their main duty is to sell goods. They become so engrossed in other details, such as arranging or dusting stock, that they lose sight of the fundamental fact that they are there to serve the customers. Others are timid about approaching a customer and need to have their courage strengthened. Be alert for the customer's first words, as it places a damper on a sale to ask, "What did you say?" or "I beg your pardon?"

MAKING THE SALE

Those All-Important First Words

Top-notch retail salespeople try to develop short sentences that will open the sale favorably. These selling sentences state or imply a customer benefit or gain from buying the item. They are not mere statements of product facts; they interpret such facts in terms of customer benefits.

A sporting goods salesperson sold skis to a reluctant customer who had entered the store for the sole purpose of buying a parka. He opened his sales presentation on a package deal the store was featuring with the words, "These skis and bindings are for the man who can't afford a broken leg." He had read the prospect correctly.

What Goods to Show First

In an effort to determine the customer's needs, the retail salesperson often wonders what merchandise to show first. If a low price item is shown, the customer may be offended, whereas if an expensive line is shown, it may scare the shopper away.

This last point it not understood by all salespeople, many of whom reason that showing high-grade goods will flatter a customer and induce the purchase of a better grade. Frequently, however, the customer, who cannot afford to pay such a price and is unwilling to admit poverty, decides to play the role which the sales rep has assigned, haughtily looking over the best good in stock but finding nothing suitable.

It may be argued that the customer who does not see the better grade of goods will never buy them, so they should be exhibited. This may be true, but they need not always be shown *first*. The practice in most stores is to lay before the customer a good medium grade, if the person's desire is not evident from his or her appearance or inquiry. From this point it is easy to work up or down the price scale, as the situation demands.

One caution: It is a mistake to show a customer too many items at once; it will only cause confusion. When a customer indicates dissatisfaction with one item, it should not lie around to confuse the issue.

Not Too Many Questions at First

In its place the question is a powerful tool, but it should not be dulled by hard usage. It is easy to overdo questioning in opening a sale. For example, if a man walks in and asks for a shirt, the following dialogue might take place:

"What size, please?"
"Sixteen."
"What length sleeve?"
"Thirty-three."
"Do you have a color in mind?
"Blue."
"Do you have a preference in collars?"
"Nothing too large."

And so it goes, at some length if the salesperson is so inclined. But we hope not. This opening is poor, because too many questions are asked.

First, it conveys an impression of laziness on the part of the clerk. The customer may feel that the salesperson is unwilling to show goods, as if to say, "If you know just what you want, I'll get it for you, but don't expect me to haul out a lot of stuff for you to look over while making up your mind." Many customers expect help in making up their minds on matters of style or design and hence may resent this appearance of reluctance to be of service.

Second, it commits the prospect too definitely. In the foregoing case, after the clerk had asked the questions about the shirt, if a search of the stock revealed none that met the specifications, it would be easy for the prospect to walk out without buying. He had defined the shirt he wished, the store did not have it, so what else was to be done?

Third, if the salesperson produced a $20 shirt of the required size, color, and style, the opportunity is lost to sell a better one. Once a customer commits himself to a price, it is hard indeed to induce him to purchase a better article. He has confessed his poverty; he has "rated" himself and has nothing to lose by sticking to his original decision. Particularly in a period of rising prices it is poor selling to ask just what price the prospect wishes to pay, as the buyer may not have kept pace in his mind with the trend.

Truly expert salespeople need not ask some of these questions about size because they can judge the answers from observation. Moreover, the impact of such expertise upon the prospect helps establish a good relationship between them. People prefer dealing with those professionals who really know their business.

It may be concluded, therefore, that it is usually best not to ask many questions at the opening of a retail sale but rather to rely on showing the goods and discovering from the customer's reaction which ones offer the strongest appeal. In any event the questions should be asked somewhat casually and not too many at a time but, rather, introduced while showing goods. Care must be exercised against appearing to be either unwilling to show goods or too curious about the customer's personal affairs.

Using Questions and Suggestions to Define Customer's Needs

There is a right way and a wrong way to ask questions. For example, a customer enters a store to buy paint for new garage doors. If you bluntly ask, "What are you going to do with it?" the customer may think you impertinent. But if you smilingly remark that you could help choose the right paint better if you knew what sort of job it was for, following up quickly with, "Is it for an inside or outside job?" the customer will see that you are trying to help. Other questions can be used, such as "What kind of surface is it—wood, metal, or plastic?" "In what condition is the surface now—painted or unpainted?" "Do you have in mind a gloss, semi-gloss, or flat finish?" Between questions, you could suggest, "You see there are several ways you can do this job, and I'd like to help you pick the paint that would give you the best results."

PROBLEMS IN RETAIL SELLING

Knowledge of Stock

One of the most common failings of the typical clerk is not being knowledgeable about the goods in stock. One clerk in the dinnerware department of a large department store, when asked for a certain item, said, "We don't carry that line." The customer replied, "But you advertised it." The reply, "Oh! Well, I'll call the buyer and see." The parting words: "Don't bother."

A manager of an auto parts store complained "Every time I go to Denver for buying my sales drop 50 percent. I see why every day. A customer comes in and asks for a widget. The clerk says that we don't have it. I have to butt in and say, 'Yes, we do. Right over here.' The clerk just will not take the trouble to learn the stock. If something is in the backroom or in the warehouse, they will deny its existence to save themselves the trouble of going after it." Good retail salesmanship starts with a knowledge of the stock and product knowledge of the items carried.

More Than One Customer at the Same Time

One of the most difficult situations a retail salesperson must face is serving more than one customer at the same time. This situation arises in several ways.

You may be waiting on one customer when a second enters. Of course, if it is practicable, you should call another salesperson, but if not, you may do one of two things. First, you may continue to serve the first customer, acknowledging, however, the presence of the new arrival by a nod or a low-spoken word of greeting. Care must be exercised to avoid giving the first customer the impression that she or he is in the way. This unfortunate result is sometimes unwittingly accomplished by saying to the second, "Good morning. I'll be with you in just a minute." If the first customer has not decided on a purchase, this may cause him or her to leave without buying. However, if the sale is obviously near completion, such tactics may be proper. Usually, this greeting should be offered somewhat out of the first customer's hearing as the salesperson moves about in search of stock or for other purposes. A better greeting is, "Good morning. Someone will wait on you soon."

Before leaving a customer with prior claim to your attention, you should excuse yourself, making it clear that you expect to return very soon. If it is impossible to complete the sale to the second customer quickly, the sales clerk faces the touchy situation of handling two or more customers at once. This is done in many stores selling shoes or clothing. As one customer examines and deliberates over a pair of shoes or tries on a suit, the sales clerk serves another customer. On a busy day a shoe clerk has been known to keep six customers occupied at once, making more sales than he or she would have made waiting on one at a time.

Often customers can be quickly handled by answering a question or taking their money or directing them to the goods they are interested in.

A deliberate, careful-thinking customer may be served first and left to examine the merchandise, while the salesclerk approaches the other quickly with "I'm sorry to have kept you waiting." He should then try hard to please. If he sees that the first customer has stopped examining the goods and wants him again, he should try to return to her. Perhaps some question to her will reveal where the transaction stands and point the way to the next move. Any way he handles it, he has a problem that challenges his ingenuity and ability to maintain his poise.

The Technique of Substitution

Every salesperson encounters situations that make it necessary to try to sell something other than the article requested. There are two conditions under which substitution may be attempted: (1) where the salesperson *has* in stock the article asked for and can, therefore, meet the demand, and (2) where *it is not* in stock and the seller is, therefore, compelled to substitute in order to make a sale.

Substitution for Items in Stock   *"This is just as good."* The salesperson who uses this weak comment in attempting to substitute, when the article asked for is carried, is inviting defeat. It is a poor expression at best, and meaningless here; for unless the article offered is *better* than the one asked for, the salesclerk is only asking for trouble by confusing the customer.

This problem of judicious substitution is unusually troublesome when customers want something *apparently* unsuited to their needs. It seems evident that they will regret the selection and harbor a distrust of the store in the future as a result of the unfortunate purchase. Under these circumstances it is wise for the salesperson to ascertain, first, just what the customer's *real* needs are, and second, whether or not she will accept suggestions made in her interests.

Determining the customer's needs requires tact. There is danger of giving serious offense by a seeming inquisitiveness. The customer may be buying for someone else, as is frequently the case, and would resent prying questions.

Regarding the second point—the customer's willingness to heed suggestions—one must judge by watching reactions to minor suggestions. If the customer combats your ideas, it is best to avoid an argument and give the customer what was requested.

Substitution for Items Not Carried   When you *cannot* supply the article asked for, you should try to substitute what is carried in stock for the requested item. It can be done. Mack Davis (see the profile at the beginning of this chapter) claims that in his clothing store, The Regiment, he only had trouble substituting for one brand—Levi. So he had to bring in Levis and drop the Lee brand which he preferred.

The first impulse is to say, "I'm sorry we don't have it. Was there something else today?" If you're a bit more adept, you probably say, "No, we don't have it, but we have something just as good." This expression has been so grossly overworked that it is best to avoid it.

Another pitfall to be avoided is, "No, we don't carry that any more. We had so few calls for it that we dropped it." This makes the buyer feel that he has asked for something that is badly out of style or that he has revealed extremely poor taste. He is uncomfortable and in no mood to accept suggestions as to alternatives.

A better way to handle this: A customer may ask, "Have you any silk shoe laces?" (Not in stock.) So the clerk promptly replies, "No, we haven't, but we have these rayon laces which look almost exactly like silk and wear much longer. They are less expensive too. Just feel how soft and silky they are!" As soon as possible the salesperson has handed a pair of these laces to the customer, pointing out the feature he wants the customer to examine.

Some tactless salespeople even deny that there is any such article made as that asked for. "They don't make that size platter," asserted the salesperson to a woman, who retorted, "I had one that size and broke it this morning." Many clerks, ignorant of their line, attempt to conceal their ignorance in this way.

When offering substitutes for goods demanded but not in stock, the salesperson has to act quickly, although the appearance of haste should be avoided. If one is selling a tangible article, it is advisable to place the substitute article in the hands of the prospect at once, thus delaying his departure long enough to make it possible to present a few of its advantages. When the prospect is ready to leave, merely *telling* him about these advantages will avail little in comparison with *showing* them.

Frequently the salesperson need not say that the article is not in stock but may show something very nearly like it in the hope that the prospect will become interested and buy. This may happen if the prospect does not have too definite an idea as to what he or she wants.

In showing a substitute, it is sound psychology to point out first those features in which it *resembles* the article asked for. This makes the transaction in the customer's mind easier than if the substitute were represented as something entirely different. After the points of similarity have been explained, the seller may focus the prospect's attention on certain points of superiority or on exclusive advantages.

Lest the salesperson feel guilty about substituting when a customer requests a specific brand of goods, she or he should be aware that in most instances customers use brand names as symbols to communicate their thoughts about goods to others. Hence the customer who wants to know where the Jell-O is kept, in reality, is asking for the location of the gelatin desserts. Most experienced retail salespeople claim that there are few truly strong brand preferences. Even though the customer requests a specific brand, substitution is usually easy if the right goods are in stock. In instances where substitution is difficult, the smart retailer sees to it that the brand is carried so that no substitution is needed. The critical factor in substituting is the protection of the customer's ego. The seller must be sufficiently adroit to get the goods into the customer's hands without communicating in some manner, "No, you don't want your brand; you want my brand."

Increasing the Sale by Suggestion

Most salespeople have at one time or another had their attention called to the desirability of increasing the size of the purchase through the use of suggestion. Suggestive selling can take three forms:

- Suggesting a larger quantity of the item being purchased
- Suggesting some related or complementary item
- Suggesting some unrelated item

Suggesting a Larger Quantity Selling the customer more than what was asked for is often a real kindness and not merely a selfish effort on the part of the salesperson to increase sales for the day.

The salesperson should try for an associate sale *before* the goods are wrapped and change made, for the customer often does not wish to start an entirely new transaction.

Some ways of suggesting buying more at a time are

- "There's a saving in buying three."
- "Shall I get you the larger one? It's really more economical."

A regular customer of your swimming pool supply store says, "I need some large chlorine tablets. I'm out again. Give me one of those 25-pound pails."

The alert manager asks, "Why don't you buy a 50-pound pail and save some money?"

The customer quickly jumps on that suggestion. "I don't want to lift a 50-pound pail in and out of the truck."

The manager saved the day by saying, "Then I'll sell you two 25-pound pails for the same price. Then you won't run out so often."

"Let's do it!" the customer smiled. And the manager carried the two pails to the truck to boot. That's selling!

Suggesting Related Items When the salesperson has sold a suit, he should make some effort to interest the buyer in ties, handkerchiefs, hose, or whatever. Indeed, this principle has been recognized by most retail merchants in the planning of their stores and the arrangement of the various departments in relation with each other. Thus related items are grouped together to allow them to exercise their silent persuasion on the customer and to facilitate the salesperson's efforts in that direction.

Suggesting Unrelated Items Occasions arise when one can logically suggest some unrelated item. Usually such suggestions focus either upon goods that are on sale or those that for some reason are desirable. If the store has some article on sale for an attractive price, that fact could certainly be mentioned. Or perhaps some new, unusual merchandise has just arrived that is worthy of mention.

Observation may provide a clue to a meaningful suggestion. Many auto accessories, such as tires, windshield wiper blades, and headlights, are sold as a result of a suggestion made by an observant gas station attendant who notes a need. Seasonal events are potent precipitators of suggestion sales. During the week or so prior to Mother's Day the likelihood of success of a suggestion focusing on some appropriate gift item for Mom is great. Perhaps impending bad weather may suggest an item—rainwear, overcoats, snow tires, etc. These ideas appear axiomatic and self-evident. But do salespeople follow this course? They do not.

The Willmark Service reported a test of this point in which 100 women were given a $5 bill and instructed to go to their favorite drugstore and purchase a 49-cent tube of toothpaste, after which they were to spend as much of the remaining $4.51 as the salesperson *suggested*. An overwhelming majority of the women left the stores with the toothpaste and $4.51 in change, emphasizing once more the fact that an untold volume of sales is lost daily by lazy salespeople.

Some excuse themselves by pleading that such tactics would constitute high-pressure selling. The chief distinction between high-pressure selling and proper selling methods is found in the effect on the customer. If the customer will truly benefit from buying, the salesperson is trying to help him much as a dentist may try to help a patient by urging him to have a tooth fixed before it is too late to save it.

We see that most efforts to suggest to customers that they buy more than they had planned to buy fall into one of four classes. Each of these should be mentally checked by the salesperson whenever a sale is made.

1 The purchase of more than one unit. This may effect a saving to the customer or it may be merely a matter of convenience to him to have a spare on hand when badly needed.

2 The purchase of a larger size, which often saves money to the buyer. It also saves time in shopping and makes less likely the embarrassment of running short of the product.

3 The purchase of a tie-in product, already discussed in detail.

4 The purchase of something distinct from the item asked for or bought. This may be a special offering at a special price, or it may be something new, just received.

Adjusting Complaints

Here is a situation calling for real sales expertise! The customer is unhappy, dissatisfied, and perhaps angry. Unless treated properly he or she is apt to be lost as a customer.

Even in stores that have complaint or adjustment departments, the salesperson is apt to be drawn into the affair, as the typical customer heads straight for the salesperson from whom the article was purchased. Even though the fault may lie with the wrapping or delivery or accounting or advertising, the salesperson is appealed to first.

The chief rule to bear in mind is that "a soft answer turneth away wrath." No matter how insulting the irate customer may be, the salesperson must maintain a calm and sympathetic attitude, showing a willingness to see the problem from the customer's viewpoint. From there the selling job starts, but first it is necessary to find out the reason for the patron's dissatisfaction.

A word of warning! When the fault lies with some other department of the store, such as delivery, the salesperson is tempted to join the customer in roundly condemning this department. This temptation should be resisted, as it merely reflects on the store and injures its reputation. Nothing is gained by commenting "We're always having trouble with those delivery truck drivers. They can't seem to get anything straight." And much may be lost. All through the conversation with the complaining customer the salesperson should seek to convey the impression that such incidents are decidedly rare. The idea is to send the customer away pleased and convinced that the store and the salesperson were very nice—so nice that the customer is friendlier than ever.

Many a sale goes sour because the buyer fails to read instructions on the package or tag. He mixes the paint with water instead of paint thinner. She insists on washing a fabric when the tag says "Dry Clean Only." Not the salesperson's fault? But it may have been! He or she should have called attention to these things or at least have stressed the fact that the instructions should be read and followed.

This is particularly true today in all fields selling anything made of fabric. There are so many different fabrics, each with its own washing instructions, that great care must be taken lest the goods be ruined in the first wash.

If the product is mechanical and the customer claims it won't work, it may be necessary to test it right there. If it does work when properly operated, the sale is nicely saved. If it does not work, it should be put in working order or a new machine given the buyer. Whatever is done should be done promptly and not grudgingly.

Sometimes the salesperson can calm an angry customer by the use of a question. The customer shouts the complaint and then yells, "Well, what are you going to do about it?" To which the salesperson may reply smilingly, "What do you feel would be the fair thing for us to do?"

Strictly speaking, *exchanges* are complaints, inasmuch as the customer is not satisfied. Here, too, a similar reselling job must be done.

The handling of a complaint is not something distinct from selling; it is primarily and definitely a selling problem.

This point is illustrated by the following incident. A business executive entered an exclusive men's shop in the financial district of the city. He carried a suit which he complained had not given good service. It had been purchased 2 years previously and looked as if it had seen hard wear. The customer figured that some adjustment should be made. The clerk agreed without argument and suggested that the man pick out another suit in place of the one he had brought in. This sounds incredible and as if the clerk had lost sight of his employer's interests and was intent only upon keeping a customer for himself. But the suit had cost $600, and that customer spent at least $6,000 a year in that store and had never before complained. He probably would be even more loyal after such a generous adjustment. Was this too great a price to pay for his continued patronage and the word-of-mouth advertising he would give the store? The store proprietor took the matter up with the manufacturer and received an adjustment on the grounds that the particular fabric in that suit was inferior. The handling of this complaint was a piece of fine, long-range selling.

Contrast that smooth adjustment with the record of the clod in the following tale. A young couple bought a $2,000 stereo system of advanced design only to discover upon plugging it in that it was seriously defective; the amplifier went up in smoke. They immediately returned to the store with their burned-out unit, only to encounter a strangely indifferent salesperson who said, "Leave it here. We'll call in 3 or 4 weeks when it's done." The shocked couple replied, "Look, we just laid out two grand for a stereo unit and now you tell us to wait 3 weeks. I think $2,000 buys some music now."

The cold reply was, "I'm sorry, that's the best I can do." And the salesperson walked away. The couple immediately called the bank and stopped payment on the check. Now the shoe was on the other foot. The salesperson called the couple upon notification of the bank's rejection of the check and could not understand their attitude; they told him in no uncertain terms that he could forget the whole matter.

From the consumer's viewpoint, one of the advantages of buying on some form of credit is that if the product turns sour, payments can be stopped, which places great pressure upon the seller to make some equitable settlement. From the seller's viewpoint, credit sales place a great burden upon the firm to keep the customer happy.

COMPLETING THE TRANSACTION

The customer has made her decision. "I'll take that and that!" Now get into action! Complete the transaction while gently trying to suggest additional merchandise. Unfortunately, in today's retailing it takes more time to complete the sale than it does to make it. And far more work.

The computer was supposed to free us from such mundane work. Computerized point-of-sale transaction stations were to make the transaction a

Computerized point-of-sale transaction stations such as those used in supermarkets speed up transactions and eliminate errors. Although delays can occur when the system breaks down or when a product code cannot be deciphered by the scanner, the technology is here to stay.

"breeze." So much for theory. Reality is often a different matter. The customer cannot walk up with money and merchandise in hand and have the goods sacked for a quick exit.

Yet the computer is here to stay. Complex transaction systems will be with us from now on. The best that salespeople can do is be sensitive to the strong desire of the customer to move on and not wait for the store to play its computer games. Moreover, the scenario becomes even more serious when customers are waiting in line for access to the system. Often several salespeople may be waiting to use the computer system, which for any one of several reasons is not working as intended. Any efforts to expedite the flow of customers is not only greatly appreciated by them but also increases the selling capacity of the staff.

You can't sell goods while using the computer. So minimize your transaction times. Alert store management so they can try to solve this problem by allowing their good salespeople to stay on the selling floor while cashiers complete the sale. While this does have advantages, it also creates some problems. Some cashiers alienate the customers, who then leave behind the goods they want and walk out of the store.

Moreover, additional suggested sales are missed by such systems. Obviously, there is no one answer to the checkout dilemma. Just be aware of it and do what you can to move the transaction along.

SUMMARY

Retail selling suffers a serious image problem that impairs its efficiency in most stores. Poor attitudes toward the job of retail selling hinder the performance of salespeople.

Since many people visiting a store are just looking, the approach used by the clerk is critical if rejection is to be avoided. Merchandise approaches are to be recommended in many cases. A service approach is good if the customer seems to have something in mind.

Knowledge of the store's stock as well as product knowledge will produce many sales that would otherwise be missed.

Two keys to building a good sale are the techniques of substitution and suggestion. Good retail salespeople are adept at both.

Above all, never forget that retail selling is selling; thus all of its basic principles apply.

DISCUSSION QUESTIONS

1 A woman cannot make up her mind between two dresses she likes. She has been vacillating between them for more than 30 minutes. What are some of the tactics you could use in assisting her?
2 What do you think is the most important facet of retail selling that should be taught to new clerks?

3 Should a clerk ever recommend that a customer go to a competitor's store? If so, under what circumstances?

4 A furniture salesperson is doubtful that her prospects will be able to qualify for credit. She has perceived many danger signals. What course of action should she take?

5 Late Saturday afternoon a couple walks into an appliance store, and after briefly looking at a washing machine, dryer, refrigerator, stove, and color television set, they give the salesperson an order for each of them. They explain that they have just moved to town and have just gotten possession of their new house; they need immediate delivery of the goods. They are buying on installment credit, but the late hour makes it impossible to check with the bank or credit bureau. What should the salesperson do?

6 Should an automobile sales rep accompany the prospects on a test ride, or should they be allowed to take the car alone?

7 A young man walks into your apparel store and asks to see some Speedo swimwear. You do not handle this brand but instead carry a line you believe to be its equal at a more attractive price. What are some of the statements you could make to substitute your brand for his request?

8 It is Christmas time in your women's apparel store; a man in his early twenties enters. When you approach him, he tells you that he is just looking. What are some of the tactics you could use in this situation?

9 Shoplifting has in recent years become a major problem in most retail stores. Many articles have been written about it, and merchants have instituted training programs to enlist the aid of their salespeople in combating shoplifting. What rules should the clerk follow in protecting against theft?

10 Throughout the book, various references have been made to consultative selling. How do some of those principles apply to retail selling?

REFERENCES

1 Lawrence R. Chonko, Marjorei J. Cahallero, and James R. Lumpkin, "Do Retail Salespeople Use Selling Skills?" *Review of Business & Economic Research,* Spring 1990, pp. 36–46, stress the need for more training of retail salespeople.

2 Stephanie Della Cagna, "The Invasion of the Nordies," *New England Business,* January 1990, pp. 24–25, discusses the Nordstrom phenomenon in retailing, namely, a department store marketing strategy based on personal selling.

3 "Handling Customers," *American Salesman,* April 1990, 29–30, reviews the retailing sales process, stressing the need for courtesy and promptness.

CASE 20-1: Brako—Selling a Service

As Jim Lund forcefully applied the brakes in his car in an emergency stop, he noted with some concern that they were rough and not particularly effective. A glance at the 46,000 miles on the odometer confirmed his diagnosis—he needed new brakes. A forthcoming motor trip urged Jim to take immediate action, for he had no desire to nurse a car around the country with inadequate brakes.

Jim first contacted a nearby Eaton's Auto Service Center, with which he had had four satisfactory auto-servicing experiences during the past year. He was well pleased with their service. He discovered that Eaton's had a special price on brake jobs for the week—$80 for a car with front disc brakes and rear drum brakes. While the price seemed fair to Jim, he wanted to check with another firm before buying.

Brako was a small chain of brake and alignment shops in Dallas, Texas, that was promoted heavily on local television. Jim was curious about Brako's operation because not only had he never been in their shops but he had heard nothing about them. He telephoned to get their price and was most politely informed, "We can't give a price over the telephone. We must inspect your brakes to see exactly what needs to be done. Bring your car in and let us look at it." Although irritated with this policy, Jim was still curious, so he drove to their closest outlet.

He was promptly waited upon and escorted to an air-conditioned office. The manager asked Jim to write his name, address, and particulars about his car on an inspection form. Jim asked, "What does the inspection cost?" He was afraid that this might be a flimflam operation in which he was going to get stuck with an inspection fee.

The reply was, "No charge, sir." The manager immediately directed one of his people to drive the car up onto a lift rack, whereupon all four wheels were removed, thus exposing the brake mechanism in rapid order. The man doing the work commented, "I can see that no one has previously looked at these brakes."

"How can you tell?" asked Jim.

"See these little metal rings that I'm taking off around the lug bolts? They hold the brake drum in place while the car is on the production line so the guy working on it doesn't get a broken foot by it dropping off on him. It's the only reason for them."

Once the brakes were exposed, the manager escorted Jim on a wheel-by-wheel inspection, during which the manager explained the exact state of Jim's brakes. In each case the brakes needed replacing; in two instances they had started gouging the brake drum. The two men then adjourned to the office, at which time the manager began punching some numbers into an adding machine. Finally he tore off the tape and approached Jim with it. Now he went down the list, saying, "Now, here's what you need: front wheel disc pads, $39.95; turning the steel discs, $25; realigning the front calipers, $27; hardware for the front wheels, $9.95; reseals, $4.50; rear wheel brake shoes, $24.95; refurbishing the brake cylinders, $12.50; hardware for the back brakes, $6.95; turning the brake drum, $6; total $155.70."

Jim gave a low whistle and said, "Well, let me think about this for a while. I really can't leave the car right now anyway. How long does it take?"

The manager said, "Give us two and a half hours."

Jim said, "Thank you," and returned to his car, which was being returned to its former state by a fast–working repairer. As the car was ready to leave, the repairer checked the brake fluid reservoir and said, "You're low on brake fluid, sir," and filled it free of charge. Jim drove away pleased with everything but the price. He thought he should check with Eaton's to see exactly what they included in their $80 price.

Upon returning to his office, Jim called the service manager at Eaton's and asked him about their brake service. He was assured that they realigned the calipers, turned the brake drums, and did a first-class job for the $80, although they did not go down the list item by item. The next morning Jim left his car at Eaton's.

1 With such a great discrepancy in the price between these outlets, how does a firm like Brako prosper and grow to such size?

2 What principles of personal selling were in evidence at Brako?

CASE 20-2: Mandrin Gems—The Case of the Broken Bishop

Marie noticed an older couple carefully studying something in one of the store's display windows. She had only been working in the store for 2 months. It was a slow Tuesday afternoon. She and the store's assistant manager had the floor responsibility. There were no other customers in the store as the couple finally strolled through the door.

The man asked, "How much is that glass chess set in the window?"

Marie replied, "Isn't that a marvelous set? You know it's one of only twelve sets made by the artist. He has signed them. It's priced at $3,300."

The man conferred with his wife for awhile then asked, "What is your best price for it?"

Marie knew that she could lower the price to $3,000, but she replied, "I'll call the owner and find out." The store's owner had instructed her carefully about using the so-called "higher authority" method for handling price negotiations. "Never let the customer know that you have the power to lower price. If you do, you'll be blamed by the customer for not lowering the price enough."

Six minutes later, Marie returned and said, "The owner said that she could let you have it for $3,000, but that is the lowest she could possibly go."

The couple conferred, and then the man said, "We'll take it. Can I use VISA?"

"Of course."

"We're going to be shopping in the mall for a while. Can we pick it up in an hour or so?"

"Certainly, I'll have it all wrapped for your trip home. I see that you live a good distance away."

The couple returned in 2 hours to pick up their purchase. It was in two packages. The glass board was wrapped separately and put in one sack. The tall glass chessmen were individually wrapped and put into several boxes which were then put into a sack that was a bit too small. One box stuck out of the top. The woman took the board and the man took the sack. On the way out of the store, the box that stuck out of the top of the sack fell out onto the floor.

Quickly, everyone picked up the box and opened it to see what, if anything, had been broken. It could have been disastrous. Fortunately, only one item, a bishop, had been broken.

The clerk said, "We can have the artist fix this quickly. He lives nearby. I'm not sure of the cost, but it won't be much."

1 Evaluate Marie's handling of the price request.
2 Evaluate Marie's handling of the broken bishop.

CHAPTER TWENTY-ONE

BUSINESS-TO-BUSINESS SELLING

CHAPTER TWENTY-ONE

BUSINESS-TO-BUSINESS SELLING

If you want to make big bucks in selling, then go where the big money is.

Anonymous

After studying the material in this chapter you should:

☐ Appreciate that the business-to-business sales representative is often involved in sales worth millions of dollars—the stakes are high

☐ Understand that often a great deal of preapproach work and research is necessary before making a formal presentation to the business-to-business customer

☐ Comprehend that the key to continued success in business-to-business selling depends upon rendering service

PROFILE OF AN INDUSTRIAL

SALES REP

Ron Rope

Co-owner
Rope & Williamson
Denver, Colo.

After five years working for Beech Aircraft in Boulder, Colorado, Ron ventured out to Los Angeles to work in marketing for Rohr Corporation. However, a seed that had been planted in his mind by a marketing professor, who suggested that Ron could best serve himself if he were to abandon his bureaucratic corporate desk and "go out and sell something," took root. He formed Rope & Williamson with an associate to represent small manufacturers of electronic components. Their efforts were highly successful.

So successful, indeed, that they joined some other successful entrepreneurs in forming The Masters Fund, a venture capital group that furnishes seed money for starting high-tech enterprises. Rope & Williamson, in effect, is financing the start-ups of firms they will represent in the marketplace. Thus the technoid who is the brains behind the new venture has its marketing arm in place before beginning operations. Moreover, who better to judge the market for a new concept than a marketing institution selling to that market?

When asked to what he attributed his success, Ron replied, "I know it's a cliché. Everybody says it, but it's true. Hard work and long hours. I don't know what a clock looks like. And persistence must be in there. I won't quit until I get the job done."

The next day he called back and stated, "You know that stuff I gave you yesterday, it's just the usual pap that everybody spouts. I've been thinking about it all night. You know making money is the easiest thing in the world if you have a good plan for doing it and then work the devil out of that plan. Success is a mindset. It's self-inflicted determination. But don't fool yourself with a bad plan. So many people try to force a bad plan to work. The key is in developing a good plan and then sticking to it."

Suppose you go into an automobile dealership to buy a new car. Rather obviously, a salesperson will be involved in the transaction. Not so obviously, an army of salespeople were involved in selling all of the things that went into making that car. Mentally wander through the manufacturing plant and visualize the hundreds of machines used to make the car. Sales representatives were involved in selling those machines. Then picture the hundreds of other sales representatives involved in selling the various subassemblies and component parts, such as spark plugs, tires, batteries, and hundreds of little things. Then there are the sellers of raw materials such as steel, aluminum, and glass. For every dollar spent at the retail level, $3.93 was purchased at the various wholesale and industrial levels.[1] Thus there is an army of unseen salespeople operating behind the scenes.

Business-to-business selling deserves your attention for several reasons. First, the business sales rep typically earns considerably more money than does the seller of consumer goods; thus the rewards of industrial selling deserve your attention. Second, business-to-business selling is particularly attractive to college-trained people. By their very nature most business sales jobs require more education and a higher level of skill than do positions

Business-to-business and industrial sales provides diverse opportunities for college-trained business students—from selling large equipment to major corporations to selling office systems or supplies to professionals such as doctors and dentists.

selling consumer goods. Most college graduates who select sales careers prefer to sell industrial or business goods. Relatively few go into selling directly to consumers. Third, many people find business-to-business selling more rewarding psychologically. The sales are larger and the problems more challenging.

Business-to-business selling encompasses a wide range of activities from selling huge installations or large equipment to major corporations to selling office systems or supplies to doctors and lawyers. It includes all of the people who sell goods and services to distributors, retailers, and professionals.

It's IBM selling computer systems to the government. It's Apple Computer selling PCs to computer stores. It's Eli Lilly selling pharmaceuticals to physicians and pharmacists. It's Procter & Gamble selling its consumer package goods to supermarket chains. It's Weyerhaeuser selling wood products to lumber yards and manufacturers. In short, it is selling things that somehow, in some form, are resold to other people or firms. It is the field that interests many college marketing graduates because the jobs are fascinating and challenging while generally well rewarded.

CHARACTERISTICS OF THE MARKET[1]

Perhaps it will help in understanding the tasks facing the business-to-business sales representative if we examine how the business markets and their buying processes differ from those of consumer buyers and their buying methods. We will examine 14 factors:

Size of market
Buying motives
Buying process
Contractual relationships
Negotiations
Long-term relationships
Length of time
Need for service
Intercompany relationships—reciprocity
Geographic concentration
Available funds
Derived demand
Inelastic demand
Technical assistance

Size of Market

While it is true that some consumer goods sales (such as houses, cars, and appliances) may be as big, if not bigger, than some business sales, such overlaps are exceptions. Usually business transactions are many times larger than the average consumer transaction. Indeed, it is not at all unusual for business sales reps to write orders for hundreds of thousands of dollars, and there are those who count their sales in the millions. The business representative is dealing with large markets. The point is that there is enough money involved that it is worth the representative's time to do the job properly. Neophyte business sales reps have "clutched" because the stakes were so high. A young man was developing a proposal to sell a $10 million shopping center to a potential investor. His commission would have been $300,000. The young man couldn't sleep at night and was paralyzed by his incessant worry over losing that $300,000 commission. He just couldn't play for those stakes and lead a normal life.

In a very real sense you determine the size of the market in which you wish to play. It's much like Las Vegas, in which you can choose to play with $1, $5, $20, $100, or even $1,000 chips. It's your choice. If you don't want to play in the big-money games, stay out of the big-money industries. If you're going to sell oil refineries, you're going to be dealing with huge sums of money. If you are not comfortable doing this, choose a different market.

While the consumer may be preoccupied with image or status or low price, a professional purchasing agent knows better. This is not to intimate that price is not important in business-to-business selling, for in many situations it most certainly is. However, the proper word to use is not "price" but "value." The professional purchasing agent learned long ago that the cheapest item will not be the best value if it fails to hold up in use. The professional buyer knows that the most important thing is to get a product that does the job properly. There is no point in buying something that will not do the job or will not hold up in use. Thus the term "assured quality" looms large in professional purchasing agents' vocabularies. They want assurance that the vendor will deliver the proper quality of goods. Many times, the cheapest manufacturer has poor quality control procedures and uses inferior materials; the product will not give the desired service. If the rep can prove that the product has the value and quality wanted, professional purchasing agents will buy.

"Assured supply" is a term also held in reverence by the industrial buyer. Visualize, for a moment, a manufacturing plant with all sorts of people busy at their machines turning out goods. For this to become real, all sorts of components and raw materials must flow into the plant constantly. One item not being there on time may shut down the whole plant, with financially disastrous results. The goods must be there on time as promised. Professional buyers have little patience with firms unable to deliver on schedule.

In buying equipment, particularly productive equipment, the industrial buyer is overwhelmingly concerned with costs of operation, durability, reliability, and availability of quick repair service. Such items are usually purchased quite rationally. It's only an inconvenience when the Xerox machine

Industrial buyers for manufacturing plants are particularly concerned with timely delivery of raw materials, quality, and durability. Raw materials must flow into plants constantly. Why are these factors so important?

breaks down, but the whole plant may be out of work if a generating plant gives out. Productive equipment is subjected to unbelievably hard use. Thus it must be extraordinarily durable. Examine the situation of a large earth-moving contractor with a multimillion-dollar freeway project. The earth-moving machines (purchased from Caterpillar) are expensive beasts, man-ufactured to be just as rugged as it's possible to make them. But they take such a beating that they still need repair. The earth-moving contractor cannot afford to have one of the monsters idle for long. Taking it into the nearest town with a Caterpillar distributorship could cost too much money and take too much time, and it's physically difficult. No, the servicing has to be done on the job. The Caterpillar distributor must be prepared to render such service. If not, he can rest assured that the contractor will buy future equip-ment from Deere & Co. or one of the other equipment companies. A business buyer with a broken machine is not someone to trifle with. There's only one thing needed, and that's for you to fix the machine—yesterday. Just re-member that the average business buyer you encounter is behind schedule and over budget. The author cannot remember ever having met a businessperson who was ahead of schedule or who was coming in under costs. Perhaps there are some—there *must* be—but if so, they keep it a secret.

Buying Process

Buying processes vary from company to company, depending upon the size of the operation and its managerial inclinations. Usually there are several people involved. Perhaps a requisition starts in the engineering department or in the factory and is forwarded to the purchasing department. Then perhaps some general manager may get into the picture to make the final decision if the purchase is out of the ordinary. Several people may be involved at different stages of the process. For example, in the engineering department alone, perhaps a committee of engineers has been formed to pass judgment on your item.

In small businesses usually the owner or manager—the boss—is the person who makes practically all the buying decisions, although minor routine purchases may be relegated to help. But do not be deluded into believing that the small operator's people are not important in the decision-making process, for they most certainly are. While the boss may make the final decision on buying a new typewriter, the chances are the secretary decided upon which brand to buy and has been the instigator of the purchase. While the boss may have the final approval on the forklift truck purchase, the warehouse manager probably had a great deal to say about it. One of the facts of life in a small company is that the people talk to one another; they all have inputs into any significant purchase.

Consequently, while the seller of consumer goods can usually focus upon one or two people who are involved in the buying process, the business sales rep is faced with a more complex task of sorting out the various people on the scene and determining what roles they play. Many times the business salesperson must see many people and touch many bases in making a sale. Sometimes the process becomes almost farcical as the rep is kicked around from one person to another, each saying another party is the one to see. It can be frustrating trying to find out who has the real authority to buy in some situations.

Contractual Relationships

Many business sales involve establishing contractual relationships which bind the parties to some promises for a length of time. A small publishing company just getting started needed a photocopier. Its vice-president of operations, for various reasons—largely because of the efforts of the IBM sales representative—signed a contract with IBM for their Model 1. The contract binds the publisher to rent the IBM machine for a year. The insertion of a contract into the picture may make things a bit stickier. Inevitably there are some things in the contract to which the buyer may object, thus causing more difficulty in closing the sale.

If the thought of extensive use of contracts in sales bothers you, try to look at it in a different light. Instead of regarding a contract as something bad or binding, look at it as a friend whose job it is to clarify the deal. We know that the spoken word is a poor medium for communication. Many things are said in the course of a sale by which the seller meant one thing but the buyer heard something else. In a large percentage of cases buyers do not clearly understand the proposition—exactly what it is they are buying and what they are promising to do. The written contract tries to clear up those ambiguities, although admittedly many written contracts are difficult to comprehend. Nevertheless, sound business practice dictates putting agreements on paper in order to minimize misunderstanding. Bear in mind that, as a good business representative, you do not want misunderstandings with your customers. No matter how right you may have been in the matter, if the customer feels misled, that account is in jeopardy. Thus written contracts are widely used in business marketing.

Negotiations

While it is true that in selling many standard business products the seller has a fixed price from which it will not deviate, in many other situations the price is negotiable, particularly for large buyers. Large firms have a great deal of power in the market. When they dangle a large order in front of you, the temptation to negotiate price with them is strong. It's not unknown for salespeople working on a commission to give part of their commission to such buyers in order to get the business.

In other instances the buyer may want some modification of the product, and the cost of that work must be negotiated. In selling such things as raw materials, components, subassemblies, and some services, prices are openly negotiated. A small advertising agency sought the account of a national concern that had in the previous year paid its advertising agency $500,000 of commissions on the advertising placed for it. The new agency was able to obtain the account by agreeing to refund $200,000 of those commissions to the advertiser, thus agreeing to do the work for $300,000—a negotiated price.

Indeed, negotiations make life miserable for some business sales representatives. Visualize being trapped between a business buyer offering a large contract if only you will shave your price somewhat and a management that adamantly refuses to do so. It is emotionally trying. (Negotiations are so important that the subject is covered separately in Chapter 12.)

Long-Term Relationships

Someone observed that in business marketing one does not have customers but relationships. That comment reflects one of the key problems encountered by the sales rep who is trying to break into a new account—the prospective customer already has established relationships with some competitor and is happy with them.

On the other side of the coin, once you have established such relationships with your accounts, you have a good measure of protection from competitive intrusions *if* the account is properly serviced.

Length of Time

Some business negotiations span a long period of time, perhaps years. Many times, you cannot walk through the door and immediately obtain a company's business. They have contractual obligations and are not free to buy until the contracts expire. A sales rep for the American Can Company spent 8 years trying to sell his first order of tin cans to a large food processor in eastern Washington. He worked long and hard during those years cultivating that account, but it still took 8 years to pay off.

Need for Service

Previously we emphasized the necessity of good servicing facilities. This is often overlooked by many industrial marketers. An examination of the firms that dominate their industries, such as IBM, Xerox, Caterpillar, and NCR, will disclose that all of them provide excellent repair service. When a computer won't work, it must be fixed now, not a week from now.

Indeed, in many instances your ability to furnish quick repairs may be the main reason the buyer is doing business with you. Few things will kill an industrial relationship quicker than having your equipment fail and having

Firms such as Xerox and IBM put great emphasis on providing prompt and reliable repair services—a factor that figures greatly in their market dominance.

difficulty obtaining the necessary parts or labor for repairing it. Sometimes these matters are so critical that the buyer is willing to maintain an inventory of repair parts on the premises at the buyer's cost to make certain that repairs can be made promptly.

Intercompany Relationships—Reciprocity

"You scratch my back and I'll scratch yours" has long been established in business. It simply makes good sense to buy from the people who buy from you, if it is possible to do so. Suppose you are selling lubricants to oil well drilling contractors. You'll not likely sell much lubricant to a contractor who is working for another company. The contractor working for Texaco feels he or she must buy from Texaco. It's smart business to do so. When the business rep comes up against such reciprocal arrangements, he or she may find it difficult, if not impossible, to do business with that buyer.

Another type of business relationship can be even more frustrating. For many years, all of the tires going on General Motors cars were made by the U.S. Rubber Company. If you were a sales rep for Firestone or Goodyear, you would have been wasting your time calling on General Motors. They were all locked up because of an intercompany relationship (one that has now disappeared because of a U.S. Supreme Court order). The relationship was the result of Du Pont's large share holdings in both General Motors and the U.S. Rubber Company. Very early the Du Pont family recognized General Motors as a good investment, not only in its own right but also as a market for Du Pont products—upholstery materials, paints, and the like. What sane General Motors purchasing agent was going to do business with a competitor of Du Pont when Du Pont owned a significant portion of General Motors? The courts were not of the opinion that General Motors's purchasing agents were feeble-minded, and so they ordered Du Pont to divest itself of the General Motors holdings. You will encounter many other *sub rosa* relationships which will keep you from doing business no matter how good your sales proposal may be. One insurance agent spent 3 years and much money wining and dining a business executive, trying without success to get his insurance business. Finally, the insurance agent learned through a mutual friend that he was not likely to get any insurance business from that company because the president's brother-in-law was the insurance agent handling the account. The business was all locked up. A good preapproach would have saved a lot of time and money. It is important to learn whether the prospect's business *can* be obtained.

Geographic Concentration

Business markets are highly concentrated geographically. Thus most business-to-business reps work in the large industrial cities. If you sell blast furnaces, you work in cities in which there are steel companies. You're not going to sell many blast furnaces in Ames, Iowa. As one man who entered the business of selling steel pipe to the oil industry said, "I never have to leave Houston. There's more business than I can possibly handle right here." In some instances, the market is so concentrated that the rep may only have to cover one building or one company.

Available Funds

Many times a consumer goods salesperson is frustrated because the prospect hasn't sufficient money to buy the goods. Most of the time the business sales rep does not encounter this problem. The company has the money for the things it needs. If it doesn't have the money, it knows where it can get it. If you persuade the management of the Ford Motor Company to buy something, they will have the money for the deal.

In the case of small businesses, this can be different. Some small firms would like to buy from you but are short of funds.

Derived Demand

Always bear in mind that the demand for business goods is totally derived from consumer demand. There is no inherent demand for lathes. The basic demand is for the product the lathe makes. It's derived from the ultimate consumer product. No one would be foolish enough to buy a blast furnace simply to own one. The demand comes from the demand for steel created by all the consumer products made from it. This is not an academic point; its implications are important. If consumer demand for goods declines, business demand is greatly affected. In the early 1990s, car production dropped significantly. The suppliers to the automotive industry suffered. General Motors is not going to buy steel or tires or paint except for the cars it can sell. The demand for capital equipment is even more severely affected, as business executives are reluctant to make investments during adverse times. Business customers buy only when they can turn about and sell goods in one form or another to someone else and make a profit doing so.

Terry Scanlon, who graduated in marketing in 1972, went into the steel pipe business in Houston with great personal success. Selling pipe to the oil industry was most lucrative during the 1970s. Terry has not sold much pipe lately since there is a glut of oil on the market.

Inelastic Demand

One result of the dependence of business demand on consumer sales is that the demand for business products tends to be inelastic in total. Automobile manufacturers can buy only as much steel as they can sell cars. Since their demands in the short run are fixed, they must pay whatever price is being asked for steel at that time. True, in the long run if steel prices are out of line, the firm's engineers will try to design steel out of the car by substituting less costly materials.

Technical Assistance

In many instances your customer will come to you and stay with you because you are in a position to render the technical advice and assistance needed. This is particularly true of concerns that are not primarily manufacturers. A young woman formed a small company to sell a printed plastic disk to the health food industry. She was not a printer and knew nothing of silk screening on plastic. Instead, she sought out a supplier who furnished a total service—art work, silk screening, and everything—a finished product for a firm price. Such customers are ideal in one respect in that they are almost totally dependent upon you, and thus they are not easy prey for competition.

THE PURCHASING AGENT

The key executive in the business-to-business sales representative's life is usually the purchasing agent, for whom most salespeople have few kind words. However, if you are going to be successful in industrial sales, you need to accept some realities about the purchasing agent.[2]

First, purchasing agents are professional buyers who see thousands of salespeople a year and have had every conceivable ploy tried on them. They've heard most stories that you're apt to think of and are not about to be influenced by a free lunch or two martinis. The representative who tries to outwit the purchasing agent is a fool who will not last long in selling.

Second, purchasing agents are employees of the buyers and thus are legally and morally obligated to strive for the best possible deal for their employers. Purchasing agents are looking out for the buyer's interests and will push for as hard a deal as possible. This is to be expected. Their careers depend upon how well they do it. A p.a. who pays too much for purchases will not have the job for long. The p.a. who buys a machine for $1,200 when you are selling the same thing to a competitor for $1,000 will be in trouble if top management ever learns of it.

Third, the p.a. is a busy person and does not want to waste time with pointless banter. If you haven't got some business to talk about, don't be there. The p.a. is not interested in courtesy calls or fishing expeditions.

Fourth, don't try to short-circuit the p.a. by going through someone else. Wise industrial salespeople learn to cultivate their contacts in the purchasing department, even though most of their work is actually done with other people in the organization.

Fifth, don't be afraid of purchasing agents. You must remember that they have their problems, too. It's difficult to find the right items. There are thousands of things to buy, so if you can save them time and effort, they'll appreciate it. If you can help the purchasing agent do a better job, you'll have won a lifelong ally.

One purchasing agent disclosed a common attitude of p.a.s that hinders the efforts of those salespeople representing firms that are not considered dominant in their industry.[3]

> If you are considering a product or service, you are not looking for the best buy. You're looking for the safest buy. You are not going to put your reputation on the line to recommend one product or service against someone else's. Why should you? . . . at some point in the life of every business something goes wrong with the product or service. . . . Somebody somewhere yells, "Why are we doing business with them?" At that point as a buyer, you want to be able to smile and say, "But everybody knows they're the best in the business even if they did make this mistake."

Thus the representative of the untried or marginal firm poses a threat to the purchasing agent's career, a threat that can be avoided if the p.a. deals only with the firms whose reputations can be used to defend buying decisions if something goes wrong later.

THE SPECIFIER

Many business purchases are made according to specifications, and the key to who gets the business is frequently a matter of how those specifications are drawn up. Consequently, one strategy is to identify the specifier and then influence that individual. Frequently the specifiers are in the engineering department, particularly design engineering. A great deal of work is done with those people. If the sales rep can influence the engineer to design the product in such a way that it incorporates a particular product, and *only* that product, the seller has a lock on that business. An electronics manufacturer was trying to sell the prime contractor for a missile system one of the countermeasures components incorporated in the "bird." Three salient factors emerged. First, the amount of electrical power available inside the "bird" was severely limited because the fuel cells had a small output and there were many devices aboard, all demanding some juice. There was not much power on which to operate the countermeasure device. Moreover, space was at a premium. There was not much room aboard for all the necessary gear. And finally, weight was a critical factor; each additional gram required more fuel. In working with the missile's designers, the electronics company's rep was able to use these three factors to sell his wares; his particular product was the smallest, lightest one on the market and required fewer microwatts of power than the others. The engineer designed the missile in such a way that the seller's device was the only product that would do the job. Once the design was accepted, the order was automatic. Industrial sellers love to be sole sources of an item; p.a.s hate it.

THE DECISION MAKER

Many times the decision maker is a person other than the specifier. In most instances decision making is done at high levels for any significant purchase. Do not be deluded by everything you read about decentralization of authority and delegation of power. When it comes to spending the company's money, such decisions go right to the top. Frequently, it is the president who is the decision maker. Many times it is the board of directors. Many large concerns place an absolute dollar limit on the amount of money that can be spent by an operating executive, and the limit can be surprisingly low, sometimes only $500 or $1,000. Companies just don't like to give middle management much power to spend money. Upper management typically keeps things under tight control.

Many times when middle management executives seem reluctant to go ahead with an approval on a project, what they may fail to disclose is that they do not have the power to give an approval. You've been talking to the wrong person.

In many organizations, decisions about significant purchases are made at the highest levels—the board of directors or the company president—not at the middle management level. If you are selling industrial equipment, be certain you are talking to the right person.

Government Buying

At no time are salespeople faced with such a complex buying structure as when they are selling to the government. Who has the power to buy? Who do you see? How does it work? How do we get paid?

The sheer size of the potential sales volume awaiting the adept sales rep who can penetrate government buying offices makes the task of selling to them well worthwhile in most cases.[4]

THE BUSINESS-TO-BUSINESS SELLING PROCESS

While most of what has been previously written applies directly to business selling, some unique aspects of industrial buying need amplification. We will deal only with these and not try to review material already covered elsewhere.

Business Prospecting

As a general rule, business prospecting is relatively easy compared to the problems facing the sellers of many consumer wares.[5] If you sell earthmoving equipment, your prospects are earth movers, who are easily located in any one of several directories. If you sell a compound for cleaning out oil wells, your prospects are oil well operators. If you sell corrugated boxes, just about every manufacturer is a prospect. Sit on the docks of a trucking company and study the boxes being shipped out to learn their origins—you will discover local prospects.

One reason business prospecting is relatively easy is that many times the prospects will seek you. They have a problem and go to some directory for a lead as to who might solve their problem. The Yellow Pages are widely used for this type of situation. If someone suddenly needs a cylinder of oxygen, looking in the Yellow Pages under "Oxygen" is the logical thing to do. Thus the business marketer is usually wise to be well represented in the Yellow Pages. Many times, sales result directly from the telephone call. Remember, business buyers can be busy people; they do not want to spend a lot of time looking for needed items, particularly for relatively minor items.

But let us not mislead you; there are situations requiring sophisticated prospecting systems. Suppose you are a management consultant. How would you locate firms needing your talents? To provide a contrast, let's examine the prospecting systems used by two different consultants. The first consultant developed a philosophy that management changes trigger a demand for consulting work; when a new president or new hierarchy assumes control of a company, the new people would likely want a study made of the situation to use as a basis or justification for making whatever changes they may want to make. This consultant relied mainly upon newspapers and trade journals for leads to corporate changes in power.

The second consultant had a different strategy. He had learned early in his career that the obvious customer for consulting—the firm in financial trouble—was *not* a good prospect. The problem was that they usually did not have the money to pay for the service. Moreover, he had discovered that it was not good policy to associate with losing situations, because many of these concerns were headed for bankruptcy and there was nothing any consultant could do about it. Instead, this consultant had discovered that highly successful, growing concerns would hire him to study special problems that they were encountering. Sometimes they felt that they did not have the staff to tackle the problem or that it was beyond them technically. These people had the money to afford the help, and their rapid growth had created the need.

There are several sources of information for business prospecting, among them directories, advertising, trade shows, and the SIC system.

Directories Just about every business has a directory of some sort. Usually trade associations compile directories of their members. Some private concerns furnish excellent information on prospects; Fairchild Publications annually publishes an excellent directory with the names of the buyers for each department store in the nation. Anyone selling to department stores would find this publication most helpful. Not only do most directories furnish names and addresses, but often they include much preapproach information on the firms and their officers.

We have already mentioned the biggest directory of all—the Yellow Pages—and we urge you to undertake an experiment. Sit down with the Los Angeles or New York or Chicago Yellow Pages and go through them page by page. You will learn about types of business you had no idea existed.

Advertising One school of thought maintains that it is a waste of money for the business rep to make cold calls. Instead it is suggested that it is much easier, and cheaper, to let advertising bring in qualified leads and then have the salespeople call upon those responding prospects. The advertising has located the prospect and paved the way for the salesperson.[6] By all means the sales manager should master the material in Chapter 6 on lead-generation systems. It is the way to generate qualified leads to excellent business sales prospects. Let the prospects identify themselves.

Trade Shows Business marketing relies heavily upon the trade show as a major promotional tool because shows can be so effective and inexpensive. Because of their interest in the goods shown, good prospects will aggressively seek out those suppliers selling what they need. An able business sales rep can pinpoint and qualify numerous excellent prospects at a good trade show if the firm has provided an effective exhibit. The major problem facing representatives working at trade shows is separating the live prospects from the idle lookers. It is too easy to get tied up with someone who is not a prospect and never will be one and miss talking with a good prospect. The business rep working a trade show must develop a series of questions that quickly screen out nonprospects. "When will you be replacing your present equipment?" "Would you like us to study your situation?" Such questions usually ferret out the real prospects.

SIC System   The *Standard Industrial Classification* (SIC) system has been established by the federal government to classify our economy into industry groupings.[7] The SIC system places each business organization into a broad industrial grouping and then subdivides each major group into subgroups. Let us examine the division of one broad industry group—the chemical process industry—to gain a clearer picture of the system. The first digit of the four-digit SIC number for most of the chemical process industry is 2 (see Figure 21-1). Note all the different industries that are included as chemical

FIGURE 21-1   Standard Industrial Classification System.

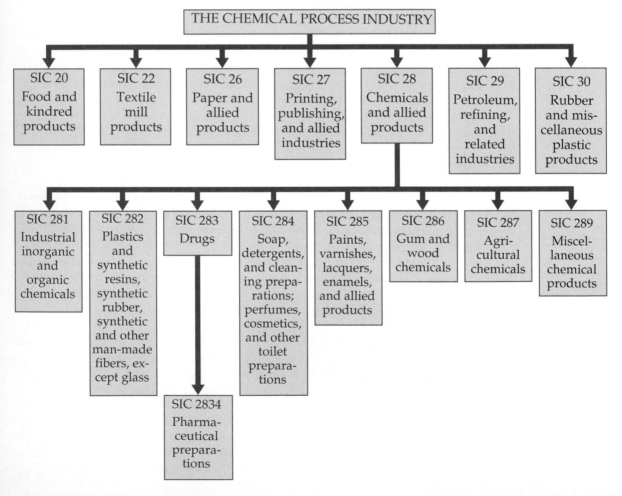

processors—food, textiles, paper, printing, chemicals, oil, and rubber. Each of those subgroups is assigned a two-digit number; for example, the chemicals and allied products organizations' SIC numbers begin with 28. Within that "28" group, a number of subgroups are identified as shown, each having an SIC number beginning with three numbers, for example, 283. Finally, firms making pharmaceutical preparations have been assigned the four-digit number 2834.

These SIC numbers are fully described in the *Standard Industrial Classification Manual* by the Department of Commerce. Each firm is classified by the principal products in which it deals, thereby posing a problem: What about firms making a number of different products? Answer: The industrial sales rep must realize that SIC numbers will not provide a clue to every maker of some goods but only to those firms whose principal product falls within that classification.

Once you have identified the SIC numbers of good customers, you can refer to a Department of Commerce publication entitled *County Business Patterns*, which lists by county every business firm in the United States by its SIC number. It provides facts on each reporting firm: payroll and employment, value added by manufacture, new plant expenditures, and value of shipments.

Not only can you determine how many firms in each county within your territory are prospects for goods but you also can learn a great deal about the size of their operations.

The Preapproach

Business sales representatives will typically do a more thorough preapproach than will the seller of most consumer goods. First, the stakes are higher. Since much more money is involved in the transaction, it makes it more worthwhile to prepare properly for the presentation. If you have a sale that can mean several thousands of dollars in commissions, you will be motivated to do your homework with care. Second, there are many more factors to be learned about an industrial situation than is the case in most consumer sales. The business sales representative wants to learn as much as possible about the problem to be solved, what the company is doing about it, from whom they have been buying, how much they have been buying, when the account will be open, who will be the critical people involved in the transaction, and other similar information needed to make an intelligent presentation. Third, it's usually easier to do a good preapproach on a business firm than on a consumer. Many times the business prospect fully cooperates by furnishing the information needed. After all, it is to the buyer's benefit to have as good a job as possible done in developing a proposal. You are trying to make them more money. It is not uncommon to have help from a sponsor inside the organization who wants to buy from your company but hasn't the power to do so without approval. The sponsor must work through you to get your product or service and therefore will provide you with excellent preapproach information.

The Written Proposal

Often, the situation requires a written proposal. Such a proposal usually contains the following elements:

    I An analysis of the problem and its dimensions as perceived by the seller
    II How the seller proposes to solve the problem
    III Specifications of equipment proposed
    IV Cost-benefit analysis
    V Financial aspects
    VI Timetable
    VII Contract

The development of such proposals can absorb much of the sales rep's time. Certainly a thoroughly professional proposal is a key element in the success of such reps.

The Approach

Usually the approach will be focused around the problems the rep hopes to solve. The approach tells the buyer what the salesperson intends to do for the company.

Admittedly, there are times when showmanship will pay off, particularly if the buyer is a marketing type who appreciates promotional flair. A business sales rep who was finding it difficult to get to the right person in a large corporation rented a large billboard located on the route from the buyer's office to his home. On it was the message, "Mr. Jones, if you had seen me a month ago, when I first called, your company would have already saved $25,000. Are we going to let another $25,000 go down the drain this month? Call me at . . ." It got results. Of course, agents using such techniques must be able to deliver what they promise.

The Presentation

Chapters 9 and 10 discussed the presentation, and we need not repeat that material here. However, business presentations pose a special problem in believability.

As we have mentioned, if prospects don't believe what you say, there is little likelihood that they will be persuaded to buy. You must at every opportunity work to create and build the impression that you are telling the truth.

The Problem The major problem you face in getting the prospect to believe you has three parts. First, the prospect has been lied to previously by a long line of sales reps, to the point of becoming exceedingly wary of anything anyone says. This is an unfortunate occupational hazard. One enterprising sales rep recognized this situation in answering a purchasing agent who said, "Look, you, I have dozens of reps through here a day, and most of them are lying about something or other. Now, why should I believe what you say?"

Although inwardly shaken by this attack, the sales rep had sufficient composure to reply, "Unfortunately, I know what you say is true. It is simply a cross that I have to bear. The burden is on me to prove to you that what I tell you is so. In the meantime I'll simply have to work that much harder. All I ask is a chance to prove that you can rely on me." What's the purchasing agent to say in response to that?

Second, there is a natural skepticism among buyers, as there should be, about what is claimed for a product. After all, a seller is going to put the firm's best foot forward while trying to hide its deficiencies. It's not realistic to expect a sales rep to tell everything that's wrong with a proposition, although one imaginative rep did. He would begin by saying, "Let me first tell you what is wrong with my equipment, then I'll show you why it shouldn't matter to you."

Third, there is a natural reluctance to make a buying decision. By not believing what the sales rep says, a decision can be avoided. In essence, buyers choose not to believe. It's easier that way.[8]

THE REAL BASIS FOR BELIEVABILITY— TRUTHFULNESS AND FAIR DEALING WITH THE PROSPECT OVER THE LONG HAUL

Credibility Tactics

Believability was previously discussed in Chapter 9. That material is relevant to the problems of the business-to-business sales rep, but let us review it here and apply it specifically to business selling.

Business sales presentations are built around an extensive use of facts, case histories, demonstrations, and trial uses. The last technique should be stressed, for there are few things more potent in selling than to let the prospective customer use the product. The manufacturer of a new type of underground oil well pump that could do the job more cheaply and out of sight (unlike the big grasshopperlike oil pumps seen in the oil fields) was finding it difficult to get it accepted. The inertia blocking the adoption of any radically new industrial product is usually difficult to overcome. People just don't change their ways easily—and for good reason. They've seen all sorts of new products come along with great promises which failed to deliver. Thus they are leery of the claims made for innovations. The sales technique which the inventor finally had to adopt was to install the product free of charge in an oil well and let the company discover its advantages through use. The only problem with this technique was that it was time-consuming and costly. He had a big investment in the trial units and it would take several months before the evidence was in to make a sale. The strategy slowed down the diffusion of the unit into the field.

Even so, many business buyers are reluctant to allow even a trial, for they are afraid of harming their production process in some manner if the new product fails to work as promised. It's not always easy to get a trial placement.

A substitute for a trial use is to install one unit somewhere and then bring the buyer to see that unit's performance. Potential customers will travel great distances to see a new product if the potential savings are sufficient. Bear in mind that at times there are millions of dollars in potential profits to be made if the product turns out to be everything that is being claimed for it. So take your business prospect to see the product in use and to talk to the people using it.

The sales library in each Xerox sales office has a large number of loose-leaf binders which contain case histories of applications of the firm's machines. A Xerox sales rep planning to call upon a university librarian could go to the archives to locate a case history of a Xerox machine being used in the library at the University of Colorado. After studying that particular application the rep could show it to the prospective buyer.

All of this is not to deny that there are many emotional appeals used in business selling. Never think that noneconomic factors do not play an important role in business buying. Many times the only reason a company is doing business with a certain vendor is that the buyer is an old friend of the seller and intends to do business with an old friend come what may, facts notwithstanding. Personal friendships are important. In industries in which all sellers are selling essentially the same product for the same price, much business is done on the basis of friendship.

Objections

We have already delved deeply into the matter of objections. Only three other types of objections need to be mentioned here: budgetary restraints, fear of organizational disruption, and career threats.[9]

Budget   Inevitably in business selling one comes face to face with that economic reality, the budget. Almost all organizations operate on a budget. At the beginning of each fiscal period funds are allocated for operations, new equipment purchases, and the like. If funds for your product are in the budget, all is well; if they are not, you have a problem. The buyer has to appeal to higher authorities to obtain budgetary approval, which may be difficult to do. If you are selling something whose cost easily falls within the budget, and the prospect has not spent the money, there is no financial problem with the purchase. The money's there, so it is a matter of persuading the buyer to spend it.

This last factor can actually be used to the rep's advantage late in the budgetary period. Most executives try to obtain more funds than they need to perform their tasks. It is a comfortable administrative feeling. Thus there is a distinct tendency to overbudget. At the end of the fiscal period there are apt to be uncommitted funds left which will usually revert to the general fund if not spent. Moreover, the administrator is fearful that if all of this year's budget is not spent, next year's budget will be reduced commensurately. Thus the bureaucratic mind is strongly motivated to spend all of the money in the budget. If you are an industrial sales rep who happens on the scene at the end of a budgetary period in which the buyer has money left, you will likely find it easy to sell almost anything you have that makes sense.

Even in the exceedingly tight budgetary system of the California State Universities, one department head had to spend the department's modest equipment budget by late April. A 3M sales rep called and found it easy to sell a small grading machine. The department did not really need it, but the money was there, and if not spent, it would be lost.

One office supplies rep obtained a large order for an assortment of supplies at the end of the year with the appeal, "Why not load up on all of your supplies for next year now while you have the money? You don't know what they're going to do to your budget next year. Since prices will be going up, you'll save money to boot." That appeal did the job.

Fear of Upsetting Operational Routine   The workings of a large organization are somewhat like a watch. All the cogs work together and must accommodate each other. Wise executives know that changes in the organization's routine can be upsetting. Shorthand stenographers became upset with the intrusion of the dictating machine, for it seemingly stripped them of some of their status. Even though your product may be clearly superior to the system being used in the company, do not be surprised at the reluctance of the executive to switch to your way of doing things. The executive is sure of what the organization now has but fearful that somehow your new system will disrupt operations.

A new executive coming into an organization that is having trouble may not be particularly loyal to old systems and may want to install new systems or equipment. The alert industrial rep should be on the lookout for such situations.

Career Threats   Business buyers implicitly consider how each purchase may affect their careers with their companies. Should some purchase prove to be unwise, their careers might be jeopardized. If you represent an old reliable company with proven products and a well-established track record you have a great advantage over a sales rep for a new concern whose claims have yet to be proven. The new firm is a threat to the business buyer's career. Why should that individual take such a risk? It is the task of the business sales rep to overcome such threats and replace them with rewards.

The Close

There are no particularly unusual aspects about the business close. Typically, the standard assumptive close works well and is quite natural. A word needs to be said, however, about using the standing-room-only close because in business situations it is frequently appropriate. There can be substantial delays in deliveries. The sooner an order is placed, the sooner it will arrive. Frequently operations will be jeopardized in some way if prompt delivery cannot be made. A standing-room-only close is effective if deliveries are important or if goods may become scarce.

The Follow-Up

It is in business selling that the follow-up achieves its greatest importance. Getting the order only begins the sale. It is what happens afterward that determines the sales rep's success. Is the delivery made on time? Are people properly instructed in the product's use? Is satisfaction delivered? The business sales rep has to master all of the follow-up, particularly for large accounts, for the advantages are far too important to lose.

SUMMARY

Business selling represents a fascinating opportunity for the individual who seeks opportunities and challenges that can lead to lucrative careers.

For the most part, the business-to-business sales representative's position is strong; the rep is there to solve some problem, make the customer more profits, or show how something can be done better or more easily. While price is important in many instances, such factors as service, durability, performance, and operating costs are usually the deciding forces in most significant transactions.

While it may take time initially to gain an industrial account, once relationships have been established they can continue for years if excellent service is rendered.

DISCUSSION QUESTIONS

1 Why is a technical background needed for selling many goods?
2 Contrast the difficulties encountered by the representatives who call upon small- to medium-size concerns with the problems met by those who focus their efforts on large enterprises.

3 Why are purchasing agents so intent on *assured quality* and *assured supply?*

4 Under what circumstances is brand image important to the purchasing agent?

5 What is meant by a purchasing agent who talks about making a "safe buy"?

6 Why has the existing vendor an advantage over a new firm?

7 Why is the industrial buying process so complicated?

8 Why does management place so much pressure upon the purchasing department to buy more cheaply?

9 How should the sales rep go about cultivating the favor of a purchasing agent?

10 Why does top management keep so much power over expenditures?

11 Why are trade shows such a popular promotional tool?

REFERENCES

1 Clifton J. Reichard, "Industrial Selling: Beyond Price and Persistence," *Harvard Business Review*, March/April 1985, pp. 127–133, provides an excellent insight into a sales program.

2 Paul R. Bergaust, "Buying Is Selling," *American Salesman*, March 1988, pp. 24–27, advises that by focusing on both selling and buying, sales staffs can use their time and resources in a more productive way and judge their effectiveness.

3 Donald L. Pagels, "Are You Seeing More Salesmen and Enjoying It Less?" *Administrative Management*, April 1973, p. 84.

4 David E. Gumpert and Jeffry A. Timmons, "Penetrating the Government Procurement Maze," *Harvard Business*, May/June 1982, pp. 14–20.

5 Robert E. Hite and Joseph A. Bellizzi, "Differences in the Importance of Selling Techniques between Consumer and Industrial Salespeople," *Journal of Personal Selling*, November 1985, pp. 19–30.

6 Robert W. Bly, "Public Relations as a Direct Response Tool," *Direct Marketing*, August 1987, pp. 110–111, describes public relations as one of the most cost-effective lead-generation tools available to business-to-business marketers and advises using press releases and writing and publishing articles in trade press journals. Jill Okun, "Lead Generation Media Usage in Business-to-Business," *Direct Marketing*, October 1987, pp. 142–146, discusses following up on leads produced by direct marketing media; she says that industrial products and equipment marketers generally mail out information first and follow it with a phone call. Karen Blue, "Closing the Loop: Hewlett-Packard's New Lead Management System," *Business Marketing*, October 1987, pp. 74–78, discusses establishing a Customer Information Center with three objectives: (1) to acquire timely, qualified sales leads; (2) to integrate and improve the productivity of all national direct-marketing activities; and (3) to automate a feedback and promotion evaluation process. Richard F. Reagan, Jr., "Industrial Prospecting: Sales Lead Generation, Qualification & Evaluation," *Agency Sales Magazine*, December 1986, pp. 25–28, points out that industrial prospecting is a means of sales lead generation whereby original equipment manufacturers can use the media establishment to attain publicity for new products, services, or general announcements. Kevin Brown, "Direct Marketing: Mail, Phone Sell Business-to-Business," *Advertising Age*, May 18, 1987, pp. S1–S4, asserts that most business-to-business marketers rely heavily on direct marketing, such as direct mail, telemarketing, and direct selling through print advertisements, to help generate leads and build sales.

7 "Data Supplement: U.S. Totals for 4-Digit SIC Industries," *Sales & Marketing Management*, June 1990, pp. 136–148, describes a statistical overview of the nation's economic output, showing establishment, employment, and shipment or receipt totals for more than 700 individual industries.

8 Roderick Wilkinson, "The Business World Is a 'You' World," *American Salesman*, September 1990, pp. 16–20, discusses the rules for getting along well with other people and gaining their respect, including telling the truth, speaking with understanding and compassion, keeping quiet when there is nothing to say, trying to understand the other person's point of view, and empathizing.

9 Christopher J. Chlon, "Tips to Reduce Rejections in Selling," *American Salesman*, September 1989, pp. 23–25, advises a salesperson to learn as much as possible about a purchasing agent's company and have a fundamental knowledge of the customer's product; make an appointment, calling ahead to confirm the appointment; and have a professional approach.

CASE 21-1: The Southwest Paper Company— Targeting Key Accounts

Ken Griffey, sales manager for the Southwest Paper Company, had just come from an unpleasant meeting with his boss, Mr. Davis. The subject had been the company's inability to meet sales forecasts for the previous 2 years. Mr. Davis was most emphatic and stated that unless Ken developed a viable sales plan to obtain a larger market share for the company, a new sales manager would soon have the opportunity to do so.

The Southwest Paper Company, located in Houston, was a paper wholesaler selling a wide line of products to just about every conceivable type of business. While it carried a full line of chipboard and paper boxes, it did not carry any corrugated boxes because management felt that the corrugated box industry was a separate industry in which it could not compete. The large corrugated box users bought directly from manufacturers and not from wholesalers.

The firm's sales reps (six men and two women) were assigned to designated geographic areas in the Houston trade area and were responsible for selling to all concerns in their territories. While none of the salespeople had achieved their sales quota for the past 2 years, they all sold sufficient volume to earn enough to live on from their commissions, which were fairly standard for the industry. As a general principle, wholesale paper sales reps are not among the better-paid people in the sales world—the average Southwest Paper sales rep earned $19,241 in 1980. In addition, the company paid each rep an expense allowance of $400 a month to cover all field selling expenses.

That night Ken pondered his fate and tried to figure out what he should do about it. He recalled a study a group of college students from a local university had done for him as one of their class projects for a course in sales management. The nub of their recommendations was that the firm's sales force was spending too much time with small accounts, submitting too many small orders, and selling items that were easy to sell. The company was missing out on large orders from key accounts. Not one single fast food chain in the area purchased its paper products from the company. Not one large retailer purchased from Southwest. Ken remembered confronting the sales force with the results of the study. Their response was that they felt they could sell more goods by taking several small orders than by fighting for one big one. Moreover, a few of the sales reps declared that the big accounts were all sewed up by competitors. They thought it was a waste of time to try to crack the big accounts. Besides, they said, "When you do, you have to give away your profit to buy their business." The sales force had continued to concentrate on small accounts, particularly small retail stores that were owner-managed.

While Ken had been inclined to go along with the sales force at the time, now he *had* to do something about the firm's inability to meet its sales goals. And it seemed clear that the firm would have to either expand its sales to larger accounts or find new areas in which to do business. Perhaps it could expand its geographic coverage of Texas or take on new lines of goods, such as corrugated boxes.

The next day Ken lunched with a friend who was the sales manager for an industrial supply wholesaler. Ken talked about his problem and mentioned that he was thinking of expanding the company's geographic coverage. The friend stared at him for a few seconds, then said, "You're not going to like what I am going to say, but you asked for it. You're crazy. You aren't doing a good job here, so you think you can do a job out in the boondocks and do it better. You go to your boss with that plan and you'll be in the breadline by nightfall. That sales force of yours sold you a load of garbage. They just don't know how to sell large accounts and are grasping at every old cliché to justify their ineptitude. You need to give them some training on selling to larger concerns and then force them to do it. If they don't learn, fire them and find others who know how it is done."

Ken's friend was right: Ken did not like what he was told. The rest of the lunch was a little strained. Nevertheless, the impact of the advice was not lost. Ken kept wondering how he could attack the big account problem. Should he train his present sales force to do it, or should he hire some specialists to do nothing but sell to large accounts?

1 What would you recommend Ken do?

2 If he chooses to train his people to sell to large accounts, how should he go about doing it?

3 If he decides to hire large-account specialists, how should he do it? Where will he get them, how will he pay them, how will he handle the objections of the present sales force to intrusions into their territories?

CASE 21–2: Mark Bryan—Selling a Promotional Format

To say that things had not been going well for Mark Bryan would be an understatement. While he was blessed with an ample supply of promises, he was dreadfully short of signed purchase orders. He had none for the 1987 season.

His small, inexpensive, one-station ear radio had been test-marketed in the 1986 baseball season as a joint promotion of WGN, the Chicago Cubs, and the Burger King restaurants in the Chicago trading area. Burger King bought the radios for $1.29 and sold them for $1.99 with a strong advertising program. The radios were tuned to WGN, which broadcast the Cubs baseball games each day. The promotion was well received and most successful. People liked it.

As of February 1987, Mark had no firm orders for the forthcoming season. Even the Chicago market had not yet signed to repeat. WGN and the Cubs supported the program, but Burger King management was in transition. The company had recently replaced its top management, and the new executives were not keen to repeat something from the old management's program. ''We want our own programs, not hand-me-downs from the previous management.''

Bryan had several excellent prospects who all loved the promotion, but for one reason or another had not issued a purchase order. Pepsico was interested in it on a world basis. Several baseball cities were also prime prospects. The other fast food franchises were not responsive to Bryan's overtures.

The firms all had ample money in their advertising budgets for the promotion. Money was not the problem. ''There are always so many people in the deal. I have to talk to the advertiser, the agency, the baseball club, and the radio station. Trying to get these guys together is a real problem.'' Bryan was agonizing over his plight to his direct-marketing consultant. They were searching for a key to open the market.

''Keep in mind that it takes time for a large company to make such a commitment to an outside promotion,'' the consultant observed.

''But I don't have the time. The season is about to open and I'm broke. I need action now.'' Bryan's desperation was showing.

''Let's search for the barriers in the decision making process. Perhaps we can isolate who or what is blocking the deal.'' The consultant began to work.

''I don't have any trouble with the baseball teams or the radio stations,'' Bryan mused. ''They love it. The problem seems to be with the advertising people both in the company and in the agency. I had one top executive with this large firm tell me, 'I'm tired of making young punks like you rich!' How do you like that! The jerk really said that, right to my face. How can I get around *that* objection? Then the purchasing agent of another large firm objected to my making any money on the deal. She tried to go around me and buy directly from my manufacturers in Hong Kong. They told me all about it. I have them tied up so they can't sell the radio to others. I feel like telling her boss just to let him know what a snake she is. All the time she was leading me on to find out everything she could about the deal. She even bought me dinner one evening.'' Bryan was not happy with the people he had been calling upon.

"And what about the agency people? Are they supportive?" asked the consultant.

"I don't know. It's difficult to read them. They are cordial and businesslike. They seem interested in it. They don't throw me out."

"But is there any one of them who is really pushing your promotion to a client?"

Bryan thought for a moment and responded, "Not really. I have to do all the pushing."

1 What is blocking Bryan's sales?

2 Why did the p.a. try to go around Bryan?

3 Why did the top executive tell Bryan that he would not help make him rich?

PHOTO CREDITS

NAME INDEX

SUBJECT INDEX